EVERY DAY WITH JESUS

ONE YEAR DEVOTIONAL

A Fresh Vision of God

CONTENTS

Foreword

Selwyn Hughes
Further Study by Trevor J Partridge

Foreword

Well over 30 years ago now, when I was pastor of a church in central London, I was asked by a member of my congregation how I went about the task of drawing spiritual strength and encouragement on a daily basis from the Word of God. I explained that every week I set out to explore a Scriptural theme like the bloodline in the Bible or looking at the encounters which some Bible characters had with the Lord on mountain tops.

He asked me if I would write on a card a few Scriptural references relating to the theme I was pursuing so that he could follow it with me. I responded to his request and after a few weeks more people were requesting the cards and soon I found myself writing a dozen of them a week. One night after a church service a group of people asked if I would add some of the comments and thoughts that came to me as I meditated on the theme. This is how the idea for *Every Day with Jesus*, a monthly study on a biblical theme, was born.

The first *Every Day with Jesus* was on the theme of Revival, a subject very close to my heart and one which has also been included in this book. Other themes followed that first edition in 1965 and it soon became clear that a month was too short to develop a subject so I decided to expand a theme over two months. Today these two-monthly themes are read daily by about half a million people around the world.

Devotional reading it needs to be said is designed not simply to inform the mind, but to fire the spirit. My prayer is that the six carefully selected themes in this first edition – themes which have nourished and fired my own soul – will nourish and fire yours also.

Selwyn Hughes

The Vision of God

Needed - a new vision

"In the year that King Uzziah died, I saw the Lord ..." (v.1)
For reading & meditation – Isaiah 6:1-13

We begin by focusing on a theme of deep spiritual importance. It is my conviction that *the Christian Church needs a fresh vision of God*. Almost without our realising it, a spiritual myopia has afflicted us; we are not seeing life clearly because we do not see God clearly. A right perspective on God gives us the right perspective on everything else – life, work, money, service, relationships, and so on.

There is possibly no greater vision of God and His glory in the whole of the Bible (apart from John's encounter with the Almighty in the book of Revelation) than the vision we find recorded in Isaiah chapter 6. It is with this chapter that we are to be concerned. We shall depart from it at times to look at other related aspects, but the thrilling vision of God that was given to Isaiah is to be central to our study. Isaiah came face to face with the living God and found that his whole life was transformed. I trust the same thing will happen to us as we pursue this theme together.

The reason our problems often seem overwhelming is because we allow the things of time to loom larger in our gaze than the things of eternity. The tiniest of coins, when held close to the eye, can blot out the sun. I invite you, therefore, on this very first day of our journey to begin to lay hold on the truth that life works better when we know how to *glance at things but gaze at God*. Seeing Him clearly will enable us to see all other things clearly.

FURTHER STUDY

Psa. 99:1-9; 21:13;
57:11; Isa. 33:5

1. What does the
psalmist affirm?

2. What does the
psalmist exhort us to
do?

Prayer

O God, give me, I pray, a fresh vision of Yourself. I need it and need it badly. Fill my whole horizon with the splendour of Your love, Your power and Your glory. In Christ's peerless and precious Name I ask it. Amen.

How sad!

"... for God is with us." (v.10)
For reading & meditation – Isaiah 8:1-10

Before concentrating on the dramatic vision given to Isaiah in the Temple, we must take a few moments to acquaint ourselves with his personal history.

We do not know exactly when Isaiah was born but we do know that he prophesied during the time of Uzziah, Jotham, Ahaz and Hezekiah. This puts his ministry from around 740 to at least 687 BC. The name "Isaiah" means "the Lord saves", and the passage before us today shows that he was married to a "prophetess" (v.3) and had two sons – Shear Jashub (7:3) and Maher-Shalal-Hash-Baz. The prophet, you remember, introduced his vision of God to us by informing us that "in the year that king Uzziah died, I saw the Lord." Just who was Uzziah? Uzziah was king of Judah from 791 to 740 BC. At first he was a godly king, but when he burned incense in the Temple (2 Chron. 26:16-21) he was struck with leprosy and remained leprous until his death.

When Uzziah died, a period of darkness descended on Judah. In the midst of this spiritual despondency Isaiah was given a vision of the Lord high and lifted up. Was the fact that Isaiah's vision occurred soon after Uzziah's death a mere coincidence? I don't think so. In some way Uzziah's death triggered in Isaiah a spiritual crisis that made him more ready to lift his gaze from earth to heaven. How true to life this is. We look up only when something happens that knocks us flat on our backs. How sad that sometimes earthly securities have to be removed before we can see the glory of Him who sits upon the throne.

FURTHER STUDY

Job 42:1-5;
Psa. 141:1-10

1. What did Job say after he saw God's greatness?

2. What did the psalmist say on observing the evildoers?

Prayer

Father, I am deeply sorry that I go through life with my gaze focused more on that which is around me than on that which is above me. Forgive me and help me develop a more heavenward gaze. In Jesus' Name I pray. Amen.

When props are knocked out

"The eternal God is your refuge, and underneath are the everlasting arms." (v.27)

For reading & meditation – Deuteronomy 33:20-29

Some commentators believe that many in the nation at that time, including Isaiah, had allowed their hopes and expectations for Judah to become so entwined around King Uzziah that when he died they were filled with despair. One modern-day commentator compares it to the shock that reverberated around the world when President Kennedy was assassinated in 1963.

If Isaiah had been pinning his hopes for the spiritual survival of Judah on Uzziah rather than on God then it is easy to see how disappointed and disillusioned he would have become on hearing that King Uzziah had died. Perhaps it wasn't until he came to recognise the impotency of the one who lay in the coffin that he was prepared to lift his eyes to gaze at the One who sat on the eternal throne. How we need to learn the solemn lesson that our trust must always be in God. If it isn't, then God will knock the props out from beneath our feet, not because He is angry at our lack of confidence in Him but because He knows we cannot function effectively unless we are fully dependent on Him.

I wonder, am I talking to someone right now who over the past year has had the props knocked from beneath their feet? The things you have depended on for so long are no longer there. Then listen to me: God is not angry with you. He just wants you to rest your weight fully on Him. You may have to be willing to see your earthly securities laid in a coffin, so to speak, before you can see the glory of the One who sits upon the throne.

FURTHER STUDY

2 Chron. 20:1-30;
Psa. 34:5; 123:1

1. What circumstances did Jehoshaphat find himself in?

2. What did he confess and affirm in his prayer?

Prayer

O Father, help me see that all Your actions toward me have my highest interest at heart. You allow things to happen not to demean me but to develop me. You strip me in order to sustain me. Give me a trusting heart. In Christ's Name I ask it. Amen.

<table>
<tr><td>

Day

4

</td><td>

Unchanging and Unshakeable

</td></tr>
</table>

"Jesus Christ is the same yesterday and today and for ever." (v.8)

For reading & meditation – Hebrews 13:1-16

We saw yesterday that whenever God knocks the props from beneath our feet it is in order that we might rest more securely on Him. The sooner we learn how to make God our security the better, for we are going to face some dark and difficult days up ahead.

During the period when the newspapers were filled with reports of the upheaval in Europe and the great changes taking place in Russia, I turned to my Bible and read these words: "... let us be grateful for receiving a kingdom that cannot be shaken ..." (Heb. 12:28, RSV). The message seemed so appropriate. All around us right now nations are being shaken and almost everything is in the stage of upheaval and change. I am not a prophet, but I think more international unrest and change is on the way. This is a time when God wants His people to look up and see that He is still on the throne.

Every kingdom is shakeable except the kingdom of God. The kingdom of Communism is shakeable. It has to be held together by force. Relax the force and, as the world has witnessed, it goes to pieces. The kingdom of finances is shakeable. The stock market goes up and down with the events of the day. The kingdom of health is shakeable. The doctor says: "I am afraid you have an incurable illness." Shakeable! But in a world of flux be assured of this: Christians are people who belong to an unchanging Person and who dwell in an unshakeable kingdom. God is allowing kingdoms to be shaken so that they might discover the unshakeable kingdom – the kingdom of God.

FURTHER STUDY

Psa. 102:27;
Mal. 3:6;
Heb. 1:10-12;
James 1:1-18

1. What has the Lord declared?

2. What did James confirm?

Prayer

Father, what a comfort it is to realise that I belong to an unchanging Person and an unshakeable kingdom. Passing events cannot shake me. In You I am more than a match for anything. I am eternally grateful. Amen.

"I saw the Lord"

"... and saw the God of Israel." (v.10)
For reading & meditation – Exodus 24:1-18

I remind you that the thought occupying our minds in these opening days of our meditations is this: God allows the props to be knocked out from beneath our feet in order that we might rest our weight fully upon Him. And this is as true for nations as it is for individuals.

We are in the midst of a great international shake-up at the moment – ideologically, politically, and economically. Every programme for the running of God's universe which is an alternative to His own is being shown to be ineffective. I love the story of the little boy in Sunday school who, when asked to make an acrostic from the word Easter, came up with this: "Every Alternative Saviour Takes Early Retirement." All systems that leave out Jesus Christ are doomed to failure for they are not in harmony with the universe. Probably the greatest form of evangelism that is going on at the moment is the shaking of the nations. What is shakeable is being shaken so that the unshakeable might appear. God is preparing the world for the revelation of His kingdom in a way that many cannot discern.

But what about your own personal life? Is that being shaken? What kind of experiences have you had recently? Have you seen, as Isaiah did, your hopes and expectations put in a coffin? Then take heart – all this could be the prelude to a new vision of God. God has often to empty the throne of our hearts before He fills it with Himself. You may yet say: "In the year that all my hopes and expectations came crashing down, I saw the Lord."

FURTHER STUDY

Gen. 32:1-31;
Ex. 24:9-11

1. What did the man say to Jacob?

2. What did Jacob say of the place where he met the man?

Prayer

O Father, how I long that the months ahead will become for me ones of vision and venture. Show me Your glory, I pray, in a way I have never known before. I ask this in and through the Name of Christ my Lord. Amen.

Whose universe is this?

"But about the Son he says, 'Your throne, O God, will last for ever and ever ..." (v.8)

We move on now to consider the fact that when Isaiah received his vision of God he saw the Almighty "seated on a throne" (Isa. 6:1).

Why a throne? Have you noticed in your study of the Scriptures that the seers and apostles in their times of perplexity were often sustained by a vision of the heavenly throne? When Ezekiel was comforting the forlorn exiles he saw the eternal throne (Ezek. 43:7). Daniel, during the rule of Belshazzar, saw the Ancient of Days sitting on His throne (Dan. 7:9). When John was exiled on the island of Patmos and had his great vision of the future, he too saw the throne many times. And in the year that King Uzziah died and Isaiah saw the Lord, he beheld Him "seated on a throne." Why was there given to these men in their hour of great need a vision of the eternal throne? To remind them whose universe it was.

A king reigns from his throne – the symbol of might, power and authority. By revealing His throne to Isaiah it was as if God was saying to him: "There may be no one on the throne of Judah at this moment, but My throne is never unoccupied." We too need at this critical hour in human history to be sustained by the vision of the Almighty seated upon the throne. Earlier this century Communist leaders were declaring: "We have deposed kings from their thrones; now we will depose the King from the skies." What foolishness. How can creatures whom God has made hope to pull the Creator from His throne? No rocket can ever reach it and no atomic bomb can blast it. The throne of God is unassailable.

FURTHER STUDY

Psa. 45:1-6;
103:19; Isa. 66:1

1. What did the psalmist declare?

2. What did the Lord declare about Himself?

Prayer

My Father and my God, just as You have sustained others with a vision of Your throne – sustain me too, I pray. Your throne is unassailable. I draw deep comfort and security from that. Thank You, Father. Amen.

Our God reigns!

*"... you have sat on your throne, judging
righteously." (v.4)*

For reading & meditation – Psalm 9:1-20

We said yesterday that earlier this century Communist leaders were declaring: "We have deposed kings from their thrones; now we will depose the King from the skies." Following the Revolution in 1917, atheism was adopted in Russia – but what is the result? There are more Christians in the Russian Federation than there are in the British Isles! Not only that, many Christians feel Russia and Eastern Europe constitute some of the greatest spiritual harvest fields in the world at the moment.

The kingdoms of Europe have been shaken in order that from the dust the unshakeable kingdom might appear. Christians need ever to keep this in mind: it is from the throne of heaven that the final decisions are made regarding the world's affairs, not the thrones of earth. I am well aware that there are times when it looks as if the authority of heaven's throne has little to do with what transpires on planet earth. Murder, pillage, lust, greed, rape, selfishness, pride and jealousy are spread wide across it, and the battle between good and evil seems as sharp as ever. But don't be taken in by what you see with your eyes or read in your newspapers. Whatever the appearances, our trust must be in the Scriptures which are God's written Word. He tells us in its pages that this is His world – and that He reigns from the central throne of the universe.

God is King! See Him on the throne! And crown Him again in your heart.

FURTHER STUDY

Psa. 47:1-9; 93:1;
96:10; 97:1-2

1. Why can we
rejoice?

2. What is the
conviction of the
psalmist?

Prayer

Father, I bow in Your presence and acknowledge You as the ruler of the universe and the captor of my heart. I have no crown of gold to cast at Your feet but I do more – I cast my heart. I am Yours and You are mine – for ever. Thank You, my Father. Amen.

Why doesn't God do something?

"Why, O Lord, do you stand far off? Why do you hide yourself in times of trouble?" (v.1)

For reading & meditation – Psalm 10:1-18

Many people, most of whom live their normal lives in neglect of God, complain in times of distress or national emergency that God never seems to do anything. Even Christians struggle and ask questions similar to the ones raised by the psalmist: "Why doesn't God intervene to prevent rail crashes, stop babies being battered, or prevent earthquakes wiping out whole communities?"

The problem is a very old one. It puzzled the psalmists, the prophets, and it has perplexed the people of God in every age. It baffled poor Peter in the Garden of Gethsemane. When he stood helpless and ineffectual, and watched soldiers march his betrayed Master away, something came nigh to bursting in his heart. He knew that it was devilry, but why should Christ allow Himself to suffer it? Surely the same word that cured the leper, gave sight to the blind, and summoned the dead to life could blast these evil men for their wickedness? Yet the Master allowed men to lead Him away. As Peter stumbled into the darkness, the question must have hammered in his reeling brain: "Why? ... Why? ... Why?"

There is only one answer to be given to this question: God does not work in our way. This may not satisfy some, but it is an answer nevertheless. His might finds fitting expression not in the power to wound but in the power to woo. His power does not coerce but constrain. Never does He violate the personalities He has made. It would be easy for Him to intervene, but another purpose is at work – the purpose of constraining love. Hard though it may be, we must have patience with the patience of God.

FURTHER STUDY

Isa. 55:1-11;
Psa. 18:30; 145:17;
Hosea 14:9

1. What is God's promise concerning His Word?

2. What conclusion did Hosea come to?

Prayer

O Father, help me understand this important truth, that in running the world You do not work our way. I am big enough to ask questions but not big enough to know the answers. Hold me fast even when I doubt. In Jesus' Name. Amen.

Unassailable – but accessible

"Let us then approach the throne of grace with confidence …" (v.16)

For reading & meditation – Hebrews 4:1-6

We continue meditating on the fact that ultimate authority rests with God who sits upon His throne. Years ago congregations frequently sang a chorus that goes like this:

> God is still on the throne,
> And He will remember His own;
> Though trials may press us
> And burdens distress us
> He never will leave us alone.

The story is told of a little boy who, when introduced to this chorus for the first time in his Sunday school, came home and told his mother: "We learned a new song in Sunday school today." "Oh yes," said his mother, "what was it?" "God is still on the phone," said the little lad. Well that wasn't exactly what he had been taught, but the thought contained in those words was equally true. Though God reigns from a majestic throne, He is accessible to us at all times of day and night. The lines of communication that lead from us to Him are never blocked and never "down". When a man or woman, boy or girl says, "God be merciful to me a sinner," the message goes straight through to the throne and they receive this personal reply: "You are forgiven, redeemed, and set free from your sin."

The throne of God, you see, is not only a throne of righteousness but a throne of grace! Righteousness says: "Stay back until you are good enough to approach." Grace says: "I will put on you the robes of righteousness that are provided for you by Christ – now you are good enough." Too good to be true? Too good not to be true!

FURTHER STUDY

Eph. 1:1-7; 2:7;
Phil. 4:19;
1 Tim. 1:14

1. What will God meet according to His riches?

2. What was Paul's testimony?

Prayer

Father, I draw near again today to Your throne of grace, and with the redeemed all around the world sing: "How marvellous, how wonderful, this my song shall ever be; how marvellous, how wonderful is my Saviour's love to me." Amen.

The sceptre of righteousness

"So Esther approached and touched the tip of the sceptre." (v.2)

For reading & meditation – Esther 5:1-14

We continue meditating on the fact that the throne of God is also a throne of grace. I know of no more wonderful picture to illustrate this than the passage before us today.

Queen Esther approaches the king in order to put into operation the first part of her plan to outwit Haman in his desire to massacre the Jews. In those days no one would enter into the king's presence uninvited, not even the queen. So she dresses as attractively as possible and stands where the king can catch sight of her. As soon as the king spots her in the entrance to the king's hall, he invites her to approach him and holds out the royal sceptre toward her as a sign that she is welcomed and accepted. Esther touches the top of the sceptre in acknowledgement of the king's welcome and proceeds to outline her request.

What a beautiful picture this is of the way we sinners are accepted into the presence of the King of kings. We are told in Hebrews 1:8 that God too has a sceptre – a sceptre of righteousness – which soiled sinners would never be able to touch. However, the good news of the gospel is this: we can approach the throne of a holy God with the assurance that

FURTHER STUDY

Psa. 65:1-13; 48:10; 97:2; 145:17-18

1. What are the foundations of God's throne?

2. What accompanies the righteousness of God?

through the sacrifice on the cross, God has given us His righteousness – the consequence of the finished work of Christ. As we move forward and touch it, in other words acknowledge our acceptance of it, we are welcomed into His presence as if we had never sinned. Can anything be more wonderful in earth or heaven than to be accepted at the throne of a righteous and holy God? And it's all because of Jesus. Blessed be His name for ever!

Prayer

O Father, how can I sufficiently thank You for extending to me Your offer of salvation in Christ? What amazing mercy! What wondrous grace! Help me witness to it both by my lips and by my life. In Jesus' Name I pray. Amen

"His Majesty!"

"For the Lord is the great God, the great King above all gods." (v.3)

For reading & meditation – Psalm 95:1-11

What is the word that comes to mind when you think of a throne? Is it not the word "majesty"? Our word "majesty" comes from the Latin *majestas* and means greatness. Jim Packer says: "When we ascribe majesty to someone we are acknowledging greatness in that person and voicing our respect for it; as for instance, when we speak of 'Her Majesty, the Queen'." "Majesty" is a word that is often used of God. "The Lord reigns, he is robed in majesty" (Psa. 93:1). "They will speak of the glorious splendour of your majesty" (Psa. 145:5). Christ, we are told, at His ascension, "sat down at the right hand of the Majesty in heaven" (Heb. 1:3).

Why was it necessary for Isaiah to see God "seated on a throne"? Because his instincts of trust and worship would be stimulated by a vision of God's majesty. And so will it be with us. One of the reasons why our faith is so feeble is because our thoughts of God are not great enough. Do we picture God "seated on a throne" or just sitting upon a cloud?

The trouble with many in today's Church is that, although they cherish great thoughts about men, they have only small thoughts about God. I love the song written by Jack Hayford that begins "Majesty! Worship His Majesty". But it is possible to sing that with great gusto in church and then revert to our inadequate thoughts about God when we kneel down to pray. Learn to associate God with majesty. I promise you, filling your mind with thoughts of "His Majesty" will set your devotional life on fire!

FURTHER STUDY

1 Chron. 29:10-13;
Psa. 96:4-6;
Job 37:22-23

1. What did David proclaim in the presence of the whole assembly?

2. What did Elihu proclaim to Job?

Prayer

O Father, as I turn my gaze upward to focus on Your greatness and Your glory, stimulate my instincts of trust and worship and set my soul on fire. I look at You and my heart cries out in godly reverence and fear: "Your Majesty". Amen.

Difficulties are not almighty

"… the Lord, the Lord Almighty, has told me …" (v.22)
For reading & meditation – Isaiah 28:16-29

There can be little doubt that the vision Isaiah received in the Temple transformed his life. The young prophet might not have known it at the time but on the River Tiber a city was being built which was to be called Rome. As we know, that city became the focal point of a great empire which in 63 BC overcame Isaiah's beloved city of Jerusalem. The vision he saw of the One who was "seated on a throne", however, would remain with him throughout his entire ministry and give within the conviction that, no matter who or what would hold the centre stage of earth's affairs, the Lord alone was sovereign and ruled over all. After that, whenever other prophets drew back from speaking the Word of the Lord because of fear, Isaiah never hesitated. We have an example of this in the passage before us today.

Now that's an important lesson for your life and mine. It is so easy for us to allow the problems of life to loom large in our thinking. When we do so we soon lose the right perspective. Our obsession with our problems can become an issue that almost blots out God. Maybe someone you trusted has hurt you, and that problem has become so large that

FURTHER STUDY

Matt. 19:16-26;
Jer. 32:17;
Luke 1:37

1. What did Jesus say to the disciples?

2. What did Gabriel say to Mary?

it reaches almost cosmic proportions. Well, I want to tell you today that, big though it may be, it is not bigger than God. Don't lose your perspective.

The Lord is on His throne, high and exalted. See how big God really is and set your problems over against that vision. Your difficulties are not almighty. The Lord alone is almighty.

Prayer

O God, fill my vision with Yourself for I see that when I do not view You as almighty I can so easily view my problems in that way. Keep my gaze and my focus fully on You. In Jesus' Name I ask it. Amen.

Seeing God as God

"Whom did the Lord consult to enlighten him … Who was it that taught him knowledge …?" (v.14)
For reading & meditation – Isaiah 40:1-20

We said yesterday that Isaiah's vision of God's majesty remained with him throughout his entire ministry. See how, in this fortieth chapter of his prophecy, Isaiah applies the truth of the majesty of God, which he learned in the vision in the Temple, to the lives of the disillusioned and downcast people of Judah. In God's Name he puts several questions to the people.

First: "Who has understood the mind of the Lord, or instructed him as his counsellor?" (v.13). This question is designed to correct false notions of God. Luther once said to Erasmus: "Your thoughts of God are too human." This may be our trouble too. We think of God in the same way that we think about ourselves – as limited and fallible, Because we are limited and require information and counselling, we think God does too. We think of God as too much like ourselves. Put the mistake right, says Isaiah. Learn to acknowledge the majesty and greatness of God.

A second and similar question is also posed: "To whom, then, will you compare God? What image will you compare him to?" (v.18). This question is also designed to correct wrong concepts of God. Isn't it sad that because we ourselves are limited and weak, we imagine that, at some points, God is too. Isaiah does here what a doctor would do when entering the room of a sick patient who has closeted himself behind shuttered windows. He opens the windows, lets in the fresh air and light, and says: "No wonder you are sick. You are not taking advantage of the resources that bring healing." Spiritual health comes from seeing God as He is.

FURTHER STUDY

Job 38:1-42:16

1. How does God bring perspective back to Job?

2. How did Job respond?

Prayer

My Father and my God, if I am mistakenly making You in my image instead of seeing that I am made in Yours then forgive me, I pray. Help me see You as You really are – ruling and reigning with all might, all power and all authority. Amen.

Strength like the eagle's

"They will soar on wings like eagles ..." (v.31)
For reading & meditation – Isaiah 40:21-31

We continue looking at the questions which Isaiah poses to the people of Judah and indeed to the whole nation of Israel, on behalf of God, here in this gripping fortieth chapter.

A third question is this: "Why do you say, O Jacob, and complain, O Israel, 'My way is hidden from the Lord; my cause is disregarded by my God'?" (v.27). The questions we looked at yesterday were designed to correct their false concepts of God; this one is designed to correct the wrong ideas they had concerning themselves. They were allowing themselves to think that God had abandoned them. How absurd! Let me ask you a personal question: Do you believe God has abandoned you? If you do, you ought to be ashamed of yourself. Such unbelieving pessimism dishonours the Almighty.

A fourth question is this: "Do you not know? Have you not heard? The Lord is the everlasting God, the Creator of the ends of the earth. He will not grow tired or weary, and his understanding no-one can fathom" (v.28). This question is intended to rebuke them for their slowness to believe in God's greatness and majesty. God talks to them in a way that is calculated to shame them out of their unbelief. How ridiculous it is for us to imagine that God can get old and tired. How slow we are to believe in God as God – sovereign, all-seeing, and all-powerful. The need to "wait upon the Lord" and contemplate His majesty is one of our greatest needs in the Church. For it is when we do so, and only when we do so that our strength will be renewed and we will soar on wings like eagles.

FURTHER STUDY

1 Kings 8:14-24;
1 Chron. 17:20;
Psa. 89:1-52

1. What was at the heart of Solomon's prayer of dedication?

2. In what ways does the psalmist describe God?

Prayer

My Father and my God, write these truths upon my heart, so that I shall be gripped and mastered by these important convictions. I don't just want to hold them as ideas, I want them to hold me. Help me, dear Father. In Jesus' Name. Amen.

"He is exalted ..."

"But you, O Lord, are exalted for ever." (v.8)
For reading & meditation – Psalm 92:1-15

We move on now to focus on a further phrase that Isaiah uses when describing his vision of God: "I saw the Lord ... high and exalted" (Isa. 6:1). These words take us beyond the fact that God is seated on a throne and show us that His throne is situated far above the boundaries of space and time. The words "seated on a throne" introduce us to the majesty of God; the words "high and exalted" introduce us to the transcendence and loftiness of God. Oh how desperately we need a new vision of the transcendence of God in the Church today.

Earlier this century A.W. Tozer shook the Church of his day when he wrote: "The Church has surrendered her once lofty concept of God and has substituted for it one so low, so ignoble, as to be utterly unworthy of thinking, worshipping men. This she has done not deliberately but little by little and without her knowledge, and her very unawareness only makes her situation all the more tragic." Tozer went on to point out that a low view of God is the underlying cause of many of our problems. He said: "A whole new philosophy of the Christian life has resulted from this one basic error of our thinking." I would have to agree.

When we lose our sense of God's transcendence then a hundred different ills arise within us. Take this for example: with the loss of the sense of God's transcendence comes the further loss of understanding the significance of worship. To truly worship God we need to see that we are worshipping Someone who is not only above us, but far above us. He is the Creator – we are merely creatures.

FURTHER STUDY

Ex. 15:1-21;
Job 36:22;
Isa. 33:5-6; 5:16

1. What did the song of Moses begin and end with?

2. What does the word "awesome" mean?

Prayer

Father, help me see that while You are nearer to me than the breath I breathe, You are also a God who is high and exalted. And help me understand that these two truths are not contradictory but complementary. In Jesus' Name I pray. Amen.

Immanent – yet transcendent

"I live in a high and holy place ... with him who is contrite and lowly in spirit ..." (v.15)

For reading & meditation – Isaiah 57:11-21

The thought occupying our attention at the moment is what theologians call the transcendence of God. The idea behind transcendence is that of distinctiveness, separateness – that God is uniquely other than everything in creation.

We said yesterday that the words "high and exalted" show us that God's throne is situated far above the boundaries of space and time. Too much must not be made of this, however, for although the transcendence of God is frequently expressed biblically in terms of time and space (see Psalm 90:2 and 1 Kings 20:28, for example), we must not think that God lives in a time and space like ours, only beyond that of creation.

Over against that thought we must hold the truth of God's immanence, and by that we mean that He dwells in the lives of those who have repented of their sin – a truth our text for today brings out so clearly. Yet the fact God indwells us must not be allowed to cloud the truth that He is above us, infinitely exalted above all creation. To think of God as transcendent inspires adoration and worship. Without this idea in our minds then worship is a mere ritual and a formality. In days past, men and women who knew what it was to walk in the fear of the Lord had, as a basis for their lives, the concept of God as "high and exalted". However intimate their communion with God, they were gripped by the fact that God was high and lifted up. Why is it that in the modern-day Church we do not meet many of this ilk?

FURTHER STUDY

Gen. 14:17-20;
Heb. 7:1; Psa. 21:7;
Mark 5:7

1. How was God described by Melchizedek?

2. How did the evil spirit address Jesus?

Prayer

O God, forgive me if, in my desire to have You close to me, I have lost sight of Your majesty, Your greatness and transcendence. Help me understand that to see You as high and exalted is not a loss but a gain. In Jesus' Name I ask it. Amen.

"The proper study of mankind ..."

"Now this is eternal life: that they may know you, the only true God ..." (v.3)

For reading & meditation – John 17:1-19

We ended yesterday with the thought that, in days past, men and women who knew what it was to walk in the fear of the Lord had, as a basis for their lives, the concept of God as "high and exalted". We finished with the question: Why is it that in the modern-day Church we do not meet many of this ilk? The answer I think is that, notwithstanding all the good things happening in the Church today, there is not enough teaching and emphasis on the nature and character of God.

The great preacher C.H. Spurgeon made this statement: "It has been said that the proper study of mankind is man. I will not oppose the idea, but I believe it is equally true that the proper study of God's elect is God." The contemporary Church, generally speaking, focuses more on issues like "how to gain a good self-image", or "how to be more effective in prayer" than it does on how to know God. Not that these other issues are unimportant, but, as Jim Packer says in his book *Knowing God*: "Knowing God is crucially important for the living of our lives. The world becomes a strange, mad, painful place, and life in it a disappointing and unpleasant business, for those who do not know about God."

Of course, it takes time to know God. Determine right now that in the coming months you will commit yourself to knowing God in a deeper way; first by spending more time with Him in prayer and meditation, and second by increasing your understanding of Him through more thorough study of His Word.

FURTHER STUDY

Eph. 1:1-17;
Phil. 3:1-11

1. What did Paul pray for the Ephesians?

2. What did Paul desire for himself?

Prayer

Father, I see that knowing You better involves increased time – time to talk to You and time to study Your Word. Guide me so that I can make the coming months yield great gains in my knowledge of You. In Jesus' Name I pray. Amen.

Our prayers reveal us

"O Lord, the great and awesome God …" (v.4)
For reading & meditation – Daniel 9:1-19

When dwelling on the fact that God is "high and exalted" we must be careful not to think of Him as highest in an ascending order of beings, starting with a single cell and going on up from, say, a fish to a bird, to a man, to an angel, to an archangel, and then – God. This would be to see God merely as eminent, perhaps even pre-eminent. He is so much more than that. He is transcendent.

That means He stands apart from creation. He is as high above an archangel as He is above an amoeba, for the gulf that separates the amoeba from the archangel is finite, whereas the gulf separating God from an archangel is infinite. The amoeba and the archangel, though far removed from one another in the scale of created things, are, nevertheless, one in that they are both created. They belong in the category of what one theologian describes as "that which is not God" – separated from God by infinitude itself.

Even a casual reader of the Scriptures could not help but notice that those who appear to have a great knowledge of God have lofty thoughts concerning Him. This comes out most clearly in the prayers of God's people – Daniel's prayer which we have ready today being just one example. If you want to know how a person views God, listen to him or her pray! It's interesting to note that those who know God intimately invariably begin by acknowledging His greatness. They know that when they accord God His rightful place then it is more likely that everything else will be put in its rightful place.

FURTHER STUDY

Neh. 1:1-11;
4:1-15; 9:32

1. What was Nehemiah's view of God?

2. How did this affect the rebuilding of the wall?

Prayer

O God, slowly the light is dawning – when You are not accorded Your rightful place then nothing else is in place. You can get along without me, but I can't get along without You. Help me never to forget this. In Jesus' Name I ask it. Amen.

God help grammar!

"Be still, and know that I am God ..." (v.10)
For reading & meditation – Psalm 46:1-11

A famous preacher once preached from the text that is before us today and entitled his message: "Have you a God you can be still with?" It was reported that most of the congregation, being well educated, tuned out a lot of what he was saying because they could only think of the fact that he ended a sentence with a preposition. How sad that when eternal issues were at stake their only thought was of grammar. The great preacher D.L. Moody often split an infinitive when preaching. Once, when a retired schoolteacher took him to task for this lapse of grammatical correctness, he replied: "Madam, when I see souls going to hell and grammar gets in the way – then God help grammar!"

At the risk of repeating the unfortunate mistake of the first minister to whom I referred, I would like to ask you that same question: Have you a God you can be still with? In other words, is your life such a ceaseless round of activity that when you come to focus your mind on God you cannot give yourself to the task for very long, so you blurt out a few prayers and then you are gone? You won't get to know God – really know God – that way.

You see, what our text is saying is this: you cannot get to know God until you are willing to stay still before Him. Knowing God means contemplating Him, worshipping Him, and studying Him. It should be a cause for deep spiritual concern that the words of our text mean next to nothing to the self-confident bustling worshippers who move in and out of our churches nowadays.

FURTHER STUDY

Job 37:1-24;
Psa. 131:2;
Isa. 30:15

1. What did Elihu counsel Job?

2. What was the psalmist able to say?

Prayer

Loving heavenly Father, how blessedly You put Your finger on our problems. Help me face up to the question "Have I a God with whom I can be still?" and not rush past it. Slow me down, dear Father, so that I face this issue. In Jesus' Name. Amen.

Knowing God as He is

"God is spirit, and his worshippers must worship in spirit and in truth." (v.24)

For reading & meditation – John 4:1-26

Modern-day Christianity, generally speaking, is not producing the kind of person who can appreciate what it means to withdraw from the hustle and bustle of life and focus on worshipping God. And one of the reasons for that is the loss of the concept of God's transcendence.

You see, it is impossible to keep up the practice of Christian principles and perform our Christian duties in the way they should be performed when our attitude to God or our view of Him is erroneous. If we are to see spiritual power flowing through our lives then we must begin to think of God as He is. "Worship is as pure or as base," said Tozer, "as the worshipper entertains high or low thoughts of God." Because of this the most important issue for the Church is not "How can we evangelise?", but "How can we know God better?" Evangelism is important, but not half as important as knowing God. Worship must always come first, and work must always come second. Today's Christian teachers should be focusing (among other things) on making clear who God is, for the Church of tomorrow will depend largely on what kind of concept of God we have today.

FURTHER STUDY

1 Cor. 3:1-11;
Eph. 2:19-20

1. What had Paul taken trouble over?

2. What are we to be careful about?

A true understanding of God is as important to our worship of God, our work for God and our witness to God as a foundation is to a building. If the foundation is not right then the building will be lopsided, or worse – topple over. Thus we must ask ourselves: What kind of building will the Church of the next generation inherit from us? A strong one or an unsteady one?

Prayer

O God, I long with all my heart to worship you "in spirit and in truth". And whatever the road blocks on that journey, help me remove them and overcome them. For your own dear Name's sake I pray. Amen.

Christian idolaters

*"Within your temple, O God, we meditate on your
unfailing love." (v.9)*

For reading & meditation – Psalm 48:1-14

We touched yesterday on an issue which I now want to expand upon because I believe it to be one of the most crucial aspects of Christian living – seeing God as He is, not as we would like Him to be. Unless we have an understanding of God *as He is*, not as we wish Him to be, then our lives will lack spiritual force and power. This is because our lives will never rise higher spiritually than our vision of God.

Among the sins which are hateful to God is the sin of idolatry, for idolatry, at its heart, is a libel on His character. Yet consider how many of us in the Church may be committing the sin of idolatry without realising it. The idolatrous heart assumes that God is other than He is, and substitutes for the true God one made after its own imagining. But a god who is created out of darkness of our hearts is not the true God. The greatest affront we can give to the Almighty is to view Him other than He really is.

God has gone to great lengths in the Scriptures to give us a clear picture of Himself, but when we continue to hold wrong ideas of Him, preferring to see Him the way we think He should be rather than the way He is, we demean Him. If we try to worship the god of our own imagining we then commit idolatry, for we are worshipping our idea of Him drawn from the darkness of our minds. Credal statements about God are fine – I have nothing against them – but if, in the secret chamber of our soul, we have an image of God which differs from the one we profess with our lips, then it is that core image which will have the greatest influence on our lives.

FURTHER STUDY

Acts 17:29;
Gal. 4:1-11;
2 Tim. 3:1-5

1. What were the
Galatians doing?

2. What did Paul ask
the Galatians?

Prayer

O Father, forgive me if I have been thinking of You as I want You to be rather than as You really are. Help me draw my concept of You from Your Word and from Your revelation in Christ, not from my own imaginings. In Jesus' Name. Amen.

Our biggest single problem

"Anyone who has seen me has seen the Father." (v.9)
For reading & meditation – John 14:1-14

We continue with the thought that we have to see God as He is, not as we would like Him to be. In a radio interview I was asked this question: "Over the years in which you have been a minister and counsellor, what has been the biggest single problem you have come across in the lives of fellow Christians? And what is the cause of that biggest single problem?" Unhesitatingly I replied: "Disappointment with God because of something He did not do, or something He did not provide. The cause – a wrong understanding of God and His ways."

Multitudes of Christians go through life with suppressed disappointment and anger because at some point in their experience God did not come through for them in the way they thought He should. I have heard people say: "I asked God to give me patience and instead He allowed the pressures to increase." "I asked God to take away my anger toward my wife and children, but He failed to answer my prayer." Time, it is said, is a wonderful healer, and many Christians recover from these negative feelings about God. But so often there is no real healing, just a covering over of the emotions. Then when some crisis hits and God does not come up to expectations the submerged feelings break the surface and the problem begins all over again.

The sooner we learn to accept God as He is, and do not imagine Him as we would like Him to be, the sooner we will move from the path of confusion to confidence. I tell you, this is a matter of supreme importance.

FURTHER STUDY

Psa. 22:1-5;
Rom. 5:5

1. What did David say about his fathers?

2. What was the result?

Prayer

O Father, I confess that I struggle when You don't seem to move in the way I want You to or do the things I want You to do. Help me know You better so that my expectations are based on truth, not on wishful thinking. In Jesus' Name. Amen.

The bottom line

"How long, O Lord, must I call for help, but you do not listen …?" (v.2)

For reading & meditation – Habakkuk 1:1-17

We continue focusing on the importance of seeing God as He really is, not as we would like Him to be.

The reason so many Christians become disappointed with God is because they do not have what can best be described as a "bottom line" – a line we draw under God. When we cannot make sense of a situation, the "bottom line" explains Him. So what is this "bottom line"? Is it the fact that God is Healer? I suggest not, for, if it was, then everyone should be healed. Is it that God is our Deliverer? No, not even that, for there are times when, despite our demands to be delivered, He makes no attempt to rescue us. Now I am not saying that God does not heal, or that He does not deliver us, but these aspects of His character are not the "bottom line". If we make them the "bottom line", we will become as confused as Habakkuk was in today's passage, when he confessed that he could not understand why God did not come through for His people.

The "bottom line", as it relates to God, is not deliverance, or healing, or protection, or any similar thing. He demonstrates His ability to do these things from time to time, but they are not to be seen as inevitable. Sometimes He heals and sometimes He doesn't. Sometimes He delivers and sometimes He doesn't. Sometimes He protects us from afflictions and accidents, and other times He allows them to happen. How do we make sense of all this? We can't unless we have a "bottom line"? So what is this "bottom line"? I will tell you tomorrow.

FURTHER STUDY

Eccl. 7:15
Psa. 73:1-28;

1. To what point had the writer of Ecclesiastes come?

2. What was the psalmist struggling with?

Prayer

My Father and my God, help me move, as Habakkuk did, from confusion to confidence, and give me the understanding and convictions I need to trust You even when I cannot trace You. In Jesus' Name I ask it. Amen.

Steady as you go!

"The Sovereign Lord is my strength; he makes my feet like the feet of a deer …" (v.19)

For reading & meditation – Habakkuk 3:1-19

We acknowledged yesterday that if we see the "bottom line" concerning God as the fact that He is a Healer, or Protector, or a Deliverer, then we are often going to be disappointed, because every one of us knows that there are times when He does not come through for us in the way we expect. If He lets something happen to us that we think He shouldn't have let happen, then we will find it very difficult to trust in Him should we have the same requirement again. Often in these situations we end up developing a deep rage or disappointment with God which, in the interests of the Christian faith, we learn to suppress. This is largely because we do not understand God's "bottom line".

So what is the "bottom line" as regards God? I suggest it is His justice. By that I mean the truth that whatever God does, He does because it is right. Not that it is right because God does it, but that God does it because it is right. There is a world of difference between those two things. Most Christians find it difficult to believe in the justice of God. They say they do, but when questioned it is clear they believe only in justice on their terms.

FURTHER STUDY

Jer. 12:1-17;
Psa. 98:8-9; 99:4

1. What issue did Jeremiah take up with God?

2. What motivates God's justice?

In the passage before us today, Habakkuk comes to see that whatever God does is just, and it is his new-found confidence in the justice of God that holds him steady as he contemplates the judgment that God is about to bring on His people. I tell you with all the conviction of my heart that unless we are gripped by the belief that God acts justly in everything – everything – then we will not have the sure-footedness we need to negotiate the rocky slopes that are up ahead.

Prayer

Father, I see that if I am to move upwards in my Christian life with the sure-footedness of a deer, then I can only do so as I am gripped by the conviction that everything You do is right. Burn that conviction into me. In Jesus' Name. Amen.

"My comfort is My justice"

"They will come to you, and when you see their conduct and their actions, you will be consoled …" (v.22)

For reading & meditation – Ezekiel 14:12-23

We continue emphasising the point that the "bottom line" as regards God is justice – the fact that everything that God does is right.

In our reading today God tells Ezekiel that He is going to judge Jerusalem but that He would provide comfort during that destruction. But what was that comfort? It was to spare a few people and bring them before Ezekiel, so that he could see how evil they were and realise that God had a just cause for everything He did. In other words, God was saying: "My comfort is My justice." You see the point? If your "bottom line" is "comfort", if that is more important to you than anything else, then when God acts justly it will be no comfort to you. When you cry out for comfort and think that is the most important thing you need from God, it may be that, from His point of view, your biggest need is justice. Then, when God acts justly but not according to your idea of justice, you get totally confused. But the problem is not with God, it is with you. You have not got the "bottom line" drawn clearly enough. Your "bottom line" is being drawn at *your idea of justice,* not His, and therefore His actions are anathema to you.

Most of us don't really believe in God's justice, only justice on our terms. It is easy to believe in God's justice when other people or other families are on the receiving end; but the true test of spiritual maturity is when in our own lives things do not go the way we expect them to go, and we say with Abraham, when pleading with God for the deliverance of Sodom: "Shall not the Judge of all the earth do right?" (Gen. 18:25, AV)

FURTHER STUDY

Gen. 18:22-25;
Psa. 33:4;
Hosea 14:1-9

1. What question did Abraham ask?

2. What was Hosea's conviction?

Prayer

Father, help me resolve this tension between my idea of justice and Yours. For I see that if it goes unresolved then I shall continue to misunderstand – even rebel. Teach me to accept that Your way is right – always. In Jesus' Name I ask it. Amen.

"See His glory come down"

"I will not yield my glory to another." (v.11)
For reading & meditation – Isaiah 48:1-11

Why do we find it difficult to draw the "bottom line" concerning God at the level of His justice? Perhaps we are able to do it when things are going well, but immediately disaster strikes we draw the line at a different level – at the level of His compassion, His ability to heal or His power to deliver. We then tend to demand from God not real justice but justice on our own terms – our terms being deliverance, healing or divine protection.

Now I am not saying that God is disinterested in us, but we must never put our well-being before His. There is a much higher value in this universe than our glory – it is God's glory. This is why we read over and over again in the book of Ezekiel words to the effect that "My glory is at stake."

The nation of Israel didn't see things that way and took a different, even a rebellious attitude toward God, saying: "No, it is our glory that is at stake." Don't we do something similar? When our problems loom large, and our welfare is under threat, we tend to argue with God when He says, "My glory is at stake," and retort, "No, Lord, it is not Your glory that is at stake; it is mine." What arrogance! What insanity! I tell you, if we are to develop any degree of spiritual maturity in our lives we have to put a higher value on God's glory than our own well-being. If we don't, then we will never come to know the depth of trust that Job exhibited when he said: "Though he slay me, yet will I hope in him" (Job 13:15).

FURTHER STUDY

Isa. 42:1-9;
1 Chron. 16:28-29;
Psa. 29:1

1. What will God not give to another?

2. What did David exhort to be ascribed to the Lord?

Prayer

Father, help me understand that in putting Your glory before my well-being I do not demean myself but develop myself. For in glorifying You I too am glorified. Help me grasp this. In Jesus' Name. Amen.

Where is our trust?

Day
27

"Trust in him at all times ..." (v.8)
For reading & meditation – Psalm 62:1-12

We continue meditating on this matter of God's glory being more important than our own well-being. The serious problem is not the pain that others have inflicted upon us, but the pain we have inflicted (and continue to inflict) upon God. Let me spell out as clearly as I can exactly what I mean.

Many Christians are far more interested in focusing on how they can get God to comfort them when they have been hurt than considering how much they have hurt Him. Not that it is wrong to seek His comfort – Scripture encourages us to do this – but it is only one side of the picture. The most popular books in our bookshops today are titles such as these: *How to be Healed of Life's Hurts* or *How to Overcome the Pains of the Past*. I repeat that this is a legitimate emphasis, but we must not lose sight of the fact that the important issue is not how badly people have behaved toward us, but how badly we have behaved (and continue to behave) toward God.

Take this for example: someone hurts us or upsets us and we decide to become the architects of their judgment. But what does God say? "Do not take revenge, my friends, but leave room for God's wrath ... 'It is mine to avenge; I will repay,' says the Lord" (Rom. 12:19). Don't you think God is hurt when He sees us ignoring His Word? We may have been sinned against, but is that any justification for sinning against God? Let's not mince words here, for any violation of a divine principle must be called by its rightful name – sin. And no sin ought to be treated lightly – especially a sin against God.

FURTHER STUDY

Matt. 21:12-13;
23:37-39;
Luke 19:41

1. What pain was inflicted on Jesus as He observed the Temple area?

2. What pain did Jesus feel as He approached the city?

Prayer

O God, forgive me that so often I am more concerned about how others have treated me than the way I treat You. I see that a failure to trust You is a failure in love. I say, "I love You," but only so far. Forgive me and help me. In Jesus' Name. Amen.

Close – but not close enough

"Teach me your way, O Lord ... give me an undivided heart ..." (v.11)

For reading & meditation – Psalm 86:1-17

We continue with the important issue we raised yesterday, namely, that the significant problem is not the hurts that others have given to us, but the hurts that we have given (and continue to give) to God. We looked at one direction we might go when hurt by others; look with me now at another.

Instead of trying to get back at them, we withdraw from them and decide to never again give them an opportunity to hurt us. Hence, in future, we relate to them at a superficial level – close enough to be considered friendly or sociable, but not close enough to get hurt. Notice what God says we ought to do when we become victims of spitefulness or animosity: "If your enemy is hungry, feed him; if he is thirsty, give him something to drink ... Do not be overcome by evil, but overcome evil with good" (Rom. 12:20-21). What this text is saying, you see, is this: be concerned about the person who has hurt you and put that concern into action; get close to them again and risk being hurt again.

To cling to our hurts and use them as a justification for avoiding close relationships is tantamount to saying: "God expects too much of us." Such an attitude is sinful. Why sinful? Because it reflects self-interest more than God-interest. It says to God: "It is not Your glory that is at stake here – it's mine." How sad that we are more keen to preserve our own well-being than trust God and His Word. I tell you, if we don't correct this imbalance we are never going to know God as He really is. We will see His justice only in terms of what it means for us, not in terms of what it means for Him.

FURTHER STUDY

Matt. 5:38-48;
Ex. 23:4-5;
Prov. 25:21-22;
Luke 23:34

1. What did Jesus teach in His sermon on the mount?

2. How did He demonstrate this?

Prayer

O God, we do not see ourselves, for we look at the sins that others commit against us with open eyes and then turn a blind eye upon the sins we commit against You. Help us to be as honest about ourselves as we are about others – and more. In Jesus' Name. Amen.

"Come on Lord, act justly"

"… all his ways are just. A faithful God … upright and just is he." (v.4)

For reading & meditation – Deuteronomy 32:1-12

Can you see now why it is so hard to draw the "bottom line" concerning God in terms of His justice? We feel much more passionate about how we have been sinned against than how we sin against Him. "To dwell only on the fact that we have been victimised," says psychologist Larry Crabb, "is to develop a demanding spirit." We tend then to say to God: "Come on Lord, start acting justly and defend me against my adversaries." Once we give up our demandingness, however, we are at the mercy of other people and have to go through life trusting God to deal with them on His terms. Can we handle that kind of vulnerability?

I am not suggesting, by the way, that people who experience serious physical or sexual abuse should not report it to the authorities. What I have in mind as I write is the kind of situation when someone wounds our spirit by an insensitive word or action. When we focus on the sins of others toward ourselves it becomes hard to give up our rebellion against God, because, in the light of how we are hurting, we see it as justified. But when we focus on how much we have hurt Him, and how we continue to hurt Him by our self-centredness and our refusal to trust His power and love, our rebellious spirit dissolves of its own accord. Then what others have done to us seems of much lesser significance than what we have done to Him. Our perspectives are corrected and we are more ready to recognise the universal rightness of things and make eternal justice the "bottom line".

FURTHER STUDY

Eccl. 3:1-14;
Psa. 18:30;
Matt 5:48

1. What did the writer of Ecclesiastes know?

2. What did Jesus exhort in His sermon on the mount?

Prayer

Gracious Father, forgive us for the wrongs we inflict upon ourselves by trying to live in ways other than Your ways. Your ways produce rhythm; our ways produce ruin. Your ways produce freedom, our ways produce folly. Help us to take Your ways unreservedly. Amen.

Hearing *and* seeing!

"My ears had heard of you but now my eyes have seen you." (v.5)

For reading & meditation – Job 42:1-17

Perhaps the person who best illustrates what we have been talking about over the past few days – a failure to understand God's justice – is God's servant Job.

Following his suffering received at the hands of Satan, Job came to believe that the whole of life was unfair. He makes this point to God in chapter 27 verse 2: "As surely as God lives, who has denied me justice, the Almighty, who has made me taste bitterness of soul ..." What is God's response to this? He confronts Job with these words: "Where were you when I laid the earth's foundation? Tell me, if you understand. Who marked off its dimensions? Surely you know!" (Job 38:4-5). Then, after listening for a long time to God outlining His greatness and His majesty, Job responds with the marvellous words that form our text for today: "My ears had heard of you but now my eyes have seen you." Job begins to see that any movement against God's justice is sin. His previous problem of being mistreated is forgotten in the light of the greater problem that he had misjudged the Almighty.

Then came the moment when Job prayed for the friends who hadn't

FURTHER STUDY

Psa. 17:1-15; 34:5; 123:1

1. What was David asking God to honour?

2. What result was David convinced of?

been much help to him, and as he turned the focus from himself to others something big and beautiful took place within him – his rebellion dissolved and he was delivered from all his problems. Job came to see God as He is, not as he wanted Him to be, and with all the conviction of which I am capable I tell you that same revelation must come to us if we are to worship God and serve Him correctly.

Prayer

O Father, to hear of You by ear is indeed wonderful, but to "see" You is bliss beyond compare. Bring me to the same place You brought Your servant Job – no matter what lies in between. In Jesus' Name. Amen.

Too far to turn back

"Whom have I in heaven but you? And earth has nothing I desire besides you." (v.25)

For reading & meditation – Psalm 73:1-28

We pause at this point to gather up some of the things we have been saying.

The most important need for the Church at this present time is a fresh vision of God. The vision which the young Isaiah received as he entered into the Temple must also become ours. It transformed him and it will also transform us too. Many Christians come to the Bible, however, not to discover God as He is, but to confirm their own view of Him. Thus they hold fast to a concept of the Almighty that is completely false, and so, lacking a true knowledge of God, they stumble through life rather than striding through it. When God is accorded His rightful place, "high and exalted", then we acknowledge our rightful place and worship becomes not a mere ritual but a deep and rich encounter with our Creator.

One of the things that prevents us from seeing God as He really is, is our preoccupation with how others behave toward us, when we should be worrying about the way we have behaved toward God. History shows that those who have really known God seem to have exhibited little concern about what others have done to them; they have been too busy focusing on how they could arrive at a better knowledge of Him. Every one of us must get hold of the fact that a little knowledge *of* God is worth more than a great deal of knowledge *about* Him. Thus we must pursue the vision which Isaiah received in the Temple still further. One thing is certain, we have come too far to turn back now.

FURTHER STUDY

John 6:53-71;
Matt. 19:21

1. What did Peter respond to Jesus' question?

2. Why?

Prayer

O God, at last the doors of my life are beginning to turn outward instead of inward. I am beginning to focus more on You than on myself. This feels so right. Lead me on, my Father. I shall follow. In Christ's Name I pray. Amen.

The exclusiveness of God

"… and the one who trusts in him will never be put to shame." (v. 6)

For reading & meditation – 1 Peter 2:1-12

As we continue looking at Isaiah's vision we come to the phrase: "… and the train of his robe filled the temple" (Isa. 6:1). The thought being conveyed here is of the exclusiveness of God. There is no room for anyone else in this high-exalted place. God is all in all.

A.W. Tozer, in his book *The Pursuit of God*, said: "When religion has said its last word, there is little that we need other than God Himself." So many of us have a faith in God which expresses itself something like this: God and a good job; God and good health. These things are fine as desires, but when they become demands we are revealing where our real trust lies. Let me ask you: Is God sufficient in your life? Maybe you have just learned that you have a terminal illness and you feel desperately alone. Is God enough? Or perhaps you have worked all your life to build up a business that has come crashing down and now you feel absolutely alone. Is God sufficient? Maybe your spouse has walked out on you and all you have left is God. Is He sufficient? Is He enough? As C.S. Lewis once put it: "You will never know how much you believe something until it is a matter of life and death."

FURTHER STUDY

Phil. 3:1-21;
John 12:24-25;
Mark 8:35

1. What was Paul's pursuit?

2. What was he willing to give up?

The moment comes to us all when we find that the gods of this world are not gods. When that moment hits us where is our trust to be placed? At the highest point of the universe there is room for no one else but the Lord our God. Is He sufficient? Is He enough? With all my heart I say – He is. I hope you are able to say it too.

Prayer

O Father, with all my heart I affirm You are my sufficiency. You are enough! Forgive me that so often I rely on my own self-sufficiency or the sufficiency of others instead of depending on You. Forgive me and release me now. In Jesus' Name. Amen.

God "and"...

"... and you have been given fulness in Christ ..." (v.10)
For reading & meditation – Colossians 2:1-15

If, as we said yesterday, we have a faith in God which maintains we need God plus something else, the result will be that we will never discover God in all His fulness. In the "and" lies our greatest woe. If we omit the "and" we shall make some discoveries about God that will surprise us, and one of those surprises will be that He is perfectly capable of sustaining us in the most difficult situations. And we need not fear that by putting our trust fully in God we restrict our potential. As Augustine put it: "Thou hast formed us for Thyself and our hearts are restless till they find their rest in Thee."

When the Lord divided Canaan among the tribes of Israel, the Levites received no share of the land. God said: "I am your share and your inheritance" (Num. 18:20). Those words made the Levites richer than all their brethren, and this principle holds good for every child of God. The man or woman who knows God has the world's greatest treasure. He or she may not have many earthly treasures, but it will not make much difference, for in having Him they have everything that matters.

Imagine the Levites saying to God: "That's fine Lord, I want You to be my portion ... but what about that lake over there. And that mountain. Could we just have those?" Do we look at the Lord who promises to be our portion and find that He is sufficient? Or are we still caught up with the idea that we need God plus something else? If we do then we do not really know God. We simply know about Him.

FURTHER STUDY

Col. 1:1-29;
Eph. 3:19;
John 1:16

1. What was Paul's prayer for the Colossians and Ephesians?

2. What did John testify of Jesus?

Prayer

O Father, help me remember that I belong to You, the all-creative, all-sufficient God. Make this truth come alive for me, not just in my head but in my heart. Let it become a conviction, not just an opinion. In Jesus' Name I pray. Amen.

No other gods

"You shall have no other gods before me." (v.3)
For reading & meditation – Exodus 20:1-21

Continuing the thought we have been examining over the past two days – that God wants to be our sufficiency – we look today at the opening statement of the Ten Commandments.

Why did God say: "I am the Lord your God … You shall have no other gods before me"? And why does He still challenge us with that word when we want to make our gods of wood or stone? Of silver and gold? Of fame or fortune? The reason is that there *are* no other gods. We are fooling ourselves. We can give ourselves to them but they can't give themselves to us. Many of you will have come to the point (perhaps even today) when you discovered that the gods of this world are no gods. You pinned your hopes on something, gave yourself to it with the same energy as you would in worship, but it has let you down. This is how it is with the gods of this world.

I remember hearing Golda Meir, when she was Prime Minister of Israel, say: "The Jews have a fundamental problem with Moses. He led them through the wilderness for forty years and then brought them to the only place in the Middle East where there is no oil." When I heard her make that remark I thought to myself: "That's exactly why God did that – He wanted the Israelites to be dependent on Him, not on the earth's natural resources." So I ask you again: Do you look to the Lord who promises to be your inheritance, your portion, and see Him as sufficient? Or do you sometimes look to other gods? Let this truth sink deep into your soul – there are no other gods.

FURTHER STUDY

Ex. 3:1-21;
Gen. 15:1-21

1. What was God's response to Moses' first question?

2. What was God's response to Moses' second question?

Prayer

O God, forgive me when I have turned from You to other gods. You alone are God, and all life, individual and corporate, must finally bow the knee to You. I do so now gladly and willingly. Keep me bowed before You – always. In Jesus' Name. Amen.

God – the Enough!

"... 'I am God Almighty [El-Shaddai] ...' " (v.1)
For reading & meditation – Genesis 17:1-22

We have been seeing that the phrase "and the train of his robe filled the temple" taken from Isaiah's vision suggests to us that there is room for no other in this exalted place. God is all in all. The Hebrew term for God, "El Shaddai", means "God – the Enough!" I like the thought that underlies that name – the Enough – because it brings home the truth that there is no situation in which we will ever find ourselves where God will not be enough.

God is much more than enough, of course. His sufficiency so immeasurably surpasses our demands. Nevertheless, it is marvellously comforting to know that however much more than enough God is to meet our needs, He is at least enough; nothing less than that.

There are many things in the world of which we think we do not have enough – money, power, status, education, and so on. And it is generally assumed that if only it were possible to have a sufficiency of "things", satisfaction would immediately result. But that is not so. The real trouble is not that people do not have enough "things", but that "things" in themselves are not enough. The plain fact is that there is ultimately only one way in which the human heart can have enough, or to be more exact, one Being who is enough for men and women, and that is God! As Dr Henry Van Dyke expressed it: "There is absolutely nothing that man cannot do without – except God." Remember – God is Enough. Only He is sufficient for us; only He can truly satisfy our souls. He, and only He is enough.

FURTHER STUDY

Eph. 3:14-21;
2 Cor. 9:8;
Psa. 36:8;
John 10:10

1. What is the heart of the apostle's prayer?

2. What has God promised?

Prayer

O Father, save me from thinking that anything can ever be a substitute for You. Just as Your glory filled all the Temple in Isaiah's day, so let Your glory fill me – exclusively. In Jesus' Name I ask it. Amen.

An encounter with the holy One

"Who of us can dwell with the consuming fire?" (v.14)
For reading & meditation – Isaiah 33:10-24

We look now at the next section of Isaiah's vision: "Above him were seraphs, each with six wings: With two wings they covered their faces, with two they covered their feet, and with two they were flying" (Isa. 6:2).

Seraphs are heavenly beings who serve above the throne of God. The sixth chapter of Isaiah contains the only references to seraphs in Scripture, but many commentators link them with the "living creatures" described in Revelation 4:8. The Hebrew word for "seraphs" means "burning ones" or "noble ones" and their specific ministry is to lead the continuous worship at the throne of God. One commentator suggests that they are described as "burning ones" because they are illuminated with the glory that comes from God's holy presence. He says: "It is not their own glory they display. It is rather a reflected glory – the glory of incandescent eternal holiness."

Ancient Christian writers often likened a close encounter with God to entering a danger zone. What did they mean? A contemporary author interprets it thus: "If we are sinful and God is holy, if God is a fire and we are straw, how can it be safe for us to enter His presence? The fact is, it is not safe. It is exceedingly dangerous." Why dangerous? The word "dangerous" is used because we differ from seraphs in that they are pure and we are not. Hence, the closer we get to God the more we run the risk of all that is unlike Him being consumed and destroyed. But when you think of it – isn't that the very reason why we ought to yearn to draw close to Him?

FURTHER STUDY

1 Cor. 3:10-17;
2 Cor. 4:18;
Heb. 12:27-29

1. What will be revealed with fire?

2. What will God remove by shaking?

Prayer

O Father, I see that this is something I cannot have too much of – an encounter with the holy One. I cannot be too much like You or have too much of Your holiness. Draw me, for I want to get as close as I can to Your holy fire. In Jesus' Name. Amen.

Lost & found

"…let us be thankful, and so worship God acceptably with reverence and awe …" (v.28)

For reading & meditation – Hebrews 12:14-29

We are told that the seraphs who stood above the throne in Isaiah's vision had six wings: "With two wings they covered their faces, with two they covered their feet, and with two they were flying" (Isa. 6:2). Why cover their faces? Clearly they dared not look upon this One whom they were worshipping. The implication here is that what we do for God must be done with reverence.

One of the tragedies of modern-day Christianity is that quietly and almost unnoticed we are losing the spirit of reverence. Holy things are becoming common and are losing their sacredness. This is not happening everywhere, of course, but there is no doubt in my mind that the cynicism of the age is making its impact on the Church. If we do not resist it, the generations that follow will feel its effect in a hundred different ways.

I remember, as a teenager attending a Christian youth camp and taking part along with some others in a humorous "send up" of angels. The youth director hit the roof. He said: "You young people have trivialised something that is deeply sacred. I doubt whether you will have a correct view of angelic ministry ever again." He was right. Deep within me there has been a cynicism toward the ministry of angels for several decades, and it was only quite recently, while in Malaysia, that it was overcome. I was privileged to experience some awesome supernatural encounters that convinced me of the ministry of angels. It took several decades to undo what a few flippant moments had etched into my heart and mind. We dare not lose our reverence for holy things.

FURTHER STUDY

1 Pet. 1:1-17; 2:17;
Psa. 33:8

1. How are we to live our lives?

2. What are all the people of the world to do?

Prayer

O God, help me develop respect and reverence for holy things, but not to become over-spiritual about these matters and bore my friends with my solemnity and heaviness. That is not healthy either. Keep me balanced. In Jesus' Name. Amen.

"God's beautiful people"

"How beautiful ... are the feet of those who bring good news ..." (v. 7)

For reading & meditation – Isaiah 52:1-15

We continue thinking about the seraphs who stood above the throne in Isaiah's vision. We saw yesterday that with two wings they covered their faces, and now we consider the fact that with two they covered their feet. What is the significance of this? The implication here is that what is to be done for God must be done with humility.

The passage before us today draws our attention to the truth that the feet of God's heralds have a special importance, presumably because they speed the messengers of God's love on their way. Someone has pointed out that the only thing that is said to be "beautiful" about the followers of the Lord in Scripture is not their faces, or their figures, but their feet! That ought to keep us humble – if nothing else does. When worldly individuals talk about "beautiful" people they usually mean film, television or pop stars who live hedonistic lives – here today and burnt out tomorrow. God has His "beautiful" people too – those who carry the good news of the gospel wherever they go.

But the seraphs seem to be saying: "Oh, don't look at our feet. We want to focus the attention not on ourselves but on the Lord whom we

are serving. This is true humility. Humble believers, while glorying in their task, seek to turn attention away from self to the Saviour and maintain the attitude which John the Baptist demonstrated when he said: "He must increase, but I must decrease" (John 3:30, AV). We should never forget that as far as our service for Christ is concerned, our task is not to draw attention to ourselves but to Him.

FURTHER STUDY

Matt. 18:1-9;
Prov. 22:4; 29:23;
Rom. 12:3

1. Who is the greatest in the kingdom of heaven?

2. How are we to think of ourselves?

Prayer

My Father and my God, grant in all my service to You that I will be hidden behind the cross, and the voice that people hear will not be mine alone, but the still small voice of the Holy Spirit speaking to them. In Christ's Name I pray. Amen.

Pursuing with passion

"The sorrows of those will increase who run after other gods." (v. 4)

For reading & meditation – Psalm 16:1-11

Now that we have examined the fact that the seraphs in Isaiah's vision had two wings covering their faces and two wings covering their feet, we focus on the phrase that says "with two they were *flying*". The implication here is that our service for God must be done with urgency.

As I considered the verse that is before us today, which points out how the ungodly chase after their gods, I thought how different it is with Christians. Few chase after God; they choose rather to saunter after Him. Christian service, generally speaking, is characterised more by lethargy than urgency, more by indolence than inspiration, and more by fitfulness than fervour. We say: "Yes, Lord, I'm available to You, providing it's convenient, providing it doesn't cost me anything." Contrast this with the attitude of people who serve the gods of sex, pleasure, fame, money, and so on. There is hardly a demand their gods make upon them that seems to be too much. They are willing to give up sleep, stay out until the early hours, and spend any amount they have to in order to satisfy their gods. Many Christians are like the young man who told his girlfriend: "Darling, I would go through fire and water for you." Then a few minutes later he said: "I'll see you tomorrow night if it isn't raining."

The seraphs of Isaiah's vision remind us that what we do for God must be done with urgency and passion. There is something terribly wrong when our Christian lives lack those qualities. God moves toward us with urgency and passion; do we move with urgency and passion toward Him?

FURTHER STUDY

2 Cor. 5:1-15;
Psa. 42:1-2

1. What did Christ's love do to Paul?

2. How did the psalmist describe his spiritual desire?

Prayer

O God, how can I ever thank You enough for pursuing me with urgency and passion? It meant so much to You to win me to Yourself. Grant that my passion might match Your passion, if not in degree, in kind. In Jesus' Name. Amen.

Our primary task

*"Ascribe to the Lord the glory due to his name; worship the
Lord in the splendour of his holiness." (v.2)*
For reading & meditation – Psalm 29:1-11

We come now to a marvellous section of Isaiah's vision where he
speaks of the seraphs in this way: "… they were calling to one
another: 'Holy, holy, holy is the Lord Almighty; the whole earth is full of
his glory.' At the sound of their voices the doorposts and thresholds
shook and the temple was filled with smoke" (Isa. 6:3-4).

What a moment this must have been for Isaiah as he watched the seraphs darting and hovering above the throne, and listened to them calling
to one another and worshipping God with voices so strong that the
sound shook the Temple! Is it any wonder that echoes of the time he
spent in the Temple are heard in almost every one of the later chapters of
his prophecy? The lofty throne, the attending seraphs and the words
they utter all combine to spell out one message: worship is the highest
function of any of God's created beings.

What is worship? The essential meaning of the word in both Old and
New Testaments is that of reverential service – a truth we see illustrated
by the conduct of the winged seraphs above the eternal throne. Our present-day English word "worship" has evolved from the Anglo-Saxon
weorthscipe which means to give worth to someone or
something. Worship can best be understood by thinking of the word in this way: worth-ship. The worship
of God, then, is attributing worth to Him – and only
Him.

The primary reason for our existence on this earth
is to worship God. When we understand all that is
involved in this then our faith will throb with a new
power and prove itself sufficient for any task.

FURTHER STUDY

Psa. 84:1-12;
95:1-7;
1 Chron. 16:29

1. What did the
psalmist say is
better?

2. How are we to
come in worship?

Prayer

Father, I ask myself in Your presence: How much of my life is spent in worship?
How much time do I give to thinking of You and only You? Help me draw near to
You, not to ask for things, but just to worship You. In Jesus' Name I pray. Amen.

"A constant pageant of worship"

"… and serve him day and night in his temple …" (v.15)
For reading & meditation – Revelation 7:1-17

We pick up from where we left off yesterday when we considered the nature and importance of worship. We must be careful not to fall into the trap of differentiating between worship and service, and thinking to ourselves that when we kneel in private we are at worship and when active in the church – teaching, preaching, or being of some practical help – we are then engaged in service. All service is worship, and all worship is service.

This thought is brought out not only in the symbolism of the seraphs whom Isaiah saw above the throne but it is found also in the passage before us today. In the book of Revelation heaven is described as a place that is filled with worship, but it is also a place where the saints "serve … day and night". I love the story of the young housewife who, having been converted to Christ and realising that everything she did was an act of worship, put a sign over her kitchen sink which read: "Divine service conducted here three times a day." Later she saw that her acts of worship were not confined to washing the dishes but included everything. So she took down the sign because it was too limiting.

Someone asked a friend of mine once: "Where do you worship?" He replied "I worship in Woolworths, in the bank, in my car, in the supermarket … My life is a constant pageant of worship." The person got the message. Worship is not something we keep for special occasions or do at certain times and periods. We worship both day and night.

FURTHER STUDY

Rom. 12:1-8;
John 4:24

1. What is to be our spiritual act of worship?

2. How are we to worship God?

Prayer

Father, forgive me that I have been thinking of worship as something that goes on only at certain times or seasons. Help me to worship You everywhere and in everything. May my life too be a constant pageant of worship. In Jesus' Name. Amen.

Worship, praise and thanksgiving

"Yet you are enthroned as the Holy One; you are the praise of Israel." (v.3)

For reading & meditation – Psalm 22:1-11

We ask ourselves now: What is the scriptural relationship between worship, praise and thanksgiving?

All the biblical words for worship, whether in Hebrew or Greek, indicate an attitude of the heart or a posture of the body. Worship starts as being spiritual but also affects us physically. This is why devout Jews rock backward and forward when they pray; they regard worship as both physical and spiritual. The Bible describes such physical postures as lying face downwards before the Lord, kneeling in His presence, or standing before Him with uplifted hands as worship. Praise, on the other hand, has to do with utterance, and while it is not exclusive to our lips (we can praise God in our hearts), it is generally related to the words of our mouth. When we come to thanksgiving we come again to the thought of utterance, the difference being this: we praise God for who He is, but we thank Him for what He does. These are only general categories, of course, and we must not think in rigid terms when we praise, give thanks, or worship. Nothing could be worse than saying to yourself: "I have spent enough time in praise now. Perhaps I should spend an equal time in thanksgiving."

FURTHER STUDY

1 Thess. 5:1-18;
Psa. 100:4; 107:22

1. What is the will of God for us?

2. In what circumstances are we to give thanks?

All three words relate very much to three characteristics of God – again, speaking generally. In worship we relate to God's holiness. In thanksgiving we relate to God's goodness. In praise we relate to God's greatness. Although the distinction between these three words can be clearly seen in Scripture, it must not be regarded as hard and fast. The three are tributaries that flow together to form one great river.

Prayer

Father, may all these three – worship, thanksgiving and praise – be present in my life not in a mechanical way but in a natural way. All I want, dear Lord, is for You to be glorified in me. Help me to do just that. In Jesus' Name. Amen.

"The joyful exchange"

"Give, and it will be given to you." (v.38)
For reading & meditation – Luke 6:27-38

Before leaving the subject of worship, we must come to grips with the question of why God requires us to worship Him. Many struggle with this thought, especially in the early days of their Christian life. I can remember as a young Christian wondering: Why does God insist on us worshipping Him? Is it because He has an ego problem?

One of those who grappled with this problem was C.S. Lewis. He recalled how at one stage he thought God was really saying: "What I want most is to be told I am good and great." He came to see, however, that, in asking for our worship, God has in mind our enjoyment more than His own. He wrote: "In commanding us to worship Him, God is inviting us to enjoy Him." He went on to point out that, because of the great respect God has for every human will, He will not force Himself upon us. He is, therefore, unable to give Himself to us until we first give ourselves to Him.

The law of giving and receiving is fundamental, and relates just as much to God as it does to us. As we go through the door of giving ourselves to God in worship we find that God comes through that same door and gives Himself to us. God's insistence that we worship Him is not really a demand at all but an offer – an offer to share Himself with us. When God asks us to worship Him, He is asking us to fulfil the deepest longing in Himself, which is His passionate desire to give Himself to us. It is what Martin Luther called "the joyful exchange".

FURTHER STUDY

Matt. 10:1-8;
Acts 20:35

1. What were the disciples to do?

2. Why?

Prayer

O Father, how can I thank You sufficiently for coming through the door of Your own self-giving to stand at the door of my heart? You have given Yourself to me; now I give myself to You. This is truly a "a joyful exchange". Amen.

The one thing

"I am the Lord, your Holy One, Israel's Creator, your King."
(v.15)

For reading & meditation – Isaiah 43:14-28

We continue focusing our thoughts on Isaiah's vision of the worshipping seraphs above the throne and today we ask ourselves: What is the one thing above all others that true worshippers think of when approaching God? His Almightiness? His goodness? His faithfulness? The answer is: His holiness! You have only to comb the record of the Scriptures – particularly the Old Testament – to discover that those who were closest to the Lord thought more about His holiness than about any other attribute.

What exactly do we mean when we talk about the holiness of God? Theologians tell us that, strictly speaking, we should not think of divine holiness as an attribute but as the essential ingredient that holds God together. "Holiness," says J. Muilenburg, "is the distinctive mark and signature of the divine. More than any other, the term 'holiness' gives expression to the essential nature of the sacred. It is therefore to be understood, not as one attribute among other attributes, but as the innermost reality to which all others are related." These are powerful words because they point out that holiness is the way God is. Because He is holy, all His attributes are holy. Whatever we think of as belonging to God must be thought of as holy. This is why theologians insist that, whenever we talk about the love of God, we talk about it as *holy* love. If we remove God's love from the thought of holiness we can easily come out with sentimentalism, and a clear example of that can be seen in the vapid theorising about God that goes on in some of the liberal churches of our day.

FURTHER STUDY

Rev. 15:1-8;
1 Pet. 1:15;
Lev. 11:44-45

1. What did the angels sing?

2. What is the standard God requires?

Prayer

O Father, as I survey the wonder of Your holiness I too, like the worshipping seraphs, want to join in the refrain and say: "Holy, holy, holy is the Lord Almighty. The whole earth is full of Your glory." I worship Your holy Name. Amen.

The divine emphasis

"I am the Lord … your God; therefore be holy, because I am holy." (v.45)

For reading & meditation – Leviticus 11:26-47

Did it surprise you to discover yesterday that the holiness of God is emphasised more than any other aspect of His nature? Stephen Charnock, a renowned theologian, says this: "God is oftener styled Holy than Almighty and set forth by this part of His dignity more than by any other. This is more fixed on as an epithet to His name than any other. You never find expressed 'His mighty name' or 'His wise name' but His *great* name and most of all His *holy* name." He goes on to make a statement that I pray will make as deep an impression upon you as it did upon me:

"As it seems to challenge an excellency above all His other perfections, so it is the glory of all the rest; as it is the glory of the Godhead, so it is the glory of every perfection of the Godhead; as His power is the strength of them, so His holiness is the beauty of them; as all would be weak without almightiness to back them, so all would be uncomely without holiness to adorn them. Should this be sullied, all the rest would lose their honour, as at the same instant the sun should lose its light, it would lose its heat, its strength, its generative and quickening virtue. As sincerity is the lustre of every grace in a Christian, so is purity the splendour of every attribute in the Godhead. His justice is a holy justice. His wisdom a holy wisdom. His arm of power 'a holy arm' (Psa. 98:1). His truth or promise a 'holy promise' (Psa. 105:42). His name which signifies all attributes in conjunction is 'holy' (Psa. 103:1)."

FURTHER STUDY

Rom. 1:1-7; Ex. 16:23; Deut. 26:15; 1 Chron. 29:3; Neh. 11:1; 2 Thess. 1:10

1. What other things are described as holy?

2. Would you describe yourself as

Prayer

O Father, if ever Your Church needed a fresh vision of Your holiness it is today. Fill our pulpits with prophets and teachers who have a knowledge of the Holy. This we ask in Christ's peerless and precious Name. Amen.

"The attribute of attributes"

"… 'Holy, holy, holy is the Lord God Almighty, who was, and is, and is to come'." (v.8)

For reading & meditation – Revelation 4:1-11

We see from the threefold cry of the winged seraphs – "Holy, holy holy" (Isa. 6:3) – that the holiness of God is celebrated as no other attribute is celebrated before the throne of heaven. God Himself singles out this perfection to be honoured in a way that shows it to be, as John Howe put it, "the attribute of attributes".

The cry of the seraphs is significant because this is the only place in Scripture, apart from the passage before us today, where the word "holy" is repeated three times. Emphasis in Hebrew (as in English) is sometimes conveyed by repeating a word. Jesus, you remember, often used this device when He introduced a subject by saying "Verily, verily, I say unto you …". But the word "holy" is repeated not just twice but three times – the implication being, we are in the presence of something profound. And indeed we are – the ineffable holiness of God.

Try something with me. Read slowly through the following texts, and see what happens. "Who will not fear you, O Lord, and bring glory to your name? For you alone are holy" (Rev. 15:4). "Who among the gods is like you, O Lord? Who is like you – majestic in holiness, awesome in glory, working wonders?" (Ex. 15:11). "For I am God, and not man – the Holy One among you" (Hosea 11:9). "'Do not be afraid, O worm Jacob … for I myself will help you,' declares the Lord, your Redeemer, the Holy One of Israel" (Isa. 41:14). Is it not a fact that the more you make yourself aware of God's holiness the more honour and respect you want to give Him?

FURTHER STUDY

Matt. 6:5-13;
Luke 1:49;
Psa. 30:4; 105:3

1. What is the first thing Christ focused on in His prayer?

2. What are we to glory in?

Prayer

O Lord my God, there is none like You in heaven above or in the earth beneath; glorious in holiness, mighty in splendour, and wondrous in majesty. I worship You my Father. Words die on my lips but my heart is Yours for ever. Amen.

Holiness is healthiness

"... let us purify ourselves from everything that contaminates body and spirit, perfecting holiness out of reverence for God." (v. 1)

For reading & meditation – 2 Corinthians 7:1-16

We said a few days ago that when we study the Scriptures, particularly the Old Testament, we find that those who got closest to God thought more of His holiness than any other thing. Why should this be? I think in the nature of things it cannot be any other way, because, more than anything else, God wants us to be holy. Over and over again in the Bible we are told: "Be holy even as I am holy." We are not directed to be omnipotent (all-powerful) or omniscient (all-wise) as God is, but we are to be holy. This is the prime way of honouring God. We do not glorify Him by eloquent expressions or pompous service, but by aspiring to converse with Him with unstained spirits and live to Him in living *like* Him.

Are you seeking to be holy? God has made holiness the moral condition necessary to the health of His universe. Sin's temporary presence in the world only accentuates this. Whatever is holy is healthy, and evil is a moral sickness that must ultimately end in death. The formation of the language itself suggests this, the English word "holy" deriving from the Anglo-Saxon *halig* meaning "well" or "whole". To be whole in Christian terms means to be holy. Can you say "I am holy – truly holy"? I am afraid I can't. I don't think any honest Christian would say "Yes" to that question. But neither would any honest Christian ignore these solemn words: "Make every effort to live in peace with all men and to be holy; without holiness no-one will see the Lord" (Heb. 12:14).

FURTHER STUDY

Luke 1:67-80;
2 Pet. 3:11;
2 Cor. 7:1

1. Why has God raised up a horn of salvation?

2. What kind of people ought we to be?

Prayer

O Father, help me to be as concerned for the moral health of the universe as You are. But more, help me to focus first on my own moral health and to be rid of all in my life that is contrary to You and Your nature. In Jesus' Name I ask it. Amen.

The divine X-ray

"The Israelites said to Moses, 'We shall die! We are lost, we are all lost!' " (v.12)

For reading & meditation – Numbers 17:1-13

We move on now to consider the fact that Isaiah's revolutionary vision of the holiness of God results in him crying out in great agony of soul: "Woe to me … I am ruined! For I am a man of unclean lips, and I live among a people of unclean lips …" (Isa. 6:5).

The thing that strikes Isaiah as he stands in the presence of God is not just the ineffable holiness of God, but, by contrast, his own personal depravity. Up to this moment Isaiah probably thought of himself as a good, upright, moral man. And no doubt he was. If someone was to compare the young Isaiah's character with that of most of the other men and women in Israel, I feel confident that he would have stood out head and shoulders above most of them. However, Isaiah is not being compared to the creatures whom God had made; he is being compared to the Creator Himself. He is face to face with the Holy One of Israel. Suddenly, all his goodness and everything he had esteemed falls to pieces, and he stands naked, exposed and afraid.

I have always thought it interesting that the people who are farthest away from the Lord are those who are impressed with their own goodness, while those who are closest to Him seem to be more conscious of their sin. Why, I wonder? Is it because the white light of God's holiness acts like an X-ray that enables people to see more clearly what is going on at the core of their beings? If so, then how vital it is that sin-sick human beings have an encounter with a holy God.

FURTHER STUDY

Eph. 5:1-20;
1 John 1:5-7;
2 Pet. 1:19

1. How are we to live?

2. What are we to pay attention to?

Prayer

O God, let the X-ray of Your holiness reveal the insidious disease of sin that is deep within me. Show up the pride and arrogance that lies hidden in my nature. Make me more like You, dear Lord. In Jesus' Name. Amen.

Invest now!

"But just as he who called you is holy, so be holy in all you do." (v.15)

For reading & meditation – 1 Peter 1:3-25

We acknowledged yesterday that those who see the holiness of God most clearly see themselves most clearly. The white light of God's holiness is like an X-ray that enables them to discern the sin that is deeply hidden in their nature. We all know in an intellectual way that to catch sight of God's ineffable holiness would make us conscious of our own sin, but how many of us are willing to draw near enough to God for Him to show us what His holiness is like? It is one thing to imagine what it might be like; it is another thing to experience it. Dr John White, in *The Shattered Mirror*, puts the same thought in this way: "We can get some idea of the matter by imagining what it would be like to find ourselves, say, at a royal garden party, surrounded by impeccably dressed royal guests, while we were still unwashed and wearing the old, rough clothes in which we had just finished gardening. The difference between that imaginary experience and Isaiah's encounter with God is not merely one of degree, but a quality we could know only by experiencing it ourselves."

How can we experience it ourselves? We can begin by looking at the nature of God's holiness as outlined in His Word. Then continue by waiting before God in fervent, believing prayer and inviting God to reveal Himself to you. This takes time, of course, but any time spent with God is spiritual investment. But remember, a vision of God and His holiness will be emotionally overwhelming. It will cause you not only to cry out "Holy, holy, holy," but also, "Woe to me! I am ruined!"

FURTHER STUDY

Luke 18:9-14;
1 Cor. 10:12;
Prov. 28:26

1. What did Jesus teach in this parable?

2. What did Paul warn the Corinthians?

Prayer

O Father, I am afraid as I draw near, yet I draw near because I am afraid. Show me even more clearly that the time I spend with You will yield more than it costs. Whatever sacrifice is needed, help me make it. In Jesus' Name. Amen.

Fearing for one's life!

"Anyone who even comes near the tabernacle of the Lord will die." (v.13)

For reading & meditation – Numbers 17:1-13

Today we ask ourselves: What did Isaiah mean when, following the vision of God's holiness, he said: "I am a man of unclean lips, and I live among a people of unclean lips …" (Isa. 6:5)? Some commentators believe he was confessing here to a struggle with profanity. Probably a more likely explanation is that Isaiah is acknowledging his unworthiness to be a prophet – the spoken word being a prophet's business.

Which of these is the true explanation we cannot be certain, but what we do know for sure is this: when Isaiah saw the holiness of God he feared for his life. This is evident in his statement: "My eyes have seen the King, the Lord Almighty" (Isa. 6:5). Why should such seemingly innocuous words reflect a fear for his life? To understand what is being said here we need to look at today's text once again: "Anyone who even comes near the tabernacle of the Lord will die." It was a well-known fact in Israel that no one could get close to God and live. Anyone who saw God expected to die immediately. In fact, God said on one occasion: "You cannot see my face, for no-one may see me and live" (Ex. 33:20).

Perhaps now we can understand something of the concern that reverberated beneath the words: "My eyes have seen the King, the Lord Almighty." Isaiah's cry reflects much more than an ordinary conviction of sin; it is one of unspeakable horror. He had seen the King, the Lord Almighty. Now he must die! But does he? No, for as we shall see, God is not only a God of holiness – He is also the God of grace.

FURTHER STUDY

Ex. 33:12-21;
1 Tim. 1:17;
6:11-16

1. What was Moses' prayer?
2. How did Paul describe the Lord to Timothy?

Prayer

Father, help me see even more clearly the principle that is at work here, namely that before I can be saved I must admit my lostness – my utter helplessness. I freely confess, Father, that salvation is all of grace. And I am deeply, deeply thankful. Amen.

"Surprised by joy!"

"For it is by grace you have been saved ..." (v.8)
For reading & meditation – Ephesians 2:1-22

O ne thing ought to be clear by now – the more we know of God the more we will discover that He is holy, and that we are unholy. It doesn't hurt us to know that; it helps us. Something occurs in the contrast that prepares us to open ourselves more fully to His grace. Listen to how Tozer put it: "No one can know the true grace of God who has not first known the fear of God. The presence of the Divine has always brought fear to the hearts of sinful men. Always there was something about any manifestation of God that ... struck them with a terror more than natural. Until we have been gripped by that nameless terror which results when an unholy creature is suddenly confronted by that One who is the holiest of all, we are not likely to be much affected by the doctrine of love and grace."

How illuminating are those words. It isn't that God delights in striking fear into our hearts by the revelation of His holiness; it is just that being who He is, He cannot reveal Himself to us without this happening. But always His mercy and grace come to our aid to sustain us and cleanse us. Watch now as God moves toward Isaiah, not in judgment, but in grace. In the vision He inspires one of the seraphs to take a live coal from the altar, place it on the prophet's lips and declare: "Your guilt is taken away and your sin atoned for." Isaiah does not tell us what effect the seraph's action had on him. But if it was anything like the experience I had when He cleansed me then Isaiah would have been, as C.S. Lewis expressed it, "surprised by joy".

FURTHER STUDY

Titus 3:1-8;
Lam. 3:22-23;
Micah 7:18

1. What is the basis of our salvation?

2. What does God delight to do?

Prayer

Thank You, my Father, that I too have been "surprised by joy". When I expected to be consigned to hell You showed me the way to heaven. How can I ever sufficiently thank You for Your grace? All honour and glory be to You for ever. Amen.

Forgiven!

"He himself bore our sins in his body on the tree …" (v.24)
For reading & meditation – 1 Peter 2:11-25

We must spend at least one more day reflecting on the wonder of the grace and forgiveness that flowed toward Isaiah at that significant moment in the Temple. Listen to the words once more: "See, this has touched your lips; your guilt is taken away and your sin atoned for" (Isa. 6:7).

In Christian circles we talk so easily about forgiveness. But do we really understand what it cost God to forgive? David Seamands points out that forgiveness is always at great cost to the forgiving one. He says: "When someone hurts us and we forgive them we take the hurt and indignation we feel and turn it back upon ourselves. Instead of putting it upon them we bear it in ourselves." Some people require of others that they be put on probation before forgiveness is given. I knew a man who, whenever his wife hurt him, would make her almost beg for days for his forgiveness. How different is real forgiveness. No marriage can properly operate without it – and no friendship either. Forgiveness means taking your own pride, your own indignation, your own hurt, holding it to your heart and quenching it in the flame of your love. This is what God does with us when He forgives.

We are now moving beyond Isaiah's vision to consider the genius of the gospel, namely that in God there is not only holiness but forgiveness also. Divine forgiveness, however, is costly. It cost God His only Son. Our text for today puts it powerfully when it says: "He himself bore our sins in his body on the tree." Can anything in earth or heaven be more wonderful?

FURTHER STUDY

1 John 1:5-10;
Psa. 130:4;
Eph. 1:7;
Isa. 43:25

1. How do we deceive ourselves?

2. What is the condition for receiving forgiveness?

Prayer

O God, nothing that anyone has done or can do against me compares to what I have done against You. Yet You have forgiven me. Help me now to forgive others, and to forgive graciously, not grudgingly. In Jesus' Name I ask it. Amen.

"An ounce of experience"

"Some time later God tested Abraham. He said to him, 'Abraham!' 'Here I am,' he replied." (v.1)

For reading & meditation – Genesis 22:1-19

As soon as Isaiah has been cleansed, he hears God's voice crying out: "Whom shall I send? And who will go for us?" Isaiah immediately responds: "Here am I. Send me!" (Isa. 6:8).

It is always a mystery to me that God wants stubborn and recalcitrant human beings on His team when He has ranks of angels who delight to do His bidding. But when you think of it, angels are limited by the one thing that is needful for God's ambassadors on earth – experience. Angels could put God's truth more eloquently, and present the divine arguments more powerfully, but they know nothing of the experience of grace, at least subjectively. They witness it at work in our lives, but they have never experienced it at work in themselves.

An old saying goes like this: "An ounce of experience is worth a ton of theory." How true. I can almost guarantee that the person who influenced you to come to Christ was himself or herself someone who had experienced the grace of God. I know people have been converted when listening to other people talk about the gospel who were not converted themselves. However, that is more the exception than the rule. The implication behind the words "Who will go for us?" is that the task on earth has to be done by the men and women on earth. Isaiah didn't hesitate. What about you? Is God calling you to some task, and you feel hesitant and uncertain? Perhaps it is because you have not had a powerful enough vision of the Lord. Those who see Him – really see Him – cannot help but say: "Here am I. Send me!"

1 Cor. 1:18-31;
John 15:16;
Acts 9:15;
James 2:5

1. What sort of people has God chosen?

2. What did the Lord say to Ananias?

Prayer

O God, day by day I am seeing more of Your glory, but give me an overwhelming vision of Yourself that will shatter every one of my self-concerns. Help me say in response to whatever You are calling me to: "Here am I. Send me!" Amen.

"The strange predicament of God"

"The Lord sent me to prophesy against this house and this city … " (v.12)

For reading & meditation – Jeremiah 26:1-16

We spend another day reflecting on the cry of God: "Whom shall I send. And who will go for us?" Someone has described this as "the strange predicament of God" – the Almighty asking help of human beings. Probably nothing is more difficult to understand as regards Christian truth than this, that the Almighty God, who holds the world in the hollow of His hand, seeks to enlist our support in relaying His truth.

Did this confuse Isaiah, I wonder? He had seen a vision of the majesty of God, and now this Almighty God was asking for Isaiah's co-operation. Why does He suddenly appear to be so powerless? Well, it isn't because God is powerless that He asks our help. He chooses to do so because that is His way. He wants us to be involved with Him in redeeming the world.

But we ask again: Why has God tied His own hands in this way? What is His rationale for wanting us on His team? John Wesley is reported to have said: "God does nothing in the world redemptively except through prayer." He seems to be saying in this statement that in bringing about redemptive changes in the universe, God moves, and only moves, through the prayers of His people. These are staggering words of Wesley's but I am in agreement with them fully and wholeheartedly. God could do His redemptive work here on earth without us, but He chooses not to because He wants it to be a team effort. Does that mean that if you and I do not make ourselves available to Him then some things just might not get done? I wonder.

FURTHER STUDY

Haggai 2:20-23;
1 Pet. 2:1-10

1. What was Haggai to tell Zerubbabel?

2. How does Peter describe God's people?

Prayer

Father, it humbles me to think that You want me on Your team. I am overwhelmed by the invitation, but my heart cries out "Yes, Yes, Yes!" Use me in any way You want to and to go anywhere You want me to go. Here I am. Send me!

A call to failure!

*"Hear this, you ... who have eyes but do not see, who have
ears but do not hear." (v.21)*

For reading & meditation – Jeremiah 5:18-31

Once Isaiah has responded to the call of God with the words "Here
am I. Send me!" the task he has been set is given in these words:
"Go and tell this people: 'Be ever hearing, but never understanding; be
ever seeing, but never perceiving.' Make the heart of this people calloused; make their ears dull and close their eyes. Otherwise they might
see with their eyes, hear with their ears, understand with their hearts,
and turn and be healed!" (Isa. 6:9-10). What a depressing commission.
This is none other than a call to failure! God clearly tells Isaiah that his
message will have the ironic but justly deserved effect of hardening the
callous hearts of the rebellious people of Judah, thus rendering the warn-
ings of judgment sure.

How do you think Isaiah felt about the fact that after offering himself
as a messenger of God he is told that his message will have a hardening
rather than a softening effect? He is given not so much a saving word as
a searing word. Whatever he felt, we know one thing for certain – he set
out to faithfully preach the word he had been given.

How many of us, I wonder, would respond to God
with the words "Here I am. Send me!" if we thought
God would commission us to failure? Speaking personally, I think I would have a big struggle with that.
When the chips are down, few of us are willing to do
what God says when we don't know whether the outcome will be successful or not. Perhaps it is because
we don't know God well enough. We have seen Him
only in part.

FURTHER STUDY

Matt. 26:36-45;
6:10; Rom. 6:13

*1. How did Jesus
respond to what
seemed a path to
failure?*

*2. What do we need
to continually echo
in the Lord's Prayer?*

Prayer

O God, I am Your disciple, but sometimes I am afraid to follow where You lead me.
Help me do Your bidding whatever the outcome. And help me evaluate success not
by what my senses say, but by what You say. In Jesus' Name. Amen.

No excuse

"You will be ever hearing but never understanding; you will be ever seeing but never perceiving." (v.14)

For reading & meditation – Matthew 13:1-17

How are we to understand the strange words God spoke to Isaiah that we looked at yesterday: "Make the heart of this people calloused; make their ears dull … close their eyes"?

The full flavour of the Hebrew language is drawn upon to describe the condition of those who harden their hearts against the Word of the Lord. We have to understand that the gospel is not only good news but also bad news. Good news to those who receive it; bad news to those who reject it. The gospel heard and accepted is life; the gospel heard and refused is death. As Dr Martyn Lloyd-Jones put it: "The same sun that melts ice, hardens clay." It is interesting that these words of Isaiah are quoted by Jesus in our reading today, and they are applied by Him to the people of His time. In fact, these words of Isaiah (in part) are found in every one of the four Gospels. The apostle Paul also quotes these words in the last chapter of the Acts of the Apostles, when explaining that God was turning the focus away from Israel to the Gentiles, and outlining the fact that, unlike the stubborn Israelites, the Gentiles "will listen" (Acts 28:28).

FURTHER STUDY

Rom. 1:18-23;
John 15:22

1. Why does Romans say that people are without excuse?

2. Why did Jesus say that people are without excuse?

Now, it is important to realise that neither God in Isaiah 6:9 nor Jesus in the passage before us is saying that some hearers will not understand but, rather, that those who are not willing to hear the Word of the Lord will find the truth hidden from them. But why preach the gospel to those who will not receive it? It is to expose and highlight their hard-hearted resistance in such a way that no one will be able to say they did not hear, and so that they will be absolutely without excuse when judgment comes.

Prayer

O Father, I see even more clearly that Your Word is not only a saving Word but a searing Word; it heals but also hardens. Save me from allowing my own feelings to hinder its accomplishment – positively or negatively. In Jesus' Name. Amen.

One ray of hope

57

"… there is hope for a tree: If it is cut down, it will sprout again …" (v.7)

For reading & meditation – Job 14:1-12

As we draw to the close of the great passage in Isaiah 6 we examine the final words: "Then I said, 'For how long, O Lord?' … 'Until the cities lie ruined and without inhabitant, until the houses are left deserted and field ruined and ravaged, until the Lord has sent everyone far away and the land is utterly forsaken. And though a tenth remains in the land, it will again be laid waste. But as the terebinth and oak leave stumps when they are cut down, so the holy seed will be the stump in the land' " (Isa. 6:11-13).

Clearly Isaiah is going to witness Israel becoming like a wasteland. He has a long hard job ahead of him, prophesying to a people who, in the main, just do not want to hear. There is one ray of hope which we see in the last phrase of the chapter. *The Living Bible* puts it most effectively: "Yet a tenth – a remnant – will survive; and though Israel is invaded again and again and destroyed, yet Israel will be like a tree cut down, whose stump still lives to grow again."

When would the people listen? Only after they had come to the end and had nowhere to turn but to God. This would happen when the land was destroyed by invading armies and the people taken into captivity. The remnant referred to are those who either remained in the land after the captivity, or those who returned from Babylon to rebuild Jerusalem.

Rom. 9:22-10:1;
11:1-36

1. What has been the result of Israel's unbelief?

2. What was Paul's prayer for the Israelites?

Oh, why don't we listen to God? Will we, like Israel, pursue our own paths and come back to Him only when we have nowhere left to turn? Is God speaking to you about this today? If so, consider what He may be telling you and obey Him while there is time.

Prayer

O Father, when will I learn that Your way is the only sure way. Forgive me for the times when I prefer my way to Your way, and kill within me all those desires that put self-interest before Your interests. In Jesus' Name I ask it. Amen.

Enjoying majority status!

"So too, at the present time there is a remnant chosen by grace." (v.5)

For reading & meditation – Romans 11:1-12

We linger a little longer on the last two sentences of Isaiah 6: "And though a tenth remains in the land, it will again be laid waste. But as the terebinth and oak leave stumps when they are cut down, so the holy seed will be the stump in the land."

The prophet is being told that Israel will become a sick society and will finish up like a wasteland, but there will be a remnant who will hold on to God and be faithful. He is told also that there will be one tree left, indeed, one stump, and out of that stump will come a new tree! Even a felled tree leaves a stump behind which may produce fresh growth. The phrase "the holy seed" refers, without doubt, to the coming of the Messiah, the One who would redeem Israel and extend the offer of salvation beyond its borders to the whole world.

We should never be concerned that those who uphold God's cause always seem to be in the minority. Those who were truly spiritual were in the minority in Old Testament times and in New Testament times too. I am not an alarmist, but I have to say that I see a parallel between Isaiah's day and the day in which we live. What a state we are in at the present moment – and things are destined to get worse. But God has His remnant in this age as He has had in every age. If you are a committed follower of Jesus Christ then you are part of that remnant. And God has always used a redeemed remnant to change the world. You and I may be in the minority as far as the world is concerned, but as someone once pointed out: "One person with God is in the majority." We are minorities with a majority status! Hallelujah!

FURTHER STUDY

Isa. 63:7-16;
Deut. 14:2;
John 1:12;
Rom. 8:15; Gal. 4:6

1. What have we received the Spirit of?

2. What does this cause us to do?

Prayer

Father, I am thankful that I am part of today's remnant but I am even more thankful that that remnant is part of You. By myself I am nothing but with You I am a number. And what a number! Amen.

It's Jesus!

"Isaiah said this because he saw Jesus' glory and spoke about him." (v.41)

For reading & meditation – John 12:37-49

On this, our final day of meditating on the sixth chapter of Isaiah, we look at something quite astonishing. John tells us in the passage we have just read that the vision Isaiah received that day in the Temple was really a vision of Jesus and His glory. John is telling us that hidden in the darkness and smoke of the Temple our Lord was present – and present in all His glory. Right now I want to challenge you to open yourself up to a new vision of the glory of the Lord. Why? Because it is only when we see God as He is that we can see ourselves as we are and then, and only then, are we equipped to move out and minister to others. Our God calls us to serve Him, but He calls us to serve Him in holiness.

We live in a day that is similar in many ways to that of Isaiah – times of great confusion, great strife and great uncertainty. The balance of power is shifting from one nation to another, and every day something appears in our newspapers that makes us wonder what will happen next. Personally, I do not know what the next few years are going to hold for the nations of the earth, or for our witness as the Christian Church around the world. But we do know that the Lord is Lord. He is sovereign. He rules over all. He is high and exalted. He is holy and supreme. And all our problems pale in the light of His sufficiency.

We need to remind ourselves over and over again – *there are no other gods.* The leaders of the nations may strut around on the world's stage but they are not gods – just creatures of whom the Creator can easily dispose. Lift up your eyes to the eternal throne – and keep them there. Our God reigns – but He reigns in holiness.

FURTHER STUDY

Rev. 1:10-18;
2 Cor. 12:2-4

1. How does John describe himself on the Lord's Day?

2. What was Paul's testimony?

Prayer

Father, may the vision of Your glory that transformed Isaiah also transform me. Help me to walk through the earth with my gaze firmly fixed on You. Thank You for what You have taught me. To You be all the honour, all the glory and all the praise. Amen.

From
Confusion to
Confidence

Sure-footedness

"The Lord God … will make my feet like deer's feet …" (v.19, NKJ)

For reading & meditation – Habakkuk 3:17-19

Today we embark upon a journey that will reveal the steps we must take in order to move from confusion to confidence, or from fear to faith. There can be no doubt, to my mind at least, that we are facing one of the most momentous times in human history. Millions of the earth's inhabitants are bewildered. They are not sure that the political leaders and scientists know what they are doing. One of the most recent scares to hit humanity – the dreadful disease "AIDS" – is causing growing consternation in all parts of the world. However we look at our generation, something appears to have snapped and life is left dangling at loose ends.

The question that faces us at this hour is this: How can we, as God's people, walk through life with confidence and poise? Is there some formula we can discover, that will prevent our feet from slipping and sliding as we traverse the rocky slopes of this sick and confused world? I believe there is – and that formula is brought clearly into focus in the prophecy of Habakkuk. Although he begins his book in utter confusion, he ends, as we see from our text for today, in a spirit of abounding confidence.

FURTHER STUDY

Psa. 40:2;
Eph. 6:10-18;
Isa. 52:7

1. What was the psalmist's testimony?

2. What is to be on our feet?

How did Habakkuk discover the formula that enabled him to walk with the sure-footedness of a deer across the rough terrain of his times? We shall discover the answer to that question in the days to come. Permit me to give you a word of advice, however, before we start: don't be too anxious to find that answer. For the deeper the search the more joyous the eventual discovery.

Prayer

O Father, help me to be patient and painstaking in my search for the answer to spiritual confusion. Show me that there are no quick answers to life's big problems. Slow me down so that I keep pace with You. In Jesus' Name. Amen.

A serious stumbling-block

"How long, O Lord, must I call for help, but you do not listen?" (v.2)

For reading & meditation – Habakkuk 1:1-4

Yesterday we said that we are starting out on a journey that will reveal the steps we need to take in order to move from confusion to confidence, or from fear to faith. Our map for this special journey is a small but significant book of the Old Testament – the prophecy of Habakkuk. We know very little about the personal details of Habakkuk's life – his home, his parents or his occupation – but we do know that he was a Hebrew and a contemporary of the prophet Jeremiah.

Habakkuk, it seems, began his prophetic ministry by asking God a pointed question – the one posed in our text today. Like many other prophets of the Old Testament, Habakkuk was perplexed and frustrated by the continuance of evil. He could not understand why God did not intervene to restrain the godless nations around him. The Almighty's apparent slowness in dealing with this issue produced within him a good deal of confusion and concern. "Confusion," says Dr Clyde Narramore, "is one of the biggest stumbling-blocks in the Christian life. It has brought many a Christian to the edge of despair."

Some years ago I met a man in the United States of America wearing a badge on which were inscribed the initials B.A.I.K. When I asked him what they meant he said: "Boy Am I Confused". I countered: "But you don't spell 'confused' with a K." He promptly replied: "Well, that shows you how confused I am." Are you confused about something in your spiritual life at this moment? Then take heart – God helped Habakkuk to move from confusion to confidence. And what He did for Habakkuk, He will also do for you.

FURTHER STUDY

Psa. 71:1-24;
James 3:16;
1 Cor. 14:33

1. What was the psalmist's request?

2. What was his positive confession?

Prayer

Father, I am grateful that when confusion surrounds me and I stumble – I can stumble onto my knees. Drive deep into my consciousness today the truth that the darkest hour is always the hour that precedes the dawn. Amen.

The first vital step

"Be honest and you will be safe ..." (v.18: GNB)
For reading & meditation – Proverbs 28:16-28

Although it is my intention to take you verse by verse through the prophecy of Habakkuk, there will be times, such as today, when we will turn into a side road and pause to focus on a different, but relevant part of Scripture. This will add to our overall understanding of the theme.

We saw yesterday that Habakkuk was confused and frustrated over God's inaction in the face of evil. Perhaps a similar confusion exists in your heart as, day after day, you pick up the newspaper and read about the appalling things that are going on in the world – rape, murder, corruption, violence, political intrigue, lust, vice, lawlessness, and so on. What do we do when confusion hits us in the way it hit the prophet Habakkuk? How do we handle ourselves at those times when nothing makes sense?

The first step is this: we must honestly admit to ourselves that we are confused. That might seem to some to be stating the obvious, but you would be amazed how difficult it is for some Christians to acknowledge and admit to what is going on inside them. This is because there is a sub-conscious desire in the hearts of many believers to present to the world the image of being people who have the answer to all of life's problems – and so whenever they feel confused, they tend to deny the fact and pretend that everything is fine. But that is dishonest – and few things cause more anxiety than dishonesty. The first thing, then, is honesty – honesty with God, honesty with others and honesty with ourselves.

FURTHER STUDY

Psa. 51:1-17;
Eph. 4:25;
Prov. 12:19

1. What does God desire?
2. What are we to speak?

Prayer

My Father and my God, I open up my depths to Your honesty. Let it search me and try me and see if there is any devious way in me – anything that dodges or denies. Help me to be an honest person. Amen.

Four ways to cope with confusion

"The Lord is my light and my salvation — whom shall I fear? The Lord is the stronghold of my life …" (v.1)

For reading & meditation – Psalm 27:1-14

Whenever we are faced with confusion – or, for that matter, any difficult situation that confronts us – we will usually take one of four measures: 1. Flee it! 2. Fight it! 3. Forget it! 4. Face it! The first three end in failure – only the fourth will get us anywhere.

So fix it clearly in your mind that the first step in dealing with confusion is admit it. Acknowledge the fact that you are feeling confused. Don't be like the minister who, when faced with a difficult passage in Scripture, would say to his congregation: "This is an interesting text – and now having looked it full in the face, let us pass on!" Be careful that you don't pass on until you have looked confusion fully in the face, acknowledged its reality and felt its pain.

Why is it necessary to feel its pain? Because any unpleasant thought or situation will, of necessity, have some impact upon our feelings. Depending on the type of person we are (our temperament, early training, and so on), we will choose either to face that feeling in all its fullness or push it down inside us – unacknowledged. But note this: to the extent that an emotion is not acknowledged, to that extent it will stay within us and cause trouble at some future point in our lives. One of the laws of the personality is this: unacknowledged emotions stay within us to cause trouble, acknowledged emotions don't. How good are you at acknowledging your feelings? Believe me, if you are not in charge of them, they will soon be in charge of you.

FURTHER STUDY

2 Cor. 12:1-10;
Isa. 40:31;
Psa. 81:1

1. How did Paul respond after acknowledging his situation?

2. What is the key to facing life's pain?

Prayer

O Father, here I am entering an area where I need Your special help and direction. You have told me to "fear nothing". Help me to face all my feelings in the knowledge that You, not my feelings, are my Lord and Master. Amen.

The way to real growth

"Be strong and courageous. Do not be terrified; do not be discouraged, for the Lord your God will be with you ..." (v.9)
For reading & meditation – Joshua 1:1-9

We must spend another day looking at this important matter of being willing to acknowledge our feelings. The truth is, most of us are unwilling to "feel" a negative emotion and we try to get rid of it as quickly as possible.

Our personalities are equipped with adaptive devices called "defence mechanisms" which come to our aid at such times and help us rid ourselves of negative feelings by either suppressing them or repressing them. Suppression involves pushing them down just below the level of our conscious mind into the subconscious, where we say: "I won't think about that now – it's too hurtful." Repression involves pushing them down into the unconscious where they are completely forgotten. These "defence mechanisms" may get us temporarily off the hook by relieving the anxiety we feel at having to face an unacceptable emotion, but they don't really solve the problem.

The only way to real growth and wholeness is a willingness to face feelings, no matter how terrifying and threatening they may be. It's not easy, of course – I still struggle in this area myself. I know I am better at facing unacceptable feelings than I was, say, twenty years ago – but I still have a long way to go. Keep in mind what I said yesterday, for it is a vitally important matter: to the extent that we push an unacceptable emotion away from us, fearing to face it and feel it, to that extent it will go on working within us counter-productively. For the sake of our mental and spiritual health, we must realise that any emotion that is buried within us is never buried dead – but buried alive.

FURTHER STUDY

Psa. 32:1-5;
Jer. 14:20;
Hosea 5:15

1. What happened when the psalmist kept silent?

2. What happened when he acknowledged his position?

Prayer

My Father and my God, since it seems my emotions are a vital part of me, give me the courage to be able to face them in the knowledge that when I am mastered by You, I can be mastered by nothing else. Amen.

Stepping off the cliff

"The eternal God is your refuge, and underneath are the everlasting arms." (v.27)

For reading & meditation – Deuteronomy 33:1-29

I know that some will feel threatened by the subject we have been looking at over these past few days because, by reason of past hurts and traumas, they feel they do not have the inner strength to cope with any more unpleasant and uncomfortable feelings. Such people find it far easier to repress unacceptable feelings than to face them. We have to face the fact, however, that if Habakkuk had done this, he would never have risen to the heights of confidence which we see him enjoying in his final chapter.

If you are terrified to face your feelings, then let me encourage you to make the conscious decision now that you will attempt to move forward in this matter – if only a little. Make up your mind the next time an unacceptable feeling comes your way, you will choose to face and feel it in the strength that God provides.

Picture yourself standing on the edge of a cliff, looking down into a deep abyss. The abyss represents your fear of experiencing your emotions. Now visualise a strong rope tied securely to your waist – a rope that represents God's love and that is held in His hands directly above the abyss. While you remain on the cliff, the rope hangs limp around your waist. Note, it is the cliff, not the rope, that is supporting you. The only way you can experience the tightness of the rope and know the power of the Lord to uphold you in the presence of unpleasant feelings is to jump off the cliff and trust yourself to the rope. In other words, if you face your feelings, you will not fall into the abyss – you will be supported by God's unbreakable rope of love.

> **FURTHER STUDY**
> Isa. 41:1-10;
> Ex. 19:4; Psa. 18:35
>
> 1. What was God's promise to Israel?
>
> 2. Take a pencil and paper and draw the above illustration to help you visualise it.

Prayer

O Father, the thought of facing the things I am afraid to face draws me to hold back and remain on the cliff of safety. But I long to experience Your mighty strength and power. Help me step off that cliff – today. In Jesus' Name. Amen.

Evasion solves nothing

"I can do everything through him who gives me strength."
(v.13)

For reading & meditation – Philippians 4:8-20

The advice I have been giving – to be willing to face your confusion and feel it – runs counter to the view that is held by many in the Christian Church. It is a view with which I am very familiar, for at one time I held it myself. It says: "Whenever you see a problem coming toward you, turn your back on it, begin to praise the Lord, and it will go away." Some go even further and say: "Once you confess you have a problem, you allow it to have a foothold in your life and you will not be able to get rid of it. Confession leads to possession – you will get what you confess."

I am heartily in agreement with the belief that we can look so long at our problems that we lose our spiritual perspective – the problem becomes bigger and God grows smaller. But we must not fall into the trap of thinking that refusing to acknowledge a problem makes it go away. Gene Autry, the famous singing cowboy (and a boyhood hero of mine) said: "I have always followed the rule of one hundred per cent honesty in everything – honesty toward God, honesty toward others, and honesty toward myself."

FURTHER STUDY

Matt. 26:36-45;
Luke 2:49;
John 5:19-20;
Heb. 4:15

1. What did Jesus do with His pain and confusing circumstances?

2. Why was He able to face them?

Once again I suggest that if we are not willing to admit to a problem, then we are denying reality and being dishonest. Those whose method of coping with problems is to pretend they don't have them are taking the first step toward mental ill-health. Nothing is solved by evasion, for whatever we try to evade comes back to pervade. It comes back as hidden complexes within – an undertow of discord that restrains our spiritual progress.

Prayer

O Father, drive this thought deep into my spirit – whatever I try to evade comes back to pervade. Make me a person of courage – able to face anything and stand up to anything. In Jesus' Name. Amen.

A dialogue with God

"Cast all your anxiety on him because he cares for you."(v.7)

For reading & meditation – 1 Peter 5:1-11

We pause to gather up what we have been saying over the last few days. The Christian way is a way of complete honesty – we must be willing to face and feel unpleasant situations and feelings. There must be no attempt to deceive ourselves or pretend that things are different from the way they really are – no attempt to entice the mind into a fool's paradise of make-believe. No one can play tricks on the universe – let alone the universe of a personality. So there must be no waving of a magic wand over negative feelings – no telling the mind they are not there. We must be willing to face things in the knowledge that when we are linked to Jesus Christ, nothing can master us or overwhelm us.

Now for the second step: bring all your questions, doubts and feelings directly to God and talk to Him about them. Some regard Habakkuk's direct questioning of God (1:1-4) as impertinent, but I do not see it in that light. God does not fall off His throne every time one of His children confronts Him with a searching question. Believe me, whatever question you ask of God – He can take it!

Habakkuk did what every one should do whenever they fail to comprehend the ways of the Almighty – he talked directly to God about it. So whenever you feel confused about the state of the world – and who doesn't? – don't become too concerned about entering into a dialogue with other people. First enter into a dialogue with God. Problems must always be talked out – and who better to talk to than God?

FURTHER STUDY

2 Kings 19:8-37;
Psa. 91:15;
Phil. 4:6

1. How did Hezekiah deal with his problem?

2. What was the result?

Prayer

O Father, forgive me for running to others with my problems when I should first be running to You. Help me in future to share my burdens and my problems with You before I share them with anyone else. In Christ's Name I pray. Amen.

"What have you done about it?"

"But may all who seek you rejoice and be glad in you ..." (v.16)

For reading & meditation – Psalm 40:1-17

We continue thinking about the second step we must take – bringing all our questions and feelings to God and talking directly to Him about them. Dr Jay Adams, a well-known Christian counsellor, says that whenever anyone comes to him for counselling, he begins by asking three preliminary questions: (1) What is your problem? (2) What have you done about it? (3) What do you expect me to do about it?

He says that one of the things that has amazed him about the replies he gets to the second question – "What have you done about it?" – is the fact that although many say they have sought help from friends, family or even books, few say that they have talked to God about their problem. My own experience would bear this out. In the early days of my ministry I remember being somewhat nonplussed when I asked a brother or sister who had come to me with a personal problem, "Have you talked to God about this?" to hear so often this response: "No, I thought I would talk to you about it first."

I have often wondered whether there would be such a demand for Christian counselling if people made it a habit to talk to God about their problems before talking them over with anyone else. That does not mean, of course, that the ministry of counselling is invalid for, according to Scripture, it is a God-ordained gift (Rom. 12:8). I am convinced, however, that if Christians developed the habit of first going to God with their problems, they would make the surprising discovery that on most occasions, they would have no need to consult anyone else.

FURTHER STUDY

1 Chron. 28:9;
Psa. 27:8;
Prov. 8:17;
Jer. 29:13

1. What does it mean to "seek the Lord"?

2. What does God promise?

Prayer

My Father and my God, help me to develop a prayer-habit so that whenever I am faced with a problem, the first One I think of talking to is You. I ask this in and through Your Son's peerless and precious Name. Amen.

Why put God first?

"You shall have no other gods before me." (v.3)
For reading & meditation – Exodus 20:1-17

We are saying that if we would learn to bring our doubts, our fears and our confusion to God and talk to Him about them in believing prayer, there would be fewer problems in the Church and less need for personal counselling.

This does not mean, as we said, that the ministry of counselling is invalid for, as Scripture clearly shows, it ought to play a vital part in every Christian congregation: "I am satisfied about you, my brethren, that you yourselves are rich in goodness, amply filled with all spiritual knowledge and competent to admonish and counsel and instruct one another also" (Rom. 15:14, Amplified Bible). There will be times when, even though we have spoken to God about our problems and our confusion, the guidance and enlightenment we need will come not directly from Him but through the lips of a minister, a friend or a counsellor.

The point I am making is that we must learn the spiritual principle of having a dialogue with God before we enter into a dialogue with anyone else. Why is this so important? Because our spiritual dependence must be rooted in God and not in anyone else. It is so easy to move away from a sense of dependence on God, and anything that contributes to that must be resisted. After all, what is the essence of sin? Is it not independence – man seeking to find his own solutions to his problems rather than discovering God's perspective on them? Of course, if God directs us to another member of His family for help and advice, then fine. The roots of our dependence, however, must be firmly fixed in Him.

FURTHER STUDY

Psa. 27:1-14;
Hosea 12:6;
Isa. 8:17

1. What is the admonition of the psalmist?

2. How often do you "wait" on the Lord?

Prayer

O God, open my eyes to see the dangers of being centred in myself or in others. If I am to move from confusion to confidence, then I must be centred in You. Help me make You the centre of my life – today and every day. Amen.

More tolerant than His people

"How long, O Lord? Will you forget me for ever? How long will you hide your face from me?" (v.1)

For reading & meditation – Psalm 13:1-6

Now that we have seen the importance of bringing all our doubts and confusion directly to God, the next question we must settle is this: How do we go about the task of telling the Almighty exactly what is in our hearts? Do we address Him in ecclesiastical language and in pious tones? No, we must talk to Him naturally, openly and honestly – telling Him precisely what we think and how we feel.

Look again at the first four verses of Habakkuk's prophecy and what do we find? We find a man addressing God in a manner that at first seems irreverent and impertinent. We see something similar in the passage that is before us today. Have you noticed how, when some of the Old Testament personalities felt confused or angry with God, they told Him exactly what they thought and felt – sometimes in language that is blunt almost to the point of rudeness?

Habakkuk was upset because God had not answered his prayers. You can almost hear the anger and frustration in his words as he hammers on the door of heaven: "Lord, I'm confused. Why don't You answer my prayer? How much longer are You going to allow this? When will You do something about these tremendous problems?" Does God tell him to shut up or rephrase his questions in more acceptable language? Does He withdraw from the prophet in an attitude of disgust? No, for as I said before – God can take it. It may not have occurred to you before, but it is a truth that is exemplified over and over again in Scripture – God is more patient and tolerant than any of His people.

FURTHER STUDY

1 Kings 19:1–21;
Rom. 15:5;
Psa. 86:5

1. How did Elijah express himself to the Lord?

2. How did the Lord respond?

Prayer

My Father and my God, when I think how I react when people show anger toward me, I stand in awe and amazement at the way You respond to those who are angry with You. Teach me to be more like You, dear Lord. In Christ's Name. Amen.

Be real

"My God, my God, why have you forsaken me? Why are you so far from saving me, so far from the words of my groaning?" (v.1)
For reading & meditation – Psalm 22:1-24

We ended yesterday by saying that God is more patient and tolerant than His people. We have only to look at Habakkuk remonstrating with God to see this. One thing we must learn about God it is this: He would prefer us to be real rather than pretend to be what we are not. Be assured of this: beneath confusion there is usually an element of anger. It may not be recognised, but it is there nevertheless.

I remember on one occasion a man telling me that he had just come through "a spiritual revolution". When I pressed him to share it with me he told me that all his life he had been brought up to believe he must address God in polite tones, and on no account should he ever show any sense of frustration or annoyance. But one day, while going through a time of spiritual confusion, he forgot himself, and in language that was stripped of all pious phrases told God exactly what he thought about Him and the way He was handling His world.

For two hours he argued with God, and when he had finished the Lord said to him: "You would never let anyone talk to you like that, would you? Why? Because you cannot see into the depths of another's heart. But I see everything – the pain, the hurt and the anger. I love you and I understand." The tender response of the Lord broke him and there followed three days of communion with Him that produced in him a deep spiritual transformation. God always responds to reality – even when that reality is couched in feelings of anger and hurt.

FURTHER STUDY

Luke 24:13-36;
Rom. 12:17

1. Why was Jesus able to respond to these disciples?

2. What was the result?

Prayer

O God, something is being burned into my consciousness – You are a God who delights in reality. Help me to be a real person – with no subterfuge, no phoneyness, no pretence. I ask this in and through the precious Name of Jesus. Amen.

"The silences of God"

"Why are you like a man taken by surprise … You are among us, O Lord, and we bear your name …" (v.9)

For reading & meditation – Jeremiah 14:1-9

Before moving on to examine the third step we must take if we are to move from confusion to confidence, we must spend a day on the question: What was the cause of Habakkuk's deep inner confusion? There were several reasons for it, but the major one was the fact that God did not appear to be interested in answering his prayer: "How long, O Lord, must I call for help, but you do not listen? Or cry out to you, 'Violence!' but you do not save?" (Hab. 1:2).

No confusion can be greater than that which comes through what we call "unanswered prayer" – especially when we know that what we are praying for is according to the divine will. Some of you who are reading this may be in that very situation. You have prayed for things that God has promised to give – but still the answers do not come.

The question I am asked more than any other is this: "Why has God not answered my prayer when I know I am praying according to His will?" Teresa of Avila is reported to have told God on one occasion when she did not receive an answer to a prayer which she knew to be in line with the divine will: "Lord, it's no wonder You have so few friends if You treat them all this way." How strangely silent and inactive God appears to be at times. If you are experiencing the "silence of God" at this moment in your life, then you will have some sympathy for the way Habakkuk felt. It may not be much help to say that others have felt the way you feel – but it is true nevertheless.

FURTHER STUDY

John 11:1-44;
Psa. 55:1-2; 77:9

1. What happened when Jesus received the sisters' request?

2. How did Martha view this?

Prayer

Father, help me to find comfort in the time of spiritual silence in knowing that others have passed this way too. They have come through to insight and understanding – so will I. Thank You, dear Father. Amen.

The reason for God's silences

*"For I am going to do something in your days that you
would not believe, even if you were told." (v.5)*
For reading & meditation – Habakkuk 1:5

We come now to the third step we need to take in our progression
from confusion to confidence: give God an opportunity to reply. It
is to Habakkuk's credit that after telling God what he thought of Him, he
sat back and listened to the divine response. One of the things we must
remember is this: prayer involves not only talking to God but also God
talking to us.

As soon as Habakkuk had finished speaking and was ready to listen,
God started answering the prophet – but not in the way that he expected. First, God tells him that despite all appearances to the contrary, He is
not inactive: "I am going to do something in your days ...". And if He
had been silent, it was only because of an unwillingness on the part of
the prophet and the people he represented to receive the solution which
God proposed: "You would not believe, even if you were told."

It is obvious that God was not doing what the prophet imagined –
standing back and allowing things to proceed unchecked. He had
already put into operation His plans and purposes, but in a way that
Habakkuk would find unbelievable and unacceptable.

Can we begin to see now that one of the reasons why
we go through times of spiritual confusion and frustration is because, although we are big enough to ask
the questions, we are not big enough to receive the
answers? What is the point of God unfolding to us His
plans and purposes when He knows that our hearts are
unwilling and unready to follow the path which He
sees is best for us?

FURTHER STUDY

Matt. 13:24-58;
Mark 16:14;
Heb. 4:11

*1. What prevented
Jesus from doing
many miracles?*

*2. What prevents us
from receiving from
God?*

Prayer

O Father, I recognise that Your silences are not due to petulance but to my own preconceived ideas – ideas which make me unready and unwilling to receive Your
answers. Help me overcome this problem, dear Lord. In Jesus' Name I pray. Amen.

The pain of answered prayer

"I am raising up the Babylonians [or Chaldeans], that ruthless and impetuous people, who sweep across the whole earth ..." (v.6)

For reading & meditation – Habakkuk 1:6-11

When the Lord announced that He was about to use the evil and cruel Chaldeans to prune His people and to bring them to heel, Habakkuk was astounded. The Chaldeans, a tribe from southern Babylonia, were terrorists who loved to plunder and torture their enemies. Listen to God's description of the Chaldean armies in the passage we are looking at today: "... they are a law to themselves and promote their own honour. Their horses are swifter than leopards, fiercer than wolves ... They fly like a vulture swooping to devour ..." (vv.7–8).

Habakkuk had his prayer answered, but not in the way he expected. The prophet is now more confused than ever. First, God took an exceptionally long time to answer him, and when He did, the answer He gave was more difficult to receive than the silence. People have often said to me: "What can be greater than the pain of unanswered prayer?" I usually respond: "the pain of answered prayer."

Habakkuk was quite clear in his mind what he wanted God to do – chastise the nation of Israel and send revival. But when God replied that He was going to use the evil and cruel Chaldean army to punish them, the prophet was nonplussed. This is not an uncommon experience in the Christian life – getting an answer we do not expect. When Augustine pleaded with God for light to overcome the dark problems he faced, God gave him light – but the first thing it revealed was Augustine's unchastity and sensuality. We take certain risks when we pray, for God sometimes tells us things we might not want to know.

FURTHER STUDY

Jonah 1:1 – 4:11

1. Why was Jonah disgruntled?

2. What was he expecting?

Prayer

My Father and my God, help me to understand that when my prayers are answered in ways that I do not expect, it is because You desire my highest good. And help me not simply to understand it – but accept it. In Jesus' Name. Amen

"We are not saved from hurt"

*"When he heard this, he became very sad, because he was
a man of great wealth." (v.23)*

For reading & meditation – Luke 18:18-30

We are seeing that the answer our prayers receive is not always the
answer our hearts desire. One preacher has said: "He who asks
God for light must not complain if the light scorches at times with its
fierce and naked heat, and he who asks for guidance must not be surprised if God points him to paths he would rather not tread."

Oliver Wendell Holmes says that it is a rule which admits of few
exceptions that when people ask for our opinion, they really want our
praise. God will not deal with us like that. If we plead for light, then providing He sees that it will not devastate us, He will grant us the petition
we ask. Note, I use the word "devastate" and not "hurt". God will not
save us from getting hurt – if that pain is part of His purpose for making
us better.

We see that principle illustrated in the story of the rich young ruler.
He said to Jesus: "Good teacher, what must I do to inherit eternal life?"
And Jesus said: "Sell everything you have and give to the poor, and you
will have treasure in heaven. Then come, follow me" (vv.18, 22). The
young man delighted in his wealth. It was the most
important thing in his life. That is why Jesus asked
him to put it on one side. The first place in any person's life is God's place. The answer the rich young
ruler got was not the one he wanted, but it was certainly what he needed. The account says that he
"became very sad". He got his answer – but failed to
receive it.

FURTHER STUDY

Mark 14:26-42;
Matt. 20:22;
Psa. 80:5; 126:5

1. What was the cup
Christ faced?

2. How does God use
suffering?

Prayer

O God, forgive me that so often I am like this rich young ruler – I ask for light, but
when it comes I am not ready to receive it. Lord, teach me to pray – and also to
receive. In Christ's Name I ask it. Amen.

Trembling in the light!

"My heart falters, fear makes me tremble; the twilight I longed for has become a horror to me." (v.4)

For reading & meditation – Isaiah 21:1-10

We continue discussing the subject of the pain that sometimes results from answered prayer. Not only Habakkuk, but also Isaiah knew something of this.

Isaiah asked for light on the political situation of his day – a religious matter to a Hebrew prophet as well as a political one. He asked God to give him insight and understanding that he might see and comprehend what was hidden from others. He prayed for a divine illumination whereby his gaze might pierce the future so that he might speak forth a prophetic word to his people. And God gave him light! His prayer was answered! The darkness turned to a growing twilight. He saw – but what he saw filled his soul with terror. When he knew, he almost wished he did not know. The light glimmered all around him, but the pain of its revelation made him wish that he was back in the darkness of ignorance once again.

What did he see? He saw the people he loved broken by the might of the enemy. He saw their homes and cities shattered by the most ruthless of foes. God had truly answered his prayer and given him the insight he desired, but he turned from it sick with foreboding and with his body quivering in fearful anticipation. Listen to how the Living Bible paraphrases our text for today: "My mind reels; my heart races; I am gripped by awful fear. All rest at night – so pleasant once – is gone; I lie awake trembling." Perhaps, at times, it is better to remain in the darkness of ignorance than to tremble in the light of illumination.

FURTHER STUDY

Daniel 10:1–21;
Lam. 3:22-23;
Rev. 1:17

1. How did Daniel and John respond to the vision of God?

2. How is God's mercy expressed?.

Prayer

O Father, help me to be in closer touch with Your ways and Your purposes. Teach me the difference between desiring and demanding – a desire to know may leave me wondering, but a demand to know may leave me trembling. Amen.

The light scorches ...

*"As the heavens are higher than the earth, so are my ways higher
than your ways and my thoughts than your thoughts." (v.9)*

For reading & meditation – Isaiah 55:1-13

N ow that we have looked at how Habakkuk and Isaiah experienced
the pain of answered prayer, we turn to consider some examples
drawn from more modern times.

When the great Methodist preacher Thomas Champness was first
appointed district evangelist to Newcastle upon Tyne, he got on his
knees and asked God for further light and illumination. The Lord said:
"You are to concentrate exclusively on winning men to Me ... and you
must be careless of your reputation as a preacher." Thomas Champness
was known as one of the greatest preachers of his day – a reputation of
which, according to his biographer, he was mildly proud. And God said:
"Give it up." He asked for light but the light scorched with an intense
and fierce heat.

Have you heard of Hugh Price Hughes? He was another great
preacher of modern times – and a man with a scholar's mind. When, as a
young man, he asked God for direction concerning his career, the Lord
said: "I want you to be a preacher of the gospel." He was quite startled,
for he had not expected that. He realised at once what
the call to the ministry meant – a lower income, the
abandonment of the delights of scholarly research, and
so on. It took him some time to receive the divine call
and adjust to it, but once he had he became a mighty
preacher and a choice servant of God. Mrs Hugh Price
Hughes was once asked what was the greatest sacrifice
her husband had ever made, and she replied: "He
could have been a scholar, but he chose under God to
be a simple preacher of the gospel."

FURTHER STUDY

Psa. 40:1-17;
139:17; Jer. 29:11

*1. How did the
psalmist describe
God's thoughts?*

*2. What is the
essence of God's
thoughts?*

Prayer

My Father and my God, day by day I am being exposed to the truth that You always
give the best to those who leave the choice to You. Help me to put Your way before
my Way – for then, and only then, will I experience true freedom. Amen.

"I just won't do that"

"He cuts off every branch in me that bears no fruit, while every branch that does bear fruit he prunes ..." (v.2)

For reading & meditation – John 15:1-11

W e are spending time meditating on the fact that the answers our prayers receive are not always the answers our hearts desire. This we are calling "the pain of answered prayer". A preacher tells how he preached a series of sermons to his congregation on the subject of guidance, and in the last message of the series he encouraged them to put the matter to personal test. "Follow the principles I have laid before you," he said, "and let me know what happens."

Several weeks later, he noticed that one woman who had attended the whole of the series on guidance no longer attended the services – so he decided to call on her. During the course of his visit, he asked what was the reason for her non-attendance at church. She said that it was due to the disappointment she had experienced after putting into operation the principles he had taught on guidance. "What happened?" asked the minister, anxiously. "Did you hear nothing?" "Oh, yes," she replied, "I heard something all right. It came to me that I ought to write to my sister-in-law, the cat, with whom I quarrelled seven years ago. I just won't do that ..."

FURTHER STUDY

James 4:1-17;
Psa. 52:3;
Prov. 2:14

1. How does James define sin?

2. What is the personal application?

The verse that comes to my mind as I tell that story is one I am sure you will know well: "This is the verdict: Light has come into the world, but men loved darkness instead of light because there deeds were evil" (John 3:19). At the risk of being repetitive, the point is so important that it must be made yet again: never forget that when you pray for light, it may reveal far more than you wish.

Prayer

"Dear Lord, these three things I pray: to see Thee more clearly, love Thee more dearly, follow Thee more nearly – day by day." In Christ's peerless and precious Name I ask it. Amen.

"March on …"

"My grace is sufficient for you, for my power is made perfect in weakness." (v.9)

For reading & meditation – 2 Corinthians 12:1-10

We spend one more day discussing the "pain of answered prayer". What do we do when we receive an answer to our prayers that causes us to tremble in the blinding light of a new revelation? We must go into the light with God. Pain or no pain – there must be no going back – we must march on.

Augustine tried to run away from what God had shown him, but he was driven out of every false place of refuge. We must do what Thomas Champness – the preacher we referred to the other day – did: we must yield to what God has shown us and come to terms with the fact that, after all, God knows best. When God said to Thomas Champness: "You must be careless of your reputation as a preacher," he struggled for a while but eventually he yielded. Speaking of the effort it cost him, he said: "I threw my reputation into the Tyne as I crossed the high-level bridge." In return for his obedience, God made him a glorious harvester of souls.

I remind you again of the risks you take when you enter into dialogue with God. The light you ask for may reveal more than you wish. It may be turned to trembling within you. But I plead with you, when that happens – go on. If you will live up to the demands God makes and face squarely what the light reveals, the trembling will pass and you will prove the truth of Isaiah's words: He will "strengthen the feeble hands, steady the knees that give way; say to those with fearful hearts, 'Be strong, do not fear; your God will come …' " (Isa 35:3–4).

FURTHER STUDY

1 John 1:1–10; 2:9;
Eph. 5:8;
2 Cor. 4:6

1. How are we to walk?

2. What will be the result?

Prayer

O Father, in those moments when I am overwhelmed by the light that I asked for but which brought answers I did not expect, help me not to pull back but to walk in the light … as You are in the light. Amen.

Knowing God

"Your eyes are too pure to look on evil; you cannot tolerate wrong." (v.13)

For reading & meditation – Habakkuk 1:12-14

Now we come to the fourth step we need to take to move from confusion to confidence: establish a spiritual context in which to think through the problem.

Look how Habakkuk sets about doing this as illustrated in the verses that are before us today. He focuses his attention, not on his feelings or his circumstances, but on the nature and character of God. One by one, he singles out some of the attributes of God and reminds himself of the characteristics of God's nature: "O Lord, are you not from everlasting?" – His eternal nature; "We will not die" – His faithfulness; "You have appointed them to execute judgment" – His justice; "Your eyes are too pure to look on evil" – His holiness; "You have made men like fish in the sea" – His omnipotence.

Some commentators believe that the reason Habakkuk identifies God's attributes here is simply to build up an argument that the course proposed by God is contrary to His character. I think there is some truth in that as evidenced by his question in verse 17, but another reason why he sets about identifying God's attributes – so I believe – is to attempt to steady himself by reminding himself who God is. You see, it is only when we understand who God is that we will understand what He does. Habakkuk was saying, in effect: "I don't know what You are doing, Lord, but I know this – You are a God of justice, of faithfulness, of holiness, of purity and of power." It is a law of the spiritual life that the more we understand God's character and nature, the more certain we will be about the rightness of His decisions.

FURTHER STUDY

Isa. 40:1–31;
Psa. 89:6;
1 Chron. 17:20

1. What question does Isaiah ask?

2. How does he answer it?

Prayer

My Father and my God, help me to know You better. I know You – yet I do not know You. Enable me over these next few days to build a spiritual context for my problems – one that will stay with me for the rest of my life. In Jesus' Name. Amen.

Pygmy Christians

*"Do you not know? Have you not heard? ... Have you not
understood ...? (v.21)*

For reading & meditation – Isaiah 40:21-31

Yesterday we ended with the statement that the more we understand God's nature, the more certain we will be about the rightness of His decisions. Have you ever wondered how it is that over the centuries, men and women have stood for God in the most unenviable circumstances? The answer is this: they were familiar with the nature and character of God.

One of the things that concerns me about many modern-day Christians is that they know little about the nature of God. The very first series of Bible studies I attended after I became a Christian was on the subject of the attributes of God. It was tough going for a young Christian, but those weeks of teaching built under me a foundation which has stood solid over the years. It was there that I heard for the first time statements that have stayed with me all my life. Statements such as: "It is only when we understand who God is that we will understand what He does." And: "We must be careful not to interpret God's character by what we see, but what we see by God's character."

J.I. Packer, in his book *Knowing God*, says: "The ignorance of God – ignorance both of His ways and of the practice of communion with Him – lies at the root of much of the church's weakness today." I agree. The modern Church, generally speaking, looks at God through the wrong end of a telescope and ends up reducing the Almighty to pygmy proportions. And what is the result? Our pews are filled with pygmy Christians who have only a superficial knowledge of the God they are pledged to serve.

FURTHER STUDY

Isa. 6:1-8; 9:6;
Psa. 97:6

1. What aspect of God's character did Isaiah witness?

2. How did he describe Christ?

Prayer

Father, I begin to see the framework in which I must win or lose the battle of life. And that framework is Your nature and Your character. Help me to know You better – then I shall be better. In Christ's Name I ask it. Amen.

"Only small thoughts of God"

"… ask for the ancient paths, ask where the good way is, and walk in it, and you will find rest for your souls." (v.16)

For reading & meditation – Jeremiah 6:16

We continue making the point that the more we understand the nature and character of God, the more secure we will feel and the better equipped we will be to handle life's serious problems. Unfortunately, few preachers today expound the great truths concerning God's nature. They prefer instead to give clever little talks – ten minutes and no more – on topical issues and current events. There are notable exceptions to what I am saying, of course, but as Jim Packer points out: "The trend these days is for Christian minds to conform to the modern spirit – the spirit that spawns great thoughts of man and leaves room for only small thoughts of God."

A century ago, pulpits were occupied by men who left their hearers in no doubt as to the nature of God. But not any more. When, for example, did you last hear a sermon on the attributes of God? But let me ask you a more pointed question: When did you last read a book on that important subject? When I asked one publisher why he was not producing books that come to grips with the basic issues of the faith, he answered: "People are not writing them, and if they did few people would want to read them." How sad.

FURTHER STUDY

Psa. 8:1-9; 102:25;
Job 26:7; Heb. 11:3

1. What question does the psalmist ask?

2. How was the universe formed?

Let me make a plea for the return to old-fashioned thinking on the nature and character of God. If you have not read the book *Knowing God* by J.I. Packer, then purchase a copy today. Focus on knowing who God is and you will never again be at the mercy of the winds of doubt and uncertainty.

Prayer

O Father, with all my heart I cry out today: "Take me deeper into You." I am tired of superficiality. Help me to know You and understand You – to deeply know and understand You. In Jesus' Name. Amen.

The importance of fixed points

"… the Father of the heavenly lights, who does not change like shifting shadows." (v.17)

For reading & meditation – James 1:12-25

Over these past few days we have been saying that one of the things we must do if we are to move from confusion to confidence is to establish a context in which to think through our problems – and that context, we said, must be the nature and character of God.

The art of navigation depends to a large extent on the existence of fixed points. The fixed point can be a star, a lighthouse, or a headland; it does not really matter what it is providing it is fixed and solid. Granted the certitude of a fixed point, the navigator can take his bearing and steer his course. He cannot take his bearing from a cloud: it moves – it is vaporous and changing and, in the course of time, disappears. Navigation is possible because of the existence of fixed points, and by constant reference to these points, seamen make their way around the world.

The voyage of life is like that – one must have fixed points from which to take a bearing. The attributes of God are fixed points. His love, faithfulness, justice, purity, holiness and power – to name but a few – are established parts of God's nature. And the more we focus on them and the more we understand them, the more safely and reliably we will make our way across the sea of life. Many things in this universe are subject to change – but not the attributes and nature of God. What He was, He is, and what He is, He was. And what He was and is He ever will be – world without end.

FURTHER STUDY

Heb. 13:1-8;
Psa. 102:27;
Mal. 3:6; Heb. 1:12

1. What is the foundation of our faith?

2. What was the psalmist's testimony?

Prayer

O Father, help me to grasp the exciting truth that is implied in the thought before me today, namely, that because Your nature cannot change, Your Word will never fail. I am eternally grateful. Amen.

God's eternal nature

"Let those who fear the Lord say, 'His love endures for ever.' " (v.4)

For reading & meditation – Psalm 118:1-21

W e continue looking at how to establish a spiritual context in which to think through a problem. Dr Martyn Lloyd-Jones, when speaking on a similar matter, said: "When you start to think about any particular difficulty, you must not focus on your immediate problem. Begin further back. Apply the strategy of the indirect approach."

The phrase, "strategy of the indirect approach" is a military one, and can be illustrated by the way the Allies overcame Germany in World War II. For a while the military campaign of the Allies focused, not on Germany, but on German forces in North Africa. When Germany was defeated there – through the strategy of the indirect approach – it was the beginning of the end. The problem of spiritual confusion must be dealt with in the same way – we must begin, not so much with the present problem, but further back.

How do we do that? We must do what Habakkuk did and remind ourselves of the things about which we are absolutely certain, things which are entirely beyond doubt. In other words – the fixed points. For example, the eternal nature of God is a fixed point. "Are you not from everlasting?" (Hab. 1:12). As Habakkuk focuses on God's eternal nature, he forgets for a moment his immediate problem and reassures himself that God is not like the gods whom the heathen nations worship – idols they have made themselves – but He is from everlasting to everlasting, without beginning and without end. By reason of this, He has preceded history and will continue beyond it. In fact, as it has been said, history is really His-story.

FURTHER STUDY

Psa. 145:1-13;
Deut. 33:27;
Rev. 1:8

1. What did Jesus declare to John?

2. What does this mean for you?

Prayer

O Father, fill my heart today with the consciousness of Your eternal nature. There was never a time when You began and there will never be a time when You will end. Help me drop my anchor in this reassuring revelation. In Jesus' Name. Amen.

God – the great "I Am"

"God also said to Moses, 'I am the Lord' " (v.2)
For reading & meditation – Exodus 6:1-8

We are looking at the way in which Habakkuk established a spiritual context in which he could think through his problem, and we are seeing that his strategy was to reassure himself with those things which are reliable and beyond dispute – the nature, the character and the attributes of God.

Yesterday we saw how he reassured himself by focusing on the eternal nature of God. Next he reminds himself of God's self-existence. He calls on the "Lord my God" (Hab. 1:12, AV). Here, as can be seen from the original Hebrew, he uses that great name for God – Jehovah. That name tells us that God is the self-existing One, the eternal "I Am". This was the name which God gave to Moses when He told him to say to the Israelites: "I Am has sent me to you" (Ex. 3:14). The name "I Am who I Am" means "I am the Absolute, the self-existent One." Self-existence means that God is dependent upon no one. Just think of that! He is the only being in eternity (apart, of course, from the other members of the Trinity) who does not depend upon anyone or anything for His existence.

Habakkuk's next step is to reassure himself with the thought of God's holiness: "My Holy One" (Hab. 1:12). Here is another fixed point – God is absolutely righteous. The moment you focus on a Scripture like that, you are forced to ask: Can the Lord do anything that is unrighteous? Of course not; such a thing is unthinkable. What is the effect of this on the prophet? His problem begins to fade. And why? Because the bigger our view of God, the smaller our view of our problems.

FURTHER STUDY

John 10:1-36; 6:35;
8:23; 8:58; 11:25

1. List the "I Am's"
of Christ in the
above verses.

2. Find 5 more in
John's Gospel.

Prayer

O God, help me to set all my problems within the framework of Your nature and Your character. I know that if I can do this, then I will see them no longer as unsolvable, but as solutions in disguise. Amen.

How to avoid panic

*"I will establish my covenant as an everlasting covenant between
me and you and your descendants ... to be your God ..."* (v.7)

For reading & meditation – Genesis 17:1-9

The next attribute of God on which Habakkuk focuses is that of faithfulness: "We will not die" (Hab. 1:12). What is the significance of
these interesting words? Habakkuk is recalling that God is the God of
the covenant.

Although the Almighty is eternal and beyond time, He condescended
to make a covenant with men. His original covenant was with Abraham
and was later renewed with Isaac and Jacob. Later still, He renewed it
with David. It was this covenant which entitled the people of Judah to
turn to God and say: "Lord, You cannot let us die, for You have made a
covenant with us, one that can never under any circumstance be broken." Whatever the Chaldean army might do, it could never exterminate
Judah, because God was bound and committed to His people in a
covenant relationship that could never be broken.

Having focused on these four aspects of God's character – His eternal
nature, self-existence, holiness and faithfulness – Habakkuk is now able
to see his problem from a different perspective: "... you have appointed
them to execute judgment ... you have ordained them to punish ..."

(v.12). Can you understand what he is saying? He is
beginning to perceive an answer to his problem and
reasons thus: "God must be raising up the Chaldeans
for Judah's benefit. Of this I can be certain. It is not
that God is incapable of restraining them. In the light
of His nature and attributes, such a thing would be
impossible. I am not able to understand it fully, but I
know that God cannot and will not do anything that is
contrary to His character." If that is true – then why
panic?

Prayer

O Father, I see You are trying to teach me Your ways – the ways written in Your
Word and exemplified in the lives of Your servants. Help me to learn this lesson of
how not to panic. In Christ's Name I ask it. Amen.

Put it to the test

*"I am still confident of this: I will see the goodness of the
Lord in the land of the living." (v.13)*

For reading & meditation – Psalm 27:1-14

We now summarise what we have been saying over the past few days
in relation to the need to establish for ourselves a spiritual context
in which to think through a problem. The secret, as we have seen, is not
to focus on the immediate problem, but to take the indirect approach
and remind ourselves of the "fixed points" in God's nature – His eternal
nature, His self-existence, His holiness, His faithfulness, and so on.

What happens when we do this? Well, try it for yourself. If you are
confused about something that God is doing – or not doing – in your life,
then I invite you to apply the principles we have been discussing over
these past days. Take the indirect approach – focus not so much on your
problem as on the nature and character of God. Remind yourself of who
and what He is – and that He can do nothing contrary to His character.
Gaze one by one upon His glorious attributes. If you do exactly as I suggest, I promise you that you will see your problem from a different perspective. Gradually you will find it shrinking to its rightful proportions.

Believers in every age have been using this method of handling spiritual confusion – and it has never failed. If, on the voyage of life, we need fixed points from which to take
our bearings, then we Christians have the most reliable of them all – one of them being the goodness and
graciousness of God. As John Greenleaf Whittier put
it:

FURTHER STUDY

Psa. 57:1-7; 108:1;
112:7

1. Where was the
psalmist's heart
fixed?

2. On what is your
heart fixed?

> *Here in this maddening maze of things,*
> *When tossed by storm and flood,*
> *To one fixed ground my spirit clings,*
> *I know that God is good.*

Prayer

O Father, I stand in awe of Your goodness. Help me to know it and understand it
more and more. And not only this, but every other aspect of Your great and glorious
character. In Christ's Name I ask it. Amen.

God answers every prayer

"And therefore the Lord earnestly waits – expectant, looking and longing – to be gracious to you ..." (v.18, Amplified Bible)

For reading & meditation – Isaiah 30:15-26

W̲e move on now to consider the fifth step we must take in order to move from confusion to confidence: recognise that sometimes God will keep you waiting for an answer.

First we must make the point that learning how to wait quietly for God to answer prayer and bring about His purposes is one of the hardest lessons in the Christian life, and can mean the difference between peace and panic in your life. I am not quite sure myself which is the more difficult situation to be in – getting an answer from God that one does not like, or having to wait interminably for the divine reply. Christian friends to whom I have put that question over the years are almost unanimous in saying that waiting is by far the most difficult thing to endure.

God answers every prayer, but it has been said that the answer may come in one of four forms: (1) Yes; (2) No; (3) Here is something better; (4) Wait to see what I will do. The first is easy to handle – we just open our hands and take what God gives. The second response is a little more difficult – but just as kind as the first. As Tagore, the great Indian thinker, said: "Sometimes the Lord has to save us by hard refusals." The third is also easy to receive. The fourth reply – "Wait" – is the most difficult to handle, but just as loving as the others. God delays His answers for many reasons but the most common reason is this: to deepen our characters so that we won't become spiritual crybabies when we don't get everything at once.

FURTHER STUDY

Acts 1:1-14; 2:1-4;
Psa. 37:7; 40:1

1. What was Jesus' instruction to His disciples?

2. What was the eventual result?

Prayer

O Father, I know in my intellect that the waiting time can prove transformative to my whole being, but I confess that I find it so hard to endure. You have helped me before – help me now with this. In Jesus' Name. Amen.

Still struggling

*"Why are you silent while the wicked swallow up those
more righteous than themselves?" (v.13)*

For reading & meditation – Habakkuk 1:13

Yesterday we said that those times when God leaves us waiting for an
answer to our prayers and questions are some of the most difficult of
our Christian life. Do the heavens seem like brass to you right now?
Have the urgent questions you have put to God gone unanswered? Then
look with me at how Habakkuk found himself in this same situation –
and how he came through it.

It is obvious from the verse before us today that although Habakkuk
had come a long way in dealing with the fact of spiritual confusion, his
perspective is still not clear. After affirming the fact that God is of "purer
eyes than to behold evil, and cannot look on wickedness" (v.13, NKJ), he
presents another provoking question. *The Living Bible* puts it like this:
"Will you, who cannot allow sin in any form, stand idly by while they
swallow us up? Should you be silent while the wicked destroy those who
are better than they?"

Clearly Habakkuk is still struggling with this idea that God is going
to use the cruel Chaldeans to punish His people. What he is really saying
is this: "If it is true, O Lord, that Your eyes are too
pure to look on evil, then how can You allow the
Chaldeans to do this to Your people? Judah might be
bad, but the Chaldeans are a thousand times worse."
Habakkuk is not the only one to be perplexed over the
fact that God uses the unrighteous to refine the righteous. If God can't get to us one way, then He will try
another. He loves us too much to let us stay as we are.

FURTHER STUDY

Luke 18:1-8;
Isa. 25:9; 33:2;
Gen. 49:18

1. What did Jesus
teach in this parable?

2. What does this
encourage us to do?

Prayer

Father, I am so grateful that You love me too much to let me get away with things
that deprive and demean me. You will develop me – even though You may have to
resort to most unusual means to accomplish it. Thank You, Father. Amen.

A prophetic protest

"Are they going to use their swords for ever and keep on destroying nations without mercy?" (v.17, GNB)

For reading & meditation – Habakkuk 1:13-17

The words before us now show that the prophet is really getting worked up about the idea of God using the cruel Chaldeans to discipline the people of Judah. And he makes his protest in the most extravagant language: "Are we but fish, to be caught and killed? Are we but creeping things that have no leader to defend them from their foes? Must we be strung up on their hooks and dragged out in their nets, while they rejoice? Then they will worship their nets and burn incense before them! 'These are the gods who make us rich,' they'll say." His outburst comes to a head with this challenging question: "Will you let them get away with this for ever? Will they succeed for ever in their heartless wars?" (vv.14-17: TLB).

We said yesterday that the fact that God uses the unrighteous to discipline the righteous has always been a problem to the people of God. Throughout the ages, believers from all walks of life have grappled with it, and so now must we.

First, let's pose the question in its modern form: Why does God use unbelievers to discipline believers – non-Christians to refine Christians?

FURTHER STUDY
Luke 12:13-21;
Psa. 73:3; 73:12;
Jer. 5:28; 12:1

1. What is the end of seemingly prosperous but godless men?

2. What did Jeremiah find

Why does He use an unconverted wife or husband to chasten a partner who is a believer, a non-Christian parent to discipline a Christian son or daughter? What possible reason can God have for taking up an impure instrument to accomplish a holy purpose? I am sure you will agree with me when I say that few things are more humbling than God using someone whom we know is godless and lacking in character to chasten and refine us. Humbling – but necessary.

Prayer

O God my Father, how relentless is Your love. You stop at nothing to make me what You want me to be. Help me see that Your humbling is not designed to cripple me but to correct me. In Jesus' Name. Amen.

Well worth waiting for ...

*"I wait for the Lord, I expectantly wait, and in His word
do I hope."* (v.5, Amplified Bible)
For reading & meditation – Psalm 130:1-8

We continue pursuing the question: Why does God use an impure instrument to accomplish a holy purpose? Or to apply it more personally: Why does God use our non-Christian relatives, acquaintances or workmates to reprove and correct us? It is extremely humbling to be on the receiving end of God's discipline at any time, but more so when it is brought to us by someone whom we regard as being below us in character and integrity.

In the days when I was an engineering apprentice, I worked for a while alongside a man who became my pet hate. He was coarse, rude, loud-mouthed, boorish and blasphemous. One day I felt I could not put up with his behaviour any longer and went to a quiet place to pray. I said: "Lord, why have You put me in this position? This man greatly irritates me, and what is more – he delights in taking Your Name in vain. Get him away from me – or get me away from him. Or give me some explanation of why You are letting me go through this."

I had to wait twelve whole months for an answer. During that time I prayed that God would respond in a positive way to my request. Sometimes I would get so angry with God because He kept me waiting for a reply that I would refuse to read His Word. A year later the answer finally came, and when it did, God showed me that He had used the waiting time to prune me of a tendency to want my own way in everything. Believe me, the experience of that year yielded far more than it cost.

FURTHER STUDY

Gen. 15:1-17:27;
21:1-34

1. What happened as a result of Abraham's impatience?

2. What are we often tempted to do?

Prayer

O Father, I am so thankful that You are strong enough not to yield to my every demand. Help me understand that there is always a good and wise purpose behind everything you do. I ask this in Christ's peerless and precious Name. Amen.

What time is it?

"… it is time to seek the Lord, until he comes and showers righteousness on you." (v.12)

For reading & meditation – Hosea 10:12

We are seeing that one of the surprising features of God's ways with us is that He sometimes uses the strangest instruments to discipline His people. This is a fact which is illustrated not just in the life and times of Habakkuk but throughout the whole of history. And we must not miss the point that He might well be doing the same in our own day and age.

Consider with me for a moment the state of the Church right now. Though there are evidences of spiritual advance in certain quarters and in certain countries, generally speaking, the Church is in a bad way. It is lethargic, indolent, prayerless, unrepentant and resistant to the Holy Spirit's control.

What can God do to bring it to the place of conformity to His will? Well, He can do many things, but one sure way of getting the Church's attention is to allow it to come under pressure from hostile forces. It is a sad admission to have to make, but the Church has always been at its best when fighting with its back to the wall.

We must now ask ourselves this piercing and pointed question: If God saw it necessary to discipline His Church by allowing hostile forces to put it under pressure, what could He use? Atheistic communism could be one possibility; humanism another. But one of the most hostile forces to Christianity in the world at the moment is that of Islam. I am not a prophet, but I suspect that this is one of the instruments the Lord will use to refine His people unless the Church moves quickly to repentance.

FURTHER STUDY

Isa. 55:1-6;
Deut. 4:29;
Psa. 105:4;
Matt. 7:7

1. What is the difference between seeking and asking?

2. What is the condition for finding the Lord when we seek Him?

Prayer

O Father, how foolish we are in that we have lived so long yet learned so little. Help us to see that we either take Your way – or take the consequences. And we know from history that the consequences can be costly. Save us, O Lord. Amen.

What do we learn from history?

"For it is time for judgment to begin with the family of God ..." (v.17)

For reading & meditation – 1 Peter 4:12-19

One person has said that "the only lesson we learn from history is that we learn nothing from history". That is certainly true of the Christian Church. You would think, with the truth of Scripture staring us in the face – namely, that when other means fail, God will use hostile forces to punish His people – we would be more careful with our spiritual inheritance. But what are the facts?

The Church, generally speaking, seems to have little or no concern about its spiritual condition. It is playing when it ought to be praying, compromising when it ought to be convicting. The Church must accept the fact that if it does not respond directly to the gentle reproofs of the Word and the Spirit, then it will have to face the harsher reproofs of circumstances. And as history records, those circumstances can be most bitter and severe. It may seem strange and contradictory to us that God will use the unrighteous to refine the righteous, but as Scripture and history both show, this is what He does. God uses the strangest instruments to discipline His people – sometimes the last we would expect.

This principle applies not only to the Church as a corporate body but we see it illustrated in our individual lives also. You may, at this very moment, be in the position where God is using the last person you would expect, such as a non-Christian relative, acquaintance or workmate, to chasten and correct you. It's humbling, isn't it, to see someone who doesn't know the Lord being used by Him to help you know Him better?

FURTHER STUDY

Deut. 8:1-8;
Zech. 13:9;
Mal. 3:3;
1 Pet. 1:6-7

1. What was God's purpose in the wilderness?

2. What is the purpose of the testing periods we experience?

Prayer

O God, forgive us that although we are Your followers, we fail to follow You. Help Your people, myself included, to stay in the place of yieldedness and repentance. For we would rather be chastened by You than by circumstances. Amen.

The willingness to wait

"Let integrity and uprightness preserve me, for I wait for and expect You." (v.21, Amplified Bible)

For reading & meditation – Psalm 25:1-22

All of us have times when, although we feel we deserve a clear answer from God in relation to a certain circumstance or situation, we do not get it. Sometimes God gives us an answer and sometimes He doesn't. Indeed, a Christian may be kept in the position of waiting for a week, a month, a year – or even a lifetime. What does one do when this happens? We must do what Habakkuk did – leave the issue with God.

I feel myself that the division between chapters one and two of Habakkuk's prophecy is misplaced. Scripture is inspired but the chapter divisions are not. The first verse of chapter two is not the start of a new section but a continuation of the previous chapter. In verse 17 of chapter 1, Habakkuk asks God a question to which he gets no reply. So what does he do? He does not attempt to rationalise his position or form a premature conclusion. He certainly does not say: "I do not understand all this so therefore I am bound to conclude that God doesn't have an answer to give."

No, he acted in the way every one of us ought to act when faced with this situation – he committed the problem to God and left it with Him.

Ignore the chapter division and you will see how naturally and easily Habakkuk moves from the place of questioning to the place of waiting. There is no petulance, no sense of being ignored by God. He simply says: "I will climb my watchtower now, and wait to see what answer God will give to my complaint" (2:1, TLB). Habakkuk's willingness was the turning point in his spiritual confusion. Today it can be yours too.

Prayer

Forgive me, dear Lord, that when answers do not come, I too quickly come to the wrong conclusions about Your purposes and designs. I see the lesson Habakkuk illustrates is a deeply important one. Help me to learn it. In Jesus' Name. Amen.

The example of Jesus

"Commit your way to the Lord; trust in him, and he will do this." (v.5)

For reading & meditation – Psalm 37:1-11

We spend one more day on the issue of learning how to commit a problem to God and wait for Him to answer in His own good time. Do you find it hard to take something you do not understand to God and leave it with Him? If you do, then believe me, you are not alone. Throughout time, as we said, the people of God have found this one of the most difficult lessons they have had to learn.

The method which Habakkuk employed of committing a problem to God and leaving it with Him was the same method Jesus used in that dramatic episode at Gethsemane. The problem which Jesus had to wrestle with was not just the problem of being crucified on a cross, but of being separated from His Father by being "made sin" for us. The thing from which the Son of God recoiled was separation from His Father. This was, without doubt, the greatest perplexity of His life.

What did He do in this situation? He prayed and said: "My Father, if it is possible, may this cup be taken from me. Yet, not as I will, but as you will" (Matt. 26:39). He took the problem with which He was wrestling – the problem of being "made sin" – and left it with God. Then He moved on in the confidence that God's will is always right and that a holy God will never command anything that is wrong. If you are struggling right now with something that you do not understand – something that is causing you considerable confusion – then get up into the watchtower and just keep looking to God. But don't just share it with Him – leave it with Him.

> **FURTHER STUDY**
>
> 2 Tim. 1:1-12;
> Psa. 31:5; Phil. 1:6;
> 1 Pet. 2:23; 4:19
>
> 1. Of what was Paul convinced?
>
> 2. Of what can we be confident?

Prayer

Gracious and loving Father, I see that if I am to enjoy peace in the midst of my problems, I must learn this lesson of leaving my problems with You. Help me begin practising it this very day. In Jesus' Name. Amen.

Write it down

"Write on a scroll what you see ..." (v.11)
For reading & meditation – Revelation 1:9-20

N ow we move on to consider the sixth step we must take to move
from confusion to confidence: understand what it means to live by
faith. Remind yourself that the future is in God's hands and that He
always knows the end from the beginning. First we shall focus on the
manner in which God's answer came to the prophet. We do not know
how long Habakkuk had to wait for his answer, but immediately prior to
receiving it, the prophet is commanded to "write down the revelation
and make it plain on tablets so that a herald may run with it" (Hab. 2:2).

The words "write down the revelation" indicate that God's answer is
to be in the form of a supernatural revelation. The words "make it plain
on tablets" indicate that the revelation is not only for Habakkuk, but for
others as well – hence it has to be in a permanent form. And the words
"so that a herald may run with it" indicate that it must be written clearly. A further reason why the revelation must be recorded in writing
could be to emphasise the immutability of its content, for future circumstances can very often appear to deny a Word that God has given and
suggest that He has changed His mind.

FURTHER STUDY

2 Pet. 1:1–21;
Jer. 36:2;
Deut. 6:6; 6:9

*1. Why did Peter put
his words in writing?*

*2. What were the
Israelites
commanded to do?*

Arising out of this, let me make a practical suggestion: whenever you feel that God has spoken to you
about anything to do with the future, do what
Habakkuk did and write it down. Delay and changing
circumstances can sometimes cause God's Word of
promise to be forgotten. So I suggest, whenever God
speaks a Word to your heart concerning the future that
you record it in a permanent form.

Prayer

Heavenly Father, help me not to be so heavenly minded that I lose a sense of practi-
cality. Help me remember that "the faintest ink can sometimes be better than the
strongest memory". Amen.

A sure word of prophecy

"For prophecy never had its origin in the will of man, but men spoke from God ... by the Holy Spirit." (v.21)
For reading & meditation – 2 Peter 1:16-21

The words "write down the revelation and make it plain" (Hab. 2:2) show that God was about to reveal to Habakkuk something that was going to take place at a future time and, as you know, that is what we call "prophecy".

Prophecy occupies a large place in Scripture – in fact, over half the Bible is devoted to predicting future events. It is my conviction that nothing brings greater comfort and consolation to a Christian than to understand the nature of a prophecy. It is something that is basic to God's relationship with human beings and that is why those who have doubts about God's concern over humankind concentrate their attacks on the subject of prophecy. "Unbelief," said Dr Martyn Lloyd-Jones, "is always critical of Bible prophecy."

In today's Church, we have teachers who tell us that the Old Testament prophets were simply men of political genius who had clear insight into situations. They take exception to the view that God revealed things to them. Our text for today in the Amplified Bible reads: "No prophecy ever originated because some man willed it to do so – it never came by human impulse – but as men spoke from God who were borne along (moved and impelled) by the Holy Spirit." What would we get out of our Bible reading today, I wonder, if all it contained were the thoughts of men? I venture to say, no more than we would get out of reading the thoughts of Kipling or of Shakespeare. My writings are exhausted of meaning after a few years but you will never exhaust the meaning of divine revelation. God comes out of it because God has gone into it.

Heb. 1:1;
2 Tim. 3:1-17;
Job 32:8;

1. How has God spoken in the past?

2. How was the Scripture given to us?

Prayer

My Father and my God, I am thankful that the Bible is not just a book, but the Book. Help me to drop my bucket into the well of Scripture and drink from its clean and pure waters. In Jesus' Name I pray. Amen.

The elements of prophecy

"... being fully persuaded that God had power to do what he had promised." (v.21)

For reading & meditation – Romans 4:1-22

Yesterday we saw that prophecy is a revelation of God to humankind. Another element of prophecy is the fact that it will take place at exactly the right time: "For the revelation awaits an appointed time; it speaks of the end and will not prove false" (Hab. 2:3). The time for the fulfilment is fixed by God and it will come to pass at the exact moment that God foreordains.

Yet another element is that of foretelling the future. Here again, some Bible teachers object to this and say that prophecy is forth-telling rather foretelling. It is quite true, of course, that prophecy is a form of teaching and therefore contains an element of forth-telling (speaking out the truth), but the true nature of prophecy lies in the fact that it is predictive. God told Habakkuk things that would happen long before they came to pass.

The last element of prophecy is that it will be fulfilled: "Write down the revelation and make it plain ... for the revelation awaits an appointed time." The events God foretells are certain to take place – and in God's time. The revelation may seem to be delayed, but nothing can prevent or frustrate its fulfilment.

How does all this relate to the more practical aspects of daily Christian living? Let me put the answer in the form of two questions: Has God given you a word or a promise that is yet to be fulfilled? And does the delay cause you to wonder whether or not He has forgotten His promise? Then take heart – there are trains on His line until 11:59. What God has promised, He will most certainly perform.

FURTHER STUDY

Matt. 5:1-18;
1 Kings 8:56;
Psa. 111:7-8;
Ezek. 12:25

1. What did Christ promise concerning God's Word?

2. Reaffirm your trust in His ability to fulfil His promise to you.

Prayer

O God, I bring to You my doubts and uncertainties for You to put them to rest – for ever. Today I want You to burn deep into me the conviction that nothing can ever stop Your Word from being fulfilled. Nothing. I am so thankful. Amen.

When tempted to doubt ...

*"But I the Lord will speak what I will, and it shall be
fulfilled without delay." (v.25)*
For reading & meditation – Ezekiel 12:21-28

Once we grasp the principles that underly Biblical prophecy, they
enable us to face the future with confidence and poise. What is the
point of being unduly anxious when we know that God is committed to
keeping His Word – not in just one thing, but in everything? Remember
God's prediction concerning the Flood? It was 120 years before it
happened (Gen. 6:3) – but it came to pass exactly as God foretold.

But perhaps the most striking illustration of this is found in the life
of Abraham in Genesis 15:13-14: "Then the Lord said to him, 'Know for
certain that your decendants will be strangers in a country not their own,
and they will be enslaved and ill-treated four hundred years. But I will
punish the nation they serve as slaves, and afterwards they will come out
with great possessions.' " Later, in Exodus 12:40-42, we read: "The sons
of Jacob and their descendants had lived in Egypt 430 years, and it was
on the last day of the 430th year that all of Jehovah's people left the land.
This night was selected by the Lord to bring His people out from the
land of Egypt" (TLB).

The first text is a general statement, but then God
narrows it down more precisely to not just the year,
not just the month, but the very night on which the
deliverance is to take place. Keep these remarkable
texts in mind when next you begin to doubt the relia-
bility of God's personal word to you. Wait upon God.
Be assured – everything He has promised will come to
pass. It will be difficult at times to understand the
delay. But wait for the vision – it is certain, it is sure, it
can never, never fail.

FURTHER STUDY

Mark 1:1-15;
Gal. 4:4; Eph. 1:10;
1 Tim. 2:6

*1. What did John
declare?*

*2. When did God
send His Son?*

Prayer

Father, help me to look out at the future, not through the eyes of chilling doubt, but
through the eyes of ever-increasing faith. And when I cannot understand, help me
just to stand. In Jesus' Name. Amen.

"The Great Divide"

"But my righteous one will live by faith …" (v.38)
For reading & meditation – Hebrews 10:19-39

We come today to one of the most wonderful statements in Scripture: "the just shall live by his faith" (Hab. 2:4, AV). The verse is quoted several times in the New Testament and is familiar to almost every Christian. What is not so familiar is the statement prior to it: "See, he is puffed up; his desires are not upright …". And if we fail to focus on that first statement, then we will miss the sense of what God is saying to Habakkuk. Join the two statements together and you will notice that they present two sides of a picture – the man who is full of unbelief and the man who is full of faith.

You see, there are only two basic attitudes we can adopt to life in this world – one is the attitude of faith, the other the attitude of unbelief. One commentator puts it like this: "Either we view our lives in terms of our belief in God and the conclusions we are entitled to draw from that; or our outlook is based upon a rejection of God and the corresponding denials."

It is quite clear that this verse is a Biblical watershed, or, as it is sometimes called, "a Great Divide", with every single person being on one side or the other. Our lives are either based on faith – or they are not. So this is what life comes down to: we accept the government of God in the universe or we do not. Those who reject His rule, whether they realise it or not, live lives that are shot through with doubt and fear. Those who receive His rule live lives of quiet confidence and faith.

FURTHER STUDY

Luke 17:1-5;
Mark 9:14-27;
Heb. 11:6

1. What was the apostles' request?

2. What was the request of the boy's father?

Prayer

Gracious Father, I see that whether I like it or not, I have to stand on one side of this Great Divide. I stand on Your side, dear Father, for nothing lies outside the domain of Your Kingdom – at least, nothing worth having. Amen.

What is faith?

"For as he thinks in his heart, so is he." (v.7, NKJ)
For reading & meditation – Proverbs 23:1-16

"A man's belief," says Dr Albert Ellis, a well-known modern-day psychologist, "determines both his conduct and his character." Our text for today, written almost 3,000 years before Ellis, puts the truth in an even more succinct form.

There are two possibilities before each of us as we look at life: we can base our conclusions about the meaning of life on what the humanistic philosophers, poets and historians tell us, or we can base them on what God tells us in His Word. Either we take the Word of God and live by it – or we do not. If we take the attitude that the prophets didn't know what they were talking about and there are no such things as miracles in the universe, then we do what the writer to the Hebrews told us about yesterday – we draw back from the godly way of life. The Biblical way is living by faith.

Listen to the word given to Habakkuk once again: "The just shall live by his faith" (Hab. 2:4, AV). Faith is taking the Word of God and relying on it. It involves believing what God says, simply and solely because He said it. The heroes of faith listed in Hebrews 11 did just that – they had no real reason for believing what God told them, other than the fact that He had spoken. Why did Abraham take his son Isaac to Mount Moriah? Why did he prepare to offer him as a sacrifice? Simply because God had spoken. A little boy, when invited to comment on the statement, "Faith is having confidence in what God has spoken," said: "God has confidence in what He has said – so must we."

FURTHER STUDY

Heb. 11:1-40;
Gal. 3:6; Phil. 3:8-9

1. How does this chapter describe faith?

2. Write out your definition of faith.

Prayer

O Father, forgive my doubts and hesitancies – and help me to have an unshakeable confidence in the truth and power of Your Word. Show me how to link my littleness to Your greatness. In Jesus' Name I ask it. Amen.

The only way to live

"He follows my decrees and faithfully keeps my laws. That man is righteous; he will surely live …" (v.9)

For reading & meditation – Ezekiel 18:1-18

We spend one more day looking at the text: "The just shall live by his faith" (Hab. 2:4, AV). Many think that the life of faith is reserved only for those Christians who go into full-time Christian work, trusting God to meet their financial and physical needs. The life of faith, however, means much more than that – it is living day by day under the controlling principle that God is true to His Word. And that is to be the position of every Christian – at all times.

Permit me to ask this personal question: What is the controlling principle in your life? Is it the expertise you have gained from years of education and training? Is it a shrewd understanding of finances? Or is it the Word of God and its clear portrayal of the fact that the things of time are merely a preparation for what is to come?

The Bible, of course, does not encourage us to turn our backs on the world, but it does tell us that we must have a right view of the world. It categorically states that what really matters is the eternal kingdom of God. Living by faith means that we live on God's side of the Great Divide that we talked about the other day. In other words, we take our view of life and the world not from what the politicians or the scientists say about them but from what God says about them. And when we are willing to stake everything on the fact that what we read in the Bible is true, then and only then will we fulfil the statement: "the just shall live by his faith". This is the only true way to live – anything else is just existence.

FURTHER STUDY

Matt. 8:1-13; 9:29-30; 17:20;
Mark 11:22

1. What did Jesus say to the centurion?

2. What did he say to the blind men?

Prayer

O Father, now I see that faith is not something that comes in fits and starts but something that underlies the whole of my life, help me understand it even more clearly. For I want to live, dear Lord, truly live – not just exist. Amen.

"The five woes"

*"Woe to him who ... makes himself wealthy by extortion! ...
Woe to him who builds his realm by unjust gain ..."* (vv. 6, 9)
For reading & meditation – Habakkuk 2:5-11

We continue examining the steps we must take in order to move from confusion to faith, and now we come to the seventh: keep in mind that no matter how dark and difficult things may appear, God is always in control.

The verses before us today are the first of "the five woes" (2:5–20). These "woes" spell out not only the doom of the Chaldeans, but the end of all those who choose the way of sin. Everything that is evil is under God's judgment. Though the Chaldeans would rise up and flourish, the boundaries of their prosperity were clearly drawn up by God.

The first woe (vv. 6-8) has to do with the way in which the Chaldeans will find their attempts at the sequestration of God's people flung back in their faces as they themselves experience what it means to be stripped of their possessions. The second woe (vv. 9-11) spells out the punishment the Chaldeans will receive for getting rich at the expense of the poor. The very houses they have built through unjust gain will cry out against them and the eventual cost of their sinful lifestyle will be the forfeiture of their own lives.

The Chaldeans would learn – and through them the other nations – that righteousness always has the last word. I once heard a young man say on television: "I would like to get this generation acquainted with this guy called 'Kick' – he gives you lots of thrills." I felt like saying: "Young man, I suggest you get acquainted with another guy called 'Kick Back'. He is always a little behind the first guy – and always has the last kick."

Prayer

O Father, I know You have designed the universe to respond with either results or consequences. When I obey Your laws I get results, when I break them I get consequences. I am determined to get results. Help me. In Jesus' Name. Amen.

"As surely as night follows day"

*" For the earth will be filled with the knowledge of the glory
of the Lord, as the waters cover the sea." (v.14)*

For reading & meditation – Habakkuk 2:12-14

We continue looking at the five woes which God pronounces on the evil Chaldeans. The third woe (vv.12-14) pronounces God's verdict on them for the prosperity they have gained through murdering and plundering other nations.

We cannot read these woes without once again thinking: Why does God allow it? Why does He permit nations to rise up and inflict such cruelty and horror on others? He allows it for a wise and particular purpose – a purpose that many find difficult to comprehend. What is that purpose? This: He allows evil nations to arise so that the rest of the world might see in them a visual aid of what happens when people attempt to pit their strength against God and His moral laws. And what does happen? They are brought down and smashed into the ground.

Isn't this the reality of history? Think of great and powerful empires such as Egypt, Babylon, Greece and Rome. What happened to them? They rose in great glory but eventually they fell. Nation after nation has risen, only to fall. The time came when God's woe was pronounced against them and put into effect. And remember this: that principle is still in effect today. God's woe is still being pronounced on all those nations who have chosen their own way instead of God's. They may have temporary success – we must be prepared for that – but as surely as night follows day, they will fall. The ultimate triumph of good over evil is certain. Let there be no doubt about it: "For the earth will be filled with the knowledge of the glory of the Lord, as the waters cover the sea."

FURTHER STUDY

2 Sam. 1:1–27;
Prov. 14:12;
Judg. 17:6

1. What was David's lament?

2. What is the end of our natural thinking?

Prayer

My Father and my God, something is quietly being burned into my consciousness – You are the One who has the last word in everything. Help me to face all that comes in the light of this great and glorious fact. Amen.

Finding out how not to live

*"What profit was there in worshipping all our man-made idols?
What a foolish lie that they could help! ..." (v.18, TLB)*
For reading & meditation – Habakkuk 2:15-19

Today we look at the last two woes which God pronounced on the evil
and cruel Chaldeans. The fourth woe (vv.15-17) had to do with the
"scorched earth" policy operated by the Chaldeans, which involved
deforestation and the destruction of animals. (Both are a matter of divine
concern – see Deuteronomy. 20:19 and Jonah 4:11.) Such outrage, says
God, carries within it the seeds of its own destruction: "You cut down
the forests of Lebanon – now you will be cut down! You terrified the
wild animals... Now terror will strike you" (v.17, TLB).

The recurrent theme of the five woes, namely that sin recoils upon
the sinner, sounds once more in the fifth and final one (vv.18-19). This
woe is uttered upon the idolater and exposes the inexplicable folly of his
practice. The words, "Woe to those who command their lifeless wooden
idols to arise and save them, who call out to the speechless stone to tell
them what to do" (v.18, TLB), demonstrate that idolatry is not something that is innocuous; indeed, it is deeply injurious because it destroys
man's basic intelligence. As someone has put it: "The worst thing about
idolatry is to be the one who practises the idolatry."

How sad that, right before our eyes, we see history
repeating itself as, once again, humanity looks to the
idols which it has set up in the world to save itself
from death and destruction. We cannot trust ourselves
to any other power but God – not even the United
Nations. The world has had so many lessons in how
not to live, you would think its people would now be
ready to try the Way.

FURTHER STUDY

Rom. 1:18-32;
Ex. 20:4-5;
Lev. 26:1;
Deut. 11:16

1. For what did men
exchange the glory of
God?

2. What was the
result?

Prayer

O Father, how sad it is that despite the fact that people have had so many lessons in
how not to live – lessons that have left them exhausted and frustrated – they still do
not turn to the Way. Help them find it – and find it soon. In Jesus' Name. Amen.

Sin has no future

"… you may be sure that your sin will find you out." (v.23)
For reading & meditation – Numbers 32:20-33

No one can read the five woes which God pronounced upon the Chaldeans without coming to the conclusion that sin has no future. The Moffatt translation of Amos 2:13 says: "I will make your steps collapse." Is this fact or fiction? It is fact. The more evil advances the more its "steps collapse".

The same thought comes across in 1 Kings 21:21: "Because you have sold yourself to no purpose in doing what is evil in the sight of the Eternal" (Moffatt). Note the phrase, "to no purpose". Does the doing of what God cannot approve always end in futility? Is it all "to no purpose"? Most certainly. Take another text: "Your doom appears; your sin has blossomed, your pride has budded" (Ezek. 7:10, Moffatt). Notice how sin blossomed and pride budded – and the fruit? Doom!

Look with me at one more Scripture: "The Beast which was and is not" (Rev. 17:11, Moffatt). Note the words, "was and is not": evil has a past, but it has no future. It "was", but it will not be. No matter if "the Beast" is spelled with a capital "B": it will shrivel; it is under the law of decay. Give evil enough rope and it will hang itself. If it is not being constantly bolstered up by the surrounding good, it will go to pieces. All evil is a parasite upon good. You have to throw enough good around evil to keep it going. When it is total "Beast", it is total blight. Sin has no future. It may get away with things at the moment, but inevitably it is doomed. The seeds of its own destruction are carried within its bosom.

FURTHER STUDY

1 Cor. 4:1-5;
Job 20:27;
Eccl. 12:14;
Luke 12:2

1. What will God bring to light?

2. What does the verse at the top of the page actually say?

Prayer

Gracious Father, this age through which we are passing has looked upon evil until its eyes are tired. Turn people's gaze in the direction of Yourself, I pray. Help them see that evil is the great illusion – and God the great Illumination. Amen.

"The long view"

"… no weapon forged against you will prevail …" (v.17)
For reading & meditation – Isaiah 54:4-17

Having now considered the five woes which God pronounced on the cruel Chaldeans, what is our conclusion? We come back to what we said at the beginning of this section – no matter how dark and difficult things may appear, God is always in control. The Chaldeans would rise and be permitted to commit great atrocities, but God would use those atrocities to discipline Judah. The Chaldeans had no direct knowledge of God's will. They would plan their attacks, ravage the cities, marshall their armies simply to satisfy their own lust for power, but God would use their purposes to carry out His. When, however, it was all over, they would have to face the judgment of God for their inhuman practices.

It is of the utmost importance that we, the people of God, learn how to become people of what has been described as "the long view". What does it mean to have "the long view"? It means, quite simply, to see things from God's perspective. If you take the short view of what is happening around you, then you come to your own conclusions. If you take the long view, then you come to God's conclusions.

God takes the long view of history and is quietly bringing all things to a predetermined end. My Christian friend, don't be a human ostrich – burying your head in the sand because you are afraid to face tomorrow. Nothing can happen in the future that God cannot control. Catch the sweep of His mind and the glory of His long-range purposes, and realise, as our text for today says, that no weapon forged against you can prevail.

FURTHER STUDY

Col. 1:13-22;
John 1:1-3;
1 Cor. 8:6

1. Where should we focus our gaze?

2. What does Colossians 1 reveal to us?

Prayer

O God, help me to look at life with "the long view". Drive deep into my spirit the thought that because You know the end from the beginning, nothing that is evil can work successfully against me. I am so thankful. Amen.

Ask "what?" not "why?"

"But the Lord is in his holy temple; let all the earth be silent before him." (v.20)

For reading & meditation – Habakkuk 2:20

The last part of God's answer to Habakkuk is as forceful as it is brief. It is that He knows what He is doing, even when circumstances seem to be speeding downhill like a car out of control. The phrase "let all the earth be silent before him" includes everything and everybody – the godly as well as the heathen. Sometimes God speaks pretty straight to us – just as He is doing here – and tells us things that we might not want to know, but things we certainly need to know.

If I understand this verse correctly, God is saying, in effect: "Stop asking endless questions such as: 'Why does God do this?' and 'Why does God do that?' Understand the fact that I know what I am doing and that I am the Lord of history." Once we make up our minds that God knows what He is doing, then all confusion vanishes. And that applies not only to the personal issues of life but to the global ones as well.

The same Word that brought comfort and illumination to Habakkuk's heart can, if we let it, comfort our own hearts. If you look at almost any day's newspaper you will find reports of rape, murder, crime, injustice and corruption. But if you turn from your newspaper and look up at God you will find yourself looking at the Ultimate, the Absolute. And what will happen? Instead of your heart being filled with fear, it will become strangely peaceful. Why? Because you will realise that God is at the centre of His universe and He is working out His purposes. And as someone said: "He who knows what God is doing need never ask why."

FURTHER STUDY

Matt. 19:16-26;
Job 42:2;
Psa. 115:3;
Isa. 43:13;
Luke 1:37

1. What did Jesus declare?

2. What can you declare today?

Prayer

Gracious and loving heavenly Father, help me this day to catch the sweep of Your purposes and become a part of them. Deepen my conviction that You are in control, for I see that then I will focus more on the "what" than the "why". Amen.

Focusing on God

*"O Lord, I have heard the report of You and was afraid
…" (v.2, Amplified Bible)*

For reading & meditation – Habakkuk 3:1-2

Having examined the nature of God's revelation to Habakkuk, we
now ask: What is the prophet's response to the divine unfolding? He
draws near to God in an attitude of reverential worship and praise. This
suggests the eighth step we must take if we are to move from confusion
to confidence: make it a daily habit to worship the Lord and open your
heart to Him in fervent prayer and praise.

Habakkuk confesses himself to be overwhelmed by the things which
God has revealed to him: "I worship you in awe for the fearful things you
are going to do" (v.2, TLB). One of the inevitable results of spending
time in God's presence, contemplating Him and listening to His voice is
that there arises within the heart a spontaneous desire to worship Him.

It was this thought that inspired me to launch the *Every Day with
Jesus* study notes in the beginning. I realised that if I could focus people's
minds on to a small portion of God's Word every day, it would inevitably
result in a greater understanding and devotion to Him. The results have
been astonishing. Someone who wrote to me said: "My life has been
turned right around since I have begun to focus my
thinking on God before I focus on the day."

You see, it is one of the laws of life that you
become like the thing on which you focus. Focus on
money and you will become like it – hard and metallic.
Focus on getting even with those who act spitefully
toward you and you will become like them – mean and
inconsiderate. Focus on God and you will become like
Him – good, gracious and generous.

FURTHER STUDY

John 4:1-24;
1 Chron. 16:29;
Psa. 96:9

1. How are we to
worship?

2. Spend time today
focusing your
worship on Christ.

Prayer

O Father, if it is true that I become like that on which I focus, then help me to focus
fully on You. Help me to maintain daily contact with You – through worshipping
You and reading Your Word. In Jesus' Name I ask it. Amen.

"Worth-ship"

"I want to know Christ and the power of his resurrection ..." (v.10)

For reading & meditation – Philippians 3:1-14

Yesterday we saw that one of the inevitable results of contemplating God and listening to His voice is a spontaneous desire to worship Him. Habakkuk, after having been closeted with God and receiving the staggering revelation of His power and sovereignty, finds his heart filled to overflowing.

You have only to read the third chapter of Habakkuk to see how his emotions are set on fire. It's interesting to notice that so strong is the emotional content in this chapter that it begins with the words: "A prayer of Habakkuk the prophet. On *shigionoth*." The word "*shigionoth*" (plural of *shigaion*; see heading to Psalm 7) is believed to indicate the tempo at which this prayer was originally meant to be sung. The tempo was to be strong one, corresponding to the profound emotions raised through the words and concepts of this chapter.

Why were Habakkuk's emotions so aroused? Because his soul had been set ablaze by a thrilling revelation of God. One of the things we must understand about the Christian life is that our worship of God is largely determined by our understanding of Him. So permit me once again to ask you a personal question: How do you see God? What is the depth of your understanding of Him? Today, comparatively few know how to really worship God. This is a direct result of the superficial preaching and teaching that comes from so many modern pulpits. Our worship of God depends, as the word suggests, on how much "worth" we ascribe to Him. The greater "worth" you see in Him, the greater worship you will give to Him.

FURTHER STUDY

Col. 1:1-12;
Jer. 9:24;
Hosea 6:3;
John 17:3

1. What was Paul's desire for the Colossians?

2. Write a psalm describing what your God is like.

Prayer

O God, if it is true that my worship of You flows from my understanding of You, then help me to know You more. As I spend time reading Your Word and in prayer, reveal Yourself to me – in a fresh and living way. In Christ's Name I ask it. Amen.

The highest form of prayer

"O Lord, listen! O Lord, forgive! O Lord, hear and act! … do not delay, because your city and your people bear your Name." (v.19)

For reading & meditation – Daniel 9:1-19

Ｗe look now at how Habakkuk moves from worship to prayer – a prayer, by the way, which has become one of the best-known petitions of Scripture: "O Lord, revive Your work in the midst of the years! In the midst of the years make it known; In wrath remember mercy" (Hab. 3:2, NKJ).

We cannot help but notice, in this prayer the prophet's attitude toward God has completely changed. There is no longer any questioning of His way. He does not even protest at what God has told him about the terrible things that are going to happen. Nor does he petition God to reverse His judgment. Instead, there is a humble recognition that what God says He is about to do is perfectly proper and that the punishment that is to come upon Judah is one that she deserves. Habakkuk's prayer contains an attitude of complete submission to the will of God.

I have chosen the prayer of Daniel for today's reading because he too displays this attitude. Like Habakkuk, Daniel also came to a place of humiliation and submission to the divine will. But how did Habakkuk arrive at this position? I think it was because he had changed his spiritual focus from gazing at Judah to gazing at God. When Habakkuk focused his gaze on Judah and the Chaldeans he was troubled, but when he focused his gaze on God, he moved into the realm of spiritual light and illumination. He saw things from God's point of view. Thus he is concerned for the glory of God – and nothing else. We practise the highest form of prayer when our concern for God's glory transcends all other priorities.

> **FURTHER STUDY**
> Eph. 6:1-7;
> Psa. 40:8; 143:10
>
> 1. How are we to carry out the will of God?
>
> 2. How did the psalmist respond to God's will?

Prayer

O God, help me lift my praying to this high place. Teach me how to bring my priorities in line with Your priority and how to make my primary concern the glory of God. In Jesus' Name. Amen.

A plea for revival

"Why don't you tear the sky apart and come down? ..."
(v.1, GNB)

For reading & meditation – Isaiah 64:1-8

We ended yesterday with the thought that the highest form of prayer is when we are concerned about the glory of God – and nothing else. Habakkuk did not petition God to give up the idea of using the Chaldeans to refine the people of Judah. Nor did he ask that there would be no sacking of Jerusalem. There was no such petition because he had come to see that the forthcoming events were well deserved.

Now that the prophet had begun to see the whole issue from God's point of view, his burden was for God's cause and God's glory. His petition – so I believe – can be paraphrased in these words: "Lord, whatever we, Your people, have to put up with is of no concern so long as Your work is revived and kept pure." His one great plea is that God will "revive [His] work in the midst of the years!" (Hab. 3:2, NKJ). Most commentators believe that the expression "in the midst of the years" means "while these terrible things that are predicted are going on among us".

Oh, that we could hear more of this kind of praying in our churches today. Most prayers we hear are concerned with topical issues – the nuclear threat, world economy, violence, corruption, and so on. These issues are important, of course, and most certainly there is a need to keep them in the focus of our praying. But these matters should not be our biggest concern. I have no hesitation in saying that the chief concern of the Church in this present age should be the spiritual restoration of God's people through a world-wide Holy Spirit revival.

FURTHER STUDY

Isa. 26:1-9;
2 Chron. 15:15;
Psa. 38:9; 73:25

1. Why did Isaiah seek God?

2. What was the psalmist's confession?

Prayer

My Father and my God, forgive us that we have allowed ourselves to slip into the depths of spiritual poverty and emptiness. Breathe once again into the midst of us – and begin, dear Lord, in me. Amen

"In wrath remember mercy"

*"Correct me, Lord, but only with justice – not in your
anger, lest you reduce me to nothing." (v.24)*

For reading & meditation – Jeremiah 10:12-25

W̶e are seeing that Habakkuk's chief concern in prayer was not that
God should call a halt to His plans, but that there should be a spiritual revival in Judah. The prophet's great fear was that Judah might be
overwhelmed, and so he prays, in effect: "Preserve Your witness in our
midst, O Lord – keep it alive, don't let it be destroyed."

The Hebrew word "revive" contains the idea of God bending down
to the dying embers of a fire and breathing into them until they burst
into flame. What an appropriate prayer this is for the Church today. If,
like Habakkuk, we would make the Name and glory of God, rather than
world events, the prime focus of our praying, we would come closer to
the Biblical pattern and be more likely to see His glory revealed.

Before we turn aside from Habakkuk's great prayer and examine the
final section of this chapter, we must spend a few moments looking at
the final statement in his prayer: "In wrath remember mercy" (Hab. 3:2).
The great devotional Bible commentator Matthew Henry says of this
phrase: "Habakkuk does not say 'Remember our merit', but 'Lord,
remember Thy own mercy'." The prophet uses a
method which seems to be characteristic of that of
many of the Old Testament saints when at prayer,
namely, to remind God of His own nature. This was
not a technique but showed a deep and profound
understanding of the nature of importunate prayer.
Modern-day praying lacks the depth and understanding that we see illustrated in the lives of the ancient
prophets. When the Church gets back to powerful
praying, then and only then will it get powerful
results.

FURTHER STUDY

Micah 7:1-18;
Psa. 103:18; 108:4

*1. How did Micah
view God?*

*2. Write out a
definition of
"mercy".*

Prayer

Gracious and loving heavenly Father, breathe on the dying embers of Your Church
this day – myself included – until out of the ashes comes a new and living flame. This
I ask in Christ's peerless and precious Name. Amen.

"Self-talk"

"… let your mind dwell on these things." (v.8, NASB)
For reading & meditation – Philippians 4:1-9

We come now to the ninth step in our progression from confusion to confidence: remind yourself of the evidences of God's faithfulness in the past and constantly talk to yourself about them.

At this point, we are going to leave Habakkuk just for a moment to lay down a foundation for our thinking over the next few days. Let me ask you: Do you ever talk to yourself? No? Then permit me to correct you. Although you don't realise it – because it goes on just below the threshold of awareness – you talk to yourself almost every minute of your waking day. Whatever event takes place in our lives, we respond to that event by talking to ourselves about it. Psychologists call this the "theory of propositional control" – we talk to ourselves in sentences. And what we tell ourselves, even subconsciously, will determine the way we feel about issues.

Have you heard someone ask the question: Why do I feel this way? Well, why do people feel a particular way about things? It is because our feelings are largely the direct consequence of our thinking. If you respond to a negative or unpleasant event by saying to yourself "Why should this happen to me?" then it is not difficult to predict how you will feel – sad and depressed. But if you respond by telling yourself, "God loves me and will never allow anything to happen to me unless it accords with a wise and loving purpose", you will feel quite different. Why? Because your feelings follow your thinking – just like little ducklings follow their mother.

FURTHER STUDY

Psa. 42:1-11;
94:19; Prov. 23:7
(footnote)

1. What are some of the statements the psalmist made to himself?

2. What are some of the statements you make to yourself?

Prayer

O Father, if what I say to myself is powerful and determinative in my personality, then help me to control my self-talk so that it serves me rather than enslaves me. In Christ's Name I ask it. Amen.

Feeling better!

"You came out to deliver your people, to save your anointed one …" (v.13)

For reading & meditation – Habakkuk 3:3-15

Now we have established the idea that what we tell ourselves, consciously or unconsciously, greatly influences how we feel, we look at how this is illustrated in the prophet Habakkuk's life and experience. The section before us today is dominated by remembrances of God's deliverances in the past. It is helpful to take in the whole section at one time so that we catch the sweep and force of the prophet's thinking.

First, he consciously focuses on the thought that God is mighty and all-powerful (vv. 3-7). He says: "His splendour was like the sunrise; rays flashed from his hand, where his power was hidden … He stood, and shook the earth; he looked, and made the nations tremble." Next, he concentrates on the facts which surrounded Israel's deliverance from Egypt (vv. 8-15): "You split the earth with rivers; the mountains saw you and writhed … the deep roared … Sun and moon stood still … you strode through the earth … in anger … You trampled the sea with your horses …".

Can you see what Habakkuk is doing here? He is calling to mind the way in which God has come to the aid of His people in times past, and the more he focuses on God's faithfulness and power, the more the remaining mists of fog and confusion are dispelled. This, then, is the divinely provided way of handling all fear and confusion – consciously to focus on the facts of God's deliverances in the past. When the prophet did this, he began to feel better. And why? Because positive thoughts about God led to positive feelings about God. They always do.

FURTHER STUDY

Psa. 89:1;
2 Tim. 2:1-13;
Deut. 7:9;
1 Cor. 1:9

1. What was the psalmist able to sing about?

2. List some ideas of God's faithfulness in your own life.

Prayer

Father, help me not to view this principle merely as an interesting idea, but help me put it to the test in my daily life and experience. Show me even more clearly that how I think greatly influences how I feel. Amen.

Happy remembrances

"… a scroll of remembrance was written in his presence concerning those who feared the Lord and honoured his name." (v.16)

For reading & meditation – Malachi 3:8-18

Yesterday we looked at some of the things which the prophet brought to mind concerning God's past deliverances and we saw how these remembrances filled his heart with hope and consolation.

Today we are in a better position than Habakkuk, for we have even more wonderful facts on which to focus our thinking. We can see, for example, how everything that was revealed to the prophet was literally fulfilled. The Chaldeans did indeed invade Judah and carried people into captivity in Babylon. But at the appointed time, God brought judgment on the Chaldeans and destroyed them and caused a remnant of His people to return to Jerusalem.

However, we can go still further. We can focus not just on the fact of how God made a way for His people to come out of Egypt and Babylon, but on the greater deliverance which He engineered when He made a path to bring us from the dominion of Satan to the very doors of heaven. In the Old Testament, a sacrificial lamb could provide redemption for an individual or a family. But in the New Testament, the Lamb of God purchased redemption not just for an individual or a family but for the sins of the whole world!

FURTHER STUDY

Rom. 8:1-39;
2 Cor. 9:15;
Eph. 2:8

1. What can we now cry out to God?

2. What is available to us through Christ's sacrifice?

And there is yet more. We can focus on the glorious fact that our Lord has overcome the darkness of death, and by His glorious resurrection has given us the eternal pledge that because He lives, we shall live also (John 14:19). Keep these thoughts in mind throughout this day, and I promise you – you will know the effect of them in your feelings.

Prayer

Glorious Father, I come to You to ask for Your help in keeping these remembrances of Your faithfulness and power before me this day. I give You my mind – so that You can give me Yours. In Christ's Name I ask it. Amen.

On being human

*"I heard and my heart pounded, my lips quivered ... and
my legs trembled ..."* (v.16)

For reading & meditation – Habakkuk 3:16

It seems strange that after recalling and reciting so many of the facts
relating to God's strength and power, Habakkuk should be in the state
we see him in at the moment. *The Living Bible* puts it thus: "I tremble
when I hear all this; my lips quiver with fear. My legs give way beneath
me and I shake in terror. I will quietly wait for the day of trouble to come
upon the people who invade us."

If it is true that what we think about greatly influences the way we
feel, then why, after focusing on such a catalogue of good things, does
Habakkuk feel the way he does? The answer, I believe, is this: although
calling to mind God's goodness is a proven and reliable method of dealing with fear and producing positive feelings within us, it does not completely eliminate all negative emotions.

It is terribly important that we understand this. Some preach that
once we become Christians, we need never experience any negative or
uncomfortable feelings. That simply is not so. The Christian faith does
not promise us that once we become Christians we will never again
experience negative emotions, but it does promise that
the negative emotions will be manageable and brought
under control. Habakkuk has been brought to the
place where he sees everything perfectly clearly, but as
he contemplates the trouble that is coming upon
Judah, he trembles like a leaf. We should note, however, that though he feels strong emotions, he is not
overcome by them. If this ever happens to you, don't
see it as a lack of faith. Like Habakkuk, you are simply
being human.

FURTHER STUDY

Phil. 2:1-13;
1 Cor. 2:3;
2 Cor. 7:15

1. How are we to
work out our
salvation?

2. What feelings did
Paul admit to?

Prayer

Thank You, Lord, for reminding me that fear and trembling do not cancel out my
faith, but serve as a reminder of my humanity. Help me to understand this – and not
be overwhelmed by it. In Jesus' Name. Amen.

How to treat trouble

"Yet I will rejoice in the Lord, I will exalt in the victorious God of my salvation!" (v.18, Amplified Bible)

For reading & meditation – Habakkuk 3:17-18

We have now reached the tenth and final step in our progression from confusion to confidence: decide to face everything that comes not in a spirit of resignation but in a spirit of rejoicing. The passage before us today shows quite clearly that it is possible to rejoice, even in the face of the most disturbing circumstances: "Though the fig-tree does not bud and there are no grapes on the vines … yet I will rejoice in the Lord, I will be joyful in God my Saviour."

There are three responses we can make in the presence of trouble: we can rebel against it, resign ourselves to it, or we can rejoice in it. Many take the way of rebellion when confronted by trouble – they cry out against the heavens and question the justice of God, believing they have good cause to do so. It is an understandable reaction, of course – but it is not the Christian way. Others resign themselves to the situation and say such things as: "Well, what will be will be." "There's no point in crying over spilt milk." "I will just have to grin and bear it." But resignation is not the Christian way either – although many believers think it is. Beneath all resignation simmers an unconscious resentment. It cannot always be observed and it is sometimes so deeply repressed that it cannot even be felt – but it is there nevertheless.

The Christian way of facing trouble is the way of rejoicing. When the worst comes to the worst, we are not just to put up with it, but rejoice in it. And if we can't – then we still have a vital lesson to learn.

FURTHER STUDY

Acts 16:16-40;
5:41; 2 Cor. 6:10

1. How did Paul and Silas respond to their circumstances?

2. What was the result?

Prayer

O Father, I have learned so many lessons through the life of Your servant Habakkuk – help me not to miss this last but vital one also. Teach me how to rejoice in all things. For Jesus' sake. Amen.

"All times" – a mistranslation?

"Rejoice at all times." (v.16, Moffatt)
For reading & meditation – 1 Thessalonians 5:12-24

Many Christians find this text so challenging that they cannot allow their minds to focus on it. But as we have been saying – evasion will never get us anywhere. A letter I once received asked: "Did Paul really mean we should rejoice at all times? Didn't he mean sometimes? Can this be a mistranslation?" No, it is not a mistranslation – it is a true and accurate translation of the apostle's words.

But is it really possible to rejoice at all times? I believe it is. Here's the secret: we can rejoice in everything only to the extent that we see God in everything. Some might have difficulty with this, and respond: "There are some things which come from the devil; how can what you say be applied to that?" It is true that God may not be in the genesis of something, but He can certainly be in its exodus. Your circumstances or problems may have begun with the devil, but by the time they get to you and through you, they have a divine purpose running through them.

An old lady was praying for bread. Some boys, hearing her, decided to play a trick on her. They climbed up on her roof and threw some loaves down the chimney. "Praise the Lord," shouted the old lady, "God has heard my prayer." The boys then knocked on her door and said: "But it was not God who gave you the bread – it was us." She laughingly replied: "Well, the devil may have brought it, but it was God who sent it." Wherever an event comes from, by the time it gets to you, you can be sure it has got God's permission – and thus has the potential of becoming not a source of trouble but a source of triumph.

FURTHER STUDY

1 Pet. 4:1-13;
Phil. 4:4; Psa. 33:1;
James 1:2-3

1. Why does God
   allow us to go
   through trials?

2. Why can we
   rejoice in our trials?

Prayer

O Father, thank You for imparting to me the secret of continuous rejoicing – we can rejoice in everything when we see God in everything. Imprint these words indelibly on my spirit so that I may for ever live in the light of them. In Jesus' Name. Amen.

Hinds' feet on high places

*"... He makes my feet like hinds' feet, and will make me to walk
... upon my high places ..." (v.19, Amplified Bible)*

For reading & meditation – Habakkuk 3:18-19

What a transformation has taken place in the heart of Habakkuk. Now he no longer stumbles in the darkness of doubt and spiritual confusion, but leaps from one revelation to another with the sure-footedness of a deer. He walks on high places where others fear to tread. By climbing his watchtower and entering into a dialogue with God, and by listening to His replies, Habakkuk has learned and discovered so much that his soul is lifted above the doubts and uncertainties that once plagued his mind. The prophet began in confusion – but ends in confidence.

What made the difference? Summing it all up in a single sentence – he saw that God was in charge of earth's affairs, no matter how things looked to the contrary, and he trusted Him to do what was right. When we learn to drop our anchor into the reassuring depths of God's nature and character and learn to trust Him even when we cannot trace Him, then we too will know the sustaining joy that Habakkuk experienced back there long centuries ago.

If we believe in God, really believe in Him, then we will not disintegrate when world events take a disastrous course, or when our newspapers tell us that society is falling apart at the seams. We believe in God's Word and therefore have inside information about the future that no news commentator (unless he is Christian) can possibly possess. Christ is Lord of history – and nothing can hinder His perfect purposes from coming to pass. So step out with confidence on the high places of life. God is the One with the last Word.

FURTHER STUDY

Psa. 37:1-40;
118:8; Prov. 3:5;
Isa. 50:10

1. How does David depict the short-lived prosperity of the wicked?

2. Where is your trust placed?

Prayer

Father, how can I sufficiently thank You for showing me the ten steps which brought Habakkuk from confusion to confidence? Help me ever to remember them and thus turn theory into fact. In Christ's Name I ask it. Amen.

The
Beatitudes

A prescription for health

"His disciples came to him, and he began to teach them…"
(vv.1-2)

For reading & meditation – Matthew 5:1-11

Today we begin a study of one of the most powerful and profound passages in Scripture – the Beatitudes. They form the first part of the Lord's teaching in what is known as the Sermon on the Mount and were addressed to His disciples. My hope is that our study of the Beatitudes will have a great impact on our spiritual lives and that we will be blessed by the discoveries we make together.

We begin our theme by laying down the thought that the eight principles which comprise the Beatitudes are the best prescription for mental and spiritual health it is possible to find. Dr James Fisher, a well-known and widely travelled psychiatrist, went throughout the world looking for the positive qualities that make for good mental health. He said: "I dreamed of writing a handbook that would be simple, practical, easy to understand and easy to follow; it would tell people how to live – what thoughts and attitudes and philosophies to cultivate, and what pitfalls to avoid in seeking mental health. And quite by accident I discovered that such a work had been completed – the Beatitudes."

What an amazing admission! I would go so far as to say that once a person absorbs the principles which underlie the Beatitudes – and lives by them – then that person will never again fall prey to serious depression or despair. How sad that so often the Christian Church has to refer its depressed and discouraged people to the mental experts of the world when we hold in our hands the blueprint for healthy and abundant living.

FURTHER STUDY

Luke 6:20-38; Psa. 32:1-2; 41:1

1. What does "blessed" mean to you?

2. How would you define the word "beatitude"?

Prayer

My Father, help me to come to You at the beginning of these studies like a little child – open and receptive. Show me how to open my heart and my hands to receive Your prescription for mental and spiritual health. Amen.

"The psychology of Jesus"

"He did not need man's testimony about man, for he knew what was in a man." (v.25)

For reading & meditation – John 2:12-25

Yesterday we touched on the statement of a psychiatrist, Dr James Fisher, who said that when searching for the positive attitudes which made for good mental health, he came across the Beatitudes and realised that he need search no longer.

After nearly fifty years' experience of helping people with mental, emotional and physical problems he concluded: "If you were to take the total sum of all authoritative articles ever written by the most qualified of psychologists and psychiatrists on the subject of mental hygiene – if you were to combine them and refine them and cleave out the excess verbiage – if you were to take the whole of the meat and none of the parsley, and if you were to have these unadulterated bits of pure scientific knowledge concisely expressed by the most capable of living poets, you would have an awkward and incomplete summation of our Lord's Beatitudes – and it would suffer immeasurably through comparison."

Dr Raymond Cramer, a minister and a Christian psychologist, says something similar when he describes the Beatitudes as "the psychology of Jesus". Some may find that expression unacceptable when applied to

FURTHER STUDY

Col. 1:1-20; 2:9-10;
John 1:16;
Eph. 1:22-23

1. Where is fulness found?

2. What does this mean for us?

the Beatitudes, but remember, this is a scientist who is speaking. In studying the laws of human behaviour and seeking to discover what brings a person to his highest point of integration, he came to see that the words of Jesus in the Beatitudes are the clearest and most succinct expression of the principles by which a person can know contentment and inner happiness. In an age which is fascinated with the study of human behaviour, there is only one true psychology – the psychology of Jesus.

Prayer

Father, I see that psychology, as well as all other "-ologies", are only valid as they are brought to Your feet. Show me, dear Lord, not just how to live, but how to live abundantly. In Jesus' Name I pray. Amen.

"The beautiful attitudes"

"Rather, clothe yourselves with the Lord Jesus Christ ..." (v.14)

For reading & meditation – Romans 13:7-14

We continue considering on the fact that the Beatitudes are the finest prescription for mental and spiritual health that has ever been given. It is helpful to keep in mind at this stage in our meditations that the Beatitudes are *be*-attitudes, not *do*-attitudes; the doing comes out of the being. Some ministers and commentators refer to them as "the beautiful attitudes" – a description I find greatly appealing.

Our attitudes have a tremendous and powerful influence upon every part of our being – physical as well as emotional. A missionary from the Philippines tells how, during the war, he and his wife were ordered into prison camps by the Japanese, and were instructed that they could take with them all they could carry in their suitcases and no more. His wife, weighing just over 100 pounds, and not at all strong, carried a load of 200 pounds, mostly tinned food, a distance of five miles – a load neither of them could even lift after they arrived. Mannheim, a famous scientist, says that we normally use about one-eighth of our physical reserves, and that these reserves are only called upon when we employ the right attitudes.

If our attitudes can help tap hidden physical reserves, then think of what our experience can be if we adopt the "beautiful attitudes" which our Lord expounds for us in His Sermon on the Mount. We can maximise our potential and multiply our effectiveness, not only in the physical area of our being, but in our mental and emotional areas also. Many doctors and scientists agree that it is not our arteries but our attitudes which have the biggest say in our personal well-being.

FURTHER STUDY

1 Pet. 2:21;
Matt. 11:29;
John 13:15;
Heb. 12:2

1. What did Jesus do besides expounding these attitudes?

2. How should our lives be?

Prayer

Loving heavenly Father, help me to do as Your Word commands and "clothe myself with the Lord Jesus Christ". Show me how to have His attitudes – the "beautiful attitudes" – so that I might live fully and abundantly. Amen.

The inner affects the outer

" 'All things are lawful for me'? Yes, but not all are good for me ..." (v.12, Moffatt)

For reading & meditation – 1 Corinthians 6:12-20

We are still focusing on this important thought that our attitudes play an important and determinative part in our physical health. One doctor told me that immediately he receives the current edition of *Every Day with Jesus*, he quickly scans it to see if I have written anything along the line of the relationship between attitudes and health – a favourite topic of mine – and then orders a small supply for those of his patients who need to have their attitudes changed. He wrote to me on one occasion and said: "Keep coming back to this subject every time you can – you just don't know how much good you are doing in my medical practice."

According to an article in the *British Medical Journal*, "there is not a tissue or an organ in the body that is not influenced by the attitude of mind and spirit". Man is a unit made up of spirit, soul and body, and he cannot be sick in one part without passing on the sickness to other parts. The attitudes we hold in our minds do not stay merely as attitudes – they pass over into definite physical effects.

God has so designed our beings that the right attitudes produce the right effects in our bodies. Suppose they produced the wrong effects. Then the body and morality would be alien to one another. An outstanding surgeon said: "I've discovered the kingdom of God at the end of my scalpel; it's in the tissues. The right thing morally is always the right thing physically." The laws of morality and the laws of health are written by the same God for the same purpose – healthy and happy living.

FURTHER STUDY

2 Cor. 4:1-16;
Prov. 20:27;
Matt. 15:18-19;
Mark 7:21-23

1. How did Paul need to be daily renewed?

2. What is it that defiles a man?

Prayer

O Father, You have made us so that we can either damage or deliver ourselves in this matter of health. Help me to have Your attitudes in everything I say and everything I do. For Your own dear Name's sake. Amen.

Christ's first word ...

"Be happy ... at all times." (v.16, Phillips)
For reading & meditation – 1 Thessalonians 5:12-24

Now that we have spent a few days meditating on the fact that the Beatitudes provide us with the right mental and spiritual attitudes for healthy and abundant living, we are ready to begin focusing on the first of these profound statements: "Blessed are the poor in spirit, for theirs is the kingdom of heaven." (Matt. 5:3).

Some translations read, "Happy are the poor in spirit ...", and one goes so far as to say, "Congratulations to the poor in spirit ..." It is important to keep in mind that the word "happy" (Greek *makarios*) carries a far richer tone than we commonly attach to the word. It suggests a deep, abiding happiness, not just a temporary emotional lift.

In the very first words of the Sermon on the Mount, therefore, Jesus puts His finger on one of life's most vital issues – individual and personal happiness. We all want to be happy – and rightly so. The longing for lasting happiness is a deep-rooted instinct that has been built into us by the Creator Himself. The God who made the sunset, painted the rose, put the smile on a baby's face, gave the gift of playfulness to a kitten and put laughter in our souls is surely not happy when we are unhappy.

Although it is a God-given instinct to be happy, we must also see that it is only God who can make us happy. Apart from Him and His redemptive love as expressed through the cross and the resurrection, we would be "most miserable" (1 Cor. 15:19, AV). As someone once confessed: "Now that I know Christ, I'm happier when I'm sad than before when I was glad."

FURTHER STUDY
Rom. 14:1-18;
Isa. 12:3;
John 16:24;
1 Pet. 1:8

1. What is the kingdom of God?
2. What is this joy full of?

Prayer

Thank You, my Father, that You not only command me to be happy but provide me with the resources which make it gloriously possible. One touch of Your gladness and my heart sings for ever. I am so deeply, deeply thankful. Amen.

You cannot *make* happiness

"And he saw them toiling in rowing ..." (v.48, AV)
For reading & meditation – Mark 6:45-51

Yesterday we said that we all want to be happy – and rightly so. This is a deep-rooted instinct which God has built into us. But happiness is not something you make but something you receive. You cannot make happiness any more than you can make love. You can express love but you cannot make love.

So it is with happiness. You cannot make it. She is a coquette: follow her and she eludes you; turn from her and interest yourself in something or someone else and you may win her. The Scriptures and psychology are at one here, and the experience of millions confirms their findings. The most miserable and fed-up people I know are those who are most bent on being happy. They are saying to themselves what the old lady said to the frightened child whom she had taken to the circus: "Now enjoy yourself, do you hear? I brought you here to have a good time, so make sure you do" – as she shook him till his teeth rattled.

In the passage before us today, it is said that the disciples were toiling, rowing in the dark and getting nowhere. The wind and the waves were against them and the whole venture was ending in futility. Then Jesus came. In John's account of the same event, we are told that they took Him into their boat and immediately the boat reached the shore where they were heading (John 6:21). This is the way it is with happiness. We strive to achieve it, but we "toil in rowing". Then we let Christ in – and lo, we reach the shore where we were going.

FURTHER STUDY

Isa. 61:1-10;
Luke 10:21;
John 15:11;
Psa. 16:11;
Neh. 8:10

1. What was Isaiah's testimony?

2. Where does our strength come from?

Prayer

Father, I see that to get happiness, I must for-get it. It is not an achievement, but a by-product – a by-product of knowing You. Help me to know You better, not just today but every day. In Jesus' Name I pray. Amen.

"Poor enough to receive"

"I tell you the truth, anyone who will not receive the kingdom of God like a little child will never enter it." (v.15)

For reading & meditation – Mark 10:13-31

Today we ask ourselves: If happiness is not something we can create but something we receive, how do we go about receiving it? Listen again to the words of Jesus: "Blessed are the poor in spirit, for theirs is the kingdom of heaven."

What does it mean to be "poor in spirit"? There are those who tell us that the words should read, "Blessed in spirit are the poor" – an idea derived from Luke 6:20, which reads: "Blessed are you who are poor, for yours is the kingdom of God." Our Lord, however, is not thinking here of material poverty, but spiritual poverty: "Blessed are the poor in spirit." The word for "poor" in the Greek is *ptochos* and refers to a chosen poverty. It implies a voluntary emptying of the inner being and is used of those who by choice are so poor that they become poor enough to receive. One translation puts it: "Blessed are those who are receptive in spirit" – those who are willing to empty their hands of their own possessions and have them filled with the riches of God.

Jesus' first prescription for happiness, then, is a voluntary act of self-renunciation. This reverses the usual prescriptions for happiness, which begin with words such as "assert", "take", "release" or "affirm". The first step, therefore toward mental and spiritual health is self-renunciation. It is the decision we must take to reach out and receive Christ – with empty hands. Note that – with empty hands. The reason why so many fail to find Christ is because they are so unreceptive. Christ cannot give Himself to them because they do not give themselves to Him.

FURTHER STUDY

Mark 9:30-37;
Matt. 10:40;
Luke 8:40;
John 1:12

1. What was the attitude of the disciples?

2. What was Jesus' response?

Prayer

O Father, help me to fling everything else away so that I might find You. I will take this first prescription: I will be humble enough to acknowledge my need and receive. In Jesus' Name I pray. Amen.

Receptivity – the first law of life

"… as many as received him, to them gave he power to become the sons of God …" (v.12, AV)

For reading & meditation – John 1:1-14

We ended yesterday by saying that the first step toward mental and spiritual health is self-renunciation and receptivity. I must be willing to acknowledge my need of Christ, stop striving to find happiness and instead receive Him into my life then, like the disciples we talked about the other day, I have reached the shore where I was going.

It should not be considered strange that entrance into the kingdom of God begins with receptivity – isn't that where all life begins? Our scientists tell us that the ovum and the sperm have to receive each other before they can begin the positive business of producing active life. The seed in the ground receives moisture and nutrition from the earth before it can begin to give forth in flower and fruit. If it doesn't begin with receptivity, it doesn't begin. The scientist who doesn't sit down before the facts as a little child and who is not prepared to give up every preconceived notion and follow to whatever end nature will lead him will know nothing.

The first law of life is receptivity, and that is also the first law of the kingdom of God. Look at our text once again: "As many as received him, to them gave he power to become the sons of God."

FURTHER STUDY

Matt. 13:1-23;
Acts 17:11;
1 Thess. 2:13

1. To what must we be receptive?

2. What was said of the Bereans?

How do we get power? First by receptivity: "as many as received him". At the very threshold of Christ's kingdom, then, we are met with the demand for self-emptying and receptivity. Have you made your own personal response to this demand? If not, I urge you to do so today. If you are not willing to do this, then nothing else can follow; if you are willing, then everything else follows.

Prayer

O God, You wrap me around as the atmosphere wraps itself around my body. Help me to respond to You as my physical body responds to its environment and lives. Through Jesus Christ my Lord. Amen.

Flinging away your garment

*"And throwing aside his garment, he rose and came to
Jesus." (v.50, NKJ)*

For reading & meditation – Mark 10:46-52

We are seeing that the first step to mental and spiritual health is receptivity – we must be willing to empty our hands of whatever we are holding and receive Christ.

Life has been defined as response to environment. You and I live physically when we respond to our physical environment – we take in food, light and air. When response is shut off, we die physically. Our spiritual environment is the kingdom of God. When we respond to it, surrender to it, receive our very life from it – then we live happily and abundantly. Take a plant – how does it live? By being proud, self-sufficient, unrelated and unresponsive? No; it lives by surrendering, adjusting, receiving. Suppose a plant tried to live by asserting itself, by trying to "lord" it over the other plants – what would be the result? It would lose its life, for it lives only as it responds to its environment. When it is properly adjusted, it takes in from the air, sun and soil and lives abundantly.

The plain truth of what Christ is saying, then, in the words, "Blessed [or happy] are the poor in spirit", is that we must choose to give up whatever we are holding and allow Him to fill our lives with His forgiveness, love and power. A highly cultured and beautiful woman, after reviewing her life, said with a sigh: "I have everything – and nothing." Everything in the way of comfort and riches – yet she was empty in heart. To find happiness, we must find Christ. And how do we find Him? We do what the blind man did in the passage today – fling away our "garment" and run to Jesus.

FURTHER STUDY

Matt. 19:16-29;
16:25; John 12:24

1. What was the
   young man's
   problem?

2. What did Jesus
   teach must come
   before life?

Prayer

Blessed Lord Jesus, where else can I run? If I run from You, I shall run away from life, from release, from forgiveness, from freedom and from eternal happiness. So I come, humbly, willingly – and receive. Amen.

As many as *touched* Him ...

"She came up behind him and touched the edge of his cloak ..." (v.44)

For reading & meditation – Luke 8:40-56

We continue meditating on Christ's first prescription for happiness: "Blessed are the poor in spirit, for theirs is the kingdom of heaven." Over the past few days we have seen that the phrase "poor in spirit" refers not to material poverty, but spiritual poverty – a willingness to throw away our own self-sufficiency and open our hands to receive Christ.

The passage before us today shows how on one occasion as Jesus passed along the road, a multitude thronged around Him. A woman in deep need came timidly through the crowd and touched His garment. "Who touched Me?" asked Jesus as He felt power go forth from Him. The disciples replied: "Master, the multitudes throng You, so why do you say, 'Who touched Me?' " "Somebody touched me", said Jesus. He knew that there was a great difference between thronging Him and touching Him. Those who throng Jesus get little, those who touch Jesus get everything.

Sunday after Sunday, thousands of people go to church and listen; they throng Jesus but never touch Him. If you are one of those who constantly throng Jesus but never touch Him, then I pray that over these few days in which we are meditating on the opening words of the Beatitudes, you will reach out and touch Christ in a definite and personal way. Touch Him now – today. Touch Him for forgiveness, for cleansing, for power over temptation, over fears, over anxieties, over everything that stands in the way of your personal happiness. As Christ gave Himself to those who needed Him when He was here on earth, so He does today. Cease thronging Him – touch Him.

FURTHER STUDY

Mark 10:1-16;
Matt. 14:35-36;
8:3; 8:15; 9:29-30;
Luke 6:19

1. What are some of the occasions when Jesus touched people?

2. What was the result?

Prayer

O Lord Jesus, as You pass by I move up from those who throng You to boldly touch You – and I do it now. By the touch of faith I receive into my being Your forgiveness and Your power. Thank You, dear Lord. It's done. Amen.

Come ... today

"For the Son of Man came to seek and to save what was lost." (v.10)

For reading & meditation – Luke 19:1-10

We spend one more day meditating on the first of the Beatitudes: "Blessed are the poor in spirit, for theirs is the kingdom of heaven." Dr Raymond Cramer, the minister and psychologist whom I mentioned earlier, says that in the psychology of Jesus, it is the one who has a problem that gets the Master's attention.

When our Lord was here on earth, everyone needed Him, but only those who realised their need got His attention. It is often said that God rushes to the side of a person in need. That is not quite true. It would be more correct to say that God rushes to the side of the person who recognises and acknowledges their need. Those who recognise their need are to be congratulated, they are to be envied – they are candidates for the kingdom of heaven.

We could translate this first Beatitude in the following manner without doing any injustice to the original statement of Jesus: "Congratulations to those who are humble and willing enough to recognise their need – for they are candidates for the help of God." Take it from me, there is no one in the kingdom of God who is not "poor in spirit". You cannot be filled until you are first empty. Salvation is not something earned, but something received. It is by grace we are saved, through faith, and that not of ourselves, it is the gift of God (Eph. 2:8). The old hymn puts it in a way that is powerful and effective:

> *Nothing in my hand I bring,*
> *Simply to Thy cross I cling ...*
> *Foul, I to the fountain fly;*
> *Wash me, Saviour, or I die.*

FURTHER STUDY

Phil. 3:1-9;
Mark 10:28;
Luke 5:27-28;
18:29-30

1. What was Paul's attitude?

2. What did Jesus require of the first disciples?

Prayer

Father, thank You for helping me understand that to be "poor in spirit" is to recognise my utter helplessness in trying to save myself. I have nothing to give, but everything to receive. Humbly I bow and receive You now. Amen.

Not just a code of ethics

*"I have been crucified with Christ and I no longer live, but
Christ lives in me …" (v.20)*

For reading & meditation – Galatians 2:15-21

We turn now to consider the second of our Lord's Beatitudes:
"Blessed are those who mourn, for they will be comforted" (Matt.
5:4). It is important to note that there is a very definite order in these
sayings of Christ. Every one is carefully thought out and is given a precise place in the spiritual sequence. Once we see that entrance into the
kingdom of God is through the acknowledgement of one's spiritual
poverty and the acceptance of Christ's riches and resources, we are then
ready to consider the next: "Happy are those who know what sorrow
means, for they will be given courage and comfort" (Phillips).

Before pondering the meaning of this Beatitude, we pause to make
clear that the Beatitudes must not be viewed simply as a code of ethics,
but as a description of character. Many people view these sayings of
Jesus, as well as the rest of the Sermon on the Mount, as a set of regula-
tions which they must follow in order to become a Christian – a kind of
New Testament "Ten Commandments".

The simple truth is that to try to live out these principles in our own
unaided strength would be about as possible as trying to move the Rock
of Gibraltar with a pea-shooter. Dr Martyn Lloyd-Jones
said: "We are not told, 'Live like this and you will
become a Christian', but rather, 'Become a Christian
and you will live like this.'" Advocates of the "social
gospel" – the belief that we become Christians by
attempting to live out Christ's principles – are seriously in error. We must first know Christ as a Person
before we can fully live out His principles.

FURTHER STUDY

Eph. 3:1-19;
John 14:20;
Col. 1:27;
1 John 3:24

1. Of what does the
indwelling Christ
bring a full
knowledge?

2. What is the "hope
of glory"?

Prayer

Father, how tragic that, down the centuries, so many have got Your truth the wrong
way round – they have tried to follow Your principles before first knowing You in
Person. Help me never to go wrong here – ever. Amen.

The purpose of sorrow

"… the Father of our Lord Jesus Christ … who so wonderfully comforts and strengthens us …" (vv.3-4, TLB)

For reading & meditation – 2 Corinthians 1:1-11

We continue meditating on our Lord's second Beatitude: "Blessed [or happy] are those who mourn, for they will be comforted." The word "mourn" has reference to more than just sorrowing over the death of a loved one; it includes all those experiences in life where we may feel crushed, broken or sorrowful. I feel the best translation of this verse is the one given by J. B. Phillips which I quoted yesterday. Permit me to quote it once again: "Happy are those who know what sorrow means, for they will be given courage and comfort."

Why should people who are caught up in the throes of distressing and sorrowful experiences be congratulated? The conclusion of the verse gives the answer: "for they will be comforted". And what then? Out of the comfort they receive, they are able to give comfort to others. Examine the text at the top of this page again, or listen to it as J. B. Phillips paraphrases it: "For he gives us comfort in all our trials so that we in turn may be able to give the same sort of strong sympathy to others in their troubles."

One of the things which often intrigues me in my work of training Christian counsellors is the fact that the best counsellors are those who have known the deepest hurts. Has the Lord allowed you to go through deep waters? Congratulations! You are a candidate for receiving the divine comfort which, in turn, will deepen your sensitivity to others and enrich your ministry in the Body of Christ. Don't, whatever you do, ask God to deliver you from painful or sorrowful experiences – they are worth much, much more than they cost.

FURTHER STUDY

John 16:1-16;
14:26; 15:26;
1 Cor. 14:31;
1 Thess. 5:11-14

1. From where do we receive our comfort?

2. What does the word "comfort" mean to you?

Prayer

Blessed Lord, help me to grasp this fact, not just with my mind, but with the whole of my spirit. I see that if I can learn this truth, my entire approach to problems can be transformed. In Jesus' Name I pray. Amen.

"It's not worth an argument"

Day
134

"Dear brothers, is your life full of difficulties and temptations? Then be happy." (v.2, TLB)

For reading & meditation – James 1:1-12

We are meditating on the second of Christ's Beatitudes: "Blessed are those who mourn, for they will be comforted." Yesterday we saw that the meaning of this statement is that when we are willing to experience sorrow and grief, then God is able to use these encounters to sensitise our spirits and make our ministry to others more effective and more fruitful.

I am afraid, however, that the majority of Christians, myself included, greatly fear this truth. Some years ago after I had expressed this same truth a woman wrote to me thus: "I am terribly afraid of what you said concerning grief and sorrow being the means in God's hands of deepening our sensitivity to others. I have not found this to be so. I find that grief and sorrow make me more concerned about myself than about others. Thus I cannot pray the prayer you suggested: 'Lord, put all the pressure on me You want; I know that the pressure You permit is all part of Your purpose – to make me the kind of person You want me to be.'"

We must always be careful that we do not interpret Biblical truth by human experiences; we must interpret human experiences by Biblical truth. Scripture tells us that God permits pressure for a purpose, and that sorrow and grief will produce tremendous benefits in our lives – providing we let them. There's the rub! Whenever Biblical principles don't seem to work for us, then don't question the principle – question whether or not you are open to it, and whether you are applying it in the way God directs. There is very little point in arguing with God – He's *always* right.

FURTHER STUDY

Job 23:10;
1 Pet. 1:1-9;
Isa. 48:10;
2 Cor. 4:17

1. What was Job's testimony?

2. What does our suffering bring about?

Prayer

O Father, help me to see that when things are not working out the way Your Word decrees, the problems are not on Your side – but on mine. And help me to side with You and against myself in such issues – for You are always right. Amen.

The dangers of denial

"Surely you desire truth in the inner parts …" (v.6)
For reading & meditation – Psalm 51:1-12

We are looking at the Beatitudes as containing the principles which enable us to experience good mental and spiritual health. I cannot think of anything more psychologically in harmony with the best thinking of today's social scientists than the words of Jesus: "Happy are those who mourn, for they will be comforted." We would not be taking any undue liberty with the text of Matthew 5:4 if we translated it thus: "Congratulations to those who are willing to face and feel sorrow, for they will discover in and through the comfort that I impart to them a new ministry and a new joy."

A mentally and spiritually healthy person is someone who is willing to face and feel sorrow, and recognise that it can be made to deepen one's life – not devastate it. You are familiar, I am sure, with the terms "neurotic" and "psychotic". A "neurotic" is someone who is afraid to face reality, while a "psychotic" is someone who is unaware of reality.

If we draw back from being willing to face and feel any emotion that rises up within us, then the denial of this feeling will have negative results within our personality. A woman once said to me: "I have problems with the second Beatitude because I don't know how to mourn; I am too happy to mourn." As we talked, it became clear to her that it wasn't so much that she didn't know how to mourn, but that she didn't want to mourn. She was afraid to face or feel any negative emotions – grief, sorrow, and so on – and thus, despite her claim to happiness and lightheartedness, she was a stunted soul.

FURTHER STUDY

Psa. 139:14-24;
1 Chron. 28:9;
Jer. 17:10

1. What was David's prayer?

2. Make that your prayer today.

Prayer

Loving heavenly Father, how wonderfully You help me to put my finger on my need. Help me, I pray, to be willing to feel and face my emotions, and show me that when You are by my side I need be afraid of nothing – myself included. Amen.

Why pretend?

*"For we do not have a high priest who is unable to
sympathise with our weaknesses …"* (v.15)
For reading & meditation – Hebrews 4:12-16

Yesterday we ended with the case of the woman who said that she
didn't know how to mourn, when in reality her problem was that she
didn't want to mourn. Whenever we are unwilling to face a negative
emotion, it implies that we are not in control of it, but that it is in control
of us.

Christians are often taught to pretend that they feel joyful when
really they are miserable. Our text today, however, tells us that we have
a great High Priest who can sympathise with us in our weaknesses. How
pointless it is to conceal our weaknesses from the Lord and deny ourselves the comfort of His uncritical compassionate understanding. This
is very important, for I would say that eight out of ten Christians have a
completely wrong view of how to handle hurts and sorrows.

The typical Christian reaction to negative emotions is either denial
or expression. We dealt yesterday with the issue of denial – refusing to
face them and feel them – so let's consider for a moment what we mean
by the term "expression". The expression of emotions is the act of letting
our emotions out. This is a popular approach with many of today's counsellors and therapists. They say, when you feel upset,
hurt or angry, then shout and scream or punch a pillow until you have released those pent-up emotions.
There is no doubt that some relief can be gained in this
way, but it is not a very Biblical or mature way of dealing with our negative feelings. The right way of handling negative feelings is neither to deny them or
express them, but to acknowledge them. But more of
that tomorrow.

FURTHER STUDY

Luke 10:25-37;
7:13; Matt. 9:36;
20:34; Mark 1:41

1. What was Jesus
always
demonstrating?

2. How did He
graphically illustrate
this?

Prayer

O Father, I see that this whole issue of emotions is a minefield in which I must tread
carefully and cautiously. Take my hand as I move through this area and lead me to
clear and Biblical conclusions. For Jesus' sake. Amen.

Moving toward maturity

*"Search me, O God, and know my heart; test me and know
my anxious thoughts."* (v.23)
For reading & meditation – Psalm 139:1-24

We continue meditating on the right way to handle our negative
feelings. We said yesterday that the two wrong ways to handle
hurting emotions are to deny them or express them. Denial pushes them
down inside us, while expression dumps them on to other people or
things. Neither of these, in my view, is a Biblical way of dealing with negative emotions. In fact, recent research by some psychologists shows that
the uncontrolled expression of negative feelings can compound, rather
than clear up, one's emotional difficulties.

In my judgement, the correct and Biblical way to handle negative
emotions is to acknowledge them fully before God and share with Him
how we feel. Now understand clearly what I am saying, for at this point
many have responded to this advice by coming to God when they are
hurt or sorrowful and saying: "Lord, please forgive me for feeling hurt."
That misses the point entirely. A Christian psychologist puts the issue
most effectively when he says: "We are not to pretend that we feel peni-
tent when we feel hurt."

When our stomachs are churning with grief, sorrow or hurt, we
must come before the One who sees and knows everything, and pray a prayer something like this: "Lord,
right now I am hurting more than I think I can endure.
I feel like screaming, running away or hitting somebody. I don't want to feel like this, dear Lord – but I
do. Thank You for loving me as I am. Help me now to
handle my feelings in a way that glorifies You and
honours Your Name." When we pray a prayer like that
– *and mean it* – we are on the way to maturity.

FURTHER STUDY

Psa. 51:1-19; 69:1-
36; 46:1-11

1. How did David
deal with his
feelings?

2. Write a short
psalm expressing
your true feelings.

Prayer

O Father, help me not just to receive this concept into my mind and do nothing
about it, but enable me to put it to work in my daily Christian living. I ask this for the
honour and glory of Your peerless and precious Name. Amen.

"Wounded healers"

"I, even I, am he who comforts you ..." (v.12)
For reading & meditation – Isaiah 51:1-16

We spend one last day meditating on Jesus' words: "Blessed [or happy] are those who mourn, for they will be comforted." Facing negative feelings such as grief, sorrow, hurt and emotional pain is essential if we are to know our Lord's purpose for our lives. When we are willing to go down into the hurt and feel it, then something glorious and transformative happens – we experience the loving comfort and compassion of our Lord. "Blessed are those who mourn, *for they will be comforted.*" Comforted? By whom? By the Triune God. He comes alongside us in our pain, and through the comfort He pours into our beings, enables us to become more sensitive to Him, to ourselves, and to others.

After a lifetime of dealing with people and their problems, I have no hesitation in saying that the happiest people on earth are those who have been hurt but have had those hurts healed through the power of Christ's transforming love. They are what someone has called "wounded healers". Having been healed themselves, they go out to heal others. Going down into the pain of hurt feelings is not a very pleasant journey, but coming back from it with the comfort of God in your soul is an experience that is positively exhilarating and enriching. You return, not only with a new sensitivity in your soul, but with a new potential for ministering to others.

Remember this: great sorrow leads to great happiness – and without the sorrow, there can be no genuine happiness. This might sound to many like a contradiction in terms. It is not a contradiction, but a paradox – and a blessed one at that!

FURTHER STUDY

2 Cor. 1:1-7;
Psa. 86:17;
Isa. 12:1; 66:13

1. What has God promised?

2. How are we to respond?

Prayer

O Father, I take again this second prescription for happiness and ask that You will enable me to take the "medicine", not just today, but every day of my life. Then I will be whole – truly whole. In Jesus' Name I pray. Amen.

"Subdued puppies"?

*"For the Lord taketh pleasure in his people: he will
beautify the meek with salvation." (v.4, AV)*
For reading & meditation – Psalm 149:1-9

We come now to Christ's third prescription for happiness: "Blessed
are the meek, for they will inherit the earth" (Matt. 5:5). How we
have shied away from that word "meek". We have thought of meekness
as weakness and thus have a totally wrong concept of what Jesus meant.
The Amplified Bible translates it thus: "Blessed are the meek (the mild,
patient, long-suffering), for they shall inherit the earth."

The dictionary defines "meek" as "humble, compliant and submissive". Does this mean that Jesus expects the children of the kingdom to
be like subdued puppies who crawl into their master's presence and
cower at his feet? Or to become the type of people who lack inner fortitude and gumption, who can be easily pushed around and manipulated?

The truly meek person – in the Biblical sense of the word – is not
timid, shy, hesitant and unassuming, but trusting, confident and secure.
The root meaning of the word "meekness" is that of yieldedness or surrender – a characteristic without which no real progress can be made in
the Christian life. What happens, for example, to the scientist who
approaches the mysteries of the universe in a manner
that is aggressive and belligerent? He discovers nothing. But what happens to the scientist who approaches
the mysteries of the universe in a spirit of meekness?
He finds its richest secrets unfolding themselves to
him and he is able to harness the mighty forces around
him to advantage. The Christian who approaches life
in the same spirit – the spirit of meekness and submission – discovers the true meaning of his existence and
the purpose of God in all his affairs.

FURTHER STUDY

James 1:12-21;
Zeph. 2:3;
Gal. 5:22-23;
1 Pet. 3:4

1. What are we to
receive with
meekness?

2. Does the Biblical
definition of
meekness fit you?

Prayer

Gracious Father, help me to understand clearly the difference between meekness and
weakness. And show me how to apply this principle in all I say and in all I do. This I
ask in Christ's powerful and precious Name. Amen.

Meekness – a *spiritual* quality

*"And that is what some of you were. But you were washed,
you were sanctified …"* (v.11)

For reading & meditation – 1 Corinthians 6:1-11

Yesterday we touched on the point that the universe will not respond to the aggressive, who approach it in a demanding spirit. It is the meek – those who are yielded, submissive and compliant – who inherit the earth. Thomas Huxley is quoted as saying something which we commented on earlier: "Science says to sit down before the facts like a little child, be prepared to give up every preconceived notion, be willing to be led to whatever end nature will lead you, or you will know nothing."

Today we must focus our thinking on the fact that the quality of meekness (sometimes translated as humility or gentleness) described in the Beatitudes is not the result of natural temperament, but comes from knowing Christ and abiding in Him. That goes, of course, for all the qualities enunciated in the Beatitudes – they are spiritual characteristics, not natural ones. This point needs elaborating, for there are many Christians who say: "I am aggressive by nature, so it is not possible for me to be a meek and mild person."

Every Christian, whatever their natural temperament, is meant to be meek. It is not a matter of natural disposition; it is a quality produced by

FURTHER STUDY

Num. 12:1-13;
Psa. 22:26; 147:6;
Luke 6:29

1. What was Moses' great characteristic?

2. How does meekness reveal itself in practice?

the Spirit of God. Think of the powerful and extraordinary nature of a man like David – and yet observe his meekness. Look at a man like Paul the apostle, a master mind, a powerful and outstanding personality, yet consider his great humility and gentleness. How did these men get to be like this? Not because of a natural proneness toward meekness, but because they were indwelt by Christ and the Holy Spirit. It is not a matter of genes; it is a matter of grace.

Prayer

My Father and my God, help me to face up to the fact that whatever I am by nature, I can be changed by the power of Your grace. Show me how to absorb that grace so that I become more and more like You. For Your own dear Name's sake. Amen.

What meekness is not

*"… the unfading beauty of a gentle and quiet spirit, which
is of great worth in God's sight." (v.4)*

For reading & meditation – 1 Peter 3:1-12

We are seeing that meekness is not a natural quality, but a spiritual one, and by reason of this all Christians should possess it. Over the past couple of days we have examined the importance of meekness and seen something of its nature; today, we examine what meekness is not.

First, meekness (or humility) is not indolence. There are people who appear to be spiritually meek, but really they are not so at all – they are indolent. Again, meekness is not an easy-going type of attitude – the attitude seen in those who just take life as it comes. That is not meekness; that is flabbiness. There are some Christians who have such a casual air about them that one can easily mistake this for the quality which Jesus is referring to in the Beatitudes.

Another thing that meekness ought not to be confused with is niceness. There are people who are nice by nature. Dr Martyn Lloyd-Jones said of such people: "Natural niceness is something biological, the kind of thing you get in animals. One dog is nicer than another, one cat nicer than another." Finally, meekness is not passivity, or a desire to obtain peace at any price. How often is the person regarded as meek who adopts the attitude that anything is better than a disagreement. This is the kind of passivity which does not make for good mental or spiritual health. The most greatly used men and women of God down the ages have been people who were meek without being weak – strong men and women, yet meek men and women. They were meek enough to absorb the resources of God.

FURTHER STUDY

2 Tim. 4:1-16;
Psa. 37:11; 149:4;
Isa. 29:19

1. How did Paul display meekness?

2. What does meekness increase?

Prayer

O Father, I see that so much depends on my understanding of what meekness really is. I pray yet again for Your continuing light to be shed around me as I pursue these thoughts day by day. I ask this in Jesus' Name. Amen.

The meek are the assured

"Put on then, as God's chosen ones … meekness …"
(v.12, RSV)

For reading & meditation – Colossians 3:1-15

It is time now to focus more precisely on what Jesus meant when He said: "Blessed are the meek, for they will inherit the earth." Meekness, as Jesus is using the word here, refers to an attitude of heart and mind that is entirely free from a spirit of demandingness and accepts the will of God in its entirety.

I think J.B. Phillips gets close to the meaning in Jesus' mind when he translates His statement thus: "Happy are those who claim nothing, for the whole earth will belong to them." I must stress once again that the thought here is not of passivity, but of active compliance and obedience to the will of God. If I might be permitted to embark upon a translation of my own, I would put it this way: "Congratulations to those who do not feel the need to be over-assertive, for they will inherit the earth."

The meek are so sure of their resources and their goals that they can afford to be meek. Others have to become aggressive simply because they are unsure of themselves and their goals – hence the universe is closed to them. The meek could be called the assured, for they are meek enough to rest confidently in the resources of God. I realise, of course, that this is directly opposite to the world's view of things. The world thinks of strength, power, ability, self-confidence and self-assurance as the keys to success. The more you assert yourself and the more you affirm yourself, says the worldly person, the more you will get. But such people do not inherit the earth: they just inherit dirt.

FURTHER STUDY

Isa. 53:1-7;
Matt. 26:62-63;
27:14; Luke 23:9

1. How did Jesus display meekness?

2. How do you display meekness?

Prayer

O Father, more and more as I hang upon Your words, I realise that You have "hidden these things from the wise and learned, and revealed them to little children." Unfold Your truth in even more new and exciting ways to my heart. In Jesus' Name. Amen.

"All things serve"

*"… By his good life let him show his works in the
meekness of wisdom." (v.13, RSV)*
For reading & meditation – James 3:1-18

We continue meditating on the meaning of the word "meek" as used
by Jesus in His third Beatitude. "Meekness," said one commentator, "is essentially a true view of oneself, expressing itself in attitude and
conduct with respect to others."

If that is so, then meekness involves two things: (1) our attitudes
towards ourselves, and (2) our attitudes toward others. The meek person
is so sure of himself that he does not need to demand anything for himself. He does not see his rights as something to be rigidly held on to, but
follows the spirit of Jesus as outlined in Philippians 2:6-7: "Who,
although being essentially one with God … did not think this equality
with God was a thing to be eagerly grasped or retained; but stripped
Himself of all privileges … and was born a human being" (Amplified
Bible).

That is the place to which you and I must come if we are to understand the principle of meekness. The Christian who is meek will not be
over-sensitive about himself, or defensive; he realises that he has no
rights at all and delights to leave everything in the
hands of God. When he is called upon to suffer unjustly, he remembers the Word of the Lord that says, "It is
mine to avenge; I will repay" (Rom. 12:19), and trusts
God to work out the situation in His own time and in
His own way. The poet Browning put the same truth
in these words: "He who keeps one end in view makes
all things serve." When that one end is the purpose of
God, then indeed – all things serve.

FURTHER STUDY

1 Pet. 2:18-25;
Matt. 11:29; 26:52

1. What was Peter's
exhortation?

2. Why was Jesus
able to display
meekness?

Prayer

O Father, instil into me such a spirit of meekness that such things as anger, impatience, irritation, distrust, suspicion and unbelief die within me. Help me to see that
only meekness must survive. For Jesus' sake. Amen.

What an example!

"Take my yoke upon you ... for I am gentle and humble in
heart, and you will find rest for your souls." (v.29)

For reading & meditation – Matthew 11:28-30

Today we ask ourselves: What is there about this famous saying of
Jesus which engenders good mental health? Mental health, after all,
is more than a medical term. It is a concept that goes beyond the walls of
a hospital or a doctor's clinic and applies also to the home, the church
and the world of everyday living.

Mental health is concerned with the dynamics of relationship and
adjustment – the way we handle such things as anxiety, hostility and
frustration. "Mental health," says one authority, "concerns itself with the
everyday troubles of everyday people – helping them to solve their problems or face them bravely when they cannot be warded off." The statement of Jesus we are focusing on at the moment contributes to good
mental health because it encourages us to be free from the attitude of
demandingness – the attitude that says: "Things must go my way", "I
ought to have some consideration", "People should respect my rights."

One psychologist goes as far as to say that if we could eliminate the
shoulds and the *woulds* from our vocabulary and our inner attitudes, we
could become transformed people overnight. He was not referring, of

FURTHER STUDY

2 Cor. 10:1-18;
11:18-21;
Phil. 4:11-12

*1. Why could Paul
be bold?*

*2. How did Paul
highlight the
difference between
weakness and
meekness?*

course, to the moral compass which God has placed
within us that cries out for obedience to that which is
right ("I ought not to lie", "I should always do right",
and so on) but to the attitude of demandingness that
insists on having one's rights irrespective of any other
considerations. One of the biggest causes of mental
and emotional illness is the attitude of demandingness
and over-concern. Do we wonder any longer why
Christ congratulates the meek and promises them the
earth?

Prayer

Blessed Lord Jesus, deliver me, I pray, from a spirit of demandingness that insists on
having my rights rather than being willing to give them up for the sake of others.
Help me to take Your yoke upon me and learn from You. Amen.

"Sand in the machinery"

"For by him all things were created: things in heaven and on earth … all things were created by him and for him." (v.16)

For reading & meditation – Colossians 1:15-27

We spend one more day meditating on the text: "Blessed are the meek, for they will inherit the earth." Today we ask ourselves: What did Jesus mean by the phrase, "for they will inherit the earth"? It means, so I believe, that when we develop the attitude of meekness, the whole universe is behind us. If, for example, we decide to manifest the attitude of anger and hostility rather than cultivating a meek and quiet spirit, then the anger and hostility becomes, as someone put it, "sand in the machinery of life".

The universe has been made in a Christlike fashion. Our text for today shows that when God made the world, He made it to work in the way of Christ: "All things were created by him [Christ] and for him." Edison, the scientist, tried eleven hundred experiments, all of which turned out to be failures. Someone said to him: "You must feel that you have wasted your time." "Oh no," answered Edison, "I simply found out eleven hundred ways how not to do things."

This is what is happening in the world right now – humanity is finding out how to live. People are discovering that there are some things which the universe will not approve and some things it will approve. The meek are those who have come to terms with reality and know that they cannot twist it to their own ends or make it approve of what cannot be approved. Whoever has the first word in this universe must always remember that the universe has the last word. The Christian who adopts the attitudes of his Master finds the universe backing him in everything he does.

FURTHER STUDY

Phil. 2:1-11;
John 1:3;
1 Cor. 8:6;
Heb. 1:1-2

1. How did Jesus demonstrate meekness?

2. How does this apply to you?

Prayer

Father, thank You for reminding me that life works in one way only – Your way. When I live life as You designed it, then the whole universe works with me. I inherit all things – all that is Yours is mine. Blessed be Your Name for ever. Amen.

What's your goal?

"But seek first his kingdom and his righteousness, and all these things will be given to you as well." (v.33)

For reading & meditation – Matthew 6:19-34

We turn now to the next of our Lord's Beatitudes: "Blessed are those who hunger and thirst for righteousness, for they will be filled" (Matt. 5:6). One of the axioms of life is this: everyone thirsts after something. Some thirst for success, some thirst for fame, some thirst for stable relationships, and some thirst for financial security. But there is a thirst which is common to every human heart – the thirst for happiness. Notice, however, that Jesus does not say: "Happy are those who thirst for happiness", but "Happy are those who thirst for righteousness."

Happiness, therefore, is a by-product – to get it, you must focus on something else. Dr W.E. Sangster, the famous Methodist preacher, when dealing with this point in one of his sermons, gave this illustration: "Do you enjoy a game of golf or tennis? Then this pleasure is strictly proportioned to the degree to which you lose yourself in the game. While it lasts, it must absorb you: your whole mind should be on the game. If you stop in the midst of it and ask yourself precisely what degree of pleasure you are deriving from this particular stroke, the pleasure will evaporate and you will begin to feel rather foolish in following a wee white ball over a mile or two of turf."

FURTHER STUDY

John 4:1-14; 6:35; Psa. 36:8; Isa. 55:1

1. What did Jesus promise?

2. What do you thirst for?

To experience happiness, one must forget it and focus on something other than its pursuit. Those who reach out for happiness are for ever unsatisfied – the more they strive, the less they find. Happiness, I say again, is a by-product; it is not something you find, but something that finds you.

Prayer

My Father and my God, I see so clearly that if my goal is wrong, then all of life turns out wrong. Help me to make my goal, not the pursuit of happiness, but the pursuit of righteousness. In Jesus' Name I pray. Amen.

An important key to living

*"And we pray this in order that you may live a life worthy
of the Lord and may please him in every way ..."* (v.10)

For reading & meditation – Colossians 1:1-14

Yesterday we saw that when we make it a goal to hunger and thirst
after happiness, we get nowhere, but when we make it our goal to
hunger and thirst after righteousness, we get everywhere.

Once again Jesus touches on an aspect of good mental health when
He teaches us through these words to focus on right goals. Those who
study human behaviour tell us that everything we do has a goal. "We are
not conditioned animals that act automatically and unthinkingly in pro-
grammed response," says a psychologist, "... neither are we the hapless
victims of internal forces that drive us relentlessly in unwanted directions." It may sometimes feel as if we do things we don't want to do, but
the truth is that everything we do represents an effort to reach a goal that
somehow, albeit at an unconscious level, makes sense. In fact, one of the
ways in which you can better understand why you do the things you do
is to ask yourself: What's my goal?

A woman I once counselled and who was extremely frustrated
because her husband would not change to meet her requirements said to
me: "My husband is so stubborn and obstinate that I
just can't see any future for us together." I shared with
her the concept that everything we do represents a
goal, and asked her to put into words what she
thought her goal might be in her marriage. Without a
moment's hesitation she replied: "To change my husband." Her daily prayer was: "Lord, You love my husband and I'll change him." I suggested she altered her
goal to: "Lord, You change my husband and I'll love
him." She did, and instantly found a new freedom –
and a new happiness in her marriage.

FURTHER STUDY

Eph. 5:1-16;
Rom. 6:4;
2 Cor. 5:7;
Gal. 5:16

1. How are we to
live?

2. Do you make the
most of every
opportunity?

Prayer

O Father, I see what I need – I need to bring my goals in line with Your goals. Unfold
more of this important truth to me as I pursue it over the next few days. In Jesus'
Name I ask it. Amen.

Why we get angry

"Run in such a way as to get the prize." (v.24)
For reading & meditation – 1 Corinthians 9:15-27

We continue meditating on the idea that everything we do represents a goal. In fact, most of the frustration we experience in life comes from wrong goals and blocks to those goals. Let me illustrate. Cast your mind back to the last time you were angry. If you can identify your goal and what blocked your goal, then you have the clue to what produced your anger and frustration.

A man once asked me if I could explain what caused his deep-seated anger. It soon became apparent that his anger was due to a blocked goal. His goal in life was to make money. He reasoned: "If I can make plenty of money, then everyone will see that I am a successful and important person." When he encountered blocks to this goal, such as his wife's insistence that he cut down on the amount of time he was spending in his business, he would erupt in anger.

I pointed out that the way to deal with the anger was to establish a goal that no-one could block. And what was that? To please the Lord. He resisted that idea at first, but when he came to realise that his goal in life was unbiblical and that his anger resulted from others blocking his unbiblical goal, he made a new commitment to God and found happiness and release. From then on his goal was not to make money, but to please the Lord. I hasten to point out that there is nothing wrong with wanting to make money – it is a legitimate human desire – but it must remain a desire and never become a goal.

FURTHER STUDY

James 1:9-20;
Psa. 37:8;
Prov. 14:17; 16:32

1. What does an impatient man do?

2. Who will "take the city"?

Prayer

O God my gracious Father, help me never to turn what can be a legitimate human desire into a life goal. Save me from pursuing unbiblical objectives, and guide me toward the truth which alone can make me free. In Jesus' Name. Amen.

Desires versus goals

*"… who for the joy set before him endured the cross,
scorning its shame …"* (v.2)

For reading & meditation – Hebrews 12:1-13

We ended yesterday by saying that some things in life, such as the desire to have money, can be legitimate concerns but they must be looked upon as desires and never become goals.

Permit me to differentiate between the two. A goal is a purpose to which a person is unalterably committed and something for which he or she assumes unconditional responsibility. A desire is something wanted and which cannot be obtained without the co-operation of another human being. A desire must never become the motivating purpose behind our behaviour, for if it does, then it becomes a goal – and a goal that is likely to be blocked, causing negative emotions to arise. Remember the man we talked about yesterday? His goal, we said, was to make money. Once he changed his goal to pleasing the Lord and then saw his concern to make money as merely a desire, he found instant release.

Keep in mind that what causes emotional problems to arise is invariably a blocked goal. Take another illustration that might help to mark the difference between goals and desires more clearly.
Have you ever found yourself talking to another Christian who seems to have difficulty in applying what seems to you a simple biblical principle? You point out the need to do as God says, but your friend fails to see the truth that to you is as clear as daylight. If you get frustrated, the chances are that you are allowing a desire to become a goal. To want your friend to listen is a legitimate desire, but to get frustrated over it means you are determined to make him listen – and that becomes a goal.

> **FURTHER STUDY**
> Psa. 37:1-11; 21:2;
> 73:25; Prov. 10:24
>
> 1. What was the psalmist's desire?
>
> 2. What happens when we delight ourselves in the Lord?

Prayer

Gracious Father, I come to You again to help me sort out this important issue of desires versus goals. I see that if I can resolve this problem, then a new chapter in my life is about to be written. Help me, dear Lord. In Jesus' Name. Amen.

Happiness is a by-product

"… in Your presence is fullness of joy, at Your right hand
there are pleasures for evermore." (v.11, Amplified Bible)
For reading & meditation – Psalm 16:1-11

Having seen the importance of differentiating between goals and desires, we return to the thought that we can experience happiness only as a by-product. If we make obtaining happiness a goal, it eludes us like a will-o'-the-wisp, but if we give up the chase and hold it only as a desire, then it takes up residence in our heart.

Let me repeat: there is nothing wrong in wanting to be happy; it is a natural and valid desire. But the paradoxical truth is that I will never be happy if I am primarily concerned with becoming happy. My overriding goal in every circumstance must be to respond biblically, to put the Lord first and seek to behave as He would want me to. The wonderful truth is that as we devote our energies to the task of becoming what Christ wants us to be – righteous – He responds by filling us with unutterable happiness and joy. I must, therefore, firmly and consciously by an act of the will, refuse to make obtaining happiness my goal, and instead adopt the goal of becoming more like the Lord.

An obsessive preoccupation with "happiness" will obscure our understanding of the biblical route to eternal peace and joy. And what is that route? Our text for today tells us: "At Your right hand there are pleasures for evermore." It follows that if we are to experience those pleasures, then we must learn what it means to be at God's right hand. Paul tells us that Christ has been exalted to God's right hand (Eph. 1:20). Can anything be clearer? The more we abide in Christ, the more we shall experience true happiness.

FURTHER STUDY

Psa. 139:1-12;
140:13; Ex. 33:14;
Isa. 43:2

1. What did the psalmist feel about God's presence?

2. How much time are you spending in His presence?

Prayer

O God, forgive us that we have made the pursuit of happiness our goal, and the pursuit of righteousness merely a desire. Help us to get our values straightened out, and to set the goal of becoming more and more like You. In Jesus' Name. Amen.

At God's right hand

"Therefore let us ... go on to maturity ..." (v.1)
For reading & meditation – Hebrews 6:1-12

Quietly we are coming to see that it is only as we learn to dwell at God's right hand in fellowship with Christ that we can experience true happiness and joy. Despite the clear teaching of Jesus that happiness is a by-product of righteousness (becoming more and more like Christ), there are still thousands of Christians paying no more than lip service to this truth. Happiness is their goal, righteousness merely their desire.

I am speaking generally when I make this next point, but sit down with any Christian who does not experience true happiness and you will find, deep within that person's heart, that they have never come to a clear understanding of this important principle uttered by Jesus: "Blessed are those who hunger and thirst for righteousness, for they will be filled." The same condition can be noted in nine out of ten people who seek help through Christian counselling. Ask them what they want to experience as they go through counselling, and they say, "I want to feel good", or "I want to feel happy."

I imply no criticism or condemnation of these people, for I know that the same tendency exists in my own heart. Whenever I am struggling or hurting over some issue, my immediate desire is to get rid of the negative feelings and recover my lost happiness. But to try to find happiness is like trying to fall asleep. As long as you consciously and zealously try to grasp it, it fails to come. There is only one way: it is to do whatever you have to do in the situation to glorify Christ. Then happiness inevitably bubbles upward – as it must.

FURTHER STUDY

Phil. 3:1-11;
2 Cor. 13:11;
Eph. 4:13;
Col. 1:28

1. What was Paul's desire?

2. What was Paul's goal?

Prayer

Father, I am so grateful that, as my Lover and my Redeemer, You corner my soul. Don't let me wriggle and apologise and slip past You. Help me to take my medicine, however bitter to the taste of self it may be. In Jesus' Name. Amen.

Spiritual/psychological problems

*"I want to know Christ and the power of his resurrection
…" (v.10)*

For reading & meditation – Philippians 3:7-21

Today we ask: What happens to those who hunger and thirst after
righteousness? The answer is clear: they will be filled. Make righteousness your goal and you will be eternally satisfied. If, once again, I
might venture upon a paraphrase of my own, I would put it like this:
"Congratulations to those who ardently crave to become more and more
like Me and to know My righteousness, for they shall find a satisfaction
that will never vanish or be destroyed."

May I be permitted to ask you this personal question: What are you
most hungering and thirsting for? Is it health? Is it relief from pain? Is it
freedom from anxiety? Is it financial security? All of these are legitimate
cravings, but if your primary hunger and thirst is not to become more
and more like Christ, then you will experience an inner emptiness that
nothing you chase after can fill.

Let me point out one more thing – something that might astonish
you: to the extent that your deepest hunger and thirst is not for God, to
that extent you will experience spiritual and psychological problems. If
you are not hungering and thirsting after Him, you will hunger and
thirst after something else. When we make it our goal
to glorify God, then we will enjoy Him. We must not
make it our goal to enjoy Him in order to glorify Him.
Remember the goal of happiness is elusive, regardless
of how well-thought-out is our strategy. But the by-
product of happiness is freely available to those whose
goal is to know God and be found in Him.

FURTHER STUDY

Psa. 38:9; 73:25;
Isa. 26:1-9;
1 Pet. 2:2-3

*1. What was the
psalmist's
confession?*

*2. What did Isaiah's
desire cause him to
do?*

Prayer

Father, You are teaching me Your ways – written in Your Word and also in me.
Help me to surrender to Your purposes so that I might be the vehicle of victory.
Amen.

The meaning of mercy

"Mercy and truth are met together ..." (v.10, AV)
For reading & meditation – Psalm 85:1-13

We continue our study of the Beatitudes – the study of Jesus' declarations of how to become "the happy ones". Today we come to the fifth of Christ's famous sayings: "Blessed are the merciful, for they will be shown mercy" (Matt. 5:7).

What does our Lord mean when He uses the word "merciful"? The thought underlying the word is that of compassion and concern for the plight of others. The Greek word used in this fifth Beatitude is also used to describe the high priestly ministry of Christ in Hebrews 2:17. One authority, W.E. Vine, says that a "merciful" person is "not simply possessed of pity but actively compassionate".

It is important to stress once again that the characteristic of being merciful of which our Lord spoke here is not something that arises from our natural temperament, but something that is endowed on us when we abide in Christ. As Dr Martyn Lloyd-Jones said: "This is not a gospel for certain temperaments – nobody has an advantage over anybody else when they are face to face with God." Again, mercy is not turning a blind eye to moral violations – the attitude that pretends not to see things. This can be seen most forcefully when we consider that the term "merciful" is an adjective which is applied especially and specifically to God Himself. This means that however the word applies to God, it applies equally to man. God is merciful, but He is also truth: "Mercy and truth are met together." If we think of mercy at the expense of truth and law, then it is not true mercy; it is merely a caricature.

FURTHER STUDY

Titus 3:1-7;
Psa. 103:17; 108:4;
Lam. 3:22

1. What is the quality of God's mercy?

2. How merciful are you?

Prayer

O God, help me, I pray, to have within me the right blend of mercy and truth. Save me from becoming a lopsided Christian – someone who manifests one characteristic at the expense of another. In Jesus' Name I pray. Amen.

Grace and *mercy*

"… and when he saw him, he took pity on him. He went to him …" (vv.33–34)

For reading & meditation – Luke 10:25–37

We continue focusing our thoughts on what it means to be "merciful". One of the best ways to understand the word is to compare it with grace. Have you ever noticed, that the introduction to every one of Paul's epistles from Romans through to 2 Thessalonians, includes the words: "Grace and peace to you from God our Father and the Lord Jesus Christ"? The phrase usually appears in the second or third verse of these epistles. However, when he comes to what are described as the pastoral epistles (1 and 2 Timothy and Titus), he changes the phrase to read: "Grace, mercy and peace from God the Father and Christ Jesus our Lord."

When Paul inserted the word "mercy" after the word "grace", he implied an interesting distinction. Someone has defined the two words thus: "Grace is especially associated with men in their sins; mercy is especially associated with men in their misery." While grace looks down upon sin and seeks to save, mercy looks especially upon the miserable consequences of sin and seeks to relieve. This helps us to see mercy in a wider dimension. *Mercy is compassion plus action.*

FURTHER STUDY

Prov. 3:3; 11:17;
Micah 6:8;
John 8:1-11

1. What does the Lord require?

2. How did Jesus show mercy without compromising truth?

A Christian who is merciful feels such compassion and concern that he is not content until he does something about the plight of the one with whom he comes in contact. The story of the Good Samaritan is a classic illustration of being merciful. Others saw the man but did nothing to help him in his plight. The Samaritan, however, crossed the road, dressed the man's wounds, took him to an inn and made provision for his comfort. I say again: mercy is compassion *plus* action.

Prayer

Merciful and loving heavenly Father, make me in Your own image. One thing is sure – I cannot be a merciful person without Your help. So come and think in me, love in me and live in me. For Your own dear Name's sake. Amen.

Most misunderstood Beatitude

"Give, and it will be given to you …" (v.38)
For reading & meditation – Luke 6:27-40

The fifth Beatitude – "Blessed are the merciful, for they will be shown mercy" – is quite different from the ones that precede it. In the first four, there is a contrast between the need and the fulfilment. The "poor in spirit" receive the kingdom; those "who mourn" are comforted; "the meek" inherit the earth; those who "hunger and thirst" are satisfied; but in the fifth Beatitude the theme changes: "the merciful will be shown mercy". It is as though we cannot receive mercy without first giving it.

We must move carefully here, for no Beatitude has been more misunderstood than this one. There are those who take these words to mean that we can only be forgiven by God to the extent that we forgive others. They bring alongside this Beatitude such passages as: "Forgive us our sins, for we also forgive everyone who sins against us" (Luke 11:4), and "This is how my heavenly Father will treat each of you unless you forgive your brother from your heart" (Matt. 18:35).

Putting all these Scriptures together, they claim that it is the clear meaning of the Bible that we are forgiven by God only to the degree that we forgive others. If this is so, then salvation is by works and not by grace. We must never interpret Scripture in a way that contradicts other Scriptures. What our Lord means in this fifth Beatitude is that when we demonstrate mercy to others, we make it possible for God's mercy to penetrate deeper into our own lives and personalities. The act of giving makes us more able to receive.

FURTHER STUDY

2 Cor. 9:1-6;
Prov. 11:25; 22:9;
Matt. 10:8

1. What is the law of sowing and reaping?

2. What was Jesus' instruction to the disciples?

Prayer

O Father, help me not to stumble over this truth. Show me that although my forgiveness of others is not a condition of salvation, it must be a consequence of it. In Jesus' Name I pray. Amen.

Forgiven!

"… forgiving each other, just as in Christ God forgave you." (v.32)

For reading & meditation – Ephesians 4:17-32

We must spend another day considering whether or not it is a condition of our salvation that we first forgive those who have sinned against us. We said yesterday that to believe this contradicts the teaching that we are saved by grace, through faith. What, then, is Scripture getting at when it seems to encourage us to forgive in order that we might be forgiven? I think it refers to the matter of realised forgiveness.

I know many Christians, as I am sure you do, who, although they have been forgiven by God, are never really sure of it. And one of the major reasons for this is that they have never taken the steps to get rid of the resentment they hold in their hearts toward others. The problem they experience in not feeling forgiven is not God's fault, but their own. He has forgiven them on the basis of their own personal repentance, but His forgiveness is unable to reach the centre of their spirit and dissolve their feelings of guilt because they harbour an unforgiving attitude toward others.

C.S. Lewis said something similar in relation to praise. He explained that we do not really receive something unless we give thanks for it. The very action of saying "thank you", and meaning it, opens up the spirit to a true sense of appreciation. In giving thanks, something moves inside the centre of our spirits and allows the wonder of what has been done for us to invade us. It is the same with mercy and forgiveness. When we adopt these attitudes toward others, we not only express mercy and forgiveness – we experience it.

FURTHER STUDY

Luke 17:1-4; 23:34;
Mark 11:25;
Col. 3:13

1. How often should we forgive?

2. How did Jesus set us an example?

Prayer

O Father, I see that You have fashioned me in my inner being for mercy and forgiveness, and when I demonstrate it, I allow it to invade me to my deepest depths. I am so grateful. Amen.

Some things bitter to digest

"Woe to them! They have brought disaster upon themselves." (v.9:)

For reading & meditation – Isaiah 3:1-11

Now we pause to ask ourselves how this fifth Beatitude, when practised, engenders within us good mental and spiritual health. Psychologists have shown that those who lack the qualities of mercy and compassion are more likely to develop physical problems. Harsh, judgmental attitudes may bring a sense of satisfaction to the person who does not know the meaning of mercy, but it is a false sense of satisfaction.

A verse that, strictly speaking, does not apply to what I am saying here, but nevertheless has some application is this: "It did taste sweet, like honey, but when I had eaten it, it was bitter to digest" (Rev. 10:10, Moffatt). That is what happens whenever we adopt any attitude that is not in harmony with Jesus Christ. At first it does "taste sweet, like honey" – its beginnings are apparently sweet, but it is "bitter to digest" – it cannot be assimilated. Our human constitution is not made to function effectively on any attitude that is foreign to the spirit of Jesus Christ.

A Christian doctor says: "We are allergic to wrong attitudes just as some people are allergic to shrimps." I am physically allergic to red and green peppers. I have tried them scores of times, but the result has always been the same – I get sick. I am just as allergic to harsh, judgmental attitudes. I can't assimilate them. They disrupt me – body, soul and spirit. And what goes for me goes also for you When we fail to practise the principles which our Lord outlined for us in the Beatitudes, then our sense of well-being is lowered, depleted and poisoned. Goodness is good for us – spiritually, mentally and physically.

FURTHER STUDY

Psa. 23:1-6; 31:9;
Ex. 34:6; Gal. 5:22;
Eph. 5:9

1. Of what is
goodness a
characteristic?

2. Can you make the
same declaration as
the psalmist?

Prayer

Father, something is being burned into my consciousness: there is only one healthy way to live – Your Way. When I break with You, I break with life. Help me always to maintain a close connection with You. In Jesus' Name. Amen.

Getting back what you give

*"He who seeks good finds goodwill, but evil comes to him
who searches for it."* (v.27)

For reading & meditation – Proverbs 11:16-31

Those who know how to be merciful are men and women to be envied. They get back what they give. Psychologists are always pointing out that our attitudes and emotions are contagious. Scripture puts the same truth in these words: "A man that hath friends must shew himself friendly" (Prov. 18:24, AV). And what's more, a merciful attitude can encourage others to themselves be merciful. People who are merciful are not so apt to arouse harsh feelings or awaken enmities – they receive what they give.

Within the act of mercy is the power to effect change. When you demonstrate mercy toward someone, it calls forth the same feeling tones from the other person, and there will be an exchange that will reinforce the importance of the quality of mercy in your own spirit. So you do not lose anything, for they, in turn, give you something of themselves that can enrich your life.

It does not always happen, of course, that the demonstration of mercy evokes a positive response in others, but whether it does or not, you are all the better for being merciful. The pay-off is in you. Have you noticed how a person with this quality always seems to have good personal relationships? And when he or she has need of mercy from others, then it is instantly forthcoming – for as we give, so shall we receive. And not only do they enjoy good personal relationships – they enjoy (other things being equal) good physical health. The right thing morally is always the healthy thing physically. For morality is one – whether it is written in our tissues, or whether it is written in the Testaments.

FURTHER STUDY

Matt. 18:23-35;
6:15; James 2:13

1. What was Jesus teaching in this parable?

2. How is this sometimes a picture of us?

Prayer

Gracious Father, I am finding Your way amid my own ways. Daily, hourly, it is being disclosed before my astonished gaze. Help me to follow Your way, Your attitudes and Your lifestyle. For all other ways defeat me. Yours develops me. Amen.

Through Christian eyes

*"Each of you should look not only to your own interests,
but also to the interests of others." (v.4)*

For reading & meditation – Philippians 2:1-13

As we conclude our study of the phrase, "Blessed are the merciful, for they will be shown mercy", we ask ourselves: What would happen if we really put into practice this important principle? It would mean that we would look at everyone through Christian eyes. We would see sinners, not merely as the victims of sin and Satan, but as men and women who are to be pitied. We would see a fellow Christian who falls by the way, not as someone to come down on, but as someone to be lifted up.

Far too many of us walk about with judgmental attitudes, and whenever anyone slips up, we either harangue them with a Bible text or wither them with a look of scorn. We have the philosophy of an eye for an eye and a tooth for a tooth. Failure is met with derision and wrong is met with contempt. I have no hesitation in saying that such attitudes ought not to be found among the people of God. Wherever they are present, they will eat like acid into the soul. Being merciful means letting Christ have control of our lives so that His gentleness overcomes our vindictiveness, His kindness our unkindness, and His bigness our littleness.

Are you a merciful person? Do you look upon those who have fallen with concern and compassion – or is your attitude one of contempt and scorn? Can you feel pity for those who have been duped by the world and the devil? If so, then – congratulations! You have passed the test and are on your way to experiencing spiritual health and happiness. Blessed indeed are those who are merciful – for they will obtain mercy.

FURTHER STUDY

Luke 18:1-14;
2 Cor. 8:1-9;
Heb. 2:17-18

1. How did Jesus
show mercy?

2. How do you show
mercy?

Prayer

O my Father, with all my heart I cry out – help me to be a merciful person. Touch my whole being today by Your blessed Holy Spirit so that I might be changed into Your image. In Jesus' Name I pray. Amen.

Spiritual heart surgery

"But the things that come out of the mouth come from the heart, and these make a man 'unclean'." (v.18)

For reading & meditation – Matthew 15:1-20

Today we come to the Beatitude which is considered by many to be the most sublime of them all: "Blessed are the pure in heart, for they will see God" (Matt. 5:8).

First we ask: What is meant by the term "heart"? According to the general use of the word in Scripture, it has reference to what goes on in the core of our being. The heart is more than just the seat of the emotions; it is the fount from which everything proceeds. In our reading today, our Lord put it thus: "For out of the heart come evil thoughts, murder, adultery, sexual immorality …" and so on (v.19). Dr Oswald Chambers said: "If a sinner really wishes to understand his heart, then let him listen to his own mouth in an unguarded frame for five minutes." Luke put it this way: "… the evil man brings evil things out of the evil stored up in his heart. For out of the overflow of his heart his mouth speaks" (Luke 6:45).

It has been pointed out that the gospel is a religion of new things. It offers us all a new birth, a new life, a new hope, a new happiness, and, at the end of time – a new name. However, out of all these fascinating new things which Christ offers His children, none is perhaps more intriguing than His offer of a new heart. The promise is first given in the prophecy of Ezekiel: "I will give you a new heart and put a new spirit within you" (Ezek. 36:26). Quite clearly, when it comes to spiritual things, the heart of the matter is the matter of the heart. Christ's offer of changing our hearts is one of the greatest promises of the Bible. Be encouraged: our Lord is not content with tinkering about on the surface of our lives – His goal is to purify our hearts.

FURTHER STUDY

Psa. 51:1-10;
19:12-13; 79:9

1. What was the psalmist's prayer?

2. Make it your prayer today.

Prayer

My Father and my God, slowly but surely I am coming under the sway of Your "beautiful attitudes". But I see You have more for me to discover. Hold me close as I go through your spiritual heart surgery. In Jesus' Name I pray. Amen.

Purity – not a popular thought

"… he purified their hearts by faith." (v.9)
For reading & meditation – Acts 15:1-11

N ow that we understand what Scripture means by the term "heart" – the core of our being – we ask ourselves another important question: What does our Lord mean when He uses the word "pure"? "Blessed are the pure in heart, for they will see God."

The word "pure" (Greek: *katharos*) means a heart that is clean or clear. Unfortunately, purity does not seem to be popular in contemporary Christianity. The emphasis nowadays seems to be more on power than on purity. Most Christians I talk to want to know how they can possess and develop spiritual gifts. Few, generally speaking, want to know how to experience the blessing of what our text today calls a heart purified by faith.

Sixteen hundred years ago St Augustine expressed a sentiment in words which might well sum up the thoughts of many – thankfully, not all – in today's Church: "Lord, make me pure … but not just yet." Most of us would be willing to identify ourselves with the conditions laid down in the first five of our Lord's Beatitudes, but how do we feel about the condition of being pure in heart? Are we ready and willing to pray:

> *I want, dear Lord, a heart that's true and clean*
> *A sunlit heart, with not a cloud between.*
> *A heart like Thine, a heart divine.*
> *A heart as white as snow.*
> *On me, dear Lord, a heart like this bestow.*

FURTHER STUDY

John 13:1-17;
2 Cor. 7:1;
James 4:8;
1 John 3:3

1. What was Peter's request?

2. Make it your request today.

Prayer

O yes, dear Father, from the depths of my being I cry – make me clean. I have come so far with You – how can I turn back now? I'm a candidate for both power and purity. Give me the deep inner cleansing I need – today. For Jesus' sake. Amen.

Whiter than snow!

"Cleanse me with hyssop, and I shall be clean; wash me, and I shall be whiter than snow." (v.7)

For reading & meditation – Psalm 51:1-15

As we continue discussing what it means to be pure in heart, we ask: How do we ensure that our hearts are made pure? Great controversy has raged over this issue in every century of the Church. Those who see sin as having made deep inroads into human nature say that the only thing God can do with sin is to forgive it. Others see the soul as a battle-ground on which long-drawn-out hostilities take place between the flesh and the Spirit. And there are those who claim, as did John Wesley, that inner purity can be imparted by a sudden influx of divine grace.

Adherents of these views fall into three main groups: (1) those who believe that purity is imputed; (2) those who believe that purity is imparted; and (3) those who believe that purity is developed. Those who believe that purity is imputed say that Christ flings His robe of right-eousness around a sinner and then God for ever sees him in the spotless garments of His Son. Those who believe purity is imparted claim that there is an experience awaiting all believers, usually subsequent to con-version, whereby, through a crisis experience, God imparts the gift of purity. This belief received great prominence under John Wesley. Those who believe purity is developed see the work of God in the soul proceeding along the lines of a slow but steady improvement.

FURTHER STUDY

1 Pet. 1:1-22;
Psa. 24:3-4;
1 Tim. 1:5; 5:22

1. To what else does
Peter relate purity?

2. What was Paul's
exhortation to
Timothy?

Which of these is right? I believe that each view has something to contribute; it is when the emphasis is disproportionately placed that problems arise. God both imputes and imparts purity, and then helps us apply and develop these truths in our daily life and experience.

Prayer

O God my gracious Father, I am so thankful that You have provided for my deepest needs – and especially my need for inner cleansing. Wash me so clean on the inside that I will be whiter than the whitest snow. Amen.

Lord – make me clean

*"… through Christ Jesus the law of the Spirit of life set me
free from the law of sin and death." (8:2)*

For reading & meditation – Romans 7:14-8:4

Yesterday we ended by saying that God can impart purity as well as
impute it, and He then helps us apply it in our daily life and experience. Permit me to share my own personal experience in this connection, not as a model for you to follow, but simply to illustrate how
God revealed Himself to me.

Following my conversion in my mid-teens, friends assured me that I
ought to ask God to baptise me in His Holy Spirit. This, they told me,
would give me the power I needed to become an effective witness for
Him. I asked God to do this – and in a remarkable encounter with Him,
I found the power I sought. But although this experience transformed
me overnight from a shy, timid follower of Christ into a fearless witness
for Him, I still felt deeply troubled by sinful forces. I fought hard with
such things as lust and sensuality until one night, worn down by the
inner conflict, I got down on my knees and prayed: "Lord, reach deep
inside me and make me truly clean."

Again, something wonderful took place – not so much an invasion of
power as an invasion of purity. It did not result, I
found, in placing me beyond the possibility of a carnal
thought, a stab of pride, a trace of envy, but it meant
that from that moment to this, I have been more conscious of the Holy Spirit's presence than I have been of
sin's presence. Evil was not eradicated in me, as some
proponents of imparted holiness believe, but I found
that the eagerness for it had gone, and the hunger for
it was no longer a clamour. Now, fifty years later, I
never cease to thank God for His Spirit's cooling and
cleansing touch.

FURTHER STUDY

Gal. 5:1-26;
Matt. 5:29;
Rom. 6:6; 13:14

1. How did Paul
   exhort the
   Galatians?

2. How drastically
   did Jesus put it?

Prayer

My Father and my God, although I realise I have to walk my own personal path to
holiness and inner cleansing, help me to know at last that same cooling, cleansing
touch in the depths of my heart. I ask this for Your own dear Name's sake. Amen.

A divine catharsis

"And he will be called Wonderful Counsellor …" (v.6)
For reading & meditation – Isaiah 9:1-7

We continue meditating on the word "pure" as used by Jesus in His sixth Beatitude. I discovered when researching this theme that the word "catharsis" – meaning to cleanse or make pure – is derived from the same Greek root as the word "pure".

In psychology, the word "catharsis" is used to describe the feeling of release and cleansing a person experiences in the presence of a trusted friend or counsellor when they empty out many of their repressed feelings or ideas. In the right circumstances and under the right conditions, a person who does this often feels purged, renewed and released. I have seen this happen myself on countless occasions when counselling. A person comes with deep hurts, and when they are sure they are in the presence of someone who understands them, someone they can trust, they open up their repressed feelings in such a way that afterwards they sit back and say: "I feel so different. It's like someone has reached deep down inside me and scraped my insides clean."

What produces this feeling of purging and release? It is difficult to explain because the inner release a person feels is not obtained simply by sharing; it comes only in the atmosphere of mutual confidence and trust. When a counsellor shows signs of disapproval or shock, then no release (catharsis) is experienced. If, as mental health experts claim, this only happens when a counsellor is warm and accepting, as opposed to harsh and judgmental, then it becomes immediately obvious that in the presence of Jesus, the Wonderful Counsellor, we have the possibility of experiencing the deepest catharsis it is possible to know.

FURTHER STUDY

1 John 1:1-7;
Psa. 65:3;
Ezek. 36:25;
Zech. 13:1

1. How are we to walk?

2. What does this result in?

Prayer

Blessed Lord Jesus, my Counsellor and my Friend, help me to open up the whole of my being to You so that I might experience a divine catharsis. I long not just to be clean – I long to be wholly clean. For Your own dear Name's sake. Amen.

"No condemnation now I dread"

"So if the Son sets you free, you will be free indeed."
(v.36)

For reading & meditation – John 8:21-36

We saw yesterday that the phenomenon of catharsis comes about not simply through telling someone else our troubles, but when that other person is a warm, accepting and understanding individual. Psychologists believe the explanation for this to be the fact that the warm, accepting manner of the helper is so directly opposite to the harsh, judgmental attitudes of those who caused the hurts that repressed feelings easily surface and are released.

What has this law of the personality to do with the subject now under discussion? A great deal, I believe. In Jesus Christ we find Someone who not only yearns for our trust, but is worthy of our trust. To sit in His presence is to hear words similar to those He spoke to the woman caught in adultery: "Neither do I condemn you … go now, and leave your life of sin" (John 8:11). Such acceptance, such compassion, such concern, cannot fail to produce within every heart a willingness to open up those hurts and fears which have been so deeply repressed.

As I said yesterday, I have witnessed on countless occasions this strange and mysterious phenomenon of catharsis take place as, in the presence of love and acceptance, repressed hurts and ideas are discharged from the personality. But beautiful and wondrous as this natural phenomenon is, it is as nothing compared to the glory and radiance that a person shows when they stand in the presence of Jesus Christ, the Wonderful Counsellor, and experience a catharsis that reaches, not merely into the outer regions of the heart, but to its greatest depths. To have such an experience is not just to be free – it is to be free indeed.

FURTHER STUDY

John 3:1-18; 5:24;
Rom. 8:1; 8:34;
Rev. 12:10

1. Who brings condemnation?

2. What is the promise to the believer?

Prayer

My Father and my God, slowly things are coming into focus. I am beginning to understand what You mean when You say: "If the Son sets you free, you will be free indeed." Purge me to the depths of my being. In Jesus' Name. Amen.

Seeing God

*"Who may ascend the hill of the Lord? Who may stand in
his holy place?" (v.3)*

For reading & meditation – Psalm 24:1-10

We spend one more day meditating on the words: "Blessed are the
pure in heart, for they will see God." The concluding words of this
Beatitude are often misunderstood. Many believe them to have reference
to the saints' eternal reward in heaven. Tennyson expressed this thought
in his famous lines: "I hope to see my Pilot face to face when I have
crossed the bar."

The thought contained in this phrase, however, is not so much related to seeing God in heaven, but to seeing God *now*. Seeing God means
seeing God in everything. Let me put it another way: not to see God is to
fail to find the meaning of life and to see no purpose in anything. Such a
condition, one must admit, produces an emotional overload on the personality that leads inevitably to despair. Some who fall prey to this mood
can end up committing suicide. As one person commented: "Those who
can't see the why have little energy to cope with the what."

Seeing God is being acquainted with Him, sensing His acceptance,
comprehending what it means to be forgiven and made anew. Raymond
Cramer puts it beautifully when he says: "To the pure in heart, seeing
God is viewing a stained glass window from the inside
rather than the outside. The pure in heart are aware of
a reality which most people miss. They are sure of
God." Seeing God must be connected with purity of
heart, for we must see and sense God first in our own
inner being before we can see Him and sense Him elsewhere. See Him within and you will not fail to see Him
without.

FURTHER STUDY

Isa. 6:1-8;
Psa. 99:9;
Heb. 12:14;
Rev. 15:4

1. What was Isaiah's
experience?

2. What is a
prerequisite for
seeing the Lord?

Prayer

Gracious and loving Father, I recognise that an uncleansed heart causes more ill
health and more unhappiness than anything else. Help me take the prescription You
have given me with a thankful heart. Amen.

Peace in our time

*"Therefore, since we have been justified through faith, we
have peace with God through our Lord Jesus Christ." (v.1)*
For reading & meditation – Romans 5:1-11

We have come now to the seventh positive attitude that makes for
good spiritual and mental health: "Blessed are the peacemakers,
for they will be called sons of God" (Matt. 5:9). This Beatitude seems to
have a special relevance to the age through which we are passing, for if
there is one thing the world needs at this moment, it is peacemakers.

Our generation has never known peace worldwide. One authority
says: "During most of our recent history the air has been filled with rum-
blings of pending war until today, at the so-called peak of scientific
enlightenment, the menace of a global conflict threatens our atomic age
with suicide." The uncertainty caused by being on the brink of nuclear
confrontation, despite the end of the cold war between the East and
West, has taken its toll on people of all nations, spiritually and psychologically. Studies show that living in a generation which has the power to
annihilate itself in global destruction has a crippling effect upon the
minds of thousands, if not millions of people.

There was never a time when peacemakers were as important as they
are now. And more and more are standing up to be
counted on the side of peace. The peace organisations
report increasing memberships and their attempts to
alert the world to the need for international treaties
continues to gain the attention of every section of the
media. Yet how strange that most of those who are so
concerned for peace between nations fail to see the
need for peace between themselves and their Creator.
The solemn truth is that no man or woman can
become a peacemaker – at least in the biblical sense of
the word – until they have found peace within their
innermost being.

FURTHER STUDY

Rom. 12:9-18;
14:19; Prov. 12:20;
Mark 9:50

1. What are we to
do?

2. Are you a
peacemaker?

Prayer

O my Father, help people to come to the realisation that before they can enjoy the
peace of God, they must first enjoy peace with God. In Jesus' Name. Amen.

How much do we "project"?

*"Search me, O God, and know my heart; test me and know
my anxious thoughts." (v.23)*

For reading & meditation – Psalm 139:1-24

We ended yesterday by saying that no one can become a peacemaker – in the biblical sense of the word – until they have found peace within their innermost self. As we are looking at the Beatitudes from the point of view of how effective they are in producing good spiritual and mental health, it is interesting to see how the psychology of Jesus is always ahead of the findings of those who study human behaviour. The view of many psychologists and psychiatrists is that much of the talk and activity by the masses in relation to international peace is actually a projection whereby they take the pressure off themselves. I am not convinced that all the concern can be dismissed in this way, but a lot of it can be explained in terms of the mechanism known as psychological projection.

Listen to what Louis Linn and Leo Schwartz say in their book *Psychiatry, Religion and Experience:* "A psychological origin of an adolescent's social idealism lies in his yearning for peace within himself. He tends to project his feelings of helplessness and turmoil on to the outer world, so that his yearning for peace may take the form of a wish for world peace." Many of the activists who work for world peace may find this difficult to accept, but the truth is that if they did not have a world crisis on which to project their feelings, they would have to create some other condition. As long as we are not at peace within ourselves, we will create situations on which we project our insecure feelings.

FURTHER STUDY

Lam. 5:1-5;
Isa. 48:22; 57:20;
Deut. 28:67

*1 Which of these
statements could be
written about this
generation?*

*2 Make this a matter
for prayer today.*

Prayer

Dear Father, help me to understand this strange mechanism of projection. For I see that I can do the right things for the wrong reasons. Only You can probe my heart. I pray today with the psalmist, "Search me, O God, and know my heart." Amen.

Discord within – discord without

" 'There is no peace,' says the Lord, 'for the wicked.' " (v.22)
For reading & meditation – Isaiah 48:12-22

We are seeing that the reason why people get caught up in activist measures to gain the attention of world leaders in relation to the need for securing international peace is due, in part, to the mechanism of projection. If we do not know peace within, then we will tend to focus on finding ways of securing peace in our outer circumstances and environment.

I hasten to add that not everyone who is involved in peace movements is motivated by this reason. I know a number of genuine Christians – people who already have the peace of God in their hearts – who are active in such organisations and have a genuine concern to bring pressure on world governments to do everything that must be done to address these problems. Nevertheless, I have no hesitation in saying that the majority of those involved in the peace organisations are motivated by this strange mechanism we introduced into our discussions yesterday – projection. Since they do not possess peace within themselves, they talk at length about international peace.

It is easier to blame the world leaders, the political parties, the presidents and prime ministers than to look into one's own heart and accept individual accountability. Actually the reason why there is so much war and hostility in the world is because, generally speaking, we do not possess peace within ourselves. We create an environment that reflects our inner conflicts – the outside world reflects our inner world. Peace between nations does not guarantee peace within nations, nor does peace between two people guarantee peace within an individual.

FURTHER STUDY
John 14:15-27;
Psa. 29:11;
119:165; Isa. 26:3
1 What keeps us in
peace?
2 What does the
peace of Christ
resolve?

Prayer

Gracious and loving Father, I bow my head in gratitude for the exquisite peace You have given me. Now that I am at peace with You, help me to be at peace with others – and to bring peace to others. In Jesus' Name. Amen.

"What a beautiful day!"

"For he himself is our peace, who has made the two one, and has destroyed the barrier, the dividing wall of hostility …" (v.14)

For reading & meditation – Ephesians 2:11-22

Our meditations over the past few days have shown us that before we can become peacemakers in the true sense of that word, we must first know peace in our own minds and hearts.

The Bible is not content to leave the nature of the peace Christ purchased for us in doubt. Our reading today tells us that Christ made peace by the blood of His cross. He bore the sins of men so that those who know Him and accept His meritorious sufferings on the cross need no longer be troubled by them. The greatest message the world has ever heard – or will ever hear – is this: Christ interposed Himself between sinful humanity and a holy God so that men and women could be eternally redeemed. Have you been redeemed? Have you accepted Christ's sacrifice for you on the cross? If so, good – your mission now in life is to be a peacemaker. You are to share His peace with others.

A little girl who, a few weeks earlier, had become a Christian came down from her bedroom one morning and said to her mother: "What a beautiful day." The surprised mother said: "What do you mean? It's raining like I've never seen it rain before, and the weather forecast is that we are going to have several more days of this. How can you call such weather beautiful?" "But Mother," the little girl replied, "a beautiful day has nothing to do with the weather." In those simple but powerful words, she reconciled her mother to the weather – and had a more beautiful day herself. You see, this is what peacemaking is all about. The peacemakers make a new world around them and within them.

FURTHER STUDY

Matt. 11:20-30;
Ex. 33:14;
Psa. 116:7;
Heb. 4:3

1 What did Jesus promise?

2 What must we do?

Prayer

O Father, help me today to be a peacemaker wherever I go, and to reconcile people, not just to the weather – but to You. That which reaches the heart must come from the heart. Let the peace in my heart overflow. In Jesus' Name. Amen.

Let every Christian begin ...

*"… those who are peacemakers will plant seeds of peace
and reap a harvest of goodness." (v.18, TLB)*
For reading & meditation – James 3:1-18

We continue making the point that we cannot be peacemakers until we first find peace within ourselves. A psychiatrist was interviewing a man full of conflicts. In the middle of the interview the telephone rang, and because the receptionist had put a call through to him when he had given instructions not to be disturbed, the psychiatrist swore. He lost his peace and he lost his patient, for the patient saw that he had little to give except verbal advice.

The fact is that when we lose our peace with others, it is usually the projection of an inner conflict within ourselves. A church in the Far East has this statement engraved over the door: "Let every Christian begin the work of union within himself." This is the place to begin – within yourself. For, as the Chinese saying puts it: "He who has peace in himself has peace in the family; he who has peace in the family has peace in the world."

A prominent member of a peace movement in the British Isles who said he was dedicated to peace wrote a stinging letter to a member of the British Parliament which was published in the press. As a result, his advocacy of peace was blurred. People said: "This man's idea of peace needs an overhaul. It is simply verbal, and not vital." A missionary said: "God and I are not at peace; we seem to be at cross purposes. And my relationships with others are becoming more and more difficult." Of course – for when we are not in harmony with God, then we are not in harmony with ourselves or others.

FURTHER STUDY

John 16:25-33;
Luke 1:78-79;
Rom. 8:6; 14:17

1. What does peace spring from?

2. Why can we take heart?

Prayer

O Father, I long to become so harmonised with You that my life becomes an example of harmony to others. Make me a peaceful and peaceable person. For Jesus' sake. Amen.

What peacemaking is not

*"Encourage and rebuke with all authority. Do not let anyone
despise you."* (v.15)

For reading & meditation – Titus 2:1-15

Today we go a step further and affirm that no one can be spiritually or
mentally healthy until they know what it means to have peace in
their inner beings. A psychologist says: "If we could only measure the
amount of emotional energy that is dissipated within the human personality by lack of peace, we would be surprised to find that physical, mental and emotional loss would represent our greatest deficit within the
human economy." He is simply saying that inner conflict tears us apart –
physically, mentally and spiritually.

The intriguing thing is that as we make peace with God, a change
comes about in our own lives and this, in turn, is reflected in the lives of
others. We are not only at peace – we become peaceable. But even more
– we become peacemakers. To be a peacemaker means, quite simply,
that we become reconcilers. We reconcile people to God and to each
other.

We should be careful not to misunderstand the meaning of the word
"peacemaker", so let's examine for a moment what it is not.
Peacemaking is not just keeping the peace. Some strive to keep the peace

FURTHER STUDY

Eph. 6:1-15;
Psa. 119:165;
Phil. 4:7

*1. What is the
essence of the
gospel?*

*2. What keeps our
hearts and minds?*

because they do not wish to risk any unpleasantness
that might be involved in trying to put matters right.
They avoid a conflict by smoothing over the surface,
but this is not peace. The true peacemaker sometimes
has to be a fighter. Paradoxically, he or she is called,
not to a passive life, but an active one. Those who pursue this ministry must realise that peacemaking is not
patching things up, but getting to the roots of the
problem. Peacemakers sometimes have to stir up trouble before they can resolve it.

Prayer

Father, thank You for reminding me that peacemaking is not cowardice or the love of
quiet. Give me the courage I need to risk any unpleasantness that may be involved in
the cause of putting matters right. In Jesus' Name I pray. Amen.

Like our Father

*"How great is the love the Father has lavished on us, that
we should be called children of God!" (3:1)*

For reading & meditation – 1 John 2:28-3:11

Peacemaking is a positive attitude that produces good spiritual and mental health, and the one who has this attitude, according to Jesus, is to be envied and congratulated. The promise of the seventh Beatitude is that peacemakers "will be called sons of God". Why *called*? Because they *are* sons of God. This is their lot in life. Dr Martyn Lloyd-Jones put it like this: "The meaning of being called the sons of God is that the peacemaker is a child of God and that *he is like his Father.*"

If I were to pick out the one verse that most perfectly expresses the meaning of the Christian gospel, it would be this: "in Christ God was reconciling the world to himself … and entrusting to us the message of reconciliation" (2 Cor. 5:19, RSV). Ever since man sinned, God has been engaged in the positive business of an outgoing love – seeking to reconcile those who did not want to be reconciled. God wants us to do what He does – He commits to us the same task of reconciliation.

Those who are inwardly reconciled to God and seek to reconcile others to Him and to each other are the healthiest and the happiest people on earth. In two outstanding passages in the Bible, we are called sons of the Father – and for the same reason: Matthew 5:9 and Matthew 5:45. What do we conclude from this? We are most like God when we are bringing people together in reconciliation. And those who try to reconcile others are doing the work of heaven – for it is heaven's work to reconcile us.

FURTHER STUDY

Gal. 4:1-7;
John 1:12;
Rom. 8:14;
Heb. 2:10

1. As sons, what have we become?

2. How are we led?

Prayer

O God my Father, I pray that You will help me become more and more like You. You are a Father who reconciles – make me into Your own divine image. Help me to breathe "peace" upon all I meet. For Your own dear Name's sake. Amen.

When society kicks back

*"For it has been granted to you on behalf of Christ not only
to believe on him, but also to suffer for him." (v.29)*

For reading & meditation – Philippians 1:12-30

We come now to Christ's eighth and final prescription for good spiritual and mental health: "Blessed are those who are persecuted because of righteousness, for theirs is the kingdom of heaven" (Matt. 5:10). The inevitable result of bringing our attitudes in line with Christ's attitudes is that our lives become a silent judgement upon others. And men and women do not like to be judged, so they kick back in persecution. "Society," said someone, "demands conformity: if you fall beneath its standards, it will punish you; if you rise above its standards, it will persecute you. It demands an average, grey conformity."

The true Christian, however, does not conform – he stands out. "Woe to you," said Jesus, "when all men speak well of you" (Luke 6:26). If they do speak well of us, then it could be that we are too much like them. Let there be no mistake about this, the righteous will be persecuted – inevitably so. Once we adopt the principles which Christ presents, the men and women of the world are going to react with hostility and indignation.

Dr E. Stanley Jones was close to the mark when he said that the first thing a person must get used to when he or she becomes a Christian is the sight of their own blood. Are you being persecuted for righteousness' sake at the moment? Is the world venting its hatred and hostility upon you because of your stand for the Lord Jesus Christ? Then take heart – the persecution is the final proof, if one is needed, that you are a true disciple of your Master, a child of God and a citizen of heaven.

FURTHER STUDY

Matt. 10:16-42;
24:9; Luke 21:12

*1 How are we sent
out?*

*2 What was Jesus'
promise?*

Prayer

My Father and my God, help me not to miss the deep underlying truth in this, the last of Your prescriptions for happiness. Strengthen me so that I am unafraid of seeing my own blood. In Jesus' Name I ask it. Amen.

Collision course

"… everyone who wants to live a godly life in Christ Jesus will be persecuted." (v.12)

For reading & meditation – 2 Timothy 3:12-17

We continue from where we left off yesterday in saying that persecution is one of the proofs that we are true disciples of the Lord Jesus Christ. Many Christians find great difficulty in coming to terms with this issue of persecution, and because they have never understood that those who reject Christ will also reject those who follow Christ, they become entangled in such things as conciliation and compromise.

If you have never done so before, face the fact right now that when you identify yourself with Jesus Christ, the world will persecute you. The degree of persecution differs from one Christian to another, but in one way or another the world will react against you with hostility and contempt. Once you recognise this, you are nine tenths of the way toward overcoming the fear which cripples so many Christians – the fear of witnessing.

Not long after my conversion, an elderly Welsh miner gave me some advice that greatly helped to overcome my fear of rejection. He said: "Keep ever before you the fact that those who reject Christ will reject you. And the more like Christ you become, the more the world will resent you. Remember also that when they do reject you, it is not you personally whom they are against, but Christ who is alive and who is being seen in you." Never shall I forget the release that came through those wise words. Once I understood that becoming identified with Christ meant I was on a collision course with the world, I came to terms with the inevitability of this fact and was set free from fear. And what happened to me can happen to you – today.

FURTHER STUDY

John 17:1-26;
15:20; 16:2

1. How did the world respond to the first disciples?

2. What was Jesus' prayer?

Prayer

Lord Jesus Christ, I bring to You my fear of persecution and ask You to set me free from it right now. Help me to face the world's hostility in the knowledge that just as it could not overcome You, it cannot overcome me. Amen.

"My neighbours won't talk to me"

"… be wise as serpents and innocent as doves." (v.16, RSV)
For reading & meditation – Matthew 10:1-20

We are saying that many Christians are ineffective witnesses because they attempt to water down their testimony to avoid persecution – and end up achieving nothing. Once we accept that those who reject Christ and His teaching will also reject us, we will then be free to throw our whole weight on the side of Christ and become fully identified with Him.

In following this principle, however, we must be careful that our freedom from fear of rejection does not lead us to become objectionable. I know some Christians who have a hard time from their non-Christian acquaintances, not because of their likeness to Christ, but because of their tactlessness and lack of wisdom. I once met a man who told me he had convincing evidence that he was a true disciple of Christ. I was intrigued to know his reason for thinking this way, and in answer to my question "Why are you so sure?" he replied: "My neighbours won't talk to me and cross to the other side of the road when they see me coming. I take this persecution as proof that I am a true citizen of the kingdom."

Some time later, I had occasion to talk to some of this man's neighbours, who told me that the reason they avoided him was because he continually accosted them with questions like "Do you know you are going to hell?" or "What if you were to drop dead at this moment – where would you spend eternity?" The neighbours thought it good policy to avoid him rather than to be faced continually with his belligerence. The man was suffering, not for Christ's sake, but for his own sake.

FURTHER STUDY

2 Tim. 3:1-13;
1 Cor. 13:3;
Rev. 2:10

1. What is the result of living a godly life?

2. What is promised for faithfulness?

Prayer

O God my Father, I see how easy it is to bring suffering and persecution upon myself by my own tactlessness and folly. Help me to object without being objectionable and to disagree without being disagreeable. In Jesus' Name. Amen.

No compulsions in Christianity

*"If you suffer, it should not be as a murderer or thief or
any other kind of criminal, or even as a meddler." (v.15)*

For reading & meditation – 1 Peter 4:7-19

We continue focusing on the fact that many Christians are persecuted, not because of identifying with Christ, but because of their
tactlessness and folly. This eighth Beatitude – "Blessed are those who are
persecuted because of righteousness, for theirs is the kingdom of heav-
en" – does not apply to such people. Let us be quite clear about that.

There is a great difference between persecution for the sake of righteousness and persecution for the sake of self-righteousness. Many
Christians are foolish in these matters. They fail to realise the difference
between prejudice and principle, and thus bring unnecessary suffering
upon themselves. The same applies to those who are over-zealous in
their witnessing. They make a nuisance of themselves and interpret the
persecution that comes as persecution for righteousness' sake.

The Scripture teaches us to be "wise as serpents and innocent as
doves". The writer of the Proverbs puts it powerfully when he says: "He
who wins souls is wise" (Prov. 11:30). We are not told in this eighth
Beatitude, "Blessed are those who are persecuted because they are over-
zealous", neither are we told, "Blessed are those who
are persecuted because they are fanatical." I was once
asked by a church to counsel one of their members
who had a compulsion to witness. The man got into so
many difficulties because of this that the church
threatened to discipline him unless he agreed to
receive counselling. I found his compulsion to
witness came not from Christ, but from his own inner
drives. He needed to witness so as to feel significant.
Witnessing should be a constraint, never a
compulsion.

FURTHER STUDY

Acts 9:1-29;
1 Cor. 4:12;
2 Cor. 4:9

1 Who was Saul
really persecuting?

2 What was his early
experience of
proclaiming Christ?

Prayer

O Father, show me how to distinguish between what is a compulsion and what is a
constraint. And help me to see that if I don't find my significance in my relationship
with You, then I will attempt to find it in other ways. Amen.

A martyr complex

"… you are complete in Him …" (v.10, NKJ)
For reading & meditation – Colossians 2:1-15

We are seeing the suffering and persecution we experience can be due to our own tactlessness and folly. Today I want to go a stage further, and suggest that in relation to this matter of suffering and persecution, some Christians have developed a "martyr complex".

A "martyr complex" is an attitude of mind that finds strange emotional satisfaction in being persecuted. Why should this be? Well, if, for example, a person does not experience a good sense of personal worth, they become motivated to secure that worth in other ways. And one of those ways can be that of making an impact upon their immediate environment or society through taking a stand on some "Christian" issue.

Now I am not saying, of course, that all of those who take a stand on such issues as pornography, violence, and other serious moral problems are motivated to do so because of a "martyr complex". That would be foolish to suggest and foolish to deduce. But it must be seen that some Christians strike out on issues, not because of an overriding concern for Christian values, but because of the satisfaction they get out of being noticed. And when being noticed leads to severe persecution, they draw from this the emotional charge they need to compensate for their low sense of worth. Such people almost court suffering and persecution, but it has to be said that they are not suffering for righteousness' sake – they are suffering for their own sake. May God give us grace and wisdom to understand when we are doing things to meet our own emotional needs, rather than out of love for Him.

FURTHER STUDY

2 Cor. 11:16-33;
2 Tim. 2:8-9;
3:10-11

1. List some of Paul's sufferings.

2. What was Paul's testimony?

Prayer

Father, I see even more clearly that unless my needs are met in a close relationship with You, then I am a vulnerable person – and prone to go astray. Draw me closer to You this day. In Jesus' Name. Amen.

"Xenophobia"

"... you do not belong to the world, but I have chosen you out of the world. That is why the world hates you." (v.19)
For reading & meditation – John 15:12-27

We continue meditating on the eighth and final Beatitude. One of the questions that has often puzzled people concerning this matter of suffering and persecution is this: Why is it that Christians, when they do good, are often persecuted, while non-Christians who do the same kind of good are adored?

One commentator suggests the reason for this is that when non-Christians do good, other non-Christians find it easy to identify with them and say to themselves: "These people are just like me when I am at my best." The thinking that goes on below the threshold of a non-Christian's mind when he sees other non-Christians doing good is along the line of: "I am probably capable of the same thing myself if the opportunity came my way." The admiration that is then given is a way of paying a compliment to oneself.

The Christian who does good has about him or her the atmosphere of another world, and because of this, the non-Christian observes, not just their act of good, but the different motivation that underlies the act. They sense that there is something different about this person, and because they cannot understand or explain the difference, they react with fear and the fear then turns to hostility. Psychologists have a name for this fear – xenophobia. It means fear of someone we do not know or understand. This is why the scribes and Pharisees hated our Lord so much. It wasn't because He was good; it was because He was different. This is the effect Jesus Christ always has upon the world. And to the extent that you reflect His spirit, to that extent you will experience the same reaction.

FURTHER STUDY

Phil. 1:1-14;
Col. 4:3;
2 Tim. 1:7-8

1. How did Paul view persecution?

2. What was his charge to Timothy?

Prayer

O Father, I see that if I just try to do good, the world will applaud me, but if I try to become Christlike, it will hate me. Nevertheless I long to be Christlike. Help me, dear Father, for apart from Your grace, I know it is not possible. Amen.

Stand – and be healthy

"… I have set before you life and death, blessings and curses. Now choose life …" (v.19)

For reading & meditation – Deuteronomy 30:1-20

We spend one last day meditating on the eighth and final Beatitude. Some feel that the verses which follow this Beatitude (verses 11 and 12) constitute a ninth Beatitude, but really they are an amplification of what our Lord has been saying in verse 10. It must be pointed out in passing that more is said about this eighth Beatitude than is said about the others – a fact that surely underlines its supreme importance.

The question we ask ourselves today is this: How does this eighth Beatitude contribute to good mental and spiritual health? It does so by encouraging us to stand up and be counted. The famous missionary doctor and scientist Dr Albert Schweitzer, when addressing a group of medical men in Africa many years ago, is reported to have said: "You cannot be healthy unless you stand for something – even at a cost."

The person who unashamedly identifies with Christ and stands up for Him, knowing that their stand will produce, in one form or another, inevitable persecution experiences an inner release from fear that affects every part of the personality in the most positive way. The positive may be persecuted, but they are also the most productive – they survive when others fall by the way. So stop wearing out your nervous system. Cease using up precious energy trying to find ways to make it through this world. Follow God's blueprint as laid out in the eight Beatitudes and yours will be a life which, through the psychology of Jesus, will bring you maximum effectiveness with minimum weariness. Choose any other way and you will experience minimum effectiveness with maximum weariness. I choose life.

FURTHER STUDY

Philemon 1-25;
Eph. 3:1;
1 Pet. 3:15-16

1. How did Paul view his imprisonment?

2. When were you last persecuted?

Prayer

Father, I, too, choose life. Help me to absorb and assimilate Your attitudes until they become my attitudes. Then life will always have to be spelt with a capital "L". With Your help, dear Lord, I'm on my way to real living. Hallelujah!

How do I rate?

"Examine yourselves to see whether you are in the faith; test yourselves." (v.5)

For reading & meditation – 2 Corinthians 13:1-14

As we conclude our study of the Beatitudes it is time for us to take a simple test. Ask yourself the following questions and see how many of Christ's "beautiful attitudes" have been assimilated into your life:

1. Am I trying to grasp things from God's hands or are my hands relaxed and empty so that I might receive?

2. Do I shrink from painful experiences or do I welcome them in the knowledge that they will make me a more sensitive person?

3. Am I so sure of God and His resources that I am free from a spirit of demandingness and over-concern?

4. Is my goal to be happy, or is it to be holy? Am I more taken up with getting pleasure out of God than I am with giving pleasure to God?

5. Do I have a deep compassion and concern for the plight of others?

6. Is my heart clean and pure? Have I experienced an inner cleansing that has reached to the deepest depths?

7. Am I a reconciler – one who seeks to reconcile others to God and, where necessary, to each other?

8. Am I so identified with Christ that I experience the hatred which the world gives to those who remind them of Him?

Don't be discouraged if you can't see all of these "beautiful attitudes" at work in your life. Remember, we *grow* in grace. Ask God, however, to help you absorb more and more of His "beautiful attitudes" day by day. The more you have, the more you are to be envied. Possess them all – and you are truly blessed.

FURTHER STUDY

Eph. 4:1-15;
Heb. 6:1;
2 Pet. 3:18

1. What are we to go on to?

2. What "beautiful attitude" will you reflect today?

Prayer

Lord Jesus, I have listened to Your words and I realise now the Word must become flesh – in me. I want the balance of my days here on earth to reflect, not my attitudes, but Yours. Help me, for Your own Name's sake. Amen.

How to use the Bible

A question I am often asked especially by young Christians is this: why do I need to read the Bible?

We need to read the Bible in order to know not only God's mind for the future but how to develop a daily walk with Him. God uses His Word to change people's lives and bring those lives into a deeper relationship with Himself and a greater conformity to His will. For over four decades now I have spent hours every week reading and studying the Scriptures. God has used this book to transform my life and to give me a sense of security in a shifting and insecure world.

How do we read the Bible? Do we just start at Genesis and make our way through to the book of Revelation? There are many ways to go about reading the Scriptures; let me mention the three most popular approaches.

One is to follow a reading plan such as is included in the *Every Day with Jesus Devotional Bible* or *Through the Bible in One Year*. The great advantage of following a reading plan is that your reading is arranged for you; in a sense you are being supervised. You are not left to the vagaries of uncertainty: what shall I read today, where shall I begin, at what point shall I end?

A second approach is to thread your way through the Scriptures by following a specific theme. It is quite staggering how many themes can be found in Scripture and what great spiritual rewards can be had by acquainting yourself with them. When I started writing *Every Day with Jesus* in 1965 I decided to follow the thematic approach and I wondered how long I would be able to keep it up. Now, over thirty years later, I am still writing and expounding on different themes of the Bible, and the truth is that I have more biblical themes and subjects than it is possible to deal with in one lifetime!

A third approach is by reading through a book of the Bible. This enables you to get into the mind of the writer and understand his message. Every book of the Bible has something unique and special to convey and, as with any book, this can only be understood when you read it from start to finish.

It is important to remember that all reading of the Bible ought to be preceded by prayer. This puts you in a spiritually receptive frame of mind

How to use the Bible

to receive what God has to say to you through His Word. The Bible can be read by anyone but it can only be understood by those whose hearts are in tune with God — those who have come into a personal relationship with Him and who maintain that relationship through daily or regular prayer. This is how the Bible puts it: "The man without the Spirit does not accept the things that come from the Spirit of God, for they are foolishness to him, and he cannot understand them, because they are spiritually discerned" (1 Cor. 2:14).

Praying before you open your Bible should not be a mere formality. It is not the *act* that will make the Bible come alive but the *attitude*. Prayer enables us to approach the Scriptures with a humble mind. The scientist who does not sit down before the facts of the universe with an open mind, is not prepared to give up every preconceived idea and is not willing to follow wherever nature will lead him, will discover little or nothing. It is the same with the reading of the Scriptures; we must come to it with a humble and receptive mind or we too will get nowhere. Prayer enables us to have the attitude that says, "Speak, for your servant is listening" (1 Sam. 3:10).

If we are to grow in the Christian life then we must do more than just *read* the Bible — we must *study* it. This means that we must give time to poring over it, considering it, thinking about what it is saying to us and assimilating into our hearts and minds its doctrines and its ideas.

I have already pointed out that one of the ways of reading the Bible is by taking a theme and tracing it through the various books of the Bible. The pleasure this brings can be greatly enhanced by using this as a regular means of Bible study. When we study the Bible with the aid of concordances, lexicons and so on, we feed our minds but when we study the Bible devotionally, we apply the Word of God to our hearts. Both exercises are necessary if we are to be completely rounded people but we must see that it is at the place of the devotional that we open up our hearts and expose ourselves to God's resources.

Let me encourage you also to take advantage of a reading plan as a further basis of study. Following this will enable you to cover the whole of the Bible in a set period. Those who have used this method tell of the most

How to use the Bible

amazing spiritual benefits. One person who had read through the whole of the Bible in a year said to me, "It demanded more discipline than I thought I was capable of, but the rewards have been enormous." When I asked her what these rewards were, she said, "I used to have a partial view of God's purposes because I dipped into my Bible just here and there as it suited me. Now, however, I feel as if I have been looking over God's shoulder as He laid out the universe, and I feel so secure in the knowledge that He found a place for me in that marvellous plan." There can be no doubt that reading through the entire Bible in a set period enables one to gain a perspective that has tremendous positive spiritual consequences.

The third form of study — reading through a book of the Bible at a time — has the advantage of helping you understand the unity and diversity of the Bible. It is quite incredible how so many writers sharing their thoughts at different times of history combine to say similar things and give a consistent emphasis. Reading and pondering on this gives you such an appreciation of the wisdom of God in putting together this marvellous volume that it fires your soul and quickly brings praise and adoration to your lips.

I have found the best way to study a book of the Bible is to read it through once for a sense of the whole, and then to read it again, making a note of anything that strikes me such as a principle to be applied, an insight to be stored away in my heart, or a thought to be shared with someone who is struggling.

One thing is sure, time spent with the Bible is not wasted. The more one loves God the more one will love the Bible. And the more one loves the Bible the more one will love God. Always remember this unique volume — God's one and only published work — yields its treasures only to those who read it, study it and obey it.

Selwyn Hughes

The Power
of a New
Perspective

"Footholds for faith"

"… I have put my trust in the Lord God …" (v.28, NKJ)
For reading & meditation – Psalm 73:1-28

We begin today a verse-by-verse examination of one of the great passages in the Bible – the seventy-third psalm. If you were to ask any group of Christians to name their favourite psalm most would probably reply: "The twenty-third." And it is not difficult to understand why. The simplicity and beauty of its language, together with its comforting content, has endeared it to millions. Unfortunately the seventy-third psalm is not so well known, but in my opinion it deserves to be. The truths and insights it contains provide us with some of the most steadying and encouraging revelations to be found anywhere in the Word of God.

The issue with which the psalmist struggles in this psalm is this: Why do the godly suffer so much when the ungodly, generally speaking, seem to get off scot-free? So deeply does this question cut into his soul that he is brought to the point of near despair: "My feet had almost slipped; I had nearly lost my foothold" (v.2). Whilst there, however, he discovers some spiritual principles that bring him step by step to the heights of spiritual assurance.

Are you puzzled by the fact that though you are following the Lord, life is extremely difficult? Do you wonder why those who live in opposition to the Almighty seem to have an easier time than those who are committed to His cause? Take heart. It is possible to find a foothold on this slippery path of doubt. The psalmist found it, and so can you. Follow me day by day through this thrilling psalm and you will discover a few more footholds for your faith.

FURTHER STUDY
Ezek. 18:24-32;
Jer. 12:1;
Hab. 1:1-4

1. What was the complaint of the Israelites?

2. What was the Lord's response?

Prayer

Gracious and loving heavenly Father, help me as I begin this quest for greater light and illumination on life's problems, for I know that a faith which does not hold my intellect will not hold my heart. I would have both held by You. Amen.

A lost emphasis

"Then those who feared the Lord talked with each other ..."
(v.16)

For reading & meditation – Malachi 3:13-18

A lthough in Psalm 73 the psalmist is beset by doubt, he begins, never-theless, on a triumphant note: "Surely God is good to Israel, to those who are pure in heart." Preachers usually leave their conclusion until the end of their sermon – but here the psalmist begins with it! It might seem strange to some that the psalmist should begin with a conclusion, but this is often seen in the book of Psalms. And the reason is this: the psalmist is so convinced of the fact that God is good that he decides to start right there. It is as if he is saying: "I want to tell you how I moved from doubt to faith, but the thing I want you to get right away is this: God is good."

Some commentators believe that in the Temple services there was a time of open testimony and worship, similar to that which featured in the old Methodist class meetings, when individuals gave testimonies to their fellow believers of God's dealings with them. This is one of the most powerful ways of building the spiritual life of the Church, but regrettably it does not seem to be widely practised today.

If this psalm was part of the psalmist's testimony during an open time of worship, one can imagine the impact it would have made upon the hearers as he related how he emerged from crippling doubt to renewed confidence in the goodness of God. I know of nothing more motivating in the Christian life than for believers to identify and share the spiritual principles which have enabled them to overcome attacks on their faith. When we ignore this principle we do so at our peril.

FURTHER STUDY

John 3:25-36; 5:39;
15:26; Acts 20:24

1. When was the last time you publicly testified to the goodness of God?

2. When will be the next time?

Prayer

O Father, show us clearly how sharing with each other what You are doing in our lives not only inspires and motivates us, but greatly strengthens the Body. Help us restore this lost emphasis wherever it is missing. In Jesus' Name. Amen.

How strong convictions come

*"... that you may be mature and complete, not lacking
anything." (v.4)*

For reading & meditation – James 1:2-8

We continue meditating on the first verse of Psalm 73: "Surely God is good to Israel, to those who are pure in heart." The psalmist has gone through an experience of crippling doubt but the great thing is this: he has emerged from it spiritually enriched and with a deeper confidence in the goodness of God. So he starts with that conclusion and then tells us how he got there.

This is one of the great values of the psalms – they reflect and analyse the experiences that we are called upon to face. Ray Steadman says of the psalms: "They are an enactment of what most of us are going through, have gone through or will go through in the walk of faith." Every one of us will be able to understand the psalmist's struggle: we start off with a positive faith in God's goodness and then something happens which causes us to be plagued with doubts. The problem then is how to get back to where we were. This is what the psalmist does in this psalm – he shows us how to return to the place where the soul finds true peace.

We should not forget that the strongest convictions are born in the throes of doubt. The statement "God is good to Israel" is a statement grounded in experience. In a similar vein, Dostoevsky, the famous Russian novelist, could say: "It is not as a child that I believe and confess Christ. My hosannah is 'born of a furnace of doubt.'" Doubts may discourage but they need not demoralise you. It is not what happens to you, but what you make of it that matters.

FURTHER STUDY

Psa. 13:1; 69:3;
119:82

*1. What
characteristic did the
psalmist display?*

*2. What was his
confession of faith?*

Prayer

Gracious and loving Father, I pray that You will do for me what You did for the psalmist and help me turn my strongest doubts into my strongest beliefs. I offer You my willingness – now add to it Your power. In Jesus' Name I ask it. Amen.

"A great soul battle"

"I sink in the miry depths, where there is no foothold." (v.2)
For reading & meditation – Psalm 69:1-12

Having shared with us the conviction that God is good, the psalmist now proceeds to tell us what caused him to move away from that belief so that his soul became filled with such desolating doubt: "But as for me, my feet had almost slipped; I had nearly lost my foothold. For I envied the arrogant when I saw the prosperity of the wicked" (Psa. 73:2-3).

Here begins what Spurgeon described as "a great soul battle, a spiritual marathon, a hard and well-fought fight in which the half-defeated became in the end wholly victorious". The psalmist seems bothered by the apparent contradiction between what he had been taught in the Scriptures – that God is good to those who are pure in heart – and his experience in life. He was envious, he says, of the arrogant and deeply upset over the fact that the wicked appeared to be more prosperous than the godly. He had been told that when you were righteous, then God would take care of you and prosper you. Obviously things had not been going too well for the psalmist and when he compared his situation with that of the ungodly who appeared to be so prosperous, he came close to giving up his faith.

FURTHER STUDY

1 Kings 19:1-21;
Psa. 31:10;
42:5-6, 11

1. What point did
Elijah come to?

2. How did God deal
with him?

Am I talking to someone who is in a similar situation at this moment? Is your faith so badly shaken by what you see around you that you are tempted to give up? Then this is the word of the Lord to you today: hold on. It is a dark tunnel you find yourself in at this moment, but God will bring you through. He never fails. Never.

Prayer

Father, thank You for speaking to me today. Help me not to form my conclusions from what I see around – the immediate – but from what I see above, in You, the Ultimate. I wait in quiet confidence for Your word to come to pass. Amen.

Be honest with yourself

"Surely you desire truth in the inner parts ..." (v.6)
For reading & meditation – Psalm 51:1-9

Even the most casual reader of Psalm 73 cannot help but be struck by the openness and honesty of the psalmist. He says: "My feet had almost slipped ... for I envied the arrogant" (vv. 2-3). This again is one of the great values of the book of Psalms – it brings home to us the importance of acknowledging what is going on in our hearts when we are caught up in the midst of conflict. I cannot stress enough how spiritually damaging it is to ignore or deny our true feelings.

There is a form of teaching going around in some Christian circles today which holds that one should never admit or acknowledge a negative thought or feeling – not even for a single second. Life must be lived positively, it is said, and that means refusing to consider or even glance at anything negative. What nonsense! The people who advocate this approach to life can never have read the book of Psalms.

I am all for a positive approach to life, but positivism first involves facing things realistically no matter how negative they may be. How can you know what you need to be positive about until you have clearly seen what is troubling you? Once an issue is faced, and faced realistically, then the matter can and must be dealt with in a positive way. But to try and be positive without bringing into clear focus what is wrong is like building a house on sand. No matter how much cement is poured into the foundations, and no matter how well the walls are reinforced, when a storm comes it will sink without trace.

FURTHER STUDY

Prov. 12:15-22;
Lev. 19:11; Mal. 2:6

1. What word does the Bible use for denial?

2. What delights the Lord?

Prayer

Father, drive this truth deeply into my spirit, for I see that it is not enough to be honest with You and others, I must also be honest with myself. Help me get there and stay there. In Jesus' Name I ask it Amen.

If you're thrown – admit it

"My God, my God, why have you forsaken me?" (v.1)
For reading & meditation – Psalm 22:1-11

We continue looking at the attitude of the psalmist, who does not hesitate to tell the truth about himself. As we saw, he admits that his feet had well-nigh slipped and his faith had almost gone. I find the psalmist's honesty both stimulating and refreshing, especially when compared to the tendency of many in today's Church to pretend that things are not as they are. Dr Martyn Lloyd-Jones said in one of his sermons: "I know of nothing in the spiritual life more discouraging than to meet the kind of person who seems to give the impression that he or she is always walking on the mountain top." I agree.

You see, it is far more important to be honest than to appear to be the sort of person who is never thrown by problems. If you are not thrown, then fine; but if you are then admit it. But can't openness be a form of exhibitionism? Yes, it can. Some people may confess to failure as a means of drawing attention to themselves. But I do not believe that this was the psalmist's motive, for quite clearly he wrote the psalm to glorify not himself but God.

The pathway to spiritual growth begins when we realistically and honestly face up to the struggles that are going on inside us. If we are so concerned about developing or preserving pleasant feelings that we ignore the negative feelings within us or pretend that they are non-existent, then we end up demeaning ourselves. An honest look may involve a struggle, but there is more hope in that for growth than there is in pretence or denial.

FURTHER STUDY

James 5:1-16;
Prov. 28:13;
Acts 12:5

1. What are we to do with our faults?

2. How are we to respond to those who share their struggles?

Prayer

O God, teach me to be unafraid to look at anything – myself included. Make me strong enough in You not to need the defences of pretence and denial. You are on the side of honesty; I am on its side too. Help me. In Jesus' Name. Amen.

Death? Who cares?

"Why do the wicked live on, growing old and increasing in power?" (v.7)

For reading & meditation – Job 21:1-9

Before moving on, we pause to remind ourselves once more of the question with which the psalmist struggles in Psalm 73: Why is it that the wicked seem to prosper while the path of the righteous is beset by so many difficulties? Look now at how the psalmist views the condition of the ungodly: "They suffer no violent pangs in their death, but their strength is firm. They are not in trouble as other men; neither are they smitten and plagued like other men. Therefore pride is about their neck as a chain; violence covers them as a garment – as a long, luxurious robe" (Psa. 73:4-6, Amplified Bible).

What a graphic description this is of the person who has no time for God, yet goes on from day to day with few troubles. It is probably the most perfect picture in all literature of the so-called successful man of the world. Note that the psalmist begins his description of the ungodly with a reference to the way they die: "They suffer no violent pangs in their death." Throughout time the notion has been universally present that a good life ends in a good death, but the psalmist makes the observation that in his experience the reverse is true.

Have you not struggled with these same feelings whenever you have heard of a Christian dying in great agony while a non-Christian passes away peacefully in his sleep? What do you do with those feelings? Ignore them? Deny them? Repress them? Remember, it is only exposed problems that can be resolved. I say again, if you are not willing to face a problem, how can you go about getting it resolved?

FURTHER STUDY

Luke 12:15–21;
16:19–31;
Psa. 14:1; 53:1;
Prov. 12:15

1. What is the danger
of worldly
prosperity?

2. How did Jesus
draw the contrast in
his parables?

Prayer

O God, save me from denying the difficult problems and feelings I encounter in life. Help me understand that it is easier to deal with things when they are up and out than when they lie buried within. In Jesus' Name. Amen.

Why we are sometimes drained

"… Clear me from hidden and unconscious faults."
(v.12, Amplified Bible)
For reading & meditation – Psalm 19:7-14

We said yesterday that exposed problems are the only ones that can be resolved. Is this just an interesting theory, or is it something that can be supported from Scripture? Let me see if I can convince you that this statement has a biblical basis.

Come back with me to the Garden of Eden and think again about the questions which God put to the first human pair: "Where are you? … Who told you that you were naked? … What is this you have done?" (Gen. 3:9-13). Does anyone believe that God needed to ask those questions in order to gain information for Himself? Of course not; being omniscient (that is, having all knowledge), He already knew what they had done. Then why did He put those searching personal questions to them? Surely the answer must be that the direct questions encouraged them to face something that they preferred not to look at. God knew that before the problem could be dealt with it must be brought out into the open.

Some people may think that by far the best way of dealing with unacceptable thoughts and feelings is to push them back into the unconscious but, as we are now seeing, that is a fallacy. Problems that are buried inside us rather than brought out into the light work to drain us of spiritual energy. It takes a lot of emotional energy to keep things repressed. This is why people who repeatedly use the defence of repression end up feeling overtired. Healthy people are those who, like the psalmist in Psalm 73, bring their thoughts and feelings into awareness – no matter how "unspiritual" those thoughts and feelings may appear to be.

FURTHER STUDY

Psa. 139:13-24;
1 Cor. 11:27-28;
Lam. 3:40

1. What was the psalmist's prayer?

2. Why is the communion service so important?

Prayer

Father, I now begin to see why You bring me face to face with so many disturbing questions, for You know the havoc that is wrought within when issues are ignored or denied. Help me face anything and everything. In Your Name. Amen.

The roots of some perplexities

*"'For my thoughts are not your thoughts, neither are your
ways my ways,' declares the Lord." (v.8)*
For reading & meditation – Isaiah 55:6-13

We continue examining the psalmist's graphic description of the so-called successful "man of the world": "Their eyes stand out with fatness, they have more than heart could wish, and the imaginations of their minds overflow with follies. They scoff and wickedly utter oppression; they speak loftily – from on high, maliciously and blasphemously. They set their mouths against and speak down from Heaven, and their tongue swaggers through the earth – invading even Heaven with blasphemy and smearing earth with slanders" (Psa. 73:7–9, Amplified Bible).

How perfectly these words describe the person who brazenly flaunts his arrogance and rides roughshod over the rights of others. Note the phrase, "their eyes stand out with fatness", or, as the *International Bible Commentary* puts it: "Their beady eyes bulged through folds of fat as they busily schemed. Superior and cynical, they engaged in malicious talk and threats." We see the same kind of people today – irreligious, self-centred men and women who live only for themselves and view God as an irrelevance.

Why does God allow them to get away with such attitudes and behaviour? Perplexing, isn't it? We must realise, however, that it is only perplexing because we are dealing with the ways of an eternal Being whose thoughts and designs are infinitely greater than our own – as the text at the top of this page clearly tells us. Think about this as you make your way through the day: half our perplexities would never arise if we were prepared *not* to understand immediately the things that God does or the things that God allows.

FURTHER STUDY
Dan. 4:1-37;
Hosea 14:9;
Hab. 3:6

1. How did God deal
with
Nebuchadnezzar?

2. What was his final
conclusion?

Prayer

O Father, what unnecessary perplexities we carry within us because we try to trace the reasons that lie behind Your designs rather than just trust them. Help us in our quest for a more confident faith. In Jesus' Name. Amen.

What's happening!?

"… perplexed, but not in despair …" (v.8)

For reading & meditation – 2 Corinthians 4:7-12

Today we stay with the thought that half our spiritual perplexities would never arise if we started out by being prepared not to understand immediately the things that God does or allows. We must accept that one of the fundamental principles of the Christian life is the truth that there will be many times when God will work things out in a manner exactly opposite to the way we think He should. If I had been taught this in the early days of my Christian life, it would have saved me from many spiritual struggles. Most of my perplexities arose because I failed to realise that I was dealing with a mind that is omniscient – that God's mind is not like my mind.

The ways of God are inscrutable; His mind is infinite and eternal and His purposes are beyond understanding. When we are dealing with such a great and mighty God it should not surprise us that He allows things to happen which we find perplexing. If we insist that everything in life should be plain, we shall soon find ourselves in the state in which the psalmist found himself – full of doubt, disillusionment and fear.

We should note, however, that perplexity is not necessarily sinful. It only becomes wrong when we allow our perplexity to drive us to despair. The apostle Paul, as our text for today shows us, was perplexed but he was not in despair. Make sure you understand the distinction. It is not foolish or wrong to say: "I don't know what is happening." It is only foolish to say: "God doesn't know what is happening."

FURTHER STUDY

Josh. 1:1-6;
Isa. 54:10;
Heb. 13:5

1. What was God's promise to Joshua and Isaiah?

2. What is God's promise to us?

Prayer

O Father, how comforting it is to realise that I can be perplexed and yet not fall into sin. Help me to keep this distinction clear. Drive the truth deep into my spirit today that You always know what is happening. In Jesus' Name I ask it. Amen.

"I hadn't even seen the accident!"

"When a land falls into the hands of the wicked, he blindfolds its judges ..." (v.24)

For reading & meditation – Job 9:21-35

The more the psalmist contemplates the condition of the ungodly, the more his perplexity increases. The next verses show him to be upset over the fact that people treat the ungodly with such admiration: "Therefore their people turn to them and drink up waters in abundance. They say, 'How can God know? Does the Most High have knowledge?' This is what the wicked are like – always carefree, they increase in wealth" (Psa. 73:10-12). He observes that because they are so well-admired and well-treated such people say: "Look at how good life is to us! If there is a God, then He doesn't appear to have much interest in the way we live."

A Christian tells of a work colleague, a successful man of the world, who said to him one day: "On my way to work this morning a man stopped me and said 'Are you a Jehovah's Witness?' Why would he ask me that? Why, I hadn't even seen the accident!" The man was quite unaware of who Jehovah was and the question had him completely puzzled.

This is what troubles the psalmist in this section of Psalm 73 – he sees people living with no concern for God, yet everything seems to be going so well for them. One can feel his indignation burning through the words he writes. Do you feel indignant about this, or a similar problem? It's not surprising if you do. Be careful, though, that you don't allow it to become your focus of concentration, for it is a law of the personality that you become like the thing you dwell upon.

Deut. 32:1-15;
Psa. 37:35;
Jer. 5:27-28

1. What did Moses declare?

2. What did prosperity do to Jeshurun?

Prayer

O Father, if it is true that I become like the thing I focus upon, then help my focus of life not to be indignation at the prosperity of the ungodly but gratitude for the fact that I am an heir to eternity. Amen.

The heart of the issue

"Yet they say ... 'Who is the Almighty, that we should serve him?'
... But their prosperity is not in their own hands ..." (vv. 14-16)

For reading & meditation – Job 21:11-16

We come now to the heart of the issue with which the psalmist is struggling in Psalm 73: "Surely in vain have I kept my heart pure; in vain have I washed my hands in innocence. All day long I have been plagued; I have been punished every morning" (Psa.73:13-14). Permit me to paraphrase what I think he is saying: "Here I am, living a godly life, keeping my heart and hands clean, avoiding sin, meditating on the things of God and devoting myself to a life pleasing to God, yet despite this I am facing all kinds of troubles. What's the advantage in serving God if He doesn't protect me?"

The problem, then, is not so much the prosperity of the wicked as the fact that he himself is passing through a period of great trial while they are getting off scot-free. We begin now to see the roots of the envy to which the psalmist referred earlier: "For I envied the arrogant when I saw the prosperity of the wicked" (v.3). Envy is born out of two things: ignorance and a wrong comparison.

Take, first, a wrong comparison. "Almost all our problems," said Dr W.E. Sangster, "begin in a wrong comparison." How true this is. We

FURTHER STUDY

Psa. 37:1-40;
Prov. 3:31; 14:30

1. What is envy?

2. What is the result
of envy?

compare our looks, our height, our income, our homes, our training and our abilities with those of others and soon we lose sight of our own individuality and specialness. To compare ourselves with Christ is a healthy spiritual discipline, but to indulge in comparison with those we think are more prosperous and fortunate than we are is the direct road to envy.

Prayer

O God, save me, I pray, from the habit of wrongly comparing myself with others. Help me to satisfy the impulse I have for making comparisons only in a way that will yield spiritual gain – by comparing myself only with You. In Jesus' Name. Amen.

Don't forget the parenthesis

"He will not judge by what he sees with his eyes …" (v.3)
For reading & meditation – Isaiah 11:1-9

Yesterday we said that envy is born out of two things: ignorance and making wrong comparisons. Having seen how a wrong comparison can produce envy, we focus now on ignorance. How can ignorance give rise to envy? Far too often our judgments of people are based only on what we see, and we fail to take into account other things that may be going on in their lives. Years ago, A.C. Gardiner wrote a little essay on Lord Simon and spoke at length of his many successes. In one place he described him as "prancing down a rose-strewn path to a shining goal". Gardiner thought that success, in the measure Lord Simon had experienced it, was free of all sorrow. Then he remembered some of the bitter disappointments that Lord Simon had faced and so he added in parenthesis: "I speak here only of his public career."

Many of us forget the parenthesis. We see simply the surface of our neighbours' lives and know nothing of their secret sorrows. If we saw beneath the surface of those lives we tend to envy – the hidden hurts, the emptiness, the heartaches, the guilt and the fears – then I doubt whether the emotion of envy would ever rise within us.

But even if there were no secret sorrows we would still have no reason to envy others. God is the rightful Lord of all life: "It is He who has made us, and not we ourselves" (Psa. 100:3, NKJ). Let us keep our eyes fixed only on Christ and resist all other attempts at comparison. Practise comparing yourself with Him, and only good will come out of it.

FURTHER STUDY

2 Cor. 10:1-18;
1 Cor. 2:13;
Psa. 89:6

1. What is it not wise to do?

2. What is the right way to make comparisons?

Prayer

Blessed Lord Jesus, I see how easily the spirit of envy can filch away my peace and happiness. Uproot this rank weed in my heart and teach me to compare myself with none other but You. For Your own dear Name's sake. Amen.

A recital of experiences

"No temptation has seized you except what is common to man." (v.13)

For reading & meditation – 1 Corinthians 10:1-13

Having spent the past days identifying the nature of the problem which almost caused the psalmist to give up, we pause today to focus on another great value of the book of Psalms – the fact that it presents its teaching in the form of a recital of experiences. We have exactly the same kind of teaching in the New Testament, but there it is presented in a more directive fashion.

Sometimes our hearts grow weary under the stresses of life and we are not open to receiving direct instruction from anyone. I remember when I was a young Christian going to church one evening feeling tired and worn down by the strong temptations I was experiencing. As the visiting preacher announced the title of his sermon – "Fifteen Principles for Overcoming Temptation" – I felt my heart sink within me. His sermon might have been what I needed but at that moment I was too weary to concentrate on principles.

When I got home that evening I turned to the book of Psalms, and as I read the experiences of some of those men and found that they too had been through what I was going through, my strength returned and my spirit revived. This is why the book of Psalms is one of the most important and valuable books of the Bible. Learn to turn to it whenever you feel battered and beaten by the waves of life. You will find, as millions have found before you, that it speaks to your condition because the men who wrote it have been in your condition.

FURTHER STUDY

2 Pet. 1:15-21;
Eph. 1:17-19;
2 Cor. 4:6

1. What is God's Word like?

2. What did Paul pray for the Ephesians?

Prayer

O Father, I am grateful to You beyond words for giving me that part of Your Word that reaches me when perhaps nothing else might reach me. Help me to make good use of it and avail myself of its unfailing resources. In Jesus' Name. Amen.

Starting at the bottom

"… my soul is downcast within me. Yet this I call to mind and therefore I have hope." (vv.20-21)

For reading & meditation – Lamentations 3:19-27

Now we come to the turning point of the seventy-third psalm – the point where the psalmist takes the first step toward the resolution of his problem. We must not forget that the purpose of this psalm is to show us how the writer solved his problem, so that when we get into the same kind of difficulty we can apply the same solutions.

Here, then, is his first step: "If I had said, 'I will speak thus,' I would have betrayed your children. When I tried to understand all this, it was oppressive to me" (Psa. 73:15-16). We see in these words what it was that arrested his feelings of doubt and despair – the thought that if he were to speak out of his discouraged heart he would put a stumbling-block in someone else's path. "If I did that," he thinks to himself, "I would be untrue to the generation of God's children. So, rather than discourage others with my doubts, I will not say anything at all."

Some might regard it as strange that the first step the psalmist took on the road to recovery should be one with such a low motivation. Indeed, there are those who have said it was unworthy of him and that he should not have allowed himself to get into that condition. Similarly, when people in the Church today confess to having "unspiritual" feelings, I am sure you have heard judgmental advice-givers address them with words like: "You ought not to feel like that!" But the point is that they do feel like that, and reality demands that we begin right where they are and not where we would like them to be. Personally, I do not care how low a person's stand might be as long as he or she is *standing* and not slipping.

Prayer

Gracious and loving Father, teach me how to handle myself in a crisis and help me not to be too proud to begin at the lowest level. Better to have my feet on the lowest rung of the ladder than to be struggling in the mire. Amen.

Stop and think!

*"… Everyone should be quick to listen, slow to speak and
slow to become angry …"* (v.19)

For reading & meditation – James 1:12-20

Yesterday we saw that the first step the psalmist took, the step which
helped to save him from spiritual disaster, was most surprising. In
the midst of overwhelming temptation, he says to himself: "If I give
expression to my doubts and speak out of my envious, discouraged
heart, I will put a stumbling-block in someone else's path – hence I will
not say anything at all" (paraphrase mine). Now as we said yesterday,
many people may find it difficult to accept this as the first step on the
road to recovery – but it worked, nevertheless.

Listen to what one commentator says about this first step: "Our reaction to the discovery of what his first step was in his process of recovery
will be a very good test of our spiritual understanding." What does he
mean? He means that if we fail to see that the steps of faith are sometimes very ordinary, then we are not as spiritual as we imagine. It's all
right to have your head in the clouds, but make sure your feet are firmly
planted on the earth!

Keep in mind, then, that the thing which stopped the spiritual slide
of the psalmist was very simple and ordinary – he made a decision not to
say what was on the tip of his tongue. He stopped to
think. Rather than spread his unbelief, he determined
to keep his mouth shut; rather than threaten someone
else's spiritual understanding, he resolved not to act on
impulse. It might not have been a particularly high
spiritual motive, but it was the thing that prevented
him from falling.

FURTHER STUDY

1 Pet. 3:8-15;
Prov. 13:3; 21:23

*1. What are we to do
with our tongue?*

*2. How are we to give
an answer?*

Prayer

Gracious and loving Father, help me grasp this point that sometimes the first step
towards spiritual recovery is one that is simple, practical and ordinary. Save me from
becoming so super-spiritual that I neglect the commonplace. In Jesus' Name. Amen.

We do what we choose to do

"The tongue has the power of life and death ..." (v.21)
For reading & meditation – Proverbs 18:15-21

We are seeing that the first step the psalmist took to save himself from falling was stopping himself from saying what was on the tip of his tongue. In other words, he took himself in hand.

This is an extremely important issue. What a lot of heartache would be saved if Christians would take heed to this and learn to put a bridle on their tongues. Expressions which convey the idea that the Lord acts unjustly or unkindly, especially if they fall from the lips of men and women who have a long experience in the Christian life, are as dangerous as sparks in a timber factory. Despite his doubts, the psalmist recognised the importance of self-discipline, and that proved to be a saving virtue.

People sometimes claim: "It is impossible for me to control what I say. It slips out before I realise what I've said." This is nonsense, of course, for what we say is the result of what we choose to say. Sometimes we may feel as though we have no control over what we say, but that is all it is – a feeling. Dr Lawrence Crabb, a Christian psychologist, tells us: "The loss of felt choice does not mean the loss of real choice." When you give a person "a piece of your mind", as we say, there is always a moment, albeit a split second, when you can choose to speak out or stay quiet. We cannot hide behind the excuse that our tongue is not under our control. What we do is what we choose to do. The psalmist, though beset by many doubts and difficulties, chose to control his tongue – and so can you.

FURTHER STUDY

James 3:1-18; 1:5;
Luke 21:15

1. What does James
teach about the
tongue?

2. What are we to
ask God for?

Prayer

O Father, help me see that the things I do and say are not the result of compulsion but of choice. I am free to obey or free to disobey. Help me to use my freedom in the right way. In Jesus' Name I ask it. Amen.

"Selective expression"

"How dare you turn my Father's house into a market!"
(v.16)

For reading & meditation – John 2:13-17

We continue thinking about the psalmist's decision to take himself in hand and refrain from relaying his doubts to others. I feel it important at this point to say a further word about repression and expression. Christians, we said earlier, are never to pretend about anything. Whether we worry, covet, resent, hate, we are to acknowledge the reality of who we are at any given moment. Fully admitting to ourselves and to God that we are angry, worried or full of doubts, is not sin. It becomes sin when we constantly focus on it and allow it to drag us down into despair.

But does this mean that in order to experience emotional health we must let everything out and tell everybody exactly how we feel? The clear answer to that question is "No", but it is an answer that must be qualified. For example, when seeking help from a counsellor or minister, it would be right to share exactly how you feel. The principle I suggest we adopt in relation to this is as follows: we may express our acknowledged emotions only when such expression is consistent with God's purposes.

FURTHER STUDY

Luke 24:13-35;
Gal. 6:2-5

1. What did Jesus encourage as He walked with the disciples?

2. How did He bring perspective to them?

This is a critical point and it must be understood. The cure for repression is not to "let it all hang out" but to be selective, expressing only those emotions that are in harmony with God's will. We must freely admit to ourselves and to God what is happening to us, but then we must carefully and selectively consider whether it is right and in line with God's purposes to share what we feel with others.

Prayer

Gracious and loving Father, help me to be honest with my feelings, yet willing to subordinate the expression of them in both timing and manner to Your perfect will. In Jesus' Name I ask it Amen.

A mature response

"But the fruit of the Spirit is ... self-control." (vv.22-23)
For reading & meditation – Galatians 5:16-26

So important is the point we raised yesterday – the need for selective expression – that we will spend another day considering it. Listen to how the Amplified Bible translates Psalm 73:15: "Had I spoken thus and *given expression to my feelings*, I would have been untrue and have dealt treacherously against the generation of your children" (emphasis mine). Notice that although the psalmist experienced strong feelings of uncertainty, he refrained from expressing these emotions because they would have had a negative effect upon his brothers and sisters. He acknowledged his emotions, but he refused to express them because he knew they would hurt and hinder the family of God.

Expression of our feelings with no thought of another's welfare amounts to sinful, selfish indulgence. We must allow ourselves to feel the full weight of our emotions but then subordinate their expression to the purposes of God. Only if it is God's will for us to share those feelings with others must we do so. Thus the apostle could write stinging words of rebuke to the Corinthian church because his words were in harmony with God's purposes.

We have to be on our guard here, because whenever we feel angry, and vent our anger on someone, it is so easy to justify our angry feelings by saying, "God wanted to use me to teach you a lesson." But more often than not, if we examine our hearts we will find that our goal was not the will of God but the desire to get those angry feelings out from inside us. Selective expression of feelings is a mature and spiritual response; indiscriminate expression is immature and unspiritual.

FURTHER STUDY

Eph. 4:15;
Prov. 16:32;
2 Pet. 1:3-7

1. What is to govern our sharing?

2. Why are we to be self-controlled?

Prayer

Gracious God and loving heavenly Father, forgive me for the times I have hurt others by the indiscriminate expression of my negative feelings. Help me understand and apply this principle of "selective expression". In Jesus' Name. Amen.

Consider the consequences

"But I said, 'Should a man like me run away? ... I will not go!'" (v.11)

For reading & meditation – Nehemiah 6:9-13

We continue meditating on the fact that the psalmist, though filled with doubts about the goodness of God, nevertheless refrained from expressing those doubts to others. He carefully considered what effect his action might have on the family of God. Nothing that we do in life is without consequences. Someone has put it like this: "Every effect has a cause and every cause produces an effect."

Many of our difficulties in life arise from the fact that we forget the principle that consequences follow our actions. The devil often inveigles us into thinking that the situation we are in is an isolated event, and he gets us to believe that what we do, or are about to do or say, will have little or no effect upon others. He is exceedingly skilful at getting us to become preoccupied with the thing he puts before us. This one thing on which we focus then takes up our whole attention and we become oblivious of everything else, including the results that may follow our actions.

Troubled though the psalmist was, in his heart he considered the consequences of his actions. And this is what Nehemiah did in the passage before us today. A false "friend" came to him and told him that he

FURTHER STUDY

Gal. 6:1-9;
Hosea 8:7;
Isa. 17:11;
James 3:8-9

1. What is the principle of sowing and reaping?

2. What are words like?

should not risk his life. The proposition undoubtedly appealed to him, but Nehemiah considered the consequences and stayed where he was. If he hadn't, the whole course of Israel's history would have been changed. Believe me, this one principle alone – of carefully considering consequences – would be the means of saving us from endless difficulties if we were to take it and consistently apply it.

Prayer

Father, how grateful I am that Your inspired Word teaches me the importance of consequences. Help me absorb this truth and apply it when next I am tempted. May I obey Your Word and not just hear it. In Christ's Name I pray. Amen.

Say nothing unless it is helpful

*"Let your conversation be always full of grace, seasoned
with salt ..." (v.6)*

For reading & meditation – Colossians 4:2-6

From what we have been seeing over the past few days, it is clear that
although the psalmist was struggling with doubts about the goodness
of God, he took a stand on something he knew to be right. He realised
that if he were to speak as he was tempted to speak, the immediate consequence would be the hurt of God's people – so he chose to keep his
thoughts and feelings to himself. He was not sure about the goodness of
God but he *was* sure it would not be right to be a stumbling-block to
God's children – and he held on to that fact.

Dr Martyn Lloyd-Jones said in one of his sermons: "When you are
puzzled and perplexed the thing to do is to try and find something of
which you are certain, and then take your stand on it. It may not be the
central thing; that does not matter." Note the words: "it may not be the
central thing". We can struggle in the midst of our doubts, waiting for
some great revelation to hit us, and fail to apply the remedy that is
immediately to hand. The psalmist saved himself from slipping by saying
to himself: "My heart is full of uncertainties and I cannot say with conviction that God is good. But one thing I am certain of: it is wrong to
hurt others because of my own doubts. Therefore I
will say nothing."

We should be careful about how we express our
doubts to other Christians, especially those who are
immature. This principle applies also to non-Christian
friends, partners, or family members. If we can say
nothing helpful we should say nothing at all. The
psalmist determined to say nothing until he could say:
"God is good to Israel." Then he was entitled to speak.

FURTHER STUDY

Mal. 2:1-8;
Isa. 57:14;
Rom 14:13;
1 John 2:10

1. What had the
words of the priests
become?

2. What are we not
to put in our
brother's way?

Prayer

Gracious and loving God, I can do no better today than frame my prayer in the
words of Your servant David: "Set a guard, O Lord, over my mouth; keep watch at
the door of my lips." Help me, my Father. In Jesus' Name. Amen.

When you fall – others fall

"For none of us lives to himself alone and none of us dies to himself alone." (v.7)

For reading & meditation – Romans 14:5-13

It seems almost unbelievable that the thing which stopped the psalmist's feet from slipping and sliding was not the awareness of his relationship with God but the awareness of his relationship with his brothers and sisters. It might not have been the highest spiritual principle he could have held on to, but it saved him from disaster.

It is this matter – our relationship with one another – that Paul is speaking about in today's passage. You will be familiar, I am sure, with the passages in 1 Corinthians 8 and 10 where Paul enlarges on this subject and where, in a remarkable statement, he says: "I mean for the sake of his conscience, not yours, do not eat it. For why should another man's scruples apply to me, and my liberty of action be determined by his conscience?' (1 Cor. 10:29, Amplified Bible). He is saying, in other words, that you might see no need to refrain from eating meat offered to idols for your own sake, because your conscience is not offended, but what about your weaker brother for whom Christ also died?

You see, "none of us lives to himself alone", so when next the devil tries to convince you that you are an isolated case and that what he is suggesting concerns you and you alone, quote this verse to him. We do not act in isolation; if you fall, you do not fall alone, the whole Church falls also. If nothing else can stop you from doing wrong, remember the people to whom you belong, remember you are part of a heavenly family, and that when you fall, others fall with you.

FURTHER STUDY

1 Cor. 9:15-22;
Acts 20:35;
Rom. 15:1;
1 Thess. 5:14

1. What was Paul's approach to the weaker brethren?

2. What was Paul's word to the Thessalonians?

Prayer

Father, drive deeply into my spirit this truth that I cannot act in isolation, for I am bound up with my redeemed brothers and sisters. Help me experience an ever-growing consciousness of this important fact. In Jesus' Name. Amen.

Use everything you can

"Who despises the day of small things? ..." (v.10)
For reading & meditation – Zechariah 4:1-14

Having followed the experience of the psalmist, who was saved from a spiritual fall by thinking of his brethren, we now ask ourselves: What does all this have to say to us? I think the answer to that question must be this: to stand is more important than to understand.

We said a few days ago that the psalmist took his stand at a very low level on the scale of spiritual values. The principle he followed was this: "If I spread my doubts, I will harm my brethren." I am sure you and I could think of much higher spiritual principles with which to confront ourselves when tempted. What about the principle of reminding ourselves of the blessings of God in times past? Or actually talking to ourselves in the way the psalmist did in Psalm 42:5: "Why are you downcast, O my soul? Why so disturbed within me? Put your hope in God ...".

The psalmist employed none of these, but the one he did employ, low as it was on the scale of spiritual values, worked. And that is the point – use everything you can to stop yourself from falling, however small or insignificant it might appear to be. We are involved in spiritual mountaineering, where sometimes the slopes are like glass. When your feet slip you must reach out and hold on to anything that will stop you in your slide – even though it be only a small branch. Stop and steady yourself. Don't concern yourself about climbing, just concern yourself with stopping your slide. Once you have stopped sliding you can then plan how to climb again.

FURTHER STUDY
1 Cor. 12:21-31;
Ex. 4:2;
Judg. 15:15;
1 Sam. 17:40;
1 Kings 17:12

1. What are some of the insignificant things God uses in his purposes?

2. How does Paul put it?

Prayer

Father, I see that when I am in danger of slipping it is better to take advantage of the smallest foothold than to slide into the depths of despair. Help me grasp the full importance and value of this. In Jesus' Name I ask it. Amen.

A critical position

"These have come so that your faith ... may be proved genuine and may result in praise, glory and honour ..." (v.7)

For reading & meditation – 1 Peter 1:1-7

Today we examine the fact that although the psalmist's feet are no longer slipping and sliding, he continues to struggle inwardly with his problem. Listen to what he says: "But when I considered how to understand this, it was too great an effort for me and too painful" (Psa. 73:16, Amplified Bible). It is clear that although he has stopped himself from falling, he is still in great anguish of heart and mind; he is still perplexed over the issue of why the ungodly are prospering while he, a child of God, has to face all kinds of difficulties. He cannot bear the thought of scandalising the family of God, and yet his confusion continues.

Have you ever been in this position in your spiritual life – saved from slipping and sliding but still harassed by a giant-sized spiritual problem? You know enough to stop you falling, but not enough to start you climbing. It is a strange position to be in but one, I must confess, in which I have found myself on many occasions. Perhaps you are there right now – your feet have stopped slipping, but strong emotions continue to rage inside you.

This is a very critical position to be in – critical because the temptation at this point is to quieten the raging emotions within by settling for answers that are less than the real ones. I know many Christians who have been in this position, and because their goal has been to alleviate the pain in their heart rather than find the real solutions to their problem, they have grasped at superficial answers that do nothing more than provide temporary relief.

FURTHER STUDY

Psa. 17:3;
2 Pet. 3:9;
Job 13:1-16

1. What had the psalmist purposed?

2. What did Job declare?

Prayer

O Father, save me from settling for less than the best, even though it means struggling a little longer with some difficult and turbulent emotions. Help me be concerned with maturity, not just temporary relief. Amen.

Staying with the pain

"Though He slay me, yet will I trust Him …" (v.15, NKJ)
For reading & meditation – Job 13:13-19

We ended yesterday with the thought that the moments after we have been saved from slipping and sliding, but are left with our main problem still unresolved, are exceedingly critical. Why critical? Because, as we said, the desire to relieve the pain that is going on inside us can sometimes lead us to settle for answers that are less than the best. We feel better when we can make sense of the ways of God – even a little sense.

When we are confronted by a spiritual problem that appears to have no immediate resolution and causes strong emotions to rage within us, there are, as far as I can see, just two options: either to live with the troublesome emotions, as Job did, and wait patiently for God to give a clear answer, in His time; or to replace the confusion with some form of understanding. The first option is often difficult, for it demands something which, especially when we are confused, we find hard to do – trust. The second is a lot easier, but potentially more dangerous, for unless we are careful, it can lead us into accepting solutions that are not solutions.

The pressure to move confidently in the midst of ambiguity and uncertainty and come up with "clear" answers is a strong one. But we must be careful that we don't settle for an answer that, although it helps to reduce the level of confusion, is not a real solution. Better to stay with the pain of confusion and uncertainty than to grasp at answers that are not answers because they evade the real problem.

FURTHER STUDY

Prov. 3:1-6;
Psa. 37:5; 118:8;
Isa. 26:4

1. What are we to do?

2. What are we not to do?

Prayer

O Father, help me as I think through this issue. I sense there is something here that I need to learn, but I need Your love and wisdom and insight to support me as I learn it. Come close to me – particularly over these next few days. In Jesus' Name. Amen.

"Why do I cry over nothing?"

"Then you will know the truth, and the truth will set you free." (v.32)

For reading & meditation – John 8:31-41

You have probably sensed that the issue we have been dealing with is extremely important. In fact, I know of nothing of greater consequence for the Christian Church than the need to resolve the issue of why it is, when facing the tough questions of life, we settle for answers that are not answers. Let me illustrate what I mean.

Many years ago a woman approached me at the end of a prayer meeting and said: "Why is it that I cry so much over nothing?" I replied that there could be a number of reasons and I recommended that if this situation continued she should seek the help of a Christian counsellor. My own feeling was that the problem arose from some unresolved conflicts in her life that needed identifying. Some time later I met the woman again and she said to me: "I still have the problem, but I know now why it happens to me – it is an attack of the devil."

I felt deeply saddened by her conclusion for I sensed that she had settled for an answer that helped to reduce her confusion but was not a real solution. Yes, the devil does attack and harass, but in my opinion something else was going on inside her which needed attention. I gently suggested this to her, but she was adamant that the devil was responsible and that the problem would eventually go. I prayed much for that woman because I saw in her what I see in many parts of the Christian Church – a tendency to reach out and settle for "answers" that help reduce the confusion but do nothing to stimulate spiritual growth and understanding.

FURTHER STUDY

Psa. 51:1-6;
Jer. 17:9;
Matt. 15:16-20

1. What does God require in the inner parts?

2. What is the condition of the heart?

Prayer

O God, I do not want to live my life amid illusions. I want to be real and I want to live really. Help me face the tough questions of life and not be content until I find the true answers –Your answers. In Jesus' Name I ask it. Amen.

Some tough questions

"How long, O Lord, must I call for help, but you do not listen?" (v.2)

For reading & meditation – Habakkuk 1:1-4

We continue thinking through the issue of why it is that we settle for easy answers. Every day we face tough questions as we live our lives for Jesus Christ. Should I let my children watch a certain television programme? Is God leading me into a new job? Why am I so prone to fall under the power of temptation? Should I use anti-depressants as the doctor says I should? These and other questions demand decisions that expose our uncertainty and force us to recognise how deeply confused we are about certain issues.

The Bible addresses some issues clearly, but on others it is not so clear. Sometimes we have to struggle with uncertainty. It is unappealing to be told that we have to go on in the midst of confusion, and we feel a great inner pressure to reduce the confusion to a point where it can be ignored. Motivated by anxiety, we seek to impose an order on our world – and it is at this point that we become extremely vulnerable.

In earlier years I used to be deeply perplexed about why intelligent Christian people bought into the ideas of some of the less responsible healing evangelists, who got them to pledge huge sums of money, give up medical treatment and do the strangest things. But then I realised that these men were providing the people who came to them with hopeful "answers" about their physical condition or that of their loved ones, and this was easier than living with confusion. God does heal, but sometimes He doesn't – no matter how hard we pray. And the way we handle this confusion determines our spiritual maturity.

FURTHER STUDY

James 5:1-7;
Psa. 13:1; 69:3;
119:82; 2 Pet. 3:9

1. What does James say we are in need of?

2. What does Peter confirm?

Prayer

O Father, give me the faith to believe in You in the midst of uncertainty and perplexity. Don't let me settle for an "answer" simply because it relieves my confusion. I know You do have answers, but help me go on even when they do not come. Amen.

The curse of modern Christianity

"… and do not give the devil a foothold." (v.27)
For reading & meditation – Ephesians 4:25-32

There is a price to pay for our desire to grab at easy answers and that price is "trivialisation". Trivialisation is the acceptance of explanations that ignore the difficult questions of life in order to experience relief from confusion. I have no hesitation in saying that this is a curse of the modern Church.

One way trivialisation reveals itself is in the acceptance, by so many, of the view that the major cause of Christians' problems is demonic activity. Demonic activity can be a cause of problems (especially in those who have dabbled in the occult) but it is not the chief cause. The New Testament teaches us the importance of spiritual warfare, but it has much more to say about the influence of our carnal nature on the rise and development of problems.

In the early days of my ministry, when people came to me with problems I would frequently engage in the practice of rebuking the devil, and those prayers often brought great relief. But the mistake I made was not to sit down with the people who came to me and deal with the beneath-the-surface problems which had given Satan a foothold in their lives. By making it appear that Satan was the only problem I trivialised the issue. It's a lot easier (and less confusing) to sit down with a person and "take authority" over Satan than it is to think through together the tough and perplexing issues that lie beneath the surface, and then work towards giving some Biblical perspectives. But that is demanded of us if we are to help each other towards maturity.

FURTHER STUDY

2 Pet. 1:1-6;
1 Cor. 14:20;
13:11; Heb. 5:14

1. What are we to add to our faith?

2. What was Paul's admonition to the Corinthians?

Prayer

O Father, forgive us for the ways in which we trivialise Your truth in order to avoid facing the tough issues. It feels good to replace confusion with certainty, but help us to be sure that the certainty is Your certainty. In Jesus' Name. Amen.

The first thing to do

"These things I remember as I pour out my soul: how I used to go with the multitude ... to the house of God ..." (v.4)

For reading & meditation – Psalm 42:1-11

Over the past few days we have seen how the psalmist was caught in the hiatus between the moment when he stopped himself from sliding and the moment when he started to climb again. This, we said, is a very critical time – critical because it makes us inclined to accept easy answers. The perplexity did not end when the psalmist stopped himself from slipping. His thoughts still went around in circles and he continued to have great anguish of heart and mind.

How, then, were his thoughts concerning the prosperity of the ungodly resolved? Not by grabbing at superficial answers, but by going into the sanctuary of God, where he could begin to see the whole situation from God's point of view. Listen to how he puts it: "When I tried to understand all this, it was oppressive to me till I entered the sanctuary of God; then I understood their final destiny" (Psa. 73:16-17). The word "sanctuary" here literally means the physical house of God. Some translations use the phrase, "till I entered the secret of God", but that is incorrect. Read Psalm 74 and read Psalm 76 and you will find that they both refer to the material building where God was worshipped.

Had the psalmist, I wonder, like so many of us when we are filled with doubt and uncertainty, stayed away from the sanctuary of God? How strange that the last thing we want to do when our hearts are filled with doubts and misunderstandings is meet with our fellow believers in the house of God. Yet that is the very first thing we ought to do.

FURTHER STUDY

Heb. 10:19-25;
Matt. 12:9;
Mark 1:21;
Luke 4:16

1. What are we not to do?

2. What was Jesus' custom?

Prayer

Gracious Father, I am so grateful that You have ordained that Your people meet together. Help me understand more clearly than ever the value and benefits that flow from being with Your people. In Jesus' Name I ask it. Amen.

A redeeming, healing fellowship

"Let us not give up meeting together, as some are in the habit of doing, but let us encourage one another …" (v.25)

For reading & meditation – Hebrews 10:19-25

Yesterday we ended with the thought that the very first thing we ought to do when seeking to break out of the vicious circle of doubt is to go to the house of God. The psalmist has been prevented from falling by considering the consequences of his actions upon his brethren, so now his next step is to go and meet with them in the sanctuary.

Whether it be in a cathedral or a cottage, how wonderful it is to join with Christian brothers and sisters. It is not so much the place that is important as the redeeming and healing fellowship we find there. Oftentimes people find release just by sitting down among their brothers and sisters and feeling the healing power of their warmth and love. One famous preacher said: "The house of God has delivered me from 'the mumps and measles of the soul' a thousand times and more – merely by entering its doors."

What is it about being among our fellow believers that is so helpful and encouraging? One thing is the very fact that our fellow believers are there. You see, in our private misery and perplexity we could easily run away with the idea that there is nothing very much in the Christian faith after all, and that it is not worth our going on. But when we enter into the Lord's house and see our fellow believers coming together, often our doubts disappear. We say to ourselves, albeit unconsciously: "Here are people who think the Christian life is worth continuing with. My uncertainties must be wrong – there must be something in it after all."

FURTHER STUDY

Acts 12:12-17;
16:12-13;
Psa. 84:10

1. What was the pattern of the early Church?

2. How did the psalmist view God's house?

Prayer

O Father, help me see the power that flows towards me through Christian fellowship. Just as I am encouraged by it, help me to encourage others. In Jesus' Name I pray. Amen.

Others have suffered too

"… the Lord knows how to rescue godly men from trials …"
(v.9)

For reading & meditation – 2 Peter 2:4-10

We continue developing the thought that meeting together with our brothers and sisters can bring about a radical change in our perspective. Tell me, have you ever gone to church feeling a little disconsolate or depressed and found, as you have looked round and seen people who have gone through much greater struggles than you, that your heart has been strangely lifted and your burdens have seemed lighter?

You see a widow, perhaps, who has been left with several children, and as you watch her singing praises to God you see your problem in a different light. You notice a man whom you know has gone through the most horrifying experiences, but he is still there worshipping and magnifying God. This again works to change your perspective.

Paul reminds us in 1 Corinthians 10:13: "No temptation has seized you except what is common to man. And God is faithful; he will not let you be tempted beyond what you can bear." One of the things the devil delights to do is to persuade us that the trial we are going through is unique. When you come in contact with others in the family of God you begin to see that is just not true. You rub shoulders with people you know suffered extremely painful experiences – experiences more distressing than you have ever faced. Yet they still continue to sing God's praises. You see, in the church we have an opportunity to evaluate 1 Corinthians 10:13 in a clear light. The truth is seen in its highest form. Others have gone through what we have gone through, and the knowledge of this helps us in our suffering.

FURTHER STUDY

Psa. 10:1-7;
1 Kings 19:10;
19:14; 19:18;
2 Tim. 4:16

1. What did Elijah think?

2. What did God say to him?

Prayer

Father, the more I dwell on the benefits of Christian fellowship, the more I see how wise and considerate are Your purposes. Help me not to neglect this most marvellous and helpful means of grace. In Jesus' Name I pray. Amen.

History is His-story

*"In him the whole building is joined together and rises to
become a holy temple in the Lord." (v.21)*

For reading & meditation – Ephesians 2:14-22

There can be little doubt that meeting together with other members
of God's family is a powerful way of bringing about a changed perspective. Another thing that happens when we go to church or meet
together in Christian fellowship is that we are reminded that the very
existence of the Church in today's world is proof positive that God is on
the throne. Voltaire, the French infidel, said: "It required eleven men to
build the Church; I will prove that it needs only one man to knock it
down."

He was wrong on two counts: first, it was not eleven men who built
the Church, it was one man, the Man, Christ Jesus, and second, no one
can ever knock it down, for its omnipotent Founder declared: "I will
build my church, and the gates of Hades will not overcome it" (Matt.
16:18).

The mere existence of the Church is, I submit, decisive proof that the
living Christ is in the midst of it. Voltaire is dust; Christ lives on. Think
of the tempests the Church has weathered through the centuries. Think
also of the persecutions through which it has victoriously come, and try,
if you can, to account for this extraordinary phenome-
non apart from the fact that its Founder and Protector
is Jesus Christ.

The next time you meet together with your fellow
Christians, reflect on the fact that, although every generation has produced people who have predicted the
downfall of the Christian Church – it is still here. The
realisation of this is yet another thing, I suggest, that
helps to put our doubts into the right perspective.

FURTHER STUDY

1 Cor 3:9-17;
Eph. 1:22; 4:15;
5:23

1. What do we know
about the foundation
of the Church?

2. What does Paul
declare to the
Ephesians?

Prayer

O Father, how can I thank You enough for the times my own perspective has been
changed after meeting together with Your people. I have greater insight now why
You commanded us not to neglect assembling together. And I am grateful. Amen.

Life's greatest science

"... that you ... may be able to comprehend with all the
saints ..." (vv.17-18, NKJ)

For reading & meditation – Ephesians 3:14-21

We are seeing that once we enter the sanctuary of God our perspective changes. This can happen to us when we are alone, of course, but the chances are it will happen more swiftly in the act of corporate worship. It is a command of God that we meet together, not only that we might come to know each other better, but that we might also come to know Him better. And here's the interesting thing – the more effectively we relate to one another, the more effectively we relate to Him. We come to know God better through the act of corporate worship than when we worship on our own. That is not to say that the shut-ins, or those who for various reasons are unable to meet together in worship, cannot know God intimately, but something special flows out of the act of corporate worship.

Listen to how C.S. Lewis put it: "God can show Himself as He really is only to real men. And that means not simply men who are individually good but to men who are united together in a body, loving one another, helping one another, showing Him to one another. For that is what God meant humanity to be like; like players in one band, or organs in one body. Consequently the only real adequate instrument for learning about God is the whole Christian community, waiting for Him together. Christian brotherhood is, so to speak, the technical equipment for this science – the laboratory outfit."

Christians who neglect attendance at the church, or choose to deprive themselves of fellowship with other Christians, miss out on life's greatest science – learning about God.

FURTHER STUDY

Eph. 2:1-19;
Rom. 8:15;
2 Cor. 6:18;
Gal. 4:5

1. How does Paul describe the Church?

2. What does it mean to be adopted?

Prayer

My Father and my God, I am so thankful that, although I can know You when I am alone, I can know You even better through the fellowship of the Church. Help me to learn about You in every way I can. In Jesus' Name I ask it. Amen.

Changed perspectives in church

"Were not our hearts burning within us while he talked with us on the road and opened the Scriptures to us?" (v.32)

For reading & meditation – Luke 24:28-35

Another thing that brings about a changed perspective when we make our way to the house of God is the reading and exposition of the Scriptures. I make this statement on the assumption that the Scriptures are expounded in your church, for, sadly, in some congregations this is not so. In the days of the psalmist, of course, they did not have the Bible as we know it today, but the portions of the Word of God that they did have they recited and meditated upon.

How many times have you gone to church feeling confused about God's dealing with you, only to find that as the Scriptures are opened your view of God and life changes, causing you to leave refreshed and reinvigorated? Calvin put it like this: "As the elderly, or those with poor sight can hardly make out the words in a book, but with the help of glasses can read clearly, so Scripture crystallises ideas about God which had been very confused, scatters the darkness and shows us the true God clearly."

You could, and should, read the Scriptures at home, but there is something special about hearing the Word of God expounded in church.

FURTHER STUDY

Luke 4:16-31;
Isa. 11:2; 61:1;
Matt. 3:16

1. What did Jesus do in the synagogue?

2. What rested upon Him?

Merely to hear a well-known text spoken by someone who emphasises a word which we might not emphasise, can strike us in a way that adds new meaning to it. Do you have a jaundiced view of God and life at this very moment? Go to church on Sunday, to a Bible-believing church, and expect God to speak to you from His Word. I have it on the highest authority that He will.

Prayer

Father, forgive me for taking for granted the revelation that flows from Your Word – whether it comes privately or in church. From now on, whenever I am "talked to" by the Scriptures, help me to recognise it and to receive it with gratitude. Amen.

Missing from the meeting!

"Now Thomas … was not with the disciples when Jesus came." (v.24)

For reading & meditation – John 20:24-31

We said a couple of days ago that those who choose to deprive themselves of fellowship with other Christians miss out on life's greatest science – learning about God. I heard one preacher say: "People who neglect attendance at the house of God are fools because on some favoured occasion something special and powerful will happen – and they will not be there."

The passage we have read today tells us of that glorious post-resurrection appearance of our Lord to His disciples. The disciples thought He was dead, and although there were rumours of His resurrection, they were not convinced. Suddenly, He appeared to them – they saw Him, heard Him, and felt the impact of His mighty presence. But here is the heart-rending tragedy of it: "Thomas … was not with the disciples when Jesus came."

Why was Thomas missing from that meeting? Many preachers have speculated on the reasons for his absence, and they vary from Thomas not expecting Jesus to be there, to being afraid for his life. My own view, for what it is worth, is that there was something wrong with Thomas himself. The root cause of his defection, so I believe, was his own doubting and denying heart. My experience in the ministry has taught me that those who profess to be Christians and yet deliberately absent themselves from fellowship with their brothers and sisters, are the ones who are usually most in need of this fellowship.

FURTHER STUDY

Matt. 25:13;
Prov. 15:5; 20:24

1. What is the message of the parable of the virgins?

2. How are 5 of them described?

Prayer

Gracious and loving heavenly Father, help me realise that the very time I need to be among my brothers and sisters is when I am at my lowest spiritually. Burn this truth into my consciousness so that it will never leave me. In Jesus' Name. Amen.

Natural versus spiritual thinking

"The man without the Spirit does not accept the things that come from the Spirit of God ..." (v.14)

For reading & meditation – 1 Corinthians 2:6-16

We have been seeing that by going "into the sanctuary" – the place where God had made provision to meet with His people – the psalmist has put himself in a position where his perspectives can be changed. This section of the psalm is probably the most vital part, for it is here that his thinking begins to change from natural thinking to spiritual thinking. He had been thinking like a natural man, considering life from just one perspective, but in the sanctuary he begins to see life from God's point of view.

What is the difference between natural thinking and spiritual thinking? Natural thinking is on the level of the earth – the level of man; spiritual thinking is on a higher level altogether – the level of God. It is surprising that so many Christians think naturally about their problems rather than spiritually. The psalmist was a good and godly man but under the pressure of circumstances he had reverted to thinking naturally about his problem.

We will never learn to live effectively until we understand that the whole of life is spiritual, not just parts of it. In the chapter before us today the apostle asks, in effect, why it was that none of the rulers of this world recognised the Lord Jesus Christ when He was here. It was because they looked at Him from a natural perspective – they saw only a carpenter. Without the Holy Spirit operating upon their minds, they just could not understand. Ultimately, the problems and difficulties of life are all spiritual; so the sooner we learn to think spiritually, the better we will be.

FURTHER STUDY

Isa. 55:1-13;
Rom. 12:2;
Jer. 29:11

1. What did God declare to Israel?

2. How can we be transformed?

Prayer

Gracious and loving heavenly Father, I realise that if I am to become a spiritual thinker I must allow You to think in me. I have given You my heart, help me now to give You my mind. Think in me, dear Lord. Amen.

"Come up on this level too"

"But they do not know the thoughts of the Lord" (v.12)
For reading & meditation – Micah 4:6-13

Yesterday we ended with the statement: "Ultimately, the problems and difficulties of life are all spiritual." What exactly does this mean? Reflect again on the psalmist's problem. He says to himself: "Why does God allow the ungodly to prosper and the godly to go through great trials and tribulations?" He has trouble as he tries to understand God's ways.

Now there is really only one answer to this problem, and it is found in Isaiah 55:8: " 'My thoughts are not your thoughts, neither are your ways my ways,' declares the Lord." Whatever we might think about the ways of God, these words give us the ultimate answer – the Almighty acts in ways that are above and beyond our comprehension. It is as if God is saying: "When you look at My ways you must not approach them on a natural level, because if you do you will be baffled and over-whelmed. I act on a higher level than the natural, and if you want to understand Me, then you must come up on this level too."

How often, however, we persist in thinking naturally about life's situations – even those of us who have been in the Christian life for many years. The difference between natural thinking and spiritual thinking is the difference between heaven and earth. The very first thing we must do when we are baffled by some circumstance in our lives, is say to ourselves: "Am I approaching this on a natural level or a spiritual level? Have I reverted unconsciously to my natural way of thinking about these things." The more we learn to think spiritually about life's problems, the less perplexed we will be.

FURTHER STUDY

Rom. 8:1-6;
Prov. 12:5; Phil. 4:8

1. What does a mind controlled by the Spirit bring?

2. What things are we to think about?

Prayer

Father, I need to adopt and practise many spiritual methods, but none is as important as that which aligns me to Your thoughts and purposes. Help me come up higher – to Your level of thinking. In Jesus' Name. Amen.

One view of things

"Let this mind be in you which was also in Christ Jesus."
(v.5, NKJ)

For reading & meditation – Philippians 2:5-11

We continue meditating on the importance of learning to think spiritually. It is sometimes interesting to listen to Christians discussing together both earthly and heavenly issues. Take politics, for example. When involved in a discussion on this subject, many Christians seem to put their Christianity on one side and bring out all the prejudices and worldly arguments which they have been accustomed to use over the years.

What does this say to us? It reveals the great need we have to break with the idea that life can be viewed on two levels – the natural and the spiritual. The Christian must learn to view everything from a spiritual viewpoint or otherwise he will fall prey to the same problems that the psalmist had. The great preacher C.H. Spurgeon once told a group of theological students that after they entered the ministry they should not be surprised to find that people who prayed like angels in a church prayer meeting could act like devils in a church business meeting. Unfortunately the history of the Church proves his statement to be true.

How can this happen? It's because in a prayer meeting people think

FURTHER STUDY

James 1:1-8;
Matt 6:22;
1 Cor. 2:16

1. What makes us unstable?

2. What happens when we are single-minded?

spiritually, but in a business meeting they revert to their natural thinking, with all its prejudices and worldly assumptions. They have a party spirit within them and as soon as any one bumps against them – out it comes. Our Lord, as our text for today shows so clearly, saw everything from a spiritual point of view. This is why, in the hour of overwhelming testing, He was able to say: "Not my will, but yours be done" (Luke 22:42).

Prayer

My Father and my God, forgive me that so often my thinking is based on natural, rather than spiritual, perspectives. I think spiritually about some matters, but not all. Help me, dear Lord. In Jesus' Name. Amen.

Lop-sided Christians

*"… if anything is excellent or praiseworthy – think about
such things." (v.8)*

For reading & meditation – Philippians 4:2-9

We continue to look at the dramatic change in the life of the
psalmist when he entered into the sanctuary. It is important to
realise that it was not merely the physical act of entering the sanctuary
that brought about change. That was important, but something else happened that was even more important. Listen again to how he puts it:
"[When] I entered the sanctuary … then I understood their final destiny" (Psa. 73:17). The word to note is "understood". In the presence of
God the psalmist was given clear understanding. This is an extremely
important point and one which cannot be emphasised too strongly: what
he found in the sanctuary was not merely a nice feeling but a new understanding. He was put right in his thinking. He did not merely forget his
problem for a little while – he found a solution.

The idea that many Christians have of the house of God or Christian
fellowship is that it is a good place to go in order to forget one's troubles
for a while. They are soothed by the music and the singing, or perhaps,
in some churches, by the beauty of the architecture, and they come away
saying, "What a lovely feeling I get whenever I go to church."

There is nothing wrong with that as far as it goes,
of course, but the real issue is this: has anything happened to their minds? The psalmist was not changed
by the architecture of the Temple; he was changed
when his thinking was put right: "Then I understood
their final destiny." If the practice of our faith does
nothing more than excite our emotions and fails to
give us a better understanding of God and His ways,
then we will be lop-sided Christians.

FURTHER STUDY

Psa. 48:1-9; 119:59;
1 Sam. 12:24

1. What did the
psalmist meditate on
in the Temple?

2. What are we to
consider?

Prayer

O Father, save me from becoming a lop-sided Christian. Give me not only joy to
thrill my emotions but understanding to guide my intellect. In Jesus' Name I ask it.
Amen.

Seeing life whole

"… Always be prepared to give an answer to everyone who asks you to give the reason for the hope that you have …" (v.15)

For reading & meditation – 1 Peter 3:13-22

A s Christians we ought never to forget that the message of the Bible is addressed primarily to the understanding; it enables us to understand life. Because of the Bible, we are able to give a reason for the hope that is within us.

The psalmist found the truth of this. In the sanctuary he discovered an explanation for the way that he felt. He was not given a temporary lift that would stay with him for a few hours or a few days – he was given a solution that would stay with him for the rest of his life. It was this, in fact, that caused him to write the psalm we are focusing upon day by day. The words: *"Then* I understood their final destiny" (Psa. 73:17) suggest that previously he had not been thinking correctly. He had been seeing things from a partial and incomplete perspective, but now "in the sanctuary" he began to see the whole picture: *"Then* I understood". When? *Then* – when he came into the sanctuary.

There is a line in one of Matthew Arnold's writings that goes like this: "Who saw life steadily, and saw it whole." What a delightful phrase this is. Nothing can be more wonderful than to see life steadily and to see it whole. Much of the inner turmoil we go through in life comes about because we do not see life as a whole. Prejudice has been defined as "seeing only what you want to see". People who are prejudiced say: "I have always seen it that way." That's their problem – their eyes are fixed on just one facet of an issue and they will not allow themselves to look at the other sides.

FURTHER STUDY

Eph. 5:1-20;
2 Tim. 1:8

1. How are we to speak to ourselves?

2. What did Paul admonish Timothy?

Prayer

O Father, help me, for I don't want to be in bondage to prejudice or bigotry – I want to see life whole. We must work this issue out together over these next few days, for apart from You I can do nothing. Help me, Father. Amen.

Restoring the image

*"May your whole spirit, soul and body be kept blameless
at the coming of our Lord Jesus Christ."* (v.23)
For reading & meditation – 1 Thessalonians 5:12-28

We continue meditating on the importance of looking at life "steadily and whole". I venture to suggest that people who are not
Christians are unable to see life as a whole. How can they, when their
thinking takes place only on the level of the natural? Natural thinking is
notoriously partial and incomplete.

Take, for example, the field of medicine. A generation ago doctors
treated the symptoms that people presented to them, but now, with a
clearer understanding of how the mind affects physical health, they have
come to see that this approach was partial. One doctor said: "At long last
the medical profession has discovered that the patient himself is important." Medicine is fast moving towards what is described as a "holistic"
approach as more and more doctors begin to realise that it is not enough
to treat the problem, we must also treat the person. They are still far
from seeing that there is also a spiritual element in the person that has to
be considered, but perhaps in time that will come.

Christian counselling suffers from the same problem – it does not
see the whole picture. I am tired of reading books on Christian counselling that give just one side of the issue and suggest

FURTHER STUDY

that problems can be resolved by applying one special
technique. Man was created as a whole person and he
will never be helped back to wholeness unless every
part of his being is treated – spirit, soul and body. God
wants to restore His image in us: not in part of us but
in the whole.

2 Cor. 4:1-16;
Prov. 20:27;
Eccl. 12:7

1. What is man
   primarily?

2. What was Paul's
   testimony?

Prayer

O Father, forgive us that so often we settle for the half view of things rather than the
whole. Quicken my spiritual understanding so that I have Your view on all things –
the "whole" view. In Jesus' Name I ask it. Amen.

No need for dead reckoning

*"I too was convinced that I ought to do all that was possible
to oppose the name of Jesus of Nazareth." (v.9)*
For reading & meditation – Acts 26:1-18

The place where we can see life as a whole is in the sanctuary of God,
or, if you prefer, in the presence of God. There we are reminded of
things we have forgotten or ignored. See how the Good News Bible
translates Acts 26:9: "I myself thought that I should do everything I
could against the cause of Jesus of Nazareth." Here you see the root of
Paul's problem: "I myself thought". And is not that the underlying cause
of many of our problems too? We say, "I myself thought …" instead of
asking: "What does God think?"

Sometimes sailors will attempt to establish the position of their ships
by estimating the distance and direction they have travelled, rather than
by astronomical observation. This is called "dead reckoning". It is sometimes necessary in foul weather but it is fraught with peril. One mariner
has said: "Undue trust in the dead reckoning has produced more disastrous shipwrecks of seaworthy ships than all other causes put together."

There are people who attempt the voyage of life by dead reckoning,
but there is no need. God has charted the map for us with loving care in
the Scriptures, and our plain duty is to study the chart so that we might
become better acquainted with His purposes and His
ways. For the better we know the Scriptures, the better
we will know God. We cannot ignore the facts of
history or science – they help – but if our perspective
is not drawn from the Scriptures it will lead us astray.
We must not rely on dead reckoning but on divine
reckoning.

FURTHER STUDY

Judg. 17:1-6; 21:25

*1. What was said of
the children of
Israel?*

*2. Can the same be
said of us?*

Prayer

O Father, just as the art of navigation requires definite and fixed points from which
to take a bearing, so does my voyage through life. I am grateful, dear Father, that in
You I have all the fixed points I need. Amen.

What says the Scripture?

*"Jesus replied, 'You are in error because you do not know
the Scriptures or the power of God." (v.29)*

For reading & meditation – Matthew 22:23-33

We spend one more day considering the proposition that apart from a relationship with God and an understanding of the Scriptures, we are unable to see life as a whole. The man or woman who knows and understands the Bible will be acquainted with the facts he or she needs to have in order to come to right and sound conclusions.

So immerse yourself in the Scriptures. Understand that human nature is corrupt and that apart from the grace and power of God men and women are unable to live up to their ideals. Realise that the spiritual is more powerful than the material, and unless the spirit is in control we will be driven by carnal desires. When people say humanity is getting better and that sin and evil are just the "growing pains" of the human race – what are the facts? You get them from the Scriptures and only from the Scriptures. What does the Bible tell us about evil? It says it is part of the human condition and can never be rooted out except through the power and the grace of God.

So study the facts of Scripture. Read them, memorise them, and meditate upon them. When next you feel dispirited because you cannot make sense of something, ask yourself: What are the facts? Dig into the Scriptures and draw your perspective from what the Bible says. The root of many of our emotional problems lies in a lack of clear thinking – clear thinking based on Scripture. Think as God thinks about issues and you will feel as God feels about them. For you are not what you think you are, but what you *think* you are.

FURTHER STUDY

2 Tim. 2:1-15; 3:16

1. What was Paul's exhortation to Timothy?

2. What is Scripture profitable for?

Prayer

Father, I see now why so often my thinking about life is confused – my thinking is not based on the facts. Help me draw my deductions not from what I see in the world but from what I see in the Word. In Jesus' Name. Amen.

Where does it all end?

"Enter through the narrow gate. For wide is the gate and broad is the road that leads to destruction …" (v.13)

For reading & meditation – Matthew 7:13-20

Today we look at the special understanding the psalmist received when he came into the sanctuary of God: "Then I understood their final destiny" (Psa. 73:17). As soon as he considered the final destiny of the ungodly, everything dropped into focus for him. He had looked at the prosperity of the ungodly but he had not looked at their end – he had not taken in all the facts.

What are the facts concerning the end of the ungodly? The passage we read today tells us: the broad road which the ungodly travel leads to destruction; the narrow road which the godly travel leads to life. It is as simple as that. Though this passage was not available to the psalmist, the truth underlying it was most certainly known to him. Listen to this from Psalm 37: "The transgressors shall be destroyed together; the future of the wicked shall be cut off" (v.38, NKJ). The writer of that psalm, King David, described the wicked spreading themselves like a green tree, but when the end came they vanished off the face of the earth and no one could find them.

The trouble with us is that so often we dwell too much on the present and fail to consider the future. Do you look at the ungodly, many of whom seem to be having a marvellous time ignoring moral restrictions, and feel envious of them? Well consider their end. Give some thought to the ultimate outcome. The Bible describes it as "destruction". We ought never to forget that it is not how things are at present that is important; it's how they end that matters.

FURTHER STUDY

Luke 12:15-21;
Prov. 12:15-16;
28:6

1. What did Jesus call the man in his parable?

2. What word keeps occurring in the parable?

Prayer

Father, whenever I am next tempted to compare my life and its circumstances with that of others who do not know You, help me to remind myself of the fact that it is the end that matters, not the beginning. In Jesus' Name. Amen.

"I'm afraid of the dark"

"Wicked men are overthrown and are no more, but the house of the righteous stands firm." (v.7)

For reading & meditation – Proverbs 12:1-8

We continue thinking about the fact that as soon as the psalmist considered the end of the ungodly, everything dropped into focus. Their true position became so clear to him that his language in the rest of the psalm indicates that he not only ceased to be envious of the ungodly but began to be sorry for them. Indeed, the same thing will happen to us too – the more we focus on the ultimate end of the unconverted, the more compassion we will feel for them.

How grim and cheerless is the non-Christian view of life, especially as it relates to the end. Dr Marrett, a rationalist and head of one of the colleges in Oxford, wrote, as he neared the end of his life: "I have nothing to look forward to but chill autumn and still chillier winter and yet I must somehow try not to lose heart." H.G. Wells, who ridiculed and scoffed at Christianity with its doctrine of sin and salvation, said at the end of his life that he was utterly baffled and bewildered. The title of his last book summed up his view of things: *A Mind at the End of its Tether.* When he was dying, a noted atheist asked one of his relatives for a lighted candle to be placed in his hand. "Why a lighted candle?" asked the concerned relative. "Because I am afraid to go out into the dark," was the reply.

How foolish to look enviously at the lifestyle of the ungodly, focusing only on their present successes and the marvellous time they seem to be having, without considering their end. We should never forget that no matter how glittering their lifestyle, the death of the ungodly is a terrible thing.

FURTHER STUDY

1 Tim. 6:1-10;
Psa. 49:10;
Prov. 23:5; 27:24

1. What truth did Paul reflect to Timothy?

2. How does the same truth affect the way we live our lives?

Prayer

O Father, let this sobering thought not only free me from envy but stimulate within me a deep concern for those who do not know You. May I be used in some way to halt the progress of someone on the road to a lost eternity. In Jesus' Name. Amen.

"It's a dead certainty!"

"Now there is in store for me the crown of righteousness, which the Lord, the righteous Judge, will award to me on that day ..." (v.8)

For reading & meditation – 2 Timothy 4:1-8

There can be no doubt that the Bible presents the death of the ungodly as being terrible. How differently, however, does it portray the death of the righteous. Even a hireling prophet like Balaam, bad as he was, recognised that there was something different about the death of the godly. Listen to his words in Numbers 23:10: "Let me die the death of the righteous, and let my end be like his" (NKJ). The book of Proverbs puts the same thought in this way: "The path of the righteous is like the first gleam of dawn, shining ever brighter till the full light of day" (4:18).

I heard one preacher say that the happiest woman he had ever seen was a dying woman. She lay on her bed and clapped her hands at the approach of death. Very many people came to look at her bright countenance. "They tell me this is death," she said. "It's not death at all – it's life." People were converted by her bedside, including her son.

A theologian by the name of W. Cosley Bell, when he sensed that he was about to leave this world, sent these words to the staff of the college where he was employed: "Tell the young men that I've grown surer of God every year of my life, and I've never been so sure as I am right now.

FURTHER STUDY

2 Tim. 1:1-12;
1 Cor. 15:45-58

1. What was Paul's testimony?

2. Why is there no fear in death for the believer?

Why it's all so! It's a fact – a dead certainty. I'm so glad I haven't the least shadow of shrinking or uncertainty. I've been preaching and teaching these things all my life and I'm so interested to find that all we've been believing and hoping is so." That is the way to die. One of John Wesley's proudest claims for the early Methodists was this: "Our people die well."

Prayer

Father, the empty tomb of Jesus makes all our fears lies, and all our hopes truths. That empty tomb is the birthplace of eternal certainty. Because He lives I shall live also. I am eternally grateful. Amen.

Rougher – but more secure

"If only they were wise and would understand this and discern what their end will be!" (v.29)

For reading & meditation – Deuteronomy 32:28-38

We have been seeing that in the sanctuary the psalmist was reminded of the things he had forgotten, and thus his thinking was straightened out. There can be no real change in our personalities until there is a change in our thinking. Counselling that focuses only on changing behaviour and fails to emphasise the importance of changed thinking is partial and incomplete. We may experience some change when we change our behaviour, but we experience the greatest change, as our text for today suggests, when we change our thinking.

In the sanctuary the psalmist's thinking was put right about the ungodly: "Then I understood their end" (Psa. 73:17, NKJ). The next verses indicate how his thinking was also put right about God Himself: "Surely you place them on slippery ground; you cast them down to ruin. How suddenly are they destroyed, completely swept away by terrors" (Psa. 73:18-19). The psalmist's problem, you remember, was not so much that the ungodly prospered, as that God had arranged it that way. Had it happened by mere chance, he might not have had any difficulties, but the fact that the great Designer had planned it like this filled him with perplexity. Now, however, he sees that the divine hand had purposely placed these men in prosperous and eminent circumstances so that they could fulfil the Creator's purposes: *"You"* – note the *You* – *"You* place them on slippery ground." Note, too, the phrase "slippery ground": their position was dangerous. Therefore God did not set His loved ones in that place, but chose instead a rougher but more secure standing for their feet.

FURTHER STUDY

Psa. 16:1-11;
1 Sam. 2:9;
Psa. 18:36;
Eph. 6:13-14

1. Why are we able to stand firm?

2. What did Paul admonish the Ephesians?

Prayer

O God, I am grateful that You have set my feet in a secure place and not on slippery ground. Why I have been chosen to be a recipient of such grace and favour I do not know. Yet it is so. I am deeply, deeply thankful. Amen.

He never leaves the helm

"Surely your wrath against men brings you praise …"
(v.10)

For reading & meditation – Psalm 76:1-12

We touched yesterday on the truth that the reason why the ungodly are set in eminent places is because God arranges it. The psalmist goes on to say that not only does God raise up the ungodly, but He also brings them down: "You cast them down to ruin. How suddenly are they destroyed …" (Psa. 73:18-19). The hand that led them up to the top of the slope is the hand that also casts them down. Why does God act in this strange and mysterious manner?

One reason is that God is able to demonstrate how unreliable and insecure are the ways of those who choose not to walk with Him. This explains why we so frequently read of some prominent godless person, such as a film star whom everyone is acclaiming, being suddenly removed from the face of the earth. The feet of such people were set in slippery places. Some reading these lines will remember how everyone stood in dread of Adolph Hitler. He had the whole world frightened, but now he is gone and almost forgotten.

The psalmist's words "You cast them down … how suddenly are they destroyed" are really an exclamation of godly wonder at the suddenness and completeness of the sinner's overthrow. God makes a spectacle of those who persist in rejecting His love and grace. They make a splash for the moment of their lives, but after that they are gone and soon forgotten. Keep that fact before you as you look out upon the world. It may sometimes seem as if God is not in control, but in actual fact His hand is ever upon the helm of human affairs.

FURTHER STUDY

Rom. 1:18;
Rom 3:19-20;
2 Tim. 2:1-19;
1 Pet. 4:18

1. What does the law expose?

2. How is God's wrath averted?

Prayer

Gracious and loving Father, my heart bows in silent wonder as I contemplate the awesomeness of Your ways. Open my eyes that I might see that You are at work all around me and that Your face is constantly set against evil. In Jesus' Name. Amen.

"Hang him on it!"

"… for the evil man has no future hope, and the lamp of the wicked will be snuffed out." (v.20)

For reading & meditation – Proverbs 24:15-22

Today we look at another reason why God allows the ungodly to flourish – to illustrate by contrast the horror of an eternity without God. Spurgeon commented: "Eternal punishment will be all the more terrible in contrast with the former prosperity of those who are ripening for it." The seeming joy and splendour of the prosperous ungodly actually renders the effect of being cast aside by God more awful, just as vivid lightning does not brighten but intensifies the thick darkness around.

You will no doubt remember the story of Haman, who prepared a gallows for Mordecai but finished up by being hanged upon it himself. The ascent to the gallows was an essential ingredient in the terror of the sentence: "Hang him on it!" (Esth. 7:9). The wicked are raised high so that all might see how great is their fall.

A preacher tells how he read the story of the rich man and Lazarus, in Luke 16, to a group of young people who were hearing it for the first time. He stopped at the part where Lazarus lay at the gate, the dogs licking his sores, while the rich man ate in splendour in his house, and said: "Which would you rather be, the rich man or Lazarus?" With one voice the young people shouted: "The rich man." He then read on, and after telling the story of how both died and the rich man was in torment while Lazarus was carried to Abraham's side, he asked: "Now which would you rather be?" This time they responded more quietly and soberly "Lazarus." That is the truth the psalmist saw as he sat quietly in the sanctuary of God.

FURTHER STUDY

Luke 16:19-31;
Matt. 13:24-30;
13:49

1. What is Jesus'
teaching in the
parable of the rich
man and Lazarus?

2. What is the
message of the
parable of the weeds?

Prayer

Father, the more I see the whole picture and realise what I have been saved from, the more I feel like flinging myself at Your feet in adoring worship and praise. Thank You for saving me, dear Lord. Words cannot fully express my gratitude. Amen.

Alexander the Great

"Surely the nations are like a drop in a bucket ..." (v.15)
For reading & meditation – Isaiah 40:12-17

Now we come to look at a section of the psalm which suggests that the reason why the ungodly continue to prosper as they do is because God is asleep. Listen to the psalmist's exact words: "As a dream when one awakes, so when you arise, O Lord, you will despise them as fantasies" (Psa. 73:20). The truth is, of course, that God does not sleep, but the psalmist has used a figure of speech which pictures our limited human perception of God's actions. God does not sleep, but at times He appears to do so.

But what happens when God stirs from His apparent sleep? The ungodly man, who has seemed so eminent and prosperous, vanishes as a dream. It is as if he had been a phantom or an illusion. The passage before us today puts this whole matter in context when it tells us that the nations are but "a drop in a bucket" to the Creator. Now they may look powerful and mighty, with their stockpiles of nuclear weapons, but when God arises they are as "grasshoppers".

Do you remember being told in your history class at school about Alexander the Great? He was one of the greatest generals of all time and conquered almost the entire known world. Did you know that he is referred to in the Bible? You will not see his name written in the Scriptures, but reference to him can be found in Daniel. Look at what the Bible calls him – a "goat" (Dan. 8:5-8). Walter Luthi puts it like this: "He who to the world is Alexander the Great, is to God nothing more than a he-goat." When God arises, the great become nothing.

FURTHER STUDY

Psa. 121:1-8;
2 Chron. 6:20; 16:9

1. What does the psalmist assure us?

2. How does God show Himself strong?

Prayer

Father, thank You for reminding me over these past few days of Your greatness and eternal power. I so easily forget that I am linked to a God who is not just powerful but all-powerful. Let the wonder of that fact sink deep into my soul today. Amen.

Take an inside look

"A man ought to examine himself …" (v.28)
For reading & meditation – 1 Corinthians 11:27-34

From what we have seen over the past few days, it is clear that the psalmist has come to the place where his views have changed. He sees that God is ruling over human affairs and that the ungodly are not in such an enviable situation after all. We come now to see that he was not only put right in his thinking about the ungodly and about God, but he was also put right about himself: "When my heart was grieved and my spirit embittered, I was senseless and ignorant: I was a brute beast before you" (Psa. 73:21-22).

What a different view he has of himself now compared to previously, when he so evidently felt very sorry for himself: "Surely in vain have I kept my heart pure; in vain have I washed my hands in innocence" (v.13). Outside the sanctuary, he felt full of self-pity; inside the sanctuary, he had an entirely different view of himself. This is a moment when the psalmist honestly faces himself – something that is very difficult to do.

Most of us don't mind working our way through our problems, but the moment we get relief, we want to stop right there. We do not go on to face up to what caused us to come to the wrong conclusions in the first place. This is why we keep going through the same problems over and over again – we fail to take an inside look. A schoolteacher claimed to have twenty-five years of experience, but her head teacher said of her: "She has just one year of experience twenty-five times." She worked long but learned little.

FURTHER STUDY

1 Chron. 28:1-10;
Jer. 17:10; 23:24;
Psa. 44:20-21

1. What did David reflect to Solomon?

2. What question did the Lord ask?

Prayer

Father, I see why it is that so often I go through the same problems over and over again – I stop short of learning why they happened in the first place. Help me today to think through why it is that I get so tied up. In Jesus' Name I pray. Amen.

"Far too 'healthy' spiritually"

"Search me, O God, and know my heart; test me and know my anxious thoughts." (v.23)

For reading & meditation – Psalm 139:17-24

We said yesterday that the task of honestly facing ourselves in self-examination is often the hardest thing for us to do. We are all very prone to pass quickly over this point. We are quite happy to hear how God has set the ungodly in slippery places but we are not happy to be invited to take a look at ourselves and uncover the things within us that cause us to go astray.

It must be said, however, that two dangers arise whenever the question of self-examination is considered. One is over-emphasis and the other is under-emphasis. Some engage in it too much and become unhealthily introspective, while others fail to look at themselves at all and thus live on the surface. The important thing to remember is this – self-examination should always be carried out in the presence of God. If this is not adhered to, then the exercise can become harmful and counter-productive.

I meet many Christians who strongly oppose the idea of self-examination. They say: "the moment you see that you have sinned and then put your sin 'under the blood' you are all right. To stop and think about it is an indication that you are not spiritually healthy and that you lack faith." Dr Martyn Lloyd-Jones once said: "The trouble with most of us is that we are far too 'healthy' spiritually." He meant by that that we are much too glib and much too superficial. Nothing is more characteristic of a true Christian than a willingness to examine himself; not too much, not too little, but in an appropriate and balanced way.

FURTHER STUDY

Dan. 2:19-23;
Amos 9:3;
Psa. 139:7-8

1. What did Daniel receive from the Lord?

2. How did David feel about God's presence?

Prayer

O Father, the reason I am afraid to examine myself is because I might find something I do not like. However, help me be honest no matter what the cost – honest with You and honest with myself. In Jesus' Name I pray. Amen.

"Emotional reasoning"

"The heart is deceitful above all things, and desperately wicked; who can know it?" (v.9, NKJ)

For reading & meditation – Jeremiah 17:5-13

We continue focusing on the thought that one of the reasons why we go through the same difficulties and problems year after year is that we never stop to examine ourselves and find out what makes us act the way we do. The psalmist examined himself in the presence of God and discovered that three things had led him astray.

First, he saw that he had allowed his heart to rule his head: "When my heart was grieved and my spirit embittered, I was senseless and ignorant" (Psa. 73:21-22). Notice the psychology of this – he put the heart before the head. Many of our troubles are due to the fact that we are governed by the feelings that arise in our hearts rather than the clear thinking that should be going on in our heads. When the heart gets in control, it bludgeons us into believing things that are not true. It makes us stupid. The psalmist thought that his feelings about the ungodly were facts, but this was nothing more than what psychologists call "emotional reasoning" – believing that what you *feel* is the way things really are. The moment the psalmist's feelings were corrected by the facts, the feelings disappeared. There was no real problem at all. He had "worked himself up", as we say, into a self-induced frenzy.

I have done this myself (and so, I am sure, have you) when I have allowed my feelings to dominate me to such an extent that I have begun to believe that molehills were mountains. The real trouble in the psalmist's life was not what was going on in his outer world, but what was going on in his inner world. In other words, the real source of his trouble was himself.

FURTHER STUDY

Mark 2:1-8;
Heb. 3:12;
2 Pet. 2:14

1. What did the teachers of the law fail to realise?

2 What are we to watch out for?

Prayer

Father, I see more clearly every day that most of my problems are the ones I make for myself by my wrong thinking and wrong perceptions. Help me keep my heart under control by biblical thinking. In Jesus' Name I ask it. Amen.

"Think, man, think"

"… be transformed by the renewing of your mind …" (v.2)
For reading & meditation – Romans 12:1-8

The second thing the psalmist learned about himself as he paused in self-examination was this: "I saw myself so stupid and so ignorant" (Psa. 73:22, TLB). There were things he knew which he had foolishly chosen to forget. He forgot that God was in control. He forgot the temporary nature of success and prosperity. He forgot the whole purpose of godly living. He forgot that God always has the last word. If you and I react as the psalmist did to trials, then there is only one thing that can be said about us – we are stupid and ignorant.

The third thing the psalmist learned about himself was that he had reacted like an animal – instinctively: "I was a brute beast before you" (Psa. 73:22b). What is the difference between a beast and a human being? A beast lacks the faculty of reason. It is unable to stand outside itself to consider itself and its actions. An animal responds to any stimulus instinctively without any interval for thought. The psalmist had been doing that – he had failed to put an interval of thought between the stimulus and the response. Once he did stop to think, and put the situation in a different context, his negative feelings immediately dissolved.

FURTHER STUDY

Psa. 105:5;
Deut. 6:12;
Psa. 50:22

1. What is a basic human tendency?

2. What does the psalmist exhort us to do?

Is not this the value of the Scriptures? As we read them they reason with us. They tell us not to react instinctively to things, but to think them through. They give us a new framework for our understanding, a new context in which to reason. The more we draw our understanding from the Scriptures and learn to think God's thoughts after Him, the more secure and the more effective our lives become.

Prayer

Father, I am grateful that You have made me with the ability to think. My thoughts can lead me astray or they can lead me to You. Help me to draw my thought patterns not from the world but from Your Word. In Jesus' Name I ask it. Amen.

"Nevertheless"

*"In my alarm I said, 'I am cut off from your sight!' Yet you
heard my cry for mercy …"* (v.22)

For reading & meditation – Psalm 31:19-24

O nce the psalmist reached the place of utter abandonment before God
there came into his heart an instant reassurance: "Yet I am always
with you" (Psa. 73:23). Some translations put it like this: "Nevertheless I
am continually with you". Personally I prefer the word "nevertheless" as
it conjures up to my mind a movement in the soul of the psalmist that
was vital to his spiritual recovery. He did not stop at the point of self-
examination and turn in upon himself – he looked into the face of his
heavenly Father and realised that he was accepted and loved.

If we end at the point of self-examination and don't remember the
next words, "Nevertheless I am continually with you," then we will stay
locked into the negative feelings of guilt and self-condemnation. This is
why I said earlier that self-examination must not be undertaken except
in the presence of God. Many have spent time examining themselves,
and because they have judged themselves to be worthless and useless,
they have gone out and committed suicide.

Am I talking to someone like that today? If so, put your foot on this
next rung of the ladder and realise that although you may be feeling useless and worthless *nevertheless* you are still in the presence of God. He still permits you to come into His
presence, even though you have forgotten His promises and misunderstood His ways. God does not cast you
away. Let the wonder of this break afresh upon you
today. Whatever has gone wrong in your life, confess
it to Him and look into His face and say: "Nevertheless
I am continually with you."

FURTHER STUDY

Gen. 28:15;
Isa. 43:1-7;
Ex. 33:14;
Heb. 13:5

1. What was God's
promise to Israel?

2. What is the
assurance we have?

Prayer

Father, how can I sufficiently thank You for giving me the right word at the right
time? You knew how much I needed this today. It is a lifeline to my spirit. As I hold
on to it let it bind me closer to You. In Jesus' Name. Amen.

What of the future?

*"… he who began a good work in you will carry it on to
completion until the day of Christ Jesus." (v.6)*
For reading & meditation – Philippians 1:3-11

We saw yesterday how the psalmist sensed that despite his doubts and failures he was still accepted by God. But there's more – he realises also that God's restraining hand has been constantly with him: "You hold me by my right hand" (Psa. 73:23). What was it, after all, that prevented him going over the brink? It was the protecting hand of God. God Himself had put it in his mind to go into the sanctuary and had thereby turned him round.

Realising that, he thinks of the future. What is the future going to be like? His conclusion is that the future is going to be just as secure, for: "You guide me with your counsel, and afterwards you will take me into glory" (v.24). Can you sense the psalmist's security as he contemplates the future? He is saying, in effect: "You are doing this now, holding me by my right hand, protecting me, restraining me, restoring me and delivering me, and I know You will keep on doing this right up to the time when I meet with you in glory."

How does God guide us? Through circumstances, through reason, through the fellowship of Christians, but mainly through the Scriptures. The Word of God, when we consult it, unfolds reality, dispels illusion and guides us safely through the snares and problems of this earthly way until we eventually arrive in glory. The psalmist had seen the end of the ungodly and it had helped to change his perspective. Now he sees the end of the godly and thus his perspective becomes even more clear. And what is the end of the godly? It is glory!

FURTHER STUDY

1 Pet. 1:1-6;
Jude v.24;
Gen. 28:15

1. Of what was Peter convinced?

2. How did Jude put it?

Prayer

O Father, let the prospect of coming glory fill and thrill my soul this day and every day. Help me never to forget that no matter how hard and difficult my earthly pilgrimage may be, it is as nothing compared to the glory that lies ahead. Amen.

No satisfying substitute

*"Lord, to whom shall we go? You have the words of
eternal life." (v.68)*

For reading & meditation – John 6:60-71

We come now to what is without question the topmost rung of the
ladder which the psalmist began to ascend when he entered the
sanctuary of God. Here, in view of his experience, he can do nothing but
give himself to the adoration of God. This is what he says: "Whom have
I in heaven but you? And earth has nothing I desire besides you" (Psa.
73:25).

The inevitable consequence of working through our problems in the
presence of God is that we worship Him. Countless times I have seen
people fall upon their knees at the end of a profitable counselling session
and worship God. In fact, this is one of the great purposes of Christian
counselling – to enlighten people about their spiritual resources and
help free them to draw closer to God. The psalmist has found that there
is no one in earth or heaven who can do for him what God has done. He
has come to realise that when he plays truant with the Almighty there is
simply no way in which he can make sense of life; that, as Othello put it:
"Chaos is come again."

Have you come to this same place in your own life? Can you say that
you have seen through everything in this life and have
come to the conclusion that nothing can satisfy you
but God? Then you are in the happy position of the
disciples who, pausing to consider how they could
replace Jesus, said "Lord, to whom shall we go? You
have the words of eternal life." They saw, as hopefully
you have seen, that there is no satisfying substitute for
Jesus.

FURTHER STUDY

Jer. 2:1-13;
Isa. 55:1-3

1. What had the
children of Israel
done?

2. What did God offer
them?

Prayer

O Father, how can I ever be grateful enough for the realisation that no one can do for
me what You can do? You are my centre and my circumference; I begin and end with
You. May the wonder of it go deep within me today and every day. Amen.

The desire for God

"My soul thirsts for God, for the living God ..." (v.2)
For reading & meditation – Psalm 42:1-11

Yesterday we looked at the words: "Whom have I in heaven but you?".
Now we examine the second part of that text: "And earth has noth-ing I desire besides you" (Psa. 73:25b). Personally, I find these some of the most enchanting words in the whole of the Old Testament. The first part of the verse is put in a negative, and the second in a positive form. Having looked around and seen that there is no satisfying substitute for the Almighty, the psalmist goes on to make the positive assertion that from the bottom of his heart he desires to know God. He has come to see (so I believe) that it is more important to desire God for who He is than for what He does or what He gives.

In a sense, the psalmist's entire problem arose out of the fact that he had put what God gives in the place of God Himself. The ungodly were having a good time while he was having a bad time. Why was he having to suffer like this? His trouble was that he had become more interested in the things God gives than in God Himself, and when he didn't have the things he wanted, he began to doubt God's love. Now, however, he has come to the place where he desires God for Himself.

FURTHER STUDY

Psa. 63:1; 38:9-10;
Luke 6:21

1. What was the psalmist thirsting for?

2. What is the result of thirsting and hungering?

The ultimate test of the Christian life is whether we desire God for Himself or for what He gives. Each one of us must ask ourselves: "Do I desire God more than forgiveness? More than release from my prob-lems? More than healing of my condition? More than gifts and abilities?" How tragic that our prayers can be full of pleadings that show, when they are examined, that we are more interested in enjoying God's blessings than we are in enjoying God.

Prayer

O Father, forgive me that so often I am concerned more with Your gifts than I am with You – the Giver. Help me to long after You, not because of what You give me, but because of who You are. In Jesus' Name I ask it Amen.

The Rock of Ages

*"To you I call, O Lord my Rock … if you remain silent I
shall be like those who have gone down to the pit." (v.1)*

For reading & meditation – Psalm 28:1-9

Now that the psalmist's faith is no longer conditioned by material factors, and he is confidently resting in God, he makes this interesting statement: "My flesh and my heart may fail, but God is the strength of my heart and my portion for ever" (Psa. 73:26). Some commentators say he is referring here to the time when his flesh will decay through old age, while others say he was experiencing some physical problems at that very time. Both may be right. When he looks into the future he knows a time will come when he will be an old man when his heart and flesh will fail. He will be unable to look after himself but it will still be all right, says this man, "For whatever may happen, God will still be the strength of my heart."

A commentator who feels the psalmist's words have a direct bearing on his physical condition at that time says this: "You cannot pass through a spiritual experience such as this man passed through without your physical body suffering. His nerves would be in a bad state and his heart would have been affected by the strain. Nevertheless he still affirms that God is his strength."

It is generally agreed that the word which is translated "strength" is the word for "rock", and so the verse may justifiably be translated: "God is the rock of my heart and my portion for ever." What a thrilling thought this is – God is my Rock. As one Welsh preacher put it: "There are many occasions when I tremble as I stand upon the Rock, but there are never any occasions when the Rock trembles under me."

FURTHER STUDY

Isa. 40:21-31;
41:10;
Eph. 3:16-17

1. How are we to
receive strength?

2. What was Paul's
prayer for the
Ephesians?

Prayer

O Father, help me this day to go out into life aware that although I may not know much about the ages of the rocks I know much about the Rock of Ages. And everything I know makes me feel deeply, deeply secure. I am so grateful. Amen.

"Nearer my God to Thee"

"Come near to God and he will come near to you." (v.8)
For reading & meditation – James 4:1-10

The final two verses of Psalm 73 form a conclusion and a resolution. Listen to them once again: "Those who are far from you will perish; you destroy all who are unfaithful to you. But as for me, it is good to be near God. I have made the Sovereign Lord my refuge; I will tell of all your deeds" (vv.27-28). The psalmist has finished his review of the past and is now hammering out a philosophy with which to face the future. He is resolved that no matter what anyone else may do, he is going to live in close companionship with God. He helps us to see the importance of this resolution by putting it in the form of a contrast: "Those who are far from you will perish … but as for me, it is good to be near God."

Really, when it comes down to it, there are only two positions in life – close to God or far away from Him. I wonder, as the psalmist penned these words was something like this going through his mind: "What caused me so much trouble in recent days and accounted for all my difficulties was the fact that I did not keep close to God. I erroneously believed that the cause of my problems was the prosperity of the ungodly, but having entered into the sanctuary of God I see that this was not the cause of my problems at all. My problems came because I had chosen not to remain close to Him. For me there is now only one thing that matters – staying close to God."

How are things with you at this moment? Do you feel close to God? If you don't, then let me put what I want to say in the words of a wayside pulpit that arrested my attention some years ago: "If you feel that God is far away guess who moved?"

FURTHER STUDY

Psa. 46:1-11;
2 Sam. 22:3;
Psa. 9:9;
Psa 62:1-12

1. What does the psalmist affirm?

2. What does the psalmist exhort the people?

Prayer

Father, I am grateful for the promise of Your Word to me today that when I draw near to You, You will draw near to me. Help me put those words to the test by moving closer to You than I have ever done before. In Jesus' Name. Amen.

Take and tell

"Go ... to my brothers and tell them ..." (v.17)
For reading & meditation – John 20:10-18

Today, on this penultimate day of our meditations on Psalm 73, we face the important practical question: How do we go about the task of keeping close to God? Firstly, we do so by prayer. The person who keeps close to God is the one who is always talking to God. Many definitions of prayer have been given; I add another: prayer is co-operation with God. In prayer you align your desires, your will, your life to God. You and God become agreed on life desires, life purposes, life plans, and you work them out *together*.

Secondly, we do it by constant study of the Scriptures. God's Word is alive with meaning, and when you read it something will happen to you, for "the word of God is living and powerful, and sharper than any two-edged sword" (Heb.4:12, NKJ). Expect it to speak to you – and it will. Faith is expectancy: "According to your faith will it be done to you" (Matt. 9:29). Remember also to surrender to the truth that is revealed: "If anyone wills to do His will, he shall know ..." (John 7:17, NKJ). In a moral universe the key to knowledge is moral response. The moment we cease to obey, that moment the revelation ceases to reveal.

We do it, thirdly, by sharing with others. Remember, nothing is ours if we do not share it. When we share, the things go deeper inside us. We must share what God is doing, both with our fellow Christians and with non-Christians also. The psalmist's last words are these: "I will tell of all your deeds." We take and we tell – we take and we tell; these, we must never forget, are the two heartbeats of the Christian experience.

FURTHER STUDY

Jer. 20:1-9;
Psa. 66:16;
Isa. 63:7

1. What was God's Word like in Jeremiah's heart?

2. What did the psalmist say he would do?

Prayer

Gracious Father, I don't want nearness to You to be an occasional experience – I want it to be a perpetual experience. Help me to pay the price, no matter what it costs. In Jesus' Name I ask it. Amen.

Reflections

"But as for me, it is good to be near God ..." (v.28)
For reading & meditation – Psalm 73:1-28

A tinge of sadness is upon my spirit as I come to this last day of our meditations on Psalm 73. In all my years of writing, never can I remember being so personally blessed. The truth this psalm conveys has gripped my own heart and life in a most unusual way.

Let's remind ourselves of what the psalmist has taught us. Life is filled with many painful and perplexing problems which at times cause us to cry out: "Lord, why don't You intervene?" Yet just as our feet are about to slide, something always comes to us – an idea or a thought, which, if we hold on to it, serves to halt our downward progress. We discover that when we act responsibly and do what is right, even though we do not feel like it, we put ourselves in the way of experiencing inward change.

But it is not God's purpose to bring about only a little change – He desires to bring about a lot of change. How does He achieve this? He does it by bringing us into His presence and revealing to us His Word. There we discover that our greatest problems are not the ones that are outside us but the ones that are inside us – our perspectives are wrong.

FURTHER STUDY

Psa. 57:1-7; 108:1; 112:7

1. What did the psalmist mean by "steadfast"?

2. Where is your heart fixed?

Real change comes about not when our feelings are soothed but when our thinking is changed. Changed thinking leads to changed desires. When our perspectives are controlled by the Word rather than by the world, then we will experience inner peace. The psalmist resolved to draw near to God and stay close to Him so that he could "see life steadily, and see it whole". Let's make that our resolution too.

Prayer

O Father, I see that the secret of effective living is looking at life from Your point of view. I resolve by Your grace to give myself more and more to learning this secret. Help me, my Father. In Jesus' Name I ask it. Amen.

The Corn of Wheat Afraid to Die

No death – no life

"… But if [a grain of wheat] dies, it produces many seeds." (v.24)

For reading & meditation – John 12:20-36

Today we begin to examine one of the most profound truths in the Bible – the principle that life is always preceded by death. It is not difficult to bring together a host of corroborative Scriptures to prove this point, but let the one that is before us suffice for now. The order is unmistakable – it is *only* when a grain of wheat falls into the ground and dies that it produces more seeds. No death, no life – it is as simple as that. Understanding this issue is so important that I would go as far as to say that Christians who don't grasp the concept can easily lose their way spiritually.

Some years ago I read of a pilot whose plane crashed in a field outside a small town in Africa. Investigators looking for the cause of the crash surmised that the pilot thought he was landing at his intended destination when in fact he was approaching a town with a similar name. The difference in spelling was a matter of just one letter. His planned destination was a thousand feet lower than where he actually landed, and he was killed (so it is thought) because he believed he had a thousand feet more than was actually the case. He worked from the wrong map.

If we have the wrong "mental map" of the issue that is before us – that life is preceded by death – then we can miss our way and end up as a spiritual casualty. If we are to live – really live – then we must be willing to die to all self-interest. A missed step here may mean a miss-spent life.

FURTHER STUDY

Rom. 6:1-23;
Luke 9:24;
1 Cor. 15:36

1. What is the significance of baptism?

2. What is "spiritual" death?

Prayer

Gracious and loving heavenly Father, help me I pray not to work from the wrong "mental map". Give me a clear understanding of the fact that life must be preceded by death. In Christ's Name I ask it. Amen.

Caught in the cross-currents

"But striking a reef where two seas met, they ran the vessel aground ..." (v.41, NASB)

For reading & meditation – Acts 27:27-44

We made the point yesterday that when we fail to understand, or misunderstand, the highly important issue that life on this sin-stained planet is preceded by death, we could do more than just miss our spiritual destination – we could end up in spiritual difficulty. Am I over-stating the issue? I think not. During my Christian life, I have had many occasions to observe firsthand the struggles of the saints, and if I had to narrow those struggles down to the biggest single problem in Christian experience, I would express it in these words – an unwillingness to die to self-interest and self-concern.

The story of Paul's shipwreck which we have read today is a picture of what happens to Christians who have not understood or come to grips with the truth that we must die in order to live. The New English Bible translates verse 41 thus: "But they found themselves caught between cross-currents and ran the ship aground, so that the bow stuck fast and remained immovable, while the stern was being pounded to pieces."

"They found themselves caught between cross-currents." That is the dilemma in which many Christians find themselves – the bow of their ship is caught up in the Christian cause, but because they have never learned how to die to self-interest, the rest of their life is being pounded to pieces by the breakers. I guarantee you this; if you get hold of the truth around which our present theme is built, you will always find yourself in a manoeuvrable position. Cross-currents may strike you and breakers may pound you – but you will stay in one piece.

FURTHER STUDY

James 1:1-8; 4:8;
Luke 16:13;
Eph. 6:5

1. What causes instability?

2. What makes us stable?

Prayer

O Father, help me not to get stuck in the sands of a half-hearted commitment, so that my life remains fixed and useless. I don't want to go to pieces, I want to go places – with You. Amen.

To die – or not to die?

"… as dying, and behold we live …" (v.9, RSV)
For reading & meditation – 2 Corinthians 6:1-13

Today we ask: What is the meaning of this strange spiritual paradox that before we can live, we must first be willing to die? The best illustration of this truth can be seen in the passage from John 12 that we read on the first day of our meditations and which we will now look at in greater detail.

One day a group of visitors from Greece arrived in Jerusalem, and hearing of the fame of Jesus sought out Philip, one of His disciples, and said to him: "Sir, we would like to see Jesus" (John 12:21). When Philip informed Jesus that some Greeks wanted to interview Him, this precipitated a spiritual crisis in our Lord's heart: "The hour has come for the Son of Man to be glorified … unless a grain of wheat falls to the ground and dies, it remains only a single seed. But if it dies, it produces many seeds" (John 12:24).

Why should the Greeks' simple request precipitate such a crisis in Jesus' heart – a crisis in which dying or not dying seemed to be the vital issue? Could it have been that He sensed that the Greeks were coming with an invitation for Him to bring His message to Athens – the centre of philosophy and learning – where it might be more readily received? Did He sense that in wanting to interview Him, they were going to say: "Sir, if You go on the way Your face is set, the Jews will kill You. Don't stay here in Jerusalem and die: come to Athens and live"? If this was the situation, then how dramatically it would have underlined the issue that was constantly before Him – to die or not to die.

FURTHER STUDY

Gal. 2:1-20;
Rom. 8:36;
2 Tim. 2:11

1. How did Paul view life?

2. What analogy did he use?

Prayer

Blessed Lord Jesus, it is clear that I face a similar issue to the one You faced when here on earth – to die, or not to die. Help me, dear Lord, for I can only face it in Your strength. Amen.

"Come to Athens and live"

"... Will he go where our people live scattered among the Greeks, and teach the Greeks?" (v.35)
For reading & meditation – John 7:25-39

We ended yesterday by suggesting that the issue which the Greeks might have wanted to talk over with Jesus was that of taking His message to Athens – the centre of philosophy and learning. Were they intent on saying to Him: "Put Your marvellous message of the kingdom of God into the medium of Greek thought, and in no time it will spread throughout the world. Don't stay in Jerusalem and die; come to Athens and live"?

We have no way, of course, of knowing for sure that this was the situation, and I am simply suggesting that this is what may have been in their minds. The idea is not as far-fetched as you might imagine when placed against the verse that is before us today: "Does he intend to go to the Dispersion ... and teach the Greeks?" (v.35, RSV). Had other nations beyond Israel's boundaries showed interest in His revolutionary approach to life? Tradition says that the king of Edessa once sent a message to Jesus inviting Him to come to his country and present His message concerning the kingdom of God.

Whether or not this was so, one thing is certain – the coming of the

FURTHER STUDY

Matt. 16:24-28;
27:32; John 19:17

1. What does the cross signify?

2. What does it mean to "take up your cross"?

Greeks precipitated a crisis in Jesus' soul: "Now my heart is troubled, and what shall I say? 'Father, save me from this hour'? ... Father, glorify your name!" (John 12:27-28). He would not rationalise or compromise; He would face the issue to which He had always been committed. It was not to be a philosopher's chair in Athens, but a grisly cross in Jerusalem. He would fall into the ground and die, and bear a harvest richer than anything the world could offer.

Prayer

Lord Jesus, help me to catch something of Your spirit as I face the challenges that lie ahead of me in the coming days. I want to make my life count for the utmost – show me how we can work things out together. Amen.

"A blank cheque"

*"Father, if you are willing, take this cup from me; yet not
my will, but yours be done."* (v. 42)

For reading & meditation – Luke 22:39-48

We have seen over the past two days how Jesus, when faced with the
news that some Greeks wanted to interview Him, appeared to be
precipitated into a spiritual crisis. Whatever we make of this incident in
the life of our Lord, it is fairly obvious that some deep struggle is going
on inside Him. And the terms of that struggle are also clear: "What shall
I say? 'Father, save me from this hour'? No, it was for this very reason I
came to this hour" (John 12:27). This passage in John 12 underlines
most powerfully the humanity of Jesus. We see Him recoiling for a
moment – and only for a moment – from the grim ordeal that He was
about to face on Calvary, but He comes through to reaffirm His unswerv-
ing commitment to His Father's eternal will and purpose.

Note once again the truth that seemed to sustain Him in this dark
and crucial hour: "I must fall and die like a grain of wheat that falls
between the furrows of the earth. Unless I die I will be alone – a single
seed. But my death will produce many new wheat grains – a plentiful
harvest of new lives" (John 12:23-24, TLB). He gave a blank cheque to
God signed in His own blood. He would fall into the ground and die and
bear a rich and bountiful harvest. He aligned Himself
with self-giving and not self-saving. The momentous
issue with which our Lord struggled in that hour is
similar to the one which you and I are being called
to face in these meditations – to die or not to die.
The way we respond to it will determine our life-
direction.

FURTHER STUDY

Phil. 2:1-8;
Psa. 40:8; 143:10;
Eph. 6.6

1. What was God's
will for His Son?

2. How did Jesus
respond?

Prayer

Father, I sense that quietly things are heading toward a moment of crisis in my life –
a crisis of commitment. Help me to see these things, not merely as a matter for discussion, but a matter for decision. In Jesus' Name I pray. Amen.

"The deepest law"

"Whoever finds his life will lose it, and whoever loses his life for my sake will find it." (v.39)

For reading & meditation – Matthew 10:24-39

Out of this incident of the Greeks seeking an interview with Jesus came these great truths that Jesus uttered. We have already looked at some of our Lord's famous statements in John chapter 12 – here is another: "The man who loves his life will lose it, while the man who hates his life in this world will keep it for eternal life" (John 12:25).

What does it mean – "The man who loves his life will lose it"? It means that when you focus on your interests alone, your life will disintegrate. Those who have no one to centre on other than themselves and live only to have their own way finish up bankrupt, beggared and defeated. Dorothy Sayers put the same truth most effectively when she said: "Hell is the enjoyment of having one's own way for ever."

But the rest of the verse is just as true: "The man who hates his life in this world will keep it for eternal life." In other words, lose your life in the plans and purposes of God and you will find the true meaning of your existence. It is a paradox, but nevertheless true, that you are never so much your own as when you are most His. Bound to Him, you walk the earth free. Low at His feet, you stand straight before anything or anyone else. You suddenly realise that you have aligned yourself with the creative forces of the universe, so you are free – free to create, free to love, free to be at your best, free to be all that He desires you to be. And this is not just mere acquiescence. It is co-operation with the power that raised Jesus from the dead. No wonder someone called this principle, "the deepest law in the universe".

FURTHER STUDY

Matt. 19:21-30;
Mark 8:35;
Phil. 3:8

1. What was Jesus teaching?

2. How does this work out in your life?

Prayer

O God, once again You are boring deep – but You have my permission to keep going. When Your drill strikes hard resistances in me, don't hold back. I want the deep living waters of Your presence and power. Amen.

What is the Father's "glory"?

*"This is to my Father's glory, that you bear much fruit,
showing yourselves to be my disciples." (v.8)*

For reading & meditation – John 15:1-11

Over these last few days, we have been seeing that just as Christ came face to face with the issue – To die or not to die – so also must we, His disciples, face a similar challenge. It is one of the axioms of the Christian life that in order to realise God's purposes in our lives, we must be prepared to die to all self-interest.

Why is this so necessary? What possible purpse can our Lord have in making such a demand? Our text for today gives us the answer: "This is my Father's glory, that you may bear fruit in plenty and so be my disciples" (NEB). The Father's "glory" is what? Rainbows? Waterfalls? Chanting angels? No, the Father's "glory" is men and women who bring forth fruit in plenty. Is your life fruitful? Does it yield a rich harvest from which your Lord will derive eternal pleasure? If not, then perhaps the reason is that your are "a corn of wheat afraid to die". You draw back from experiences which are designed, not to demean you, but to develop you. And if you are afraid to die, then, as Jesus put it, you "remain only a single seed".

A women once came up to me after I had preached a sermon on this theme, and said: "Why is God so cruel in demanding so much of us?" She meant: Why does God demand the one and only thing I own – me, myself? It seemed to her that she would be consenting to her own extinction. She saw only what she had to give up – not what she had to gain. If we are to win this battle, then we must do as Jesus did and continually focus our gaze on the fact that beyond the chosen way of the cross lies ultimate power and victory.

FURTHER STUDY

Col. 1:1-10;
Psa. 1:3;
Matt. 13:23;
Rom. 6:22

1. What is God's purpose for us?

2. What does that entail?

Prayer

My Father and my God, I do not want to shirk, to dodge, or to put things off. Help me, and help me now, to face this issue of the death of my self-interests so that it is settled once and for all. Amen.

The greatest loneliness

"I will obey thee eagerly, as thou dost open up my life."
(v.32, Moffatt)

For reading & meditation – Psalm 119:17-32

Now that we have seen how crucial is the spiritual principle that life is preceded by death, we move on to consider some of the areas into which God leads us so that this principle may be put to work. If, as we said, this principle is "the deepest law in the universe", then we should not be surprised when God provides us with opportunities to demonstrate its effectiveness.

The first area we consider is *loneliness*. Is this a situation in which you find yourself at the moment? If so, then you can respond to it in one of two ways: you can rebel against it and wallow in self-pity, or you can face it in the knowledge that God is with you in your loneliness and will help you turn it into something positive. Geoffrey Bull, when speaking of his lonely life in Tibet in his book *When Iron Gates Yield*, said: "The Lord had appointed me to stand in solitude upon the threshold of crisis, yet the only loneliness I had need to fear was that of a corn of wheat afraid to die."

A corn of wheat afraid to die – that is the greatest loneliness. Just as there is one sin – the sin of making yourself God (all the rest are *sins*), so there is just one loneliness – the loneliness of being alone with a self that is not surrendered to God. You see, if you do not understand the principle that going God's way is always the best route to spiritual fruitfulness, then loneliness will hold tremendous terror for you. I say again: there is no greater loneliness than a self that is afraid to die.

FURTHER STUDY

Psa. 102:7; 38:11;
John 16:17-33;

1. How did the psalmist feel?

2. What was Jesus' testimony?

Prayer

O God, if You see that I am "a corn of wheat afraid to die", then uproot that fear – in Jesus' Name. May I echo the psalmist's words: "I will obey thee eagerly, as thou dost open up my life." Amen.

"His-appointment"

"Listen to this wise advice; follow it closely, for it will do you good … Trust in the Lord." (vv.17-19, TLB)

For reading & meditation – Proverbs 22:17-29

Are you afraid of loneliness? If so, then it is likely that there is a greater fear than that in your life – the fear of "a corn of wheat afraid to die". Settle that fear, and all other fears are as nothing in comparison. When our attitude is that of complete and utter surrender to God and confidence in the outcome of His purposes, then we can face anything that comes – good, bad or indifferent.

An extremely prominent minister who was greatly used by God got caught up in a spiritual conflict because he had his eye upon a position in his denomination which he desired for himself. He shared his desire with a prominent laymen and tried to get him to use his influence in securing the position. The layman said: "I do not think it right to use my influence in the way you ask. The decision must be with those who have been selected for that purpose."

The minister was deeply upset by his friend's remarks and became extremely bitter and morose. In due course the position was given to someone else, and the minister, unable to cope with the disappointment, withdrew from the ministry and now lives in a big house all by himself – terribly alone. He was "a corn of wheat afraid to die". Had he been willing to die to the desire for self-aggrandisement, position and prestige, he would have seen the disappointment as "His-appointment". Now he is lonely with the loneliness that comes to all who fail to realise that God always gives the best to those who leave the choice to Him.

FURTHER STUDY

Prov. 3:1-6;
Psa. 37:3-5; 118:8

1. What does "trust" mean?

2. What is promised to those who trust?

Prayer

My Father and my God, I see that there is no greater loneliness than the loneliness that comes from being locked into my own purposes and my own desires. Help me to be continually centred in You and not in myself. In Jesus' Name I pray. Amen

"See Mrs Noby Jo first"

"My food … is to do the will of him who sent me and to finish his work." (v.34)

For reading & meditation – John 4:27-42

We continue meditating on the thought that the greatest loneliness is that of a "corn of wheat afraid to die."

A story from China tells how a young woman, Mrs Noby Jo, went out into the hills to pray. Soon the Lord began to show her that His plans for her life led in a different direction to her own. Petulantly she cried: "Lord, why do You always have to have Your way; what about my way for a change?" Gently the Lord whispered into her heart: "My child, it is not that your way is wrong; it is rather that My way is best." She surrendered her will to His, and came away with these words ringing in her ears: "You belong to the discouraged and broken people who commit suicide at the bend of the railway track."

Confused by this message, she made enquiries and discovered that outside the town where she lived was a notorious spot at the bend of the railway track where people intent on committing suicide would throw themselves over a cliff into the deep ravine below. She arranged to put up a sign near the spot that read: "Don't: see Mrs Noby Jo first. God loves you." She added her address and the very first day the sign was put up, several people knocked on her door and said they had come in response to the notice. She was "promoted to glory" at the age of 92, having saved 5,000 people from suicide. When she died to her own desires and took God's way, the grain of wheat that had fallen into the ground and died brought forth fruit a hundredfold. It always does.

FURTHER STUDY

Phil. 3:1-21;
Prov. 23:26;
Rom. 12:1

1. What was Paul's attitude?

2. How did he work it out?

Prayer

Father, help me not to get so caught up in my own plans that I become entangled in myself. I want to start with You, not with myself. It is then, and only then, that I will be able to do what You want me to do. Help me – in Jesus' Name. Amen.

"God of remarkable surprises"

"O thou Eternal, thou wilt light my lamp … thou wilt make my darkness shine." (v.28, Moffatt)

For reading & meditation – Psalm 18:20-40

If you have not yet taken hold of the truth we have been discussing over the past few days, then grasp it with both hands today: the greatest loneliness is the loneliness of "a corn of wheat afraid to die". If we are afraid to die to our own purposes and allow God's purposes to become supreme, then we finish up pleasing ourselves but not liking the self we have pleased. And again, being willing to face any situation that comes with the conviction that God will make it contributive enables us to face life with an inner fortitude and poise.

Understanding this truth and being willing to apply it to all circumstances and situations is one of the greatest safeguards against emotional or personality problems. In fact, I would go further and say that it is one of the greatest defences against reactive depression that I know. I say "reactive" depression because there are some forms of depression which are chemically based and result from malfunctioning of the body's chemical systems. Reactive depression is the depression that comes from the way we interpret the knocks and hardships that crowd into our lives. And what greater hardship can there be than loneliness?

The Bible teaches us, however, that God will never allow one of His children to find themselves in any situation where He is not able to help them – loneliness included. Someone has referred to our heavenly Father as "the God of remarkable surprises". What a fascinating description – and how true. In the midst of life's loneliest moments, God has a way of approaching us and revealing Himself in ways that we would never have conceived possible.

FURTHER STUDY

1 Kings 19:1-8;
Psa. 91:11;
Heb. 1:14

1. How did God deal with Elijah's loneliness?

2. Whom did He send to him?

Prayer

Father – surprise me. In some way today, let the wonder of Your concern and care for me break through the ordered routines and duties of my life. Pull aside the curtain and give me a fresh glimpse of Your face. In Jesus' Name I pray. Amen.

Knowing God

"When my spirit grows faint within me, it is you who know my way." (v.3)

For reading & meditation – Psalm 142:1-7

We referred yesterday to our heavenly Father as "the God of remarkable surprises". We must stay with that thought a little longer and draw from it further inspiration. Who hasn't seen the scenario in the old silent movies in which a victim is tied to a railway track by a handlebar-moustached villain? But the story isn't over: invariably, moments before the train comes thundering around the corner, someone rescues the hapless victim from what looks like certain death – and often in the most surprising manner.

Have you not often found a similar scenario in your own life? Just when it looks as if you are facing what seems like unmitigated disaster, the "God of remarkable surprises" turns a desperate situation into an opportunity for unparalleled joy. How does He do it? Just when we are feeling as if there is no one in the world who cares and that we will not be able to get through the day, He draws close to us and wraps the warmth of His presence around us in a way that makes the experience of temporary isolation worthwhile.

You see, sometimes our knowledge of God is just theoretical – we know Him in our heads, but we don't really know Him in our hearts. In the depths of loneliness, however, this undergoes a deep change – the theory is turned into reality. Someone has defined loneliness as "the surprising opportunity to know God". It is. When there is no one but God – those are the times when we learn to know God – and *really* know Him. The experience of loneliness is not easy to go through, but believe me, it is worth far more than the cost.

FURTHER STUDY

Luke 24:13-35;
Psa. 139:2;
Matt. 6:8

1. What was the problem of these 2 disciples?

2. How did Jesus deal with them?

Prayer

Father, something within me still shrinks away from the challenge that You are putting before me. Help me to understand, however, that in order to know You – *really* know You – I must be willing, not just to trust, but obey. Amen.

From holy ground

"One thing I ask of the Lord ... that I may dwell in the house of the Lord all the days of my life ..." (v.4)

For reading & meditation – Psalm 27:1-14

We said yesterday it is in times of deepest loneliness, when there is no one there but God, that we learn to know Him most fully. Not long after my conversion in my mid-teens, a preacher I greatly admired came to stay in our home. I had the opportunity to sit with him for many hours asking him some of the spiritual questions which, up until then, had greatly perplexed me. During one period of discussion I said to him: "Tell me, what is the secret of your great and powerful ministry?"

It was quite a while before he answered, and as I waited I pondered what his answer might be. Would he say, "It is the way I use words", or "My skill at chiselling attractive and appealing phrases", or perhaps, "My insight and understanding of the Scriptures"? It was none of these. He said quite simply: "If there is any power in my ministry, it has come out of walking with God through the valley of loneliness."

I cannot remember in the whole of my life ever hearing a more compelling and moving statement than that. It introduced me to a truth that I myself had to learn – that the route to knowing God often passes through the valley of profound loneliness. The depth of character that is developed through loneliness is something that not only enriches the life of the individual concerned, but spills over into the lives of many others also. In periods of loneliness, the Master draws us into His presence so that later, when we speak to others, they sense we are speaking to them from holy ground.

FURTHER STUDY

1 Kings 19:9-21; Josh. 1:5; Isa. 54:10

1. What did Elijah wrongly believe in his loneliness?

2. How did God use his loneliness?

Prayer

O God, help me to commit my will to Your will, not to be borne but to be done. If knowing You – really knowing You – means walking through the valley of loneliness, then lead on, dear Lord – I will follow. Amen.

Lonely – but not alone

"… you will be scattered, each to his own home. You will leave me all alone. Yet I am not alone, for my Father is with me." (v.32)

For reading and meditation – John 16:19-33

We spend one last day looking at the issue of loneliness. Our meditations on this subject have made one thing clear – it is in the periods of loneliness that we most abandon ourselves to God and learn how to depend upon Him utterly and completely.

The more I read the biographies of those who have achieved great things for God, the more I realise that their deep knowledge of Him came, in part, out of moments of profound loneliness. It was in such moments that "the God of remarkable surprises" revealed Himself and gave them an understanding of His grace and power such as they could never otherwise have known. Is it not true that God's glory bursts through most powerfully when the sky is at its darkest? Does not His strength uphold us most when we are feeling weak and inadequate? And does not His love penetrate most deeply when we feel unloved or isolated from others?

When we are prepared to die to our own interests and are willing to follow our Lord fearlessly along the path which He sees is best for us, we experience, not just temporal, but eternal rewards. The seed that falls into the ground and dies is the one that yields a rich and bountiful harvest. Many of us fail to be fruitful in our Christian life and experience because we are afraid or unwilling to face the issues which demand a wholehearted commitment to the will of God. We save ourselves – and then what? We finish up by not liking the self we have saved. Make no mistake about it – God's way is best, even though a thousand hardships beset the path.

FURTHER STUDY

John 11:1-46;
14:18; Heb. 13:5

1. How did it seem to Mary and Martha in their moment of loneliness?

2. What did Jesus say to them?

Prayer

O God my Father, give me the courage of Jesus who, despite His loneliness and isolation, went on to achieve Your perfect will. Quicken within me today the sense that when I am walking with You I may feel lonely, but I am never alone. Amen.

"Wait! Wait! Wait!"

*"How great is your goodness, which you have stored up
for those who fear you …" (v.19)*

For reading & meditation – Psalm 31:1-24

As we move on we start to think about some of the red furrows of life
from which we often draw back. At such times we become "a corn of
wheat afraid to die". But as we are seeing, where there is no death, there
can be no life. Outside the furrow we remain safe, warm, comfortable –
and unfruitful.

First we shall consider what I am calling "divine delays" – those
periods of life to which God leads us when it seems that nothing is happening and that His purposes for our lives are temporarily shelved.
Perhaps you are at this point at this very moment. If so, don't panic –
God's delays are not His denials. Our Master has a purpose in everything He does. You must believe that, even though your fears scream the
opposite.

One of the most difficult things to do in the Christian life is to wait
for God's purposes to come to pass. Sometimes they take so long to
materialise that we find ourselves getting vexed and frustrated. Have you
heard about the Christian who prayed: "Lord, give me patience … and I
want it right now"? Wouldn't you rather do anything than wait? A man
told a Christian counsellor I know: "Waiting for God
to bring His purposes to pass is the biggest problem I
face in my Christian life; there is something within me
that would rather do the wrong thing than wait." As
waiting for God to bring about His purposes is more
the rule than the exception in the Christian life, we
had better learn what God has in mind when His red
light flashes out the signal, "Wait! Wait! Wait!"

FURTHER STUDY

Acts 1:4-8; 2:1-8;
Gen. 49:18;
Isa. 25:9

*1.What was the
result of the disciples'
time of waiting?*

*2.What will be the
result of our
waiting?*

Prayer

O Father, teach me to trust You when Your plans and purposes for my life are seemingly delayed. I confess that impatience is one of the most difficult things for me to
"die" to. I cannot do it on my own. Help me, my Father. In Jesus' Name. Amen.

Catching a vision

*"If it pleases the king … let him send me to the city in Judah
where my fathers are buried so that I can rebuild it."* (v.5)

For reading & meditation – Nehemiah 2:1-10

We ended yesterday with the thought that waiting for God's purposes to come to pass is more the rule than the exception in the Christian life. Does this mean that for most of our Christian life we should do nothing but wait for God to move? No. Clearly there are certain aspects of the Christian life which require immediate and daily attention, and for which we have all the guidance we need. We don't need to wait on God, for example, to know what we should do about forgiving those who have hurt us, or sharing our faith with the unconverted. Those purposes of God are to be seen as standard operating procedure and are clearly set out in His Word.

I am referring here, not so much to His general purposes, but to His individual purposes – those special plans which He wants to achieve through us personally. Every Christian has the responsibility of coming before God to seek to discover just what it is that the Lord wants to achieve through his or her life. And as we are faithful in reading His Word, obeying His commands, and communing with Him in prayer, we can expect Him to reveal those special plans for our lives.

FURTHER STUDY

Gen. 15:1-21;
21:1-5; Heb.2:3;
Prov. 29:18

1. What vision did God give Abraham?

2. How long did it take to be fulfilled?

Take our reading today: Nehemiah served the king faithfully, but when he heard about the disgraceful condition of God's city, Jerusalem, he caught a vision of rebuilding the walls. God then worked in the king's heart to give him a desire to assist Nehemiah in achieving that vision. Have you caught the vision of what God wants to achieve through your own individual life and witness on this earth? If not, why not?

Prayer

Gracious Father, give me, I pray, a clear picture of what You want to achieve through my own personal life and witness for You. I have kept myself in the dark too long; now I want to step out into the light – Your light. Amen.

The special thing

"Where there is no vision, the people perish ..." (v.18, AV)

For reading & meditation – Proverbs 29:1-18

What is the point we are making? It is this: as we are faithful in following the Lord, we can expect Him to reveal His special plan for our lives. Just as Nehemiah caught the vision of rebuilding the walls of Jerusalem, so we, too, if we are ready and alert, will catch the vision of what God has specially equipped us to do.

Many years ago, I asked God to give me a vision of the special thing He wanted me to achieve for Him. He gave me the vision of launching a daily Bible reading programme which is now read by half a million people daily. He also, so I believe, inspired the choice of the title, *Every Day with Jesus.* I sometimes tremble at the awesome responsibility I now have of developing a spiritual theme month by month which will minister to the needs in people's lives.

What if I had not asked God to give me a vision of what He wanted me to do? I might have continued in a ministry that would have been good, but not the best. I believe there are many of you now reading these lines who are living faithful lives for God, but you have never asked Him to show you the special thing He wants you to achieve for Him. And don't think of that special calling in terms of something that will bring you prestige and glamour – to do that will take you right off the track. If you have never done so before, ask the Lord right now to give you a vision of what He wants you to achieve for Him. Who knows – this could be, not just a new day, but a new beginning.

FURTHER STUDY

Acts 26:1-19;
Eph. 1:9; 3:11

1. What was Jesus'
message to Paul?

2. What was Paul
able to testify to
Agrippa?

Prayer

O Father, I don't just want to achieve the good – I want to achieve the best. If I have not yet caught the vision of that special thing You want to achieve through my life, then reveal it to me today. In Jesus' Name I pray. Amen.

Everyone is special

"Though it linger, wait for it; it will certainly come and will not delay." (v.3)

For reading & meditation – Habakkuk 2:1-14

A rising out of what we said yesterday – that God has a special calling for each of us – the thought occurs to me that some might view that statement as applying only to those who have the opportunity of working in "full-time Christian service". I don't much like the phrase, "full-time Christian service" – hence the quotation marks. Every Christian is in full-time Christian service – every hour of the day and every day of the week.

Let me make it perfectly clear that in saying God has a special purpose for every one of us, I mean just that – every one of us. The trouble is, when we talk about Nehemiah catching the vision of rebuilding the walls of Jerusalem, or Moses catching the vision of leading his people out of bondage, we tend to think that such visions apply only to those who are specially chosen and gifted.

As you read these lines today ask yourself: "Have I taken the time to ask God what He especially wants me to do?" A man may catch the vision today of a special ministry to other men. A woman may catch the vision of teaching other women how to be discreet, to manage their homes and to love their husbands and children (Titus 2:4-5). A married couple may catch the vision of ministering to singles. And those who are single may catch the vision of embarking on some project for God to which they can give their time and energies in a way that married people cannot. Open your heart and mind to what God is saying to you today. God sees everyone as special, and has a special task for everyone.

FURTHER STUDY

Rom. 12:1-21;
1 Cor. 12:1-31;
Eph. 4:1-16

1. What does Paul teach about the body of Christ?

2. Have you discovered where you fit in?

Prayer

Gracious Father, You continue to stretch my faith and my expectancy. I am so grateful. If I have not yet caught the vision of what You want me to do, then help me to do so today. In Jesus' Name I pray. Amen.

God's wonderful ways

*"How unsearchable his judgments, and his paths beyond
tracing out!"* (v.33)

For reading & meditation – Romans 11:25-36

Now that we have spent a few days discussing the importance of catching a vision of the special contribution God wants us to make through our lives, we ask ourselves: What happens next? Usually, the next step after catching a vision is to see it die. There is a special reason for this: our vision often contains a combination of godly concerns and human perspectives, so God has to engineer a way whereby the godly concerns remain and the human perspectives are changed to divine perspectives. His way of doing this is to cause the vision to die.

This is a Biblical principle that can be traced from Genesis to Revelation. The vision Abraham received of being the father of a great nation "died" when he found his wife was barren. The vision Moses received "died" when he was rejected by his people and was forced to flee into the desert for forty years.

Why, we ask, does God bring a vision to birth and then allow it to die? For this reason: the waiting time in which we find ourselves during the death of a vision is God's classroom for the development of godly character in us. It is in the waiting time, as the vision "dies", that such qualities as patience, persistence, perseverance and self-control are built into us. Has God given you in the past a vision of something that you knew was definitely from Him – but now the vision has died? Then don't be discouraged. This is the way God works. He is using the waiting time to change your ideas to His ideas and your perspectives to His perspectives.

FURTHER STUDY

John 21:1-25; 6:27;
Isa. 55:2

1. What had Peter
decided to do?

2. Why did Jesus
challenge him?

Prayer

O my Father, I stand in awe at the wonder of Your ways. Forgive me that so often I have viewed the time of waiting as tedious rather than transformative. Now my perspectives are different. Lead on, dear Father – I want to learn more. Amen.

The hour of temptation

"… he rebuked Peter, and said, 'Get behind me, Satan! For you are not on the side of God, but of men.' " (v.33, RSV)

For reading & meditation – Mark 8:27-38

We are seeing that once we have been given a vision of what God wants us to do for Him, the next thing that happens is that the vision dies. The reason for this is that Christian character must be developed in us before God can accomplish His purpose in our lives, and this can only be done by God bringing our vision down into death. Many Christians have been baffled by this strange strategy which God uses to develop Christlikeness in us, but it is yet another illustration of the principle that death must precede life.

An important thing to remember is that Satan is extremely operative at this time, for his purpose is to get you to fulfil the vision by your own human effort. And whenever you do this, you will finish up in conflict. Remember what happened to Abraham? Rather than waiting for God to bring the vision into being at His own time, he tried to "help" God by having a son through Sarah's maidservant, Hagar (Gen. 16:3-4). The result of that was conflict between Isaac and Ishmael – a conflict that has continued to this day.

In our reading today, we see Peter being used by Satan to talk Christ out of facing death on Calvary, but Jesus recognised the true source of his ideas and responded with the words: "Get behind me, Satan!" One writer comments on this passage: "Satan often uses those who are closest to us to 'protect' us from what we know God has called us to do." Even close Christian friends sometimes fail to understand that before we can live for God's purposes, we must die to our own.

FURTHER STUDY

Eph. 6:10-18;
2 Cor. 2:11; 11:3

1. How can we withstand Satan's schemes?

2. Do it today.

Prayer

O Father. I sense that Your ways are written, not only in Your Word, but also in me. Something within me echoes to truth. Help me to be always willing to die to my own purposes so that I can be alive to Yours. Then I will live abundantly. Amen.

The power behind these pages

"I will not yield my glory to another." (v.11)
For reading & meditation – Isaiah 48:1-11

Today we ask ourselves: What happens after God causes our vision to "die", and His purpose of building into us the characteristics of Christ has been achieved? This: He then resurrects the vision and brings it to joyous fulfilment. His purpose in doing this is not just to fulfil the vision, but to do so in a way that points to His supernatural intervention. In that way no onlooker can be in any doubt as to whose power lies behind the success of the ministry – everyone recognises it to be God.

While the disciples were with Christ, they received a vision of the coming kingdom, but on the cross they saw that vision die before their eyes. What happened then? Three days later, they witnessed the supernatural power of God bring Christ back from the dead – an event that turned them upside down.

I referred a few days ago to the vision which God gave me – the vision of putting together a daily Bible reading and meditation programme which would motivate Christians. That took place in 1965. In 1968, three years after the vision was launched, it "died". I do not mean that it discontinued, but for a whole year it was on the verge of collapse. My own enthusiasm for it slowly ebbed away until I came to the place where I said: "Lord, it's not mine – it's Yours." Then came resurrection. From that time to this, God has been seen to have the greatest part in its compilation. The constant stream of letters telling of changed lives, changed families and changed attitudes point to the fact that Jesus Christ is the power behind these pages – not me.

FURTHER STUDY

Isa. 14:12-15;
Micah 6:8;
1 Cor. 1:19-29

1. What was Lucifer's downfall?

2. What was Paul's conclusion?

Prayer

O God, now that I understand this principle of the birth, death and resurrection of a vision, help me to apply it to those periods in my life when it seems as if nothing is happening and Your purposes are temporarily shelved. Amen.

"Men cry out against the heavens"

"Yet man is born to trouble as surely as sparks fly upward."
(v.7)

For reading & meditation – Job 5:1-16

We now focus on yet another aspect of our theme – *The Corn of Wheat Afraid to Die*. Slowly we are coming to grips with one of the greatest truths of Scripture, namely that life comes through the giving of life, and fruitfulness through falling into the ground and dying. When we remain by ourselves, using only human resources, our lives will turn out to be shallow and fruitless. Refusing to pay the ultimate price of giving ourselves, we find ourselves paying the price of the deadness of life itself.

Another area of life from which we often cry out to be exempted, but one which, if we are willing to give ourselves, yields great spiritual fruitfulness, is the area of unmerited suffering. Our text for today reminds us that "man is born to trouble as surely as sparks fly upward", and there are few of us who have not had cause to lament the truth of those words. A more modern observer of the human condition puts it thus:

> *My son, the world is dark with griefs and graves*
> *So dark that men cry out against the heavens.*

FURTHER STUDY

Psa. 116:1-19;
71:20;
Jer. 8:15

1. What did the psalmist do in trouble?

2. What was his testimony?

I suppose there is nothing that makes people "cry out against the heavens" so much as the anguish that comes through unmerited suffering. Horace Walpole said: "To those who think, life is comedy; to those who feel, life is tragedy." There are few of us who do not "feel" – so is life a tragedy to most? God did not deliver His Son from suffering – He did something better. And it is along this line of the "something better" that we will find the answer to unmerited suffering.

Prayer

O God my Father, I must find the key to this issue of unmerited suffering. For the doors of life and fruitful service will be closed to me unless I know how to open them and walk through to victory. Help me to find that key. In Jesus' Name. Amen

The world's answers to suffering

*"For with much wisdom comes much sorrow; the more
knowledge, the more grief." (v.18)*
For reading & meditation – Ecclesiastes 1:1-18

Today we look at the various answers – so called – which the world
has offered in relation to the problem of suffering. Omar Khayyam,
the poet, looked upon the world of suffering and said:

*To grasp this sorry scheme of things entire …
Shatter it to bits – and then remould it to my heart's desire.*

His answer was to remake the world with the possibility of suffering left
out.

Another answer is to accept the fact of suffering and meet it with
resigned anticipation. You say to yourself: "I knew it would come, I was
not caught unawares, for everything I hold can be taken away." This is
the attitude of disillusioned cynicism. Then another response is to give
way to self-pity. Those who follow this method of dealing with suffering
get pleasure out of feeling sorry for themselves. And many exaggerate
their troubles in order to increase the possibility of gaining others' sympathy.

Yet another way is the way of stoicism. This is the attitude of accepting the fact of suffering and steeling oneself against it.
I read about an Indian tribe in South America who
teach their children: "You are born into a world of
trouble. Shut your mouth, be quiet and bear it." You
can see how this type of thinking produces the stoical
Indian. The Eastern religions, such as Buddhism and
Hinduism, have complex answers to suffering, but
they, along with the others, lack one important thing –
there are no wounds that answer our wounds, no
death that will answer our death. Christ and Christ
alone gives us the final answer to suffering.

> **FURTHER STUDY**
>
> 1 Pet. 4:1-13;
> Job 11:16; Psa. 30:5
>
> 1.How are we to face
> suffering?
>
> 2.What is the
> assurance we have?

Prayer

O God, as I move from day to day in search of an answer to the problem of unmerited suffering, I see clearly that the world has found no satisfying solution to this
problem. My trust and confidence is in You. Lead on, dear Father. Amen

The Christian answer to suffering

"Look, the hour is near, and the Son of Man is betrayed into the hands of sinners. Rise, let us go!" (vv.45-46)

For reading & meditation – Matthew 26:36-46

Yesterday we looked at some of the world's ineffectual answers to the problem of unmerited suffering. In them there are no wounds to answer our wounds, no death to answer our death.

Their so-called answers remind me of a cartoon I once saw which depicted two toddlers in a children's boxing ring. Stripped for action, with nothing on but shorts and boxing gloves, they were ready for the fray. The attention of one of the youngsters was caught by two butterflies flitting just above his head and he stood gazing up at them, exposing himself to the blow which his opponent was about to land on his nose. Gazing at butterflies while in the midst of a conflict is a dangerous occupation. Any system of thought that takes your attention off the grim facts of life by calling attention to butterflies is doomed inevitably to produce pessimism as the blows begin to fall.

What, then, is the Christian answer to this problem? First, we must realistically face the fact that life involves suffering. There is no escaping that fact; to deny it is a denial of reality. I have found from experience that the first thing many Christians do when caught up in a form of suffering is to deny its reality and say something like this: "I don't have any problems, for Jesus is the Great Insulator between me and everything that happens." It is not lack of faith to acknowledge a problem. You don't have to dwell upon it, but before you can deal with it, you must acknowledge it. Remember, you must first be willing to face reality before you can expect to overcome it.

FURTHER STUDY

2 Cor. 4:1-17;
Psa. 34:19-20;
2 Tim. 2:12

1. What is the purpose of our affliction?

2. What has God promised?

Prayer

O God, give me courage to face up to issues and not dodge them. Help me to be open and honest. Father, I look to You now to help me put this into daily practice. For Jesus' sake. Amen.

Is suffering the result of sin?

"Do you think that these Galileans were worse sinners than all the other Galileans because they suffered this way?" (v.2)

For reading & meditation – Luke 13:1-9

Yesterday we ended by making the point that it is only when we realistically acknowledge a problem that we can take the steps to deal with it. The teaching that says you should not admit to having a problem as the negative thought that comes from such an admission will interfere with your ability to deal with it is psychologically and spiritually unsound.

The passage we read yesterday showed how Jesus, in the Garden of Gethsemane, dealt with the problem of His impending death on the cross: He first faced it in His feelings, and then went out to face the fact. "Rise, let us go!" The second thing we must do to deal with suffering is to recognise that not all suffering is due to personal sin. Some suffering is, of course, but not all. The person who violates God's moral laws must not be surprised when these laws kick back. The fact that not all suffering is due to personal sin can be seen from the account in John 9, where Jesus pointed out that personal or parental sin is not always at the back of physical calamities such as congenital blindness.

The point is made even more clearly in the passage before us today, where Jesus points out that calamities can stem from man's inhumanity to man (Pilate's butchering of Galilean Jews) or natural accidents or disasters (the collapse of the tower in Siloam), and therefore the people who suffer from them are not especially sinful. This takes away the self-righteous attitude of those who, being free from calamities themselves, view the problems of others as being the direct punishment of God upon their sin.

FURTHER STUDY

Job 1:1-5; 4:1-5:27; 8:1-22

1. What does Scripture say about Job?

2. What did his friends say?

Prayer

Father, I'm relieved to know that suffering is not always the result of personal sin. I'm willing to take my share of the blame for the problems I face, but help me not to become plagued with false guilt. Keep me balanced. Amen.

Turning tests into testimonies

"It will lead to an opportunity for your testimony."
(v. 13, NASB)

For reading & meditation – Luke 21:1-13

We look now at the third step in the process of dealing with unmerited suffering: don't spend too much time trying to understand the reason for suffering – focus rather on how you can deal with it. Notice, Jesus spent very little time trying to explain human suffering, much less explain it away. Had He undertaken to explain it, then His gospel would have become a philosophy – in which case it would not have been a gospel. A philosophy undertakes to explain everything, and then leaves everything as it was. Jesus undertook to explain little, but He changed everything He touched. He did not come to bring a philosophy, but a fact.

What was that fact? The fact was His own method of meeting suffering and transforming it into something higher. Out of this fact, we put together our philosophy – a system of principles and procedures by which we live out our life in this world. Notice that fact comes first, and then the philosophy about the fact. The good news is not merely "good news"; it is the fact of sin and suffering being met and overcome, and a way of life blazed out through them.

FURTHER STUDY

John 17:1-26;
16:33; Rom. 5:3-4

1. What did Jesus promise?

2. What did Jesus pray?

The fourth step is this: remind yourself that in God's universe, He allows only what He can use. In the passage before us today, Jesus gives the nine sources from which suffering comes upon us: confused religionists (false Christs), wars and conflicts in society, calamities in nature, and so on. Then He says this: "It will lead to an opportunity for your testimony." In other words, you are not to escape trouble, nor merely bear it as the will of God – you are to use it.

Prayer

Blessed Lord Jesus, You who used Your suffering to beautify everything You did, teach me the art of turning every test into a testimony and every tragedy into a triumph. For Your own dear Name's sake. Amen.

Gold and silver ...

"After John was put in prison, Jesus went into Galilee, proclaiming the good news of God." (v.14)

For reading & meditation – Mark 1:14-28

Yesterday we looked at the final answer to dealing with unmerited suffering: reminding ourselves that in God's universe, He only allows what He can use. Look again at the words of our text for today: "After John was put in prison, Jesus went into Galilee, proclaiming the good news of God." *After* the finest and truest of prophets had been put in prison and his preaching silenced by a wicked and unjust king, Jesus came preaching the good news about God.

How could there be good news about the God who had allowed such a thing to happen? But that is exactly what Jesus did proclaim – and proclaimed unashamedly. And why? Because Jesus knew that everything God allowed, He would use. By His action, He rejected the idea that a man like John should be exempt from suffering, and that God isn't good when He permits such things to happen.

Can you see now why God allows us to go through suffering? He does it so that, in the fires of affliction, we learn the secret of an alchemy which transmutes the base metal of injustice, and consequent suffering into the gold of character and the silver of God's purposes. In one place in the New Testament, Jesus refers to being "perfected" by His death on the cross (Luke 13:32, AV). Just think of it: the worst thing that can happen to a man – crucifixion – turns out to be the best that can happen to Him – perfection. This is the attitude we must cultivate if we are not only to face, but use suffering.

FURTHER STUDY

Psa. 121:1-8; 50:15;
Isa. 43:2

1. What was David's declaration?

2. What is your declaration today?

Prayer

O my Father, how can I ever sufficiently thank You for showing me this way of life? Nothing stops it – permanently. When men and circumstances concentrate on doing their worst – You bring out of it Your best. I see, I follow, and I am unafraid. Amen.

The triumphant attitude

"Do not let your hearts be troubled. Trust in God; trust also in me." (v.1)

For reading & meditation – John 14:1-14

By now it should be fairly obvious to even the newest disciple of Christ that if, like a "corn of wheat afraid to die", we shrink back from being ploughed into the red furrows of suffering, we shall remain alone – alone, and unfruitful. Someone has said, "God never uses anyone unless He puts them through the test of suffering and pain." Strong words. Do you find yourself flinching as you read them? I do. Yet it is not wrong to flinch at the approach of a spiritual test. God knows how you feel.

The issue, however, is not about flinching; it is about following. Are we willing to open our hearts to the Lord and say: "Do to me as You will"? I suggest the only way we will be able to do that is when we have the thought clearly fixed in our minds that God will never allow us to go through anything without providing all the grace we need to bear it, and will turn the test into a testimony that will eternally glorify Him and make our characters more like His.

Jesus, remember, began His ministry here on earth with a wilderness experience, and ended it with an Easter morning. He told His disciples in

the text before us today, "Let not your hearts be troubled", not because they were to be protected from troubles, but because they were to "trust in God". Faith in God will not save you from suffering, but it will save you through it – the suffering can be made into an instrument of redemption. Remember, you cannot bless without bleeding, and you cannot succour until you have suffered.

Prayer

O Father, I see that refusing to pay the ultimate price of surrendering to Your purposes is to choose deadness and death. Today I choose life. I am a "corn of wheat" not afraid, but willing to die. Help me, in Jesus' Name. Amen.

Going – yet not knowing

"And now, compelled by the Spirit, I am going to Jerusalem, not knowing what will happen to me there." (v.22)

For reading & meditation – Acts 20:17-35

We come now to examine another area into which our Lord, eager to obtain fruit from our lives, may be leading us: that of ambiguity and uncertainty. By ambiguity, I mean those situations we sometimes find ourselves in where the Lord's purposes are not clear, and by uncertainty, I mean the feelings we get when we don't know which direction to take on the road ahead.

Are you the kind of person who likes to see the way ahead as far as you possibly can? Do you find yourself getting irritated and frustrated when the Lord unfolds His purposes just one step at a time? If so, then your irritation is saying something about you. What is it saying? Perhaps it is saying that in this area of your life, you are "a corn of wheat afraid to die"; you are fearful of trusting yourself to the unseen and unknown purposes of God.

There isn't a Christian reading my words now who hasn't been called to walk this path of uncertainty and ambiguity, and there may be many who are there at this moment. The apostle Paul, in the verse before us today, was in this situation when he said: "I am going to Jerusalem, not knowing what will happen to me there" (v.22, GNB). What an honest admission: going – yet not knowing. Yet there seems to be no anxiety or apprehension in that statement. And why? Because the great apostle had died to all self-interest and. Having surrendered to God, he was not at the mercy of circumstances, situations, feelings – anything. Sure of God – the one great Certainty – he needed to fear no uncertainty.

FURTHER STUDY

James 4:10-17;
Prov. 27:1; Isa.
55:8

1.What should our
attitude be?

2.What picture does
James give us of life?

Prayer

O God, I see that unless my certainty is in You – the divine Certainty – I will be at the mercy of all uncertainties. Forgive my little antics of self-dependence. Help me to live in God-dependence. Amen.

"Talking to God all night"

"Therefore, if anyone is in Christ, he is a new creation ..."
(v.17)

For reading & meditation – 2 Corinthians 5:14-21

We ended yesterday by saying that because Paul had died to all self-interest, he was not at the mercy of ambiguity and uncertainty. Sure of God, he was sure of the future. You see, if you don't surrender to God, don't think you don't surrender. Everybody surrenders to something. If you don't surrender to God, then you will surrender to something else – your moods, your circumstances, your fears, your self-centred concerns. And if you do, you will end up becoming downcast and disillusioned.

A doctor tells of being called to see a patient, the head of a large company, who was having increasing attacks of asthma. The doctor could find no physical basis for the asthma, and so he asked the man: "Is there anything troubling you?" The patient replied: "No, doctor, I'm a member of a church, in fact an official in the church – nothing is troubling me."

The next day the patient again sent for the doctor and said to him: "Yesterday I told you nothing was troubling me, but I've been talking to God all night. I looked at the ceiling and saw the words: 'Seek first the kingdom of God.' Doctor, I've been seeking my own kingdom. I've been a completely self-centred man. But last night something happened to me. I'm seeking first the kingdom of God." The doctor said: "I went away with tears streaming down my cheeks. I had seen the birth of a soul." Surrender means not just the birth of a soul, but the birth of everything – new relationships, new perspectives on life, new power to face whatever comes, and a new sense of certainty and belonging – a new everything.

FURTHER STUDY

2 Cor. 8:1-9;
Matt. 19:21;
1 Cor. 10:24;
Phil. 2:4

1. What was Christ's example?

2. How can we imitate Him?

Prayer

O Father, it is obvious that unless my confidence is placed in the Ultimate, then I will not be able to cope with the immediate. Help me to be a fully surrendered person. For surrendered to You, I need surrender to nothing else. Amen.

The future – safe with Him

"For you died, and your life is now hidden with Christ in God. (v.3)

For reading & meditation – Colossians 3:1-15

We are discovering that when we are surrendered to the certain, we need never surrender to the uncertain. Sure of God, we do not have to be sure of anything else. A Christian who shrinks from walking the road of ambiguity and uncertainty in company with his Lord is saying, in effect: "My trust is in myself and not in Him." We don't like to put it in those terms, of course, because it challenges our self-interest. And if there is one thing we must learn about the self, it is that it does not like to be challenged, confronted or dislodged.

The self, however, must be disciplined to die. It must die to being first in order to live as second. That is why the centre of the kingdom of God is a cross. We must go through spiritually what Jesus went through physically – we must die and be buried in order to experience a resurrection into freedom and fullness of life.

A man who was part of a small group who had met together to deepen their spiritual understanding said: "I see what I need, and I see that I don't want what I need." In those words, he identified the struggle we all have with this business of self. Who is to be first – myself or God? That decision decides all other decisions – it is a seed decision. The moment you fully surrender to Christ, you automatically die to your own intentions and purposes and you gain a new perspective on life. From then on, you live in a state of Christ-reference – not self-reference. You look out at ambiguity and uncertainty and say: "I may not know what the future holds – so what? I know *who* holds the future."

FURTHER STUDY

2 Tim. 2:1-13;
Rom. 6:6;
2 Cor. 4:11

1. Which saying is trustworthy?

2. How does this apply to you?

Prayer

My Father and my God, I see now that I've been out of focus, and all of life's pictures have been blurred and distorted. Help me to see life from a new point of view – Your point of view. In Jesus' Name I ask it. Amen.

Strangers and pilgrims

"… Therefore God is not ashamed to be called their God, for he has prepared a city for them." (v.16)

For reading & meditation – Hebrews 11:8-16

We continue meditating on the fact that one of the reasons why we find it so difficult to cope with ambiguity and uncertainty is because we have never really died to self-interest. We are more concerned about our own purposes than we are about His – hence we are uncertain and insecure.

Today we look at Abraham and the way he handled his situation of ambiguity and uncertainty. He was almost seventy-five years old when God called him to step out on the pathway of uncertainty. There he was, loading up his camel caravan with his wife and nephew, bound for … somewhere. The Amplified Bible puts if most effectively when it says: "… he went, although he did not know or trouble his mind about where he was to go."

Charles Swindoll humorously pictures a conversation between Abraham and his neighbours going something like this: "Abraham, where are your going?" "I'm moving." "Why? Why ever would you want to leave Ur?" "God has made it clear that I should go." "God? You've been talking to Him again?" "Right. He told me to leave. I must go."

FURTHER STUDY

Gen. 12:1-9;
Psa. 25:9, 48:14;
Matt. 1:1

1. What was the result of Abraham's obedience?

2. What followed his first step of obedience?

"Well, where are you going?" "I don't know; He didn't tell me that." "Wait a minute, you know you ought to go, but you don't know where you ought to go?" "Yes." "Abraham, you really have gone off the deep end." And so it continues. It isn't easy to obey without understanding. It is the same thing that we talked about two days ago – going – without knowing. It might help to remind ourselves of the term God sometimes uses to describe us – strangers and pilgrims. People on the move, free to follow Him wherever He leads – regardless.

Prayer

O God, You who wrap me around as the atmosphere wraps itself around my body. Let me respond to You as my physical body responds to its environment – and lives. Help me to trust You even when I cannot trace You. In Jesus' Name. Amen.

A personal word

"But by the grace of God I am what I am ..." (v.10)
For reading & meditation – 1 Corinthians 15:1-11

Today we ask ourselves: Why is it that even though we may have a fairly mature faith in God, we still find it frustrating to be caught up in situations where we have no clear direction or control? The root cause of this is misplaced dependency – we depend too much upon ourselves and not enough upon God.

As I examine my own life, I am constantly amazed that after over fifty years' experience in the Christian faith, I am still sometimes prone to take the way of independence rather than dependence. Do you not find a similar tendency in yourself? I want God's way – so very much – but I want it on my own terms. Granted, this is less of a problem now than it was, say, thirty years ago, but it is still sometimes a struggle nevertheless.

What does this say about me? It says that in this area of my life, there is still a need to die to my own self-concern, and even before these lines were written I had to get down on my knees and acknowledge this before the Lord. I may still have struggles with this issue in the future, but I know for sure that at this moment, my will is more yielded to Him than ever. Perhaps this is the last battle I shall have to fight on this matter, and when I find myself facing situations in the future that are vague and ambiguous without fearing the outcome, I will know the issue has been settled once and for all. I have exposed my heart to you in obedience to the prompting of the Spirit. I need Him as much as you.

FURTHER STUDY

Rom. 8:1-14; 15:1;
Gal. 5:24;
1 Pet. 2:24

1. What happens if we live according to the sinful nature?

2. How do we know we are sons of God?

Prayer

O Father, as we see yet again where we should be centred – in You – help us to die in those areas of life where we have established our independence. Only in You can we be safe and steady and growing. Help us, dear Lord. Amen.

The crucified "self"

"I have been crucified with Christ and I no longer live, but Christ lives in me ..." (v.20)

For reading & meditation – Galatians 2:15-21

If there is one note ringing through these pages, it is this: to the extent that we are afraid to die to our self-interest, to that extent will our Christian lives be unfruitful. We remind ourselves again: "Unless a grain of wheat falls into the earth and dies, it remains just one grain; never becomes more but lives by itself alone. But if it dies, it produces many others and yields a rich harvest" (John 12:24, Amplified Bible). It is easy to say but difficult to put into practice – difficult but not impossible.

Today we ask ourselves: What exactly happens when we "die" to self? Does it mean that the "self" undergoes annihilation? No. The death to which we are called is the death of the false life we have been living, the false ideas and values we have set up, the false world of sin and evil, and the false self, organised around self-concern. When Paul said, "I have been crucified with Christ", he meant that he had died to all the purposes in his life except Christ's purposes.

This whole passage telling of Paul's burial and resurrection is one of the most exciting in the New Testament. He goes on to say: "I no longer live, but Christ lives in me." Paul discovered that life was much more positive and powerful when he pursued God's purposes rather than his own purposes. He got on better with Christ than he did with himself. This may take some thinking through, but the truth is, if you won't live with God, you won't be able to live harmoniously with yourself – nor, for that matter, with anyone else.

FURTHER STUDY

Gal. 5:1-25;
Rom. 6:2; Col. 3:3

1. To what have we been called?

2. How is this achieved?

Prayer

O God, I just can't go through life with this ghastly contradiction – the self – at the centre of my being. I cannot bear this constant civil war within me. Command it to cease and command me to be free. In Jesus' Name. Amen.

"Grace upon grace"

"And from his fullness have we all received, grace upon grace." (v.16, RSV)

For reading & meditation – John 1:1-17

Today we ask: What purpose does God have in leading us into situations which are uncertain and ambiguous? He does so in order that we might learn to depend on Him and not on ourselves. Just as in times of loneliness we learn to realise His presence, so in times of uncertainty we learn to realise His power.

The major reason why our lives are unfruitful lies right here: we depend more on our own strength than we do on His. How can God teach us dependence unless He puts us into situations which are so uncertain that we are compelled either to choose the way of frustration or the way of faith? And if we draw back from entering such situations, we will miss a valuable spiritual education and our lives will become barren.

A statement I came across some time ago sums up what I want to say cocncerning ambiguity and uncertainty. It is this: "God's purposes are always God's enablings." In other words, when God steers you into strange and uncertain situations, He will keep you very much in the dark concerning His purposes, but He will not leave you bereft of His grace. The purpose of God and the grace of God are two sides of the one coin. If you accept the purpose, you get the grace; if you refuse the purpose, you annul the grace. Anything God purposes for you, He gives you the grace to perform. John speaks in our text for today of "grace upon grace". One preacher I know translates that text like this: "Use the grace I give you and rest assured – there will always be more to follow."

FURTHER STUDY

2 Cor. 12:1-10;
Eph. 2:6-7;
Phil. 4:19

1. How did Paul view his "thorn in the flesh"?

2. What was his attitude?

Prayer

O Father, how wonderful it would be if I could master this lesson today, and become a living illustration of "grace upon grace". May it be so, to the honour and glory of Your peerless and precious Name. Amen.

The final battle

"For the love of money is a root of all kinds of evil …"
(v.10)

For reading & meditation – 1 Timothy 6:3-11

We now start examining some of the areas of life into which we are led by God in order that He might make our lives more fruitful and profitable to Him. First we focus upon the problem of cramped financial circumstances.

No one can deny that money plays an enormous part in our lives. It was Balzac who said more than a century ago: "The final battle for Christian discipleship will be over the money problem: till that is solved there can be no universal application of Christianity." It comes as a great surprise to many new Christians that the Bible talks a good deal about money, and more than one preacher has pointed out that when Jesus was here on earth, this was one of the subjects He talked about most.

One of the most interesting aspects of money to a Christian is that through either the giving or the withholding of it, God is able to steer our lives into the areas in which He wants us involved. Do you find yourself in financial straits at the moment? Does your bank account need month-to-month resuscitation? Then don't panic – God may be allowing this financial stringency in order to teach you some valuable lessons about Himself. Thousands of Christians will testify that God has no more certain way of getting our undivided attention than by withholding money or putting us into tight financial circumstances. How strange that when our pockets are full, often God has to shout to get our attention, but when they are empty, we are alert and ready to hear His faintest whisper.

FURTHER STUDY

James 5:1-5;
Eccl. 5:10;
Jer. 17:11

1. What is avarice?

2. What is the lesson of the partridge?

Prayer

O Father, if it is true that the final battle for Christian discipleship will be over the money problem, then help me resolve this issue once and for all in these next few days. Help me to make whatever I own the instrument of Your purposes. Amen.

God's four purposes for money

"But if we have food and clothing, we will be content with that. (v.8)

For reading & meditation – 1 Timothy 6:6-19

Before we can understand what God may be trying to achieve in our lives by putting us into tight financial circumstances, we must know something of our Lord's purposes for money. Many Christians think that the purpose of money is to provide security, establish independence, or create power and influence, but this is a very worldly view of the subject. The Bible shows us that God has four basic purposes which He wants to achieve through money – and understanding these purposes is crucial if we are to be fruitful and productive Christians.

The first purpose of money is to provide basic needs. It's surprising how little money we need in order to sustain the basic needs of life. These needs can be summed up in the words food, clothing and shelter. And God demonstrates His loving care by assuring us of His help in obtaining these basic essentials: "And why do you worry about clothes? See how the lilies of the field grow. They do not labour or spin … will he not much more clothe you, O you of little faith?" (Matt. 6:28-30).

Since the dawn on time, humankind has tried to become independent of God. There are tendencies in our fallen nature to be self-sufficient and self-supporting. We would much rather pray, "Give us this month our monthly pay cheque" than "Give us this day our daily bread." And why? Because it doesn't bring us face to face with our need to be daily dependent on the Lord. How wise was our Lord in including that phrase in the model prayer He gave His disciples. He knew the recognition of daily needs would help to produce daily dependence.

FURTHER STUDY

Matt. 6:19-34,
10:29-31; 1 Pet. 5:7

1. What are we to seek first?
2. What will follow?

Prayer

Father, I pray that You will bring me under the complete sway of Your Spirit so that my spiritual dependence will not be year by year, month by month or week by week – but day by day. This I ask in Jesus' Name. Amen.

True contentment?

"But godliness with contentment is great gain."(v.6)
For reading & meditation – 1 Timothy 6:6

We continue meditating on the first of God's four purposes for money – to provide our basic needs. We saw yesterday that God longs for us to be dependent on Him. This is not because God is possessive, but because He knows that we experience our greatest happiness and freedom when we rely on Him alone. When we fail to recognise our need for God, we tend to lose our love for God. And the more we lose our love for God, the more we come to depend upon ourselves.

Permit me to remind you again of the text we looked at yesterday: "If we have food and clothing, we will be content" (1 Tim. 6:8). Contentment is the satisfaction we get from knowing there will be provision for our basic needs. We begin to lose our contentment when we compare what we have with what others have – and then before long expectations dominate our focus. To the degree that our expectations increase, contentment diminishes.

One of the great advantages of being content with basics is that it equips us to resist the alluring advertising which seeks to convince us that we are not able really to enjoy life unless we buy some new commodity. A contented person feels wealthy because he knows that what he already possesses is all he needs for daily living. A veteran missionary, meeting some new recruits to the mission field, surprised them by saying: "The first thing I would like you to do is to make a list of all the things you think you need – then I will spend some time with you showing you how to do without them."

FURTHER STUDY

Phil. 4:1-11;
Prov. 15:16;
Heb. 13:5

1.What was Paul's testimony?

2.How should we live?

Prayer

O my Father, I see that material things can be a good servant but a bad master. Deliver me from the bondage of the material and help me to become a truly content-ed person. In Jesus' Name I ask it. Amen.

Presumption versus faith

"Be still before the Lord and wait patiently for him …"
(v.7)

For reading & meditation – Psalm 37:1-26

We look now at God's second purpose for money: to confirm His loving direction in our lives. God will use the supply of money or the lack of it to confirm His direction and guidance for many of the decisions we make in our lives. I constantly meet Christians who tell me that one of the biggest lessons they have learned in the Christian life is that of discerning God's guidance through His giving or His withholding of money.

Some years ago, a minister shared with me how he had asked God to guide him over a certain project, and part of his prayer, he said, went like this: "Lord, give me the money to do this, or else it just cannot be done." The money didn't come, so the minister went ahead and borrowed money for the project. A few weeks later, the project got into difficulties and he was declared bankrupt.

I said to him: "Do you know what made you go ahead even though God did not provide the money?" He paused for a few minutes, and said with tears in his eyes: "I had not then learned the difference between presumption and faith." "What is the difference?" I asked. He replied: "Faith is trusting God to achieve His purposes through us, presumption is deciding what we want to accomplish and trying to get God to do it for us." It is so easy to claim that Christ is Lord of our lives, but, as someone put it: "His Lordship is only confirmed when we are obedient to the promptings and limitations which He places on our daily decisions."

FURTHER STUDY

Psa. 46:1-11;40:1;
Isa. 26:8

1. How can we know God?

2. How much time will you spend waiting on Him today?

Prayer

My Lord and my God, You know my proneness to "nudge" You when I don't think You are working things out right. Make me sensitive to the promptings of Your Spirit and the limitations that You set upon my life. In Jesus' Name I ask it. Amen.

Generosity generates

"Share with God's people who are in need. Practise hospitality." (v.13)

For reading & meditation – Romans 12:9-21

Today we look at God's third purpose for money: to bless and enrich other Christians. One of the characteristics which God wants to develop in us is that of generosity, for our generosity will determine how much spiritual light we have in our being. Take this verse: "If your Eye is generous, the whole of your body will be illumined" (Matt. 6:22, Moffatt). If your "eye" – your outlook on life, your whole way of looking at things and people – is generous, then your whole personality is illuminated, is lighted up. If you have a greedy or selfish "eye", your whole being will be filled with darkness.

In Acts 11:27-30 we read about a severe famine that caused suffering to many Jewish Christians. The church at Antioch – made up mostly of Gentiles – sent an offering to their fellow believers in Jerusalem, and that offering was an important means of tearing down national and cultural barriers between them, and building bonds of genuine Christian love. God likens generous giving to reaping a harvest: "He who sows sparingly will also reap sparingly, and he who sows bountifully will also reap bountifully" (2 Cor. 9:6, RSV).

FURTHER STUDY

1 Kings 17:8-16;
Prov. 25:21; 11:25;
Eccl. 11:1

1. What is the lesson of the widow of Zarephath?

2. How will you be generous today?

Perhaps the greatest benefit of generous giving to other Christians, however, is this – it results in "an overflowing tide of thanksgiving to God" (v.12, Phillips). Yes, God will give you much so that you can give away much, and when you take your gifts to those who need them they will break out in thanksgiving and praise of God for your help. Giving to the needs of fellow Christians means that many will thank God and fill His Church with praise.

Prayer

O God, help be to become a truly generous person, for I see that when I am generous, then my generosity generates generosity in others. I ask this in the peerless and exalted Name of the Lord Jesus. Amen.

What is a financial miracle?

*" 'Test me in this,' says the Lord Almighty, 'and see if I
will not throw open the floodgates of heaven …' " (v.10)*

For reading & meditation – Malachi 3:1-12

We look now at God's fourth purpose for money: to show His divine
power. God is a supernatural God – something Christians seem to
forget – and He delights to demonstrate His reality and power among His
people. One means through which God has chosen to do this is through
His miraculous provision of money.

What is a financial miracle? It is a supernatural event whereby God
provides one of His children with the money required to meet a financial
need – and usually it involves such precise timing that it cannot fail to
point to the Lord's direct intervention. When a Christian prays about a
financial need, for example, and an unexpected gift is given to him by
someone who knows nothing about the need, the supernatural power of
God is demonstrated.

In the days of Elijah, the nation of Israel tried to worship God and
serve Baal at the same time. Elijah knew that this would inevitably lead
to God's judgment, so he proposed a simple test. The test involved building two altars, one for God and one for Baal, and whichever answered by
a display of supernatural power was the one whom they would worship.
The prophets of Baal cried out to their non-existent
deity all day, but nothing happened. Then Elijah
prayed, and in response to his prayer God sent fire
from heaven.

One of the biggest of the false gods of this age is
money. It has become an idol because people expect
from it what only God can give – true security. As the
world hankers after money, God wants to prove to
those who seek Him that they will not lack any good
thing.

Prayer

O Father, help me to see that I grow into the image of the god that I serve. I don't
want to be like money – hard and metallic; I want to be like You – gracious and
beneficent. Help me to keep my focus only on You. In Jesus' Name I pray. Amen.

The day you "die"

"Take your son, your only son, Isaac, whom you love …"
(v.2)

For reading & meditation – Genesis 22:1-14

Having seen God's four purposes for money, we are now ready to ask: What part does money play in our lives? Does it draw us closer to God, or drive us further away from Him? Is our security in silver – or in the Saviour?

Most of us would claim that we are serving God. We would strenuously deny that we have a greater love for money than we do for the Master. God, however, is aware that what we believe to be the situation is not always so. Sometimes He has to bring us into cramped financial circumstances so that we realise where our true security lies.

Although the story of Abraham and Isaac does not have a precise application to what we are saying here, there are certain similarities which I consider do apply. First, God singled out in Abraham's life the thing he most loved – his only son. God often starts His test of our character with the thing that we love the most. Is money one of your greatest loves? If so, recognise and acknowledge it right now.

Second, God pinned Abraham down to a fixed time and place. God's way of doing business always involves a specific time and place.

FURTHER STUDY

Matt. 26:1-13;
Luke 21:4;
Acts 4:34-35

1. What did Jesus say about the woman who anointed Him?

2. What was the attitude of the early Church?

"Sacrifice him *there* as a burnt offering" (v.2). Let the place where you are sitting now be your meeting place with God. God asked Abraham to sacrifice his only son. Abraham could never have lifted the knife over his son unless he had "died" to him in his emotions. Without this emotional break, the offering is only a meaningless ritual. This must be the day on which you "die" to the bondage of money.

Prayer

O Father, Your timing is perfect. Today, by faith, I "die" to all emotional attachments to money, and lay every financial bondage on Your altar. Father, it's done – I'm free. Help me now to live out that freedom. In Jesus' Name. Amen.

Problems? No, prods!

"… God … is using your sufferings to make you ready for his kingdom." (v. 5, TLB)

For reading & meditation – 2 Thessalonians 1:1-12

We pause at this point to remind ourselves of the principle we are seeking to understand, namely that in God's order of things, life is always preceded by death. A grain of wheat has within it the potential of becoming many grains of wheat, but first the solitary grain must fall into the ground and die. It is only after death that its potential is released, and out of the dying comes an abundant harvest. That principle is not just to be seen as an interesting fact of nature; if our lives are to be fruitful, then we, too, must be willing to die to our own purposes so that we might live to God's.

The next sphere of life we examine is the area of obstacles and opposition. Would you like your life to be free of those potentially frustrating situations that block your way or impede your spiritual development? Then let me say at once, you could be worse off without them. The obstacles and opposition you face can turn out to be prods – prods toward your spiritual growth.

A minister friend of mine who was going through a period of great difficulty once asked me to pray with him that God would remove all the obstacles from his ministry. I put my hand lovingly on his shoulder and replied: "If He does, it will make your ministry less effective." He saw the point, and instead asked me to pray that God would help him to die to his own concerns. I did, and from that day to this, his ministry has flourished and become extremely fruitful. And so, my friend, can yours.

FURTHER STUDY

Phil. 1:1-14;
Acts 5:41;
Rom. 8:17

1. How did Paul view his setbacks?

2. What was the positive outcome

Prayer

O Father, more and more the conviction grows that it is not what happens to me, but what I do with it, that is important. Deepen this conviction within me so that it becomes a controlling one – today and every day. In Jesus' Name. Amen.

Acquiescence – or control?

*"I am ready for anything through the strength of the one
who lives within me." (v.13, Phillips)*

For reading & meditation – Philippians 4:10-20

Day by day, as we unfold this thrilling theme of *The Corn of Wheat Afraid to Die*, it is becoming increasingly obvious that God gives us a choice – a choice of either to live or to die. We can live for the fulfilment of our own desires, or we can die to our desires and live for His.

This is perhaps the moment that we should come to grips with the question which people often ask when this issue of "dying to self" is raised: "Isn't this a terribly passive attitude to life? And doesn't it tend to diminish personal responsibility and self-control?" John Dewey, the famous American educator, held that view. Once, when lecturing to his students, he drew a line down a blackboard and on one side listed those systems of thought which teach control, and on the other those systems that teach acquiescence. On the "control" side he put "science", and on the "acquiescence" side he put "religion".

To be fair, he should have written, "Some forms of religion". The religion of Jesus Christ does not produce passive and acquiescent disciples, but surrendered disciples – surrendered to God, but surrendered to nothing else. They rise from the dust of self-surrender to lay hold on the raw materials of life – good, bad and indifferent – and use them. Would you describe the early Christians as passive and acquiescent? I wouldn't. Surrendered – yes. Acquiescent – no. Surrendering to God so that He may work in and through us may at first seem passive, but actually it represents the most amazingly positive and active method of dealing with life. Other ways are possible, but no other way is as powerful.

FURTHER STUDY

Phil. 2:12-30;
Eph. 3:16;
2 Cor. 9:8

1. What are we able to do when God works in us?

2. What does God's grace produce in us?

Prayer

Gracious and loving heavenly Father, I am so thankful that You show me a way of life that doesn't demean me, but develops me. I fall at Your feet, and lo – I rise to new purposes and new achievements. I am eternally grateful. Amen.

Rise up and walk

"In the name of Jesus Christ of Nazareth rise up and walk." (v.6, AV)

For reading & meditation – Acts 3:1-16

We said yesterday that when we die to self-interests we rise to meet life, not passively, but actively. In fact, self-surrender is the most amazingly active method of dealing with life.

Take, for example, Peter and John. When they met the man asking for alms, they were, as we say, "financially embarrassed" and unable to help in that way. Most of us would have let the incident go at that, for what can you do if you have no money in a world like this? Not these men, however – they took up this poverty into the purpose of their lives and used it. What do I mean? This: if they had had some money, they might have tossed him a coin and that would have been the end of it – their adequacy on that level would have blocked the higher good.

Instead, conscious that they could not minister to him at one level – the financial – they sought to minister to him at another level – the spiritual. The result was that the obstacle on one level was turned into an opportunity on another. "Rise up and walk," they said to the man – and rise up he did. Nothing passive about that! As one wag put it: "The lame man asked for alms, but instead he got legs!" Forgive me for extending this illustration beyond the bounds of proper biblical exposition, but there are many of us who need to look at the things lying lame around us, and perhaps even within us – higher ministries, spiritual aptitudes – and say to them, "Rise up and walk." Then together we shall walk on into the temple of wider and more effective living.

FURTHER STUDY

Matt. 9:1-8;
John 14:13, 20:31;
Phil. 2:9-11

1. Why is the Name of Jesus so powerful?

2. What will happen one day?

Prayer

O God, forgive me for failing to see the opportunities in every obstacle. Help me to understand that when I am blocked on one level, then I can break out on another. Nothing can deter me when my will coincides with Yours. Thank You, Father. Amen.

The divine-human partnership

"To this end I labour, struggling with all his energy, which so powerfully works in me." (v.29)

For reading & meditation – Colossians 1:15-29

We spend another day focusing on the question: Does self-surrender mean that we become passive and acquiescent? At first sight, it seems to be so – we surrender to Another. Do we resign ourselves to whatever comes, letting this "Another" do everything for us?

We talked a few days ago about John Dewey's suggestion that "science" encourages control, while "religion" encourages acquiescence. Actually, when we surrender to Christ, we experience, not passivity, but a new type of control. Jesus said: "My Father is always at his work … and I, too, am working" (John 5:17). In God's universe, there is always work to do – creative work. But what sort of creative work? Listen to this: "And we know that all things work together for good to them that love God" (Rom. 8:28, AV).

How can that be? We know that all things do not of themselves work together for good. The Revised Standard Version puts it like this: "In everything God works for good with those who love him." Note the change – "with those who love him". Not "to", but "with". Can you see the truth underlying this text? Given our consent and co-operation, God is able to retrieve some good out of everything that happens to us. Given our consent and co-operation – ah, there's the rub. In order to achieve good out of bad, God requires us to work "with" Him – this is not acquiescence, but control. Look again at the text for today: "I labour, struggling" – the human; "with all his energy, which so powerfully works in me" – the divine. What a picture – the human and the divine working together – in "control".

FURTHER STUDY

Eph. 3:1-19;
John 14:20; 17:23;
Rev. 3:20

1. What was Paul's prayer for the Ephesians?

2. What does this produce?

Prayer

My Father and my God, what can I say? I surrender to You, and the next thing I know is that I am taken into partnership with You. It just seems too good to be true – but too good not to be true. Thank You, Father. Amen.

There's always the "next"

"… and they went to another village." (v.56)
For reading & meditation – Luke 9:51-62

What are we discovering? We are seeing that nothing is lost when we surrender ourselves to God – indeed, everything is gained. When we lose ourselves, we find ourselves. We throw ourselves at Christ's feet, and end up by sitting with Him on His throne, where He invites us to co-operate with Him in turning chaos into cosmos and bringing good out of everything. What a way to live! I wouldn't change it for anything.

When we fully understand what "dying to self" means, we then face obstacles and opposition in an entirely different frame of mind. We see them in the way Jesus saw them – not as obstacles, but as opportunities. When the Samaritans refused to receive Jesus and His disciples, the account says that, after Jesus had rebuked the disciples for wanting to retaliate, "they went to another village". Life always has "another village". If you are opposed in this one, then you pass on to the next.

If there is one lesson I have learned in life, it is this: there is always a "next". And that next village was, in fact, nearer Jesus' final goal. He didn't have to go so far the next day. He advanced toward His goal by way of the snobbery and fear that He encountered among the Samaritans. Thank God life always has "another village". Is the way ahead strewn with endless obstacles and opposition? Then, providing you have died to your own instinct for self-preservation, you and God are able to team up and make the obstacles into new opportunities. Nothing can frustrate the Christian who has died to himself, and lives out the purposes of Another. Nothing.

FURTHER STUDY

Acts 16:1-15;
John 16:13;
Rom. 8:14

1. What happened when Paul's way was blocked?

2. Who was leading Paul?

Prayer

Lord Jesus, You who were never deterred by the blocking of Your plans, help me to approach life with that same attitude. Show me that when one "village" remains closed to me, there is always the "next". For Your own dear Name's sake. Amen.

Victim – or victor?

*"... the immeasurable greatness of his power in us who believe,
according to the working of his great might ..."* (vv.19-20, RSV)

For reading & meditation – Ephesians 1:11-23

Permit me to ask you: What will the obstacles and opposition you meet do to you today? Will they make you bitter, or will they make you better? The last word is not with them, but with you. If your own concerns and interests are well and truly "dead", and you are committed to pursuing God's purposes, then the issue is not so much what your circumstances will do to you, but what you will do to your circumstances.

The Christian who understands this has the power to say to life – do your worst, I have the resources to take every negative and turn it into a positive. Nothing successfully opposes the believer whose life is hidden with Christ in God. Jesus once faced great opposition in His ministry: "They were filled with madness, and began to discuss with one another what they should do to Jesus" (Luke 6:11, Weymouth). Here was opposition in its most terrifying form.

What did Jesus do? Listen again to the Weymouth translation: "About that time He went out ... into the hill country to pray" (v.12). Prayer, that powerful means of communicating with God and controlling, not so much the situation as the outcome of the situation, made Jesus, not a victim, but a victor. One of the major purposes of God seems to be that of producing character in His children. Not their ease, not their happiness – except as a by-product – but their character. And how is character produced? One way it is produced is through overcoming difficulties. So don't groan at the obstacles and opposition that face you today – grow in them. They help to sharpen your character – and your wits!

FURTHER STUDY

Rom. 8:28-37;
5:17; Rev. 1:5-6

1. What are we through Christ?

2. What should we be doing in life?

Prayer

O God, forgive me that so often I cry to You for tasks equal to my powers. Help me to pray instead for power equal to my tasks. I ask this, not for my sake, but for Yours. Amen.

Attacked – but not injured

*"I am sending you out like sheep among wolves. Therefore
be as shrewd as snakes and as innocent as doves." (v.16)*

For reading & meditation – Matthew 10:5-20

The gospel of Jesus Christ is the only faith that dares to say to its followers: "Behold, I send you forth as sheep in the midst of wolves" (AV). It is as if Jesus is saying: "You will have as much chance of escaping difficulties and opposition as sheep have in the midst of wolves." If you are a Christian, you can expect people to oppose you – even hurt you. Notice what I say: "hurt" you, but not "harm" you. Sometimes God may not protect us from being hurt, but He will protect us from being harmed.

One writer puts that same thought in this way: "At times God may suffer His children to be attacked, but providing they are fully abandoned to Him and His purposes, He will never suffer them to be injured." He is using the words "attack" to mean physical or verbal abuse, and "injury" to mean the scarring of the soul. In that sense, no attack from without can injure us; we can only be injured from within by wrong perspectives and wrong choices.

Some time ago I quoted a maxim that goes like this: "No man is safe unless he can stand anything that happens to him." A young student wrote to me and said: "Then there aren't many people who are 'safe' – are there?" I point you now to another verse to lay alongside our text for today: "For the Lamb in the midst of the throne will be their shepherd" (Rev. 7:17, RSV). Christ's being on the throne is the pledge that we, too – somehow, some way – shall pass out of the midst of the "wolves" of people and things, to victory over both.

FURTHER STUDY

2 Cor. 4:1-12;
Col. 3:3-4;
Rev. 1:18

1. What was Paul's testimony?

2. How did Paul view life?

Prayer

Lord Jesus, Master of every situation – even on a cross where You dispensed forgiveness to Your crucifiers – give me this mastery over circumstances. Help me to see I am not beaten until I am beaten within. Amen.

"Stay in the kitchen"

"God … will not allow you to be tempted beyond what you are able, but … will provide the way of escape …" (v.13, NASB)

For reading & meditation – 1 Corinthians 10:1-13

We turn now to another sphere of life from which many of us might long to be exempted – the area of strong and unrelenting temptation. Most of us, if we are honest, would like to be excused from having to face temptation, but temptation has its uses: it can work in God's hands to the development of character, and help perfect the image of Christ in our lives. Mark Antony was called "the silver-throated orator of Rome", but he had the fatal flaw of not being able to resist a temptation.

That indictment, I'm afraid, applies not just to Mark Antony, or to the ranks of the unconverted, but to many in the Church also. We all face temptation, and unfortunately far too many of us fall beneath its power. The root meaning of the word "temptation" (Greek, *peirasmos*) is that of testing. The dictionary defines temptation as "the act of enticement to do wrong, by promise of pleasure or gain". Charles Swindoll commented: "Temptation motivates you to be bad by promising something good."

Isn't that just like the devil? Are you facing a particularly fierce temptation at the moment? Then take heart – you have all the power you need to stand up under the blast. Harry S. Truman, a former President of the United States, is famous for saying: "If you don't like the heat, get out of the kitchen." But I've not found anyone who was able to stay strong without spending time in the "kitchen". In coming to grips with the sphere of temptation, my advice is: "If you can't stand the heat, stay *in* the kitchen – and in God's strength, learn to handle it."

FURTHER STUDY

James 1:1-15;
Rom. 8:31;
Heb. 2:18

1. When are we tempted?

2. On what basis can we face and use temptation?

Prayer

O Father, show me how to experience continual victory over temptation. And help me, in this area of life also, not to be "a corn of wheat afraid to die". I face the fire in Your strength, knowing that You never allow what You cannot use. Amen.

"The original quitters"

"They forgot what he had done, the wonders he had shown them." (v.11)

For reading & meditation – Psalm 78:1-11

We ended yesterday with the advice: "If you can't stand the heat, stay *in* the kitchen – and in God's strength, learn to handle it." The psalm before us today begins by commanding us to listen: "O my people, hear my teaching." You have only to read a few verses of this psalm to see that the psalmist Asaph is recalling the disobedience which characterised the Jews during their forty years' wandering in the wilderness. Then a strange verse appears: "The men of Ephraim, though armed with bows, turned back on the day of battle" (v.9).

These Ephraimites were equipped with all they needed for warfare, but on the day of the battle – that is, the first day of the fray – they "turned back". Although well armed, in the moment of testing they were overcome by fear. Doubtless they paraded well and looked fine as they marched out to battle, but when they came face to face with the enemy, the only weapon they used was a cloud of dust as they retreated en masse – and in a hurry.

A preacher I once heard referred to the Ephraimites in this verse as "the original quitters". What an indictment. The Ephraimites live on, you know; they are to be found in the rank and file of many a modern-day congregation. They look fine in church on Sunday mornings with a hymn book and a Bible in their hands, but let the hot rays of temptation beat upon them – and they run. They surrender to temptation because they have never learned how to surrender to God. As I've said before – when we surrender to God, then we need not surrender to anything else.

FURTHER STUDY

Dan. 1:1-21;
Rom. 6:13;
Eph. 6:13

1. How did Daniel resist the temptation to compromise?

2. What are the results of resisting temptation?

Prayer

Lord Jesus, help me clarify to myself whether I am surrendered or not. For I see that if I do not fall at Your feet, then I fall at the feet of things and circumstances. Show me at whose feet I am lying. For Your own Name's sake. Amen.

"No" to self – "Yes" to God

"... seeing that you have put off the old nature with its practices and have put on the new nature ..." (vv.9-10, RSV)

We continue from where we left off yesterday, saying that the reason why many of today's Christians surrender so easily to temptation is because they have never really learned how to surrender to God. Many (not all) of the people who come for counselling are struggling with the fact that they have never understood how to die to their own purposes and live for God's purposes. Time and time again in counselling, it has been my experience to watch a person slowly recognise that his problem is due, not so much to what is happening to him as his reactions to what is happening to him – and then decide not to do anything about it.

I am saddened by the trend to treat biblical principles as optional rather than obligatory. It is amazing to notice the casualness with which so many approach Scripture and say: "I suppose I shouldn't really be living like this; I had better try to change – if I can." When that attitude is present, there is little hope of change. You see, if there is no experienced death, there can be no experienced life.

When a person does not see the importance of recognising, albeit painfully, that God's way is the way of obedience, irrespective of whether we feel like it or not, and involves death to wrong patterns of thinking and wrong patterns of behaving, there will be no victory and no change. Putting on the new nature requires first putting off the old nature by asserting, with all the conviction possible, that one is going to go God's way no matter how much the carnal nature argues to the contrary.

FURTHER STUDY

James 4:1-8;
Eph. 6:11;
1 Pet. 5:8-9

1. What 3 steps are given in James 4 for overcoming the devil?

2. How would you apply these steps in a practical way?

Prayer

O Father, help me shout a thunderous "No" to anything that is contrary to You, and a mighty "Yes" to all You want to do in my life. And when my carnal nature argues back, help me to put it in its place – under my feet. In Jesus' Name I pray. Amen.

Be a nonconformist

"Don't let the world around you squeeze you into its own mould ..." (v.2, Phillips)

For reading & meditation – Romans 12:1-13

We must spend some more time focusing on the fact that many of today's Christians are like the Ephraimites we spoke of a few days ago – good at parading, but not so good in battle. They cry out for help with their problems, but when confronted with the demands of Scripture, one of which is to die to self, they scurry like rats down the first bolthole they can find. They want a medicine man with a quick cure, not direct advice about how to repent of their egocentricity.

I sometimes wonder to myself whether this trend in today's Church is the result of our being brain-washed by an age that tends to make quitting a way of life. Anna Sklar, in her book *Runaway Wives*, uncovered an incredible statistic of American life when she said that a decade ago, for every woman who walked away from her home and family responsibility, 600 husbands and fathers did so. Today, for each man who does that, two women do.

My purpose in making this statement is not to take sides with either group, but simply to point out that, more and more, the modern trend is to choose the way of escape as the method of dealing with problems. Things that were once viewed by society as a stigma are now accepted without the flicker of an eyelid. "Let's just quit" are almost household words. A marriage gets shaky, hits a few rough patches and the solution is: "Let's get a divorce." How much of today's worldly patterns are affecting our thinking, I wonder? And how much are we letting the world squeeze us into its own mould?

FURTHER STUDY

Matt. 6:19-24;
1 Kings 18:21;
Eph. 6:5; James 1:8

1. What does it mean to have singleness of heart?

2. How does Satan seek to divert us?

Prayer

Father, make me a nonconformist – not in a denominational sense, but in a dynamic sense. Forgive me if I have allowed the world to squeeze me into its own mould. Change my way of thinking to Your way of thinking. In Jesus' Name. Amen.

The greatest temptation

"Jesus … was led by the Spirit in the desert, where for forty days he was tempted by the devil." (vv.1-2)

For reading & meditation – Luke 4:1-13

I am often asked the question: What is the greatest temptation a Christian faces? My reply is usually this: the temptation to avoid the way of the cross. It was temptation that constantly faced our Lord Jesus Christ, and it is one that constantly faces us:

> *It is the way the Master went*
> *Should not the servant tread it still?*

There were two outstanding periods in Jesus' life when He was greatly tempted to face the sorrow and sin of the world in some way other than the one He took. One such time was the temptation in the desert, and the other was at the coming of the Greeks. As we have already looked at the latter incident – and will briefly examine it once more before we conclude – we shall focus our thinking over the next few days on our Lord's temptation in the desert.

Following His baptism in the River Jordan, Jesus was led by the Spirit into the desert to be tempted (or tested) by the devil. He got away from humanity in order to prepare Himself for the ordeal of giving Himself to humanity. In a sense, the temptation began as soon as He entered the desert. What temptation? The testing of His purposes to see whether, being the Son of God, He would also be the Son of Man. For to be the Son of Man would mean that He would take upon Himself all that falls on the sons of men. Yet on that issue, He never wavered. The Son of God willingly accepted all that was involved in becoming the Son of Man, so that the sons of men might become the sons of God.

FURTHER STUDY

Matt. 4:1-11;
Gen. 3:1-12;
Heb. 4:15

1. Compare the temptations of Jesus and Adam.

2. Why did Adam fail, and Jesus overcome?

Prayer

Lord Jesus, Son of God and also Son of Man, how can I ever sufficiently thank You for aligning Yourself with this sinful human race? I cannot understand it, but yet I stand upon it – and stand upon it for all eternity. Amen.

Feeding on the wrong bread

"… I have come to do your will, O God."(v.7)
For reading & meditation – Hebrews 10:1-18

We continue looking at Christ's temptation in the desert, but from a slightly different perspective. We are seeing how the temptation was designed to keep Him from identifying Himself with the sons of men. We saw yesterday how, He withdrew from men in order that He might give Himself to men. The issue was not so much whether He was the Son of God – He had heard that confirmed quite clearly at His baptism – but whether, being the Son of God, He would also be the Son of Man.

Once Jesus feels that His period of fasting is over, He prepares to return to feed His weakened body, but the tempter intervenes and tempts Him to turn the stones of the desert into bread. In doing this, is he really saying to Jesus: "Why go back to men? Stay here and feed Yourself. You are the Son of God, isn't that enough"? We cannot be sure, of course, but seen in this light, it is a possibility.

In all spiritual work, there is always the temptation to withdraw, to feed ourselves apart, to rejoice in the fact that we are sons of God and feast upon it. Many Christians down the ages have fallen for this, and have opted for an "escape mentality" in which they attempt to avoid the issue of death via a cross by isolating themselves from it. Mark this and mark it well: a similar temptation will come to you – the temptation to avoid the challenge of going down into the death of your self-life, by focusing on the fact that you are already a son of God, and that there is no need for any further humiliation or pain.

FURTHER STUDY

Eph. 1:1-23;
Gen. 3:15;
John 16:33;
1 John 3:8

1.How did Jesus destroy the devil's works?

2.How can we overcome the devil's works?

Prayer

Gracious and loving heavenly Father, help me, as You did Your Son, to resist every temptation that tries to keep me from coming to grips with my own personal Calvary. Abide with me, and then I can abide with anything. Amen.

The divine end

*"... that I may know him and the power of his resurrection,
and may share his sufferings ..." (v.10, RSV)*

For reading & meditation – Philippians 3:1-14

If the first temptation contained elements designed to prevent Christ from returning to humanity as the Son of Man, then the second temptation might be seen as an attempt to get Him to take a different attitude to men. Was the devil saying: "If you must go back, then do not take the attitude You took when You began. Don't stand alongside man, but stand on the pinnacle of the Temple. Be worshipped, be honoured and respected. Your place is up there, not down among those wretched multitudes"? A similar temptation will come to you, too. Satan will say: "Stay above all this talk of going down into death; escape the pain by remaining above it. You can descend to help men and women, but then let the angels carry you back to your exalted position."

Then came the subtle third temptation, which seemed to suggest this: "If You are determined to be the Son of Man and to be one with men, then adopt humanity's methods – fall down and worship me. If You are going to be like them, be like them in everything, and take a similar attitude to those who obey them."

Jesus refused this way too. He would be the Son of Man and let everything that falls on men fall on Him. But there would be this difference – He would reach the divine end only by means of the divine method, and by doing the will of His Father in heaven. At that point, He put His feet upon the way that He knew would lead ultimately to the cross. No temptation would divert Him from that. And no temptation must divert you and me either.

FURTHER STUDY

Psa. 37:1-40;
Isa. 12:2;
Luke 12:29

1. What 7 steps of trusting are in Psalm 37?

2. What are the 5 results of trusting?

Prayer

O Father, help me to do with temptation what Jesus did with it – to use it to reinforce my readiness to do Your will. I am so thankful that Your tests are not meant to catch me out, but to spur me on. Help me to meet every test – triumphantly. Amen.

A second look

"Jesus replied, 'The hour has come for the Son of Man to be glorified.' " (v.23)

For reading & meditation – John 12:20-36

Having experienced the principle that life is always preceded by death, we return now to focus again on the incident which launched us into this study – the coming of the Greeks to Jesus.

I firmly believe that this incident has been greatly overlooked by Bible expositors and commentators. We usually take the text, "Sir, we would like to see Jesus" (v.21), and leave it at that. But this is one of the most momentous events in the life of our Lord – an event that is next in importance, in my judgement, to His temptation in the wilderness. In many ways, it was more subtle than the wilderness experience, for the wilderness represents the temptation that comes at the beginning of one's ministry, while the coming of the Greeks represents the temptation that comes as one gets close to the end.

It is often as one gets close to one's goal that the temptation to compromise, or to take an easier way becomes more acute. Just as, in the desert, there was a pull to get Jesus to take another way, so here we see a similar situation. As I said at the beginning of our study, we cannot be at all sure that the Greeks arrived with the intention of enticing Christ to come to Athens, but it is significant that their arrival threw Him into a spiritual crisis. Assuming that to be so, the issue before Him was acceptance in Athens or rejection in Jerusalem. A philosopher's chair, or a grisly cross. A similar issue confronts those of us who are His followers. Do we go the way of the cross, or do we go the way of the crowds?

FURTHER STUDY

Col. 1:1-29;
Psa. 45:11;
Deut. 5:7; 6:13-15

1. What was Satan's aim in tempting Jesus?

2. What did Christ accomplish through overcoming him?

Prayer

Father, my mind is made up – I want to go Your way. Help me to come out clearly on Your side – for You and against everything that is against You. This I pray in Jesus' Name. Amen.

Living by the heartbeat

"… the Son can do nothing by himself; he can do only what he sees his Father doing …" (v.19)

For reading & meditation – John 5:16-30

Although we do not know exactly why the Greeks came to Jesus, it is clear that their arrival aroused powerful emotions. He soliloquises: "Unless a grain of wheat falls into the earth and dies, it remains alone; but if it dies, it bears much fruit" (John 12:24, RSV).

Some commentators think that although there is no record of the Greeks having actually conversed with Christ, they might have sent a message via Andrew and Philip to the effect that He could have a long and fruitful life if He brought His message to their shores. Was this so? We will never know – at least, not this side of eternity. But if it was, this was His answer: life comes through giving life, and fruitfulness through falling into the ground and dying.

Jesus did not live by the hourglass, but by the heartbeat. He knew that when we remain alone by ourselves – when we are like the "corn of wheat afraid to die" – we will find life shallow and fruitless. A refusal to pay the ultimate price – the price of giving ourselves – is to find ourselves paying the price of the deadness of life itself. Again we hear Him cry: "The man who loves his life will lose it, while the man who hates his life in this world [as I must do] will keep it for eternal life" (John 12:25). If the Greeks were coming to ask Him to love His life and save it – and thus save others – they were asking Him to bless without bleeding. Jesus knew that could not be done. There is no life without death, no gain without pain, no crown without a cross, and no victory except through surrender.

FURTHER STUDY

Luke 15:11-32;
Mark 8:36;
Matt. 25:27-28

1. What did the prodigal son have to learn?

2. What is the lesson of the man with one talent?

Prayer

My Father and my God, soon I will leave this theme and focus on another. If I have not yet settled this issue of where my allegiance lies – with myself or with You – then help me to settle it today. For Your own dear Name's sake. Amen.

The hour of decision

"I tell you, now is the time of God's favour, now is the day of salvation." (v.2)

For reading & meditation – 2 Corinthians 6:1-18

Listen to Jesus as He receives the news that the Greeks have come to interview Him: "Now is my heart troubled …" (John 12:27). The Greek word used here for "troubled" is *tarasso*, which implies extreme agitation. And well might He be troubled, for being human as well as divine, our Lord would have felt as keenly as you and I the horror of impending death.

Some of us are not troubled at this point because we fall in with the spirit of the age, and choose acceptance rather than rejection – the plaudits of men rather than the nails of a cross. We are afraid to die, and thus live on to experience only shallowness. Again our Lord cries: "And what shall I say? 'Father, save me from this hour?'" (John 12:27). Would He ask to be excused, from paying the supreme price? Some of us may be asking that at this very moment. We are asking to be "saved from this hour". Listen to how Jesus meets this moment: "No, it was for this very reason I came to this hour" (John 12:27).

Can you see what He is saying? "All the ages have matched me against this moment, all the yearnings of men have brought me face to face with this crisis. I cannot fail now, for I would fail both God and them." Can you sense in your own heart right now that God has been working to bring you to this crisis point? For some of you, particularly those of you who have not yet fully surrendered your lives to God's purposes, this is a moment of destiny. Someone has brought you to this hour – that Someone is God.

FURTHER STUDY

Acts 26:1-32;
Psa. 32:6; 69:13;
Deut. 30:19

1. What was Agrippa's response to the challenge?

2. How will you respond to God's challenge?

Prayer

O Father, what can I say? I feel a struggle going on inside me – the struggle concerning who is to be my soul's rightful Lord. Help me to make the final surrender. I do it now, fully and finally. In Jesus' worthy and wonderful Name. Amen.

"It thundered"

"The spiritual man judges all things, but is himself to be judged by no one." (v.15, RSV)

For reading & meditation – 1 Corinthians 2:1-16

The final words of our Lord in the incident we are considering are these: "Father, glorify thy name" (John 12:28, RSV). What a decision! What a moment! "Father, do not think of what it costs me – only glorify Your name." At that moment, He gave God a blank cheque, blank save that it was signed in His own blood. It is a great moment in our life, too, when we hand God a blank cheque, signed in our own blood, and invite Him to call on us for all we have and all we are.

One person described this moment as "the great renunciation". If that is so, then the moment of great renunciation is followed by a great annunciation. Listen: "Then a voice came from heaven, 'I have glorified it, and I will glorify it again' " (John 12:28, RSV). The moment Jesus made the final response, then heaven spoke. Many of us who complain we are living under a silent heaven would find it vocal with the voice of God if we would choose the Calvary way.

Of course, the bystanders missed what was really going on and "said that it had thundered" (John 12:29). To them, it was the impersonal voice of nature. Others came a little closer to reality, and said: "An angel had spoken to him." To them, it was a little more than the impersonal voice of nature, and yet something less than the voice of God. Anyone who stands on the edges of life as a bystander is bound to give a shallow interpretation of what God is doing. It is only those who have faced the alternatives – to die or not to die – who are really involved.

FURTHER STUDY

Josh. 24:1-15;
Psa. 119:30;
Luke 10:42;
Heb. 11:25

1. What challenge did Joshua bring?

2. What was said of Moses?

Prayer

My Father, I don't want to be a bystander. I want to be in the centre of all You are saying and all You are doing. Here's my cheque – signed with my own blood. Fill it in for everything You want from me. I do it willingly, gladly, happily. Amen.

The last word is *life*

"I have come that they may have life, and have it to the full." (v.10)

For reading & meditation – John 10:7-18

At the close of our meditations we look at the results of the momentous choice Jesus made when the Greeks said: "Sir, we would like to see Jesus."

Our Lord saw that three things would happen: first, the judgment of this world (John 12:31). What did choosing the cross have to do with that? This – the cross is the judgment seat of the world. I confess that the Man on the cross judges me, convicts me, challenges me. His Spirit of facing the world's sin and suffering makes my spirit tremble like a magnetic needle in a storm. At the cross, His love judges my hate, my selfishness, my desire to live only for myself. His self-sacrifice inspires my self-sacrifice.

The second thing our Lord saw would happen was the overpowering of Satan: "Now shall the ruler of this world be cast out" (John 12:31, RSV). He would overthrow Satan, not by breaking his head, but by letting him break His heart. Third, He would make the cross the magnet by which He would draw all people to Himself: "But I, when I am lifted up from the earth, will draw all men to myself" (John 12:32). His choice was made – and hopefully, ours is also. No longer will we lie on the edge of life's furrow – "a corn of wheat afraid to die" – but willingly roll over into the dark channel of death, knowing, as we do, that from our death will come a life that is well-pleasing to God – fruitful, profitable and productive. Afraid to die? No – afraid to live. For life that is not preceded by death is a life not worth living.

FURTHER STUDY

Gal. 2:16-21;
Phil.1:21;
John 5:24;
1 John 3:14

1. What was Paul's great declaration?

2. Can you make that same declaration?

Prayer

O Father, burn the message into my heart that when I try to save my life, I succeed only in losing it. And help me never to forget that the last word is not death, but life. Thank You, Father. Amen.

Heaven-Sent
Revival

On heavens

"For I will pour water on him who is thirsty, and floods on the dry ground …" (v.3, NKJ)

For reading & meditation – Isaiah 44:1-8

We begin today a study on what is without doubt one of the greatest themes of Scripture – heaven-sent revival. I say "heaven-sent" because real revival is not something that springs up or out of the normal activities of the Church but something that comes down to us from above.

There are, of course, many different and conflicting views on this subject, so I want to begin by looking at a question which I imagine no Christian will have any difficulty in facing: Has God got something bigger in His heart for us than we are at present seeing? What is your response, I wonder? Those who are privileged to be part of a vibrant church, or are actively involved in evangelism, might respond differently from those who find themselves in a spiritual backwater. But the truth is (in my opinion) that no matter how spiritually alive the community in which you work and worship, God is able to do greater and yet more wondrous things. Our God has reserves of power which we, the Church of this generation, have not fully experienced. Surely every Christian believes that.

FURTHER STUDY

Isa. 58:1-11;
Psa. 36:8; 107:9

1. What does the prophet expose?

2. What does God promise?

Although we must not be unappreciative of the fact that God is obviously sending showers of blessing upon His Church, we must not forget either that the God who sends the showers can also send the floods. In fact, revival is just that – God flooding a locality or a community of His people, stirring up the complacent, and producing the conviction and conversion of a great number of people. It has happened at various times in various places throughout history, and as sure as night follows day it will happen again

Prayer

O Father, while I see the need for a greater outpouring of Your Spirit upon Your Church, my initial prayer is not corporate but personal: Lord, send a revival and let it begin in *me*. In Jesus' Name I ask it. Amen.

Defining revival

"... that times of refreshing may come from the Lord."
(v.19)

For reading & meditation – Acts 3:11-26

Today we ask: What is revival? Unfortunately the word has no sharp edges and thus everyone who uses the word has to define what they mean by it. The first time I visited the United States (now nearly forty years ago), I was asked by a minister if I would preach at the "revival" his church would be having in a few weeks' time. I remember being overwhelmed by what I thought was my faith in predicting the exact date of a revival, until I was informed by a friend that in that part of America the term "revival" simply referred to a series of special meetings.

In these studies I am using the word in its classic sense to denote the sudden awesome flood of God's power upon a community of His people. D.M. Panton describes true spiritual revival as "an inrush of divine life into a body threatening to become a corpse". Christmas Evans, a famous Welsh preacher whom God used to stir the nation of Wales on several occasions, had this to say: "Revival is God bending down to the dying embers of a fire just about to go out and breathing into it until it bursts into flame." Quite simply, revival means "to wake up and live".

I know of no better definition of revival than that given by J. Edwin Orr who, in his book *The Second Evangelical Awakening in Britain*, wrote: "Revival takes place when we experience 'times of refreshing from the presence of the Lord'." Whichever way we look at it, revival is life at its best, life in all its fulness, life abundant, life overflowing with the grace and power of God.

FURTHER STUDY

Deut. 11:1-17;
Jer. 3:1–25;
Joel 2:23-27

1. What does the latter (spring) rain symbolise?

2. Why did God withhold the latter rain?

Prayer

O Father, this matter of revival has the feel of the real and the eternal upon it. Awaken within me a deep desire for a "time of refreshing from the presence of the Lord" – personal as well as corporate. In Jesus' Name. Amen

What revival is not

"O Lord, revive Your work in the midst of the years!"
(v.2, NKJ)

For reading & meditation – Habakkuk 3:1-19

A s it is vitally important to be quite sure what we are talking about when we use the word "revival", we must spend another day defining it. G. Campbell Morgan, the great preacher of a bygone generation, defined it like this: "Revival is the reanimation of the life of the believer, not the unregenerate as they are 'dead in sin'. There can only be revival where there is life to revive."

Revival always begins, not with the conversion of sinners, but with the reanimation of the people of God. That is why it is a mistake to see evidences of spiritual revival in the crusades where hundreds or thousands of people are converted. Evangelism is the expression of the Church; revival is an experience in the Church. Evangelism is the work man does for God; revival is the work God does for man.

Revival is much greater, also, than the restoration of backslidden Christians. There are times in church life, such as during special conventions, large rallies, conferences, camps and other activities, when large numbers of lethargic Christians make a new and deeper commitment to Jesus Christ. This, of course, is highly desirable and is something for which we ought to be deeply thankful – but it is not revival.

Again, some of the large healing services we hear about, where hundreds of people are healed and wonderful miracles take place, are not a sign of revival. We can see people converted, renewed, restored, healed, and yet these happenings fall short of revival. Revival includes all these things yet surpasses them all.

FURTHER STUDY

Isa. 32:1-33:24;
Psa. 80:18; 119:25;
119:40; 119:50;
119:88

l. What will happen when revival comes?

2. How will this affect evangelism?

Prayer

Gracious and loving Father, the more I meditate on this subject of revival, the more I long to experience it. You have visited Your people in times past in great and awesome power. Do it again, dear Lord. Do it again. Amen.

Why we need revival

"... But this happened that we might not rely on ourselves but on God, who raises the dead." (v.9)

For reading & meditation – 2 Corinthians 1:3-14

We have seen that revival is "a time of refreshing from the presence of the Lord". Today we examine the question: Why do we keep on needing such experiences? Why can't we hold on to the spiritual highs when they come and not let them go? Why, for example, did the Christians in Wales during the revival in 1904 allow the fire that swept the Principality to die out?

We can find the answer to these questions by looking more closely at the history of God's people as found in the Scriptures and in the records of the Church. In the Old Testament we see that there were times when God's people were lifted to the heights of spiritual blessing, only to plunge later into spiritual apathy and despair. Even after the great outpouring of the Spirit at Pentecost the Church one generation later lapsed into coldness so that in Revelation 2 and 3 we see our Lord confronting the seven churches of Asia with the challenge to repent and return to their first love. History tells us that there have been periods when the Church has experienced spiritual decay, for instance in the early Middle Ages, before a time of renewal occurred.

Note carefully what I am now about to say: the cause of all spiritual lapse is rooted in the desire for independence. Initially, when we enter into a new relationship with God, we are conscious of a great sense of dependence upon Him, but unfortunately after a while something rises up within us and clamours for independence. And it is this, more than any other single thing, that causes us to let go of what God gives us.

FURTHER STUDY

1 Kings 18:1-39;
Isa. 35:6-7;
Lam.3:40-42

1. In what way is Elijah's experience a picture of revival?

2. Write out your definition of revival.

Prayer

O Father, help me to look within my own heart today and evaluate to what extent the desire for independence rules my life. Show me, dear Lord, that if I do not crown You Lord of all, I do not crown You Lord at all. Amen.

"The swings of history"

"… They have forsaken me, the spring of living water, and have dug their own cisterns, broken cisterns …" (v.13)

For reading & meditation – Jeremiah 2:4-13

We continue meditating on the thought we touched upon yesterday, that one of the major reasons why we experience a spiritual lapse (and thus need to be revived) is our natural and stubborn commitment to independence. Historians talk about "the swings of history", and as far as the people of God are concerned, no swing is more evident in their history than the swing from dependence to independence.

The reason I have chosen the chapter that is before us today is because it highlights, perhaps better than any other passage in the entire Bible, this matter of independence. Note the charge which God brings against the people of Judah: "But My people have changed their Glory for what does not profit" (v.11, NKJ). This indictment bears down on the fact that the inhabitants of Judah were not as loyal to the Almighty as the pagans were to their own gods – a fact so astonishing to God that He calls on the heavens to bear witness to it (v.12). Next, He indicts them for failing to drink from the fountain of living water which He provides for His people and for turning instead to cisterns that can hold no water (v.13).

FURTHER STUDY

Acts 19:1-41;
Eph 1:15-16;
Rev. 2:1-5

1. What did the Ephesian church need?

2. What was it required to do?

Can you see what had happened to the people of Judah? They had started off in absolute dependence on God – worshipping only Him and drinking from His fresh wells – but after a while they had felt within them the urge to take control of their spiritual lives and manage them as they thought fit. And whenever God's people do this, no matter how bright and seemingly happy their religious life may be, they are desperately in need of revival.

Prayer

O God, how it must grieve You that we Your Church, like Judah of old, start off depending on You, but then hanker to put our reliance on things that are more tangible. Forgive us, dear Father. Forgive me. In Jesus' Name. Amen.

The stepping stone

*"Take words with you and return to the Lord. Say to him:
'Forgive all our sins …'" (v.2)*

For reading & meditation – Hosea 14:1-9

Nothing is more abhorrent to God than to see within His people the desire for self-control and self-dependence. This is not because of any egotism in the Almighty that requires Him to be the boss, but because He knows that when we try to run our lives on our own terms we demean ourselves and fall short of His plans and purposes for us. We must face the fact that we are helplessly dependent and that God and God alone is independent. He can exist without us but we cannot exist without Him.

The periods of revival in the Old Testament came at the high peaks of corporate worship in the life of Israel, when the people acknowledged the fact that they could not successfully run their lives on their own terms but were happy and effective only to the degree that they were dependent upon God. In the chapter before us today we see how God called His people back to dependence upon Him by encouraging them to repent: "Take words with you, and return to the Lord." This means (so I believe): "Have a clear idea of what you are repenting of."

The stepping stone from independence to dependence is always repentance. There is simply no other way that it can be done. That is why in all revivals the issue of repentance becomes paramount. In revival God underlines in a dramatic way the truth that the path to a continuous relationship with Him is through repentance. Never forget this. The key to all change is in a returning to God, for every effort to change must invoke at its core a shift in direction – away from dependence on one's own resources to dependence on the living God.

> **FURTHER STUDY**
>
> 2 Chron. 7:1-14;
> Joel 2:12; Isa. 55:7
>
> 1. When will God heal the land?
> 2. What is God's promise?

Prayer

Father, I see that if I stumble here, over this matter of dependence and independence, I stumble all down the line. Help me not to deny this issue but to face it and repent of it. I do so now in Jesus' Name. Amen.

Pentecost – the God-given norm

*" 'In the last days, God says, that I will pour out my Spirit
on all people." (v.17)*

For reading & meditation – Acts 2:5-21

W e have been seeing over the past few days that revival means "wake up and live". As you know, whenever the prefix "re" is used before a word, as in re-vival, re-animation, or re-turn, it simply means "back again". Revival, then, is the Christian Church going back again to the God-given norm. And what is that "norm"? I suggest it is nothing less than what happened on the Day of Pentecost.

Picture the scene with me on that first Whitsunday. Thousands of people fill the narrow streets of Jerusalem, drawn to the city for the celebration of the Feast of Pentecost. Spiritually, however, the nation is at an all-time low. Except for Jesus and John the Baptist, no prophet has spoken in Israel for over 400 years. The disciples are gathered in a house in secret expectancy, waiting for the fulfilment of the promise which Jesus had given them ten days earlier: "You will receive power when the Holy Spirit comes on you" (Acts 1:8). Suddenly the Spirit comes and transforms the timid disciples into men who are ablaze and invincible. They in turn go out into the streets and witness in such a powerful way that multitudes are swept into a close and thrilling relationship with God. The very atmosphere is impregnated with divine power to such an extent that one feels anything can happen.

This was the "norm" and this is what the Church returns to whenever a revival comes. Indeed, there is clear evidence for the fact that every revival that has taken place over the centuries the Church has been in existence contains some feature of the Day of Pentecost.

FURTHER STUDY

Hosea 6:1-11;
Psa. 80:7; 85:6

1. What was Hosea's exhortation?

2. What 2 things happen when God revives us?

Prayer

O Father, give us we pray another Day of Pentecost. Open the windows of heaven over all countries and all nations, and pour out Your power. In Christ's Name we ask it. Amen.

Christlike power

*"Up to that time the Spirit had not been given, since Jesus
had not yet been glorified." (v.39)*

For reading & meditation – John 7:32-39

Yesterday we said that the pattern for revival is based on what God did for His people on the Day of Pentecost. But why could the pattern not be based on the many revivals we read about in the Old Testament such as those that took place under Nehemiah, Hezekiah or even David?

I believe it was because the Old Testament revivals, while powerful and reformative, did not contain enough ingredients on which to establish a norm. The Holy Spirit – always the prime agent in any revival – operated in a limited way. His ministry was special, temporary and intermittent. He came and went, providing temporary infusions of power for temporary tasks. Also in Old Testament times He came upon people from the outside as opposed to residing permanently on the inside. It was said of Samson: "And the Spirit of the Lord began to move him at times in the camp of Dan" (Judg. 13:25, AV). Yet another reason why the Spirit's ministry was limited in the Old Testament is the fact there was no perfect vehicle through whom He could reveal Himself.

The passage before us today draws all these strands of truth together when it tells us that the Spirit could not be fully given until Jesus had been glorified. Why should this be so? It was because only through the life and death of Jesus could God's power be properly seen and understood. Eternal power must be seen not only in the context of signs, wonders and miracles, but at work on a cross, dying, suffering and overcoming sin. The power that fell at Pentecost, if it is to be the pattern for the centuries to come, must not be just power – but *Christlike* power.

FURTHER STUDY

John 16:1-16; 6:63;
15:26; Rom. 8:11

1. List several things
Jesus said concerning
the Holy Spirit.

2. What did Paul say
concerning the power
of the Holy Spirit?

Prayer

O Father, how can I ever sufficiently thank You for sending Jesus to reveal the truth about the Holy Spirit, as well as about You? I see now so clearly that not only are You a Christlike God but the Spirit is a Christlike Spirit. I am so grateful. Amen.

Sanity as well as sanctity

"Let this mind be in you which was also in Christ Jesus …"
(v.5, NKJ)

For reading & meditation – Philippians 2:1-11

We saw yesterday that the Holy Spirit could not be given until Christ had come to fix the content of the Spirit and make clear to people just what kind of Spirit He is. Jesus reveals not only the nature of the Father but also the nature of the Spirit. If God is a Christlike God, then the Spirit is also a Christlike Spirit.

Men and women have some strange ideas about the Holy Spirit and the way He works in human lives. Over the years I have met some fanatical people in the Church who have claimed that the Holy Spirit has been prompting them to do things which quite clearly were downright absurd, even bizarre. I remember talking to a man some years ago who told me the Holy Spirit had instructed him to leave his wife and go and live with another woman. Clearly his understanding of the nature of the Spirit needed correction.

The nature of the Spirit is determined by what we see in Jesus Christ. This is very important, for in some parts of the Church people have made the Spirit into someone who appears to be peculiar. Why are so many Christians afraid to surrender to the Holy Spirit? They think that to do so will expose them to emotionalism or make them off-balance. The fact that Jesus has fixed the content and nature of the Spirit guarantees that when we surrender to the Holy Spirit we will be made like Christ. If this is not the case then we are not under the guidance of Holy Spirit but some other spirit. Christ is not only sanctity – He is also sanity.

FURTHER STUDY

Acts 2:1-47;
Isa. 40:31;
Zech. 4:6

1. List 7 results of the Spirit's outpouring.

2. How do these relate to revival?

Prayer

Lord Jesus, I am so grateful that You have clarified once and for all the nature and character of the Holy Spirit. Help me never forget that He is like You, and when He comes, He comes to make me like You – balanced and sane and poised. Amen.

"In My Name"

"But the Counsellor, the Holy Spirit, whom the Father will send in my name, will teach you all things …" (v.26)

For reading & meditation – John 14:15-31

We continue with the thought we considered yesterday, that some people have strange ideas about the work and nature of the Holy Spirit. I once knew a minister who unfortunately had fallen into the grip of alcohol and could not break free. Instead of admitting the bondage he was in and seeking help and support from his fellow Christians, he rationalised the problem and said his heavy drinking opened him up to the Holy Spirit because it lifted his inhibitions and made him more susceptible to divine revelation. I suggested that all that was happening to him was that he was getting drunk. He replied: "Ah, alcohol makes some people drunk, but me it makes more available to God." What nonsense!

How thankful we ought to be that through Christ the nature and content of the Holy Spirit has been fixed. The Holy Spirit is like Jesus. As our text for today says, He is given in Christ's Name. This is why God could only give the Holy Spirit sparingly to people in Old Testament times; He waited until Jesus had fixed the content and character of the Spirit. It is only in Jesus that we see ultimate character revealed.

So take a good look at Jesus before you take a good look at the Holy Spirit, and then you will come out with the right perspectives. There was nothing weird or strange or unbalanced about Jesus. He never laid stress (as do some modern-day Christians) on getting guidance through visions and dreams. He received His guidance through prayer and waiting upon God, as you and I should. Visions and dreams may have their place in the Christian life, but not an unbalanced place.

FURTHER STUDY

1 Cor. 2:1-13;
Luke 12:12;
1 John 2:27

1. What was Paul's testimony?

2. List 5 things the Holy Spirit has taught you.

Prayer

Father, once again I want to thank You for clarifying for me the content and character of the Holy Spirit. Help me not to expect You to exercise or demonstrate in my life any power that is not power Jesus would have exercised or demonstrated. Amen.

Pentecost – the only pattern

"… the place where they were meeting was shaken. And they were all filled with the Holy Spirit …" (v.31)

For reading & meditation – Acts 4:23-37

We continue exploring the thought that Pentecost, and not the Old Testament revivals, is God's norm for the Church. It is imperative that we grasp this, because when they are praying for revival many Christians set their sights on happenings in the Old Testament. But while these contain interesting and helpful insights, they ought not to become our pattern.

As we have seen, the pattern for revival is Pentecost. The Spirit could not have been fully given in the Old Testament dispensation as this would have set a wrong pattern, and for the same reason He could not have been given in the day of our Lord's humiliation. The Spirit could only be given in the time of Christ's triumph – after He had returned to the eternal throne – for that alone was the right pattern. That is why our prayers for revival and our expectation of it must be based on Pentecost – the greatest manifestation of the Holy Spirit the world has ever known.

Do not be swayed by those who tell you that Pentecost was a one-off experience which God does not want to repeat. As I have said, throughout the history of the Church every revival that has taken place has contained one or more of the ingredients of Pentecost. In some the dominant feature has been conviction of sin; in others, abounding joy; and in others, amazing miracles brought about through supernatural power. If God sees fit to send another revival to the world, or parts of the world, perhaps the next one will contain all the ingredients of Pentecost. I don't know about you, but this is something I find myself longing for with all my heart.

FURTHER STUDY

Acts 19:1-41; Ezek. 36:27;
Acts 10:44-46

1. When the Holy Spirit fell on the 12 men, what were some results in their lives?

2. How did this affect the

Prayer

O Father, let my longing for another Pentecost be translated into a deeper and closer walk with You – by prayer, meditation on the Scriptures and sharing with others the concept of Your greatness and power. In Jesus' Name. Amen.

What Pentecost produced

"And suddenly there came a sound from heaven, as of a rushing mighty wind …" (v.2, NKJ)
For reading & meditation – Acts 2:1-4

By now it should be clear that revival is an extraordinary work of God producing extraordinary results among a large group of people. It is vitally important that we see it in these terms, otherwise we will fall for the popular notion of calling any unusual activity of the Church by the name "revival".

Consider with me what the Day of Pentecost produced. First, it produced extraordinary physical manifestations – "a rushing mighty wind" and "divided tongues, as of fire". Almost every revival in history contains accounts of extraordinary physical manifestations. In the 1859 Ulster revival people would fall to the ground in the streets or the fields and would lie there motionless for hours. So astonishing were the physical phenomena that crowds gathered just to see these manifestations take place and many were converted as they witnessed God at work.

The Day of Pentecost also produced extraordinary preaching. One sermon preached by Peter resulted in 3,000 souls coming into the kingdom. Sometimes, today, it takes 3,000 sermons to bring one soul into the kingdom! In revival, preachers experience a strange and extraordinary power pulsing through their sermons. My grandfather, who was converted in the Welsh revival of 1904, told me that many of the ministers of Wales took on a new eloquence and power during the days of revival which quite astonished those who had hitherto listened to them. You may have heard some great preaching in your time, but believe me, it is nothing compared to what one hears when revival comes again.

Simple statements bristle with power; it is preaching from hearts set on fire.

> **FURTHER STUDY**
>
> Acts 16:25-40,
> 4:31; 8:39; 9:3-4;
> 12:7
>
> 1. List some of the extraordinary events of the early Church.
>
> 2. What is the last supernatural event you remember witnesssing?

Prayer

O Father, while it is You my heart longs after, not powerful manifestations, I see how these things can make people in the world sit up and take notice. So for their sakes' – do it again, dear Lord. Do it again. Amen.

Detained before the Eternal

"No-one else dared join them, even though they were highly regarded by the people." (v.13)

For reading & meditation – Acts 5:1-16

Another outcome of Pentecost was an extraordinary sense of God's holiness. Something of this is undoubtedly present in the Church at all times but when revival comes it is greatly heightened. So great was the sense of God's holiness in the early Church that, as our text for today tells us, it was felt even by those who were outside. It would be impossible, I think, to find any revival in history where an extraordinary sense of God's holiness has not been present. During the days of the revival in the United States under Charles Finney the sense of God's holiness became so overwhelming that the entire congregation of 500 rose up as one crying out, "O God, save us – or destroy us."

Yet another outcome of Pentecost was an extraordinary interest in prayer and in the reading of the Scriptures. Prior to Pentecost, the disciples, Jews to a man, no doubt spent a good deal of time in prayer and the perusal of the Scriptures. After Pentecost, however, both prayer and the study of the Scriptures took on a new and greater importance. The disciples agreed among themselves to hand over their administrative responsibilities to others in order that they might give themselves continually to prayer and the study of the Word (Acts 6:2-4).

FURTHER STUDY

Acts 5:1-11; 8:9-25; 9:31; 10:2

1. What was the sin of Ananias and Sapphira?
2. How did the apostles maintain holiness in the Church?

In revival Christians find no activity more meaningful than praying and reading the Scriptures. Even those who gave time to prayer and daily Bible reading prior to revival find themselves gripped with a new spiritual interest and desire. As they read the Word they discover that they do not want to pull away. They are, as Moffatt translates, "detained in the presence of the Eternal" (1 Sam. 21:7).

Prayer

Father, the more my mind ponders the great things You are able to do, the more my heart cries out: "Do it again dear Lord." But don't let my desire to see the extraordinary things blind me to the joys of the "ordinary". In Jesus' Name I pray. Amen.

Dejected melancholics?

"So there was great joy in that city." (v.8)
For reading & meditation – Acts 8:1-8

Yet another outcome of Pentecost was extraordinary fervour and excitement. One has only to read the pages of Acts to feel the throb of excitement and joy that characterised the early disciples. It surfaces in many places, one of which is the text before us today.

The early Church was excited about everything that was connected with God and His kingdom. They were excited about Jesus, about the coming of the Spirit, about the establishment of His kingdom, and about the promise of His coming again. They were gripped by an intense earnestness and a spirit of expectation. The God who had raised up Jesus from the dead had raised them also from their own graves of sin. The power that had elevated Christ to the heavens and placed Him at the right hand of the Father was working in them with all its quickening might.

This is also the way it is in times of revival. Once people have repented of their sins and found peace with God there is invariably extraordinary joy. Let no one think that revival is associated with heaviness and gloom. There is always a period of mourning for sin but this is soon followed by waves of endless delight. It is surely amongst the most tragic misrepresentations of truth that historians should write that in times of revival Christians act like dejected melancholics. The reality is that in revival Christians, like their brothers and sisters in the first century, have to defend themselves against the charge of being drunk. Very few of us come under that dark suspicion nowadays, but it is hardly to our credit that there is rarely any need to stress the distinction.

FURTHER STUDY

Acts 4:1-37, 15:3;
16:25; Rom. 14:17

1. How did Peter and John stir things up?

2. What was the response?

Prayer

O Father, as far as it is possible outside of the great wave of revival, let me be gripped with the same spirit of fervour and excitement that pervaded the early Church. For Your own dear Name's sake I ask it. Amen

"The shop is always open"

*"So, because you are lukewarm – neither hot nor cold – I
am about to spit you out of my mouth." (v.16)*

For reading & meditation – Revelation 3:14-22

Having examined some of the ingredients of a spiritual revival we consider now arguments advanced by those (and there are many) who believe that revival is an irrelevant issue in today's Church. Some say the Church is essentially a religious institution not wholly unlike the institutions of law and medicine. And just as the institutions of law and medicine have the resources to meet the needs of those who wish to draw upon them, so also has the Church. The exponents of this view say that the Church possesses everything we need to live an effective life – sacraments, hallowed forms of worship, hymns, fellowship, and so on. If someone is spiritually sick, so they say, all that person has to do is make their way to the Church and they will find there the medicine they need for their soul.

Emyr Roberts and Geraint Davies in their booklet *Revival and Its Fruit* rightly take issue with this view and say of it: "In this sense the Church exists independently of the congregation; if nobody calls, the shop is always open." There can be little doubt that one's view of revival depends on one's view of the Church. Those who see the Church as an institution rather than a community of people brought into being and maintained by the Holy Spirit and the Word will regard revival as irrelevant.

FURTHER STUDY

Heb. 1:1-14; 8:4-6;
1 Cor. 10:11;
2 Pet. 2:6

1. Why has God given us a historical account of the Church?

2. What is the significance of a shadow?

But what is the Church? It is not a building but a body made alive by the Holy Spirit. And the secret of her survival is in continually opening herself to the Spirit who gave her life. She was not only born of the Spirit but survives and thrives by the Spirit.

Prayer

Father, I see that unless the red blood of the Spirit's energy and power flows through the veins of the Church she becomes weak and faint and anaemic. Give us, oh give us, a greater flow of Your life and power. Start in me today. Amen

Too cramped for comfort

"…where the Spirit of the Lord is, there is liberty."
(v.17, NKJ)

For reading & meditation – 2 Corinthians 3:1-18

We continue looking at the view of the Church as a religious or divine institution. Those who see the Church in this light believe (as we said) that the Church exists independently of the congregation. It is easy to see how anyone holding this view of the Church will have little interest in the subject of spiritual revival. They will be interested not in commotion or fervency, but in order and stability. They will not merely regard revival as irrelevant, but as downright messy, even injurious. It interferes with the smooth functioning of the services and cuts across the well-established forms and ceremonies.

The revivals of the past have always been opposed by those who have seen the Church as an institution, for the work of the Spirit cannot be brought under human control. A revival can be untidy and undignified, with people crying out in the midst of a sermon, or striking up a hymn at a seemingly inappropriate time. Whenever institutional Christianity has been faced with a movement of the Spirit that did not fit into its preconceived ideas of how the Church should function, it has immediately set its face against it.

During the Middle Ages, when the Church as an institution was at its strongest, the Spirit tried to break in and reveal Himself to His people, but as history clearly records, the leaders resisted these breezes from the Spirit. As a result, those who felt the Spirit's touch abandoned the institutional church and met together to enjoy Spirit-directed activity and worship. I do not think God despises institutional Christianity; it's just that sometimes it gets too cramped for comfort, and He has to move out.

> **FURTHER STUDY**
>
> Matt. 9:16-17;
> Acts 5:12-42; 8:6;
> Isa. 61:10;
> 1 Pet. 1:8
>
> 1. What did Jesus teach?
> 2. What does revival bring with it?

Prayer

O Father, help me to have a right view of the Church for I see that the way I look at this, and every, issue affects all my attitudes. And help me to take Your way, even though it cuts across my nature. Amen

"The pulse beat of all we do"

"So [Samson] ... said, 'I will go out as before, at other times ...' But he did not know that the Lord had departed from him." (v.20, NKJ)

For reading & meditation – Judges 16:1-22

We continue examining the view that the Church is a religious institution. The dictionary defines the word "institution" as "an establishment for the cure of souls". In a sense then, the Church is an institution, but it is not *essentially* an institution. Essentially it is a body through which life and energy must continuously flow. And the life that must flow through the Church is the life that comes from the Spirit. He and He alone gives life. I say "He" for the Holy Spirit is more than an influence. He is a Person who guides, counsels, cleanses, empowers, directs and, most of all, just abides with us. An impersonal influence, an "it", doesn't do that.

Have you ever wondered why it was that at Pentecost the Holy Spirit did not fall in the Temple but in a house? I have thought about this for many years and for what it is worth my conclusion is this: if the Holy Spirit had been given in the Temple, then His coming would be associated with a sacred place, sacred services and sacred occasions. The Holy Spirit came in the most common place – a home. He is not given for special "spiritual" occasions, but for all occasions – for all life.

The Holy Spirit is not a spiritual luxury to be imported into the unusual but a spiritual necessity at work in the usual. He is to be the pulse beat of all we do – the Life in our living. And when He is absent or not permitted to have full control, the Church, like Samson in our text today, might shake itself and make a great fuss but will accomplish nothing.

FURTHER STUDY

Acts 9:1-21;
Gen. 32:24-30;
1 Sam. 16:7; 11:13

1. Why was Saul an unlikely candidate to meet with God?

2. Why was the Damascus road an unlikely place?

Prayer

Gracious and loving Father, I am so grateful that I do not have to wander from sacred place to sacred place in search of Your Spirit. You come down to me wherever I am and turn all my seculars into sacreds. Amen.

A scandal to Christianity

"Do not quench the Spirit." (v.19, NKJ)
For reading & meditation – 1 Thessalonians 5:12-22

Today we look at another argument advanced by those who think revival is an irrelevant issue. It is sometimes stated in this fashion: "A religious revival is nothing more than a manifestation of crowd hysteria." For example, one critic of the Welsh revivals says: "Welsh people are easily moved. Their fiery nature and love of singing makes them easy prey to the emotional and the melodramatic." There is some truth in those words of course, but it takes more than emotionalism to explain the fact that during the 1904 revival in Wales crime dropped to such a degree that many of the courts were closed and some of the public houses went out of business.

Peter Price, a strong critic of the Welsh revival, saw in it nothing more than tumult, noise, play acting and imitation. Those who believe that religious worship should not contain any show of emotion are offended by the ferment of spiritual revival. Thomas Morgan, a nonconformist minister writing about the Methodists of his day said: "It appears to all true and serious Christians that they [the Methodists] are stark mad and given to a spirit of delusion, to the great disgrace and scandal of Christianity."

But those who condemn revival for what they call its extremes of emotion would do well to reflect on those occasions in Scripture when men and women appear to be beside themselves in the presence of God. Whilst we must not hesitate to condemn all excess of emotion we must make equally sure that we do not quench the Spirit by our intellectualism and our unwillingness to accept the supernaturalism that is everywhere portrayed in the Scriptures.

FURTHER STUDY

Acts 4:13-22; 5:12-16; 14:1-18

1. How did the rulers, elders and scribes react to the early disciples?

2. What effect did this have?

Prayer

O God, help me not to be one who quenches Your Spirit. Whatever it may be that causes me to draw back from asking and believing for greater and bigger things, then root it out of me today. In Jesus' Name I ask it. Amen.

The poorer language

"But the natural man does not receive the things of the Spirit of God …" (v.14, NKJ)

For reading & meditation – 1 Corinthians 2:6-16

We spend another day examining the objection we looked at yesterday, that revival is merely a manifestation of crowd hysteria. One eyewitness of a revival meeting in Anfield Road Chapel, Liverpool, in 1905, says: "… crowds were pressing against the chapel doors trying to push their way in, elderly ladies were climbing over the railings to get to the door and falling on the others, and some were being thrown inside by the police like sacks of flour."

Critics who read such reports ask: "Is there any difference between the religious madness seen in times of spiritual revival and the frenzies and ecstasies associated with the rock and pop groups of the present day?" On the surface there appears to be little difference; the immediate sensations and the conscious nervous impressions may be very similar. But, as C.S. Lewis pointed out in *Screwtape Proposes a Toast*, the tongues phenomenon on the Day of Pentecost might also have appeared to an onlooker to be nothing but an expression of nervous excitement or hysteria.

When we try to express the spiritual through the natural it is like translating from a richer to a poorer language. In the poorer language you have to use the same word to express more than one meaning, and it is the same when you try to express the richer world of the spirit through the poorer medium of the physical frame. We have only laughter to express both ribald revelry and godly joy; we have only tears to express the most selfish, worldly grief and the most godly sorrow. Therefore we must not be unduly surprised that spiritual rejoicings are mistaken for rejoicings of a very different kind.

FURTHER STUDY

Dan 3:13-30;
Num. 22:21-35;
Ex.7:20-21;
Acts 28:1-6

1. How did Nebuchadnezzar respond to the manifestation of God's power?

2. In what ways did God reveal Himself?

Prayer

Gracious and loving Father, give me that inward look, the ability to think through and see the reason for things. Quicken my spirit so that I am able to recognise the truth. In Jesus' Name I pray. Amen.

An excitement going somewhere

"One generation will commend your works to another ..."
(v.4)

For reading & meditation – Psalm 145:1-13

I remind you that the question we are looking at is this: Is revival a manifestation of crowd hysteria? We have seen that though on the surface there may appear to be little difference between the scenes reported at meetings where revival has broken out and the frenzy and excitement observed in many of today's pop and rock concerts, underneath there are great differences.

Let me deal with just one difference – the matter of final outcome. A crowd coming together for a pop concert experiences a high degree of emotion and excitement, but what does it result in? A family member of mine who is not a Christian and who attended a pop concert said to me afterwards: "It was tremendously exciting being there but the trouble is, the excitement doesn't go anywhere." Compare this with the excitement and fervour that was evident on the Day of Pentecost. It was excitement and fervour that went somewhere.

Charles Foster Kent says: "On the Day of Pentecost this pent up feeling broke out into an irresistible wave of spiritual enthusiasm that marked the beginning of the world-wide Christian missionary movement." I have a little problem with his phrase, "a pent up feeling broke out into an irresistible wave of spiritual enthusiasm", for it was not an enthusiasm worked up by circumstances but an infusion of the Holy Spirit. However, he is right when he says it "marked the beginning of the world-wide Christian missionary movement". When God moves in revival power the fervour and excitement goes somewhere – it influences and affects not just the present but also the coming generations.

FURTHER STUDY
Psa. 33:11; 45:17;
72:5; 79:13;
Acts 2:1-21

1. What was the
psalmist's testimony?

2. What did Peter
reaffirm?

Prayer

O God, whatever excitement or fervour fills my soul as a result of my contact with You – let it go somewhere. Grant that it might not stay in my feelings but be translated into light and energy by which I might walk. In Jesus' Name I ask it. Amen.

Don't get tipped off balance

"... so that the man of God may be thoroughly equipped for every good work." (v.17)

For reading & meditation – 2 Timothy 3:16-4:5

We look now at another argument advanced by those who see the issue of revival as unnecessary and irrelevant. It goes like this: "Encouraging people to believe for a revival serves only to make them spiritually discontent. They become so preoccupied with praying in a revival (which happens only infrequently) that they fail to get on with the task at hand." I have some sympathy for this argument as I too have been concerned for years over those Christians who talk a lot about a coming revival but avoid the day-to-day responsibilities of Christian living.

Many years ago, when I was a minister in Wales, I knew a church whose leaders believed that they should cancel all their activities and hold a prayer meeting every evening of the week until God sent revival to their community. Once committed to this seemingly spiritual but rather misguided idea, they simply had to keep going. They continued holding prayer meetings every evening for over a year, after which the congregation were so tired and bewildered they were obliged to call a halt. The church has never recovered to this day.

FURTHER STUDY

Luke 11:1-13;
2 Chron. 7:14;
Deut. 4:29;
Isa. 55:6

1. What is promised to those who sincerely seek?

2. How did Jesus illustrate this?

Think of all the opportunities the church missed in evangelism and outreach because they had an unbalanced view of the subject of revival. They thought they were being guided, but they failed to see that their commitment to pray every evening until revival came was more an obsessive demand than a deep spiritual desire. When the issue of revival becomes an obsession that tips us off our spiritual balance then there is something seriously wrong.

Prayer

O Father, help me differentiate between the demands that arise out of my own nature and the spiritual desires which arise out of Your inner prompting. For I see that one is an open road; the other a cul-de-sac. In Jesus' Name I pray. Amen.

Is revival an obsession?

*"Now to him who is able to do ... according to the power
that works in us." (v.20, NKJ)*

For reading & meditation – Ephesians 3:14-21

Yesterday we looked at a church whose commitment to pray every
evening until revival came was more an obsessive demand than a
deep spiritual desire. This raises the question: What is an obsession? An
obsession is a repetitive or persistent thought or idea which crowds into
the mind and thus helps to relieve one's basic anxiety. It is really a
defence mechanism which enables the personality to avoid anxiety by
focusing not on the anxious feelings but on the continuing or recurring
thought instead.

Some years ago I talked with a young psychologist who told me that
he had made a study of the temperaments of people who continually
wrote and talked about spiritual revival and had found an interesting
pattern – all of them tended to be obsessive. I offered to take the psychological test he had devised and it showed that although I was determined
and single-minded, I was also able to change – something an obsessive
person cannot do. When I saw he was convinced that I was a fairly well-
adjusted person, I talked to him about my own preoccupation with
revival. And he said I was the exception that proved the rule!

I have no doubt that by reason of their temperament some Christians can become obsessed about
anything – including revival. But I also know that
around the world there is a growing army of well-
adjusted Christians who are discovering within their
hearts at this vital time in history a deepening desire to
see God work in great and mighty power. Some may
see it as an obsession; I see it as a possession – the
thoughts of God taking hold of the thoughts of man.

> **FURTHER STUDY**
>
> 1 John 5:1-15;
> Rom. 8:25;
> Heb. 10:22;
> 1 Pet. 1:3
>
> 1. What motivates us
> to pray for revival?
>
> 2. What does the
> word "hope" mean in
> Scripture?

Prayer

O Father, while I do not want to be the victim of an obsession, I most certainly want
to be the recipient of divine possession. I give You the freedom to occupy my whole
being and to think and feel in me day by day. Amen.

How to wait for revival

"Do business till I come" (v.13, NKJ)
For reading & meditation – Luke 19:11-27

We continue looking at the argument that encouraging people to pray for revival serves only to make them spiritually discontented, so much so that they fail to get on with the tasks at hand. I recognise that this can happen, but it need not happen if clear biblical teaching is given.

Permit a personal testimony here: I have been talking and writing about revival ever since I came into the ministry nearly fifty years ago, and although it has been a major preoccupation of my life (not an obsession!), I have always encouraged people not only to pray for revival but also to be sure that other responsibilities, such as evangelism, fellowship, and Bible study, are not neglected.

In the text before us today our Lord tells us: "Occupy till I come" (v.13, AV). I take this to mean that He wants us to get on with the task of representing Him to the world no matter what may be the conditions around us. Those who say, "Let's give up working and just wait and pray for God to send revival," are violating Scripture. Evan Roberts prayed several hours a day for thirteen years for God to send revival to Wales, but he still went about his daily tasks and made sure that nothing was left undone. The same can be said of others who have figured greatly in past revivals.

A good motto to follow is one that was given to me early in my ministry. Like most mottoes, it has some flaws but it makes good spiritual sense nevertheless: Work as if it all depended on you, and pray as if it all depended on God.

FURTHER STUDY

James 2:14-26;
Heb.10:24;
1 Pet. 2:12

1. What does James admonish us?

2. What are the pagans to see?

Prayer

Gracious and loving heavenly Father, make me a responsible and balanced person, I pray. Help me to keep up my prayer life without neglecting the other responsibilities that You have given me. I want to keep occupied until You come. Amen

Taking a qualitative look

"The Lord reigns for ever, your God, O Zion, for all generations. Praise the Lord." (v.10)

For reading & meditation – Psalm 146:1-10

We look now at yet another argument advanced by those who see revival as unnecessary. Put in its simplest form it goes like this: fruits of revival do not last.

Admittedly not all who make a profession of faith during a time of revival continue to follow Christ after the fire has subsided. It would be foolish to deny that some of the fruits of revival do not last. Critics claim that out of the many converts won to Christ in the United States during the 1859 revival, only a small proportion could be found in the Church ten years later.

How do we answer this argument? The fruits of revival, I submit, ought to be looked at qualitatively and not just quantitatively. Take, for example, my native Wales. I believe that if it had not been for the revival that stirred the Principality in 1904, the Christian presence there today would be almost non-existent. During revival sometimes only one member of a family is converted, but that one person often influences a whole family.

I regard myself as a product of revival. My grandfather was converted to Christ in the Welsh revival of 1904. He influenced my mother who, together with my father, greatly influenced me to give my life to Jesus Christ. How many families who are now in the Christian Church might be outside had it not been for the fact that some distant relative or ancestor was won to Christ during a time of revival. The duration of a revival may be comparatively short and brief but its results spill over into succeeding generations.

FURTHER STUDY

Acts 8:1-40; 10:44-48; 11:19; 13:3

1. How did the coming of the Holy Spirit spread beyond Jerusalem?

2. What were the results?

Prayer

Father, I am beginning to understand that there is more to revival than I first thought. Thank You for helping me see that the influences of revival never stop – they pass from one generation to the other. I am grateful. Amen.

Fruit that lasts

"… we will tell the next generation the praiseworthy deeds of the Lord …" (v.4)

For reading & meditation – Psalm 78:1-8

We continue considering the argument that the fruit of revival does not last. While it is true that some of the fruit does not last, it is not true that none of the fruit lasts. When revival is measured qualitatively and not just quantitatively we see that its benefits spill over into the next generations.

Some of the greatest preachers have been men who were converted during the time of revival. It was said that at the funeral of Daniel Rowland of Llangeitho in October 1790 (the man who was greatly used by God to bring revival to Wales in the eighteenth century) over one hundred ministers were present, many of them having been won to Christ during the days of that revival. Sidney Evans, a man who has written a good deal about the subject of revival said: "The revivals of past history have often safeguarded the Christian ministry for a whole generation." And when you consider the influence ministers have in inspiring young men to enter the ministry you can see that a revival safeguards the ministry not just for one generation but for many generations.

Then take the staggering number of converts who have been swept into the kingdom of God during times of revival. The revival in America in 1859 claimed a million converts and a further million in the British Isles, 110,000 of these in Wales alone. These numbers are staggering, and even allowing for the fact that not all may have been genuinely converted, it is obvious to a fair-minded person that the spiritual impact of these large numbers of converts cannot help but have an influence on future generations.

FURTHER STUDY

Acts 3:11-26; 4:13; 9:29; 14:3; 19:8; Matt. 7:29

1. How was Peter's message far-reaching?

2. What was the central focus of the early Church's message?

Prayer

Father, help me to understand that the river of revival never really stops. It may disappear for a while but it continues to flow on – underground. Thank You, dear Father. Amen.

Why things are not worse

*"Let this be written for a future generation, that a people
not yet created may praise the Lord." (v.18)*

For reading & meditation – Psalm 102:18-28

Although the Church of Jesus Christ is sometimes in a sad and sorry
state, things might well be worse were it not for the fact that the
influence of previous revivals still reverberates in our midst. The same, I
think, can be said of the secular world. Here in the British Isles our society is in a bad way, morally and spiritually, but I believe things would be
much worse were it not for the continuing influence of the great revivals
of history.

This must not be taken to mean that the prayer life and godly living
of present-day Christians make no contribution to our world, for clearly
they do. We the people of God in this present generation provide "the
salt and light" that makes it more difficult for evil to prosper. That said,
however, the impact of past revivals can still be felt at work in our generation – even in our Houses of Parliament.

Several years ago I was part of a small group who visited the Houses
of Parliament to present a specially produced Bible to the prime minister
of the day – Harold Wilson. While there, we had the opportunity to talk
to several Christian MPs who, among other things, informed us that the
origins of many of the laws and statutes by which our
land is run can be traced back to the times when our
nation was in the midst of spiritual awakenings. I
know it is a sobering thought with which to begin the
day, but we might well ponder what kind of society we
would find ourselves in at this moment were it not for
the great spiritual awakenings of the past.

FURTHER STUDY

Acts 16:1-40;
10:19; Rom. 8:14

1. How did the early
Church revival
spread to Europe?

2. How were the
early apostles
directed by the Holy
Spirit?

Prayer

Gracious and loving heavenly Father, how can I sufficiently thank You for the way
You have revived Your people at intervals throughout history? I sense the past at
work right here in the present – and I am grateful. Amen.

Mixed experiences

"But grow in the grace and knowledge of our Lord and Saviour Jesus Christ ..." (v.18)

For reading & meditation – 2 Peter 3:10-18

We examine one more reason why some people regard revival as unnecessary and irrelevant – the fact that emotions kindled in revival are not unmixed spiritual experiences. Critics point out that revival brings to the fore not only the spiritual side of human nature but the baser and more carnal side too.

Here again we must listen to the truth in this criticism before attempting to answer it. It is true that in revival the spiritual is often mixed with the carnal. Williams put it like this: "When our soul came to taste the feasts of heaven, the flesh also insisted on having its share, and all the passions of nature aroused by grace were rioting tumultuously." And this was at the high point of the Methodist revival when none can deny that the Holy Spirit was mightily at work. Revival does not abolish in one fell swoop human carnality or the defects of our nature.

In the years immediately following the great outpouring of the Spirit at Pentecost there were clear evidences of carnality at work. Paul's letters are full of exhortations to resist carnality and subdue the works of the flesh. The great revivalist Jonathan Edwards said that if the Corinthian Church had been left to themselves they would have torn themselves to pieces – yet clearly the Spirit was at work in their midst. The apostle greets them as "the church of God ... called to be saints" (1 Cor. 1:2, AV).

We will never understand revival until we understand its primary purpose. And what is that? It is not to bring saints to perfection in a day, but to wake up the drowsy.

FURTHER STUDY

Rom. 8:1-17;
Gal. 5:25; 6:8

1. What does Paul teach about the Spirit and the flesh?

2. What new law does he talk about?

Prayer

Father, thank You for reminding me that revival, like conversion, does not produce "instant" saints. Help me understand that although character may come out of a crisis, more often than not it is the result of a process. In Christ's Name I ask it. Amen.

The Delectable Mountains

"… you rejoice with joy inexpressible and full of glory …"
(v.8, NKJ)

For reading & meditation – 1 Peter 1:3-12

W e continue considering that the primary purpose of revival is not
to bring saints to perfection but to wake up the drowsy. "The cul-
tivation of Christian virtues, and the building of sound and sane
Christian character," says Emry Roberts, "is the work, under the blessing
of God, of the pastor and the teacher." Sublime and joyous feelings,
however, have their place, and these are felt most keenly during revival.

Listen to what one person says about his experience of revival:
"Thursday night the 22nd December 1904 will be inscribed in letters of
fire on my heart for ever! Don't ask me to describe what I felt that night
– I can never do it! All I can say is that I felt the Holy Spirit like a torrent
of light causing my whole nature to shake. I saw Jesus Christ – and my
nature melted at His feet. I have done nothing since Thursday night but
to sing to myself that hymn: 'O, the love of Jesus'. And today I feel I
belong to everybody. Oh how the love of Christ expands a man's heart."

We readily agree with the critics of revival that such an elevated
emotional state cannot last, and it would be misguided to expect that one
could live continuously in the fever of such exaltation. This does not
mean, however, that there is no point to such feelings.
One supporter of revival says of such experiences:
"They are like a walk on the Delectable Mountains
from whose heights we are given a glimpse of Mount
Zion. We have to walk generally by faith and not by
sight but on our pilgrimage it is no small thing to
catch a glimpse of the heavenly city and to know a
foretaste of its felicity and bliss."

FURTHER STUDY

Eph. 3:14-21;
Isa. 12:3;
John 15:11; 16:20-
28; Psa. 16:11

1. What do we need
to do for our joy to
be full?

2. What was Paul's
prayer?

Prayer

O Father, day by day my appetite for revival is being whetted. I see that only an invasion from heaven can produce the impact to turn both the Church and the world in
Your direction. Grant that it may come soon. In Jesus' Name I pray. Amen.

No need for a fire extinguisher

"For Demas, because he loved this world, has deserted me ..."
(v.10)

For reading & meditation – 2 Timothy 4:9-18

The fact that Christians can come down from the ecstatic heights experienced during times of great spiritual awakening and lose their first love and joy is not a valid argument against revival. As we have seen, we have only to examine the New Testament to find that following the outpouring of the Spirit at Pentecost there were some who seemed to lose their joy. Yet none can deny the reality and genuineness of the power that surged in their midst.

Critics also draw our attention to the fact that revival can induce great spiritual pride – especially in the young. Revival history contains many accounts of young men being carried away by pride after a high peak in their spiritual experience. William Williams says of one: "He was a raw youth whom no one would entrust to shepherd his sheep and is riding high in a boldness of spirit much superior to old ministers who have borne the burden and heat of the day." But then, were there not such people in the Church that emerged after the Day of Pentecost? In one place Paul warns against appointing a novice in the faith to office in the Church, "... lest being puffed up with pride he fall into the same condemnation as the devil" (1 Tim. 3:6, NKJ). It is a failing that must be expected and guarded against.

Revival is full of dangers – let us not argue against that – but all the dangers can be handled through the principles set forth in the Word of God. When a coal falls out of the fire no reasonable person rushes for a fire extinguisher. They simply pick up the tongs and return the coal to the grate.

FURTHER STUDY

1 Cor. 4:15-21;
Prov.11:2; 28:25;
Rom. 14:17

1. How did Paul describe the kingdom of God?

2. How did he describe himself?

Prayer

O Father, help us as Your Church not to draw back from praying for revival because of the obvious dangers that accompany it. Show us that when we keep close to You we are equipped to handle anything that comes. Thank You dear Father. Amen.

Getting ready for revival

*"… exhorting one another, and so much the more as you
see the Day approaching." (v.25, NKJ)*

For reading & meditation – Hebrews 10:19-25

We spend a final day reflecting on the argument that the emotions kindled in revival are counter-productive to an effective Christian life. The answer, as we have seen, is that this can be so – but it need not be. When sound Christian teaching is available to channel the emotion seen in times of revival into productive purposes, then the sky's the limit.

Many who witnessed the 1904 Welsh revival say that it could have continued longer and made an even greater spiritual impact if there had been more teachers to lead the people into the deeper things of God. When I first learned this (just after becoming a Christian in my mid-teens), I immediately committed my life to doing everything I could to ensure that future revivals would not suffer for lack of teaching resources.

In 1965 I founded the Crusade for World Revival (now called CWR) with the primary objective of encouraging people to pray for both personal and corporate revival and deepen their understanding of the Word of God. Other objectives have been added to these over the years, but the primary goal is still that of helping God's people prepare for revival. I like to think that day by day as you follow these meditations and read the set Scriptures, you are not only building up your own spiritual resources but preparing yourself for a deeper and more effective ministry to others – now and in the future. Who knows but that in addition to your present and daily ministry for Christ you may have a part in establishing someone who has come to know Him in a time of revival?

FURTHER STUDY

2 Tim. 2:1-15;
Heb. 3:13;
Rom. 15:1

1. What was Timothy to do with the things he heard?

2. What was he to do personally?

Prayer

O Father, how wonderful it would be to witness a revival – and have a part in it. But whether I will or not, help me take the knowledge I gain from You day by day – and pass it on. In Jesus' Name I ask it. Amen.

What good is light without life?

"... when the enemy comes in like a flood, the Spirit of the Lord will lift up a standard against him." (v.19, NKJ)

For reading & meditation – Isaiah 59:9-21

From what we have been saying, it is quite clear that revival brings not only unlimited blessing but very real dangers. It is also clear that despite the dangers, the very survival of the Church depends on the timely and reviving work of the Holy Spirit.

There are some who think the Church does not need revival. A magazine article I read a few years ago said: "The Christian Church is stronger now than she has ever been throughout her entire history. Numerically, there are more people in the Church today than at any other period of her existence. She is well represented in almost every nation under the sun and if she would become aware of her strength and size and draw upon it she could dominate the world and have it sitting at her feet."

The words sound good but what are the facts? The Church may be numerically strong and well represented in different parts of the world but since when has her strength been in her numbers? The source of her strength and power is in the Holy Spirit. Without His presence in the Church, energising and reviving, there may be plenty of light, but little life. And it is *life* – the life of the Spirit – which the Church so easily loses.

Generally speaking, the Church has been good at protecting its theological position, but not so good at preserving life. That is why at certain times and in certain generations God mercifully breaks in upon His people to revive and refresh them by the Spirit. In every century the Christian Church has stood in need of a new invasion of that life. But perhaps never so much as now.

FURTHER STUDY

Matt.23:23-39;
2 Tim. 3:5;
Isa. 29:13

1. How did Jesus deal with pharisaism?

2. How did Paul put it?

Prayer

Father, help me see that no matter what else Your Church has, if it does not have life – the life of the Spirit – then it is nothing more than a religious club. Breathe upon us for we want not only to be living – but lively. In Jesus' Name. Amen.

How do revivals begin?

*"Will you not revive us again, that your people may
rejoice in you?" (v.6)*
For reading & meditation – Psalm 85:1-13

Now that we are at the half-way point in our meditations on revival
we pause for a moment to remind ourselves of some of the points
we have been considering. Revival, we have said, is God bending down
to the dying embers of a fire just about to go out and breathing into it
until it bursts again into flame. The pattern for all revivals is Pentecost,
which was an extraordinary visitation of God accompanied by extraordinary happenings. God is after the recovery of a fully-orbed New
Testament Christianity and He has invariably used revivals to this end.
The reason why we need revival is because the Church turns from its
first love and falls into decline. And when revival comes it achieves,
sometimes in a few weeks, what could never have been achieved in years
of normal Christian activity.

The next question we must consider is this: How does a revival
begin? Is it something that forms in the minds of devoted Christian people and is then brought into being through powerful intercessory
prayer? Or is it something that originates in the mind of God and comes
down to earth irrespective of the desires or the prayer life of His people?

I have no hesitation in saying that in my opinion
revival begins in the mind of God. It is something that
God plans; men and women have little to do with it.
There are many things that Christians, by dedicated
and committed spiritual effort, can bring to pass in the
Church, but revival is not one of them. For instance,
evangelism, preaching, teaching, and counselling is
work that we do for God; revival is work that God
does for us.

FURTHER STUDY

Ezek. 18:1-32;
Isa. 55:7;
Acts 17:30

1. What does God
demand before He
will send revival?

2. What does this
involve?

Prayer

Father, let the wonder of Your sovereignty and power sink deep into my soul today.
Help me see how much bigger and greater You are than my imagination could ever
conceive. In Christ's Name I pray. Amen.

The place of prayer

"Ask the Lord for rain in the time of the latter rain …"
(v.1, NKJ)

For reading & meditation – Zechariah 10:1-8

We continue considering the question: How do revivals begin? A revival is a sovereign act of God in the sense that it is initiated by Him and not by the Church. It is at this point – the sovereignty of God – that Christians tend to differ in their thinking. One school of thought says: "Revival is a sovereign act of God and there is absolutely nothing that man has to do with it. God sends revival when He wills and does not consult or confer with any of His creation." Many of the great Welsh revivalists, such as Christmas Evans, Daniel Rowlands, John Elias, Thomas Charles Edwards, and John Evans subscribed to this view.

Another school of thought says: "Revival can happen any time the Church wants it – providing she is willing to pay the price." The great revivalist Charles Finney believed this. "The Church," he said, "can have a revival whenever it wills, for revival is like a crop of wheat – the farmer sows and then in due course the wheat comes up. When we are willing to sow the seeds of prayer and travail in the red furrows of God's fields then as sure as night follows day – we will have a revival."

The truth, so I believe, lies somewhere between these two views. Revival is a sovereign act of God in the sense that He alone can produce it, but I believe that He deigns to hand over to His people the responsibility of bringing it down from heaven by fervent believing intercession. Every great outpouring of the Holy Spirit – Pentecost included – began in the mind of God but it broke through on earth at the point of passionate and persevering prayer.

FURTHER STUDY

Gal. 6:1-10;
John 12:24;
Eccl. 11:1;
2 Cor. 9:6

1. What is the principle underlying sowing and reaping?

2. How does this relate to revival?

Prayer

O Father, if so much depends upon prayer, then wake me up to its power and its importance. Help me this day to catch a new vision of what it means to be an intercessor. In Christ's Name I ask it. Amen.

Involved in government

*"... that now, through the church, the manifold wisdom of
God should be made known ..."* (v.10)

For reading & meditation – Ephesians 3:1-13

Today we ask: What does it mean when we say that God is sovereign?
Sovereignty simply means to possess supreme power. What we have
to be careful about when we talk of the sovereignty of God is that we do
not fall for the idea (as some have) that this is God's *greatest* attribute;
His greatest attribute is love. And because He is love this means (so I
believe) that He delights to have His redeemed children become
involved with Him in bringing His purposes to pass.

Anyone who writes on the subject of revival has to come to a point
where these two great and important truths – the sovereignty of God and
the involvement of man – have to be harmonised. I am at that point right
now. A way of thinking about this issue which has always satisfied me is
to see these two thoughts like two rails that run from one end of the
Scriptures to the other. One rail is the sovereignty of God and the other,
the involvement of man. If you try to keep to only one rail you finish up
being derailed. Those who focus only on the sovereignty of God
inevitably result in minimising the responsibility of man. And those who
focus only on the responsibility of man end up minimising the sovereignty of God.

When we move along both rails, making sure that
we do not place a disproportionate emphasis on either
truth, then we are more likely to arrive at sound judgements and correct conclusions. God is sovereign but
He is also a *loving* Sovereign and by virtue of this fact
delights to involve His people in the affairs of government.

FURTHER STUDY

Acts 12:1-19;
Luke 1:10;
Acts 1:14; 4:24

*1. What was the
result of corporate
prayer?*

*2. How did the
believers respond to
Peter's appearance?*

Prayer

Gracious and loving Father, how can we Your Church sufficiently thank You for the
fact that You love us enough to involve us in Your government? Help us to see that
we are there not because we deserve it, but because You desire it. Amen.

"Except through prayer"

"Devote yourselves to prayer ...." (v.2)
For reading & meditation – Colossians 4:2-15

A single sentence written by the great John Wesley has helped me more than anything else to balance the two great truths we referred to yesterday – the sovereignty of God and the responsibility of man. Here is the statement which Wesley made: "God does nothing redemptively in the world – except through prayer."

Permit me to put into my own words what I think he was saying: whenever God wants to bring His purposes to pass here on earth He does not act arbitrarily, but touches the hearts of praying people and then ushers in His purposes across the bridge of prayer. God may be sovereign but He is not dictatorial or capricious. He can no more act against His nature and the principles He has established in the world than He could make a square circle or an aged infant. There are some things impossible even for God, and acting independently of the principles of prayer is one of them. This is why prayer and revival are so inseparably linked. I know of no revival that is not connected in some way with powerful, believing, intercessory prayer.

This, then, is how I see God's sovereignty and man's responsibility being brought together in harmony: when God decides that in the interests of His people a spiritual revival is necessary, He lays a burden of prayer upon the hearts of His children – it may only be comparatively few – so that their prayers become the bridge across which revival power flows. Let Wesley's famous statement ring in your heart once again: "God does nothing redemptively in the world – except through prayer."

FURTHER STUDY

2 Kings 19:1-37;
Prov. 21:1;
Ex. 17:8-13;
Rev. 19:6

1. What caused Hezekiah to act as he did?

2. How did God show His sovereignty?

Prayer

O God, I see that Your purposes are not arbitrary or capricious but the expression of Your nature – a revelation of Yourself. Amid the splendour of Your majesty I feel a heartbeat – a heartbeat of love. Thank you, dear Father. Amen.

The wider context of revival

*"... if my people ... will humble themselves and pray ... then
will I hear from heaven and will forgive their sin ..." (v.14)*
For reading & meditation – 2 Chronicles 7:12-22

We continue meditating on the question: If revival is a sovereign act of God (and it is), does this mean that the people of God have no part to play in it? My answer to that question is a categorical "No". Revival is a sovereign act of God in the sense that He sends it where and when He wills, but a study of revivals of the past, both in Scripture and in the history of the Church, shows that revival always follows the prevailing prayers of God's people.

The central condition of the verse before us today is, "if my people ... *pray* ...". When Evan Roberts was asked the secret of revival he said: "There is no secret: ask and you shall receive." Matthew Henry, the renowned Bible commentator, wrote a good deal about this particular point and summed it up in this powerful statement: "When God intends a great mercy for His people, the first thing He does is set them a-praying." God is the only one who can produce revival, but the fervent believing intercession of His people is the ramp over which it flows into the Church.

It must be recognised that sovereignty is not the *only* thing at work in revival – love is also at work. We are dealing with a God who is beneficent as well as omnipotent. Once we see revival in this wider context – the context of love – we begin to understand why God inspires strong intercessory prayer in the hearts of His people prior to revival. He just loves His children to be involved with Him in bringing about His purposes.

FURTHER STUDY

John 15:1-17;
Jer. 29:13;
Mark 11:24;
1 John 3:21-22

1. When can we ask for whatever we want?

2. What is one of the conditions of answered prayer?

Prayer

O Father, I am grateful that You are a God who not only hears our prayers but delights to respond to them. Cause our prayers to be Spirit-inspired that we may pray aright and help build Your Kingdom. In Jesus' Name I ask it. Amen.

The burden of revival

"And the burden of the Lord shall ye mention no more: for every man's word shall be his burden …" (v.36, AV)

For reading & meditation – Jeremiah 23:33-40

We ended yesterday by saying that God loves His children to be involved with Him in bringing about His purposes, and that it is not in God's nature to ignore the great principle of prayer which He Himself has established in the universe. At the risk of being tedious, let me make the point again: although revival begins in the sovereign purposes of God, it comes into the world through the doorway of believing prayer.

John Wallace, principal of the Bible college I attended prior to entering the ministry, used to say: "Before somebody can experience a blessing, somebody has to bear a burden." He used to illustrate the point in this way: "Before deliverance came to the nation of Israel when they were in Egypt, Moses had to bear a burden. Before the great Temple of God could be built in Jerusalem, Solomon was called to bear a burden. Before the sins of the world could be removed Christ had to bear a burden. Before somebody can experience a blessing, somebody has to bear a burden."

This is a principle that can be traced throughout the whole of the Bible – from Genesis to Revelation. It can be seen at work, too, in the history of all religious revivals. Before God comes from heaven to work in extraordinary ways He places the burden of revival on the hearts of His people. And who does He choose to carry this burden? You can be sure that they will be men and women who are drawn to prayer and understand something of its power and potential. Would you, I wonder, be one?

FURTHER STUDY

Psa. 21:1-13; 38:9;
73:25; Isa. 26:9;
Mark 11:24

1. What will God grant to us?

2. How can a desire become a burden?

Prayer

Gracious Father, You know how my heart shrinks from such a great challenge as this. All I can say is – I am willing to be made willing. Help me, dear Father. In Jesus' Name. Amen.

God works through authority

*"… who has blessed us in the heavenly realms with every
spiritual blessing in Christ." (v.3)*

For reading & meditation – Ephesians 1:3-10

Another reason why God takes great care to involve His people when
He initiates a revival is because He is committed to working through
His Church – not behind her back. I said earlier, you might remember,
that our view of the Church will greatly influence our view of revival,
and now I must make the point again.

The Church (so I believe) is God's agent in the world through which
His purposes are demonstrated. She is here to model the kingdom of
God to the world. God is committed to working through her and not
around her, and no matter how lethargic His people become, He will not
withdraw from that commitment. If God wanted to exercise His sovereignty (and nothing else) then He could burst in upon His Church in
times of declension without regard to anyone. But, as we have seen,
there are other characteristics in God beside sovereignty – love and
respect being just two.

If there is one thing above all others that impresses me about God's
dealings with people in the Bible it is the fact that He greatly respects the
authority He establishes, even though that authority does not act in the
way He desires. It would have been easy for Him to
have swept aside the Old Testament kings and priests
who failed to do His bidding, but patiently and lovingly He worked to involve them in His purposes. If God
did that with His earthly people, Israel, then I cannot
conceive of Him doing any less with His heavenly people, the Church. He will make sure the Church is represented and involved in every single spiritual project
in the universe.

FURTHER STUDY

Hosea 10:1-15;
Deut. 4:29;
Psa. 105:4;
Isa. 55:6

*1. What did the
prophet exhort
children of Israel to
do?*

*2. How can we break
up our fallow
ground?*

Prayer

Gracious Father, Your commitment never to go behind the back of Your Church
to accomplish Your purposes amazes me. My heart says: a God who works like this can
have all there is of me to have. Amen.

"Revival praying"

"Oh, that you would rend the heavens and come down ..."
(v.1)

For reading & meditation – Isaiah 64:1-12

Now that we have seen the place which prayer plays in bringing about revival, without doing any injustice to the sovereignty of God, the next question we must face is this: What kind of praying is it that seems to precipitate a mighty and extraordinary move of God?

A phrase which crops up time and time again in revival literature is the phrase "revival praying". This is a term used to describe the special type of praying which observers have noticed takes place in the months or years preparatory to the outbreak of revival. Over the next few days I want to examine with you some of the characteristics of this phenomenon known as "revival praying". By doing so I hope to deepen our understanding and awareness of this mysterious but important subject.

First, "revival praying" is zealous praying. People pray with fervour and passion. It is not that they look with disdain upon formal prayers but, almost as if they cannot help it, their prayers catch alight and are uttered with what appears to onlookers to be uncharacteristic energy and enthusiasm. They become not only enthusiastic about their prayers but eager in the pursuit of them. They pray whenever they can, wherever they can and with whomsoever they can. Prayer becomes less of a duty and more of a delight. I am sure you have occasionally touched something like this in your own prayer times but prior to a revival it is not something that happens periodically but something that happens regularly, not just in a few scattered places, but generally.

FURTHER STUDY

Joel 2:1-13;
Psa. 34:18; 51:17;
Isa. 66:2;
2 Cor. 7:10

1. How should we turn to the Lord?

2. What does it mean to "rend your heart"?

Prayer

Father, I long to experience more zealousness and passion in my prayer life. I throw open every pore of my being to You today. Move into the whole of my life, but especially my prayer life, and set my prayers on fire. In Jesus' Name I pray. Amen.

The story of Jeremiah Lanphier

"… zeal for your house consumes me …" (v.9)
For reading & meditation – Psalm 69:1-15

We continue thinking about zealousness, which we said yesterday is one of the characteristics of "revival praying". An example of what I mean by zealous praying comes out of the story of the great revival which hit New York in the middle of the nineteenth century.

On 1st July 1857 a man by the name of Jeremiah Lanphier, described as "a quiet and zealous businessman", took up an appointment as city missionary in the Dutch Reformed Church in New York. He decided to hold a noon-day prayer meeting and distributed a few handbills inviting others to join him during the lunch hour every Wednesday. At the first meeting six people were present. The second week there were twenty and the third week over forty. It was then decided to hold the prayer meeting every day. Within months 10,000 people were gathering in the city every day to pray. Thus began in New York the spiritual awakening which eventually spread through America and in 1859 crossed the seas to the British Isles. Zealous praying – the kind that precedes revival – usually begins with one person in an area and then spreads to others. I know of no revival where this has not happened.

How can we explain this strange "spirit of prayer" that grips God's people prior to revival? What makes them want to be present at as many prayer meetings as they can get to and pour out their hearts in earnest supplication to God? There is only one convincing explanation – it is a supernatural phenomenon. The heart of revival is beyond psychological or sociological explanation. It has been well said that if in prayer we have great intention, then God gives greater attention.

FURTHER STUDY

Acts 3:1-10; 4:24;
12:12; 21:5

1. Where were Peter and John going?

2. What was the result?

Prayer

Father, I have already asked You to give me more zealousness in prayer; now I must go further and take it. I reach out with empty hands to receive the fullness of Your Spirit. From now on my prayer life shall be Spirit-taught and Spirit-wrought. Amen.

"Great prayer warriors"

"… I will not let you go unless you bless me." (v.26)
For reading & meditation – Genesis 32:22-31

We look now at the second characteristic of "revival praying" – tenacity and persistence. Read the record of revivals and you will find that this quality is also present. In the days prior to revival people not only pray zealously but they pray persistently. For over a period of thirteen years Evan Roberts prayed for revival to come to Wales. "There was never a day," he says, "when I didn't fling myself before God and cry out for Him to send the Holy Spirit to my native land." Dafydd Owen also prayed every day for over ten years for a great outpouring to come to the Principality. And concerning David Morgan it was recorded "that for ten years before 1858 a petition for the outpouring of the Holy Spirit was never absent from his prayers".

We must recognise that often this persistence was not something that was natural but was given by the Holy Spirit. It was said of Evan Roberts that when he was a boy, "he hardly ever saw anything through and would give up a task most easily".

Listen to what Jonathan Edwards, another great revivalist, had to say about the importance of persistence and perseverance: "It is very apparent from the Word of God that the Lord is wont often to try the faith and patience of His people, when crying to Him for some great and important mercy, by withholding the mercy sought for a season; and not only so but at first to cause an increase of dark appearances. And yet He, without fail, at last succeeds those who continue instant in prayer with all perseverance and will 'not let Him go except He blesses'."

FURTHER STUDY

Luke 18:1-8;
James 5:13-18;
1 Thess. 5:17

1. What did Jesus teach on prayer?
2. What did Elijah demonstrate?

Prayer

O Father, search my heart today and see if there is any hidden thing in me that holds me back from persistent and persevering prayer. Bring it to the light so that I can deal with it. I ask this in Jesus' Name. Amen.

"A revival is on the way"

*"And pray in the Spirit on all occasions with all kinds of
prayers and requests …" (v.18)*
For reading & meditation – Ephesians 6:10-20

We continue looking at the quality of tenacity or persistence as a
component of "revival praying". Prior to a revival this characteristic is seen even in those who were not naturally persistent or tenacious
people, and this is fairly clear evidence (so I believe) that something
supernatural is at work.

When the news of the American 1857 revival reached the shores of
Great Britain many churches (especially those in Northern Ireland and
Wales) became gripped with a desire to see the same thing happen here.
William Jenkins, the minister of a church in one of the Welsh valleys,
said in 1858: "Ever since the news of the outpouring of the Spirit upon
the American churches reached our country I longed and prayed that the
Lord would, in His infinite mercy, visit poor Wales. I immediately
brought the subject before the church and earnestly exhorted them to
'seek the Lord'. I related every fact and incident I could glean … in order
to produce in the minds of my people the desire for a similar visitation.
Some of our members prayed and *continued to pray* as I have never heard
them pray before. A new burden seemed to press upon their hearts. They
became persistent almost to the point of being
obsessed. Even before revival came there were no less
than eighty-five added to the church in about six
months" (italics mine).

Examples of persistent and tenacious praying gripping the people of God prior to a revival can be multiplied. They have made such an indelible mark in history that those who observe their occurrence are able
to say with confidence: "A revival is on the way."

FURTHER STUDY

Rom. 8:22-28;
Matt. 26:41;
John 16:24

1. What help do we
get in prayer?

2. What did the
disciples find?

Prayer

O Father, I cannot help but echo the words of Your disciples: "Lord, teach us to
pray." In this area I confess I am weak, but help me see that in You I am able for anything. So I shed my weakness and take Your completeness. Amen.

God – sleeping on the job?

"Awake, O Lord! Why do you sleep?" (v.23)
For reading & meditation – Psalm 44:13-26

A third characteristic of "revival praying" is boldness or directness. Here again I have been struck, as I have read and researched this subject, by the daring and direct language used by God's people when pleading with Him to send revival.

We can see something of this in the verses that are before us today. The psalmist appears to be accusing God of sleeping on the job. Listen to the graphic language used in the Moffatt translation of this passage: "Bestir thyself, Eternal one! Why sleep? Awaken! ah discard us not for ever! Why art thou hiding thy face, forgetful of our woe and our distress? For our soul is bowed to the dust." This language of the psalmist is forceful and direct but it is the kind of attitude and language that prevails with God.

Notice I say *attitude* as well as language. You and I can come before God and use similar language but if it is not accompanied by the kind of holy desperation that the psalmist felt, then it will sound false and hollow – even impertinent. Such was the spiritual decline around him that it looked to the psalmist as if God was asleep and needing arousing. His deep concern over the declining conditions with which he was surrounded made his language appropriate and permissible. When we feel as strongly about the moral and spiritual bankruptcy that surround us as the psalmist felt in his day, then we can speak as strongly as he did. We dare not copy the words unless we are also prepared to copy the psalmist's deep spiritual concern.

FURTHER STUDY

1 John 3:16-22;
Heb 4:16; 13:6

1. Why can we come
to God with
confidence?

2. What can we say
with confidence?

Prayer

O God, my concern at this moment is not so much whether You are awake but whether I am awake – awake to the urgent needs that lie all around me. Wake me up, dear Lord, and help me pray with boldness. In Jesus' Name I ask it. Amen.

Prayer God delights to answer

*"O Lord God Almighty, the God of Israel, rouse yourself
to punish all the nations ..." (v.5)*

For reading & meditation – Psalm 59:1-8

We must spend another day looking at this quality of boldness which seems to be a characteristic of all "revival praying". There is a fine line, of course, between impertinence and concern. To some it may appear that the psalmist has crossed this line. Telling God to rouse Himself hardly seems to be a reverent or respectful way of approaching Him. But, as we said yesterday, it is the spirit underlying the words that makes it permissible.

I have often heard people in prayer meetings try to copy the strong language of the psalmist and other Old Testament characters, but only on a few occasions have I felt that they had the psalmist's same burning concern. And lacking that concern, their prayers came across as empty and hollow. One biographer tells of listening to the great Christmas Evans praying before the outbreak of revival in a certain part of North Wales. This is what he said: "Wake up, O Lord, and shake Yourself. Can't you see what is happening to Your Church? It's shameful that You allow things to go on like this. Do anything – do something – and do it soon."

The biographer went on to say: "Those who heard him caught their breath and wondered why God did not strike him dead for his impertinence. But what they did not know was that Christmas Evans had earned the right to talk to God in this way." He was not just using language – he was expressing through that language the deep concern of his heart. And when those two things combine – passion and daring – you have the ingredients of the kind of prayer that God delights to answer.

FURTHER STUDY

Dan. 10:1-21;
Psa. 65:2; Jer. 24:7

1. How earnest was
Daniel?

2. What does "all
their heart" mean?

Prayer

O Father, once again I have to confess that my feet stumble on the path of prayer. There is so much to learn, so help me over the hard places. This is life and I must learn it. In Jesus' Name I pray. Amen.

"Pleading the promises"

"… Revive me according to Your word." (v.25, NKJ)
For reading & meditation – Psalm 119:25-32

Now we look at a fourth characteristic of "revival praying", which I am calling persuasiveness. As the word is sometimes used to convey the idea of being coercive, permit me to give it a more precise definition. One of my dictionaries defines it thus: "The art of being able to marshall one's arguments in a convincing way so as to leave the other person or persons little or no option." This exactly sums up what I have in mind when using the word in relation to "revival praying".

Here again, when examining the great prayers that precede revival, I have been struck by the way in which the men and women concerned build and develop their arguments on the basis of what God has said in His Word. You might have already noticed in the psalm before us today that the psalmist founds his plea for divine quickening on the fact that God has promised it in the Scriptures: "Revive me according to Your word." Some people call this "pleading the promises" – taking a clear promise which the Lord has made, reminding Him of it and insisting that He be held to it.

Charles Spurgeon, when teaching on prayer, used to say: "Every promise of Scripture is a writing of God which may be placed before Him in reasonable request, 'Do as Thou hast said.' The Creator will not cheat the creature who depends upon His truth; and far more, the heavenly Father will not break His own word to His own child." Our forefathers discovered that prayers which plead the clear promises of a covenant-keeping God are guaranteed success – it is time we discovered it too.

FURTHER STUDY

2 Cor. 3:1-18;
Heb. 10:16;
Rom. 2:14-15; 7:22

1. Where does God want to write His law?

2. How does He do it?

Prayer

Father, the concept that You are a covenant-keeping God fires my faith and energises my spirit as nothing else can. You are showing me a way of prayer that is breathtakingly powerful. Help me know how to use it. Amen.

What is a promise?

*"And now, Lord God, keep for ever the promise you have
made … Do as you promised …" (v.25)*
For reading & meditation – 2 Samuel 7:18-29

Yesterday we ended with the thought "prayers which plead promises
are guaranteed success". This raises this question: What is a
promise? A promise has been defined as, "a written declaration that
binds the person who makes it to do or forbear from doing a specified
act." When used of God, it is His pledge or undertaking to do or refrain
from doing a certain thing. Such promises form the basis of the prayer of
faith.

The validity and dependability of a promise rests on the character
and resources of the one who makes it, just as the validity of a bank
cheque depends on the honour and bank balance of the one who signs it.
It is the holy character and faithfulness of God that makes all His
promises credible. "Not one word has failed of all the good promises,"
said King Solomon (1 Kings 8:56). Those who have studied the great
prayers of the Old Testament are struck by the way in which the prayer
warriors continually reminded God of the promises He had made. We
see this, for example, in the passage before us today: "Do as you
promised".

It is not presumptuous to take God at His Word,
providing we are sure that the promise applies to our
particular situation. Note that last statement, for it is
extremely important. The requests in verses 25 and 26
of today's passage are built on the promises in the previous verses. In "revival praying" men and women
stretch their desires to the width of God's promises
and hold God to the pledge He has made that times of
refreshing *shall* come from the presence of the Lord.

FURTHER STUDY
1 Pet. 1:1-9;
Heb. 6:17; 11:17-19

*1. What have we
become partakers of
through the
promises?*

*2. What did
Abraham prove?*

Prayer

O Father, I see that this throws open infinite possibilities to me. But I see also the
danger of holding You to a promise that is not relevant or applicable. Give me the
wisdom to know the difference. In Jesus' Name. Amen.

"Are my hands clean?"

"O Lord, we acknowledge our wickedness and the guilt of our fathers …" (v.20)

For reading & meditation – Jeremiah 14:17-22

A fifth characteristic of "revival praying" is contrition. Even the most casual reader of the Old Testament cannot help but notice that when the leaders of the people approached God with the plea of revival they usually began by acknowledging their own sin and the sins of the people. Jeremiah does this in the passage before us today: "We acknowledge, O Lord, our wickedness and the iniquity of our fathers … Remember, do not break Your covenant with us" (vv.20-21, NKJ).

Every carefully researched report of revival I have read contains the record of people coming before God prior to the revival and openly confessing their sins. The Hebrides revival which took place in 1949 is a classic illustration of this. A group of people gathered to pray in a barn about twelve miles north of Stornaway. Kneeling in the straw one of them, a young deacon, opened up his Bible and read from Psalm 24: "Who shall ascend into the hill of the Lord? or who shall stand in his holy place? He that hath clean hands, and a pure heart …" (vv.3-4, AV).

After reading the passage twice the young man said: "Brethren, it is just so much humbug to be waiting thus night after night if we are not right with God. I must ask myself: Is my heart pure? Are my hands clean?" And at that moment something happened. Let Duncan Campbell, the man who wrote the account of the Hebrides revival, finish the story: "God swept into the barn, whereupon the group moved out of the realm of the common and the natural into the sphere of the supernatural. And that is revival."

FURTHER STUDY

2 Cor. 7:1-10;
Psa. 34:18; 51:17

1. What is godly sorrow?

2. Who is the Lord close to?

Prayer

Father, I see that prayer holds challenges for me which only a full and determined commitment can meet. I have come a long way with You, Lord. Now help me go further. In Jesus' Name. Amen.

A sure sign of revival

*"Then I acknowledged my sin to you and did not cover up
my iniquity ..." (v.5)*
For reading & meditation – Psalm 32:1-11

We are seeing that prior to revival the prayers of God's people are characterised by contrition and a desire to break with all known sin. The closest I have ever come to witnessing this came during a visit to South Korea in 1958. As you know, Korea has been experiencing religious revival since the beginning of the 60s, but in the year that I was there, although the people were greatly expectant, the Church could not be described as being in revival.

One morning I participated in a 4 am prayer meeting. As I entered the prayer venue – a large school assembly hall – I was conscious that I was about to witness something unusual. The place was crowded and there was a tense reverent expression of attention on every face. There was no singing and at a given signal people knelt for prayer. At first there was silence but soon the people began to pray aloud, one after the other, until within seconds their voices became a crescendo which then stopped as suddenly as it had begun. A man's voice rose in high-pitched tones and my interpreter told me that he was confessing his sins and the sins of the nation. No words of mine can adequately describe the intensity that was in his voice, the agony of his sobs and the penitence that seemed to grip him. Within minutes the same spirit of penitence swept through every heart in the audience – my own included.

I came away from Korea sensing that I had witnessed the first stages of a spiritual revival. When later I heard that revival had broken out I was not surprised. The signs had told me so.

FURTHER STUDY

Luke 15:1-21;
Prov. 28:13;
1 John 1:9

1. How did the prodigal son show penitence?

2. What is the result of confessing sin?

Prayer

O Father, help me never forget that Your Name is called Jesus because You save Your people from their sins. I know I am saved but now I ask – save me to the uttermost. In Christ's Name I pray. Amen.

"Labour pains"

"… I sat down and wept, and mourned for days; and I continued fasting and praying before the God of heaven." (v.4, RSV)
For reading & meditation – Nehemiah 1:1-11

We look now at the sixth and final characteristic of "revival praying": spiritual desperation. My one-time pastor, David Thomas, used to say to me when I was a young Christian: "If ever there is to be another revival in our nation, then it will be borne in on the shoulders of desperate men."

One of the best illustrations I know in the Old Testament of a person who experienced spiritual desperation is Nehemiah. When he heard of the pitiable condition of his fellow countrymen he reacted deeply. He was told: "The survivors there in the province who escaped exile are in great trouble and shame; the wall of Jerusalem is broken down, and its gates are destroyed by fire" (v.3, RSV). Look at the reaction of Nehemiah when he received this news: "When I heard these words I sat down and wept, and mourned for days; and I continued fasting and praying before the God of heaven" (v.4).

We do not read of many of the Jewish exiles reacting in this way. Nehemiah could easily have turned his attention to other things, but his heart was so sensitive to God that he became spiritually desperate.

FURTHER STUDY

Ezra.10:1-6;
Joel 2:12; Acts 13:2

1. What motivated
Ezra to fast?

2. What happened
when the early
disciples were
fasting?

Arthur Wallis, commenting on Nehemiah's reaction to the news that the walls of Jerusalem were reduced to rubble, says: "His feelings … were the labour pains out of which a new movement of God was born."

Nehemiah was so desperate to see God work that he not only prayed but fasted as well. People have to be pretty desperate to go without food! How desperate are you in connection with the need for revival? Desperate enough to do something about it?

Prayer

Father, You are probing deep. But I know You do it not to demean me but to develop me. Help me, I pray, to know something more of what it means to be spiritually desperate. In Jesus' Name I ask it. Amen.

"Desperate men"

"I spread out my hands to you; my soul thirsts for you like a parched land." (v.6)

For reading & meditation – Psalm 143:1-12

We continue looking at the characteristic of spiritual desperation which, we have been saying, usually makes its presence known in all "revival praying". I believe it was Karl Barth who once said: "We do not read our Bibles aright until we read them like desperate men." He meant, I think, that until we become spiritually desperate ourselves we will not be able to recognise the desperation that flowed in the hearts of the men and women who are portrayed in the Scriptures.

I wonder, as you read the psalm that is before us today did you feel the desperation that is present in the heart of the psalmist? Commenting on this psalm, C.S. Lewis said: "The first eleven verses were written in a strain that brings tears to the eyes. He is obviously a desperate man." Of course, the psalmist here is praying for personal revival and not national revival, but the principle to get hold of is this: desperate praying brings powerful and positive results.

Permit me once again to ask you a personal question: Have you ever felt desperate enough about the moral and spiritual conditions around you to spend a few days praying and fasting? Most people's response to the idea of fasting is: "Well, things are not desperate enough to demand *that*!" There's an old saying that goes: "Desperate situations demand desperate measures," I don't know how you view the world situation, but it seems obvious to me that things are in a desperate state. And they will only change as the desperation in the world is met and countered by a holy desperation in the hearts of the men and women who constitute the Christian Church.

FURTHER STUDY

Isa. 55:1-7;
Matt. 5:6;
Psa. 42:1-2; 63:1

1. What is promised to those who thirst?

2. How did David depict his longing for God?

Prayer

O Father, use the facts that I have read today to drive me to Your feet in a spirit of holy desperation. I cannot escape them – nor do I want to. Make me desperate – desperate enough to be a "fool for Christ" if that is necessary. In Jesus' Name. Amen.

Are you available?

"… I did not immediately confer with flesh and blood … but I went to Arabia, and returned again to Damascus." (vv.16-17, NKJ)

For reading & meditation – Galatians 1:11-24

Over the past days we have been looking at some of the marks of "revival praying" – the special characteristics that appear in the intercessions of those who feel deeply burdened for revival. We have examined six of these characteristics (though of course there are many more): first, zealousness; second, persistence; third, boldness; fourth, persuasiveness; fifth, contrition and sixth, desperation.

We now ask: What is it that causes these characteristics to manifest themselves? Is it something that God puts into people's hearts or is it something that arises out of the conditions that are around? Probably it is a combination of both. Oswald Chambers has the key to it, I think, when he says: "Whenever God plans to send revival blessing He first lays a burden for it on the hearts of those who make themselves available to Him." Note the phrase: "those who make themselves available to Him". Oswald Chambers tells the story of how an aged saint came to his pastor one night and announced: "We are about to have a revival." The pastor asked him why he thought this, whereupon the old man replied: "I went into the stable to take care of my cattle two hours ago, and the Lord has kept me in prayer until just now. Because of this I just know we are going to have a revival." Oswald Chambers continues: "Sure enough, a revival followed just as the old man had predicted."

Are we similarly available to God? Would we be spiritually sensitive enough to know when God is breaking in upon us to lay a burden of prayer upon our hearts for revival? Is this perhaps the real reason why revival tarries?

FURTHER STUDY

John 3:1-8;
Rom. 8:14;
Acts 10:19-20

1. What did Jesus say of the Holy Spirit?

2. What was Peter's experience?

Prayer

Gracious and loving heavenly Father, once again You have Your finger on a nerve centre in my life – and I wince. Help me not to draw back, for I know that here are the issues of life and death. Help me be available. In Jesus' Name I pray. Amen.

"The spirit of prayer"

"And I will pour out on the house of David and the inhabitants of Jerusalem a spirit of grace and supplication." (v.10)

For reading & meditation – Zechariah 12:1-14

One of the insights I discovered many years ago which threw a whole new light upon the subject of revival came from the phrase found in the verse before us today: "a spirit of grace and supplication". The passage refers to the days of Christ's return when God will pour out His Holy Spirit upon the people of Israel so that they recognise the One they crucified as their one true Messiah. As a result of the Spirit's work in their hearts, they will be able to approach God with a degree of prayer and supplication that they never before experienced.

I believe something similar happens in the hearts of those who carry a great burden for revival. They are lifted out of themselves into a new dimension of praying, so that their prayers become filled with a passion and an urgency that is greater than anything they ever before knew. Sometimes this is referred to in revival literature as "the spirit of prayer" or "the spirit of intercession".

Over the past few days I have asked you some deeply personal and challenging questions. Permit me to ask yet another: Are you willing to let God put upon your heart a burden for revival? Would you be prepared to be enrolled in the company of those who know what it means to be involved in what we have been calling "revival praying"? Think long before you answer, for the cost is great in terms of time, dedication, energy, commitment and effort. Keep in mind, however, that the rewards are worth more than the cost and no one can give anything to God without experiencing something greater in return.

FURTHER STUDY

Jer. 23:33-40;
Num. 11:11

1. What had Israel lost?

2. How did they make light of it?

Prayer

Father God, help me see as I face yet another challenge that You not only set before me extremely high demands but You also provide the power by which I can meet them. In Jesus' Name. Amen.

Don't wait for feelings – begin

"Call to me and I will answer you and tell you great and unsearchable things you do not know." (v.3)

For reading & meditation – Jeremiah 33:1-11

Following what we said yesterday about the "spirit of prayer", it occurred to me that some might conclude that unless one feels strongly impelled by the Spirit to pray for revival there is no real need to do so. But as our text for today implies, whenever we see that there is a need for revival, as there was in Jeremiah's day, we are instructed to pray for it. We must be careful that we do not wait for any special "moving" of the Spirit to do what the Word of God plainly tells us is our spiritual duty.

I have come across many Christians in my time who believe that prayer is of no value unless one "feels like it". They seem to think that the efficacy of prayer depends on the emotional keenness one feels as one prays. This is nonsense. D.L. Moody said: "When it is hardest to pray, we ought to pray the hardest." When we pray and do not really feel like it we bring to God not only our prayers but a disciplined spirit as well. We must be willing to recognise feelings but not to depend on them. Feelings fluctuate with our health, the weather or the news, and our communication with heaven must not depend on something as flimsy as feelings.

FURTHER STUDY

Isa. 65:17-25; 58:9; Zech. 13:9

1. What did Isaiah prophesy?
2. What has God promised when we call on His Name?

Having said that, however I must make the point that many of those who in their prayer times begin to take up the need of revival often find themselves being gripped and seized by a depth of passion and feeling they have never known before. They begin in the natural and are caught up into the supernatural. The important thing, however, is to *begin*.

Prayer

Father, show me even more clearly that I do not need to experience a "spirit of prayer" in order to pray for revival. If the spirit of prayer comes as I pray, then so be it. If it does not, I will pray anyway. Help me – in Jesus' Name. Amen.

"The magnetism of heaven"

"… they were cut to the heart and said to Peter and the other apostles, 'Brothers, what shall we do?' " (v.37)

For reading & meditation – Acts 2:36-47

An important and final question which we must look at before we close our meditations on revival is this: How great is our need at this moment in history for a great spiritual awakening? I would say that in most countries of the world it is very great. If revival is an extraordinary movement of the Holy Spirit bestowed upon the Church by a sovereign God, then when is God most likely to demonstrate this extraordinary work? Is it not at a time of extraordinary need? Such a time, I suggest, is upon us now. If I understand contemporary Christianity at all, then it is my conviction that the need for revival is not only great but urgent and desperate.

Take, for example, the issue of evangelism. It should be a matter of the deepest concern that with all its evangelistic efforts the Church is only touching a small proportion of the community. The fact that some are being converted should not obscure the fact that great masses of people remain unreached. We expend great effort and spend large sums of money on evangelistic crusades, which is right, but the results are rarely what deep down in our hearts we long for. We are thankful, of course, for those who are being won to Christ but surely it must concern us that in proportion to the population the results are but a drop in a bucket.

Revival would change all that. Although revival, as we saw, is different from evangelism, you can be sure that when revival comes the unconverted will crowd into the churches, drawn not by human persuasion but by the magnetism of heaven.

FURTHER STUDY

1 Kings 8:1-11;
Ex. 24:17; 40:34-
35; John 1:1-18

1. What happened when the glory of God filled the Temple?

2. What are 2 characteristics of God's glory?

Prayer

O Father, give us another Pentecost so that as in Bible days preachers will not call on sinners, but sinners call on the preachers asking: "What must I do to be saved?" In Christ's Name we ask it. Amen.

"A time of spiritual tragedy"

"… Jesus went out to a mountainside to pray, and spent the night praying to God." (v.12)

For reading & meditation – Luke 6:12-19

Another issue in today's Church which makes the need for revival urgent is the way in which the Church, generally speaking, has become more activity oriented than prayer oriented. There can be little doubt that today's Church has learned a good deal about how to organise events, how to get the best results from advertising, how to research and target specific objectives, how to identify trends and make predictions based on those trends … and so on. What it is not so good at is teaching people how to pray – to pray powerfully for God to make His mighty presence known in the world. I would point out again that I am speaking generally, for I know there will be many reading these lines who come from churches which are exceptions to what I am saying.

Now do not hear me speaking in condemning tones of the prowess of today's Church in the areas I have mentioned. It is good to research and study underlying principles, such as, for example, what makes for effective evangelism or how churches grow. There can be little doubt that the study of these things has greatly contributed to the life and development of the Church in this generation.

FURTHER STUDY

Prov. 6:1-11;
Eph.5:14;
Rom. 13:11;
1 Thess. 5:6

1. What can we learn from the ant?

2. What is the danger of over-activity?

Here, however, is the problem: it is so easy for us to become satisfied by our successes in the field of study and research that our satisfaction deadens our desire and robs us of a sense of need to see God work in a sovereign and extraordinary way through revival. We are in a time of spiritual tragedy when our activity becomes a blockage to His activity. Only prayer can keep our eyes fully upon Him.

Prayer

O Father, forgive us that we so easily let our successes move our focus away from what You can do, to what we can do. Bring us to our knees – metaphorically and literally. In Jesus' Name we pray. Amen.

When *we* become god

"Pride goes before destruction, and a haughty spirit before a fall." (v.18)

For reading & meditation – Proverbs 16:17-25

Another issue in today's Church which makes the need for revival urgent is unconscious self-dependence. I say "unconscious" because most Christians do not know they have this attitude – but they do, nevertheless.

This is how it develops: we learn ways of doing things for God that make us feel good. At first, the more important thing is not the feelings we get but the significance of the task in which we are engaged. Gradually, however, we become preoccupied with the good feelings that our actions give us and the significance of what we are doing takes second place. Subtly the tables have been turned – we have moved from depending on God for our significance to depending on the good feelings we get from what we are doing. Can you see the danger in this? And whatever we depend upon to hold our lives together and make them work – that is our god. So it can be said that when self-dependence rules our hearts then we become god.

Revival would change all this. In times of great spiritual awakening unconscious motives are brought into consciousness and men and women see themselves as they really are. The proud become humble, the arrogant become unassuming, and the self-dependent become God-dependent. One of the most difficult tasks of a Christian counsellor is to help people realise how they are hiding behind the defence mechanism of denial and come out from behind it. It sometimes takes months, even years, to get that point across. In revival God does it in one fell swoop.

FURTHER STUDY

Psa. 139:13-24;
1 Chron. 28:9;
Jer. 17:10

1. What was the psalmist's prayer?

2. What were David's words to Solomon?

Prayer

Gracious and loving heavenly Father, I don't want to wait for a revival in order that I might become a more real and aware person. You have my permission to do it this hour. Give me my own personal revival – today. In Jesus' Name. Amen.

The battle for the Bible

"For ever, O Lord, Your word is settled in heaven."
(v.89, NKJ)

For reading & meditation – Psalm 119:89-96

Yet another issue in today's Church which makes the need for revival urgent is a growing loss of confidence in the Scriptures. Not all churches have moved away from the authority of the Scriptures, but we must face the fact that many have.

"We are slowly reaching the position," says one writer, "where the Christian who is orthodox in his beliefs and convictions, who stands on the Bible and in the central tradition of the Christian faith is considered to be a dogmatic reactionary, a stubborn anti-intellectualist, an obscurantist to be pitied and derided. The gospel which brings men to a personal knowledge of Christ and to the joyful experience of the new birth has to be fought for in the very inner councils of the historic denominations. In conditions such as these it would be a glib and shallow mind that dared to say a revival is not our greatest need."

Revival brings with it a new confidence in the Bible. People who are moved upon by the Holy Spirit in times of great spiritual awakening invariably find their faith and understanding of the Bible being greatly quickened. An Irishman who was involved in the revival in Ireland in the mid 1800s said: "I used to read the Bible before revival came, but after I came in touch with the Holy Spirit the Bible became a new and different book. It was as if God had taken it up to heaven, rewritten it and handed it back to me. I now know it is inspired because it inspires me."

That is not the only reason, of course, why we know it is inspired but it is a good reason nevertheless.

FURTHER STUDY

2 Tim. 2:1-15;
Psa. 119:1-16;
Acts 2:42

1. What was Paul's exhortation to Timothy?

2. What did the early Church continue to do?

Prayer

Father, it is difficult to see how the battle for the Bible can be won apart from a mighty deluge of Your Holy Spirit. Your people need to be revived, refreshed and enlightened. Let it happen, dear Lord – soon. In Jesus' Name. Amen.

"The sound of marching"

"... when you hear the sound of marching in the tops of the mulberry trees, then you shall advance quickly ..." (v.24, NKJ)

For reading & meditation – 2 Samuel 5:17-25

Having recognised the urgent need for revival, we must ask: Will we see another great spiritual awakening in our own day? I cannot say with certainty, but I most definitely feel so. There are clear signs that a revival is on the way, but before looking at them, pause with me to focus on the passage before us today.

Soon after David had been made king over Israel he was threatened by the Philistines. His first concern was to find what God wanted him to do about it. After getting divine permission to proceed, he led a bold frontal attack that carried the day. Later, however, the Philistines returned and took up the position that they had occupied before. Without presuming on past guidance David again sought God's direction and obtained permission to attack. However, this time he was led to make a detour and take up a position behind the enemy, near the mulberry (or balsam) trees. God said: "When you hear the sound of marching in the tops of the mulberry trees, then bestir yourself; for then has the Lord gone out before you, to smite the army of the Philistines" (v.24, Amplified Bible).

These two battles illustrate the difference between the normal activity of the Holy Spirit in the Church and the way He operates in revival. In the first we see David acting under God's direction and with His enabling. In the second it is God who takes the field and David follows on behind gathering up the spoils of victory. We have witnessed for decades the normal operation of the Spirit; the time has now come to prepare for revival.

FURTHER STUDY

Psa. 85:1-13;
Hab. 3:1-19

1. What was the psalmist's prayer?

2. What was his expectation?

Prayer

O Father, quicken my faith to believe for an outpouring of the Spirit as great if not greater than at Pentecost. I want to live in Your Word and Your Word to live in me. Fill Your Church with Your glory – and let it overflow. In Jesus' Name I ask it. Amen.

Three signs of coming revival

"… Zion … For Your servants take pleasure in her stones, and show favour to her dust." (vv.13-14, NKJ)

For reading & meditation – Psalm 102:1-17

We saw yesterday that before God came down and intervened in the battle against the Philistines He gave David a sign that He was about to move in a supernatural way against the enemy. I am emboldened to say that I believe God is giving us at this hour in history some clear signs that He is about to move in great power throughout the world.

The first sign I see is an increasing interest in the subject of revival. Almost every Christian leader I have spoken to recently has talked to me about his or her concern for a spiritual revival. I hear it also in the new hymns and songs that are being written for the Church. God is touching the hearts of His people in a fresh and wonderful way to pray and expect a great Holy Spirit revival.

The second sign I see is a deep desire amongst Christians to forget denominational differences and identify themselves simply as brothers and sisters in Christ. The preparation of the first disciples at Pentecost came as they were all "with one accord" in one place (Acts 2:1, AV). A third sign I see is a growing desire in the hearts of believers everywhere to pray and intercede for revival. It is one thing to be interested in revival; it is another to be interested enough to give time to pray and intercede for it. When God finds those who are as concerned for revival as God's people were about the stones and dust of Zion (as our passage for today points out), it will not be long before those who mourn are comforted – by divine intervention.

FURTHER STUDY

Acts 2:1-7;
John 17:1-26;
1 Cor. 1:10

1. What was the prayer of Jesus?
2. What did Paul beseech the Corinthians?

Prayer

My Father and my God, deepen my conviction that revival is not just a dream but a reality. You have sent revival before and You can do so again. I believe – help Thou my unbelief. In Christ's Name I ask it. Amen.

"The watchman on the walls"

"Behold … new things I declare; before they spring forth I tell you of them." (v.9, NKJ)

For reading & meditation – Isaiah 42:1-9

"There is a vital faith element which is always in evidence in the days preceding a revival," says Arthur Wallis in his book *Rain from Heaven*, and the stimulus for that faith is provided by those whom we may call "the watchmen on the walls".

In Bible times watchmen stood on the walls of Jerusalem during the night so that they could report any signs of enemy activity. These watchmen were also the first to see the dawn and in its light assess the situation in a way that those in the city could not.

Just as Jerusalem had its watchmen, so too does the modern-day Church. They are the seers, the prophets, the intercessors, who are constantly on watch and report to us their findings. I do not regard myself as one of this favoured group, but I do know many who are. They tell me that like Elijah of old they see "a cloud the size of a man's hand" scudding across the heavens and know that soon we shall see a deluge such as we have never seen before. I believe them, for my own spirit witnesses to what they say.

Charles Finney tells the story of a woman in New Jersey who felt that God was about to send revival to her town. She encouraged the leaders to arrange some special meetings and when they refused she went ahead herself, getting a carpenter to make seats so that she could have meetings in her house. He had hardly finished before the Spirit of God fell upon the community. How could this woman have been so sure? She was a watchman – a watchman of God.

FURTHER STUDY

Rev. 2:1-7;
Acts 3:19; 8:22;
17:30; Luke 15:21

1. What was Jesus'
message to the
Ephesian church?

2. What does
repentance mean?

Prayer

O Father, I may not be in the category of a "watchman" but help me keep so close to You that I will be able to hear Your faintest whisper. This I ask in Christ's peerless and precious Name. Amen.

"Keep your eyes on the tide"

"Your troops will be willing on your day of battle ..." (v.3)
For reading & meditation – Psalm 110:1-7

On this our final day we ask again: Has God something bigger for us than we are at present seeing? I hope I have convinced you that He has! How can we be open to receiving it? It comes at the precise moment God appoints but it is carried down from heaven on the wings of fervent believing prayer. Dr A.T. Pierson said: "From the Day of Pentecost until now, there has not been one great spiritual awakening in any land which has not begun in a union of prayer though only among two or three, and no such outward or upward movement has continued after such prayer meetings have declined." Revivals are born in prayer and sustained by prayer.

Just as there are signs concerning the second coming, so there are signs that the Lord is not far from reviving His whole Church. In the early days of the Salvation Army in France, the eldest daughter of General Booth, known by her French rank as the "Marechale", found herself at one point in an extremely discouraging situation. She wrote to General Booth asking for his advice, which came in these words: "Take your eyes off the waves and fix them on the tide."

FURTHER STUDY

Ezek. 37:1-14;
2 Kings 3:16-17;
Isa. 40:3-5;
Rev. 22:1

1. What was God's message to Ezekiel?

2. What will you do to bring about revival?

I give you now that same advice. Don't let your eyes become focused on the waves, with their advances and retreats. Keep your eyes on the tide and ask yourself: Is it rising? If you look with the eye of faith I think you will see that it is. When it breaks I pray that it will not find you or me unprepared, but that we shall be a people who are willing in the day of God's power.

Prayer

Father, I don't know whether I will live to see a world-wide revival but I want to live to experience a personal revival. Take me on from this point to know You in a much greater way. In Christ's Name I ask it. Amen.

Index

Index

Index

Index

THE WORLD'S CLASSICS

THE ILIAD

THE ILIAD was probably composed around 750 BC, when oral verse composition was the only way of telling a story in any permanent form. Homer would almost certainly have sung his long narrative poem, to an audience who could neither read nor write. Behind him stood an ancient tradition of oral poetry, from which many of the dramatic and formulaic elements of the *Iliad* derive. But the work also clearly bears the marks of Homer's astonishing originality and genius, which has made it perhaps the greatest epic poem in world literature.

Little is known about Homer's life or personality. He probably came from one of the Aegean islands or from the mainland of Asia Minor. The *Iliad* appears to be the work of his mature years, the *Odyssey* (if indeed he was its author) of his old age. By tradition Homer was blind, which is how most of the portraits of him that survive from antiquity represent him.

THE POET Robert Fitzgerald was Boylston Professor of Rhetoric, Emeritus, at Harvard. He died in 1985.

G. S. KIRK, former Regius Professor of Greek at Cambridge, has written on Greek myths and philosophy, as well as on Homer. His books include *The Songs of Homer* and *Homer and the Oral Tradition*.

THE WORLD'S CLASSICS

HOMER
The Iliad

Translated by
ROBERT FITZGERALD

with an Introduction by
G. S. KIRK

Oxford
OXFORD UNIVERSITY PRESS

Oxford University Press, Walton Street, Oxford OX2 6DP

Oxford New York
Athens Auckland Bangkok Bombay
Calcutta Cape Town Dar es Salaam Delhi
Florence Hong Kong Istanbul Karachi
Kuala Lumpur Madras Madrid Melbourne
Mexico City Nairobi Paris Singapore
Taipei Tokyo Toronto
and associated companies in
Berlin Ibadan

Oxford is a trade mark of Oxford University Press

Robert Fitzgerald's translation first published 1974 in the USA
by Doubleday & Co. Inc.
First published in the UK 1984 by Oxford University Press as a World's
Classics paperback with a new introduction by G. S. Kirk

ISBN 0-19-281594-6

10

Printed in Great Britain by
BPC Paperbacks Ltd.
Aylesbury, Bucks

CONTENTS

THE ILIAD

CONTENTS

INTRODUCTION

G. S. KIRK

THE *Iliad* is the tale of a few days' fighting in the tenth year of the Trojan War, when the Greeks – Homer knew them as Achaeans or Argives or Danaans – had sailed across the Aegean to win back Helen and humble the great fortress-city of King Priam. Helen was wife of Menelaus of Sparta; most of the young Achaean aristocrats had wooed her, promising each other to help, if ever the need arose, the one among them who was successful. So when Paris, one of Priam's sons, abducted her (for he was as handsome as she was beautiful), this promise was brought into effect. It was left to Menelaus' brother Agamemnon, king of Mycenae 'of much gold', whose palace was in the hills overlooking the rich Argive plain in the north-west Peloponnese, to gather a great force from all the cities of Greece, which after certain difficulties sailed from Aulis in Boeotia (the 'Catalogue of Ships' in Book II is an adapted list of naval contingents there). After nearly ten years of stalemate the gods themselves became more close' involved in the war down below, as King Agamemnon offended first of all Apollo and then his own greatest warrior Achilles, whose mother was the sea-goddess Thetis and who was thus able to enlist the support of Zeus himself to restore his honour. That proved to be a costly affair, which led to the death not only of Hector the Trojan leader (which ultimately sealed the fate of Troy), but also, first, of Achilles' companion Patroclus. It is with these events, varied, tragic, and profound, that the *Iliad* is concerned.

It is an extraordinary poem, and one that makes unusual demands of the reader. Partly it is a question of style; long narrative poems in verse are bound in any case to be stylistically unfamiliar, to make heavy calls on our ability to tolerate what might appear as an unnatural way of expression. To say that when the *Iliad* was composed there was no literary prose, that verse was the only way of telling a story in any permanent form, provides some answer but raises new questions. Why was that so? What were the conditions of society and the techniques of communication that made epic hexameters the inevitable form of any ambitious tale of war and heroism? Obviously, in order to give even preliminary answers to such questions, we have to be able to assign this kind of composition to an approximate date or period, and, if not to one particular region, at least to a particular kind of social and material setting.

That runs directly counter to a recent approach to literary criticism which rejects any serious interest in the biography of the author, and in particular any reconstruction of his literary intentions, as irrelevant and misleading, together with any provision of historical glosses on the work itself. That we should be primarily concerned with literature and not history and biography – with the text before us, without too much distraction from problems over the exact conditions of its creation – is in one way obvious enough. Yet even with a relatively modern work, created under conditions we can understand (for example with full use of writing), that approach can be criticized. With a work in an unfamiliar medium like narrative verse, and in a 'dead' language, in a style that can be immediately seen as incompatible with familiar literate composition, it has to be rejected (in its severest form at least) as both restrictive and unimaginative. The kinds of archaeological and historical information that we find in a classical commentary on the *Iliad* (not that there has been a complete one in any detail for over eighty years) are admittedly often irrelevant to the poem as literature, and can sometimes interpose a barrier of pedantry and learning that the sensitive reader, Greekless or not, finds distracting and obstructive. Yet to present such a reader with the bare text, to expect him or her to understand from the internal evidence of the poem itself everything about its special idiosyncrasies of construction and style, is impractical if not worse.

What is he to make, for example (to take a minor concrete instance), of the common Iliadic practice of taking chariot and horses right into the thick of battle? Is that what people really did? If so, why do we not hear of more casualties among the horses and more isolation of warriors through the disabling of their chariots? Was that nevertheless something that really happened in this period (but then we are forbidden to think about period)? Or can it be put down to carelessness on the part of the composer (but then we are not allowed to consider evidence that might show whether he would be careless over such details or not)? Or take another difficulty that would strike any careful reader, insulated from distracting outside knowledge, of the unencumbered text whether in Greek or English: how is it that the unusual duel between Paris and Menelaus in Book III is apparently closely copied, and at equal length, so soon afterwards as the beginning of Book VII, this time between Hector and Ajax?* Certain details may differ, but the overall similarity is striking – except that this second duel seems pointless, and ends in anticlimax when the heralds intervene because night is coming on. It is not archaeological information that will help solve either problem, but rather historical knowledge in the broadest sense, particularly about the development of the technique of writing, the characteristics of the preceding 'oral' period, and the special difficulties facing an ambitious composer of a large-scale narrative without the full resources of writing.

For the Greeks had a peculiar relation to writing; they were late to acquire it from their more progressive neighbours in the second millennium BC, and then they applied their clumsy syllabary (in the so-called 'Linear B' script found on the famous clay tablets from Knossos in Crete and Pylos in the south-west Peloponnese) only to documentary purposes – whereas cuneiform, for example, had been used for literary texts in Mesopotamia for over a thousand years before. Then by the end of the Bronze Age, when the Mycenaean empire, whose last great venture is described in the *Iliad* itself, went down in ruins, that archaic syllabary became forgotten and disappeared. Infinitely more practical and accurate systems were now available around the eastern end of the Mediterranean, and it was from the Levant that the Phoenician alphabetic system was adapted and introduced, probably by way of Cyprus and near the beginning of the eighth century BC. The earliest surviving examples of Greek writing, mere scraps recording an owner's name for the most part, are from the middle of that century; quite soon, around 725 BC, the earliest 'literary' inscriptions begin to appear, but even they are mere single hexameter verses, or pairs of verses, scratched on a pot to record its role as a prize, for instance. For this new writing system to become flexible enough to be used as a serious means of literary creation seems to have taken two or three generations more. Archilochus, the soldier-poet from the island of Paros, is the earliest surviving composer of whom we can be relatively sure that he *wrote* his poems (though with many survivals of remembered 'oral' verse), one of them referring to an eclipse of the sun that can be dated to 648 BC. And his poems were short ones, quite unlike the massive *Iliad*.

How did all this affect Homer? That depends on his date; the evidence for this is complicated and not absolutely watertight,

---

* The Translation uses the exactly transliterated Greek form Aias.

x   G. S. KIRK

but by combining several different kinds of indication (Homeric
figure-scenes on vases, quotations in other poets, above all the
mention in the *Iliad* and *Odyssey* themselves of roughly datable
objects and practices) we can assign the *Iliad* to around 750 or
725 BC, with the *Odyssey* perhaps as late as around 700 or even
680 BC. The consequence is, therefore, that Homer – as
composer, that is, certainly of the *Iliad* and perhaps also of the
Odyssey – must have been active in the very early days of the
new alphabetic writing system, and its technical limitations
(including those of writing-material and book-form) would have
made it unlikely that he was able to use it as a primary and
essential aid to his monumental task.

Whatever the use he made of writing (and it is likely to
have been very limited at best), we can be certain that his
audiences made no use of it whatever – during his lifetime, that
is. He composed for people who were essentially non-literate,
who *listened* to poetry as their ancestors had, and to poetry
that was sung rather than recited; at any rate, Homer's own
word for a poet is *aoidos*, or singer. He was, in short, an 'oral
poet' in the clumsy modern phrase, composing and delivering
his poems in something of the manner of the illiterate Yugoslav
guslari, singers of heroic Serbian and Montenegrin folk-epics,
who have been intensely studied by Western romantics and
scholars from the mid-nineteenth century until today, when
they are almost extinct. Homerists had already begun to draw
conclusions about Homer's use of repeated phrases when a
talented American, Milman Parry, finally demonstrated in 1926
that his style depended on an elaborate *system* of standardized
phrases that could only have been gradually perfected, not by
one man but as a result of a whole tradition of oral poetry
going back over several generations.

These standard phrases are an important and a prominent
element of Homeric style; they are known as 'formulas', and
the 'formular style' was a keyword of Anglo-Saxon Homeric
scholarship until the quite recent reaction against an emphasis
on the traditional and supposedly mechanical aspects of Homer's
language and in favour of his obviously striking creative
powers. The truth seems to be that both the formular language
of the long-standing tradition of oral epic and the individual
imagination and brilliance of the composer of the *Iliad* itself
are essential and complementary elements of that epic. And if
this is so, then the reader cannot properly understand and
appreciate the poem unless he takes the formular, repetitive
elements into account. Admittedly many modern translators

tend to diminish the repetitions in order to reduce this particular problem; Robert Fitzgerald has certainly done so, because he does not seek complete literalness, which can be rather deadly and usually misses the special Greekness of the text it seeks to preserve and transmit. His translation seems to me wonderfully strong and Homeric in character, even though it plays down to a certain extent this formular element in the Homeric style. Readers of this translation, therefore, are not likely to be as unnerved by apparently monotonous repetitions as those of some others – of Richmond Lattimore's, for example. Even so, they need to know that the repetitions are there in the Greek, and why they are there.

Moreover, there are other results of the oral and non-literate nature of early Greek heroic poetry that are analogous and cannot be disguised. The chief of these is the use, not of standard epithets and phrases this time, but of standard motifs, which find expression often enough in whole verses or sequences of verses, themselves therefore repeated exactly from time to time; but which can also be varied in detail and so in language. Beginning or ending a speech, arriving or departing, bringing a message, travelling to a destination whether by land or sea (or air, in the case of gods visiting earth), preparing a meal and making a sacrifice, boast and counter-boast followed by blow and counter-blow in battle – these are some of the typical actions of the poem, which can be developed into typical incidents or scenes which use much of the same content and expression each time they occur. Every description in every language has, of course, some of this standard quality, some of these almost formular elements; but the oral epic developed that kind of repetitiveness to a fine art, mainly because that is the only way that an oral singer, working without a fixed text either on paper or even in memory, can develop his theme. When we read Homer we are often aware of the reuse of a standard word, phrase, sentence, or motif in circumstances a literate composer would carefully avoid. That should not cause us to compare him unfavourably with the literate poet, who sedulously avoids repetition and, moreover, tends to cultivate variety as desirable in itself, an opportunity to describe something in a fresh way.

This repetition is something that does not explain itself in the text of the *Iliad*, and so deserves discussion as an external critical factor. At the same time, the 'oral style' – a concept which should not be elevated to absurd heights, as are implied by the occasional demand for the creation of a distinct 'oral poetics' – has its own positive merits, and that is important to understand. When Homer uses a formular epithet, for example, it is not merely a necessary concession to the unlettered singer who has no time to choose a word that is fresh or unfamiliar or particularly appropriate to the individual context. It is also a response to the antiquity, the austerity, and the solemnity of the poetical tradition itself. Thus a ship may be 'black' or 'equal' or 'balanced' or 'hollow' or 'swift' – a good variety of epithets, it seems; but then one notices that the choice between them is dictated simply and solely by the particular part of the hexameter verse that needs to be filled by a word – most easily by some kind of descriptive epithet. A ship is hollow or black according to its grammatical case and exactly where in the verse it is convenient to mention it, and this sometimes over-rides literal meaning; that is why a beached ship can be described as 'swift' on occasion. But even that is not carelessness, or allowing the mechanics of oral composition to get out of hand; rather it is that these hallowed descriptions were carefully shaped and isolated in the course of time, they were functional but also carried something of the essence of the object or person to which they were applied; a ship is potentially 'swift' even when it is ashore, and when an Achaean ship drawn up on the beach before Troy is called 'swift', then that tends to carry a sinister and pathetic reminder of what it should really be doing, indeed of the whole failure and frustration of the siege as it enters its tenth year.

The repetition of epithets, of phrases, of verses and passages, of standard themes and motifs gives the *Iliad* a distinctive flavour that would become enervating if carried too far; but that does not happen. Rather this element of oral style confers a certain almost hieratic character on the poem as a whole, and one that adds to the pleasure of reading it (but even more of hearing it), especially if one knows what is happening and accepts the particular style not blindly but as something of a connoisseur. But there are other ways, too, in which an appreciation of the possible by-products of oral composition and delivery can help one perceive the poem far better than if one simply faces the text in a state of innocence or ignorance. Important among these is the whole matter of consistency and inconsistency. Occasional anomalies in this respect are to be expected even in a written text, if it is an extremely long and complicated one; but where the composer does not even have the help of a written draft, and where everything has to be kept somehow in his head as he develops his plot progressively from performance to performance, the anomalies are likely to be more far-reaching. Homer manages his extensive list of characters, many of them mere victims for the great warriors on either side, with admirable skill, but the insignificant Pylaemenes notoriously contrives to be slain twice over. That is unimportant, not even a necessarily oral mistake. A more interesting and indeed problematic case is concerned with the complex figure presented by Agamemnon.

Agamemnon 'lord of men' (this formular description is occasionally applied to others, but it is Agamemnon's special hallmark), commander-in-chief of the whole Achaean expedition to Troy, is only occasionally presented with the majesty and venerability that this role would lead one to expect. As the army prepares to march out, in Book II, he is compared to a great bull standing out from a herd of cattle, and early in Book XI he has his own moment of martial glory and success. But the preparations in Book II had been immediately preceded by a highly equivocal scene in which he tests the troops' morale by proposing immediate retreat, and which nearly turns to disaster; and that followed the whole quarrel with Achilles in Book I, which shows him as selfish and arrogant. Moreover, the call for retreat in the morale-testing episode is repeated, in different circumstances, at the beginning of the ninth book, and establishes Agamemnon as distinctly lacking in moral stamina compared with men like Diomedes, Ajax, or Odysseus. When he finally ends his quarrel with Achilles, in Book XIX, he refuses to accept responsibility for it and blames it all on Zeus. Now part of all this may reflect a stereotype of the king or tyrant (which can be glimpsed in surviving Greek tragedy, and which could have had its origins in the epic tradition even outside the Iliadic Agamemnon) as arrogant and ungenerous in the face of bad news, or of advice contrary to his own wishes. Another part of it may have been deliberate; most of the great leaders have their own special characteristics, amounting at times almost to idiosyncrasy – Nestor's garrulity, Achilles' impetuosity, Ajax's imperturbability, for instance. Why should not Agamemnon have been depicted by the poet as rather unstable? Well, perhaps he was, although it is surprising for such a key role in the poem to be made so equivocal and disconcerting. But close study of, for example, the morale-testing episode in the second book suggests that his actions may sometimes result from other causes, in fact from the reshuffling of scenes and motifs or the conflation of different variant accounts. That sort of thing only rarely obtrudes in the *Iliad* – it probably

accounts for the division of the not wholly successful 'Battle of
the Gods' between Books XX and XXI – and may be the
result of either of two different kinds of manipulation: attempts
at expansion and elaboration of the poem after Homer's own
time (especially by rhapsodes in the seventh century BC), or the
relocation, adaptation, and development of traditional materials
by the monumental composer, Homer, himself. For I repeat that,
like other heroic singers, he can be shown to have used not
merely phrases and sentences from the tradition – that is, which
had been invented and refined by earlier singers – but also
themes and episodes. This introduces a new dimension into the
problem of Agamemnon's erratic behaviour and peculiar personality, for the reader has to consider whether part of it, at least,
may not be the unintended result of the kind of manipulation
and selection of earlier versions that the monumental *oral*
composer was inevitably committed to, here and there. Scholars
have not succeeded in determining the exact combination of
factors in such a complex equation, and the ordinary reader
may be no more successful; but at least he will understand the
poem better, and perhaps enjoy it more, if he has an idea of
the full range of possibilities in a case such as that of
Agamemnon.

Taking all that into account, what will the reader find? A
poem of truly heroic length that obviously aimed, among other
things, at conveying the quality of the whole Trojan expedition.
It does so by taking an episode in its tenth year that begins in
a clash of personalities on the Achaean side and develops into
a massive conflict between the two opposing armies which
leaves Patroclus and Hector dead, Achilles in despair, and Troy
on the verge of final collapse – this last was to be achieved by
the stratagem of the Trojan Horse, to which Homer alludes but
which lies outside his strictly envisaged scheme for the whole
epic. For one of the more remarkable characteristics of the poem
is the discipline it reveals on the part of a composer who had at
his disposal an enormous store of legendary material about Troy,
but steadfastly refused to dissipate the severe concentration of
his chosen theme and its immediate consequences. That theme
is stated in a deliberately limited form in the opening verses:

> Anger be now your song, immortal one,
> Achilles' anger, doomed and ruinous,
> that caused the Achaeans loss on bitter loss
> and crowded brave souls into the undergloom.

But that anger, that wrath (*mēnis* is the Greek word), infected
Agamemnon as well as Achilles, and involved the whole Greek

army in confusion and frustration. It brought out the tensions and contradictions that underlay the whole 'heroic' view of what matters most in life; that, by itself, makes the *Iliad* a fascinating exercise in moral self-analysis (if that is not too pedantic a way of describing one aspect of a work of art). For these heroes – the Greek word is *hērōes* and implies great men of the almost mythical past who were ultimately descended from the Olympian gods themselves – are kings and princes, royal leaders in peace and war, proud aristocrats whose life and pleasures were founded on wealth, display, prowess at hunting and fighting, and feasting among their equals. That may be too crude a picture – as kings, they also concerned themselves with dispensing justice – but it is one confirmed in the *Iliad* by Achilles, who in his rage against Agamemnon rejects both the warfare itself, as he fumes in his quarters among his followers, and even the urgent appeals of his close friends in the powerful embassy-scene of the ninth book. Why should a man risk his life in battle on behalf of other men's womenfolk, when his own Briseis has been taken from him in an act of despotic spite? The Trojans have done him no particular harm; they have not rustled his cattle or (one may infer) damaged his honour in the way Agamemnon has. That will all change when Patroclus, his great friend and protégé, is at last permitted by Achilles to wear his armour and fight in his place, and is subsequently killed by Hector. Now the heroic character, questioned and rejected by Achilles in his own case, reasserts itself in its most violent form as the hero goes half mad with rage and despair and slaughters Trojans by the dozen to make up for his own miscalculations and their consequences. Zeus himself has to bring him to his senses, and in its closing book the epic shows an unexpected and even sublime resolution of Achilles' inner conflicts. One kind of modern Homeric criticism has been concerned to show that the epic tradition did not have the resources, either conceptual or linguistic, for describing mental tensions or even the process of making up one's mind. That is wrong, as Achilles in the *Iliad* and Odysseus in the *Odyssey* clearly reveal; yet it is of course true that psychological insight is not an ordinary or a developed tool of the epic tradition. More usually a hero relieves his feelings by his actions, and action is the dominant mode of the poem as a whole; yet the action, especially in the long scenes of fighting, is given meaning and depth by the questioning of heroic aims that underlies it all.

Nevertheless many readers will find the descriptions of

fighting, especially in the central part of the epic from Book XI
to Book XVII, quite hard to accept without effort. Until then
the warfare has been punctuated by diversions, designed no
doubt to create a certain kind of suspense (even though the
audience knew the eventual outcome, if not of the quarrel
between Achilles and Agamemnon, at least of the war as a
whole). Fighting does not even begin until the fourth book;
before that has come the great quarrel in Book I, the preparations and catalogues in Book II, the formal duel and Helen's
identifying of the Achaean princes in Book III, Pandarus' breaking of the truce and Agamemnon's final inspection in Book IV
itself. The long fifth book is mainly devoted to Diomedes'
prowess in battle (for he is the most formidable attacking
fighter, Ajax being best in defence, after Achilles); but that is
given variety by his remarkable wounding of two deities,
Aphrodite and then Ares. No book hereafter, until close to the
end of the poem, is entirely free from fighting, but the sixth is
mainly concerned with Hector's return to Troy (ostensibly to
organize prayers for Trojan success) and the unusual scenes, for
the *Iliad*, of domestic life there; the ninth is centred round the
embassy to Achilles, and the tenth devoted to a dramatic night
patrol by Diomedes and Odysseus in which they capture the
Trojan spy Dolon and then kill the newly arrived Rhesus. Then,
in the eleventh book, after early successes by Agamemnon himself, he and Diomedes and Odysseus are all wounded and put
temporarily out of action. The threat from the Trojan forces
becomes even more urgent, and the severest part of the fighting
begins.

Hector breaks through the defences of the Achaean encampment at the end of Book XII after heavy fighting – in the *Iliad*,
that means after a long series of individual encounters in which,
after an almost ritual exchange of spear-thrusts or -throws,
the weaker and less god-protected warrior is struck down and
dies. The variety of fatal wounds is enormous (no formular
simplification here), and these anatomical descriptions are often
placed in deliberate and stark contrast with moving little
biographies of the victim as he expires. Yet every Homeric duel
ends as destiny has decreed and the particular hero's status
makes appropriate. These vignettes are more than a necessary
simplification of the complex action, a mere descriptive device;
they symbolize something important about war itself and how
in the end it destroys the individual human spirit, the only
thing (in the unsentimental Greek view) a man can count as
truly his own; but the mass fighting, with ranks of warriors

bearing down on each other across the plain, goes on in the background. Occasionally there are short evocations of the general scene, sometimes illuminated by the developed similes, here of rivers in flood or tumultuous seas or forest fires, that are one of the most brilliant and individual elements of the Homeric style. Other interludes in this austere martial core of the epic are rare, but they include the lyrical and even light-hearted episode of Hera's seduction of Zeus, to allow Poseidon a free hand in helping the Achaeans, that runs from Book XIV into XV. At the end of that book Hector sets fire to one of the ships, and Achilles at last dispatches Patroclus to relieve the hard-pressed Achaeans. He is victorious for a time and surges up to the walls of Troy, but is then dazed and stripped of his armour by the god Apollo, to fall an easy victim to Hector. Something similar will happen when Hector himself succumbs to Achilles six books later – these poets and their audiences were not really interested in a 'fair fight', or whether one great warrior was marginally tougher and more deadly than the other; they saw each encounter as a move in the complex operations of divine destiny, in which a man's success or failure depended on the gods as much as, or more than, on himself, and the important thing was to win or lose with honour, with pride, defiant or boastful as a true aristocrat should be.

That will be Hector's undoing, in a sense, in Book XXII, as he alone remains outside Troy with Achilles back in action and obsessively determined to avenge Patroclus' death. He wonders in a moment of weakness whether to retreat within the gates; his old parents Priam and Hecuba implore him from the walls, his mother baring her breast to remind him of the duty he owes her. All to no avail; he is determined, infatuated with the concept of honour, proud of himself as the Trojans' greatest defender, but destined by recurrent human weakness to turn and run as his formidable enemy, divinely inspired and with his brazen shield gleaming like fire, approaches. Just as Apollo deluded Patroclus, so Athena deludes Hector and lays him open to his inevitable death. Hector is one of the most appealing of these great princes, and the tenderness of his meeting with his wife and child back in Book VI is never forgotten. How far he was the special invention of Homer, or at least of some close predecessor in the oral poetical tradition, is uncertain – he may have been less of a solid historical figure, in origin, than Agamemnon or Odysseus, Diomedes or Cretan Idomeneus; but Troy (Ilios as Homer calls the city itself as distinct from its region) was destined to fall, and it had to

have a great fighter to match Achilles and justify the tradition
of a long siege.

At all events, the monumental poet leads his great construction into a powerful and unexpected conclusion. Troy, with
Hector's death, is doomed – let other singers tell of that in
lesser songs. What matters in the *Iliad* is the solution of the
dilemma posed by the quarrel and its consequences. That is
achieved in the most ·remarkable way. For Achilles becomes,
first, little more than an animal, as he drags Hector's body
behind his chariot round the walls of Troy in an act that was
wholly contrary to heroic behaviour, and then slaughters twelve
Trojan prisoners on the pyre of Patroclus. Then, with the
funeral games over which he presides serving as partial restoration of his heroic status, he becomes almost superhuman, an
instrument of Zeus at his most impressive, as he hands back
Hector's body to his father Priam as climax of that mysterious
and other-worldly nocturnal scene in the final, twenty-fourth
book. How the earlier stages of the epic have led up to that,
and whether Achilles, rather than, for example, warfare or the
heroic past itself, forms the true heart of the poem, are
questions critics have often posed. They are valid questions,
even important ones, but the overwhelming experience of reading
the *Iliad* as a whole may make them appear as aesthetically
irrelevant or incomplete.

SELECT BIBLIOGRAPHY

COMMENTARIES ETC.

J. C. Hogan, A *Guide to the* Iliad (based on the translation by Robert Fitzgerald) (New York, 1979)
W. Leaf, *Commentary on the* Iliad, 2 vols. (London, 1899–1901)
C. W. Macleod, Homer: Iliad *Book Twenty-Four* (Cambridge, 1982)
M. M. Willcock, A *Companion to the* Iliad (Chicago, 1976)

TRANSLATIONS

A Lang, W. Leaf, and E. Myers, rev. edn. (London, 1892)
R. Lattimore (Chicago, 1961)

STUDIES

J. Griffin, *Homer on Life and Death* (Oxford, 1980)
—, *Homer* (Oxford: Past Masters, 1980)
G. S. Kirk, *The Songs of Homer* (Cambridge, 1962), abbreviated as *Homer and the Epic* (Cambridge, 1964)
—, *Homer and the Oral Tradition* (Cambridge, 1977)
D. L. Page, *History and the Homeric* Iliad (Berkeley, 1959)
A. Parry (ed.), *The Making of Homeric Verse* (Oxford, 1971)
J. M. Redfield, *Nature and Culture in the* Iliad: *The Tragedy of Hector* (Chicago, 1975)
A. J. B. Wace and F. H. Stubbings, A *Companion to Homer* (Cambridge, 1962)

NOTE ON REFERENCES, SPELLINGS, AND PRONUNCIATION

REFERENCES to the *Iliad* are customarily given by book and line (e.g. IV 175) of the traditional Greek text. In this World's Classics edition of Robert Fitzgerald's translation the left-hand running headline states the span of lines of the Greek text rendered on the relevant double-page spread.

The translation has been completely reset in English style for this edition, and the transliteration of familiar names has for the most part been brought into line with the conventional English usage also adopted in the World's Classics *Odyssey*, translated by Walter Shewring.

It is possible that readers who do not know Greek may mistake disyllables in certain names, such as Coon and Selleis, for diphthongs, thus losing the metre of the line. Most of these names are included in the Glossary, which shows the correct pronunciation.

THE ILIAD

*

BOOK I

QUARREL, OATH, AND PROMISE

ANGER be now your song, immortal one,
Achilles' anger, doomed and ruinous,
that caused the Achaeans loss on bitter loss
and crowded brave souls into the undergloom,
leaving so many dead men – carrion
for dogs and birds; and the will of Zeus was done.
Begin it when the two men first contending
broke with one another – the Lord Marshal
Agamemnon, Atreus' son, and Prince Achilles.

    Among the gods, who brought this quarrel on?
The son of Zeus by Leto. Agamemnon
angered him, so he made a burning wind
of plague rise in the army: rank and file
sickened and died for the ill their chief had done
in despising a man of prayer.
This priest, Chryses, had come down to the ships
with gifts, no end of ransom for his daughter;
on a golden staff he carried the god's white bands
and sued for grace from the men of all Achaea,
the two Atreidae most of all:

               'O captains
Menelaus and Agamemnon, and you other
Achaeans under arms!
The gods who hold Olympus, may they grant you
plunder of Priam's town and a fair wind home,
but let me have my daughter back for ransom
as you revere Apollo, son of Zeus!'

    Then all the soldiers murmured their assent:
'Behave well to the priest. And take the ransom!'

    But Agamemnon would not. It went against his desire,
and brutally he ordered the man away:
'Let me not find you here by the long ships
loitering this time or returning later,
old man; if I do,
the staff and ribbons of the god will fail you.

Give up the girl? I swear she will grow old
at home in Argos, far from her own country,
working my loom and visiting my bed.
Leave me in peace and go, while you can, in safety.'

So harsh he was, the old man feared and obeyed him,
in silence trailing away
by the shore of the tumbling clamorous whispering sea,
and he prayed and prayed again, as he withdrew,
to the god whom silken-braided Leto bore:
'O hear me, master of the silver bow,
protector of Tenedos and the holy towns,
Apollo, Sminthian, if to your liking
ever in any grove I roofed a shrine
or burnt thigh-bones in fat upon your altar –
bullock or goat flesh – let my wish come true:
your arrows on the Danaans for my tears!'

Now when he heard this prayer, Phoebus Apollo
walked with storm in his heart from Olympus' crest,
quiver and bow at his back, and the bundled arrows
clanged on the sky behind as he rocked in his anger,
descending like night itself. Apart from the ships
he halted and let fly, and the bowstring slammed
as the silver bow sprang, rolling in thunder away.
Pack animals were his target first, and dogs,
but soldiers, too, soon felt transfixing pain
from his hard shots, and pyres burned night and day.
Nine days the arrows of the god came down
broadside upon the army. On the tenth,
Achilles called all ranks to assembly. Hera,
whose arms are white as ivory, moved him to it,
as she took pity on Danaans dying.
All being mustered, all in place and quiet,
Achilles, fast in battle as a lion,
rose and said:

          'Agamemnon, now, I take it,
the siege is broken, we are going to sail,
and even so may not leave death behind:
if war spares anyone, disease will take him . . .
We might, though, ask some priest or some diviner,
even some fellow good at dreams – for dreams
come down from Zeus as well –
why all this anger of the god Apollo?
Has he some quarrel with us for a failure
in vows or hecatombs? Would mutton burned

or smoking goat flesh make him lift the plague?'
   Putting the question, down he sat. And Calchas,
Calchas Thestorides, came forward, wisest
by far of all who scanned the flight of birds.
He knew what was, what had been, what would be,
Calchas, who brought Achaea's ships to Ilion
by the diviner's gift Apollo gave him.
   Now for their benefit he said: 'Achilles,
dear to Zeus, it is on me you call
to tell you why the Archer God is angry.
Well, I can tell you. Are you listening? Swear
by heaven that you will back me and defend me,
because I fear my answer will enrage
a man with power in Argos, one whose word
Achaean troops obey. A great man in his rage is formidable
for underlings: though he may keep it down,
he cherishes the burning in his belly
until a reckoning day. Think well
if you will save me.'
                    Said Achilles: 'Courage.
Tell what you know, what you have light to know.
I swear by Apollo, the lord god to whom
you pray when you uncover truth,
never while I draw breath, while I have eyes to see,
shall any man upon this beachhead dare
lay hands on you – not one of all the army,
not Agamemnon, if it is he you mean,
though he is first in rank of all Achaeans.'
   The diviner then took heart and said: 'No failure
in hecatombs or vows is held against us.
It is the man of prayer whom Agamemnon
treated with contempt: he kept his daughter,
spurned his gifts: for that man's sake the Archer
visited grief upon us and will again.
Relieve the Danaans of this plague he will not
until the girl who turns the eyes of men
shall be restored to her own father – freely,
with no demand for ransom – and until
we offer up a hecatomb at Chryse.
Then only can we calm him and persuade him.'
   He finished and sat down. The son of Atreus,
ruler of the great plain, Agamemnon,
rose, furious. Round his heart resentment
welled, and his eyes shone out like licking fire.

Then, with a long and boding look at Calchas,
he growled at him: 'You visionary of hell,
never have I had fair play in your forecasts.
Calamity is all you care about, or see,
no happy portents; and you bring to pass
nothing agreeable. Here you stand again
before the army, giving it out as oracle
the Archer made them suffer because of me,
because I would not take the gifts
and let the girl Chryseis go; I'd have her
mine, at home. Yes, if you like, I rate her
higher than Clytemnestra, my own wife!
She loses nothing by comparison
in beauty or womanhood, in mind or skill.

'For all of that, I am willing now to yield her
if it is best; I want the army saved
and not destroyed. You must prepare, however,
a prize of honour for me, and at once,
that I may not be left without my portion –
I, of all Argives. It is not fitting so.
While every man of you looks on, my girl
goes elsewhere.'

                    Prince Achilles answered him:
'Lord Marshal, most insatiate of men,
how can the army make you a new gift?
Where is our store of booty? Can you see it?
Everything plundered from the towns has been
distributed; should troops turn all that in?
Just let the girl go, in the god's name, now;
we'll make it up to you, twice over, three
times over, on that day Zeus gives us leave
to plunder Troy behind her rings of stone.'

    Agamemnon answered: 'Not that way
will I be gulled, brave as you are, Achilles.
Take me in, would you? Try to get around me?
What do you really ask? That you may keep
your own winnings, I am to give up mine
and sit here wanting her? Oh, no:
the army will award a prize to me
and make sure that it measures up, or if
they do not, I will take a girl myself,
your own, or Aias', or Odysseus' prize!
Take her, yes, to keep. The man I visit
may choke with rage; well, let him.

But this, I say, we can decide on later.
    'Look to it now, we launch on the great sea
a well-found ship, and get her manned with oarsmen,
load her with sacrificial beasts and put aboard
Chryseis in her loveliness. My deputy,
Aias, Idomeneus, or Prince Odysseus,
or you, Achilles, fearsome as you are,
will make the hecatomb and quiet the Archer.'

    Achilles frowned and looked at him, then said:
'You thick-skinned, shameless, greedy fool!
Can any Achaean care for you, or obey you,
after this on marches or in battle?
As for myself, when I came here to fight,
I had no quarrel with Troy or Trojan spearmen:
they never stole my cattle or my horses,
never in the black farmland of Phthia
ravaged my crops. How many miles there are
of shadowy hills between, and foaming seas!
No, no, we joined for you, you insolent boor,
to please you, fighting for your brother's sake
and yours to get revenge upon the Trojans.
You overlook this, dogface, or don't care,
and now in the end you threaten to take my girl,
a prize I sweated for, and soldiers gave me!

    'Never have I had plunder like your own
from any Trojan stronghold battered down
by the Achaeans. I have seen more action
hand to hand in those assaults than you have,
but when the time for sharing comes, the greater
share is always yours. Worn out with battle
I carry off some trifle to my ships.
Well, this time I make sail for home.
Better to take now to my ships. Why linger,
cheated of winnings, to make wealth for you?'

    To this the high commander made reply:
'Desert, if that's the way the wind blows. Will I
beg you to stay on my account? I will not.
Others will honour me, and Zeus who views
the wide world most of all.
                              'No officer
is hateful to my sight as you are, none
given like you to faction, as to battle –
rugged you are, I grant, by some god's favour.
Sail, then, in your ships, and lord it over

your own battalion of Myrmidons. I do not
give a curse for you, or for your anger.
    'But here is warning for you: Chryseis
being required of me by Phoebus Apollo,
she will be sent back in a ship of mine,
manned by my people. That done, I myself
will call for Briseis at your hut, and take her,
flower of young girls that she is, your prize,
to show you here and now who is the stronger
and make the next man sick at heart – if any
think of claiming equal place with me.'
    A pain like grief weighed on the son of Peleus,
and in his shaggy chest this way and that
the passion of his heart ran: should he draw
longsword from hip, stand off the rest, and kill
in single combat the great son of Atreus,
or hold his rage in check and give it time?
And as this tumult swayed him, as he slid
the big blade slowly from the sheath, Athena
came to him from the sky. The white-armed goddess,
Hera, sent her, being fond of both,
concerned for both men. And Athena, stepping
up behind him, visible to no one
except Achilles, gripped his red-gold hair.
    Startled, he made a half turn, and he knew her
upon the instant for Athena: terribly
her grey eyes blazed at him. And speaking softly
but rapidly aside to her he said:
    'What now, O daughter of the god of heaven
who bears the storm-cloud, why are you here? To see
the wolfishness of Agamemnon?
Well, I give you my word: this time, and soon,
he pays for his behaviour with his blood.'
    The grey-eyed goddess Athena said to him:
'It was to check this killing rage I came
from heaven, if you will listen. Hera sent me,
being fond of both of you, concerned for both.
Enough: break off this combat, stay your hand
upon the sword hilt. Let him have a lashing
with words, instead: tell him how things will be.
Here is my promise, and it will be kept:
winnings three times as rich, in due season,
you shall have in requital for his arrogance.
But hold your hand. Obey.'

The great runner,
Achilles, answered: 'Nothing for it, goddess,
but when you two immortals speak, a man
complies, though his heart burst. Just as well.
Honour the gods' will, they may honour ours.'

On this he stayed his massive hand
upon the silver pommel, and the blade
of his great weapon slid back in the scabbard.
The man had done her bidding. Off to Olympus,
gaining the air, she went to join the rest,
the powers of heaven in the home of Zeus.

But now the son of Peleus turned on Agamemnon
and lashed out at him, letting his anger ride
in execration: 'Sack of wine,
you with your cur's eyes and your antelope heart!
You've never had the kidney to buckle on
armour among the troops, or make a sortie
with picked men – oh, no; that way death might lie.
Safer, by god, in the middle of the army –
is it not? – to commandeer the prize
of any man who stands up to you! Leech!
Commander of trash! If not, I swear,
you never could abuse one soldier more!

'But here is what I say: my oath upon it
by this great staff: look: leaf or shoot
it cannot sprout again, once lopped away
from the log it left behind in the timbered hills;
it cannot flower, peeled of bark and leaves;
instead, Achaean officers in council
take it in hand by turns, when they observe
by the will of Zeus due order in debate:
let this be what I swear by then: I swear
a day will come when every Achaean soldier
will groan to have Achilles back. That day
you shall no more prevail on me than this
dry wood shall flourish – driven though you are,
and though a thousand men perish before
the killer, Hector. You will eat your heart out,
raging with remorse for this dishonour
done by you to the bravest of Achaeans.'

He hurled the staff, studded with golden nails,
before him on the ground. Then down he sat,
and fury filled Agamemnon, looking across at him.
But for the sake of both men Nestor arose,

the Pylians' orator, eloquent and clear;
argument sweeter than honey rolled from his tongue.
By now he had outlived two generations
of mortal men, his own and the one after,
in Pylos land, and still ruled in the third.

In kind reproof he said: 'A black day, this.
Bitter distress comes this way to Achaea.
How happy Priam and Priam's sons would be,
and all the Trojans – wild with joy – if they
got wind of all these fighting words between you,
foremost in council as you are, foremost
in battle. Give me your attention. Both
are younger men than I, and in my time
men who were even greater have I known
and none of them disdained me. Men like those
I have not seen again, nor shall: Peirithous,
the Lord Marshal Dryas, Caeneus, Exadius,
Polyphemus, Theseus – Aegeus' son,
a man like the immortal gods. I speak
of champions among men of earth, who fought
with champions, with wild things of the mountains,
great centaurs whom they broke and overpowered.
Among these men I say I had my place
when I sailed out of Pylos, my far country,
because they called for me. I fought
for my own hand among them. Not one man
alive now upon earth could stand against them.
And I repeat: they listened to my reasoning,
took my advice. Well, then, you take it too.
It is far better so.

                'Lord Agamemnon,
do not deprive him of the girl, renounce her.
The army had allotted her to him.
Achilles, for your part, do not defy
your King and Captain. No one vies in honour
with him who holds authority from Zeus.
You have more prowess, for a goddess bore you;
his power over men surpasses yours.

    'But, Agamemnon, let your anger cool.
I beg you to relent, knowing Achilles
a sea wall for Achaeans in the black waves of war.'

    Lord Agamemnon answered: 'All you say
is fairly said, sir, but this man's ambition,
remember, is to lead, to lord it over

everyone, hold power over everyone,
give orders to the rest of us! Well, one
will never take his orders! If the gods
who live for ever made a spearman of him,
have they put insults on his lips as well?'

Achilles interrupted: 'What a poltroon,
how lily-livered I should be called, if I
knuckled under to all you do or say!
Give your commands to someone else, not me!
And one more thing I have to tell you: think it
over: this time, for the girl, I will not
wrangle in arms with you or anyone,
though I am robbed of what was given me;
but as for any other thing I have
alongside my black ship, you shall not take it
against my will. Try it. Hear this, everyone:
that instant your hot blood blackens my spear!'

They quarrelled in this way, face to face, and then
broke off the assembly by the ships. Achilles
made his way to his squadron and his quarters,
Patroclus by his side, with his companions.

Agamemnon proceeded to launch a ship,
assigned her twenty oarsmen, loaded beasts
for sacrifice to the god, then set aboard
Chryseis in her loveliness. The versatile
Odysseus took the deck, and, all oars manned,
they pulled out on the drenching ways of sea.
The troops meanwhile were ordered to police camp
and did so, throwing refuse in the water;
then to Apollo by the barren surf
they carried out full-tally hecatombs,
and the savour curled in crooked smoke toward heaven.

That was the day's work in the army. Agamemnon
had kept his threat in mind, and now he acted,
calling Eurybates and Talthybius,
his aides and criers:

                    'Go along,' he said,
'both of you, to the quarters of Achilles
and take his charming Briseis by the hand
to bring to me. And if he balks at giving her
I shall be there myself with men-at-arms
in force to take her – all the more gall for him.'

So, ominously, he sent them on their way,
and they who had no stomach for it went

along the waste sea shingle toward the ships
and shelters of the Myrmidons. Not far
from his black ship and hut they found the prince
in the open, seated. And seeing these two come
was cheerless to Achilles. Shamefast, pale
with fear of him, they stood without a word;
but he knew what they felt and called out:

                    'Peace to you,
criers and couriers of Zeus and men!
Come forward. Not one thing have I against you:
Agamemnon is the man who sent you
for Briseis. Here then, my lord Patroclus,
bring out the girl and give her to these men.
And let them both bear witness before the gods
who live in bliss, as before men who die,
including this harsh king, if ever hereafter
a need for me arises to keep the rest
from black defeat and ruin. Lost in folly,
the man cannot think back or think ahead
how to come through a battle by the ships.'

    Patroclus did the bidding of his friend,
led from the hut Briseis in her beauty
and gave her to them. Back along the ships
they took their way, and the girl went, loath to go.

    Leaving his friends in haste, Achilles wept,
and sat apart by the grey wave, scanning the endless sea.
Often he spread his hands in prayer to his mother:

    'As my life came from you, though it is brief,
honour at least from Zeus who storms in heaven
I call my due. He gives me precious little.
See how the lord of the great plains, Agamemnon,
humiliated me! He has my prize,
by his own whim, for himself.'

                    Eyes wet with tears,
he spoke, and her ladyship his mother heard him
in green deeps where she lolled near her old father.
Gliding she rose and broke like mist from the inshore
grey seaface, to sit down softly before him,
her son in tears; and fondling him she said:
'Child, why do you weep? What grief is this?
Out with it, tell me, both of us should know.'

    Achilles, fast in battle as a lion,
groaned and said: 'Why tell you what you know?
We sailed out raiding, and we took by storm

that ancient town of Eetion called Thebe,
plundered the place, brought slaves and spoils away.
At the division, later,
they chose a young girl, Chryseis, for the king.
Then Chryses, priest of the Archer God, Apollo,
came to the beach-head we Achaeans hold,
bringing no end of ransom for his daughter;
he had the god's white bands on a golden staff
and sued for grace from the army of Achaea,
mostly the two Atreidae, corps commanders.
All of our soldiers murmured in assent:
"Behave well to the priest. And take the ransom!"
But Agamemnon would not. It went against his desire,
and brutally he ordered the man away.
So the old man withdrew in grief and anger.
Apollo cared for him: he heard his prayer
and let black bolts of plague fly on the Argives.
    'One by one our men came down with it
and died hard as the god's shots raked the army
broadside. But our priest divined the cause
and told us what the god meant by the plague.
    'I said, "Appease the god!" but Agamemnon
could not contain his rage; he threatened me,
and what he threatened is now done –
one girl the Achaeans are embarking now
for Chryse beach with gifts for Lord Apollo;
the other, just now, from my hut – the criers
came and took her, Briseus' girl, my prize,
given by the army.
                        'If you can, stand by me:
go to Olympus, pray to Zeus, if ever
by word or deed you served him –
and so you did, I often heard you tell it
in Father's house: that time when you alone
of all the gods shielded the son of Cronos
from peril and disgrace – when other gods,
Pallas Athena, Hera, and Poseidon,
wished him in irons, wished to keep him bound,
you had the will to free him of that bondage,
and called up to Olympus in all haste
Aegaeon, whom the gods call Briareus,
the giant with a hundred arms, more powerful
than the sea-god, his father. Down he sat
by the son of Cronos, glorying in that place.

For fear of him the blissful gods forbore
to manacle Zeus.

'Remind him of these things,
cling to his knees and tell him your good pleasure
if he will take the Trojan side
and roll the Achaeans back to the water's edge,
back on the ships with slaughter! All the troops
may savour what their king has won for them,
and he may know his madness, what he lost
when he dishonoured me, peerless among Achaeans.'

Her eyes filled, and a tear fell as she answered:
'Alas, my child, why did I rear you, doomed
the day I bore you? Ah, could you only be
serene upon this beach-head through the siege,
your life runs out so soon.
Oh early death! Oh broken heart! No destiny
so cruel! And I bore you to this evil!

'But what you wish I will propose
to Zeus, lord of the lightning, going up
myself into the snow-glare of Olympus
with hope for his consent. Be quiet now
beside the long ships, keep your anger bright
against the army, quit the war.

'Last night
Zeus made a journey to the shore of Ocean
to feast among the Sunburned, and the gods
accompanied him. In twelve days he will come
back to Olympus. Then I shall be there
to cross his bronze doorsill and take his knees.
I trust I'll move him.'

Thetis left her son
still burning for the softly belted girl
whom they had wrested from him.

Meanwhile Odysseus
with his shipload of offerings came to Chryse.
Entering the deep harbour there
they furled the sails and stowed them, and unbent
forestays to ease the mast down quickly aft
into its rest; then rowed her to a mooring.
Bow-stones were dropped, and they tied up astern,
and all stepped out into the wash and ebb,
then disembarked their cattle for the Archer,
and Chryseis, from the deep-sea ship. Odysseus,
the great tactician, led her to the altar,

putting her in her father's hands, and said:
  'Chryses, as Agamemnon's emissary
I bring your child to you, and for Apollo
a hecatomb in the Danaans' name.
We trust in this way to appease your lord,
who sent down pain and sorrow on the Argives.'
  So he delivered her, and the priest received her,
the child so dear to him, in joy. Then hastening
to give the god his hecatomb, they led
bullocks to crowd around the compact altar,
rinsed their hands and delved in barley-baskets,
as open-armed to heaven Chryses prayed:
  'Oh hear me, master of the silver bow,
protector of Tenedos and the holy towns,
if while I prayed you listened once before
and honoured me, and punished the Achaeans,
now let my wish come true again. But turn
your plague away this time from the Danaans.'
  And this petition, too, Apollo heard.
When prayers were said and grains of barley strewn,
they held the bullocks for the knife, and flayed them,
cutting out joints and wrapping these in fat,
two layers, folded, with raw strips of flesh,
for the old man to burn on cloven faggots,
wetting it all with wine.
                          Around him stood
young men with five-tined forks in hand, and when
the vitals had been tasted, joints consumed,
they sliced the chines and quarters for the spits,
roasted them evenly and drew them off.
Their meal being now prepared and all work done,
they feasted to their hearts' content and made
desire for meat and drink recede again,
then young men filled their winebowls to the brim,
ladling drops for the god in every cup.
Propitiatory songs rose clear and strong
until day's end, to praise the god, Apollo,
as One Who Keeps the Plague Afar; and listening
the god took joy.
                   After the sun went down
and darkness came, at last Odysseus' men
lay down to rest under the stern-hawsers.
  When Dawn spread out her fingertips of rose
they put to sea for the main camp of Achaeans,

and the Archer God sent them a following wind.
Stepping the mast they shook their canvas out,
and wind caught, bellying the sail. A foaming
dark blue wave sang backward from the bow
as the running ship made way against the sea,
until they came offshore of the encampment.
Here they put in and hauled the black ship high,
far up the sand, braced her with shoring timbers,
and then disbanded, each to his own hut.

Meanwhile unstirring and with smouldering heart,
the godlike athlete, son of Peleus, Prince
Achilles waited by his racing ships.
He would not enter the assembly
of emulous men, nor ever go to war,
but felt his valour staling in his breast
with idleness, and missed the cries of battle.

Now when in fact twelve days had passed, the gods
who live for ever turned back to Olympus,
with Zeus in power supreme among them.
Thetis
had kept in mind her mission for her son,
and rising like a dawn mist from the sea
into a cloud she soared aloft in heaven
to high Olympus. Zeus with massive brows
she found apart, on the chief crest enthroned,
and slipping down before him, her left hand
placed on his knees and her right hand held up
to cup his chin, she made her plea to him:

'O Father Zeus, if ever amid immortals
by word or deed I served you, grant my wish
and see to my son's honour! Doom for him
of all men comes on quickest. Now Lord Marshal
Agamemnon has been high-handed with him,
has commandeered and holds his prize of war.
But you can make him pay for this, profound
mind of Olympus! Lend the Trojans power,
until the Achaeans recompense my son
and heap new honour upon him!'
When she finished,
the gatherer of cloud said never a word
but sat unmoving for a long time, silent.

Thetis clung to his knees, then spoke again:
'Give your infallible word, and bow your head,
or else reject me. Can you be afraid

to let me see how low in your esteem
I am of all the gods?'
                        Greatly perturbed,
Lord Zeus who masses cloud said: 'Here is trouble.
You drive me into open war with Hera
sooner or later:
she will be at me, scolding all day long.
Even as matters stand she never rests
from badgering me before the gods: I take
the Trojan side in battle, so she says.

   'Go home before you are seen. But you can trust me
to put my mind on this; I shall arrange it.
Here let me bow my head, then be content
to see me bound by that most solemn act
before the gods. My word is not revocable
nor ineffectual, once I nod upon it.'

   He bent his ponderous black brows down, and locks
ambrosial of his immortal head
swung over them, as all Olympus trembled.
After this pact they parted: misty Thetis
from glittering Olympus leapt away
into the deep sea; Zeus to his hall retired.
There all the gods rose from their seats in deference
before their father; not one dared
face him unmoved, but all stood up before him,
and thus he took his throne.
                                But Hera knew
he had new interests; she had seen
the goddess Thetis, silvery-footed daughter
of the Old One of the sea, conferring with him,
and, nagging, she enquired of Zeus Cronion:

   'Who is it this time, schemer? Who has your ear?
How fond you are of secret plans, of taking
decisions privately! You could not bring yourself,
could you, to favour me with any word
of your new plot?'
                        The father of gods and men
said in reply: 'Hera, all my provisions
you must not itch to know.
You'll find them rigorous, consort though you are.
In all appropriate matters no one else,
no god or man, shall be advised before you.
But when I choose to think alone,
don't harry me about it with your questions.'

The Lady Hera answered, with wide eyes:
'Majesty, what a thing to say. I have not
"harried" you before with questions, surely;
you are quite free to tell what you will tell.
This time I dreadfully fear — I have a feeling —
Thetis, the silvery-footed daughter
of the Old One of the sea, led you astray.
Just now at daybreak, anyway, she came
to sit with you and take your knees; my guess is
you bowed your head for her in solemn pact
that you will see to the honour of Achilles —
that is, to Achaean carnage near the ships.'

Now Zeus the gatherer of cloud said: 'Marvellous,
you and your guesses; you are near it, too.
But there is not one thing that you can do about it,
only estrange yourself still more from me —
all the more gall for you. If what you say
is true, you may be sure it pleases me.
And now you just sit down, be still, obey me,
or else not all the gods upon Olympus
can help in the least when I approach your chair
to lay my inexorable hands upon you.'

At this the wide-eyed Lady Hera feared him,
and sat quite still, and bent her will to his.
Up through the hall of Zeus now all the lords
of heaven were sullen and looked askance. Hephaestus,
master artificer, broke the silence,
doing a kindness to the snowy-armed
lady, his mother Hera. He began:

'Ah, what a miserable day, if you two
raise your voices over mortal creatures!
More than enough already! Must you bring
your noisy bickering among the gods?
What pleasure can we take in a fine dinner
when baser matters gain the upper hand?
To Mother my advice is — what she knows —
better make up to Father, or he'll start
his thundering and shake our feast to bits.
You know how he can shock us if he cares to —
out of our seats with lightning bolts!
Supreme power is his. Oh, soothe him, please,
take a soft tone, get back in his good graces.
Then he'll be benign to us again.'

He lurched up as he spoke, and held a winecup

out to her, a double-handed one,
and said: 'Dear Mother, patience, hold your tongue,
no matter how upset you are. I would not
see you battered, dearest. It would hurt me,
and yet I could not help you, not a bit.
The Olympian is difficult to oppose.
One other time I took your part he caught me
around one foot and flung me
into the sky from our tremendous terrace.
I soared all day! Just as the sun dropped down
I dropped down, too, on Lemnos – nearly dead.
The island people nursed a fallen god.'

   He made her smile – and the goddess, white-armed Hera,
smiling took the winecup from his hand.
Then, dipping from the winebowl, round he went
from left to right, serving the other gods
nectar of sweet delight. And quenchless laughter
broke out among the blissful gods
to see Hephaestus wheezing down the hall.

   So all day long until the sun went down
they spent in feasting, and the measured feast
matched well their hearts' desire.
So did the flawless harp held by Apollo
and heavenly songs in choiring antiphon
that all the Muses sang.

               And when the shining
sun of day sank in the west, they turned
homeward each one to rest, each to that home
the bandy-legged wondrous artisan
Hephaestus fashioned for them with his craft.
The lord of storm and lightning, Zeus, retired
and shut his eyes where sweet sleep ever came to him,
and at his side lay Hera, Goddess of the Golden Chair.

BOOK II

ASSEMBLY AND MUSTER OF ARMIES

NOW slept the gods, and those who fought at Troy –
horse-handlers, charioteers – the long night through,
but slumber had no power over Zeus,
who pondered in the night how to exalt
Achilles, how in his absence to destroy
Achaeans in wind-rows at the ships.
He thought it best to send to Agamemnon
that same night a fatal dream.

Calling the dream he said: 'Sinister Dream,
go down amid the fast ships of Achaea,
enter Lord Agamemnon's quarters, tell him
everything, point by point, as I command you:
Let him prepare the long-haired carls of Achaea
to fight at once. Now he may take by storm
the spacious town of Troy. The Olympians, tell him,
are of two minds no longer: Hera swayed them,
and black days overhang the men of Troy.'

The dream departed at his word, descending
swift as wind to where the long ships lay,
and sought the son of Atreus. In his hut
he found him sleeping, drifted all about
with balm of slumber. At the marshal's pillow
standing still, the dream took shape
as Neleus' son, old Nestor. Agamemnon
deferred to Nestor most, of all his peers;
so in his guise the dream spoke to the dreamer:

'Sleeping, son of Atreus, tamer of horses?
You should not sleep all night, not as a captain
responsible for his men, with many duties,
a great voice in the conferences of war.
Follow me closely: I am a messenger
from Zeus, who is far away but holds you dear.
"Prepare the troops," he said, "to take the field
without delay: now may you take by storm
the spacious town of Troy. The Olympian gods
are of two minds no longer: Hera's pleading
swayed them all, and bitter days from Zeus
await the Trojans." Hold on to this message

against forgetfulness in tides of day
when blissful sleep is gone.'
                            On this the dream
withdrew into the night, and left the man
to envision, rapt, all that was not to be,
thinking that day to conquer Priam's town.
Oh childish trust! What action lay ahead
in the mind of Zeus he could not know – what grief
and wounds from shock of combat in the field,
alike for Trojans and Achaeans.
                                    Waking,
he heard the dream voice ringing round him still,
and sat up straight to pull his tunic on,
a fresh one, never worn before. He shook
his cloak around him, tied his shining feet
in fitted sandals, hung upon his shoulder
baldric and long sword, hilted all in silver,
and, taking his dynastic staff in hand,
he made his way among the ships.
                                    Pure Dawn
had reached Olympus' mighty side,
heralding day for Zeus and all the gods,
as Agamemnon, the Lord Marshal, met
his clarion criers and directed them
to call the unshorn Achaeans to full assembly.
The call sang out, and quickly they assembled.
But first, alongside Nestor's ship, he held
a council with his peers – there he convened them
and put a subtle plan before them, saying:
  'Hear me, friends. A vision in a dream
has come to me in the starry night – a figure
in height and bearing very close to Nestor,
standing above my pillow, saying to me:
"Sleeping, son of Atreus, tamer of horses?
You should not sleep all night, not as a captain
responsible for his men, with many duties,
a great voice in the conferences of war.
Follow me closely: I am a messenger
from Zeus, who is far away but holds you dear.
'Prepare the troops,' he said, 'to take the field
without delay: now may you take by storm
the spacious town of Troy. The Olympian gods
are of two minds no longer: Hera's pleading
swayed them all, and bitter days from Zeus

await the Trojans.' Hold on to this message."
When he had said all this, the phantasm
departed like a bird, and slumber left me.
Look to it then, we arm the troops for action –
but let me test them first, in that harangue
that custom calls for. What I shall propose
is flight in the long ships! You must hold them back,
speaking each one from where he stands.'

                       How curtly
he told his curious plan, and took his seat!
    Now stood Lord Nestor of the sandy shore
of Pylos, in concern for them, and spoke:
'Friends, lord and captains of the Argives,
if any other man had told this dream,
a fiction we should call it; we'd be wary.
But he who saw the vision is our king.
Up with you, and we'll put the men in arms.'
    On this he turned and led the way from council,
and all the rest, staff-bearing counsellors,
rose and obeyed their marshal.

                    From the camp
the troops were turning out now, thick as bees
that issue from some crevice in a rock face,
endlessly pouring forth, to make a cluster
and swarm on blooms of summer here and there,
glinting and droning, busy in bright air.
Like bees innumerable from ships and huts
down the deep foreshore streamed those regiments
toward the assembly-ground – and Rumour blazed
among them like a crier sent from Zeus.
Turmoil grew in the great field as they entered
and sat down, clangorous companies, the ground
under them groaning, hubbub everywhere.
Now nine men, criers, shouted to compose them:
'Quiet! Quiet! Attention! Hear our captains!'
    Then all strove to their seats and hushed their din.
Before them now arose Lord Agamemnon,
holding the staff Hephaestus fashioned once
and took pains fashioning: it was a gift
from him to the son of Cronos, lordly Zeus,
who gave it to the bright pathfinder, Hermes.
Hermes handed it on in turn to Pelops,
famous charioteer, Pelops to Atreus,
and Atreus gave it to the sheep-herder

Thyestes, he to Agamemnon, king
and lord of many islands, of all Argos –
the very same who leaning on it now
spoke out among the Argives:
   'Friends, fighters, Danaans, companions of Ares,
the son of Cronos has entangled me
in cruel folly, wayward god! He promised
solemnly that I should not sail
before I stormed the inner town of Troy.
Crookedness and duplicity, it is clear!
He calls me to return to Argos beaten,
after these many losses.
                          'That must be
his will and his good pleasure, who knows why?
Many a great town's height has he destroyed
and will destroy, being supreme in power.
Shameful indeed that future men should hear
we fought so long here, with such weight of arms,
all uselessly! We made long war for nothing,
never an end to it, though we had the odds.
The odds – if we Achaeans and the Trojans
should hold a truce and tally on both sides,
on one side native Trojans, on the other
Achaean troops drawn up in squads of ten,
and each squad took one Trojan for a steward,
then many squads would go unserved. I tell you,
Achaean men so far outnumber those
whose home is Troy!
                     'But the allies are there.
From many Asian cities came these lances,
and it is they who hedge me out and hinder me
from plundering the fortress town of Troy.
Under great Zeus nine years have passed away,
making ship timbers rot, old tackle fray,
while overseas our wives and children still
await us in our halls. And yet the mission
on which we came is far from being done.
Well and good; let us act on what I say:
Retreat! Embark for our own fatherland!
We cannot hope any longer to take Troy!'
   He made their hearts leap in their breasts, the rank
and file, who had no warning of his plan;
and all that throng, aroused, began to surge
as groundswells do on dark Icarian deeps

under the south and east wind heeling down
from Father Zeus's cloudland – or a field
of standing grain when wind-puffs from the west
cross it in billows, and the tasseled ears
are bent and tossed: just so moved this assembly.
Shouting confusedly, they all began
to scramble for the ships. High in the air
a dustcloud from their scuffling rose, commands
rang back and forth – to man the cables, haul
the black ships to the salt immortal sea.
They cleared the launching-ways, their hearts on home,
and shouts went up as props were pulled away.

    Thus, overriding their own destiny,
the Argives might have had their voyage homeward,
had Hera not resorted to Athena
and cried: 'Can you believe it? Tireless
daughter of Zeus who bears the shield of cloud,
will they put out for home this way, the Argives,
embarking on the broad back of the sea!
How could they now abandon Helen,
princess of Argos – leave her in Priam's hands,
the boast of every Trojan? Helen, for whom
Achaeans died by thousands far from home?
Ah, go down through the ranks of men-at-arms;
in your mild way dissuade them, one by one,
from hauling out their graceful ships to sea!'

    The grey-eyed goddess Athena obeyed her, diving
swifter than wind, down from the crests of Olympus,
to earth amid the long ships. There she found
Odysseus, peer of Zeus in stratagems,
holding his ground.

                He had not touched the prow
of his black ship, not he, for anguish filled him,
heart and soul; and halting near him now,
the grey-eyed goddess made her plea to him:
    'Son of Laertes and the gods of old,
Odysseus, master mariner and soldier,
must all of you take oars in the long ships
in flight to your old country? Leaving Helen
in Priam's hands – that Argive grace, to be
the boast of every Trojan? Helen, for whom
Achaeans died by thousands, far from home?
No, no, take heart, and go among the men;
in your mild way dissuade them, one by one,

from hauling out their graceful ships to sea.'
   Knowing the goddess' clear word when he heard it,
Odysseus broke into a run. He tossed
his cloak to be picked up by his lieutenant,
Eurybates of Ithaca, and wheeling
close to the silent figure of Agamemnon
relieved him of his great dynastic staff,
then ran on toward the ships.

                              Each time he met
an officer or man of rank he paused
and in his ear he said: 'Don't be a fool!
It isn't like you to desert the field
the way some coward would! Come. halt, command
the troops back to their seats. You don't yet know
what Agamemnon means. He means to test us,
and something punitive comes next. Not everyone
could hear what he proposed just now in council.
Heaven forbid he cripple, in his rage,
the army he commands. There's passion in kings;
they hold power from Zeus, they are dear to Zeus!'
   But when Odysseus met some common soldier
bawling still, he drove him back; he swung
upon him with his staff and told him: 'Fool,
go back, sit down, listen to better men –
unfit for soldiering as you are, weak sister,
counting for nothing in battle or in council!
Shall we all wield the power of kings? We can not,
and many masters are no good at all.
Let there be one commander, one authority,
holding his royal staff and precedence
from Zeus, the son of crooked-minded Cronos:
one to command the rest.'

                              So he himself
in his commanding way went through the army,
and back to the assembly ground they streamed
from ships and huts with multitudinous roar,
as when a comber from the windy sea
on a majestic beach goes thundering down,
and the ebb seethes offshore.

                              So all subsided,
except one man who still railed on alone –
Thersites, a blabbing soldier,
who had an impudent way with officers,
thinking himself amusing to the troops –

the most obnoxious rogue who went to Troy.
Bow-legged, with one limping leg, and shoulders
rounded above his chest, he had a skull
quite conical, and mangy fuzz like mould.
Odious to Achilles this man was,
and to Odysseus, having yapped at both,
but this time he berated Agamemnon –
at whom in fact the troops were furious –
lifting his voice and jeering:

               'Agamemnon!
What have you got to groan about? What more
can you gape after? Bronze fills all your huts,
bronze and the hottest girls – we hand them over
to you, you first, when any stronghold falls.
Or is it gold you lack? A Trojan father
will bring you gold in ransom for his boy –
though I – or some foot soldier like myself –
roped the prisoner in. Or a new woman
to lie with, couple with, keep stowed away
for private use – is that your heart's desire?
You send us back to bloody war for that?
Comrades! Are you women of Achaea?
I say we pull away for home, and leave him
here on the beach to lay his captive girls!
Let him find out if we troops are dispensable
when he loses us! Contempt is all he shows
for a man twice his quality, by keeping
Achilles' woman that he snatched away.
But there's no bile, no bad blood in Achilles;
he lets it go. Sir, if he drew his blade,
you'd never abuse another man!'

                     So boldly
Thersites baited Marshal Agamemnon,
till at his side, abruptly,
Odysseus halted, glaring, and grimly said:
    'You spellbinder! You sack of wind! Be still!
Will you stand up to officers alone?
Of all who came here to beleaguer Troy
I say there is no soldier worse than you.
Better not raise your voice to your commanders,
or rail at them, after you lie awake
with nothing on your mind but shipping home.
We have no notion, none, how this campaign
may yet turn out. Who knows if we sail homeward

in victory or defeat? Yet you bleat on,
defaming the Lord Marshal Agamemnon
because our Danaan veterans award him
plentiful gifts of war. You sicken me!
      'Here is my promise, and it will be kept:
if once again I hear your whining voice,
I hope Odysseus' head may be knocked loose
from his own shoulders, hope I may no longer
be called the father of Telemachus,
if I do not take hold of you and strip you –
yes, even of the shirt that hides your scut!
From this assembly ground I'll drive you howling
and whip you like a dog into the ships!'
      At this he struck him sharply with his staff
on ribs and shoulders. The poor devil quailed,
and a welling tear fell from his eyes. A scarlet
welt, raised by the golden-studded staff,
sprang out upon his back. Then, cowering down
in fear and pain, he blinked like an imbecile
and wiped his tears upon his arm.
                                      The soldiers,
for all their irritation, fell to laughing
at the man's disarray. You might have heard
one fellow, glancing at his neighbour, say:
'Oh, what a clout! A thousand times Odysseus
has done good work, thinking out ways to fight
or showing how you do it: this time, though,
he's done the best deed of the war,
making that poisonous clown capsize. By god,
a long, long time will pass before our hero
cares to call down his chief again!'
                                      The crowd
took it in this way. But the raider of cities,
Odysseus, with his staff, stood upright there,
and at his side grey-eyed Athena stood
in aspect like a crier, calling: 'Silence!'
that every man, front rank and rear alike,
might hear his words and weigh what he proposed.
Now for their sake he spoke:
                              'Lord Agamemnon,
son of Atreus, king, your troops are willing
to let you seem disgraced in all men's eyes;
they will not carry through the work they swore to
en route from Argos, from the bluegrass land,

never to turn back till they plundered Troy.
No, now like callow boys or widowed women
they wail to one another to go home!
    'I grant this hardship wearying to everyone.
I grant the urge to go. Who can forget,
one month at sea – no more – far from his wife
will make a raider sick of the rowing bench,
sick of his ship, as gales and rising seas
delay him, even a month! As for ourselves,
now is the ninth year that we keep the siege.
No wonder at it, then: I cannot blame
you men for sickening by the beaked ships!
Ah, but still it would be utter shame
to stay so long and sail home empty-handed.
Hold on hard, dear friends!
Come, sweat it out, until at least we learn
if Calchas made true prophecy or not.
Here is a thing we cannot help remembering,
and every man of you whom death has spared
can testify:
                    'One day, just when the ships
had staged at Aulis, loaded, every one,
with woe for Priam and the men of Troy,
we gathered round a fountain by the altars,
performing sacrifices to the gods
under a dappled sycamore. The water
welled up shining there, and in that place
the great portent appeared. A blood-red serpent
whom Zeus himself sent gliding to the light,
blood-chilling, silent, from beneath our altar,
twined and swiftly spiralled up the tree.
There were some fledgeling sparrows, baby things,
hunched in their downy wings – just eight of these
among the leaves along the topmost bough,
and a ninth bird, the mother who had hatched them.
The serpent slid to the babies and devoured them,
all cheeping pitifully, while their mother
fluttered and shrilled in her distress. He coiled
and sprang to catch her by one frantic wing.
    'After the snake had gorged upon them all,
the god who sent him turned him to an omen:
turned him to stone, hid him in stone – a wonder
worked by the son of crooked-minded Cronos –
and we stood awed by what had come to pass.

Seeing this portent of the gods had visited
our sacrifices, Calchas told the meaning
before us all, at once. He said:

"Dumbfounded, are you, gentlemen of Achaea?
Here was a portent for us, and a great one,
granted us by inscrutable Zeus – a promise
long to be in fulfilment – but the fame
of that event will never die.

                    "Consider:
the snake devoured fledglings and their mother,
the little ones were eight, and she made nine.
Nine are the years that we shall wage this war,
and in the tenth we'll take the spacious town."

'That was his explanation of the sign.
Oh, see now, how it all comes true! Hold out,
Achaeans with your gear of war, campaigners,
hold on the beach-head till we take the town!'

After the speech a great shout from the Argives
echoed fiercely among the ships: they cried
'Aye' to noble Odysseus' words. Then Nestor,
lord of Gerenia, charioteer, addressed them:

'Lamentable, the way you men have talked,
like boys, like children, strangers to stern war.
What will become of our sworn oaths and pacts?
"To the flames," you mean to say, "with battle plans,
soldierly calculations, covenants
our right hands pledged and pledged with unmixed wine"?
Once we could trust in these. But wrangling now
and high words dissipate them, and we cannot
turn up a remedy, though we talk for days.

'Son of Atreus, be as you were before,
inflexible; commit the troops to combat;
let those go rot, those few, who take their counsel
apart from the Achaeans. They can win
nothing by it. They would sail for Argos
before they know if what the Lord Zeus promised
will be proved false or true.

'I think myself the power above us nodded
on that day when the Argives put to sea
in their fast sailing ships, with death aboard
and doom for Trojans. Forking out of heaven,
he lightened on the right – a fateful sign.
Therefore let no man press for our return
before he beds down with some Trojan wife,

to avenge the struggles and the groans of Helen.
  'If any man would sooner die than stay,
let him lay hand upon his ship –
he meets his death and doom before the rest.
My lord, yourself be otherwise persuaded.
What I am going to say is not a trifle
to toss aside: marshal the troops by nations
and then again by clans, Lord Agamemnon,
clan in support of clan, nation of nation.
If you will do this, and they carry it out,
you may find out which captains are poltroons
and which are valorous; foot soldiers, too;
as each will fight before his clansmen's eyes
when clans make up our units in the battle.
You can discern then if your siege has failed
by heaven's will or men's faintheartedness
and foolishness in war.'
                                  Lord Agamemnon
made reply: 'Believe me, sir, once more
you win us all with your proposals here.
O Father Zeus, Athena, and Apollo,
give me ten more to plan with me like this
among the Achaeans! Priam's fortress then
falls in a day, our own hands' prey and spoil.
But Zeus the storm-king sent me misery,
plunging me into futile brawls and feuds.
I mean Achilles and myself. We fought
like enemies, in words, over a girl –
and I gave way to anger first. We two –
if we could ever think as one, the Trojans'
evil day would be postponed no longer.
  'Take your meal, now; we prepare for combat.
Let every man be sure his point is whetted,
his shield well slung. Let every charioteer
give fodder to his battle team, inspect
his wheels and car, and put his mind on war,
so we may bear ourselves as men all day
in the grim battle. There will be no respite,
no break at all – unless night coming on
dissolve the battle lines and rage of men.
The shield strap will be sweat-soaked on your ribs,
your hand will ache and stiffen on the spearshaft,
and sweat will drench the horses' flanks that toil
to pull your polished car. But let me see

one man of you willing to drop out – one man
skulking around the ships, and from that instant
he has no chance against the dogs and kites!'

Being so dismissed, the Argives roared, as when
upon some cape a sea roused by the south wind
roars on a jutting point of rock, a target
winds and waves will never let alone,
from any quarter rising. So the soldiers
got to their feet and scattered to the ships
to send up smoke from campfires and be fed.
But first, to one of the gods who never die,
each man resigned his bit and made his prayer
to keep away from death in that day's fighting.
As for Lord Agamemnon, their commander,
a fattened ox he chose for sacrifice
to Zeus the overlord of heaven – calling around him
the senior captains of the Achaean host:
Nestor, then Lord Idomeneus, then those
two lords who bore the name of Aias, then
the son of Tydeus and, sixth, Odysseus,
the peer of Zeus in warcraft. Menelaus,
lord of the war-cry, needed no summoning;
he knew and shared the duties of his brother.
Around the ox they stood, and took up barley,
and Agamemnon prayed on their behalf:

'O excellency, O majesty, O Zeus
beyond the storm-cloud, dwelling in high air,
let not the sun go down upon this day
into the western gloom, before I tumble
Priam's blackened roof-tree down, exploding
fire through his portals! Let me rip
with my bronze point the shirt that clings on Hector
and slash his ribs! May throngs around him lie –
his friends, head-down in dust, biting dry ground!'

But Zeus would not accomplish these desires.
He took the ox, but added woe on woe.

When prayers were said and grains of barley strewn,
they held the bullock for the knife and flayed him,
cutting out joints and wrapping these in fat,
two layers, folded, with raw strips of flesh,
to burn on cloven faggots, and the tripes
they spitted to be broiled. When every joint
had been consumed, and kidneys had been tasted,
they sliced the chines and quarters for the spits,

roasted them evenly and drew them off.
The meal being now prepared and all work done,
they feasted royally and put away
desire for meat and drink.

                    Then Nestor spoke:
'Excellency, Lord Marshal Agamemnon,
we shall do well to tarry here no longer,
we officers, in our circle. Let us not
postpone the work heaven put into our hands.
Let criers among the Achaean men-at-arms
muster our troops along the ships. Ourselves,
we'll pass together down the Achaean lines
to rouse their appetite for war.'

                              And Agamemnon,
marshal of the army, turned at once,
telling his criers to send out shrill and clear
to all Achaean troops the call to battle.
The cry went out, the men came crowding, officers
from their commander's side went swiftly down
to form each unit – and the grey-eyed goddess
Athena kept the pace behind them, bearing
her shield of storm, immortal and august,
whose hundred golden-plaited tassels, worth
a hecatomb each one, floated in air.
So down the ranks that dazzling goddess went
to stir the attack, and each man in his heart
grew strong to fight and never quit the mêlée,
for at her passage war itself became
lovelier than return, lovelier than sailing
in the decked ships to their own native land.

As in dark forests, measureless along
the crests of hills, a conflagration soars,
and the bright bed of fire glows for miles,
now fiery lights from this great host in bronze
played on the earth and flashed high into heaven.

And as migrating birds, nation by nation,
wild geese and arrow-throated cranes and swans,
over Asia's meadowland and marshes
around the streams of Caystrius, with giant
flight and glorying wings keep beating down
in tumult on that verdant land
that echoes to their pinions, even so,
nation by nation, from the ships and huts,
this host debouched upon Scamander plain.

With noise like thunder pent in earth
under their trampling, under the horses' hooves,
they filled the flowering land beside Scamander,
as countless as the leaves and blades of spring.
So, too, like clouds of buzzing, fevered flies
that swarm about a cattle stall in summer
when pails are splashed with milk: so restlessly
by thousands moved the fighters of Achaea
over the plain, lusting to rend the Trojans.
But just as herdsmen easily divide
their goats when herds have mingled in a pasture,
so these were marshalled by their officers
to one side and the other, forming companies
for combat.

       Agamemnon's lordly mien
was like the mien of Zeus whose joy is lightning;
oaken-waisted as Ares, god of war,
he seemed, and deep-chested as Lord Poseidon,
and as a great bull in his majesty
towers supreme amid a grazing herd,
so on that day Zeus made the son of Atreus
tower over his host, supreme among them.

  Tell me now, Muses, dwelling on Olympus,
as you are heavenly, and are everywhere,
and everything is known to you – while we
can only hear the tales and never know –
who were the Danaan lords and officers?
The rank and file I shall not name; I could not,
if I were gifted with ten tongues and voices
unfaltering, and a brazen heart within me,
unless the Muses, daughters of Olympian
Zeus beyond the storm-cloud, could recall
all those who sailed for the campaign at Troy.
Let me name only captains of contingents
and number all the ships.

          Of the Boeotians, 31 bttm - map
Peneleos, Leitus, Arcesilaus,
Prothoenor, and Clonius were captains.
Boeotians – men of Hyria and Aulis,
the stony town, and those who lived at Schoenus
and Scolus and the glens of Eteonus:
Thespeia; Graea; round the dancing grounds
of Mycalessus; round the walls of Harma,
Eilesium, Erythrae, Eleon,

Hyle and Peteon, and Ocalea,
and Medeon, that compact citadel,
Copae, Eutresis, Thisbe of the doves;
those, too, of Coroneia, and the grassland
of Haliartus, and the men who held
Plataea town and Glisas, and the people
of Lower Thebes, the city ringed with walls,
and great Onchestus where Poseidon's grove
glitters; and people, too, of Arne, rich
in purple wine-grapes, and the men of Mideia,
Nisa the blest, and coastal Anthedon.
All these had fifty ships. One hundred twenty
Boeotian fighters came in every ship.

 Their neighbours of Aspledon, then, and Minyan
Orchomenus, Ascalaphus their captain
with Ialmenus, both sons of Ares, both
conceived in Actor's manor by severe
Astyoche, who kept a tryst with Ares
in the women's rooms above, where secretly
the strong god lay beside her. Thirty ships
these Minyans drew up in line of battle.

 Phocians in their turn were led by Schedius
and by Epistrophus, the sons of Iphitus
Naubolides, that hero; Phocians
dwelling in Cyparissus, rocky Pytho,
Crisa the holy, Panopeus and Daulis,
near Anemoreia, Hyampolis,
and by the side of noble Cephisus,
or in Lilaea, where that river rises.
Forty black ships had crossed the sea with these,
who now drew up their companies on the flank
of the Boeotians, and armed themselves.

 The Locrians had Aias for commander,
Oileus' son, that Aias known as the Short One
as being neither tall nor great compared
with Aias Telamonius. A corselet
all of linen he wore, and could outthrow
all Hellenes and Achaeans with a spear.
His were the Locrians who lived at Cynus
and Opoeis and Calliarus,
Bessa and Scarphe and the pretty town
Augeiae; Tarphe and Thronium that lie
on both sides of the stream Boagrius.
Aias led forty black ships of the Locrians

who lived across the channel from Euboea.
    Men of that island, then, the resolute
Abantes, those of Chalcis, Eretria,
and Histiaea, of the laden vines,
Cerinthus by the sea, the crag of Dion,
those of Carystus, those of Styra – all
who had young Elephenor Chalcodontiades,
the chief of the Abantes, for commander.
Quick on their feet, with long scalp locks, those troops
enlisted hungering for body armour
of enemies to pierce with ashen spears;
and Elephenor's black ships numbered forty.
    Next were the men of Athens, that strong city,
the commonwealth protected by Erechtheus.
He it was whom Athena, Zeus's daughter,
cared for in childhood in the olden time –
though he was born of plough-land kind with grain.
She placed him in her city, in her shrine,
where he receives each year, with bulls and rams,
the prayers of young Athenians. Their commander
here at Troy was Peteos' son, Menestheus.
No soldier born on earth could equal him
in battle at manœuvring men and horses –
though Nestor rivalled him, by grace of age.
In his command were Athens' fifty ships.
    Great Aias led twelve ships from Salamis
and beached them where Athenians formed for battle.
    Then there were those of Argos, those of Tiryns,
fortress with massive walls, Hermione
and Asine that lie upon the gulf,
Troizen, Eïonae, the vineyard country
of Epidaurus, Aegina and Mases:
these Diomedes, lord of the battlecry,
commanded with his comrade, Sthenelus,
whose father was illustrious Capaneus,
and in third place Euryalus, a figure
godlike in beauty, son of Mecisteus,
Lord Talaonides. Over them all
ruled Diomedes, lord of the battle-cry,
and eighty black ships crossed the sea with these.
    Next were the men who held the well-built city,
Mycenae, and rich Corinth, and Cleonae,
and Orneiae and fair Araethyrea
and Sicyon where first Adrastus ruled;

Hyperesia, hilltop Gonoessa,
Pellene, and the country round Aegium,
and those who held the north coast, Aegialus,
with spacious Helice. Their hundred ships
were under the command of Agamemnon,
son of Atreus: he it was who led
by far the greatest number and the best,
and glorying in arms he now put on
a soldier's bronze – distinguished amid heroes
for valour and the troops he led to war.

Next, those of Lacedaemon, land of gorges,
men who had lived at Pharis, Sparta, Messe
haunted by doves, Bryseiae, fair Augeiae,
Amyclae, too, and Helus by the sea,
and Laas and the land around Oetylus:
these Menelaus, Agamemnon's brother,
lord of the war-cry, led with sixty ships,
and drawn up separately from all the rest
they armed, as Menelaus on his own
burned to arouse his troops to fight. He burned
to avenge the struggles and the groans of Helen.

Next came the men of Pylos and Arene,
that trim town, and Thryum where they ford
Alpheius river, Aepy high and stony,
Cyparisseis, Amphigeneia,
and Pteleos and Helus – Dorium, too,
where once the Muses, meeting Thamyris,
the Thracian, on his way from Oechalia –
from visiting Eurytus, the Oechalian –
ended his singing. Pride had made him say
he could outsing the very Muses, daughters
of Zeus who bears the storm-cloud for a shield.
For this affront they blinded him, bereft him
of his god-given song, and stilled his harping.
The countrymen of Pylos were commanded
by Nestor of Gerenia, charioteer,
whose ninety decked ships lined the shore.

Then came
the troops who had their homes in Arcadia
under Cyllene crag: close-order fighters
who lived around the tomb of Aepytus,
at Pheneos, and at Orchomenus
where there are many flocks; at Rhipe, too,
at Stratia, and in the windy town

Enispe; men of Tegea and lovely
Mantinea; men of Stymphalus
and Parrhasia, all of whom were led
by Agapenor, son of Ancaeus,
and he commanded sixty ships. Arcadians
able in war had thronged to go aboard,
for the Lord Marshal Agamemnon lent
those ships in which they crossed the wine-dark sea,
as they had none, nor knowledge of seafaring.

Next were the soldiers from Buprasium
and gracious Elis – all that plain confined
by Hyrmine and Myrsinus, and by
Alesium and the Olenian Rock.
These had four captains with ten ships apiece,
on which the Epeians had embarked in throngs.
Some served under Amphimachus and Thalpius,
grandsons of Actor, sons of Cteatus
and of Eurytus. Powerful Diores
Amarynceides had command of others,
and Polyxeinus led the fourth division –
son of Agasthenes Augeiades.

Then came the islanders from Dulichium
and the Echinades, all those who dwelt
opposite Elis, over the open sea,
Meges their captain, Meges Phyleides
begotten by that friend of Zeus, the horseman
Phyleus, who withdrew to Dulichium
in anger at his father long ago.
Forty black ships had crossed the sea with Meges.

Odysseus, then, commanded the brave men
of Cephallenia: islanders of Ithaca
and Neritus whose leafy heights the sea-wind
ruffles, and the men of Crocyleia,
of Aegilips the rocky isle, and those
of Samos and Zacynthus: those as well
who held the mainland eastward of the islands.
Odysseus, peer of Zeus in forethought, led them
in twelve good ships with cheek-paint at the bows.

Thoas, Andraemon's son, led the Aetolians,
inhabitants of Pleuron, Olenus,
Pylene, seaside Chalcis, Calydon
of rocky mountainsides: Thoas their leader
because the sons of Oeneus were no more,
and red-haired Meleager too was dead.

Command of all had thus devolved on Thoas,
and forty black ships crossed the sea with him.

Idomeneus, famed as a spear-fighter,
led the Cretans: all who came from Cnossus,
Gortyn, the town of many walls, and Lyctus,
Miletus and Lycastus, gleaming white,
Phaestus and Rhytium, those pleasant towns –
all from that island of a hundred cities
served under Idomeneus, the great spearman,
whose second in command, Meriones,
fought like the slaughtering god of war himself.
Eighty black ships had crossed the sea with these.

Tlepolemus, the son of Heracles,
had led nine ships from Rhodes: impetuous men,
the Rhodians, in three regional divisions:
Lindos, Ialysus, and bright Cameirus,
serving under Tlepolemus, the spearman,
whose mother, Astyocheia, had been taken
by Heracles, who brought her from Ephyra
out of the Selleis river valley,
where he had plundered many noble towns.
No sooner was Tlepolemus of age
than he had killed his father's uncle, old
Licymnius, Alcmene's warrior brother,
and fitting out his ships in haste, he sailed
over the deep sea, taking many with him
in flight from other descendants of Heracles.
Wandering, suffering bitter days at sea,
he came at last to Rhodes. The island, settled
in townships, one for each of three great clans,
was loved by Zeus, ruler of gods and men,
and wondrous riches he poured out upon them.

Nireus had led three well-found ships from Syme –
Nireus, Aglaïa's child by Lord Charopus –
Nireus, of all Danaans before Troy
most beautifully made, after Achilles,
a feeble man, though, with a small contingent.

Then those of Nisyrus and Crapathus
and Casus and the island town of Cos,
ruled by Eurypylus, and the Calydnae,
islands ruled by Pheidippus and Antiphus,
the sons of Thessalus, a son of Heracles.
Thirty long ships in line belonged to these.

Tell me now, Muse, of those from that great land

called Argos of Pelasgians, who lived
at Alos, at Alope, and at Trachis,
and those of Phthia, those of Hellas, lands
of lovely women: all those troops they called
the Myrmidons and Hellenes and Achaeans,
led by Achilles, in their fifty ships.
But these made no advances now to battle,
since he was not on hand to dress their lines.
No, the great runner, Prince Achilles, lay
amid the ships in desolate rage
for Briseis, his girl with her soft tresses—
the prize he captured, fighting all the way,
from Lyrnessus after he stormed that town
and stormed the walls of Thebe, overthrowing
the spearmen, Mynes and Epistrophus,
sons of Evenus Selepiades.
For her his heart burned, lying there,
but soon the hour would come when he would rouse.

Next were the men of Phylace, and those
who held Pyrasus, garden of Demeter,
Iton, maternal town of grazing flocks,
Antron beside the water, and the beds
of meadow grass at Pteleos: all these
were under Protesilaus' command
when that intrepid fighter lived—
but black earth held him under now, and grieving
at Phylace with lacerated cheeks
his bride was left, his house unfinished there.
Plunging ahead from his long ship to be
first man ashore at Troy of all Achaeans,
he had been brought down by a Dardan spear.
By no means were his troops without a leader,
though sorely missing him: they had Podarces,
another soldier son of Iphiclus
Phylacides, master of many flocks—
Podarces, Protesilaus' blood brother,
a younger man, less noble. But the troops
were not at all in want of a commander,
though in their hearts they missed the braver one.
Forty black ships had sailed along with him.

Next were the soldiers who had lived at Pherae
by the great lake: at Glaphyrae and Boebe,
and in the well-kept city of Iolcus.
Of their eleven ships Admetus' son

Eumelus had command – the child conceived
under Admetus by that splendid queen,
Alcestis, Pelias' most beautiful daughter.

Next, those of Methone and Thaumacia,
of rugged Olizon and Meliboea.
These in their seven ships had been commanded
at first by Philoctetes, the great archer.
Fifty oarsmen in every ship, they came
as expert archers to the Trojan war.
But he, their captain, lay on Lemnos isle
in anguish, where the Achaeans had marooned him,
bearing the black wound of a deadly snake.
He languished there, but soon, beside the ships,
the Argives would remember and call him back.
Meanwhile his men were not without a leader
though missing Philoctetes: Medon led them,
Oileus' bastard son, conceived
by Rhene under Oileus, raider of cities.

Next were the men of Tricce and Ithome,
that rocky-terraced town, and Oechalia,
the city of Eurytus: over these
two sons of old Asclepius held command –
both skilled in healing: Podaleirius
and Machaon. Thirty decked ships were theirs.

Next were the soldiers from Ormenius
and from the river source at Hypereia;
those of Asterium and those below
Titanus' high snow-whitened peaks. Eurypylus,
Euaemon's shining son, led all of these,
with forty black ships under his command.

Then those who held Argissa and Gyrtona,
Orthe, Elone, and the limestone city
Oloosson, led by a dauntless man,
Polypoetes, the son of Peirithous,
whom Zeus, the undying, fathered. Polypoetes
had been conceived by gentle Hippodameia
under Peirithous, that day he whipped
the shaggy centaurs out of Pelion –
routed them, drove them to the Aethices.
Polypoetes as co-commander had
Leonteus, son of Coronus Caeneides.
Forty black ships had crossed the sea with these.

Gouneus commanded twenty-two from Cyphus,
The Enienes and the brave Peraebi

served under him: all who had had their homes
around Dodona in the wintry north
and in the fertile vale of Titaressus.
Lovely that gliding river that runs on
into the Peneius with silver eddies
and rides it for a while as clear as oil –
a branch of Styx, on which great oaths are sworn.

The Magnetes were led by Prothous,
Tenthredon's son: by Peneius they lived
and round Mount Pelion's shimmering leafy sides.
Forty black ships had come with Prothous.

These were the lords and captains of the Danaans.
But tell me, Muse, of all the men and horses
who were the finest, under Agamemnon?
As for the battle horses, those were best
that came from Pheres' pastures, and Eumelus
drove those mares, as fleet as birds – a team
perfectly matched in colour and in age,
and level to a hair across the cruppers.
Apollo of the silver bow had bred them
both in Pereia as fearsome steeds of war.
Of all the fighting men, most formidable
was Aias Telamonius – that is
while great Achilles raged apart. Achilles
towered above them all; so did the stallions
that drew the son of Peleus in the war.
But now, amid the slim seagoing ships
he lay alone and raged at Agamemnon,
marshal of the army. And his people,
along the shore above the breaking waves,
with discus throw and javelin and archery
sported away the time. Meanwhile their teams
beside the chariots tore and champed at clover
and parsley from the marshes; the war-cars
shrouded in canvas rested in the shelters;
and, longing for their chief, beloved in war,
the Myrmidons, idly throughout the camp,
drifted and took no part in that day's fighting.

But now the marching host devoured the plain
as though it were a prairie fire; the ground
beneath it rumbled, as when Zeus the lord
of lightning-bolts, in anger at Typhoeus,
lashes the earth around Einarimus,
where his tremendous couch is said to be.

So thunderously groaned the earth
under the trampling of their coming on,
and they consumed like fire the open plain.

Iris arrived now, running on the wind,
as messenger from Zeus beyond the storm-cloud,
bearing the grim news to the men of Troy.
They were assembled, at the gates of Priam,
young men and old, all gathered there, when she
came near and stood to speak to them: her voice
most like the voice of Priam's son Polites.
Forward observer for the Trojans, trusting
his prowess as a sprinter, he had held
his post mid-plain atop the burial mound
of the patriarch Aesyetes; waiting there
to see the Achaeans leave their camp and ships.

In his guise, she who runs upon the wind,
Iris, now spoke to Priam: 'Sir, old sir,
will you indulge inordinate talk as always,
just as in peacetime? Frontal war's upon us!
Many a time I've borne a hand in combat,
but never have I seen the enemy
in such array, committed, every man,
uncountable as leaves, or grains of sand,
advancing on the city through the plain!
Hector, you are the one I call on: take
action as I direct you: the allies
that crowd the great town speak in many tongues
of many scattered countries. Every company
should get its orders from its own commander:
let him conduct the muster and the sortie!'

Hector punctiliously obeyed the goddess,
dismissed the assembly on her terms, and troops
ran for their arms. All city gates, wide open,
yawned, and the units poured out, foot soldiers,
horses and chariots, with tremendous din.

Rising in isolation on the plain
in face of Troy, there is a ridge, a bluff
open on all sides: Briar Hill they call it.
Men do, that is; the immortals know the place
to be the Amazon Myrine's tomb.
Anchored on this the Trojans and allies
formed for battle.

                    Tall, with helmet flashing,
Hector, great son of Priam, led the Trojans,

largest of those divisions and the best,
who drew up now and armed, and hefted spears.

The Dardans were commanded by Aeneas,
whom ravishing Aphrodite had conceived
under Anchises in the vales of Ida,
lying, immortal, in a man's embrace.
His co-commanders were Antenor's sons,
Acamas and Archelochus, good fighters.

Then those from Zeleia, the lower slope
of Ida – Trojans, men of means who drank
the water of Aesepus dark and still –
they served under Lycaon's shining son,
Pandarus, whom Apollo taught the bow.

Adrasteia's men, those of the hinterland
of Apaesus, Pityeia, and the crag
of Tereia – all these Adrastus led
with Amphius of the linen cuirass, both
sons of Merops Percosius, the seer
profoundest of all seers; he had refused
to let them take the path of war –
man-wasting war – but they were heedless of him,
driven onward by dark powers of death.

Then, too, came those who lived around Percote,
at Practium, at Sestos and Abydos,
and old Arisbe: Asius their captain,
Asius Hyrtacides – who drove
great sorrel horses from the Selleis river.

Hippothous led the tough Pelasgians
from Larisa's rich plough-land – Hippothous
and the young soldier Pylaeus, both sons
of the Pelasgian Lethus Teutamides.

Then Thracians from beyond the strait, all those
whom Helle's rushing water bounded there,
Acamas led and the veteran Peirous.

Son of Troizenus Ceades, Euphemus
led the Cicones from their distant shore;
and those more distant archers, Paeones,
Pyraechmes led from Amydon,
from Axius bemirroring all the plain.
The Paphlagonians followed Pylaemenes,
shaggy, great-hearted, from the wild mule country
of the Eneti – men who held Cytorus
and Sesamus and had their famous homes
on the Parthenius riverbanks, at Cromna,

Aegialus, and lofty Erythini.

Odius and Epistrophus were captains
of Halizones from Alybe, far
eastward, where the mines of silver are.

The Mysians Chromis led, with Ennomus,
reader of birdflight; signs in flurrying wings
would never save him from the last dark wave
when he went down before the battering hands
of the great runner, Achilles, in the river,
with other Trojans slain.

                     The Phrygians
were under Phorcys and Ascanius
from far Ascania – both ready fighters.

The Lydians then, Maeonians, had for leaders
Mesthles and Antiphus; these were the sons
of Talaemenes by Lake Gygaea.
They led men bred in vales under Mount Tmolus.
Nastes commanded Carians in their own tongue,
men of Miletus, Phthiron's leafy ridge,
Maeander's rills and peaks of Mycale.
All these Amphimachus and Nastes led,
Nomion's shining children. Wearing gold,
blithe as a girl, Nastes had gone to war,
but gold would not avail the fool
to save him from a bloody end. Achilles
Aeacides would down him in the river,
taking his golden ornaments for spoil.

Sarpedon led the Lycians, with Glaucus,
from Lycia afar, from whirling Xanthus.

BOOK III

DUELLING FOR A HAUNTED LADY

THE Trojan squadrons flanked by officers
drew up and sortied, in a din of arms
and shouting voices — wave on wave, like cranes
in clamorous lines before the face of heaven,
beating away from winter's gloom and storms,
over the streams of Ocean, hoarsely calling,
to bring a slaughter on the Pygmy warriors —
cranes at dawn descending, beaked in cruel attack.
The Achaeans for their part came on in silence,
raging under their breath, shoulder to shoulder sworn.

Imagine mist the south wind rolls on hills,
a blowing bane for shepherds, but for thieves
better than nightfall — mist where a man can see
a stone's throw and no more: so dense the dust
that clouded up from these advancing hosts
as they devoured the plain.

                              And near and nearer
the front ranks came, till one from the Trojan front
detached himself to be the first in battle —
Alexandrus, vivid and beautiful,
wearing a cowl of leopard skin, a bow
hung on his back, a longsword at his hip,
with two spears capped in pointed bronze. He shook them
and called out to the best men of the Argives
to meet him in the mêlée face to face.

Menelaus, watching that figure come
with long strides in the clear before the others,
knew him and thrilled with joy. A hungry lion
that falls on heavy game — an antlered deer
or a wild goat — will rend and feast upon it
even though hunters and their hounds assail him.
So Menelaus thrilled when he beheld
Alexandrus before his eyes; he thought
I'll cut him to bits, adulterous dog! — and vaulted
down from his car at once with all his gear.

But when Alexandrus caught sight of him
emerging from the ranks, his heart misgave,
and he recoiled on his companions, not

to incur the deadly clash.
                         A man who stumbles
upon a viper in a mountain glen
will jump aside: a trembling takes his knees,
pallor his cheeks; he backs and backs away.
In the same way Alexandrus paced backward
into the Trojan lines and edged among them,
dreading the son of Atreus.
                              Hector watched
and said in scorn: 'You bad-luck charm!
Paris, the great lover, a gallant sight!
You should have had no seed and died unmarried.
Would to god you had!
Better than living this way in dishonour,
in everyone's contempt. Now they can laugh, Achaeans
who thought you were a first-rate man, a champion,
going by looks – and no backbone, no staying
power is in you.
                  'Were you this way then
when you made up your crews and crossed the sea
in the long ships, for trafficking abroad?
And when you then brought home a lovely woman
from a far land: a girl already married
whose brother-in-law and husband were great soldiers?
Ruin for your father and all his realm,
joy for your enemies, and shame for you!
Now could you not stand up to Menelaus?
You'd find out what a fighting man he is
whose flower-like wife you hold. No charm would come
of harping then, or Aphrodite's favours –
the clean-limbed body and the flowing hair –
when you lay down to make love to the dust!
What slaves these Trojans are! If not, long since
you might have worn a shirt of cobblestones
for all the wrong you've done!'
                                The beautiful prince,
Alexandrus, replied to him: 'Ah, Hector,
this harshness is no more than just. Remember, though,
your spirit's like an axe-edge whetted sharp
that goes through timber, when a good shipwright
hews out a beam: the tool triples his power.
That is the way your heart is in your breast.
My own gifts are from pale-gold Aphrodite –
do not taunt me for them. Glorious things

the gods bestow are not to be despised,
being as the gods will: wishing will not bring them.
Now, if what you want from me is fighting,
make all the other Trojans and Achaeans
down their arms; let Menelaus alone
and me, between the lines, in single combat,
duel for Helen and the Spartan gold.
Whoever gets the upper hand in this
shall take the treasure and the woman home;
let the rest part as friends, let all take oath,
that you may live in peace in Troy's rich land
while they make sail for Argos and its pastures
and the land of lovely womankind, Achaea.'

Listening, Hector felt his heart grow lighter,
and down the Trojan centre, with his lance
held up mid-haft, he drove, calling 'Battalions
halt!' till he brought them to a stand-at-ease.

The long-haired Achaean soldiers bent their bows,
aiming with arrows and with stones. But high
and clear they heard a shout from Agamemnon;
'Hold on, Argives! Men, don't shoot! This means
he has in mind some proclamation,
Hector, there in the flashing helmet!'

                                        Archers
lowered their bows, and all fell silent now,
as Hector to both armies made appeal:
'Hear me, Trojans, Achaeans under arms,
hear the proposal of Alexandrus
because of whom this quarrel began. He asks
all other Trojans and Achaean soldiers
to put their arms aside upon the ground,
while he and Menelaus fight it out
between the lines alone
for Helen and her Spartan gold – the winner
to take the treasure home, and take the woman,
the rest, with solemn oaths, to part as friends.'

The armies were now hushed. Across the field,
Menelaus, clarion in war, addressed them:
'Hear me also, as the iron enters
deepest in me. Yet I agree, the Trojans
and Argives should withdraw in peace; you've borne
so many hardships, taking part with me
in the quarrel Alexandrus began. So death
to him for whom the hour of death has come!

The rest of you part peacefully and soon!
Bring down a black ewe and a snow-white ram
for sacrifice to Earth and Helios;
we here shall dedicate a third to Zeus.
And lead down Priam in his power, that he
himself may swear to peace. Reckless, untrustworthy
sons he has, but no man's overweening
should break the peace of Zeus. The younger men
are changeable; he in his age among them,
looking before and after, can see clearly
what shall be in the interests of all.'

    Now all hearts lifted at his words, for both sides
hoped for an end of miserable war;
and backing chariots into line, the men
stepped out, disarmed themselves, and left their weapons
heaped at close intervals on open ground.
Hector meanwhile had sent two runners back
to bring the sheep and summon the Lord Priam.
Agamemnon at the same time dispatched
Talthybius to the ships, bidding him bring
a sheep as well, and he obeyed.

                    Now Iris
made her way to inform the Lady Helen,
appearing as her sister-in-law, Laodice,
loveliest of Priam's daughters and the wife
of Helicaon, a son of Lord Antenor.
She found her weaving in the women's hall
a double violet stuff, whereon inwoven
were many passages of arms by Trojan
horsemen and Achaeans mailed in bronze –
trials braved for her sake at the war-god's hands.
Approaching her, swift Iris said: 'Come, dearest,
come outside and see the marvellous change
in Trojans and Achaeans! Up to now
they have made war till we were dead with weeping,
war unending, in the cruel plain.
No more now: they are resting on their shields,
each with his tall spear thrust in earth beside him.
It seems Alexandrus and the great soldier,
Menelaus, will meet in single combat
with battle spears, for you! The man who wins
shall win you as his consort.'

                    And the goddess,
even as she spoke, infused in Helen's heart

a smoky sweetness and desire
for him who first had taken her as bride
and for her parents and her ancient town.
Quickly she cloaked herself in silvery veils
and let a teardrop fall and left her chamber,
not unaccompanied, but as became
a princess, with two maids-in-waiting – one
Aethra, child of Pittheus, and the other
wide-eyed Clymene.
Soon these three women neared the Scaean Gates.

There Priam and his counsellors were sitting –
Thymoetes, Panthous, Lampus, Clytius,
the soldier Hicetaon, and those two
clearheaded men, Antenor and Ucalegon –
peers of the realm, in age strengthless at war
but strong still in their talking – perching now
above the Scaean Gates on the escarpment.

They sounded like cicadas in dry summer
that cling on leafy trees and send out voices
rhythmic and long – so droned and murmured these
old leaders of the Trojans on the tower,
and watching Helen as she climbed the stair
in undertones they said to one another:

'We cannot rage at her, it is no wonder
that Trojans and Achaeans under arms
should for so long have borne the pains of war
for one like this.'

             'Unearthliness. A goddess
the woman is to look at.'

                   'Ah, but still,
still, even so, being all that she is, let her go in the ships
and take her scourge from us and from our children.'

These were the old men's voices. But to Helen
Priam called out: 'Come here, dear child, sit here
beside me; you shall see your onetime lord
and your dear kinsmen. You are not to blame,
I hold the gods to blame for bringing on
this war against the Achaeans, to our sorrow.
Come, tell me who the big man is out there,
who is that powerful figure? Other men
are taller, but I never saw a soldier
clean-cut as he, as royal in his bearing:
he seems a kingly man.'

                 And the great beauty,

Helen, replied: 'Revere you as I do,
I dread you, too, dear father. Painful death
would have been sweeter for me, on that day
I joined your son, and left my bridal chamber,
my brothers, my grown child, my childhood friends!
But no death came, though I have pined and wept.
Your question, now: yes, I can answer it:
that man is Agamemnon, son of Atreus,
lord of the plains of Argos, ever both
a good king and a formidable soldier –
brother to the husband of a wanton . . .

or was that life a dream?'

The old man gazed and mused and softly cried:
'O fortunate son of Atreus! Child of destiny,
O happy soul! How many sons of Achaea
serve under you! In the old days once I went
into the vineyard country of Phrygia
and saw the Phrygian host on nimble ponies,
Otreus' and Mygdon's people. In those days
they were encamped on Sangarius river.
And they allotted me as their ally
my place among them when the Amazons
came down, those women who were fighting men;
but that host never equalled this,
the army of the keen-eyed men of Achaea.'

Still gazing out, he caught sight of Odysseus,
and then the old man said: 'Tell me, dear child,
who is that officer? The son of Atreus
stands a head taller, but this man appears
to have a deeper chest and broader shoulders.
His gear lies on the ground, but still he goes
like a bell-wether up and down the ranks.
A ram I'd call him, burly, thick with fleece,
keeping a flock of silvery sheep in line.'

And Helen shaped by heaven answered him:
'That is Laertes' son, the great tactician,
Odysseus. He was bred on Ithaca,
a bare and stony island – but he knows
all manner of stratagems and moves in war.'

Antenor, the alert man, interposed:
'My lady, there indeed you hit the mark.
Once long ago he came here, great Odysseus,
with Menelaus – came to treat of you.
They were my guests, and I made friends of both,

and learned their stratagems and characters.
Among us Trojans, in our gatherings, Menelaus,
broad in the shoulders likewise, overtopped him;
seated, Odysseus looked the kinglier man.
When each of them stood up to make his plea,
his argument before us all, then Menelaus
said a few words in a rather headlong way
but clearly: not long-winded and not vague;
and indeed he was the younger of the two.
Then in his turn the great tactician rose
and stood, and looked at the ground,
moving the staff before him not at all
forward or backward: obstinate and slow
of wit he seemed, gripping the staff: you'd say
some surly fellow, with an empty head.
But when he launched the strong voice from his chest,
and words came driving on the air as thick
and fast as winter snowflakes, then Odysseus
could have no mortal rival as an orator!
The look of him no longer made us wonder.'

Observing a third figure, that of Aias,
the old man asked: 'Who is that other one,
so massive and so strongly built, he towers
head and shoulders above the Argive troops?'

Tall in her long gown, in her silver cloak,
Helen replied: 'That is the giant soldier,
Aias, a rugged sea-wall for Achaeans.
Opposite him, among the Cretans, there,
is tall Idomeneus, with captains round him.
Menelaus, whom the war-god loves,
received him often in our house in Sparta
when he crossed over out of Crete. I see
all the Achaeans now
whom I might recognize and name for you,
except for two I cannot see, the captains
Castor, breaker of horses, and the boxer, Polydeuces,
both my brothers; mother bore them both.
Were these not in the fleet from Lacedaemon?
Or did they cross in the long ship, but refrain
from entering combat here because they dread
vile talk of me and curses on my head?'

So Helen wondered. But her brothers lay
motionless in the arms of life-bestowing earth,
long dead in Lacedaemon of their fathers.

Meanwhile by lane and wall the criers came
with sacrificial sheep and bearing wine
that warms the heart, gift of the vineyard ground –
a goatskin ponderous with wine. And one, Idaeus,
carrying golden goblets and a winebowl
shining, reached the side of the aged king
and called upon him: 'Son of Laomedon,
arise: the master soldiers of both armies,
Trojan breakers of horses, Achaeans mailed in bronze,
request that you be present in the plain
for peace offerings and oaths. Alexandrus
and Menelaus, whom the war-god loves,
will fight with battle spears over the lady.
She and the treasure go to him who wins.
As for the rest, by solemn pact, thereafter
in this rich land of Troy we dwell in peace
while they return to the grazing land of Argos
and to Achaea, country of fair women.'

At this announcement by the crier, a tremor
shook the old king, head to foot. He said:
'Harness the team.'

            And hastily they did so.
Stepping into his car, Lord Priam took
the reins and leaned back, tugging at the horses
until Antenor mounted at his side.
Then to the Scaean Gates and out they drove,
keeping the swift team headed for the plain.
They reined in at the battle line, set foot
upon the open ground, once cattle pasture,
and walked between the Trojans and Achaeans.

Promptly Lord Agamemnon and Odysseus,
master of stratagems, arose. The criers,
noble retainers, brought the votive sheep,
prepared the bowls of wine, and rinsed the hands
of their commanders. Then the son of Atreus
drew from his hip the sheath knife hanging there
beside his longsword scabbard; from the brows
of ram and ewe he cut the fleece, and criers
handed it out to officers of both armies.

With arms held wide to heaven, Agamemnon
prayed in the name of all: 'O Father Zeus!
Power over Ida! Greatest, most glorious!
O Helios, by whom all things are seen,
all overheard; O rivers! O dark earth!

O powers underground, chastisers of dead men
for breaking solemn oaths! Be witness, all:
preserve this pact we swear to! If in fact
Alexandrus should kill Lord Menelaus,
let him keep Helen and keep all the gold,
while we sail home in the long ships.
But if Alexandrus be killed, the Trojans
are to surrender Helen and the treasure –
moreover they must pay a tribute, due
the Argives now, renewed to their descendants.
In the event that Priam and his sons
refuse this – though Alexandrus be killed –
then I shall stay and fight for my indemnity
until I come upon an end to war.'
                He drew
the pitiless bronze knife-edge hard across
the gullets of the sheep, and laid them
quivering on the ground, their lives ebbing,
lost to the whetted bronze.
                Now dipping up
wine from the winebowls into golden cups,
the captains tipped their offerings and prayed
to the gods who never die. Here is the way
the Trojans and Achaeans prayed:
                'O Zeus
almighty and most glorious! Gods undying!
Let any parties to this oath who first
calamitously break it have their brains
decanted like these wine-drops on the ground –
they and their children; let their wives be slaves.'
    The oath ran so, but Zeus would not abide
by what they swore.
              Now Dardan Priam spoke:
'One word from me, O Trojans and Achaeans.
For my part, back I go to the windy town
of Ilium. I cannot bear to watch
my son in combat against Menelaus,
a man the war-god stands behind. No doubt
Zeus knows the end, and all the immortals know
which of the two must die his fated death.'
    He placed the carcasses of ram and ewe
before him in the chariot, and stepped
aboard in majesty, holding the horses
while Lord Antenor climbed the royal car.

Then circling back they drove toward Ilium.
Prince Hector and Odysseus together
paced off the duelling-ground. Next they took up
two tokens in a bronze helm, shaking it
to see which man would cast his weapon first.
    Meanwhile the soldiers held their hands to heaven,
Trojans and Achaeans, in this prayer:
'Father Zeus, almighty over Ida,
may he who brought this trouble on both sides
perish! Let him waste away
into the undergloom! As for ourselves,
let us be loyal friends in peace!'
                                    They prayed
as powerful Hector in his flashing helmet,
keeping his eyes averted, churned the tokens.
That of Paris quickly tumbled out.
And now, holding their lines, the troops sank down,
each one beside his horses and his gear.
    The time had come, and Prince Alexandrus,
consort of Helen, buckled on his armour:
first the greaves, well moulded to his shins,
with silver ankle circlets; then
around his chest the cuirass of his brother
Lycaon, a good fit for him. He slung
a sword of bronze with silver-studded hilt
by a baldric on his shoulder; over this
a shield-strap and the many-layered shield;
then drew a helmet with a horse-tail crest
upon his head, upon his gallant brow,
the tall plume like a wave-crest grimly tossing.
He picked out, finally, a solid spear
with his own handgrip.
                        Meanwhlie the great soldier,
Menelaus, put on his own equipment.
Armed now, each in his place apart, both men
walked forward in the space between the armies,
glaring at one another. Fierce excitement
ran through all who gazed – horse-breaking Trojans,
Achaeans in leg armour – as the champions
came to a stand inside the duelling ground
and hefted spears in rage. Without delay
Alexandrus opened the fight: he hurled
his long-shadowing spear and hit Atreides
fair on the round shield. Nothing brazen broke –

no, but the point of bronze at impact bent
in that hard armour.
                    Second to make his cast,
and rousing to it with his bronze-shod spear,
the son of Atreus, Menelaus, prayed
to Father Zeus: 'O Zeus aloft,
grant I shall make the man who wronged me first
pay for it now!
Let him be humbled, brought down at my hands,
and hearts in those born after us will shrink
from treachery to a host who offers love.'

   Hefting and aiming as he spoke, he hurled
his long-shadowing spear and hit his adversary
fair on the round shield. Formidably sped,
the spear went through the polished hide and through
the densely plated cuirass, where it ripped
the shirt forward along his flank and stuck –
but Paris, twisting, had eluded death.
Drawing his longsword then, Lord Menelaus
reared and struck him on the helmet ridge,
but saw his blade, broken in jagged splinters,
drop from his hand.
                    Lifting his eyes to heaven
he groaned: 'O Father Zeus, of all the gods,
none is more cruel to hopeful men than you are!
I thought to make Alexandrus
pay for his crime, and what luck have I had?
My spear slipped from my grip in vain: I missed him.
And now my sword is shattered in my hand!'
   But now in one bound, pouncing, he laid hold
of the horse-tail crest and spun his enemy,
then yanked him backward toward the Achaean lines,
choked by the chin strap, cutting into his throat –
a well-stitched band secured beneath his helmet.
To his own glory, Menelaus
now would in fact have pulled him all the way,
had Aphrodite with her clear eye not
perceived him – and she snapped that band of oxhide,
cut from a clubbed ox.
                    Now, at this the helmet
came away easily in the fighter's hand.
He whirled it round his head and let it fly
amid the Achaeans, where his own men caught it.
And once again, raging to kill his man,

he lunged, aiming a lance. But this time Aphrodite
spirited Alexandrus away as easily
as only a god could do. She hid him in mist
and put him down in his own fragrant chamber,
while she herself went off to summon Helen.
She came upon her on the battlement, amid
a throng of Trojan ladies. Here the goddess
plucked at a fold of her sweet-scented gown
and spoke to her. She seemed a spinning-woman
who once had spun soft wool for her, at home
in Lacedaemon, and the princess loved her.
    In this guise ravishing Aphrodite said:
'Come home with me. Alexandrus invites you.
On the ivory-inlaid bed in your bedchamber
he lies at ease, and freshly dressed – so handsome
never could you imagine the man came
just now from combat; one would say he goes
to grace a dance, or has until this minute
danced and is resting now.'
                            So she described him,
and Helen's heart beat faster in her breast.
Her sense being quickened so, through all disguise
she recognized the goddess' flawless throat,
her fine breasts that move the sighs of longing,
her brilliant eyes.
                    She called her by her name
in wonder, saying: 'O immortal madness,
why do you have this craving to seduce me?
Am I to be transported even farther
eastward, into some Phrygian walled town
or into Maeonia, if you have there
another mortal friend? Is it because
Menelaus has beaten Alexandrus
and, hateful though I am, would take me home,
is that why you are here in all your cunning?
Go take your place beside Alexandrus!
Leave the bright paths the gods take over heaven
and walk no more about Olympus! Be
unhappy for him, shield him, till at last
he marries you – or, as he will, enslaves you.
I shall not join him there! It would be base
if I should make his bed luxurious now.
There will be such whispering
among the Trojan women later –

as though I had not pain enough to bear.'
　　To this the goddess haughtily replied:
'Better not be so difficult. You'll vex me
enough to let you go. Then I shall hate you
as I have cherished you till now. Moreover,
I can make hatred for you grow
amid the Danaans and Trojans both,
and if I do, you'll come to a bad end.'
　　Now Helen shaped by heaven was afraid.
Enfolded in her shining robe of silver
she turned to go, without a word – unseen
by all the women, for the goddess led her.
　　Entering Alexandrus' magnificent house,
the maids went quickly to their work, and Helen
mounted to her high chamber. Aphrodite,
who smiles on smiling love, brought her a chair
and set it down facing Alexandrus.
　　Helen, daughter of Zeus beyond the storm-cloud,
took her seat with downcast eyes, and greeted him:
'Home from the war? You should have perished there,
brought down by that strong soldier, once my husband.
You used to say you were the better man,
more skilful with your hands, your spear. So why not
challenge him to fight again?
　　　　　　　　　　　　　　'I wouldn't,
if I were you. No, don't go back to war
against the tawny-headed man of war
like a rash fool. You'd crumple under his lance.'
　　Paris replied: 'Love, don't be bitter with me.
These are unkind reflections. It is true,
on this occasion he – and Athena – won.
Next time, I may. We, too, have gods with us.
Let us drop war now, you and I,
and give ourselves to pleasure in our bed.
My soul was never so possessed by longing,
not even when I took you first aboard
off Lacedaemon, that sweet land, and sailed
in the long ships. Not at Cranae Island
where I first went to bed with you and loved you.
Greater desire now lifts me like a tide.'
　　He went to bed, and she went with him,
and in the inlaid ivory bed these two
made love, while Menelaus roamed the ranks
like a wild beast, hunting the godlike man,

Alexandrus.
> But not a Trojan there,
not one of all the allies, could produce him
for the war-god's friend, Menelaus – and none
for love would ever hide him if he saw him,
the man being abhorred like death itself.

Now the Lord Marshal Agamemnon spoke
amid the armies: 'Give me your attention,
Trojans, Dardans, and allies;
beyond question, Menelaus is victorious.
Therefore, Helen of Argos and the treasure
are now to be surrendered; you must pay
tribute as well, the compensation due,
payable, too, in future generations.'

And to this judgement of the son of Atreus
the rest of the Achaeans gave assent.

BOOK IV

A BOWSHOT BRINGING WAR

THE gods were seated near to Zeus in council,
upon a golden floor. Graciously Hebe
served them nectar, as with cups of gold
they toasted one another, looking down
toward the stronghold of Ilium.

                          Abruptly
and with oblique intent to ruffle Hera,
Zeus in cutting tones remarked: 'Two goddesses
have Menelaus for their protégé –
Hera, the patroness of Argos, and
Athena, known as Guardian in Boeotia.
Still, they keep their distance here; their pleasure
comes from looking on. But Aphrodite,
who loves all smiling lips and eyes,
cleaves to her man to ward off peril from him.
He thought he faced death, but she saved him. Clearly,
Menelaus, whom Ares backs, has won
the single combat. Let us then consider
how this affair may end; shall we again
bring on the misery and din of war,
or make a pact of amity between them?
If only all of you were pleased to see it,
life might go on in Priam's town,
while Menelaus took Helen of Argos home.'

    At this proposal, Hera and Athena
murmured rebelliously. These two together
sat making mischief for the men of Troy,
and though she held her tongue, a sullen anger
filled Athena against her father.

                             Hera
could not contain her own vexation, saying:
'Your majesty, what is the drift of this?
How could you bring to nothing all my toil,
the sweat I sweated, and my winded horses,
when I called out that army to bear hard
on Priam and his sons? Act, if you must,
but not all here approve!'

                         Coldly annoyed,

the Lord Zeus, who drives the clouds of heaven,
answered: 'Strange one, how can Priam
and Priam's sons have hurt you so
that you are possessed to see the trim stronghold
of Ilium plundered? Could you breach the gates
and the great walls yourself and feed on Priam
with all his sons, and all the other Trojans,
dished up raw, you might appease this rage!
Do as you wish to do, then. This dispute
should not leave rancour afterward between us.
I must, however, tell you one thing more:
remember it.

      'Whenever my turn comes
to lust for demolition of some city
whose people may be favourites of yours,
do not hamper my fury! Free my hands
as here I now free yours, my will prevailing
on my unwilling heart. Of all the cities
men of earth inhabit under the sun,
under the starry heavens, Ilium
stood first in my esteem, first in my heart,
as Priam did, the good lance, and his people.
My altar never lacked a feast at Troy
nor spilt wine, nor the smoke of sacrifice –
perquisites of the gods.'

      And wide-eyed Hera
answered: 'Dearest to me are these three cities:
Mycenae of the broad lanes, Argos, Sparta.
Let them be pulled down, if you ever find them
hateful to you. I will not interfere.
I will not grudge you these. And if I should?
Why, balking and withholding my consent
would gain me nothing, since the power you hold
so far surpasses mine. My labour, though,
should not be thwarted; I am immortal, too,
your stock and my stock are the same. Our father,
Cronos of crooked wit, engendered me
to hold exalted rank, by birth and by
my standing as your queen – since you are lord
of all immortal gods.

      'Come, we'll give way
to one another in this affair: I yield
to you and you to me; the gods will follow.
Only be quick, and send Athena down

into the hurly-burly of the armies
to make the Trojans, not the Achaeans, first
to sunder the truce they swore to.'

                  This way Hera
prompted him, and the father of gods and men
complied by saying briskly to Athena:
'In all haste, down you go amid the armies
to see if Trojans, not Achaeans, first
will sunder the truce they swore to.'

                     Given orders
to do her own will, grey-eyed Athena left
Olympus, dropping downward from the crests –
as though the son of crooked-minded Cronos
had flung a shooting star, to be a sign
for men on the deep sea, or some broad army –
a streak of radiance and a sparkling track.
Down she flashed, to alight amid the troops,
and wonder held them all at gaze, horse-breaking
Trojans and Achaeans in leg-armour.
You might have heard one, glancing at the next man,
mutter: 'What is to come? Bad days again
in the bloody lines? Or can both sides be friends?
Which will it be from Zeus, who holds the keys
and rationing of war?'

                 That was the question
for Trojan and Achaean fighting men.
Athena, meanwhile, in a soldier's guise,
that of Laodocus, Antenor's son,
a burly spearman, passed among the Trojans
looking for Pandarus, if she could find him –
Lycaon's noble son. Find him she did,
waiting with troops, now covered by their shields,
who once had followed him from the cascades
of Aesepus.

            Near him she took her stand
and let her sharp words fly: 'Son of Lycaon,
I have in mind an exploit that may tempt you,
tempt a fighting heart. Have you the gall
to send an arrow like a fork of lightning
home against Menelaus? Every Trojan
heart would rise, and every man would praise you,
especially Alexandrus, the prince –
you would be sure to come by glittering gifts
if he could see the warrior, Menelaus,

the son of Atreus, brought down by your bow,
then bedded on a dolorous pyre! Come, now,
brace yourself for a shot at Menelaus.
Engage to pay Apollo, the bright archer,
a perfect hecatomb of firstling lambs
when you go home to your old town, Zeleia.'

    That was Athena's way, leading him on,
the foolish man, to folly.
                    He uncased
his bow of polished horn – horn of an ibex
that he had killed one day with a chest shot
upon a high crag; waiting under cover,
he shot it through the ribs and knocked it over –
horns, together, a good four feet in length.
He cut and fitted these, mortised them tight,
polished the bow, and capped the tips with gold.
This weapon, now against the ground, Pandarus
bent hard and strung. Men of his company
at the same time held up their shields to hide him –
not to bring any Argives to their feet
before he shot at Menelaus.
                    He bared
his quiver top and drew a feathered arrow,
never frayed, but keen with waves of pain
to darken vision. Smoothly on the string
he fitted the sharp arrow. Then he prayed
to the bright archer, Lycian Apollo,
promising first-born lambs in hecatomb
on his return to his old town, Zeleia.

    Pinching the grooved butt and the string, he pulled
evenly till the bent string reached his nipple,
the arrowhead of iron touched the bow,
and when the great bow under tension made
a semicircular arc, it sprang. The whipping
string sang, and the arrow whizzed away,
needlesharp, vicious, flashing through the crowd.

    But Menelaus, you were not neglected
this time by the gods in bliss! Athena,
Hope of Soldiers, helped you first of all,
deflecting by an inch the missile's flight
so that it grazed your skin – the way a mother
would keep a fly from settling on a child
when he is happily asleep. Athena
guided the arrow down to where the golden

belt buckles and the breastplate overlapped,
and striking there, the bitter arrowhead
punctured the well-sewn belt and cut its way
into the figured cuirass, where it stuck,
although the point passed onward through the loin-guard
next his belly, plated against spearheads,
shielding him most now; yet the point entered
and gouged the warrior's mortal skin.

    Then dark blood rippled in a clouding stain
down from the wound, as when a Maeonian
or a Carian woman dyes clear ivory
to be the cheekpiece of a chariot team.
Though horseman after horseman longs to carry it,
the artefact lies in a storeroom, kept
for a great lord, a splendour doubly prized –
his team's adornment and his driver's glory.
So, Menelaus, were your ivory thighs
dyed and suffused with running blood, your well-made
shins and ankles, too.

             Now Agamemnon,
marshal of the army, looked and shuddered
to see the dark blood flowing from the wound,
and Menelaus himself went cold.
But when he saw the lashing of the iron
flange outside the wound, and barbs outside,
then life and warmth came back about his heart.
Meanwhile the troops heard Agamemnon groan,
holding his brother's hand, and heard him say,
so that they groaned as well:

                    'The truce I made
was death for you, dear brother! When I sent you
forward alone to fight for the Achaeans,
I only gave a free shot to the Trojans.
They've ground the truce under their heels. But not
for nothing have we sworn an oath and spilt
lamb's blood, red wine, and joined our hands and theirs –
putting our trust in ritual. No, no,
if the Olympian upon the instant
has not exacted punishment, he will
in his good time, and all the more they'll pay
for their misdeed in lives, in wives and children!
For this I know well in my heart and soul:
the day must come when holy Ilium
is given to fire and sword, and Priam perishes,

good lance though he was, with all his people.
For Zeus, the son of Cronos,
benched in the azure up there where he dwells,
will heave his shield of storm against them all
in rage at their bad faith! So it must be.

　　But this for me is anguish, Menelaus,
if you have measured out your mortal time
and are to die. Backward in depths of shame
I go to the drought of Argos. The Achaeans
will turn their minds again to their far lands,
and we, I have no doubt, must leave behind
the Argive woman, Helen, for the Trojans,
for Priam's glory, while your bones decay
in Trojan plough-land, rotting where they lie,
your mission unachieved!

　　　　　　　　　　'In my mind's eye
I see some arrogant Trojan on the grave
of Menelaus, the great and famous man,
leaping to say: "Let Agamemnon's anger
in every case come out like this! Remember
he brought an army of Achaeans here
for nothing, and sailed back in the long ships
again to his own land – but had to leave
Menelaus behind!" Someone will say it,
and let the vast earth yawn for me that day!'

　　But red-haired Menelaus said: 'Be calm.
Courage, do not alarm the troops! The point
has hit no vital spot here where it lodged;
the faceted belt stopped it, and the loin-guard,
stiff with plate the smiths had hammered out.'

　　Then Agamemnon said: 'God send you're right,
dear Menelaus! But the wound –
we'll have a surgeon clean the wound and dress it
with medicines to relieve the pain.'

　　　　　　　　　　　　　　He turned
and spoke out to Talthybius, the crier:
'Go quickly as you can and call Machaon,
son of Asclepius, the great healer,
call him here to examine Menelaus.
A master bowman, Trojan or Lycian,
has wounded him – a feat for the enemy,
worry and pain for us.'

　　　　　　　　　　　　Talthybius
obeyed, making his way amid the army,

among the mailed Achaeans, everywhere
looking for the soldierly Machaon.
He found him standing ready, troops with shields
in rank on rank around him – companies
of his that came from grazing lands in Tricce.
   Approaching him, the crier said:
son of Asclepius: you are called by Agamemnon
to examine Menelaus, the co-commander.
A master bowman, Trojan or Lycian,
has wounded him – a feat for the enemy,
worry and pain for us.'
                  The message stirred him,
and back the two men hastened through the army
to where the red-haired captain had been hit.
Gathered around him in a circle stood
the Achaean peers, but through their midst Machaon
quickly gained his side, and pulled the arrow
free of the belt and clasp. As it came out,
the barbs broke off. The surgeon then unbuckled
faceted belt and, underneath, his loin-guard,
stiff with plate the smiths had hammered out,
and when he saw the arrow wound, he sucked it
clean of blood, then sprinkled it with balm,
a medicine that Cheiron gave his father.
Now while they tended Menelaus, lord
of the war-cry, Trojan ranks re-formed with shields
and the Achaeans, too, put on their armour,
mindful again of battle.
                In that hour
no one could have perceived in Agamemnon
a moment's torpor or malingering, but fiery
ardour for the battle-test that brings
honour to men. He left aside his team,
his chariot, a-gleam with bronze: his driver,
Eurymedon, a son of Ptolemaeus
Peiraides, reined in the snorting horses;
and Agamemnon gave him strict command
to bring the war-car up when weariness
should take him in the legs, after inspection
of all his many marshalled troops. On foot
he ranged around the men in their formations,
and where he saw his charioteers in units
alert for battle, he exhorted them:
   'Argives, keep your courage up, for Zeus

will never back up liars! Men who are first
to sunder oaths, their flesh the kites will feed on –
tender fare; as for their wives and children,
we'll enslave them when we take the town.'

On seeing any slack and unready still
for hated war, he lashed at them in anger:
'Rabbit hearts of Argos,
are you not dead with shame? How can you stand there
stunned as deer that have been chased all day
over a plain and are used up at last,
and droop and halt, broken in heart and wind?
That is the way you look, no fight left in you!
Will you stand by till Trojans overrun
our line of ships, beached here above the breakers,
to find out if the hand of Zeus is over you?'

So as their lord commander he reviewed them,
passing along the crowded ranks. He came
upon the Cretans, putting on their armour,
around Idomeneus. Like a wild boar,
with his great heart, this captain in the van
harangued his companies, and in the rear
Meriones did likewise.

                              The Lord Marshal
Agamemnon, elated at the sight,
said to Idomeneus in the warmest tones:
'Idomeneus, you are a man I prize
above all handlers of fast horses, whether
in war or any labour, or at feasts
whenever in their mixing bowls our peers
prepare the wine reserved for counsellors.
Achaean gentlemen with flowing hair
may down their portions, but your cup will be
filled up and filled again, like mine – to drink
as we are moved to! Now, the feast is war.
Be as you always have been up to now!'

To this Idomeneus, captain of Cretans,
answered: 'Son of Atreus, more than ever
shall I stand by you as I swore I would.
But now stir up the rest of the Achaeans
to give battle as quickly as we can!
The Trojans have dissolved the truce. Again,
death to the Trojans! Bad times are ahead
for those who overrode our pact and broke it!'

This fierceness made the son of Atreus happy

as he passed down the crowded ranks. He came
to where the two named Aias, tall and short,
were buckling on their gear. Around them armed
their cloud of infantry. Like a dark cloud
a shepherd from a hilltop sees, a storm,
a gloom over the ocean, travelling shoreward
under the west wind; distant from his eyes
more black than pitch it seems, though far at sea,
with lightning squalls driven along its front.
Shivering at the sight, he drives his flock
for shelter into a cavern. Grim as that
were the dense companies that armed for war
with Telamonian Aias and the other —
shields pitch-black and a spiny hedge of spears.

   Lord Agamemnon, heartened at the sight,
spoke to the captains warmly: 'Aias and Aias,
captains of Argos in your mail of bronze,
I have no orders for you: there's no need
to put you in a mood for war: it's clear
you've passed your fighting spirit to your troops.
O Father Zeus, Athena and Apollo,
if only every heart were strong as these!
Lord Priam's fortress would go down before us,
taken in a day, and plundered at our hands.'

   With this he left them there, and passing on
to others as they formed, he found Lord Nestor,
the Pylian master orator, haranguing
soldiers of Pylos, forming them for action
around the captains Pelagon, Alastor,
Chromius, Haemon, and the marshal, Bias.
Charioteers with teams and cars he sent
forward, and kept his infantry behind
to be the bristling bulk and hedge of battle,
placing weak men and cowardly between
brave men on either side, so willy-nilly
all would be forced to fight.
                              The chariot men
he first instructed in the way of battle —
charioteers to keep their teams in line,
not to be tangled, cut off in the mêlée:
'None of you should rely so far on horsemanship
or bravery as to attack alone — much less
retreat alone. That way you are most vulnerable.
Let any man in line lunge with his lance

when he can reach their chariots from his own;
you'll fight with far more power. In the old days
cities and walls were overthrown by men
who kept this plan in mind and fought with courage.'

So ran the old man's exhortation, shrewd
from a long lifetime in the ways of war.
It gladdened Agamemnon, who said to him:
'I wish you had the same force in your legs
as in your fighting heart; I wish your strength
were whole again. The wrinkling years have worn you.
Better some other soldier had your age,
and you were still among the young.'

                         And Nestor,
Earl of Gerenia, charioteer, replied:
'Agamemnon, I too could wish I were
the man who brought great Ereuthalion down.
But the immortal gods have given men
all things in season. Once my youth, my manhood,
now my age has come. No less for that
I have my place among the charioteers
to counsel and command them. Duties fit
for elder men, these are: the young can be
good lancers, good with spears – men who were born
in a later day, and still can trust their powers.'

The son of Atreus heard him out and passed
happily onward.

                   Next he found Menestheus,
the good horse-handler, son of Peteos, waiting,
surrounded by Athenians, good hands
in battle. Near him, too, the great tactician,
Odysseus, had his place, with Cephallenians
in ranks around him, not at all feeble; these
waited, for word of battle had not reached them,
but only a first ripple in the lines
of Trojans and Achaeans. There they stood,
as though they waited for some other troop
to move out and make contact with the Trojans.
Surveying these, Lord Agamemnon, marshal
of fighting men, in urgent speech rebuked them:
'Son of Peteos whom the gods reared! You, too,
Odysseus, hero of battle guile and greed!
Why both so deferential, so retiring?
Waiting for other troops? You two should be
among the first in action, in the blaze

of combat – as you both are first to hear
my word of feasting, every time we Achaeans
prepare a feast for our staff officers.
There is the fare you like: roast meat, and cups
of honey-hearted wine, all you desire!
But now you'd gladly see ten troops ahead of you
moving up to attack with naked bronze!'
Odysseus, the wily field commander,
scowled at him and answered: 'Son of Atreus,
what is this panic you permit yourself?
How can you say we'd let a fight go by,
ever, at any time when we Achaeans
against the Trojans whet the edge of war?
If you will make it your concern you'll see
the father of Telemachus in action
hand to hand in the enemy's front ranks.
Your bluster is all wind!'
                    Lord Agamemnon,
sure of his angry man, replied,
smiling and taking back his provocation:
'Son of Laertes and the gods of old,
Odysseus, master mariner and soldier,
I would not be unfair to you; I need not
give you orders, knowing as I do
that you are well disposed toward all I plan.
Your thought is like my own.
Come, then; in time we'll make amends for this,
if anything uncalled for has been said:
God send the sea-winds blow it out of mind!'

   He left them there, and going amid others
found Diomedes, gallant son of Tydeus,
with combat cars and horses all around him,
still at a stand. Nearby stood Sthenelus,
the son of Capaneus.
                And Agamemnon
at a first glimpse in scathing speech rebuked him:
'Baffling! Son of Tydeus the battle-wise
breaker of horses, why are you so shy?
So wary of the passages of war?
Your father did not lag like this, nor care to –
far from it: he would rather fight alone
ahead of all his men, or so they said
who saw him toil in battle. I myself
never met him, never laid eyes on him,

but men say that he had no peer.
                                    In peace,
without a fight, as Polyneices' ally,
he entered old Mycenae, hunting troops.
At that time they were marching to besiege
the ancient walls of Thebes, and they appealed
for first-rate men as volunteers. Our people
agreed and would have granted these, but Zeus
by inauspicious omens changed their minds.
Taking the road, and well along, the army
came to Asopus in his grassy bed,
a river deep in rushes; there again
they ordered Tydeus forward with a message.
Forward he went, and found Cadmeians thronging
a great feast in the manor of Eteocles,
where, though no liege nor distant friend, and though
he came alone amid so many, Tydeus
went unafraid. He challenged them to wrestling
and easily beat them all – being seconded
so well by Athena. Those goaders of horses,
the furious Cadmeians, laid a trap for him
on his retreat up-country: fifty men
deployed in a strong ambush by two leaders,
Maeon, immortal-seeming son of Haemon,
and Polyphontes, son of Autophonus.
But these, as well, Tydeus brought to grief:
he killed them all but one. Maeon he spared
and sent home, bid by portents from the gods.
This, then, was Tydeus the Aetolian.
Weaker than he in war, the man he fathered,
stronger in assembly!'
                                    Diomedes,
the rugged man, said nothing whatsoever,
accepting his commander's reprimand.

   But Sthenelus, the son of Capaneus,
made a retort: 'Atreides, why distort things
when you know well how to be just? We say
we are far better men than our fathers were.
Not they, but we, took Thebes of the seven gates,
leading a smaller force
against a heavier wall – but heeding signs
the gods had shown, and helped by Zeus. Our fathers?
Their own recklessness destroyed our fathers!
Rate them less than equal to ourselves!'

Now rugged Diomedes with a frown
turned and said: 'Old horse, be still. Believe me,
I do not take this ill from the Lord Marshal
Agamemnon. He must goad the Achaeans
to combat – for the glory goes to him
if his detachments cut the Trojans down
and take their powerful city – as the anguish
goes to him also, if his men are slain.
Come, both of us should put our minds on valour.'

As he said this he bounded from his car
in full armour, and the bronze about his chest
rang as he hit the ground, a captain roused.
Even a stout heart would have feared him then.

As down upon a shore of echoing surf
big waves may run under a freshening west wind,
looming first on the open sea, and riding
shoreward to fall on sand in foam and roar,
around all promontories crested surges
making a briny spume inshore – so now
formations of Danaans rose and moved
relentlessly toward combat. Every captain
called to his own. The troops were mainly silent;
you could not have believed so great a host
with war-cries in its heart was coming on
in silence, docile to its officers –
and round about upon the soldiers shone
the figured armour buckled on for war.

The Trojans were not silent: like the flocks
that huddle countless in a rich man's pens,
waiting to yield white milk, and bleating loud
continually as they hear their own lambs cry,
just so the war-cry of the Trojans rose
through all that army – not as a single note,
not in a single tongue, but mingled voices
of men from many countries.

                                    This great army
Ares urged on; the other, grey-eyed Athena,
Terror and Rout, and Hate, insatiable
sister-in-arms of man-destroying Ares –
frail at first, but growing, till she rears
her head through heaven as she walks the earth.
Once more she sowed ferocity, traversing
the ranks of men, redoubling groans and cries.

When the long lines met at the point of contact,

there was a shock of bull's hide, battering pikes,
and weight of men in bronze. Bucklers with bosses
ground into one another. A great din rose,
in one same air elation and agony
of men destroying and destroyed, and earth
astream with blood. In spring, snow-water torrents
risen and flowing down the mountainsides
hurl at a confluence their mighty waters
out of the gorges, filled by tributaries,
and far away upon the hills a shepherd
hears the roar. So when these armies closed
there came a toiling clamour.

                        Antilochus
was the first man to down a Trojan soldier,
a brave man in the front line, Echepolus
Thalysiades: he hit him on the ridge
that bore his crest, and driven in, the point
went through his forehelm and his forehead bone,
and darkness veiled his eyes. In the mêlée
he toppled like a tower. Then by the feet
the fallen man was seized by Elephenor
Chalcodontiades, chief of Abantes,
who tried to haul him out of range and strip him
quickly of his arms. The trial was brief.
Seeing him tugging at the corpse, his flank
exposed beside the shield as he bent over,
Agenor with his spearshaft shod in bronze
hit him, and he crumpled. As he died
a bitter combat raged over his body
between the Trojan spearmen and Achaeans,
going for one another like wolves, like wolves
whirling upon each other, man to man.

    Then Aias Telamonius knocked down
Simoisius, the son of Anthemion,
in the full bloom of youth. On slopes of Ida
descending, by the banks of clear Simois,
his mother had conceived him, while she kept
a vigil with her parents over flocks;
he got his name for this. To his dear parents
he never made return for all their care,
but had his life cut short when Aias' shaft
unmanned him. In the lead, as he came on,
he took the spear-thrust squarely in the chest
beside the nipple on the right side; piercing him,

the bronze point issued by the shoulder-blade,
and in the dust he reeled and fell. A poplar
growing in bottom-lands, in a great meadow,
smooth-trunked, high up to its sheath of boughs,
will fall before the chariot-builder's axe
of shining iron – timber that he marked
for warping into chariot tyre-rims –
and, seasoning, it lies beside the river.
So vanquished by the god-reared Aias lay
Simoisius Anthemides.

    At Aias in his turn the son of Priam,
Antiphus, glittering in his cuirass, made
a spear-cast, but he missed and hit instead
Leucus, Odysseus' comrade, in the groin
as he bent low to pull away the corpse.
It dropped out of his grasp, and he fell over it.
Odysseus, wrought to fury at this death,
with flashing helmet shouldered through the ranks
to stand above him: glowering right and left
he kept his lance in play, and made the Trojans
facing him recoil. With no waste motion
he cast and hit a bastard son of Priam,
Democoon, who had come down from Abydos
where he kept racing horses. Full of rage
over his dead companion, Odysseus
speared him in the temple, and the spearhead
passed clean through his head from side to side
so darkness veiled his eyes. When he fell down
he thudded, and his armour clanged upon him.

    The Trojan front gave way, Prince Hector, too,
while Argives raised a great yell. Dragging dead men
out of the press, they made a deep advance.

    Now looking down from Pergamus, Apollo
in indignation cried out to the Trojans:
'Forward! Trojans, breakers of horses, will you
bow in fury of battle to the Argives?
When hit, they are not made of iron or stone
to make the cutting bronze rebound! See, too,
Achilles, child of Thetis, is not fighting
but tasting wrath and wrong beside the ships!'

    The terrible god cried out thus from his tower,
and on the Achaean side Tritogeneia,
glorious daughter of Zeus, went through the ranks
to lift the hearts of those she saw dismayed.

The next on whom fate closed was Diores
Amarynceides, hit by a jagged stone
low on the right leg near the ankle. Peiros threw it,
Peiros Imbrasides, a Thracian captain,
one who had come from Aenus. With the bone
itself, the vicious stone crushed both leg-tendons
utterly, and the tall man tumbled down
into the dust, flinging his arms out wide
to his companions, panting his life away;
but on the run the man who hit him, Peiros,
came with a spear to gash him by the navel.
His bowels were spilled, and darkness veiled his eyes.

Then Thoas the Aetolian lunged at Peiros,
hitting him with a spear above the nipple,
so the bronze point stuck in his lung; and Thoas
at close quarters, wrenching the heavy spear,
pulled it out of his chest, then drew his sword
and killed him with a stroke square in the belly.
His gear he could not strip, though; friends of the dead man,
topknotted Thracians, closing round with spears,
repulsed him, huge and powerful as he was,
a noble figure; staggering, he gave ground.
As for the two, they lay there in the dust
stretched out near one another: captain of Thracians
and captain of Epeians mailed in bronze,
while others, many, fell in death around them.

Thereafter no man could have scorned that fight,
no veteran of battle who might go round,
untouched amid the action – as observer
led by Athena, with his hand in hers,
shielded by her from stones' and arrows' flight;
for that day throngs of Trojans and Achaeans,
prone in the dust, were strewn beside each other.

BOOK V

A HERO STRIVES WITH GODS

NOW Diomedes' hour for great action came.
Athena made him bold, and gave him ease
to tower amid Argives, to win glory,
and on his shield and helm she kindled fire
most like midsummer's purest flaming star
in heaven rising, bathed by the Ocean stream.
So fiery she made his head and shoulders
as she impelled him to the centre where
the greatest number fought.

                    A certain Dares,
a noble man among the Trojans, rich,
and a votary of Hephaestus, had two sons
well-trained in warfare, Phegeus and Idaeus.
These two the Achaean faced as they came forward
upon their car; on foot he braced to meet them.
As the range narrowed, Phegeus aimed and cast
his long spear first: the point cleared Diomedes'
shoulder on the left, and failed to touch him.
Then Diomedes wheeling in his turn
let fly his bronze-shod spear. No miss,
but a clean hit midway between the nipples
knocked the man backward from his team. Idaeus
left the beautiful chariot, leaping down,
but dared not stand his ground over his brother;
nor could he have himself eluded death
unless Hephaestus had performed the rescue,
hiding him in darkness – thus to spare
his father full bereavement, were he lost.
Yanking the horses' heads, lashing their flanks,
Diomedes handed team and chariot over
to men of his command, to be conducted
back to the ships. Now when the Trojans saw
how Dares' two sons fared – one saved, indeed,
the other lying dead beside his car –
every man's heart misgave him.

                       Grey-eyed Athena
took the fierce wargod, Ares, by the hand
and said to him: 'Ares, bane of all mankind,

crusted with blood, breacher of city walls,
why not allow the Trojans and Achaeans
to fight alone? Let them contend – why not? –
for glory Zeus may hold out to the winner,
while we keep clear of combat – and his rage.'

Even as she spoke she led him from the battle
and sat him down upon Scamander side.
Now Danaans forced back the Trojan lines,
and every captain killed his man.
First the Lord Marshal Agamemnon
struck from his car Odius, a tall warrior,
chief of the Halizones; he had turned,
signalling a retreat, when Agamemnon's
point went through him from the rear, between
the shoulders, driving through his chest,
and down he crashed with clang of arms upon him.
Idomeneus then killed the son of Borus,
Phaestus, who came from good farmland at Tarne.
As this man rose upon his car, Idomeneus
drove through his right shoulder, tumbling him
out of the chariot, and numbing darkness
shrouded him, as the Cretans took his gear.
Scamandrius, hunter son of Strophius,
fell before Menelaus' point – Scamandrius,
expert at hunting: Artemis herself
had taught him to bring down all kinds of game
bred in the forests on wild hills. But she
who fills the air with arrows helped him not
at all this time, nor did his own good shooting.
No, as he ran before the Achaean's lance
Menelaus caught him with a lunging thrust
between the shoulder-blades, drove through his ribs,
and down he fell, head first, his armour clanging.
Meanwhile Meriones killed Phereclus,
son of Harmonides, a man who knew
all manner of building art and handicraft,
for Pallas Athena loved him well. This man
had even built Alexandrus those ships,
vessels of evil, fatal to the Trojans
and now to him, who had not guessed heaven's will.
Running behind and overtaking him,
Meriones hit his buttock on the right
and pierced his bladder, missing the pelvic bone.
He fell, moaning, upon his hands and knees

and death shrouded him. Then Meges killed
Pedaeus, bastard son of Lord Antenor,
a son whom Lady Theano had cherished
equally with her own, to please her husband.
Meges Phyleides, the master spearman,
closing with him, hit his nape: the point
clove through his tongue's root and against his teeth.
Biting cold bronze he fell into the dust.
Eurypylus Euaemonides brought down
Hypsenor, son of noble Dolopion,
priest of Scamander in the old time, honoured
by countryfolk as though he were a god.
As this man fled, Eurypylus leapt after him
with drawn sword, on the run, and struck his shoulder,
cutting away one heavy arm: in blood
the arm dropped, and death surging on his eyes
took him, hard destiny.
          So toiled the Achaeans
in that rough charge. But as for Diomedes,
you could not tell if he were with Achaeans
or Trojans, for he coursed along the plain
most like an April torrent fed by snow,
a river in flood that sweeps away his bank;
no piled-up dike will hold him, no revetment
shielding the bloom of orchard land, this river
suddenly at crest when heaven pours down
the rain of Zeus; many a yeoman's field
of beautiful grain is ravaged: even so
before Diomedes were the crowded ranks
of Trojans broken, many as they were,
and none could hold him.
          Now when Pandarus
looked over at him, saw him sweep the field,
he bent his bow of horn at Diomedes
and shot him as he charged, hitting his cuirass
in the right shoulder joint. The winging arrow
stuck, undeflected, spattering blood on bronze.
Pandarus gave a great shout: 'Close up, Trojans!
Come on, charioteers! The Achaean champion
is hit, hit hard: I swear my arrowshot
will bring him down soon – if indeed it was
Apollo who cheered me on my way from Lycia!'
Triumphantly he shouted; but his arrow
failed to bring Diomedes down. Retiring

upon his chariot and team, he stood
and said to Sthenelus, the son of Capaneus:
'Quick, Sthenelus, old friend, jump down
and pull this jabbing arrow from my shoulder!'
Sthenelus vaulted down and, pressed against him,
drew the slim arrow shaft clear of his wound
with spurts of blood that stained his knitted shirt.

And now at last Diomedes of the war-cry
prayed aloud: 'Oh hear me, daughter of Zeus
who bears the storm-cloud, tireless one, Athena!
If ever you stood near my father and helped him
in a hot fight, befriend me now as well.
Let me destroy that man, bring me in range of him,
who hit me by surprise, and glories in it.
He swears I shall be blind to sunlight soon.'

So ran his prayer, and Pallas Athena heard him.
Nimbleness in the legs, sure feet and hands
she gave him, standing near him, saying swiftly:
'Courage, Diomedes. Press the fight
against the Trojans. Fury like your father's
I've put into your heart: his never quailed –
Tydeus, master shieldsman, master of horses.
I've cleared away the mist that blurred your eyes
a moment ago, so you may see before you
clearly, and distinguish god from man.
If any god should put you to the test
upon this field, be sure you are not the man
to dare immortal gods in combat – none,
that is, except the goddess Aphrodite.
If ever she should join the fight, then wound her
with your keen bronze.'

                    At this, grey-eyed Athena
left him, and once more he made his way
into the line. If he had burned before
to fight with Trojans, now indeed blood-lust
three times as furious took hold of him.
Think of a lion that some shepherd wounds
but lightly as he leaps into a fold:
the man who roused his might cannot repel him
but dives into his shelter, while his flocks,
abandoned, are all driven wild; in heaps
huddled they are to lie, torn carcasses,
before the escaping lion at one bound
surmounts the palisade. So lion-like,

Diomedes plunged on Trojans.
                              First he killed
Astynous and a captain, Hypeiron,
one with a spear-thrust in the upper chest,
the other by a stroke of his great sword
chopping his collar-bone at the round joint
to sever his whole shoulder from his body.
These he left, and met Polyidus
and Abas, Eurydamas' sons: the father
being an old interpreter of dreams.
He read no dreams for these two, going to war;
Diomedes killed and stripped them. Next he met
Xanthus and Thoon, two dear sons of Phaenops,
a man worn out with misery and years
who fathered no more heirs – but these
Diomedes overpowered; he took their lives,
leaving their father empty pain and mourning –
never to welcome them alive at home
after the war, and all their heritage
broken up among others. Next two sons
of Dardan Priam Diomedes killed
in one war-car: Echemmon and Chromius.
Just as a lion leaps to crunch the neck
of ox or heifer, grazing near a thicket,
Diomedes, leaping, dragged them down
convulsed out of their car, and took their armour,
sending their horses to the rear.
                                      Aeneas,
observing all the havoc this man made
amid the Trojan ranks, moved up the line
of battle and along the clash of spears,
in search of Pandarus. Coming upon him,
he halted by Lycaon's noble son
and said to him: 'Pandarus, where is your bow?
Where are your fledged arrows? And your fame?
No man of Troy contends with you in archery,
no man in Lycia would claim to beat you.
Here, lift your hands to Zeus, let fly at that one,
whoever he is: an overwhelming fighter,
he has already hurt the Trojans badly,
cutting down many of our best. Let fly!
Unless it be some god who bears a grudge
against us, raging over a sacrifice.
The anger of a god is cruel anger.'

To this Lycaon's noble son replied:
'Aeneas, master of battle-craft for Trojans
under arms, that spearman, as I see him,
looks very like Diomedes: shield and helm
with his high plume-socket I recognize,
having his team in view. I cannot swear
he is no god. If it be Diomedes,
never could he have made this crazy charge
without some god behind him. No, some god
is near him wrapped in cloud, and bent aside
that arrowhead that reached him – for I shot him
once before, I hit him, too, and squarely
on the right shoulder through his cuirass joint
over the armpit. Down to the ditch of Death
I thought I had dispatched him. Not at all:
my arrow could not bring him down.
Some angry god is in this.
                              'Teams and chariots
I lack, or I could ride. In Father's manor
there are eleven war-cars newly built
and outfitted, with housings on them all,
and every chariot has a team nearby
that stands there champing barley meal. God knows
how many things Lycaon had to tell me
in the great hall before I left! He said
that I should drive a team, a chariot,
and so command the Trojan men-at-arms
in combat. How much better if I had!
But I refused: sparing the teams, I thought,
from short rations of fodder under siege.
And so I left them, made my way on foot
to Ilium, relying on my bow –
a bow destined to fail me. In this battle
I have had shots at two great fighters: one
Diomedes and the other Menelaus;
I drew blood from both, but only roused them.
Destiny was against me on that day
I took my bow of horn down from its peg
and led my men to your sweet town of Troy,
for Hector's sake. If ever I return,
if ever I lay eyes on land and wife
and my great hall, may someone cut my head off
unless I break this bow between my hands
and throw it into a blazing fire! It goes

everywhere with me, useless.'

Aeneas said:
'Better not talk so. Till we act, he wins.
We two can drive my car against this man
and take him on with sword and spear.
Mount my chariot, and you'll see how fast
these horses of the line of Tros can run:
they know our plain and how to wheel upon it
this way and that way in pursuit or flight
like wind veering. These will save us, take us
Troyward if again Zeus should confer
the upper hand and glory on Diomedes.
Come take the whip and reins; and let me mount
to fight him from the car – or you yourself
may face the man, and let me mind the horses.'

Lycaon's noble son replied: 'Aeneas,
manage the reins yourself, and guide the team,
they'll draw the rounded war-car with more ease
knowing the driver, if we must give ground
to Diomedes this time. God forbid
they panic, missing your voice,
and balk at pulling out when Diomedes
makes his leap upon us!
God forbid he kill the two of us
and make a prize of these! No, you yourself
handle your car and team. I'll take him on
with my good spear when he attacks.'

So both agreed and rode the painted car
toward Diomedes.

Sthenelus, the son
of Capaneus, caught sight of them
and turned at once to Diomedes, saying:
'Friend of my heart and soul,
I see two spearmen who would have your blood,
a pair of big men, bearing down on you.
One's Pandarus the bowman; by repute
his father was Lycaon; and the other,
Aeneas, claims Anchises as his father;
his mother is Aphrodite. Up with you.
We'll move back somewhat in our chariot.
Now is no moment for another charge,
or you may lose your life.'

But Diomedes
glanced at him scowling. 'No more talk,' he said,

'of turning tail. You cannot make me see it.
For me there's no style in a dodging fight
or making oneself small. I am fresh as ever.
Retire in the car? I dread it. No,
I'll meet them head on as before. Athena
will never let me tremble. These two men
are not to get away behind their horses
after we hit them, even if one survives
to try it.
            'Let me tell you this thing, too:
remember it. If in her craft Athena
confers on me the honour of killing both,
you halt our horses hard upon the spot,
taking a full hitch round the chariot rail,
and jump Aeneas' horses: mind you drive them
among Achaeans, out of the Trojans' range.
They are that breed that Zeus who views the wide world
gave to Tros in fee for Ganymedes,
under the Dawn and under Helios
the finest horses in the world.
Anchises, marshal of Troy, stole their great stock
without Laomedon's knowledge, putting fillies
to breed with them, and from these half a dozen
foals were bred for Anchises at his manor,
four to be reared in his own stalls: but two
he gave Aeneas as a battle team.
If we can take that team we win great honour.'
    This was the way these two conferred. Meanwhile
the other pair behind their team full tilt
had come in range, and Pandarus called out:
'O son of Tydeus, undaunted heart
and mind of war, my arrow
could not bring you down – a wasted shot.
This time I'll try a spear. God, let me hit you!'
    Rifling it, he let the long spear fly
and struck him on the shield: his point in flight
broke through to reach the cuirass –
and Pandarus gave a great shout: 'Now you're hit
square in the midriff. Can you keep your feet?
Not long, I think. This time the glory's mine!'
    Unshaken by the blow, Diomedes answered:
'A miss, no hit. I doubt you two will quit, though,
being what you are, till one of you is down
and glutting leather-covered Ares, god

of battle, with your blood!'

                             At this he made his cast,
his weapon being guided by Athena
to cleave Pandarus' nose beside the eye
and shatter his white teeth: his tongue
the brazen spearhead severed, tip from root,
then ploughing on came out beneath his chin.
He toppled from the car, and all his armour
clanged on him, shimmering. The horses
quivered and shied away; but life and spirit
ebbed from the broken man, and he lay still.

    With shield and spear Aeneas, now on foot,
in dread to see the Achaeans drag the dead man,
came and bestrode him, like a lion at bay.
Keeping the spear and rounded shield before him,
thrusting to kill whoever came in range,
he raised a terrible cry. But Diomedes
bent for a stone and picked it up – a boulder
no two men now alive could lift, though he
could heft it easily. This mass he hurled
and struck Aeneas on the hip, just where
the hip-bone shifts in what they call the bone-cup,
crushing this joint with two adjacent tendons
under the skin ripped off by the rough stone.
Now the great Trojan, fallen on his knees,
put all his weight on one strong hand
and leaned against the earth: night veiled his eyes.

    Aeneas would have perished there
but for the quickness of the daughter of Zeus,
his mother, Aphrodite, she who bore him
to shepherding Anchises, and who now
pillowed him softly in her two white arms
and held a corner of her glimmering robe
to screen him, so that no Danaan spear
should stab and finish him. Then from the battle
heavenward she lifted her dear son.

    Meanwhile Sthenelus, the son of Capaneus,
remembered the command of Diomedes.
He brought his horse to a halt, made fast
his taut reins to the chariot rail, and flung himself
upon Aeneas' long-maned beautiful team.
Away, out of the Trojans' reach, he drove them
and gave them into the hands of Deipylus –
for he esteemed this friend more than his peers

for presence of mind – to lead them to the ships.
Remounting, shaking out his polished reins,
he turned his sure-footed horses and drove hard
in Diomedes' track – as Diomedes
moved ahead to attack the Cyprian goddess.
He knew her to be weak, not one of those
divine mistresses of the wars of men –
Athena, for example, or Enyo,
raider of cities – therefore he dared assail her
through a great ruck of battle. When in range
he leaped high after her and with his point
wounded her trailing hand: the brazen lancehead
slashed her heavenly robe, worked by the Graces,
and cut the tender skin upon her palm.
Now from the goddess that immortal fluid,
ichor, flowed – the blood of blissful gods
who eat no food, who drink no tawny wine,
and thereby being bloodless have the name
of being immortal.
                    Aphrodite screamed
and flung her child away; but Lord Apollo
caught him in his arms and bore him off
in a dark cloud, through which no Danaan spear
could stab and finish him.
                    Now Diomedes,
lord of the battle-cry, with mighty lungs
cried out to her: 'Oh give up war, give up
war and killing, goddess! Is it not enough
to break soft women down with coaxing lust?
Go haunting battle, will you? I can see you
shudder after this at the name of war!'
So taunted, faint with pain, she quit the field,
being by wind-running Iris helped away
in anguish, sobbing, while her lovely skin
ran darkness. Then she came on Ares resting
far to the left, his spearshaft leaning on
a bank of mist; there stood his battle team,
and falling on one knee she begged her brother
for those gold-bangled horses. 'Brother dear,
please let me take your team, do let me have them,
to go up to the god's home on Olympus.
I am too dreadfully hurt: a mortal speared me.
Diomedes it was; he'd even fight with Zeus!'
Then Ares gave her his gold-bangled team,

and into the car she stepped, throbbing with pain,
while Iris at her side gathered the reins
and flicked the horses into eager flight.
They came, almost at once, to steep Olympus
where the gods dwell. Iris who runs on wind
halted and unyoked the team and tossed them
heavenly fodder.

In Dione's lap
Aphrodite sank down, and her dear mother
held and caressed her, whispering in her ear:
'Who did this to you, darling child? In heaven
who could have been so rude and wild,
as though you had committed open wrong?'

    And Aphrodite, lover of smiling eyes,
answered: 'Diomedes had the insolence
to wound me, when I tried to save
my dear son from the war: Aeneas, dearest
of all the sons of men to me.
It seems this horrid combat is no longer
Trojans against Achaeans – now, the Argives
are making war upon the gods themselves!'

    Then said Dione, loveliest of goddesses:
'There, child, patience, even in such distress.
Many of us who live upon Olympus
have taken hurt from men, and hurt each other.
Ares bore it, when Otus and Ephialtes,
Aloeus' giant sons, put him in chains:
he lay for thirteen moons in a brazen jar,
until that glutton of war might well have perished
had Eeriboea, stepmother of the two,
not told Hermes: Hermes broke him free
more dead than alive, worn out by the iron chain.
Then think how Hera suffered, too,
that time Amphitryon's mighty son let fly
his triple-barbed arrow into her right breast:
unappeasable pain came over her.
And Hades too, great lord of undergloom,
bore a shot from the same strong son of Zeus
at Pylos, amid the dead. That arrow stroke
delivered him to anguish. Hades then,
pierced and stricken, went to high Olympus,
the arrow grinding still in his great shoulder,
and there Paeeon with a poultice healed him
who was not born for death. What recklessness

in Heracles, champion though he was at labours,
to shrug at impious acts and bend his bow
for the discomfiture of Olympians!
But this man, he that wounded you, Athena
put him up to it – idiot, not to know
his days are numbered who would fight the gods!
His children will not sing around his knees
"Papa! Papa!" on his return from war.
So let Diomedes pause, for all his prowess,
let him remember he may meet his match,
and Aegialeia, daughter of Adrastus,
starting up from sleep some night in tears
may waken all the house, missing her husband,
noblest of Achaeans: Diomedes.'

　　Dione soothed her, wiped away the ichor
with both her hands from Aphrodite's palm –
already throbbing less, already healing.
But Hera and Athena, looking on,
had waspish things to say, to irritate Zeus.
It was the grey-eyed goddess who began:
'Oh, Father, will you be annoyed if I
make a small comment? Aphrodite
likes to beguile the women of Achaea
to elope with Trojans, whom she so adores:
now, fondling some Achaean girl, I fear,
she scratched her slim white hand on a golden pin.'

　　He smiled at this, the father of gods and men,
and said to the pale-gold goddess Aphrodite:
'Warfare is not for you, child. Lend yourself
to sighs of longing and the marriage bed.
Let Ares and Athena deal with war.'

　　These were the colloquies in heaven.

　　　　　　　　　　　　　　　　Meanwhile,
Diomedes, lord of the war-cry, charged Aeneas
though he knew well Apollo had sustained him.
He feared not even the great god himself,
but meant to kill Aeneas and take his armour.
Three times he made his killing thrust; three times
the Lord Apollo buffeted his shield,
throwing him back. Beside himself, again
he sprang, a fourth time, but the Archer God
raised a bloodcurdling cry: 'Look out! Give way!
Enough of this, this craze to vie with gods!
Our kind, immortals of the open sky,

will never be like yours, earth-faring men.'

Diomedes backed away a step or two
before Apollo's terrible anger, and
the god caught up Aeneas and set him down
on Troy's high citadel of Pergamus
where his own shrine was built.
There in that noble room Leto and Artemis
tended the man and honoured him. Meanwhile
Apollo made a figure of illusion,
Aeneas' double, armed as he was armed,
and round this phantom Trojans and Achaeans
cut one another's chest-protecting oxhide
shields with hanging shield-flaps.

                              Then Apollo
said to the war-god: 'Bane of all mankind,
crusted with blood, breacher of walls, why not
go in and take this man out of the combat,
this Diomedes, who would try a cast
with Zeus himself? First he attempted Cypris
and cut her lovely hand, then like a fury
came at me.'

                    Apollo turned away
to rest in Pergamus, upon the height,
while baleful Ares through the ranks of Trojans
made his way to stiffen them. He seemed
Acamas, a good runner, chief of Thracians,
appealing to the sons of Priam: 'Princes,
heirs of Priam in the line of Zeus,
how long will the Achaeans have your leave
to kill your people? Up to the city gates?
Lying in dust out there is one of us
whom we admire as we do Lord Hector –
Aeneas, noble Anchises' son.
Come, we can save him from the trampling rout.'

He made them burn at this, and then Sarpedon
in his turn growled at Hector: 'What of you,
Hector, where has your courage gone?
Defend the city, will you, without troops,
without allies, you and your next of kin,
brothers-in-law and brothers? In the combat
I neither see nor hear of them – like dogs
making themselves scarce around a lion.
We do the fighting, we who are allies here
as I am – and a long journey I made of it

from Lycia and Xanthus' eddying river
far away, where I left wife and child,
with property a needy man would dream of.
Here all the same I am, sending my Lycians
forward, and going in to fight myself,
though I have no least stake in Troy:
no booty for Achaeans to carry off –
while you stand like a sheep. You have not even
called on the rest to hold their ground, to fight
for their own wives! Will you be netted, caught
like helpless game your enemies can feast on?
They will be pillaging your city soon!
Here is your duty: night and day
press every captain of your foreign troops
to keep his place in battle, and fight off
the blame and bitterness of your defeat!'

This lashing had made Hector hot with shame,
and down he vaulted from his chariot,
hefting two spears, to pace up through the army,
flank and centre, calling on all to fight,
to join battle again. The Trojans rallied
and now stood off the Achaeans, while the Achaeans
kept formation too.

          See in the mind's eye
wind blowing chaff on ancient threshing-floors
when men with fans toss up the trodden sheaves,
and yellow-haired Demeter, puff by puff,
divides the chaff and grain: how all day long
in bleaching sun straw-piles grow white: so white
grew those Achaean figures in the dustcloud
churned to the brazen sky by horses' hooves
as chariots intermingled, as the drivers
turned and turned – carrying their hands high
and forward gallantly despite fatigue.

Now coming to the Trojans' aid in battle,
Ares veiled them everywhere in dusk,
obeying Apollo of the golden sword
by rousing Trojan courage: he had seen
Pallas Athena, defender of Danaans,
depart from the other side. Apollo then
out of his sanctum, hushed and hung with gold,
sent back the marshal of Trojan troops, Aeneas,
with fighting spirit restored. He stood again
amid his peers, to their relief; they saw him

whole, without a scratch, and hot for war –
but no one there could pause to question him;
Apollo brought new toil upon them now,
with Ares, bane of men, and Strife insatiable.
Amid the Achaeans those two men named Aias,
joining Diomedes and Odysseus,
made bastion for Danaans. See these four,
all fearless of attack or Trojan power,
patient in battle – motionless as clouds
that Zeus may station on high mountain-tops
in a calm heaven, while the north wind sleeps
and so do all the winds whose gusty blowing
rifts and dispels shade-bearing cloud. So these
Danaans held their ground against the Trojans
and never stirred, while Agamemnon passed
amid the ranks haranguing troops:

                         'Dear friends,
be men, choose valour and pride in one another
when shock of combat comes. More men of pride
are saved than lost, and men who run for it
get no reward of praise, no safety either.'

    Lightning-quick, he lunged with his own spear
and hit a friend of Aeneas, Deicoon,
Pergasus' son, a spear-fighter, a man
the Trojans honoured as they did their princes,
knowing him prompt to join the battle line.
His shield hit hard by Agamemnon's thrust
could not withstand the spearhead, but the point
drove through his belt low down
and crumpled him, with clang of arms upon him.
Aeneas now, for his part, killed two champions
of the Danaans: Orsilochus and Crethon,
sons of Diocles, who owned estates
in Phere, being descended from that river
Alpheius, running broad through Pylian land.
Alpheius fathered Lord Ortilochus,
powerful over many men, and he
in his turn fathered gallant Diocles,
whose sons were twins, Orsilochus and Crethon,
skilful at every kind of fight.

                         Still fresh
in manhood they embarked in the black ships
for the wild horse country of Ilium, to gain
vengeance for the Atreidae, Agamemnon

and Menelaus. Here Death hid them both.
Imagine two young lions, reared
by a mother lioness in undergrowth
of a deep mountain forest – twins who prey
on herds and flocks, despoiling farms, till one day
they too are torn to pieces, both at once,
by sharp spears in the hands of men. So these
went down before the weapons of Aeneas,
falling like lofty pines before an axe.

    Pitying the two men fallen, Menelaus
came up, formidable in glittering bronze,
with menacing spear – for Ares urged him on
to see him conquered at Aeneas' hands.
But Nestor's watchful son, Antilochus,
advanced to join him, anxious for his captain,
fearing his loss, and failure of their cause.
The two champions with weapons tilted up
had faced each other, when Antilochus
moved in, shoulder to shoulder, with Menelaus;
and agile fighter though he was, Aeneas
shunned the combat, measuring this pair.
On his retreat they pulled away the dead
unlucky twins, and passed them to the rear,
then turned again to battle.

                    First they killed
a captain of Paphlagonians, Pylaemenes,
burly as Ares; Menelaus it was
who hit him with a spear-thrust, pierced him through
just at the collar-bone. Antilochus
knocked out his driver, Atymnius' noble son
called Mydon. As the man wheeled his horses
a boulder smashed his elbow; in the dust
his reins, inset with ivory, curled out,
as with drawn sword Antilochus leapt on him
and gashed his forehead. Gasping, down he went,
head first, pitching from his ornate car,
into a sandbank – so his luck would have it –
to stay embedded till his trampling horses
rolled him farther in the dust. Antilochus
lashed at them and consigned them to the rear.

    Surveying these Achaeans through the ranks
Hector charged with a sudden cry. Beside him
strong Trojan formations moved ahead,
impelled by Ares and by cold Enyo

who brings the shameless butchery of war.
Ares wielding a gigantic spear
by turns led Hector on or backed him up,
and as he watched this figure, Diomedes
felt like a traveller halted on a plain,
helpless to cross, before a stream in flood
that roars and spumes down to the sea. That traveller
would look once and recoil: so Diomedes
backed away and said to his company: 'Friends,
all we can do is marvel at Prince Hector.
What a spearman he is, and what a fighter!
One of the gods goes with him everywhere
to shield him from a mortal wound. Look! there,
beside him – Ares in disguise! Give ground
slowly; keep your faces toward the Trojans.
No good pitting ourselves against the gods.'

The Trojans reached them as he spoke, and Hector
swept into death a pair of men who knew
the joy of war – Menesthes and Anchialus –
both in a single car. Now, these two fallen
were pitied by great Aias Telamonius,
who moved in close, his glittering spear at play,
and overcame Selagus' son, Amphius,
a landowner in Paesus. Destiny
had sent this man to take a stand with Priam
and Priam's sons in war. Now Aias' thrust
went through his belt, and in his lower belly
the spearpoint crunched and stuck. He fell
hard in the dust. Then Aias
came up fast to strip him, while the Trojans
cast their spears in a bright hail: his shield
took one shock after another. With one heel
braced on the corpse he pulled away his point,
but being beset by spears he could not slip
sword-belt or buckler from the dead man's shoulders.
And now, too, he began to be afraid
of Trojans coming up around the body,
brave men and many, pressing him with spears.
Big as he was, and powerful and bold,
they pushed him back, and he retired, shaken.

This way the toil of battle took its course
in that quarter. Elsewhere, all-powerful fate
moved Heracles' great son, Tlepolemus,
to meet Sarpedon. As they neared each other,

son and grandson of cloud-massing Zeus,
Tlepolemus began to jeer: 'Lycian,
war-counsellor Sarpedon, why so coy
upon this field? You call yourself a fighter?
They lie who say you come of Zeus's line,
you are so far inferior to those
fathered by Zeus among the men of old.
Think what the power of Heracles was like,
my lion-hearted father! For Laomedon's
chariot horses once he beached at Troy
with only six shiploads of men, a handful,
yet he sacked Ilium and left her ways
desolate. But your nerve is gone, your troops
are losing badly: it is no gain for Trojans
that you came here from Lycia, powerful
man that you are – and when you fall to me,
down through the gates of Death you go!'

          Sarpedon
answered: 'Right enough, Tlepolemus,
he did ruin Ilium: Laomedon,
the greedy fool, gave him a vicious answer
after great labour well performed – refused
to make delivery of the promised horses
that Heracles had come for. As for you,
I promise a hard lot: a bloody death
you'll find here on this battleground,
when my spear knocks you out. You'll give up glory
to me and life to him who drives the horses
of undergloom, Lord Hades.'

          Then Tlepolemus
raised his ashen spear, and from their hands
in unison long shafts took flight. Sarpedon's
hit his enemy squarely in the neck
with force enough to drive the point clear through;
unending night of death clouded his eyes.
Tlepolemus' point, hitting the upper leg,
went jolting through between the two long bones,
but once again Sarpedon's father saved him.
Out of the mêlée men of his command
carried the captain in his agony, encumbered
by the long dragging spear. No one had time
to think of how the shaft might be withdrawn,
that he might use one leg at least, so hastily
they did their work, so pressed by care of battle.

Meanwhile Tlepolemus was carried back
by the Achaeans on the other side.
Rugged Odysseus noted it with anger
and pain for him. What should he do, he thought,
track down Sarpedon, son of thundering Zeus,
or take the life of Lycians in throngs?
It was not given to Odysseus
to finish off Sarpedon, but Athena
turned his fury upon the Lycians.
He killed Coeranus, Alastor, Chromius,
Alcandrus, Halius, Noemon, Prytanis,
and would have killed more Lycians, had not
great Hector's piercing eye
under his shimmering helmet lighted on him.
    Across the clashing line he came a-glitter
with burning bronze, a terror to Danaans,
making Sarpedon's heart lift up to see him,
so that as Hector passed he weakly said:
'I beg you not to leave me
lying here for Danaans to despoil.
Defend me; afterward let me bleed away
my life within your city. Not for me
to see my home and country once again,
my dear wife in her joy, my little son.'
    Silent under his polished helmet, Hector,
dazzling and impetuous, passed on
to drive the Argives back with general slaughter,
and those around Sarpedon
laid their commander in the royal shade
of Zeus's oak. One dear to him, Pelagon,
worrying the spearhead, pulled it from his thigh,
at which he fainted. But his breath came back
when a cool north wind, a reprieve, blew round
and fanned him, wakened him from his black swoon.
    Even though not yet routed to the ships
under attack from Ares and from Hector,
the Argives could not gain but yielded everywhere,
knowing that Ares fought among the Trojans.
One by one, who were the fighting men
that Hector slew, and Ares? Teuthras first;
Orestes, breaker of horses; a spear-thrower,
Trechus, an Aetolian; Oenomaus;
Helenus Oenopides; Oresbius
whose plated breast-band glittered – in the past

he lived at Hyle on Lake Cephisus,
fond of his wealth, amid his countrymen,
Boeotians of the fertile plain.
                                   Now Hera,
seeing those Argives perish in the fight,
appealed with indignation to Athena:
'A dismal scene, this. O untiring goddess,
daughter of mighty Zeus who bears the storm-cloud,
our word to Menelaus was a fraud –
that he should never sail for home
before he plundered Ilium! How likely,
if we allow this lunatic attack
by that sinister fool Ares? Come,
we'll put our minds on our own fighting power!'

   Grey-eyed Athena listened and agreed,
and Hera, eldest daughter of old Cronos,
harnessed her team, all golden fringes. Hebe
fitted upon her chariot, left and right,
the brazen wheels with eight shin-bones, or spokes,
around the iron axle-tree: all gold
her felloes are, unworn, for warped upon them
are tyres of bronze, a marvel; and the hubs
are silver, turning smoothly on each side.
The car itself is made of gold and silver
woven together, with a double rail,
and from the car a silver chariot-pole
leans forward. Hebe fitted to the tip
a handsome golden yoke, and added collars
all soft gold. And Hera in her hunger
for strife of battle and the cries of war
backed her sure-footed horses in the traces.

   As for Athena, she cast off and dropped
her great brocaded robe, her handiwork,
in lapping folds across her father's doorsill,
taking his shirt, the shirt of Zeus, cloud-masser,
with breast armour, and gear of grievous war.
She hung the storm-cloud shield with ravelled tassels
ominous from her shoulder: all around
upon it in a garland Rout was figured,
Enmity, Force, and Chase that chills the blood,
concentred on the Gorgon's head, reptilian
seething Fear – a portent of the storm-king.
Quadruple-crested, golden, double-ridged
her helmet was, enchased with men-at-arms

put by a hundred cities in the field.
She stepped aboard the glowing car of Hera
and took the great haft of her spear in hand –
that heavy spear this child of Power can use
to break in wrath long battle-lines of fighters.
Then at the crack of Hera's whip
over the horses' backs, the gates of heaven
swung wide of themselves on rumbling hinges –
gates the Hours keep, for they have charge
of entry to wide heaven and Olympus,
by opening or closing massive cloud.
Passing through these and goading on their team,
the goddesses encountered Cronos' son,
who sat apart from all the gods
on the summit of Olympus.
                              Reining in,
Hera with arms as white as ivory
addressed the all-highest: 'Father Zeus,
are you not thoroughly sick of Ares? All
those brutal acts of his? How great, how brave
the body of Achaeans he destroyed
so wantonly; he has made me grieve,
while Cypris and Apollo take their pleasure,
egging on that dunce who knows no decency.
Father, you cannot, can you, be annoyed
if I chastise and chase him from the field?'
    Then Zeus who gathers cloud replied: 'Go after him.
Athena, Hope of Soldiers, is the one
to match with him: she has a wondrous way
of bringing him to grief.'
                           At this permission,
Hera cracked her whip again. Her team
went racing between starry heaven and earth.
As much dim distance as a man perceives
from a high look-out over wine-dark sea,
these horses neighing in the upper air
can take at a bound. Upon the Trojan plain
where the two rivers run, Scamander flowing
to confluence with Simois, Hera halted
to let her horses graze. Around them both
she rained an emanation of dense cloud,
while for their pasturing Simois made
ambrosial grass grow soft.
                            The goddesses

gliding in a straight line like quivering doves
approached the battle to defend the Argives,
but once arrived where their best spearmen fought
at the flank of Diomedes, giving ground
like lions or boars, like carnivores at bay,
no feeble victims – Hera took her stand
with a loud cry. She had the look of Stentor,
whose brazen lungs could give a battle-shout
as loud as fifty soldiers, trumpeting:

'Shame, shame, Argives: cowards! good on parade!
While Prince Achilles roamed the field the Trojans
never would show their faces in a sortie,
respecting his great spear too much – but now
they fight far from the city, near the ships!'

This shout put anger into them. Meanwhile
the grey-eyed goddess Athena from the air
hastened to Diomedes. By his car
she found him resting, trying to cool the wound
Pandarus' arrow gave him. Spent and drenched
with sweat beneath his broad shield-strap, he felt
encumbered by his shield, being arm-weary,
and slipped the strap off, wiped his blood away.

The goddess put her hand upon the yoke
that joined his battle-team, and said: 'Ah, yes,
a far cry from his father, Tydeus' son.
Tydeus was a small man, but a fighter.
Once I forbade him war or feats of arms
that time he went as messenger to Thebes
alone, detached from the Achaean host,
amid Cadmeians in their multitude.
Bidden to dine at ease in their great hall,
combative as he always was, he challenged
the young Cadmeians – and he had no trouble
pinning them all, I took his part so well.
But you, now – here I stand with you, by heaven,
protect you, care for you, tell you to fight,
but you are either sluggish in the legs
from battle-weariness or hollow-hearted
somehow with fear: you are not, after all,
the son of Tydeus Oeneides.'

Proud Diomedes answered her: 'I know you,
goddess, daughter of Zeus who bears the storm-cloud.
With all respect, I can explain, and will.
No fear is in me, and no weariness;

I simply bear in mind your own commands.
You did expressly say I should not face
the blissful gods in fight – that is, unless
Aphrodite came in. One might feel free
to wound her, anyway. So you commanded,
and therefore I am giving ground myself
and ordering all the Argives to retire
shoulder to shoulder here, because I know
the master of battle over there is Ares.'

    The grey-eyed goddess answered: 'Diomedes,
dear to my heart: no matter what I said,
you are excused from it; you must not shrink
from Ares or from any other god
while I am with you. Whip your team
toward Ares, hit him, hand to hand, defer
no longer to this maniacal god
by nature evil, two-faced everywhere.
Not one hour ago I heard him grunt
his word to Hera and myself to fight
on the Argive side; now he forgets all that
and joins the Trojans.'

               Even as she spoke,
she elbowed Sthenelus aside and threw him,
but gave him a quick hand-up from the ground,
while she herself, impetuous for war,
mounted with Diomedes. At her step
the oaken axle groaned, having to bear
goddess and hero. Formidable Athena
caught up the whip and reins and drove the horses
hard and straight at Ares.

               Brute that he was,
just at that point he had begun despoiling
a giant of a man, the Aetolians' best,
Periphas, brilliant scion of Ochesius.
The bloodstained god had downed him. But Athena,
making herself invisible to Ares,
put on the helm of the Lord of Undergloom.
Then Ares saw Diomedes, whirled, and left
Periphas lying where he fell. Straight onward
for Diomedes lunged the ruffian god.
When they arrived in range of one another,
Ares, breasting his adversary's horses,
rifled his spear over the yoke and reins
with murderous aim. Athena, grey-eyed goddess,

with one hand caught and deflected it
and sent it bounding harmless from the car.
Now Diomedes put his weight behind
his own bronze-headed spear. Pallas Athena
rammed it at Ares' belted waist so hard
she put a gash in his fair flesh, and pulled
the spearhead out again. Then brazen Ares
howled to heaven, terrible to hear
as roaring from ten thousand men in battle
when long battalions clash. A pang of fear
ran through the hearts of Trojans and Achaeans,
deafened by insatiable Ares' roar.

Like a black vapour from a thunder-head
riding aloft on storm-wind brewed by heat,
so brazen Ares looked to Diomedes
as he rose heavenward amid the clouds.
High on Olympus, crag of the immortals,
he came to rest by the Lord Zeus. Aching,
mortified, he showed his bleeding wound
and querulously addressed him:

                        'Father Zeus,
how do you take this insubordination?
What frightful things we bear from one another
doing good turns to men! And I must say
we all hold it against you. You conceived
a daughter with no prudence, a destroyer,
given to violence. We other gods
obey you, as submissive as you please,
while she goes unreproved; never a word,
a gesture of correction comes from you –
only begetter of the insolent child.
She is the one who urged Diomedes on
to mad attempts on the immortals – first
he closed with Cypris, cut her palm, and now
he hurled himself against me like a fury.
It was my speed that got me off, or I
should still be there in pain among the dead,
the foul dead – or undone by further strokes
of cutting bronze.'

                        But Zeus who masses cloud
regarded him with frowning brows and said:
'Do not come whining here, you two-faced brute,
most hateful to me of all the Olympians.
Combat and brawling are your element.

This beastly, incorrigible truculence
comes from your mother, Hera, whom I keep
but barely in my power, say what I will.
You came to grief, I think, at her command.
Still, I will not have you suffer longer.
I fathered you, after all;
your mother bore you as a son to me.
If you had been conceived by any other
and born so insolent, then long ago
your place would have been far below the gods.'

    With this he told Paeeon to attend him,
and sprinkling anodyne upon his wound
Paeeon undertook to treat and heal him
who was not born for death. As wild fig sap
when dripped in liquid milk will curdle it
as quickly as you stir it in, so quickly
Paeeon healed impetuous Ares' wound.
Then Hebe bathed him, mantled him afresh,
and down he sat beside Lord Zeus,
glowing again in splendour.

    And soon again to Zeus's home retired
Argive Hera, Boeotian Athena,
who made the bane of mankind quit the slaughter.

BOOK VI

INTERLUDES IN FIELD AND CITY

No gods, but only Trojans and Achaeans,
were left now in the great fight on the plain.
It swayed this way and that between the rivers,
with levelled spears moving on one another.

    Aias Telamonius, Achaean
bastion of defence, attacked and broke
a Trojan mass, showing his men the way,
by killing the best man of all the Thracians –
Acamas, brawny son of Eussorus.
He hit him on the forecrest, and the spearhead
clove his frontal bone, lodged in his brain,
filling his eyes with darkness.

                  Diomedes
then slew Axylus Teuthranides
from the walled town Arisbe. A rich man
and kindly, he befriended all who passed
his manor by the road. But none of these
could come between him and destruction now,
as the Achaean killed him, killing with him
Calesius, his aide and charioteer –
leaving two dead men to be cloaked in earth.
Euryalus killed Dresus and Opheltius,
then met the twins, Aesepus and Pedasus,
borne by Abarbarea, a sea-nymph,
to Bucolion, son of Laomedon –
his first and secret child. When Bucolion
served as a shepherd he had loved the nymph,
and she conceived these twins. Euryalus
now broke their valour, cut them down, and bent
to drag from their dead shoulders belted swords
and bucklers.

              Polypoetes killed Astyalus,
Percosius Pidytes fell before
the spearhead of Odysseus, Aretaon
fell before Teucer, and Antilochus,
the son of Nestor, brought Ablerus low
with one spear-flash. Then Marshal Agamemnon
took the life of Elatus, whose home

had been in Pedasus upon the height
near Satnioïs river. Leïtus then
killed Phylacus as that man turned to run.
Eurypylus dispatched Melanthius.

But great-lunged Menelaus took a prisoner,
Adrastus. Veering wild
along the plain, this Trojan's team had caught
his hurtling car upon a tamarisk
and broken at the joint his chariot-pole.
The animals then galloped on toward Troy
with all the rest who panicked; but the driver,
flung out of his car head over heels,
landed alongside face down in the dust –
and there with his long spear stood Menelaus.
Adrastus threw his arms around his knees
and begged him: 'Son of Atreus, take me alive!
You will have all the ransom one could ask.
Plenty of precious things, gold, gold and silver
and hard-wrought iron, fill my father's house.
He would give anything, no end of ransom,
if he could only know I am alive
among the Achaean ships.'

                                Adrastus' plea
won his great captor to consent: he thought
of granting him safe conduct to the ships
by his own runner, when his brother
Agamemnon in grim haste came by
to bar his mercy and cried: 'What now, soft heart?
Were you so kindly served at home by Trojans?
Why give a curse for them, Oh, Menelaus,
once in our hands not one should squirm away
from death's hard fall! No fugitive, not even
the manchild carried in a woman's belly!
Let them all without distinction perish,
every last man of Ilium,
without a tear, without a trace!'

                                Implacably
thus he recalled his brother's mind to duty,
and Menelaus pushed away Adrastus.
Then Agamemnon speared him in the flank,
and he fell backward. Stamping with one heel
hard on his chest, he disengaged the spear.

Now Nestor in a loud voice called to the Argives:
'Friends, Danaans, fighters, companions of Ares,

no one should linger over booty now,
piling up all he can carry to the ships.
Now is the time to kill them! Later on
strip them at leisure when they lie here dead!'

    Shouting, he urged them on. And once again
the Trojans, overmastered by Achaeans
and cowed, would have re-entered Ilium –
But Helenus Priamides, an augur
better than any, halted beside Aeneas
and Hector, saying:

                    'You two bear the brunt
of Lycian and Trojan travail, always,
in every enterprise, war-plans or battle,
first among us all. Take your stand here.
Here make our troops hold fast, before the gates.
Rally them everywhere, or back again
they go pell-mell into the arms of women –
a great day for our enemies. Put heart
into all our men, into every company,
and we can hold the Danaans on this line,
dead tired as we are. We have no choice.
But you go up into the city, Hector;
speak to our mother; tell her to call together
women in age like hers, unlock the shrine
of grey-eyed Athena on our citadel,
and choose that robe most lovely and luxurious,
most to her liking in the women's hall,
to place upon Athena's knees.
Then heifers, twelve, are to be promised her,
unscarred and tender, if she will relent
in pity for our men, our wives and children,
and keep Diomedes out of holy Troy.
He is so savage in pursuit and combat
I call him most formidable of Achaeans now.
We never were so afraid of Prince Achilles,
and he, they say, came of a goddess. No,
this fellow fights like one possessed: no man
can equal him in fury.'

                      Hector agreed
and did his brother's bidding, first and last.
He vaulted quickly from his chariot,
waving his whetted spears high overhead,
as up and down he went, arousing war.
Then all those in retreat turned in their tracks

and stood against the Achaeans, who recoiled
before that stand and killed no more. It seemed
some one of the immortals out of heaven
had come down to put spirit in the Trojans,
they wheeled about so suddenly.
                                                  And Hector
in a great voice called out:
'Soldierly Trojans, allies famed abroad,
be men, remember courage, and defend yourselves,
while I go up to Ilium
to make our wives and elders pray the gods
with dedication of hecatombs.'
                                       Then Hector
turned away, under his shimmering helm,
his long shield slung behind him; nape and ankle
both were brushed by the darkened oxhide rim.
    Meanwhile, driving into an open space
between the armies, Hippolochus' son, Glaucus,
and Diomedes advanced upon each other,
hot for combat. When the range was short,
Diomedes, face to face with him, spoke up:
    'Young gallant stranger, who are you?
I have not noticed you before in battle –
never before, in the test that brings men honour –
but here you come now, far in front of everyone,
with heart enough to risk my beam of spear.
A sorrowing old age they have whose children
face me in war! If you are a god from heaven,
I would not fight with any out of heaven.
No long life remained – far from it – for
Lycurgus, Dryas' rugged son,
when he in his day strove with gods – that time
he chased the maenads on the sacred ridge
of manic Dionysus, on Mount Nysa.
Belaboured by the ox-goad of Lycurgus,
killer that he was, they all flung down
their ivy-staves, while terrified Dionysus
plunged under a sea-surge. In her arms
Thetis received him, shaking from head to foot,
after that yelling man's pursuit.
And now the gods whose life is ease
turned on Lycurgus; Zeus put out his eyes;
his days were numbered, hated by them all.
I would not fight, not I, with gods in bliss,

but you, if you are man and mortal, one
who feeds on harvest of the grainland, take
one step nearer! and before you know it
you will come up against the edge of death.'

   Hippolochus' distinguished son replied:
'Why ask my birth, Diomedes? Very like leaves
upon this earth are the generations of men –
old leaves, cast on the ground by wind, young leaves
the greening forest bears when spring comes in.
So mortals pass; one generation flowers
even as another dies away. My lineage?
If you are really bent on knowing all –
and many others know my story – listen.
Ephyra is a city on the gulf
of Argos: in Ephyra Sisyphus
Aeolides, the craftiest of men,
lived once upon a time and fathered Glaucus,
father in turn of Prince Bellerophon,
one to whom the gods had given beauty
with charm and bravery. But there came a day
when Proetus wished him ill – and Zeus had put him
under the power of Proetus. That strong king
now drove Bellerophon away from Argos:
this because Anteia, the queen,
lusted to couple with him secretly,
but he was honourable, she could not lure him,
and in the king's ear hissed a lie: "Oh, Proetus,
I wish that you may die unless you kill
Bellerophon: the man desired to take me
in lust against my will."

                         'Rage filled the king
over her slander, but being scrupulous
he shrank from killing him. So into Lycia
he sent him, charged to bear a deadly cipher,
magical marks Proetus engraved and hid
in folded tablets. He commanded him
to show these to his father-in-law,
thinking in this way he should meet his end.
Guided by gods he sailed, and came to Lycia,
high country, crossed by Xanthus' running stream;
and Lycia's lord received him well.
Nine days he honoured him, nine revels led
with consecrated beasts. When Dawn with rosy
fingers eastward made the tenth day bright,

he questioned him, and asked at length to see
what sign he brought him from his son-in-law.
When he had read the deadly cipher, changing,
he gave his first command: his guest should fight
and quell a foaming monster, the Chimaera,
of ghastly and inhuman origin,
her forepart lionish, her tail a snake's,
a she-goat in between. This thing exhaled
in jets a rolling fire.

      'Well, he killed her,
by taking heed of omens from the gods.
 'His second test was battle with Solymi,
formidable aborigines. He thought
this fight the worst he ever had with men.
A third mission was to slaughter Amazons,
women virile in war. On his return,
the king devised yet one more trap for him,
laying an ambush, with picked men of Lycia.
But not a single one went home again:
Bellerophon brought them all down.

        'His eyes
opened at last to the young man's power, godly
from godly lineage, the king detained him,
offered him his daughter, gave him, too,
a moiety of royal privileges,
and Lycians for their part set aside
their finest land for him, vineyard and ploughland,
fertile for wheatfields. The king's daughter bore
three children to Bellorophon: Isander,
Hippolochus, and Laodameia.
Zeus the Profound lay with Laodameia,
who bore Sarpedon, one of our great soldiers.
But now one day Bellerophon as well
incurred the gods' wrath – and alone he moped
on Aleion plain, eating his heart out,
shunning the beaten track of men. His son
Isander in a skirmish with Solymi
met his death at insatiable Ares' hands,
and angry Artemis killed Laodameia.
Hippolochus it was who fathered me,
I am proud to say. He sent me here to Troy
commanding me to act always with valour,
always to be most noble, never to shame
the line of my progenitors, great men

first in Ephyra, then in Lycia.
'That is the blood and birth I claim.'

                     At this,
joy came to Diomedes, loud in battle.
With one thrust in the field where herds had cropped
he fixed his long spear like a pole, and smiled
at the young captain, saying gently: 'Why,
you are my friend! My grandfather, Oeneus,
made friends of us long years ago. He welcomed
Prince Bellerophon to his great hall,
his guest for twenty days. They gave each other
beautiful tokens of amity: Grandfather's
offering was a loin-guard sewn in purple,
Bellerophon bestowed a cup of gold
two-handled; it is in my house, I left it there,
coming away to Troy. I cannot remember
Tydeus, my father – I was still too young
when he departed, when the Achaean army
came to grief at Thebes.

                  'I am your friend,
sworn friend, in central Argos. You are mine
in Lycia, whenever I may come.
So let us keep from one another's
weapons in the spear-fights of this war.
Trojans a-plenty will be left for me,
and allies, as god puts them in my path;
many Achaeans will be left for you
to bring down if you can. Each take the other's
battle-gear; let those around us know
we have this bond of friendship from our fathers.'

   Both men jumped down then to confirm the pact,
taking each other's hands. But Zeus
had stolen Glaucus' wits away –
the young man gave up golden gear for bronze,
took nine bulls' worth for armour worth a hundred!

   Now, when Hector reached the Scaean Gates
daughters and wives of Trojans rushed to greet him
with questions about friends, sons, husbands, brothers.
'Pray to the gods!' he said to each in turn,
as grief awaited many.

                 He walked on
and into Priam's palace, fair and still,
made all of ashlar, with bright colonnades.
Inside were fifty rooms of polished stone

one by another, where the sons of Priam
slept beside their wives; apart from these
across an inner court were twelve rooms more
all in one line, of polished stone, where slept
the sons-in-law of Priam and their wives.
Approaching these, he met his gentle mother
going in with Laodice, most beautiful
of all her daughters.

              Both hands clasping his,
she looked at him and said: 'Why have you come
from battle, child? Those fiends, the Achaeans, fighting
around the town, have worn you out; you come
to climb our Rock and lift your palms to Zeus!
Wait, and I'll serve you honeyed wine.
First you may offer up a drop to Zeus,
to the immortal gods, then slake your thirst.
Wine will restore a man when he is weary
as you are, fighting to defend your own.'

  Hector answered her, his helmet flashing:
'No, my dear mother, ladle me no wine;
you'd make my nerve go slack: I'd lose my edge.
May I tip wine to Zeus with hands unwashed?
I fear to – a bespattered man, and bloody,
may not address the lord of gloomy cloud.
No, it is you I wish would bring together
our older women, with offerings, and go visit
the temple of Athena, Hope of Soldiers.
Pick out a robe, most lovely and luxurious,
most to your liking in the women's hall;
place it upon Athena's knees; assure her
a sacrifice of heifers, twelve young ones
ungoaded ever in their lives, if in her mercy
relenting toward our town, our wives and children,
she keeps Diomedes out of holy Troy.
He is a wild beast now in combat and pursuit.
Make your way to her shrine, visit Athena,
Hope of Soldiers.

          'As for me, I go
for Paris, to arouse him, if he listens.
If only earth would swallow him here and now!
What an affliction the Olympian
brought up for us in him – a curse for Priam
and Priam's children! Could I see that man
dwindle into Death's night, I'd feel my soul

relieved of its distress!'

So Hector spoke, and she walked slowly on
into the megaron. She called her maids,
who then assembled women from the city.
But Hecabe went down to the low chamber
fragrant with cedar, where her robes were kept,
embroidered work by women of Sidonia
Alexandrus had brought, that time he sailed
and ravished Helen, princess, pearl of kings.
Hecabe lifted out her loveliest robe,
most ample, most luxurious in brocade,
and glittering like starlight under all.
This offering she carried to Athena
with a long line of women in her train.
On the Acropolis, Athena's shrine
was opened for them by Theano, stately
daughter of Cisseus, wife to Lord Antenor,
and chosen priestess of Athena. Now
all crying loud stretched out their arms in prayer,
while Theano with grace took up the robe
to place it on fair-haired Athena's knees.

She made petition then to Zeus's daughter: 'Lady,
excellent goddess, towering friend of Troy,
smash Diomedes' lance-haft! Throw him hard
below the Scaean Gates, before our eyes!
Upon this altar we'll make offering
of twelve young heifers never scarred!
Only show mercy to our town,
mercy to Trojan men, their wives and children.'

These were Theano's prayers, her vain prayers.
Pallas Athena turned away her head.

During the supplication at the shrine,
Hector approached the beautiful house Alexandrus
himself had made, with men who in that time
were master-builders in the land of Troy.
Bedchamber, hall, and court, in the upper town,
they built for him near Priam's hall and Hector's.
Now Hector dear to Zeus went in, his hand
gripping a spear eleven forearms long,
whose bronze head shone before him in the air
as shone, around the neck, a golden ring.
He found his brother in the bedchamber
handling a magnificent cuirass and shield
and pulling at his bent-horn bow, while Helen

among her household women sat nearby,
directing needlecraft and splendid weaving.
    At sight of him, to shame him, Hector said:
'Unquiet soul, why be aggrieved in private?
Our troops are dying out there where they fight
around our city, under our high walls.
The hue and cry of war, because of you,
comes in like surf upon this town.
You'd be at odds with any other man
you might see quitting your accursed war.
Up; into action, before torches thrown
make the town flare!'
                                    And shining like a god
Alexandrus replied: 'Ah, Hector,
this call to order is no more than just.
So let me tell you something: hear me out.
No pettishness, resentment toward the Trojans,
kept me in this bedchamber so long,
but rather my desire, on being routed,
to taste grief to the full. In her sweet way
my lady rouses me to fight again —
and I myself consider it better so.
Victory falls to one man, then another.
Wait, while I put on the war-god's gear,
or else go back; I'll follow, sure to find you.'
    For answer, Hector in his shining helm
said not a word, but in low tones
enticing Helen murmured: 'Brother dear —
dear to a whore, a nightmare of a woman!
That day my mother gave me to the world
I wish a hurricane-blast had torn me away
to wild mountains, or into tumbling sea
to be washed under by a breaking wave,
before these evil days could come! — or, granted
terrible years were in the gods' design,
I wish I had had a good man for a lover
who knew the sharp tongues and just rage of men.
This one — his heart's unsound, and always will be,
and he will win what he deserves. Come here
and rest upon this couch with me, dear brother.
You are the one afflicted most
by harlotry in me and by his madness,
our portion, all of misery, given by Zeus
that we may live in song for men to come.'

Great Hector shook his head, his helmet flashing,
and said: 'No, Helen, offer me no rest;
I know you are fond of me. I cannot rest.
Time presses, and I grow impatient now
to lend a hand to Trojans in the field
who feel a gap when I am gone. Your part
can be to urge him – let him feel the urgency
to join me in the city. He has time:
I must go home to visit my own people,
my own dear wife and my small son. Who knows
if I shall be reprieved again to see them,
or beaten down under Achaean blows
as the immortals will.'

                              He turned away
and quickly entered his own hall, but found
Princess Andromache was not at home.
With one nursemaid and her small child, she stood
upon the tower of Ilium, in tears,
bemoaning what she saw.

                              Now Hector halted
upon his threshold, calling to the maids:
'Tell me at once, and clearly, please,
my lady Andromache, where has she gone?
To see my sisters, or my brothers' wives?
Or to Athena's temple? Ladies of Troy
are there to make petition to the goddess.'

     The busy mistress of the larder answered:
'Hector, to put it clearly as you ask,
she did not go to see your sisters, nor
your brothers' wives, nor to Athena's shrine
where others are petitioning the goddess.
Up to the great square tower of Ilium
she took her way, because she heard our men
were spent in battle by Achaean power.
In haste, like a madwoman, to the wall
she went, and Nurse went too, carrying the child.'

     At this word Hector whirled and left his hall,
taking the same path he had come by,
along byways, walled lanes, all through the town
until he reached the Scaean Gates, whereby
before long he would issue on the field.
There his warmhearted lady
came to meet him, running: Andromache,
whose father, Eetion, once had ruled

the land under Mount Placus, dark with forest,
at Thebe under Placus – lord and king
of the Cilicians. Hector was her lord now,
head to foot in bronze; and now she joined him.
Behind her came the maid, who held the child
against her breast, a rosy baby still,
Hectorides, the world's delight, as fresh
as a pure shining star. Scamandrius
his father named him; other men would say
Astyanax, 'Lord of the Lower Town,'
as Hector singlehandedly guarded Troy.
How brilliantly the warrior smiled, in silence,
his eyes upon the child!

                    Andromache
rested against him, shook away a tear,
and pressed his hand in both her own, to say:
'Oh, my wild one, your bravery will be
your own undoing! No pity for our child,
poor little one, or me in my sad lot –
soon to be deprived of you! soon, soon
Achaeans as one man will set upon you
and cut you down! Better for me, without you,
to take cold earth for mantle. No more comfort,
no other warmth, after you meet your doom,
but heartbreak only. Father is dead, and Mother.
My father great Achilles killed when he
besieged and plundered Thebe, our high town,
citadel of Cilicians. He killed him,
but, reverent at least in this, did not
despoil him. Body, gear, and weapons forged
so handsomely, he burned, and heaped a barrow
over the ashes. Elms were planted round
by mountain-nymphs of him who bears the storm-cloud.
Then seven brothers that I had at home
in one day entered Death's dark place. Achilles,
prince and powerful runner, killed all seven
amid their shambling cattle and silvery sheep.
Mother, who had been queen of wooded Placus,
he brought with other winnings home, and freed her,
taking no end of ransom. Artemis
the Huntress shot her in her father's house.
Father and mother – I have none but you,
nor brother, Hector; lover none but you!
Be merciful! Stay here upon the tower!

Do not bereave your child and widow me!
Draw up your troops by the wild fig-tree; that way
the city lies most open, men most easily
could swarm the wall where it is low:
three times, at least, their best men tried it there
in company of the two called Aias, with
Idomeneus, the Atreidae, Diomedes –
whether someone who had it from oracles
had told them, or their own hearts urged them on.'
    Great Hector in his shimmering helmet answered:
'Lady, these many things beset my mind
no less than yours. But I should die of shame
before our Trojan men and noblewomen
if like a coward I avoided battle,
nor am I moved to. Long ago I learned
how to be brave, how to go forward always
and to contend for honour, Father's and mine.
Honour – for in my heart and soul I know
a day will come when ancient Ilium falls,
when Priam and the folk of Priam perish.
Not by the Trojans' anguish on that day
am I so overborne in mind – the pain
of Hecabe herself, or Priam king,
or of my brothers, many and valorous,
who will have fallen in dust before our enemies –
as by your own grief, when some armed Achaean
takes you in tears, your free life stripped away.
Before another woman's loom in Argos
it may be you will pass, or at Messeis
or Hypereia fountain, carrying water,
against your will – iron constraint upon you.
And seeing you in tears, a man may say:
"There is the wife of Hector, who fought best
of Trojan horsemen when they fought at Troy."
So he may say – and you will ache again
for one man who could keep you out of bondage.
Let me be hidden dark down in my grave
before I hear your cry or know you captive!'
    As he said this, Hector held out his arms
to take his baby. But the child squirmed round
on the nurse's bosom and began to wail,
terrified by his father's great war helm –
the flashing bronze, the crest with horsehair plume
tossed like a living thing at every nod.

His father began laughing, and his mother
laughed as well. Then from his handsome head
Hector lifted off his helm and bent
to place it, bright with sunlight, on the ground.
    When he had kissed his child and swung him high
to dandle him, he said this prayer: 'O Zeus
and all immortals, may this child, my son,
become like me a prince among the Trojans.
Let him be strong and brave and rule in power
at Ilium; then someday men will say
"This fellow is far better than his father!"
seeing him home from war, and in his arms
the bloodstained gear of some tall warrior slain –
making his mother proud.'
                                        After this prayer,
into his dear wife's arms he gave his baby,
whom on her fragrant breast
she held and cherished, laughing through her tears.
    Hector pitied her now. Caressing her,
he said: 'Unquiet soul, do not be too distressed
by thoughts of me. You know no man dispatches me
into the undergloom against my fate;
no mortal, either, can escape his fate,
coward or brave man, once he comes to be.
Go home, attend to your own handiwork
at loom and spindle, and command the maids
to busy themselves, too. As for the war,
that is for men, all who were born at Ilium,
to put their minds on – most of all for me.'
    He stooped now to recover his plumed helm
as she, his dear wife, drew away, her head
turned and her eyes upon him, brimming tears.
She made her way in haste then to the ordered
house of Hector and rejoined her maids,
moving them all to weep at sight of her.
In Hector's home they mourned him, living still
but not, they feared, again to leave the war
or be delivered from Achaean fury.
    Paris in the meantime had not lingered:
after he buckled his bright war-gear on
he ran through Troy, sure-footed with long strides.
Think how a stallion fed on clover and barley,
mettlesome, thundering in a stall, may snap
his picket rope and canter down a field

to bathe as he would daily in the river –
glorying in freedom! Head held high
with mane over his shoulders flying,
his dazzling work of finely jointed knees
takes him around the pasture haunts of horses.
That was the way the son of Priam, Paris,
ran from the height of Pergamus, his gear
ablaze like the great sun,
and laughed aloud. He sprinted on, and quickly
met his brother, who was slow to leave
the place where he had discoursed with his lady.

Alexandrus was first to speak: 'Dear fellow,'
he said, 'have I delayed you, kept you waiting?
Have I not come at the right time, as you asked?'

And Hector in his shimmering helm replied:
'My strange brother! No man with justice in him
would underrate your handiwork in battle;
you have a powerful arm. But you give way
too easily, and lose interest, lose your will.
My heart aches in me when I hear our men,
who have such toil of battle on your account,
talk of you with contempt. Well, come along.
Someday we'll make amends for that, if ever
we drive the Achaeans from the land of Troy –
if ever Zeus permit us, in our hall,
to set before the gods of heaven, undying
and ever young, our winebowl of deliverance.'

BOOK VII

A COMBAT AND A RAMPART

As Hector spoke he came out through the gateway
running, with Alexandrus beside him,
both resolved on battle.

                  Like a wind,
a sailing-wind heaven may grant to oarsmen
desperate for it at the polished oars,
when they have rowed their hearts out, far at sea,
so welcome to the Trojans in their longing
these appeared.

                  And each one killed his man. Alexandrus
brought down Menesthius from Arne, son
of a mace-wielder, Lord Areithous
and wide-eyed Phylomedusa. Hector speared
Eioneus under his helmet rim
and cut his nape, so that his legs gave way.
Young Glaucus, too, leader of Lycians,
in the rough mêlée thrust at Iphinous
Dexiades just as he swung aboard
his fast war-car: he rammed him in the shoulder,
and down he tumbled from his chariot.
Seeing these Argive warriors overthrown
in the sharp fighting, grey-eyed Athena came
in a gust downward from Olympus peaks
to the old town of Troy – and up to meet her
from Pergamus, where he surveyed the fight,
his heart set on a Trojan victory,
Apollo rose.

               By the great oak they met,
and the son of Zeus began:
'Down from Olympus to this field again?
What passion moves you now? To give Danaans
power for a breakthrough? Daughter of Zeus,
you waste no pity on the Trojan dead.
If you would listen, I know a better plan.
Why not arrange an interval in battle,
a day's respite? They can fight on tomorrow
until they find the end ordained for Ilium –
as that is all you goddesses have at heart,

the plundering of this town.'

                      The grey-eyed goddess
answered him: 'So be it, archer of heaven.
I, too, thought of a truce, on my way down
toward Trojans and Achaeans. Only tell me:
how do you plan to make them break off battle?'

    Apollo said: 'By firing the spirit
of Hector, breaker of wild horses. Let him
defy some champion of Danaans
to measure spears with him in mortal combat.
When they are challenged, let them pick a man
to stand up against Hector in his pride.'

    The grey-eyed one did not dissent from this,
and Priam's dear son, Helenus, aware
of what these gods were pleased to set afoot,
moved over to Hector and accosted him:
'Hector, gifted as you are with foresight
worthy of Zeus himself, will you consent
to my new plan? I tell you as your brother.
Make all the others, Trojans and Achaeans,
rest on their arms, and you yourself defy
whoever may be greatest of Achaeans
to face you in a duel to the death.
Your hour, you know, has not yet come to die;
I have it from the gods who live for ever.'

    At this, great Hector's heart beat high. Along
the battle line he went, forcing the Trojans
back with a lance held up mid-haft. They halted
and sank down in their tracks, while Agamemnon
brought to a halt Achaeans in their armour.
Now Athena rested, with Apollo,
god of the silver bow – both gods transformed
to hunting birds, perched on the royal oak
of Father Zeus who bears the shield of storm.
Here with delight they viewed the sea of men
in close order at rest, with shields and helms
and lances ruggedly astir. A west wind rising
will cast a rippling roughness over water,
a shivering gloom on the clear sea. Just so
the seated mass of Trojans and Achaeans
rippled along the plain.

                     Hector addressed them:
'Hear me, Trojans and Achaeans: listen
to what I am moved to say. The peace we swore to

Lord Zeus throned on high would not confirm.
He has adversity for both in mind
until you take high Troy, or are defeated,
beaten back to your deep-sea-going ships.
Knowing the bravest of Achaea's host
are here with you, my pride demands that I
engage some champion: let one come forward,
the best man of you all, to fight with Hector.
And here is what I say – Zeus be my witness –
if with his whetted bronze he cuts me down,
my armour he may take away and carry
aboard the long-decked ships; not so my body.
That must be given to my kin, committed
to fire by the Trojans and their women.
And if I kill this man, if Lord Apollo
grants me victory, his helm and shield
I shall unstrap and bring to Ilium
to hang before the Archer Apollo's shrine.
But his dead body I'll restore
to your encampment by the well-trimmed ships.
Achaeans there may give him funeral
and heap a mound for him by Helle's water.
One day a man on shipboard, sailing by
on the wine-dark sea, will point landward and say:
"There is the death-mound of an ancient man,
a hero who fought Hector and was slain."
Someone will say that someday. And the honour
won by me here will never pass away.'

He finished, and the Achaeans all sat hushed,
ashamed not to respond, afraid to do so,
until at length Lord Menelaus arose
groaning in disgust, and stormed at them:
'Oh god, you brave noise-makers! Women, not men!
Here is disgrace and grovelling shame for us
if none of the Danaans fight with Hector!
May you all rot away to earth and water,
sitting tight, safe in your ignominy!
I will myself tie on a breastplate with him.
Out of our hands, in the gods' hands above us,
ultimate power over victory lies.'

With this he began buckling on his gear,
and now – O Menelaus! – it seemed foregone
your end of life was near at Hector's hands,
as Hector was far stronger; but Achaean

officers in a rush laid hold of you,
and Agamemnon, lord of the great plains,
taking your right hand, said:

                     'You've lost your head,
my lord; no need of recklessness like this.
Galling as it may be, hold on! Give up
this wish for emulation's sake to face
a stronger fighter. Everyone else dreads
Prince Hector, Priam's son. Even Achilles
shivered when for glory he met this man
in combat – and he had more driving power
than you, by far. Go back, then, take your seat
with fellow-countrymen of your command.
The Achaeans will put up another champion.
And gluttonous though he may be for carnage,
with no fear in him – still he'll be relieved
if he comes through this deadly fight, no quarter
asked or given.'

                  Greatly had he recalled
his brother's mind to a just sense of duty,
and Menelaus complied; his own retainers
happily relieved him of his gear.

    Then Nestor stood up, saying to the Argives:
'Ah, what distress for our Achaean land!
How Peleus, the old master of horse, would grieve,
that noble counsellor of Myrmidons!
One day, questioning me in his own hall,
he took delight in learning of the Argives'
lineage and birth. If he should hear
how every man here quails before Hector now,
he'd lift his arms to the immortal gods
and pray to quit his body, to go down
into the house of Death!

                 'O Father Zeus,
Athena and Apollo! Could I be young again
as in those days of fighting by the rapids
of Celadon, between the mustered men
of Pylos and the pikemen of Arcadia,
near Pheia's walls and Iardanus riverside!
Ereuthalion was their champion,
and he stood out, foremost, magnificent,
buckled in armour of Areithous –
Areithous, the mace-wielder, so called
by fighting men and by their sumptuous women

for using neither bow nor spear: he swung
an iron mace to break through ranks in battle.
Lycurgus had defeated him, by guile
and not by force at all: in a byway
so narrow that his mace could not avail him —
there Lycurgus, lunging first,
had run him through with his long spear
and pinned him backward to the ground. He took
the arms given to Areithous by Ares
and bore them afterward in grinding war.
Then Lycurgus, when he aged, at home,
passed them on to his friend, Ereuthalion.
Equipped with these he challenged all our best,
but all were shaken, full of dread; no one
would take the field against him. Well, my pride
drove me to take him on with a high heart,
though I was then still youngest of us all.
I fought him, and Athena gave me glory.
Tallest and toughest of enemies, I killed him,
that huge man, and far and wide he sprawled.
Would god I had my youth again, my strength
intact: Lord Hector would be soon engaged!
But you that are the best men of Achaea
will not go forward cheerfully to meet him.'
    So chided by the old man, volunteers
arose then, nine in all — first on his feet
being Lord Marshal Agamemnon, second
Diomedes, powerful son of Tydeus,
and, joining these, those two who were called Aias,
rugged impetuous men, and joining these
Idomeneus and that lord's right-hand man,
Meriones, the peer of the battle-god
in butchery of war; along with these
Eurypylus, Euaemon's handsome son,
Thoas Andraemonides, and Odysseus.
These were all willing to encounter Hector
in single combat.
                    Then again they heard
from Nestor of Gerenia, charioteer:
'By lot now: whirl for the one who comes out first.
He is the one to make Achaeans proud,
and make himself, too, proud, if he survives
this bitter fight, no quarter asked or given.'
    At this each put his mark upon a stone

and dropped it in the helmet of Agamemnon.
Meanwhile the troops addressed the gods in prayer
with hands held up. You might have heard one say,
his eyes on heaven: 'Father Zeus, let Aias'
pebble jump! Or make it Diomedes!
Make it the king himself of rich Mycenae!'
    So they murmured. Then Lord Nestor gave
the helm a rolling shake and made that stone
which they desired leap out: the stone of Aias.
A herald took it round amid the nine,
showing the fortunate mark, this way and that,
to all the Achaean champions; but none
could recognize it or acknowledge it.
Only when he had come at length to him
who made the sign and dropped it in the helmet,
Aias, the giant, putting out his hand
for what the pausing herald placed upon it,
knew his mark. A thrill of joy ran through him.
    Down at his feet he tossed the stone, and said:
'Oh, friends, the token's mine! And glad I am,
as I believe I can put Hector down.
Come, everyone, while I prepare to fight,
pray to Lord Zeus the son of Cronos! Keep it
under your breath so Trojans will not hear –
or else be open about it; after all,
we have no fear of any. No man here
will drive me from the field against my will,
not by main force, not by a ruse. I hope
I was not born and bred on Salamis
to be a dunce in battle.'
                              At this the soldiers
prayed to Zeus. You might have heard one say,
his eyes on heaven: 'Father Zeus, from Ida
looking out for us all: greatest, most glorious:
let Aias win the honour of victory!
Or if you care for Hector and are inclined
to favour him, then let both men be even
in staying power and honour!'
                              So they prayed,
while Aias made his brazen helmet snug,
fitted his shield and sword-strap. He stepped out
as formidable as gigantic Ares,
wading into the ranks of men, when Zeus
drives them to battle in blood-letting fury.

Huge as that, the bastion of Achaeans
loomed and grinned, his face a cruel mask,
his legs moving in great strides. He shook
his long spear doubled by its pointing shadow,
and the Argives exulted. Now the Trojans
felt a painful trembling in the knees,
and even Hector's heart thumped in his chest –
but there could be no turning back; he could not
slip again into his throng of troops;
he was the challenger. Aias came nearer,
carrying like a tower his body-shield
of seven oxhides sheathed in bronze – a work
done for him by the leather-master Tychius
in Hyle: Tychius made the glittering shield
with seven skins of oxhide and an eighth
of plated bronze. Holding this bulk before him,
Aias Telamonius came on
toward Hector and stood before him.

Now he spoke,
threatening him: 'Before long, man to man,
Hector, you'll realize that we Danaans
have our champions, too – I mean besides
the lion-hearted breaker of men, Achilles.
He lies now by the beaked seagoing ships
in anger at Lord Marshal Agamemnon.
But there are those among us who can face you –
plenty of us. Fight then, if you will!'

To this, great Hector in his shimmering helmet
answered: 'Son of the ancient line of Telamon,
Aias, lordly over fighting men,
when you try me you try no callow boy
or woman innocent of war. I know
and know well how to fight and how to kill,
how to take blows upon the right or left
shifting my guard of tough oxhide in battle,
how to charge in a din of chariots,
or hand to hand with sword or pike to use
timing and footwork in the dance of war.
Seeing the man you are, I would not trick you
but let you have it with a straight shot,
if luck is with me.'

Rifling his spear,
he hurled it and hit Aias' wondrous shield
square on the outer and eighth plate of bronze.

The spearhead punched its way through this and through
six layers, but the seventh oxhide stopped it.
Now in his turn great Aias made his cast
and hit the round shield braced on Hector's arm.
Piercing the bright shield, the whetted spearhead
cut its way into his figured cuirass,
ripping his shirt along his flank; but he
had twisted and escaped the night of death.
Now both men disengaged their spears and fell
on one another like man-eating lions
or wild boars – no tame household creatures. Hector's
lancehead scored the tower shield – but failed
to pierce it, as the point was bent aside.
    Then Aias, plunging forward, rammed his spear
into the round shield, and the point went through
to nick his furious adversary, making
a cut that welled dark blood below his ear.
But Hector did not slacken, even so.
He drew away and in one powerful hand
picked from the plain a boulder lying there,
black, rough and huge, and threw it,
hitting Aias' gigantic sevenfold shield
square on the boss with a great clang of bronze.
Then Aias lifted up a huger stone
and whirled, and put immeasurable force
behind it when he let it fly – as though
he flung a millstone – crushing Hector's shield.
The impact caught his knees, so that he tumbled
backward behind the bashed-in shield. At once
Apollo pulled him to his feet again,
and now with drawn swords toe to toe
they would have doubled strokes on one another,
had not those messengers of Zeus and men,
the heralds, intervened – one from the Trojans,
one from the Achaean side – for both
Idaeus and Talthybius kept their heads.
    They held their staves out, parting the contenders,
and that experienced man, Idaeus, said:
'Enough, lads. No more fighting. The Lord Zeus,
assembler of bright cloud, cares for you both.
Both are great spearmen, and we all know it.
But now already night is coming on,
and we do well to heed the fall of night.'
    Said Aias Telamonius in reply:

'Idaeus, call on Hector to say as much.
He was the one who dared our champions
to duel with him. Let him take the lead.
Whatever he likes, I am at his disposition.'
    Hector in his shimmering helmet answered:
'Aias, a powerful great frame you had
as a gift from god, and a clear head; of all
Achaeans you are toughest with a spear.
And this being shown, let us break off our duel,
our blood-letting, for today. We'll meet again
another time – and fight until the unseen
power decides between these hosts of ours,
awarding one or the other victory.
But now already night is coming on,
and we do well to heed the fall of night.
This way you'll give them festive pleasure there
beside the ships, above all to your friends,
companions at your table. As for me,
as I go through Priam's town tonight
my presence will give joy to Trojan men
and to our women, as in their trailing gowns
they throng the place of god with prayers for me.
Let us make one another memorable gifts,
and afterward they'll say, among Achaeans
and Trojans: "These two fought and gave no quarter
in close combat, yet they parted friends."'
    This he said, and lifting off his broadsword,
silver-hilted, in its sheath, upon
the well-cut baldric, made a gift of it,
and Aias gave his loin-guard, sewn in purple.
Each then turned away. One went to join
the Achaean troops; the other joined his Trojans,
and all were full of joy to see him come
alive, unhurt, delivered from the fury
of Aias whose great hands no man withstood.
Almost despairing of him still, they led him
into the town.
                    On their side, the Achaeans
conducted Aias in his pride of victory
to Agamemnon. In the commander's hut
Lord Marshal Agamemnon sacrificed
a five-year ox to the overlord of heaven.
Skinned and quartered and cut up in bits
the meat was carefully spitted, roasted well,

and taken from the fire. When all the food
lay ready, when the soldiers turned from work,
they feasted to their hearts' content, and Lord
Agamemnon, ruler of the great plains,
gave Aias the long marrowy cuts of chine.
Then, hunger and thirst dispelled, they heard
Lord Nestor first in discourse. The old man
had new proposals to elaborate –
he whose counsel had been best before.
     Concerned for them, he said: 'Lord Agamemnon,
princes of Achaea, think of our losses.
Many are dead, their dark blood poured by Ares
around Scamander river, and their souls
gone down to undergloom. Therefore at dawn
you should suspend all action by Achaeans.
Gathering here, we'll bring the dead men back
in wagons drawn by oxen or by mules.
These corpses we must fire abaft the ships
a short way from the sterns, that each may bear
his charred bones to the children of the dead
whenever we sail home again. We'll bring
earth for a single mound about the fire,
common earth from landward; based on this,
a line of ramparts to defend our ships
and troops – with gates well fitted in the walls
to leave a way out for our chariots.
Outside, beyond the walls, we'll dig a moat
around the perimeter, to hold at bay
their teams and men, and break the impetus
of Trojans in assault.'
                              To this proposal
all the great captains gave assent. And now
at that same hour, high in the upper city
of Ilium, a Trojan assembly met
in tumult at the gates of Priam.
                              First
to speak before them all, clear-eyed Antenor
cried out: 'Trojans, Dardans, and allies,
listen to me, to what I am moved to say!
Bring Argive Helen and the treasure with her,
and let us give her back to the Atreidae
to take home in the ships! We fight as men
proven untrustworthy, truce-breakers. I see
no outcome favourable to ourselves unless

we act as I propose.'

                With this short speech,
he took his seat. But Prince Alexandrus,
husband of the fair-haired beauty, Helen,
rose and in a sharp tone answered him:
'What you propose, Antenor, I do not like.
You can conceive of better things to say.
Or if you take it seriously, this plan,
the gods themselves have made you lose your wits.
To all you Trojan handlers of fast horses
here is my speech: I say No to your face:
I will not give the woman up! The treasure,
all that I once brought home from Argos, though,
I offer willingly, and with increment.'

    After this declaration he took his seat.
Then Priam, son of Dardanus, arose,
sage as a god in counsel, and spoke out
in his concern amid them all: 'Now hear me,
Trojans, Dardans, and allies,
listen to what I feel I must propose.
At this hour take your evening meal as always
everywhere in the city. Bear in mind
that sentries must be posted, every man
alert. Then let Idaeus go at dawn
among the decked ships, bearing the Atreidae,
Agamemnon and Menelaus, report
of what was said here by Alexandrus
because of whom this quarrel began. Then too
let him make inquiry to this effect:
will they accept a truce in the hard fighting,
allowing us to burn our dead? Next day
again we'll fight, until inscrutable power
decides between us, giving one side victory.'

    They listened and abided by his words.
In companies the soldiers took their meal,
and then at dawn Idaeus made his way
amid the decked ships. Finding the Danaans,
companions of Ares, gathered in assembly
before the bow of Agamemnon's ship,
he took his stand among them, calling out:

    'Agamemnon and all princes of Achaea,
Priam and the noble men of Troy
direct me to report, and may it please you,
the offer of Alexandrus

because of whom this quarrel began. The treasure,
all that he brought to Troy in his long ships –
would god he had foundered on the way! – he now
desires to give back, with increment.
Menelaus' wife, on the other hand,
he has affirmed that he will not restore,
let Trojans urge it as they will. I am directed
further to make this inquiry:
will you accept a truce in the hard fighting,
allowing us to burn our dead? Next day
again we'll fight, until inscrutable power
decides between us, giving one side victory.'

  He finished, and they all sat hushed and still.
At last Diomedes of the great warcry
burst out: 'Let no man here accept
treasure from Alexandrus – nor Helen
either. Even a child can see the Trojans
live already on the edge of doom!'

  The Achaean soldiers all roared 'Aye!' to this,
aroused by Diomedes' words, and Lord
Agamemnon responded to Idaeus:
'Idaeus, there by heaven you yourself
have heard the Achaeans' answer! For my part
I am content with it. As to the dead,
I would withhold no decency of burning;
a man should spare no pains to see cadavers
given as soon as may be after death
to purifying flame. Let thundering Zeus,
consort of Hera, witness I give my word.'

  And as he spoke he gestured with his staff
upward toward all the gods. Turning around,
Idaeus made his way again to Ilium.
Upon the assembly ground Trojans and Dardans
were waiting all together for him to come.
Soon he arrived and standing in their midst
delivered his report.
                              Then all equipped themselves
at once, dividing into two working parties,
one for timber, one to bring in the dead,
as on the other side, leaving their ships,
the Argives laboured, gathering firewood
and bringing in the dead.
                              Bright Helios
had just begun to strike across the ploughlands,

rising heavenward out of the deep
smooth-flowing Ocean stream, when these two groups
met on the battlefield, with difficulty
distinguishing the dead men, one by one.
With pails they washed the bloody filth away,
then hot tears fell, as into waiting carts
they lifted up their dead. All cries of mourning
Priam forbade them; sick at heart therefore
in silence they piled corpses on the pyre
and burned it down. Then back they went to Ilium.
Just so on their side the Achaeans piled
dead bodies on their pyre, sick at heart,
and burned it down. Then back to the ships they went.
Next day before dawn, in the dim of night,
around the pyre, chosen Achaean men
assembled to make one mound for all, with common
earth brought in from landward. Based on this
they built a wall, a rampart with high towers,
to be protection for their ships and men.
And well-framed gateways in the wall they made
to leave a way out for the chariots.
Outside, beyond the wall, they dug a moat
and planted it with stakes driven in and pointed.
These were the labours of the long-haired carls
of Achaea. And the gods arrayed with Zeus,
lord of the lightning flash, looked down
on this great work of the Achaean army.

   Then he who shakes the mainland and the islands,
Poseidon, made his comment. 'Father Zeus,
will any man on boundless earth again
make known his thought, his plan, to the immortals?
Do you not see? The long-haired carls of Achaea
put up a rampart, inshore from the ships,
and ran a moat around; but they would not
propitiate us with glory of hecatombs!
The fame of this will be diffused as far
as Dawn sends light. Men will forget the wall
I drudged at with Apollo for Laomedon.'
   Hot with irritation, Zeus replied:
'By thunder! Lord of the wide sea's power, shaking
islands and mainland, sulking, you? Another
god, a hundred times feebler than you are
in force of hand and spirit, might be worried
over this stratagem, this wall. Your own

renown is widespread as the light of Dawn!
Come, look ahead! When the Achaeans take
again to their ships and sail for their own land,
break up the wall and wash it out to sea,
envelop the whole shore with sand! That way
the Achaean wall may vanish from the earth.'

  So ran their colloquy. The sun went down
and now the Achaean labour was accomplished.
Amid their huts they slaughtered beasts and made
their evening meal. Wine-ships had come ashore
from Lemnos, a whole fleet loaded with wine.
These ships were sent by Euneus, Jason's son,
born to that hero by Hypsipyle.
To Agamemnon, as to Menelaus,
he gave a thousand measures of the wine
for trading, so the troops could barter for it,
some with bronze and some with shining iron,
others with hides and others still with oxen,
some with slaves. They made a copious feast,
and all night long Achaeans with flowing hair
feasted, while the Trojans and their allies
likewise made a feast.

                 But all night long
Zeus the Profound made thunder overhead
while pondering calamities to come,
and men turned pale with fear. Tilting their cups
they poured out wine upon the ground; no man
would drink again till he had spilt his cup
to heaven's overlord. But at long last
they turned to rest and took the gift of sleep.

BOOK VIII

THE BATTLE SWAYED BY ZEUS

DAWN in her saffron robe came spreading light
on all the world, and Zeus who plays in thunder
gathered the gods on peaked Olympus' height,
then said to that assembly:

                            'Listen to me,
immortals, every one,
and let me make my mood and purpose clear.
Let no one, god or goddess, contravene
my present edict; all assent to it
that I may get this business done, and quickly.
If I catch sight of anyone slipping away
with a mind to assist the Danaans or the Trojans,
he comes back blasted without ceremony,
or else he will be flung out of Olympus
into the murk of Tartarus that lies
deep down in underworld. Iron the gates are,
brazen the doorslab, and the depth from hell
as great as heaven's utmost height from earth.
You may learn then how far my power
puts all gods to shame. Or prove it this way:
out of the zenith hang a golden line
and put your weight on it, all gods and goddesses.
You will not budge me earthward out of heaven,
cannot budge the all-highest, mighty Zeus,
no matter how you try. But let my hand
once close to pull that cable – up you come,
and with you earth itself comes, and the sea.
By one end tied around Olympus' top
I could let all the world swing in mid-heaven!
That is how far I overwhelm you all,
both gods and men.'

                       They were all awed and silent,
he put it with such power. After a pause,
the grey-eyed goddess Athena said: 'O Zeus,
highest and mightiest, father of us all,
we are well aware of your omnipotence,
but all the same we mourn the Achaean spearmen
if they are now to meet hard fate and die.

As you command, we shall indeed
abstain from battle – merely, now and again,
dropping a word of counsel to the Argives,
that all may not be lost through your displeasure.'

The driver of cloud smiled and replied: 'Take heart,
dear child, third born of heaven. I do not speak
my full intent. With you, I would be gentle.'

Up to his car he backed his bronze-shod team
of aerial runners, long manes blowing gold.
He adorned himself in panoply of gold,
then mounted, taking up his golden whip,
and lashed his horses onward. At full stretch
midway between the earth and starry heaven
they ran toward Ida, sparkling with cool streams,
mother of wild things, and the peak of Gargaron
where are his holy plot and fragrant altar.
There Zeus, father of gods and men, reined in
and freed his team, diffusing cloud about them,
while glorying upon the crest he sat
to view the far-off scene below – Achaean
ships and Trojan city.

                                   At that hour
Achaean fighting men with flowing hair
took a meal by their huts and armed themselves.
The Trojans, too, on their side, in the city,
mustered under arms – though fewer, still
resolved by dire need to fight the battle
for wives' and children's sake. Now all the gates
were flung wide and the Trojan army sortied,
charioteers and foot, in a rising roar.

When the two masses met on the battle line
they ground their shields together, crossing spears,
with might of men in armour. Round shield-bosses
rang on each other in the clashing din,
and groans mingled with shouts of triumph rose
from those who died and those who killed: the field
ran rivulets of blood. While the fair day
waxed in heat through all the morning hours
missiles from both sank home and men went down,
until when Helios bestrode mid-heaven
the Father cleared his golden scales. Therein
two destinies of death's long pain he set
for Trojan horsemen and Achaean soldiers
and held the scales up by the midpoint. Slowly

one pan sank with death's day for Achaeans.

Zeus erupted in thunder from Ida, with burning
flashes of lightning against the Achaean army,
dazing them all: now white-faced terror seized them.
Neither Idomeneus nor Agamemnon
held his ground, and neither Aias held,
the Tall One nor the Short One, peers of war;
only the old lord of the western approaches,
Nestor, stayed in place –
not that in fact he willed to. No, one horse
had been disabled, hurt by Alexandrus,
whose arrow hit him high, just at the spot
most vulnerable, where the springing mane begins.
The beast reared in agony, for the point
entered his brain, and round and round
he floundered, fixed by the bronze point, making havoc
among the horses. While the old man hacked
to cut away the trace-horse with his sword,
amid the rout Lord Hector's team appeared
and the car that bore the fierce man. Soon enough,
old Nestor would have perished in that place,
had not Diomedes of the great war-cry
seen Hector coming.

                              With a tremendous shout
he tried to rouse Odysseus, and called to him:
'Where are you off to, turning tail like a dog?
Son of Laertes and the gods of old,
Odysseus, master mariner and soldier,
someone's lance might nail you from behind
between the shoulders, god forfend. Hold on with me
to fight this wild man off the old man's back!'

Odysseus did not hear him, as he ran
far wide of him and seaward toward the ships.

Then, single-handed, Diomedes joined
the mêlée forward of the old man's horses
and called to him, in a piercing voice: 'Old man,
they have you in a bad way, these young Trojans.
Age bears hard on you, your strength is going,
your groom is wobbly and your beasts are spent.
Here, mount my chariot, and see how fast
the horses are in the line of Tros: they know
this Trojan plain and how to wheel upon it
this way and that way in pursuit or flight.
I had this team as booty from Aeneas,

and they are masters at stampeding troops.
Let the men take over yours, while we two
drive these on the Trojans! Hector will find
my spear is mad for battle, like his own.'
  Lord Nestor of Gerenia, master of chariots,
did not refuse; his team was taken in hand
by Sthenelus and noble Eurymedon.
Boarding the car alongside Diomedes,
Lord Nestor took the reins and whipped the horses
forward until they came in range of Hector,
as Hector drove upon them at full speed;
then Diomedes made his throw.
He missed his man but hit the charioteer,
Eniopeus, a son of proud Thebaeus –
hit him squarely just beside the nipple
so that he tumbled backward, and his horses
shied away as the man died where he fell.
Now a cold gloom of grief passed over Hector
and anger for the driver. Still, he left him
and wheeled to spot a replacement – but his team
would not be driverless more than an instant,
for soon he came on Archeptolemus,
Iphitus' son, and took him on,
giving him reins and horses.

                              Now at the hands
of Diomedes there might soon have been
a ruin of Trojans, irreversible rout,
and Ilium crowded like a shepherd's pen,
had not the father of gods and men perceived it.
Thundering he let fly a white-hot bolt
that lit in front of Diomedes' horses
and blazed up terribly with a sulphur fume.
The team quailed, cowering against the chariot,
and the flashing reins ran out of Nestor's hands.

                                            His heart
failed him, and he said to Diomedes:
'Give way, now; get the team to pull us out!
Do you not realize that power from Zeus
is being denied you? Glory goes today
to Hector, by favour of the son of Cronos.
Another day he may bestow it on us
if he only will. No man defends himself
against the mind of Zeus – even the ruggedest
of champions. His power is beyond us.'

Diomedes, lord of the war-cry, answered:
'All that you say is right enough, old man.
But here's atrocious pain low in my chest
about my heart, when I imagine Hector
among the Trojans telling them one day:
"Diomedes made for the ships with me behind him!"
That's the way he'll put it. May broad earth
yawn for me then and hide me!'

                              Nestor said:
'Ai, Diomedes, keep your head, what talk!
Even if Hector calls you a coward
he cannot make them think so, Trojans or Dardans,
no, nor the Trojan soldiers' wives who saw
their fine men in the dust, dead at your hands!'
    Then Nestor whipped the horses into a turn
and joined the rout.

                        With a wild yell
behind them Hector and his men let fly
their spears and grievous arrows in a shower,
and Hector towering in his bright helmet
shouted out: 'O Diomedes, once
Achaean skirmishers gave you the place of honour!
Heart of the roast, cups brimming full! But they'll
despise you now – turned woman, after all!
You empty doll, ride on!
Never will I give way to you, and never
will you climb hand over hand upon our ramparts
or load our women in your ships: you face
your doom from me!'

                         Hearing this, Diomedes
hesitated and had half a mind
to wheel his horses, face around, and fight.
Three times he put it to himself; three times
from Ida's mountain-top great Zeus who views
the wide world thundered, as a sign to Trojans
that now the tide of battle swung to them.
    And Hector could be heard among them shouting:
'Trojans, Lycians, Dardans! Fighters all!
Be men, friends, keep up your driving power.
I know now that Zeus has accorded me
victory and glory – and the Danaans
bloody defeat. What fools, to build that wall,
soft earth, no barrier: it will not stop me.
Our horses in one jump can take the ditch,

but when I reach the decked ships, one of you
remember to bring incendiary torches
burning, so I can set the ships afire
and kill the Argives round them, blind with smoke.'

Then he spoke to his team: 'Tawny and Whitefoot,
Dusky and Dapple, now is the time to pay
for all that delicate feeding by Andromache:
the honey-hearted grain she served, the wine
she mixed for you to drink when you desired –
before me, though I am her own true husband.
Press the Achaeans hard, give all you have,
and we may capture Nestor's shield whose fame
has gone abroad to the sky's rim: all in gold
they say it's plated, crossbars too. Then too
remember the enamelled cuirass worn
by Diomedes, crafted by Hephaestus.
If we can take these arms, I have a chance
to drive the Achaeans aboard ship tonight!'

While he appealed to them, Queen Hera tossed
with rancour and indignation in her chair,
making mighty Olympus quake, and said
into Poseidon's ear: 'Oh, what a pity!
God of the wide sea, shaker of the islands,
are you not moved to see Danaans perish
who send so many and lovely gifts to you
at Helice and Aegae? You had wished them
victory. If only we who take
the Achaean side would have the will to fight,
to repel the Trojans and keep Zeus away,
there he might sit and fret alone on Ida!'

But the Earthshaker growled at her in anger:
'Hera, mistress of babble that you are,
what empty-headed talk is this? I would not
dream of pitting all the rest of us
against Lord Zeus. He overmasters all.'

That ended their exchange. Meanwhile, below,
and inland from the ships, the strip of shore
enclosed by moat and rampart now was thronged
with chariots and men, rolled back
by whirlwind Ares' peer, the son of Priam,
as glory shone on him from Zeus. And soon
he would have set the ships ablaze – had not
a thought from Hera come to Agamemnon,
to rouse himself and rally his Achaeans.

Along the line of huts and ships he came,
holding a purple cloak in his great hand,
and stood beside the black wide-bellied ship
of Lord Odysseus. Midway in the line
this ship was placed; one there could send his voice
as far as Telamonian Aias' camp
at one end, or Achilles' at the other –
for these had drawn their ships up on the flanks,
relying on their valour and force of arms.
    Agamemnon's harangue reached all his troops:
'Shame, shame, you pack of dogs, you only *looked* well.
What has become of all our fighting words,
all that brave talk I heard from you in Lemnos,
when you were feasting on thick beef and drinking
bowls a-brim with wine? Then every man
could take on Trojans by the hundred! Now
we are no match for one of them, for Hector.
He will set our black ships afire, and soon.
O Father Zeus, what great prince before this
have you so blinded in disastrous folly,
taking his glory and his pride away? And yet
no altar of yours did I pass by, not one,
in my mad voyage this way in the ships.
On every one I burned thigh flesh and fat,
in hope to take walled Troy by storm. Ah, Zeus!
Grant me this boon: let us at least
escape the worst: do not allow the Trojans
to crush the Achaeans as it seems they will!'
    The father on Ida pitied the weeping man
and nodded; his main army should be saved.
And Zeus that instant launched above the field
the most portentous of all birds, an eagle,
pinning in his talons a tender fawn.
He dropped it near the beautiful altar of Zeus
where the Achaeans made their offerings
to Zeus of Omens: and beholding this,
knowing the eagle had come down from Zeus,
they flung themselves again upon the Trojans,
with joy renewed in battle. Of all Danaans
as many as were crowded there, not one
could say he drove his team across the moat
and faced the enemy before Diomedes.
Far out ahead of all, he killed his man –
Agelaus, Phradmon's son. As this man wheeled

his chariot in retreat, the spear went into him
between the shoulder blades and through his chest.
He toppled, and his armour clanged upon him.
After Diomedes came the Atreidae,
Agamemnon and Menelaus, and then
the two named Aias, jacketed with brawn;
then came Idomeneus and his lieutenant
Meriones, peer of Enyalius,
the god of slaughter. After these Eurypylus
Euaemon's son, and ninth in order, Teucer,
his bow bent hard and strung. He took his stand
behind the shield of Telamonian Aias,
and Aias would put up his shield a bit: beneath it
the archer could take aim – and when his shot
went home, his enemy perished on the spot,
while he ducked back to Aias' flank the way
a boy does to his mother, and with his shield
Aias concealed him. Whom did he hit first?
Orsilochus and Ormenus, Ophelestes,
Daetor and Chromius and Lycophontes,
Amopaon Polyaemonides, Melanippus –
one after another he brought them down
upon the cattle-pasturing earth. And Marshal
Agamemnon exulted to see him slash
the Trojan ranks with shots from his tough bow.

He moved over nearby and said to him:
'Teucer, good soldier and leader that you are,
that is the way to shoot. Your marksmanship
will be a gleam of pride for the Danaans
and for your father, too, for Telamon.
He reared you at home despite your bastard birth;
now distant as he is, lift him to glory.
And I can tell you how the case will be,
if Zeus beyond the storm-cloud, and Athena,
allow me ever to storm and pillage Troy:
I pledge a gift to you, next after mine,
a tripod or a team with car, or else
a woman who will sleep with you.'
                                        To this
the noble Teucer answered: 'Agamemnon,
excellency, I am doing all I can; no point
in promising things to cheer me on. As long
as I have it in me I will never quit.
No, from the time we held and pushed them back

on Ilium, I have watched here with my bow
for openings to kill them: eight good shots
I've had by now with my barbed shafts —
and all on target in the flesh of men.
But that mad dog I cannot hit!'
                              So saying,
he let one arrow more leap from the string
in passionate hope to knock Lord Hector down.
He missed once more, but did hit in the chest
a noble son of Priam, Gorgythion,
whom Castianeira of Aesyme bore,
a woman tall in beauty as a goddess.
Fallen on one side, as on the stalk
a poppy falls, weighed down by showering spring,
beneath his helmet's weight his head sank down.
Then Teucer, aiming hard at Hector, let
an arrow leap from the string, and yet again
he missed; this time Apollo nudged its flight
toward Archeptolemus, driver to Hector,
as he came on. It struck him near the nipple.
Down he tumbled from the car, his horses
shying back as the man died where he fell.
A gloom passed over Hector for his driver,
but angered as he was he left him there
and called out to his brother, Cebriones,
to take the reins. As he did so, Lord Hector
sprang out of the glittering chariot
with a savage cry, picked up a stone, and ran
for Teucer in a fury to strike him down.
Out of his quiver the cool archer drew
one more keen arrow, fitting it to the string,
but even as he pulled it back Lord Hector
cast the rough stone and caught him on the shoulder
just at the collar-bone, that frail cross-beam
that separates the chest and throat. A tendon
snapped; the archer's arm went numb; he dropped
on one knee, and his bow fell. Now great Aias,
seeing his brother fallen, threw himself
forward to give him cover with his shield,
and Mecisteus and brave Alastor, two
of Aias' men, reached under him and bore him
groaning toward the ships.
                              The Olympian
again at this put heart into the Trojans,

and straight into the moat they drove the Achaeans,
Hector, elated, leading the attack.
You know the way a hunting dog will harry
a wild boar or a lion after a chase,
and try to nip him from behind, to fasten
on flank or rump, alert for an opening
as the quarry turns and turns: darting like that,
Hector harried the long-haired men of Achaea,
killing off stragglers one by one, and when
the main mass had got through the stakes and ditch,
many had perished at the Trojans' hands.
Now at the ships they tried to stand and fight,
and shouted to each other, calling out
with hands held high to all the gods as well,
as Hector drove his beautiful team around them,
blazing-eyed as a Gorgon, or as Ares,
bane of men.

     But Hera, looking down,
was touched by the sight and said to Athena: 'Daughter
of Zeus who bears the storm-cloud, can it be
that we'll no longer care for the Danaans
in their extremity? All is fulfilled
to the bitter end, they are being cut to pieces
under one man's attack. No one can hold him,
the son of Priam, in his battle fury,
adding slaughter to slaughter.'

        Grey-eyed Athena
answered: 'Death twice over to this Trojan!
Let him be broken at the Argives' hands,
give up his breath in his own land and perish!
My father, now, is full of a black madness,
evil and perverse. All that I strive for
he brings to nothing; he will not remember
how many times I intervened to save
his son, worn out in trials set by Eurystheus.
How Heracles would cry to heaven! And Zeus
would send me out of heaven to be his shield.
Had I foreseen this day
that time he went down, bidden by Eurystheus,
between Death's narrow gates to bring from Erebus
the watchdog of the Lord of Undergloom,
he never would have left the gorge of Styx!
Now Zeus not only scorns me, he performs
what Thetis wills: she kissed his knees, she begged him

to give back honour to that stormer of towns,
Achilles! But in time to come he'll call me
dear Grey Eyes again. Harness the team for us,
while I go in to get my battle-gear
in Zeus's hall. Then let me see
if Hector in his flashing helm exults
when we appear on the precarious field,
or if a certain Trojan, fallen by the ship-ways,
gluts the dogs and birds with flesh and fat!'

    Hera whose arms are white as ivory
attended to her horses, their heads nodding
in frontlets of pure gold: the eldest goddess,
Hera, daughter of Cronos, harnessed them.
Meanwhile Athena at her father's door
let fall the robe her own hands had embroidered
and pulled over her head a shirt of Zeus.
Armour of grievous war she buckled on,
stepped in the fiery car, caught up her spear –
that massive spear with which this child of Power
can break in rage long battlelines of fighters.
Hera flicked at the horses with her whip,
and moving of themselves the gates of heaven
grated a rumbling tone. Their keepers are
the Hours by whom great heaven and Olympus
may be disclosed or shut with looming cloud.
Between these gates the goddesses drove on.

    Zeus, looking out from Ida, terribly angered,
roused his messenger, Iris of Golden Wings,
and said: 'Away with you, turn them around,
allow them no way through. It is not well
that we should come together in this battle!
But if we do, I swear
I shall hamstring their horses' legs and toss
the riders from their car; the chariot
I'll break to pieces: not in ten long years
will their concussions from that lightning stroke
be healed. Let Grey Eyes realize the peril
of going into battle with her father.
I cannot be so furious with Hera –
she balks me from sheer habit, say what I will.'

    At his command his emissary, Iris,
who runs on the rainy wind, from Ida's range
went up to grand Olympus. At the gate
of that snow-craggy mountain, where she met them,

she held them back and spoke the word of Zeus:
   'Where are you going? Have you lost your minds?
The son of Cronos does not countenance
aid to the Argives: here is the penalty
he threatens to impose, and will impose:
your horses he will cripple, first of all,
then toss you both out of the chariot
and break it into pieces: not in ten years
can what you suffer from that lightning stroke
be healed. So, Grey Eyes, you may learn
the peril of doing battle with your father.
With Hera he cannot be so furious:
her habit is to balk him, say what he will;
but as for you, you are a brazen bitch
if you dare lift your towering spear against him!'
   When she had finished, Iris departed swiftly,
and Hera said to Athena: 'Very upsetting.
I cannot now consent, I am afraid,
that we make war with Zeus over mankind.
No, let them live or die as it befalls them!
Let him be arbiter, as he desires,
between Danaans and Trojans. It is due
his majesty.'
               And she turned the horses back.
Then acting for the goddesses the Hours
unharnessed those fine horses with long manes
and tied them up at their ambrosial troughs.
Against the glittering wall they stood the car,
its tilted pole up-ended, and the goddesses
rested on golden chairs amid the gods,
with hearts still beating high.
                  Now Father Zeus
from Ida to Olympus drove his chariot
back to the resting place of gods. For him
the illustrious one who makes the islands tremble
freed the team, spread out a chariot-housing,
and drew the car up on a central stand.
Then Zeus who views the wide world took his chair,
his golden chair, as underfoot
the mighty mountain of Olympus quaked.
Alone, apart, sat Hera and Athena
speaking never a word to him.
                      He knew
their mood and said: 'Athena, why so gloomy?

And Hera, why? In war, where men win glory,
you have not had to toil to bring down Trojans
for whom both hold an everlasting grudge.
Such is my animus and so inexorable
my hands that all the gods upon Olympus
could not in any case deflect or turn them.
Fear shook your gracious knees before you saw
the nightmare acts of warfare. I can tell you
why, and what defeat was sure to come of it:
no riding in your chariot back to Olympus,
back to your seats here, after my lightning bolt.'

Zeus fell silent, and they murmured low,
Athena and Hera, putting their heads together,
meditating the Trojans' fall. Athena
held her peace toward Zeus, though a fierce rancour
pervaded her; Hera could not contain it,
and burst out to him: 'Fearsome as you are,
why take that tone with goddesses, my lord?
We are well aware how far from weak you are;
but we mourn still for the Achaean spearmen
if they are now to meet hard fate and die.
As you command, we shall indeed
abstain from battle – merely, now and again,
dropping a word of counsel to the Argives,
that all may not be lost through your displeasure.'

Then Zeus who gathers cloud replied to her:
'At dawn tomorrow you will see still more,
my wide-eyed lady, if you care to see
the Lord Zeus in high rage scything that army
of Argive spearmen down – for Hector shall not
give his prowess respite from the war
until the marvellous runner, son of Peleus,
rouses beside his ship – when near at hand,
around the sterns, in a desperate narrow place,
they fight over Patroclus dead. That way
the will of heaven lies. You and your anger
do not affect me, you may betake yourself
to the uttermost margin of earth and sea,
where Iapetus and Cronos rest and never
bask in the rays of Helios who moves
all day in heaven, nor rejoice in winds,
but lie submerged in Tartarus. You, too,
may roam that far, you bitch unparalleled,
I'll be indifferent still to your bad temper!'

Hera whose arms are white as ivory
made no reply.

          Now in the western Ocean
the shining sun dipped, drawing dark night on
over the kind grain-bearing earth – a sundown
far from desired by Trojans; but the night
came thrice besought and blest by the Achaeans.
Hector at once called Trojans to assembly,
leading the way by night back from the ships
to an empty field beside the eddying river –
a space that seemed free of the dead. The living
halted and dismounted there to listen
to a speech by Hector, dear to Zeus. He held
his lance erect – eleven forearms long
with bronze point shining in the air before him
as shone, around the shank, a golden ring.
Leaning on this, he spoke amid the Trojans:

    'Hear me, Trojans, Dardans, and allies!
By this time I had thought we might retire
to windy Ilium, after we had destroyed
Achaeans and their ships; but the night's gloom
came before we finished. That has saved them,
Argives and ships, at the sea's edge near the surf.
All right, then, let us bow to the black night,
and make an evening feast! From the chariot-poles
unyoke the teams, toss fodder out before them;
bring down beeves and fat sheep from the city,
and lose no time about it – amber wine
and wheaten bread, too, from our halls. Go, gather
piles of firewood, so that all night long,
until the first-born dawn, our many fires
shall burn and send to heaven their leaping light,
that not by night shall the unshorn Achaeans
get away on the broad back of the sea.
Not by night – and not without combat, either,
taking ship easily, but let there be
those who take homeward missiles to digest,
hit hard by arrows or by spears as they
shove off and leap aboard. And let the next man
hate the thought of waging painful war
on Trojan master-horsemen.

               'Honoured criers
throughout our town shall publish this command:
old men with hoary brows, and striplings, all

camp out tonight upon the ancient towers;
women in every megaron kindle fires,
and every sentry keep a steady watch
against a night raid on the city, while
my troops are in the field. These dispositions,
Trojans, are to be taken as I command. And may
what I have said tonight be salutary;
likewise what I shall say at Dawn. I hope
with prayer to Zeus and other immortal gods
we shall repulse the dogs of war and death
brought on us in the black ships. Aye, this night
we'll guard ourselves, toward morning arm again
and whet against the ships the edge of war!
I'll see if Diomedes has the power
to force me from the ships, back on the rampart,
or if I kill him, and take home his gear,
wet with his blood. He will show bravery
tomorrow if he face my spear advancing!
In the first rank, I think, wounded he'll lie
with plenty of his friends lying around him
at sun-up in the morning.

                      'Would I were sure
of being immortal, ageless all my days,
and reverenced like Athena and Apollo,
as it is sure this day will bring defeat
on those of Argos!'

                    This was the speech of Hector,
and cheers rang out from the Trojans after it.
They led from under the yokes their sweating teams,
tethering each beside his chariot,
then brought down from the city beeves and sheep
in all haste – brought down wine and bread as well
out of their halls. They piled up firewood
and carried out full-tally hecatombs
to the immortals. Off the plain, the wind
bore smoke and savour of roasts into the sky.
Then on the perilous open ground of war,
in brave expectancy, they lay all night
while many camp-fires burned. As when in heaven
principal stars shine out around the moon
when the night sky is limpid, with no wind,
and all the look-out points, headlands, and mountain
clearings are distinctly seen, as though
pure space had broken through, downward from heaven,

and all the stars are out, and in his heart
the shepherd sings: just so from ships to river
shone before Ilium the Trojan fires.
There were a thousand burning in the plain,
and round each one lay fifty men in firelight.
Horses champed white barley, near the chariots,
waiting for Dawn to mount her lovely chair.

BOOK IX

A VISIT OF EMISSARIES

So Trojans kept their watch that night. To seaward
Panic that attends blood-chilling Rout
now ruled the Achaeans. All their finest men
were shaken by this fear, in bitter throes,
as when a shifting gale
blows up over the cold fish-breeding sea,
north wind and west wind wailing out of Thrace
in squall on squall, and dark waves crest, and shoreward
masses of weed are cast up by the surf:
so were Achaean hearts torn in their breasts.

By that great gloom hard hit, the son of Atreus
made his way amid his criers and told them
to bid each man in person to assembly
but not to raise a general cry. He led them,
making the rounds himself, and soon the soldiers
grimly took their places. Then he rose,
with slow tears trickling, as from a hidden spring
dark water runs down, staining a rock-wall;
and groaning heavily he addressed the Argives:

'Friends, leaders of Argives, all my captains,
Zeus Cronides entangled me in folly
to my undoing. Wayward god, he promised
solemnly that I should not sail away
before I stormed the inner town of Troy.
Crookedness and duplicity, I see now!
He calls me to return to Argos beaten
after these many losses. That must be
his will and his good pleasure, who knows why?
Many a great town's height has he destroyed
and will destroy, being supreme in power.
Enough. Now let us act on what I say:
Board ship for our own fatherland! Retreat!
We cannot hope any longer to take Troy!'

At this a stillness overcame them all,
the Achaean soldiers. Long they sat in silence,
hearing their own hearts beat.
                                        Then Diomedes
rose at last to speak. He said: 'My lord,

I must contend with you for letting go,
for losing balance. I may do so here
in assembly lawfully. Spare me your anger.
Before this you have held me up to scorn
for lack of fighting spirit; old and young,
everyone knows the truth of that. In your case,
the son of crooked-minded Cronos gave you
one gift and not both: a staff of kingship
honoured by all men, but no staying-power –
the greatest gift of all.
What has come over you, to make you think
the Achaeans weak and craven as you say?
If you are in a passion to sail home,
sail on: the way is clear, the many ships
that made the voyage from Mycenae with you
stand near the sea's edge. Others here will stay
until we plunder Troy! Or if they, too,
would like to, let them sail for their own country!
Sthenelus and I will fight alone
until we see the destined end of Ilium.
We came here under god.'
                          When Diomedes
finished, a cry went up from all Achaeans
in wonder at his words.
                     Then Nestor stood
and spoke among them: 'Son of Tydeus, formidable
above the rest in war, in council, too,
you have more weight than others of your age.
No one will cry down what you say, no true
Achaean will, or contradict you. Still,
you did not push on to the end.
I know you are young; in years you might well be
my last-born son, and yet for all of that
you kept your head and said what needed saying
before the Argive captains. My own part,
as I am older, is to drive it home.
No one will show contempt for what I say,
surely not Agamemnon, our commander.
Alien to clan and custom and hearthfire
is he who longs for war – heartbreaking war –
with his own people.
                    'Let us yield to darkness
and make our evening meal. But let the sentries
take their rest on watch outside the rampart

near the moat; those are my orders for them.
Afterward, you direct us, Agamemnon,
by right of royal power. Provide a feast
for older men, your counsellors. That is duty
and no difficulty: your huts are full of wine
brought over daily in our ships from Thrace
across the wide sea, and all provender
for guests is yours, as you are high commander.
Your counsellors being met, pay heed to him
who counsels best. The army of Achaea
bitterly needs a well-found plan of action.
The enemy is upon us, near the ships,
burning his thousand fires. What Achaean
could be high-hearted in that glare? This night
will see the army saved or brought to ruin.'

They heeded him and did his will. Well-armed,
the sentries left to take their posts, one company
formed around Thrasymedes, Nestor's son,
another mustered by Ascalaphus
and Ialmenus, others commanded by
Meriones, Aphareus, Deipyrus,
and Creon's son, the princely Lycomedes.
Seven lieutenants, each with a hundred men,
carrying long spears, issued from the camp
for outposts chosen between ditch and rampart.
Camp-fires were kindled, and they took their meal.

The son of Atreus led the elder men
together to his hut, where he served dinner,
and each man's hand went out upon the meal.
When they had driven hunger and thirst away,
Old Nestor opened their deliberations –
Nestor, whose counsel had seemed best before,
point by point weaving his argument:

'Lord Marshal of the army, Agamemnon,
as I shall end with you, so I begin,
since you hold power over a great army
and are responsible for it: the Lord Zeus
put in your keeping staff and precedent
that you might gather counsel for your men.
You should be first in discourse, but attentive
to what another may propose, to act on it
if he speak out for the good of all. Whatever
he may initiate, action is yours.
On this rule, let me speak as I think best.

A better view than mine no man can have,
the same view that I've held these many days
since that occasion when, my lord, for all
Achilles' rage, you took the girl Briseis
out of his lodge – but not with our consent.
Far from it; I for one had begged you not to.
Just the same, you gave way to your pride,
and you dishonoured a great prince,
a hero to whom the gods themselves do honour.
Taking his prize, you kept her and still do.
But even so, and even now, we may
contrive some way of making peace with him
by friendly gifts, and by affectionate words.'

　　Then Agamemnon, the Lord Marshal, answered:
'Sir, there is nothing false in your account
of my blind errors. I committed them;
I will not now deny it. Troops of soldiers
are worth no more than one man cherished by Zeus
as he has cherished this man and avenged him,
overpowering the army of Achaeans.
I lost my head. I yielded to black anger,
but now I would retract it and appease him
with all munificence. Here before everyone
I may enumerate the gifts I'll give.
Seven new tripods and ten bars of gold,
then twenty shining cauldrons, and twelve horses,
thoroughbreds, who by their wind and legs
have won me prizes: any man who owned
what these have brought me could not lack resources,
could not be pinched for precious gold – so many
prizes have these horses carried home.
Then I shall give him seven women, deft
in household handicraft – women of Lesbos
I chose when he himself took Lesbos town,
as they outshone all womankind in beauty.
These I shall give him, and one more, whom I
took away from him then: Briseus' daughter.
Concerning her, I add my solemn oath
I never went to bed or coupled with her,
as custom is with men and women.
These will be his at once. If the immortals
grant us the plundering of Priam's town,
let him come forward when the spoils are shared
and load his ship with bars of gold and bronze.

Then he may choose among the Trojan women
twenty that are most lovely, after Helen.
If we return to Argos of Achaea,
flowing with good things of the earth, he'll be
my own adopted son, dear as Orestes,
born long ago and reared in bounteous peace.
I have three daughters now at home, Chrysothemis,
Laodice, and Iphianassa.
He may take whom he will to be his bride
and pay no bridal gift, leading her home
to Peleus' hall. But I shall add a dowry
such as no man has given to his daughter.
Seven flourishing strongholds I'll give him:
Cardamyle and Enope and Hire
in the wild grassland; holy Pherae too,
and the deep meadowland about Antheia,
Aepeia and the vineyard slope of Pedasus,
all lying near the sea in the far west
of sandy Pylos. In these lands are men
who own great flocks and herds; now as his liegemen,
they will pay tithes and sumptuous honour to him,
prospering as they carry out his plans.
These are the gifts I shall arrange if he
desists from anger. Let him be subdued!
Lord Death indeed is deaf to appeal, implacable;
of all gods therefore he is most abhorrent
to mortal men. So let Achilles bow to me,
considering that I hold higher rank
and claim the precedence of age.'

                      To this
Lord Nestor of Gerenia replied:
'Lord Marshal of the army, Agamemnon,
this time the gifts you offer Lord Achilles
are not to be despised. Come, we'll dispatch
our chosen emissaries to his quarters
as quickly as possible. Those men whom I
may designate, let them perform the mission.
Phoenix, dear to Zeus, may lead the way.
Let Aias follow him, and Prince Odysseus.
The criers, Odius and Eurybates,
may go as escorts. Bowls for their hands here!
Tell them to keep silence, while we pray
that Zeus the son of Cronos will be merciful.'
  Nestor's proposal fell on willing ears,

and criers came at once to tip out water
over their hands, while young men filled the winebowls
and dipped a measure into every cup.
They spilt their offerings and drank their fill,
then briskly left the hut of Agamemnon.
Nestor accompanied them with final words
and sage looks, especially for Odysseus,
as to the effort they should make to bring
the son of Peleus round.

                Following Phoenix,
Aias and Odysseus walked together
beside the tumbling clamorous whispering sea,
praying hard to the girdler of the islands
that they might easily sway their great friend's heart.
Amid the ships and huts of the Myrmidons
they found him, taking joy in a sweet harp
of rich and delicate make – the crossbar set
to hold the strings being silver. He had won it
when he destroyed the city of Eetion,
and plucking it he took his joy: he sang
old tales of heroes, while across the room
alone and silent sat Patroclus, waiting
until Achilles should be done with song.
Phoenix had come in unremarked, but when
the two new visitors, Odysseus leading,
entered and stood before him, then Achilles
rose in wonderment, and left his chair,
his harp still in his hand. So did Patroclus
rise at sight of the two men.

                Achilles
made both welcome with a gesture, saying:
'Peace! My two great friends, I greet your coming.
How I have needed it! Even in my anger,
of all Achaeans, you are closest to me.'
And Prince Achilles led them in. He seated them
on easy chairs with purple coverlets,
and to Patroclus who stood near he said:

   'Put out an ampler winebowl, use more wine
for stronger drink, and place a cup for each.
Here are my dearest friends beneath my roof.'

   Patroclus did as his companion bade him.
Meanwhile the host set down a carving block
within the fire's rays; a chine of mutton
and a fat chine of goat he placed upon it,

as well as savoury pork chine. Automedon
steadied the meat for him, Achilles carved,
then sliced it well and forked it on the spits.
Meanwhile Patroclus, like a god in firelight,
made the hearth blaze up. When the leaping flame
had ebbed and died away, he raked the coals
and in the glow extended spits of meat,
lifting these at times from the firestones
to season with pure salt. When all was done
and the roast meat apportioned into platters,
loaves of bread were passed round by Patroclus
in fine baskets. Achilles served the meat.
He took his place then opposite Odysseus,
back to the other wall, and told
Patroclus to make offering to the gods.
This he did with meat tossed in the fire,
then each man's hand went out upon the meal.
When they had put their hunger and thirst away,
Aias nodded silently to Phoenix,
but Prince Odysseus caught the nod.

                                        He filled
a cup of wine and lifted it to Achilles,
saying: 'Health, Achilles. We've no lack
of generous feasts this evening – in the lodge
of Agamemnon first, and now with you,
good fare and plentiful each time.
It is not feasting that concerns us now,
however, but a ruinous defeat.
Before our very eyes we see it coming
and are afraid. By a blade's turn, our good ships
are saved or lost, unless you arm your valour.
Trojans and allies are encamped tonight
in pride before our ramparts, at our sterns,
and through their army burn a thousand fires.
These men are sure they cannot now be stopped
but will get through to our good ships. Lord Zeus
flashes and thunders for them on the right,
and Hector in his ecstasy of power
is mad for battle, confident in Zeus,
deferring to neither men nor gods. Pure frenzy
fills him, and he prays for the bright dawn
when he will shear our stern-post beaks away
and fire all our ships, while in the ship-ways
amid that holocaust he carries death

among our men, driven out by smoke. All this
I gravely fear; I fear the gods will make
good his threatenings, and our fate will be
to die here, far from the pasture-land of Argos.
Rouse yourself, if even at this hour
you'll pitch in for the Achaeans and deliver them
from Trojan havoc. In the years to come
this day will be remembered pain for you
if you do not. No remedy, no remedy
will come to hand, once the great ill is done.
While there is time, think how to keep this evil
day from the Danaans!

               'My dear lad,
how rightly in your case your father, Peleus,
put it in his farewell, sending you out
from Phthia to take ship with Agamemnon!
"Now as to fighting power, child," he said,
"if Hera and Athena wish, they'll give it.
Control your passion, though, and your proud heart,
for gentle courtesy is a better thing.
Break off insidious quarrels, and young and old,
the Argives will respect you for it more."
That was your old father's admonition:
you have forgotten. Still, even now, abandon
heart-wounding anger. If you will relent,
Agamemnon will match this change of heart
with gifts. Now listen and let me list for you
what just now in his quarters he proposed:
seven new tripods, and ten bars of gold,
then twenty shining cauldrons, and twelve horses,
thoroughbreds, that by their wind and legs
have won him prizes: any man who owned
what these have brought him would not lack resources,
could not be pinched for precious gold – so many
prizes have these horses carried home.
Then he will give you seven women, deft
in household handicraft: women of Lesbos
chosen when you yourself took Lesbos town,
as they outshone all womankind in beauty.
These he will give you, and one more, whom he
took away from you then: Briseus' daughter,
concerning whom he adds a solemn oath
never to have gone to bed or coupled with her,
as custom is, my lord, with men and women.

These are all yours at once. If the immortals
grant us the pillaging of Priam's town,
you may come forward when the spoils are shared
and load your ship with bars of gold and bronze.
Then you may choose among the Trojan women
twenty that are most lovely, after Helen.
And then, if we reach Argos of Achaea,
flowing with good things of the earth, you'll be
his own adopted son, dear as Orestes,
born long ago and reared in bounteous peace.
He has three daughters now at home, Chrysothemis,
Laodice, and Iphianassa.
You may take whom you will to be your bride
and pay no gift when you conduct her home
to your ancestral hall. He'll add a dowry
such as no man has given to his daughter.
Seven flourishing strongholds he'll give to you:
Cardamyle and Enope and Hire
in the wild grassland; holy Pherae too,
and the deep meadowland about Antheia,
Aepeia and the vineyard slope of Pedasus,
all lying near the sea in the far west
of sandy Pylos. In these lands are men
who own great flocks and herds; now as your liegemen,
they will pay tithes and sumptuous honour to you,
prospering as they carry out your plans.
These are the gifts he will arrange if you
desist from anger.

       'Even if you abhor
the son of Atreus all the more bitterly,
with all his gifts, take pity on the rest,
all the old army, worn to rags in battle.
These will honour you as gods are honoured!
And ah, for these, what glory you may win!
Think: Hector is your man this time: being crazed
with ruinous pride, believing there's no fighter
equal to him among those that our ships
brought here by sea, he'll put himself in range!'

    Achilles the great runner answered him:
'Son of Laertes and the gods of old,
Odysseus, master soldier and mariner,
I owe you a straight answer, as to how
I see this thing, and how it is to end.
No need to sit with me like mourning doves

making your gentle noise by turns. I hate
as I hate Hell's own gate that man who hides
one thought within him while he speaks another.
What I shall say is what I see and think.
Give in to Agamemnon? I think not,
neither to him nor to the rest. I had
small thanks for fighting, fighting without truce
against hard enemies here. The portion's equal
whether a man hangs back or fights his best;
the same respect, or lack of it, is given
brave man and coward. One who's active dies
like the do-nothing. What least thing have I
to show for it, for harsh days undergone
and my life gambled, all these years of war?
A bird will give her fledgelings every scrap
she comes by, and go hungry, foraging.
That is the case with me.
Many a sleepless night I've spent afield
and many a day in bloodshed, hand to hand
in battle for the wives of other men.
In sea-raids I plundered a dozen towns,
eleven in expeditions overland
through Trojan country, and the treasure taken
out of them all, great heaps of handsome things,
I carried back each time to Agamemnon.
He sat tight on the beach-head, and shared out
a little treasure; most of it he kept.
He gave prizes of war to his officers;
the rest have theirs, not I; from me alone
of all Achaeans, he pre-empted her.
He holds my bride, dear to my heart. Aye, let him
sleep with her and enjoy her!
                                        'Why must Argives
fight the Trojans? Why did he raise an army
and lead it here? For Helen, was it not?
Are the Atreidae of all mortal men
the only ones who love their wives? I think not.
Every sane decent fellow loves his own
and cares for her, as in my heart I loved
Briseis, though I won her by the spear.
Now, as he took my prize out of my hands,
tricked and defrauded me, he need not tempt me;
I know him, and he cannot change my mind.
Let him take thought, Odysseus, with you

and others how the ships may be defended
against incendiary attack. By god,
he has achieved imposing work without me,
a rampart piled up overnight, a ditch
running beyond it, broad and deep,
with stakes implanted in it! All no use!
He cannot hold against the killer's charge.
As long as I was in the battle, Hector
never cared for a fight far from the walls;
his limit was the oak-tree by the gate.
When I was alone one day he waited there,
but barely got away when I went after him.
Now it is I who do not care to fight.
Tomorrow at dawn when I have made offering
to Zeus and all the gods, and hauled my ships
for loading in the shallows, if you like
and if it interests you, look out and see
my ships on Helle's waters in the offing,
oarsmen in line making the sea-foam scud!
And if the great Earthshaker gives a breeze,
the third day out I'll make it home to Phthia.
Rich possessions are there I left behind
when I was mad enough to come here; now
I take home gold and ruddy bronze, and women
belted luxuriously, and hoary iron,
all that came to me here. As for my prize,
he who gave her took her outrageously back.
Well, you can tell him all this to his face,
and let the other Achaeans burn
if he in his thick hide of shamelessness
picks out another man to cheat. He would not
look me in the eye, dog that he is!
I will not share one word of counsel with him,
nor will I act with him; he robbed me blind,
broke faith with me: he gets no second chance
to play me for a fool. Once is enough.
To hell with him, Zeus took his brains away!
His gifts I abominate, and I would give
not one dry shuck for him. I would not change,
not if he multiplied his gifts by ten,
by twenty times what he has now, and more,
no matter where they came from: if he gave
what enters through Orchomenus' town gate
or Thebes of Egypt, where the treasures lie —

that city where through each of a hundred gates
two hundred men drive out in chariots.
Not if his gifts outnumbered the sea-sands
or all the dust-grains in the world could Agamemnon
ever appease me – not till he pays me back
full measure, pain for pain, dishonour for dishonour.
The daughter of Agamemnon, son of Atreus,
I will not take in marriage. Let her be
as beautiful as pale-gold Aphrodite,
skilled as Athena of the sea-grey eyes,
I will not have her, at any price. No, let him
find someone else, an eligible Achaean,
kinglier than I.
                    'Now if the gods
preserve me and I make it home, my father
Peleus will select a bride for me.
In Hellas and in Phthia there are many
daughters of strong men who defend the towns.
I'll take the one I wish to be my wife.
There in my manhood I have longed, indeed,
to marry someone of congenial mind
and take my ease, enjoying the great estate
my father had acquired.
                        'Now I think
no riches can compare with being alive,
not even those they say this well-built Ilium
stored up in peace before the Achaeans came.
Neither could all the Archer's shrine contains
at rocky Pytho, in the crypt of stone.
A man may come by cattle and sheep in raids;
tripods he buys, and tawny-headed horses;
but his life's breath cannot be hunted back
or be recaptured once it pass his lips.
My mother, Thetis of the silvery feet,
tells me of two possible destinies
carrying me toward death: two ways:
if on the one hand I remain to fight
around Troy town, I lose all hope of home
but gain unfading glory; on the other,
if I sail back to my own land my glory
fails – but a long life lies ahead for me.
To all the rest of you I say: "Sail home:
you will not now see Ilium's last hour,"
for Zeus who views the wide world held his sheltering

hand over that city, and her troops
have taken heart.
        'Return, then, emissaries,
deliver my answer to the Achaean peers –
it is the senior officer's privilege –
and let them plan some other way, and better,
to save their ships and save the Achaean army.
This one cannot be put into effect –
their scheme this evening – while my anger holds.
Phoenix may stay and lodge the night with us,
then take ship and sail homeward at my side
tomorrow, if he wills. I'll not constrain him.'

    After Achilles finished, all were silent,
awed, for he spoke with power.

    Then the old master-charioteer, Lord Phoenix,
answered at last, and let his tears come shining,
fearing for the Achaean ships: 'Achilles,
if it is true you set your heart on home
and will not stir a finger to save the ships
from being engulfed by fire – all for this rage
that has swept over you – how, child, could I
be sundered from you, left behind alone?
For your sake the old master-charioteer,
Peleus, made provision that I should come,
that day he gave you godspeed out of Phthia
to go with Agamemnon. Still a boy,
you knew nothing of war that levels men
to the same testing, nothing of assembly
where men become illustrious. That is why
he sent me, to instruct you in these matters,
to be a man of eloquence and action.
After all that, dear child, I should not wish
to be left here apart from you – not even
if god himself should undertake to smooth
my wrinkled age and make me fresh and young,
as when for the first time I left the land
of lovely women, Hellas. I went north
to avoid a feud with Father, Amyntor
Ormenides. His anger against me rose
over a fair-haired slave girl whom he fancied,
without respect for his own wife, my mother.
Mother embraced my knees and begged that I
make love to this girl, so that afterward
she might be cold to the ageing man. I did it.

My father guessed the truth at once, and cursed me,
praying the ghostly Furies that no son
of mine should ever rest upon his knees:
a curse fulfilled by the immortals – Lord
Zeus of undergloom and cold Persephone.
I planned to put a sword in him, and would have,
had not some god unstrung my rage, reminding me
of country gossip and the frowns of men;
I shrank from being called a parricide
among the Achaeans. But from that time on
I felt no tie with home, no love for lingering
under the roof-tree of a raging father.
Our household and our neighbours, it is true,
urged me to stay. They made a handsome feast
of shambling cattle butchered, and fat sheep;
young porkers by the litter, crisp with fat,
were singed and spitted in Hephaestus' fire,
rivers of wine drunk from the old man's store.
Nine times they spent the night and slept beside me,
taking the watch by turns, leaving a fire
to flicker under the entrance colonnade,
and one more in the court outside my room.
But when the tenth night came, starless and black,
I cracked the tight bolt on my chamber-door,
pushed out, and scaled the courtyard wall, unseen
by household men on watch or women slaves.
Then I escaped from that place, made my way
through Hellas where the dancing-floors are wide,
until I came to Phthia's fertile plain,
mother of flocks, and Peleus the king.
He gave me welcome, treated me with love,
as a father would an only son, his heir
to rich possessions. And he made me rich,
appointing me great numbers of retainers
on the frontier of Phthia, where I lived
as lord of Dolopes. Now, it was I
who formed your manhood, handsome as a god's,
Achilles: I who loved you from the heart;
for never in another's company
would you attend a feast or dine in hall –
never, unless I took you on my knees
and cut your meat, and held your cup of wine.
Many a time you wet my shirt, hiccuping
wine-bubbles in distress, when you were small.

Patient and laborious as a nurse
I had to be for you, bearing in mind
that never would the gods bring into being
any son of mine. Godlike Achilles,
you were the manchild that I made my own
to save me someday, so I thought, from misery.
Quell your anger, Achilles! You must not
be pitiless! The gods themselves relent,
and are they not still greater in bravery,
in honour and in strength? Burnt offerings,
courteous prayer, libation, smoke of sacrifice,
with all of these, men can placate the gods
when someone oversteps and errs. The truth is,
prayers are daughters of almighty Zeus —
one may imagine them lame, wrinkled things
with eyes cast down, that toil to follow after
passionate Folly. Folly is strong and swift,
outrunning all the prayers, and everywhere
arriving first to injure mortal men;
still they come healing after. If a man
reveres the daughters of Zeus when they come near,
he is rewarded, and his prayers are heard;
but if he spurns them and dismisses them,
they make their way to Zeus again and ask
that Folly dog that man till suffering
has taken arrogance out of him.

                              'Relent,
be courteous to the daughters of Zeus, you too,
as courtesy sways others, and the best.
If Agamemnon had no gifts for you,
named none to follow, but inveighed against you
still in fury, then I could never say,
"Discard your anger and defend the Argives —"
never, no matter how they craved your help.
But this is not so: he will give many things
at once; he promised others; he has sent
his noblest men to intercede with you,
the flower of the army, and your friends,
dearest among the Argives. Will you turn
their words, their coming, into humiliation?
Until this moment, no one took it ill
that you should suffer anger; we learned this
from the old stories of how towering wrath
could overcome great men; but they were still

amenable to gifts and to persuasion.
Here is an instance I myself remember
not from our own time but in ancient days:
I'll tell it to you all, for all are friends.
The Curetes were fighting a warlike race,
Aetolians, around the walls of Calydon,
with slaughter on both sides: Aetolians
defending their beloved Calydon
while the Curetes longed to sack the town.
The truth is, Artemis of the Golden Chair
had brought the scourge of war on the Aetolians;
she had been angered because Oeneus made
no harvest-offering from his vineyard slope.
While other gods enjoyed his hecatombs
he made her none, either forgetful of it
or careless – a great error, either way.
In her anger, the Mistress of Long Arrows
roused against him a boar with gleaming tusks
out of his wild-grass bed, a monstrous thing
that ravaged the man's vineyard many times
and felled entire orchards, roots,
blooms, apples and all. Now this great boar
Meleager, the son of Oeneus, killed
by gathering men and hounds from far and near.
So huge the boar was, no small band could master him,
and he brought many to the dolorous pyre.
Around the dead beast Artemis set on
a clash with battle-cries between Curetes
and proud Aetolians over the boar's head
and shaggy hide. As long, then, as Meleager,
backed by the war-god, fought, the Curetes
had the worst of it for all their numbers
and could not hold a line outside the walls.
But then a day came when Meleager
was stung by venomous anger that infects
the coolest thinker's heart: swollen with rage
at his own mother, Althaea, he languished
in idleness at home beside his lady,
Cleopatra.

         'This lovely girl was born
to Marpessa of ravishing pale ankles,
Evenus' child, and Idas, who had been
most powerful of men on earth. He drew
the bow against the Lord Phoebus Apollo

over his love, Marpessa, whom her father
and gentle mother called Alcyone,
since for her sake her mother gave that sea-bird's
forlorn cry when Apollo ravished her.
With Cleopatra Meleager lay,
nursing the bitterness his mother stirred,
when in her anguish over a brother slain
she cursed her son. She called upon the gods,
beating the grassy earth with both her hands
as she pitched forward on her knees, with cries
to the Lord of Undergloom and cold Persephone,
while tears wetted her veils – in her entreaty
that death come to her son. Inexorable
in Erebus a vampire Fury listened.
Soon, then, about the gates of the Aetolians
tumult and din of war grew loud; their towers
rang with blows. And now the elder men
begged Meleager not to immure himself,
and sent the high priests of the gods, imploring him
to help defend the town. They promised him
a large reward: in the green countryside
of Calydon, wherever it was richest,
there he might choose a beautiful garden-plot
of fifty acres, half in vineyard, half
in virgin prairie for the plough to cut.
Oeneus, master of horsemen, came with prayers
upon the doorsill of the chamber, often
rattling the locked doors, pleading with his son.
His sisters, too, and then his gentle mother
pleaded with him. Only the more fiercely
he turned away. His oldest friends, his dearest,
not even they could move him – not until
his room was shaken by a hail of stones
as Curetes began to scale the walls
and fire the city.
                    'Then at last his lady
in her soft-belted gown besought him weeping,
speaking of all the ills that come to men
whose town is taken: soldiers put to the sword;
the city razed by fire; alien hands
carrying off the children and the women.
Hearing these fearful things, his heart was stirred
to action: he put on his shining gear
and fought off ruin from the Aetolians.

Mercy prevailed in him. His folk no longer
cared to award him gifts and luxuries,
yet even so he saved that terrible day.
Oh, do not let your mind go so astray!
Let no malignant spirit
turn you that way, dear son! It will be worse
to fight for ships already set afire!
Value the gifts; rejoin the war; Achaeans
afterward will give you a god's honour.
If you reject the gifts and then, later,
enter the deadly fight, you will not be
accorded the same honour, even though
you turn the tide of war!'

                                    But the great runner
Achilles answered: 'Old uncle Phoenix, bless you,
that is an honour I can live without.
Honoured I think I am by Zeus's justice,
justice that will sustain me by the ships
as long as breath is in me and I can stand.
Here is another point: ponder it well:
best not confuse my heart with lamentation
for Agamemnon, whom you must not honour;
you would be hateful to me, dear as you are.
Loyalty should array you at my side
in giving pain to him who gives me pain.
Rule with me equally, share half my honour,
but do not ask my help for Agamemnon.
My answer will be reported by these two.
Lodge here in a soft bed, and at first light
we can decide whether to sail or stay.'

He knit his brows and nodded to Patroclus
to pile up rugs for Phoenix' bed – a sign
for the others to be quick about departing.
Aias, however, noble son of Telamon
made the last appeal. He said: 'Odysseus,
master soldier and mariner, let us go.
I do not see the end of this affair
achieved by this night's visit. Nothing for it
but to report our talk for what it's worth
to the Danaans, who sit waiting there.
Achilles hardened his great heart against us,
wayward and savage as he is, unmoved
by the affections of his friends who made him
honoured above all others on the beach-head.

There is no pity in him. A normal man
will take the penalty for a brother slain
or a dead son. By paying much, the one
who did the deed may stay unharmed at home.
Fury and pride in the bereaved are curbed
when he accepts the penalty. Not you.
Cruel and unappeasable rage the gods
put in you for one girl alone. We offer
seven beauties, and much more besides!
Be gentler, and respect your own roof-tree
whereunder we are guests who speak for all
Danaans as a body. Our desire
is to be closest to you of them all.'
   Achilles the great runner answered him:
'Scion of Telamon and gods of old,
Aias, lord of fighting men, you seemed
to echo my own mind in what you said!
And yet my heart grows large and hot with fury
remembering that affair: as though I were
some riff-raff or camp-follower, he taunted me
before them all!
             'Go back, report the news:
I will not think of carnage or of war
until Prince Hector, son of Priam, reaches
Myrmidon huts and ships in his attack,
slashing through Argives, burning down their ships.
Around my hut, my black ship, I foresee
for all his fury, Hector will break off combat.'
   That was his answer. Each of the emissaries
took up a double-handed cup and poured
libation by the shipways. Then Odysseus
led the way on their return. Patroclus
commanded his retainers and the maids
to make at once a deep-piled bed for Phoenix.
Obediently they did so, spreading out
fleeces and coverlet and a linen sheet,
and down the old man lay, awaiting Dawn.
Achilles slept in the well-built hut's recess,
and with him lay a woman he had brought
from Lesbos, Phorbas' daughter, Diomede.
Patroclus went to bed at the other end,
and with him, too, a woman lay – soft-belted
Iphis, who had been given to him by Achilles
when he took Scyrus, ringed by cliff, the mountain

fastness of Enyeus.

Now the emissaries
arrived at Agamemnon's lodge. With cups
of gold held up, and rising to their feet
on every side, the Achaeans greeted them,
curious for the news.

Lord Agamemnon
put the question first: 'Come, tell me, sir,
Odysseus, glory of Achaea – will Achilles
fight off ravenous fire from the ships
or does he still refuse, does anger still
hold sway in his great heart?'

That patient man,
the Prince Odysseus, made reply: 'Excellency,
Lord Marshal of the army, son of Atreus,
the man has no desire to quench his rage.
On the contrary, he is more than ever
full of anger, spurns you and your gifts,
calls on you to work out your own defence
to save the ships and the Achaean army.
As for himself, he threatens at daybreak
to drag his well-found ships into the surf,
and says he would advise the rest as well
to sail for home. "You shall not see," he says,
"the last hour that awaits tall Ilium,
for Zeus who views the wide world held his sheltering
hand over the city, and her troops
have taken heart." That was Achilles' answer.
Those who were with me can confirm all this,
Aias can, and the two clear-headed criers.
As to old Phoenix, he is sleeping there
by invitation, so that he may sail
to his own country, homeward with Achilles,
tomorrow, if he wills, without constraint.'

When he had finished everyone was still,
sitting in silence and in perturbation
for a long time.

At last brave Diomedes,
lord of the war-cry, said: 'Excellency,
Lord Marshal of the army, Agamemnon,
you never should have pled with him, or given
so many gifts to him. At the best of times
he is a proud man; now you have pushed him far
deeper into his vanity and pride.

By god, let us have done with him –
whether he goes or stays! He'll fight again
when the time comes, whenever his blood is up
or the god rouses him. As for ourselves,
let everyone now do as I advise
and go to rest. Your hearts have been refreshed
with bread and wine, the pith and nerve of men.
When the fair Dawn with fingertips of rose
makes heaven bright, deploy your men and horses
before the ships at once, and cheer them on,
and take your place, yourself, in the front line
to join the battle.'

              All gave their assent
in admiration of Diomedes,
breaker of horses. When they had spilt their wine
they all dispersed, each man to his own hut,
and lying down they took the gift of sleep.

BOOK X

NIGHT IN THE CAMP: A FORAY

THEY slept then, all the rest, along the shipways,
captains of Achaea, overcome
nightlong by slumber; but their high commander,
Agamemnon, lay beyond sweet sleep
and cast about in tumult of the mind.
As when the lord of fair-haired Hera flashes,
bringing on giant storms of rain or hail
or wintry blizzard, sifting on grey fields –
or the wide jaws of drear and bitter war –
so thick and fast the groans of Agamemnon
came from his heart's core, and his very entrails
shook with groaning. Ai! When he looked out
in wonder and dismay upon the plain
where fires burned, a myriad, before Troy,
and heard flute-sounds and pipes, nocturnal hum
of men encamped there; when he looked again
at his Achaeans and their ships, before
high Zeus he tore his hair out by the roots
and groaned, groaned from the well of his great heart.
But this expedient came into his mind:
to visit Nestor, first of all, and see
what plan if any could be formed with him –
some well-wrought plan that might avoid the worst
for the Danaans. And, rising,
he pulled his tunic on over his ribs
and tied his smooth feet into good rawhide sandals,
took a great tawny lionskin for mantle,
dangling to his heels, and gripped a spear.

Now Menelaus, like his brother, shaken,
lay unsleeping, open-eyed, foreboding
anguish for the Argives, who had come
for his sake many a long sea mile to Troy
to wage the daring war. He rose and cloaked
his broad back with a spotted leopardskin,
picked up a bronze-rimmed helmet for his head,
and took a long spear in his fist, to go
arouse his brother, lord of all the Argives,
whom as a god the common folk revered.

He found him buckling on his handsome baldric
close to the ship-stern, and he turned in joy
to see Menelaus come.
                         Then Menelaus,
lord of the warcry, said: 'Why under arms,
dear brother? Will you call for a volunteer
to look the Trojans over? Hardly one
will take that duty on, I fear: alone
to circle and scout the dangerous enemy
in the starry night. It will take nerve to do it.'

   Agamemnon answered: 'You and I
must have some plan of action, Menelaus,
and a good one, too – some plan to keep the troops
and ships from ruin. Zeus's mood has changed;
he cares for Hector's offerings more than ours.
In my lifetime I have not seen or heard
of one man doing in a day's action
what Hector did to the Achaean army –
one man, son of neither god nor goddess,
in one day's action – but for years to come
that havoc will be felt among the Argives.
Go now, wake Idomeneus and Aias.
Go on the run along the ships, and I
will turn out Nestor, if he'll come to join us
at the first sentry-post and give commands.
He is the one they should most willingly
obey: his own son heads a company
with Idomeneus' lieutenant, Meriones.
We put the sentries mainly in their charge.'

   Said Menelaus in reply: 'But how
do you intend this order? Am I to stay
with those two, waiting till you come,
or track you on the run, after I tell them?'

   The Lord Marshal Agamemnon answered:
'Stay in their company. We might not meet,
coming and going: there are many paths
through the encampment. When you go, speak out,
tell them to rouse themselves, but courteously,
giving each man his patronymic and
his rank; and do not feel it is beneath you.
We must do service, too. That is the way
the Lord Zeus burdened us when we were born.'

   With these words, making clear what he commanded,
he sent his brother off, while he himself

went on toward Nestor. Close to his hut and ship
he found him in a bed of fleece. Nearby
his glinting arms were lying: a round shield,
two lances, and a helmet burnished bright.
There lay his many-faceted kilt or loin-guard,
girded on when the old man armed for war
to take his soldiers forward, undeterred
by doleful age.

            He heaved up on his elbow,
lifting his head, and peering in the dark,
he asked: 'Who are you, going about alone
amid the host by night when others sleep?
Looking for some stray mule or some companion?
Speak: don't stand there silent; what do you want?'
    Then the Lord Marshal Agamemnon answered:
'Nestor, son of Neleus, pride of Achaeans,
know me for Agamemnon, son of Atreus,
plunged by Zeus into the worst trouble
a man could know, for as long as I draw breath,
as long as my own legs will carry me.
I roam this way because no sleep will come
to settle on my eyes; the war stays with me
and what the army suffers. How I fear
for our Achaeans! Quietude of heart
I have none: fever of dread is in my brain,
my heart leaps from my ribs, my knees give way.
If you will act – and even you are sleepless –
let us inspect the sentries and make sure
they are not drugged by weariness,
not lying asleep, their duty all forgotten.
Hard enemies are encamped nearby. We cannot
say for sure they'll not attack by night.'
    Earl Nestor of Gerenia answered: 'Lord
Marshal of the army, Agamemnon,
Zeus the Profound will not achieve for Hector
all that the man imagines now, or hopes for.
I think he, too, will have his difficulties,
and more, if ever Achilles drops his anger.
But I will come with you, and gladly. Why not
awaken others to join us – Diomedes,
who is a wonder with a spear, Odysseus, and
Aias, the fast one, and the son of Phyleus?
Someone might go as well and waken Aias,
the tall one, and Idomeneus – their ships

are not so near, any of them. Moreover,
dear and respected as your brother is,
I have hard words for him. You may resent it;
I will not hide it: see the way he sleeps
and leaves the toil and worry to you alone!
He should be up and asking help of all
our noblest, now the inexorable need
has come upon us.'

               The Lord Marshal said:
'Sir, I should say, accuse him another time.
He often does go easy and holds off,
not out of laziness or lightness of mind
but following my lead, deferring to me.
This time, though, he was the first to rise,
and came to me. I sent him off to summon
the very men you name. Let us go on,
we'll come across them at the sentry-post
outside the gates. All were to gather there.'

  Earl Nestor of Gerenia replied:
'No Argive then can take it ill; no one
will disregard him when he calls to action.'

  With this he pulled his tunic to his waist,
tied his smooth feet into good rawhide sandals,
and gathered round him with a brooch
his great red double mantle, lined with fleece.
He picked a tough spear capped with whetted bronze
and made his way along the Achaean ships.
Coming first on Odysseus, peer of Zeus
in stratagems, he gave a call to wake him.

  Clear in the sleeper's shrouded mind it rang
and he burst startled from his hut to ask:
'Why are you out wandering through the army,
you alone, in the starry night? What brings you?'

  Earl Nestor of Gerenia replied:
'Son of Laertes and the gods of old,
Odysseus, master mariner and soldier,
do not be vexed at this. The Achaeans' peril
warrants it. Now, come along with us,
and we shall find another man to waken –
someone fit to advise retreat or war.'

  The great tactician stepped inside and picked
a painted shield to hang from his broad shoulders,
then he went after them. The next in line
was Diomedes, and outside his hut

they found him with his gear of war. Around him
his men were sleeping, pillowed on their shields,
with spears driven upright, butt-spikes in the ground:
point after point of bronze reflecting light
into the distance, like a glare of lightning
flung by Father Zeus. But the hero slept,
a bull's hide spread beneath him, and a bright
unfolded rug beneath his head.

                          Beside him
Nestor of Gerenia took his stand
and jogged him with his foot, then lectured him:
'Up, get up, Diomedes! Will you snore
the whole night through? Do you not know the Trojans
have taken up positions near the ships
where the beach rises – only a stone's throw off?'

   At this the hero, starting up from sleep,
gave back a rough reply: 'Hard as a knife
is what you are, old man. By night and day
you never rest. Are there no younger men
who might go round about to wake the captains
one by one? Can no one hold you down?'

   Then Nestor said: 'No doubt of it, dear lad,
there's reason in what you say. I have indeed
able young sons and soldiers, many of them,
any of whom could go and bear the summons.
Terrible pressure is upon us, though;
the issue teeters on a razor's edge
for all Achaeans – whether we live or perish.
Go and rouse Meges, rouse Aias the runner,
if as a younger man you'd spare my age.'

   Diomedes took for full-length cape the skin
of a great tawny lion, picked a spear,
and ran to rouse the others and conduct them.
Filing out among the sentries, then,
they found that not one captain was asleep;
each man sat up, all wakeful, under arms.
As shepherd-dogs keep bristling watch, their ears
pricked up at the approach of a wild beast
roaming down hills through woodland, toward the fold;
they hear an outcry, far away, of men
and watchdogs, and their rest is at an end:
so for these sentries rest had been dispelled
as they kept watch on that bad night, forever
facing the plain, peering when they could catch

a sound of Trojans moving.

                            And old Nestor,
in his relief at seeing them, said heartily:
'That is the way to keep your watch, dear lads,
sleep must not capture one of you, or all
may well give cause for gloating to the enemy.'

   He crossed the moat then, and the peers who came
to attend the council followed him,
as did Meriones and Nestor's son,
whom they had asked to join them. Once across,
they sat down in the clear, an open space
not littered with dead bodies – the same place
where Hector in his power had turned back
from slaughtering Argives, when the night came down
and shrouded all. Here, then, they sat and talked,
and first to speak was Nestor.

                            'Friends,' he said,
'is there no man who trusts his own brave heart
enough to make a foray on the Trojans,
killing some isolated guard, perhaps,
or picking up information – overhearing
plans they exchange among themselves? Have they
a mind to stay afield, here by the ships,
or to re-enter Troy, since they defeated us?
A man might learn these things and get away
unhurt to join us; and his feat would be
renowned among all people under heaven.
A handsome prize will be awarded him:
every commander of a ship division
gives him a black ewe, with a suckling lamb –
no token of honour like it. Afterward
he can attend all feasts and drinking parties.'

   Now at this challenge everyone grew still,
but Diomedes in their midst spoke out:
'Nestor, pride and excitement urge me on
to make a foray into the enemy camp
so close at hand here. If some other soldier
goes along, it will be better, though –
more warmth to it. Two men can make a team:
one will catch on quicker than the other
when there's a chance of bringing something off,
while one man's eyes and wit may move more slowly.'

   Volunteers aplenty desired to go
with Diomedes: Aias the Tall; Short Aias;

Meriones, and the eager son of Nestor;
the spearman, Menelaus. Then Odysseus,
that rugged man, wished, too, to pierce the lines,
bold for adventure, as he always was.

Now the Lord Marshal Agamemnon said:
'Diomedes, my own right arm, you name
your own companion; take the one you want,
the best of those whose hands are up. You have
plenty to choose from. No damned bashfulness
that might incline you to pass by the strongest
and take a lesser man, through deference
to birth or to rank higher than your own.'

He said this, fearing for his red-haired brother,
Menelaus.

                    But Diomedes said:
'If this is a command, and I may choose,
could I pass by that kingly man, Odysseus?
Shrewd as he is, and cool and brave, beyond
all others in rough work. Pallas Athena
loves that man. If he were at my side
we'd go through fire and come back,
the two of us. No man knows war as he does.'

Rejoined the Lord Odysseus: 'Diomedes,
no good flattering me, or carping, either –
not before men who know me through and through.
We should be on our way. How the night passes!
Dawn is near: high stars have all gone down.
Two thirds of night are gone; one third is left us.'

Then both men buckled on grim gear of war.
Diomedes was given by Thrasymedes
a two-edged sword – for his own was at the ship –
and a shield, too. Upon his head he pulled
a bull's-hide helmet with no ridge or plume,
a so-called 'cut down' made to guard the skulls
of rugged men-at-arms. Meriones
handed Odysseus his bow and quiver,
gave him a two-edged sword, and fitted on
a helmet that was first a cap of hide
with bands of leather criss-crossed, and on these
a boar's white teeth were thickly set, disposed
with cunning on all sides. A felt lining
padded the cap. This helm Autolycus
brought in the old days out of Eleon,
where he had made a breach in the palace wall

of Amyntor, the son of Ormenus.
He gave it to Amphidamas the Cytheran,
Scandeia-bound; Amphidamas in return
for hospitality gave it to Molus,
and Molus handed it on to his own son,
Meriones, to wear in battle. Now
it capped Odysseus' head.

                      Grimly accoutred,
the two moved out into the darkness, leaving
all their peers behind. Off to the right
along their path, Pallas Athena sent
a heron gliding down the night. They could not
see it passing, but they heard its cry;
and heartened by that fisher bird, Odysseus
prayed:

      'O child of Zeus who bears the storm-cloud,
hear me. In hard hours ever at my side
you follow every move I make: tonight
befriend me most, Athena.
Before we two retire on the ships
let us bring off some feat to gall the Trojans.'

  In his turn Diomedes, lord of the war-cry,
prayed: 'O tireless one, hear me as well:
be with me, as with Tydeus once, my father,
when he advanced as messenger to Thebes
ahead of all Achaeans – left the Achaeans
on the Asopus river under arms.
His words to the Cadmeians were like honey,
but terrible were the actions he devised
as he withdrew, bright goddess, with your blessing.
Now in the same way bless me, guard me now.
For my part I shall offer at your altar
a virgin heifer, a yearling, never yoked,
her horns all sheathed in gold.'

                 These were their prayers,
and Pallas Athena, Zeus's daughter, heard them.
Falling silent after invoking her,
they made their way like lions through black night
toward kills and carnage, braving spears and blood.

  Neither were Trojan leaders permitted sleep
by Hector, but he called them all together,
all who were lords and captains of the Trojans,
to put his plan before them: 'Who volunteers
to undertake this mission and see it through

for a great prize? He will have satisfaction!
A chariot and two mettlesome fine horses,
best of those beside the Achaean ships,
for the man who dares to win fame for himself
by a night patrol along the ships, to learn
if they are guarded as before. It may be
the Achaeans were so battered by our charge
that now they talk of sailing, and are so weary
that now they have no will for a night watch.'

The listening Trojans all grew mute and still.
Among them there was one by the name of Dolon;
rich in gold, and rich in bronze, this man
was heir to the great herald called Eumedes,
and a good runner, puny though he seemed,
an only son, with five sisters.

                                    He spoke
before the Trojans in response to Hector:
'Hector, pride and excitement urge me on
to make this night-patrol close to the ships
for information. Only, lift up your staff
and swear that my reward will be that team
and brazen car that bear the son of Peleus.
For my part, I take oath not to be blind
on this patrol, or let you down. I'll make it
straight through all the camp until I reach the ship
of Agamemnon. There the Achaean captains
must be debating battle or retreat.'

Hector complied, held up his staff, and swore:
'May Zeus in thunder, consort of Hera, witness
this: no other Trojan rides that car
behind that team. I say that you will do so.
It is to be your glory.'

                                    So he swore
an oath to incite the man – and swore in vain.
At once the runner slung his curving bow
over his shoulders, and for cloak the skin
of a grey wolf. He took a cap of weasel,
picked up a javelin, and headed down
for the line of ships, leaving the Trojan camp –
but he would not return with news for Hector.
When he had left the troops and tethered horses,
trotting eagerly on the seaward path,
Odysseus caught sight of the man coming
and whispered to Diomedes:

'Who is this,
now headed toward us from the camp? A scout,
on night-patrol along the ships, or bent
on rifling some dead body – I can't say.
Let him just pass into open ground a little
and we can catch him from behind. If he outruns us,
once we are in between him and his base,
attack with a spear-throw, force him on the ships:
not to let him cut back to the town.'

    The two conversed in whispers, then lay still,
flattened among dead bodies off the path,
while the unwary man came running by.
But when he had passed them fifty yards or so –
a field's width, say, a team of mules could plough,
being faster at this work than oxen, dragging
a bolted ploughshare in a furrow – both
ran after him. And at the sound of feet
he stood stock-still, for in his heart he hoped
that at a nod from Hector fellow Trojans
were on their way to fetch him back. Now only
a spear-throw distant from him, maybe less,
he recognized the Achaean enemies
and took to his heels. The two veered after him.
As when two hounds, well-trained in tricks of game,
hang on behind a young buck or a hare
through wooded land, and the quarry races on
emitting shrieks of dread – so Diomedes
and Odysseus, raider of cities, chased their man
after they cut him off from his own army.
Seaward he fled, and now when he seemed headed
straight into the sentries' arms, Athena
set Diomedes raging not to give
some other lucky Achaean the first shot
by being slow to catch up.

                Poising his lance,
Diomedes managed a great burst of speed
and called out: 'Halt! – or else my spear goes through you!
Plunging death is coming at my hands!
You cannot get away!'

                In fact, he threw,
but missed deliberately: the spearhead passed
above the man's right shoulder and stuck fast
before him in the ground. In panic fear
the runner tripped and stopped, a chattering noise

came from his mouth, and he turned faint and pale.
The two men, panting, soon came up with him
to pin his arms.
            But now in tears he begged them:
'Take me alive! I can arrange a ransom!
Iron and bronze and gold I have at home,
and Father will not count the cost if only
he knows me safe amid the Achaean ships!'

    The shrewd captain, Odysseus, answered him:
'Courage, you need not feel your death so near.
Tell me this, though, and plainly: what has brought you
out of your camp and this way toward the ships
alone by night, when others take their rest?
Would you despoil some corpse among the dead,
or were you sent by Hector to find out
our dispositions at the ships – or did you
wish to find out, yourself?'
                        Dolon replied,
his legs shaking under him: 'Carried away,
I was, against my own good sense, by Hector.
He said Achilles' team would be my prize,
his chariot, too, all trimmed with bronze. He told me
to go through the black night, now swiftly passing,
and to approach our enemies – to learn
if guards are posted at the ships as usual
or if the Achaeans, punished at our hands,
are in accord to sail and, being far gone
in weariness, have no will for a night watch.'

    At this the great tactician smiled. He said:
'By heaven, quite a reward was in your grasp –
the car and horses owned by the great fighter,
Aeacus' grandson. That is a fractious team
for mortal men to master! Not for Achilles,
but he was born of an immortal mother.
Tell me this now, give me a plain answer:
Where is Hector?
Where did you leave him when you took this path?
His arms, where are they lying? Where are his horses?
How have the other Trojans planned their watches
and hours for sleep?'
                    Dolon again made answer:
'Hector is with his staff, holding a council
beside the funeral mound of the patriarch
Ilus, far from the battlefield. No watches

in your sense, sir, are being stood, no sentries
chosen to guard the camp. At every fire
the necessary number are awake
and keep one another vigilant. Detachments
of allies, though, are everywhere asleep
and leave the sentry duty to the Trojans.
Allies have no families near at hand.'
    The great tactician, Odysseus, said to him:
'And how are they encamped? Mixed in with Trojans
or separately? Tell me about each one;
I must know this.'
               Dolon replied: 'I'll tell you.
Nearest the sea are Carians and Paeones
with Leleges, Caucones, and Pelasgians.
Up the Scamander are the Lycians, Mysians,
Phrygian horsemen, and Maeonians –
but why do you question me on these details?
If you are bent on raiding a Trojan company,
yonder are Thracians just arrived, far out
on the left wing, apart from everyone.
Their king is Rhesus Eionides,
his horses the most royal I have seen,
whiter than snow and swift as the sea-wind.
His chariot is a masterwork in gold
and silver, and the armour, huge and golden,
brought by him here is marvellous to see,
like no war-gear of men but of immortals . . .
You'll take me to the ships now, will you not?
Or will you leave me here, bound hand and foot,
while you go forward, testing what I told you
for accuracy and advantage to yourselves?'
    Diomedes frowned and looked at him and said:
'As I see it, you need not hold this thought
of slipping through our hands, now you are in them,
accurate though your facts may be. Suppose
we let you go, or let you go for ransom?
Later, by god, you'll come down on the ships
to spy again, or to make open war!
Resign your life now at my hands.
You make no further trouble for the Argives.'
    Even as he spoke, the man leaned forward, reaching
to touch his chin, beseeching; but he brought
his sword-blade in a flash down on the nape
and severed the two tendons. In the dust

the head of the still crying man was muffled.
Now they pulled off his cap of weasel skin,
his grey-wolf jacket, javelin, and bow,
and Lord Odysseus held these trophies high
to Athena, Hope of Soldiers.

                He appealed to her:
'Joy in this armour, goddess, first on Olympus,
first of immortals in our invocation!
Give us more luck, send us against that Thracian
bivouac and horses!'

              And at this
he rid himself of Dolon's gear by lifting it
into a tamarisk tree. He bundled it
and made it easier to see by breaking
tamarisk shoots and twigs from underneath,
so he and Diomedes could not miss it
on their way back in the night now swiftly passing.
Onward they pressed now, braving spears and blood,
and came soon to the bivouac of Thracians
at the camp's edge. Here weary troops were sleeping,
armour beside them canted on the ground
in three well-ordered rows. The chariot-teams
were tethered, each one, near their charioteer,
and in the centre Rhesus slept. Beside him
snowy horses were tethered by the reins
that ran from the chariot-rail.

              Odysseus first
distinguished him and whispered, pointing him out
to Diomedes: 'There is the man; there are
the horses Dolon whom we killed described.
Come put your back in it, your heart: why stand here
in arms for nothing? Go untie the horses,
or let me do it, while you kill the men.'

   Grey-eyed Athena filled Diomedes' heart
with fury. Whirling left and right he struck,
and pitiable sounds came from the bodies
cleft by the sword's edge. Earth ran red with blood.
As on a flock of goats or sheep, unshepherded
and undefended, a baleful lion falls,
the son of Tydeus fell upon those Thracians
until he had killed twelve. And at his shoulder
Odysseus, adept at war, moved up
to drag out by the heels each man he killed,
thinking by this to save the beautiful horses

from shying at the bodies when they passed –
being unused to dead men yet.

                              At last
when Diomedes reached the Thracian king,
he took a thirteenth precious life away
as the man gasped in sleep, nightmare upon him.
Meanwhile patient Odysseus freed the horses,
hitching them together by the reins,
and drove them off. He used his bow to whack them,
missing the whip fixed in the painted chariot
ready to his hand. With a low whistle
he made Diomedes look – but Diomedes
waited, pondering what next to try
in the way of outrage. Would he lift the pole
and pilfer the king's chariot with his weapons,
or take the life of still more Thracian men?

    His heart distended at the thought, when near him
out of the night air turning, Athena stood
and said: 'No, put your mind on getting back
to your own camp, son of great-hearted Tydeus,
unless you choose to run for it, supposing
some other god may wake the Trojans now.'

    Diomedes respected the goddess' voice
and turned to mount the chariot. Odysseus
used his bow for whip, and off they went
to the ships of the Achaeans.

                              No blind watch
was kept by Apollo of the silver bow,
who saw Athena following Diomedes.
Irritated by her, he joined a company
of Trojans, and aroused Hippocoon,
a noble cousin of Rhesus. Out of sleep
the man awoke and saw the empty ground
where once fast teams had stood; he saw the soldiers
massacred and soaking in their blood,
and cried aloud at this, calling his friends.
Soon there were other cries, and a wild din
of troops who ran up, staring at the horrors
done in that sortie from the ships.

                              Now those
who did that work had reached, on their return,
the spot where they had killed Hector's observer.
Noble Odysseus here reined in the team
while Diomedes vaulted down to sweep

the bloody trophies into Odysseus' hands
and then remounted – and he whipped the horses
into a willing run.

                    Of all Achaeans
Nestor first heard the beat of distant hooves
and said: 'Friends, lords, and captains of the Argives,
do I imagine it or is it real?
A drumming of distant hooves is in my ears.
May it turn out, already, to be Odysseus
and rugged Diomedes – back again,
with no time lost and driving Trojan horses!
I have been fearful that they might be hurt
in the Trojan outcry!'

                              He had not yet finished
all he was going to say, when up they came
and set foot on the quiet ground. Their friends
with warm handgrips and greeting gave them welcome.

    Nestor, lord of Gerenia, put the question:
'Tell me, Odysseus, great in all men's eyes,
how did you take these horses? How slip by
into the Trojan camp? Or did some god
come down to meet you and bestow them on you,
horses like the white flames of the sun!
I join the fighting every day with Trojans,
never, I think, malingering at the ships,
old soldier that I am; but teams like these
I never saw or heard of. Well, some god
who crossed your path bestowed them, I suppose.
I know both men are dear to the cloud-herder
Zeus, and to his daughter, grey-eyed Athena.'

    Odysseus, the resourceful man, replied:
'O Nestor, son of Neleus, light of Achaeans,
a god might easily give still better horses,
gods being so much stronger than ourselves.
But these you ask about were new arrivals,
Thracians, excellency. Diomedes killed
their master and a dozen fellow officers.
A thirteenth man, a scout, abaft the ships
we executed: Hector and his peers
had sent him forward to observe the army.'

    Down through the moat he drove the horses now
and laughed a rumbling laugh. Along with him
the others crossed, exulting. When they reached
Diomedes' quarters, they tied up the horses

by their own well-cut reins before the trough
where the master's chariot-horses fed on grain.
Astern upon his ship, Odysseus hung
the bloodstained gear of Dolon –
pending a proper offering to Athena.
Wading into the sea, the men themselves
splashed at their coats of sweat – shins, nape, and thighs –
until the surf had washed it from their skin
and they were cool again. Then out they came
to take warm baths in polished tubs. Being bathed
and rubbed with olive oil, the two sat down
to take refreshment. From a full winebowl
they dipped sweet wine and poured it to Athena.

BOOK XI

PROWESS AND WOUNDS OF ACHAEANS

DAWN came up from the couch of her reclining,
leaving her lord Tithonus' brilliant side
with fresh light in her arms for gods and men,
and Zeus commanded Strife down to the beach-head –
hard-bitten goddess, bearing in her hands
the storm-cloud sign of war.

                        At the dead centre
upon Odysseus' black-tarred ship she paused –
in earshot of both wings, if a man shouted,
as far as Aias' quarters and Achilles'.
Confident of their powers, these had beached
their ships at the far right and the far left.
Now from Odysseus' lugger Strife gave tongue
to a shivering cry. It stirred Achaean hearts
to battle without rest; now warfare seemed
lovelier than return, lovelier than sailing
in the decked ships to their own native land.

    The son of Atreus cried out, 'Troops in arms!'
and clothed himself in armour of bright bronze.
Upon his legs he fitted beautiful greaves
with silver ankle-straps. Around his chest
he buckled on a cuirass, long ago
a pledge of friendship from the Lord Cinyras,
who heard his fame at Cyprus, on the eve
of the Achaean sailings against Troy.
To please the Achaean king he made this gift,
a cuirass with ten bands of dark enamel,
twelve of gold, twenty of tin. Dark blue
enamel serpents, three on either side,
arched toward the neck, like rainbows that Lord Zeus
will pose on cloud as presages to men.
Across his shoulder and chest he hung a sword
whose hilt bore shining golden studs, and bands
of silver glinted on the scabbard, hooked
to a gilt baldric. Next he took his shield,
a broad one and a work of art for battle,
circled ten times with bronze; the twenty studs
were pale tin round the rim, the central boss

dark blue enamel that a fire-eyed Gorgon's
horrifying maw enclosed, with Rout
and Terror flanking her. Silver the shield-strap
whereon a dark blue serpent twined – three heads,
put forth by one trunk, flexing every way.
Then Agamemnon fitted on his brow
a helmet double-ridged, with four white crests
of horsehair nodding savagely above it.
Last, two tough spears he took, with brazen spearheads
whetted sharp, and that clear bronze reflected
gleams of sunlight far into heaven. Athena
thundered overhead, and Hera thundered
honour in heaven to golden Mycenae's lord.

Now every captain told his charioteer,
'Dress on the moat, hold hard here!' and on foot
in battle-gear, with weapons, all these fighters
moved ahead. Into the sky of dawn
an irrepressible cry went up, as lines
of men preceded war-cars at the moat
and war-cars in support came just behind.
Now Zeus the son of Cronos roused an uproar
along this host, and sprinkled bloody dew
from highest heaven, being resolved that day
to crowd great warriors into the undergloom.

Across the moat, on rising ground, the Trojans
mustered around tall Hector, noble Polydamas,
Aeneas, whom they honoured as a god,
Antenor's three sons, Polybus, Agenor,
and young Acamas – godlike prince.
Hector moved forward with his round-faced shield.
As from night-clouds a baleful summer star
will blaze into the clear, then fade in cloud,
so Hector shone in front or became hidden
when he harangued the rear ranks – his whole form
in bronze aflash like lightning of Father Zeus.

Imagine at each end of a rich man's field
a line of reapers formed, who cut a swath
in barley or wheat, and spiky clumps of grain
are brought low by the scything: even so
those armies moved to cut each other down,
and neither Trojans nor Achaeans thought
of ruinous retreat. The line of battle
held them face to face, lunging like wolves,
and Strife who thrives on groaning

looked on that field in joy, for she alone
of goddesses or gods mixed in the fighting.
   The rest were absent now and were at ease
in great halls of their own, beautiful chambers
built for immortals on Olympus' ridges,
all being bitter against the dark storm-king
for decreeing this day's battle to the Trojans.
But their father ignored them. In his chair
withdrawn from all, he gloried, looking down
on wall and ship and metal flash of battle,
men slaying others, and the quiet slain.
While the sun rose and morning grew in splendour,
javelins were launched and soldiers fell
on both sides equally. But at the hour
a woodsman takes his lunch in a cool grove
of mountain pines, when he has grown arm-weary
chopping tall timber down, and, sick of labour,
longs for refreshment – at that height of noon
Danaans calling fiercely back and forth
broke the Trojan line. First Agamemnon
charged and killed a Trojan chief, Bienor,
and Oileus, his charioteer: this man
dismounted to face him, aye! but only met
a spear-thrust square between the eyes, unchecked
by his bronze helmet-rim. Through bronze and bone
the spearhead broke into the brain within
and left it spattered. Down he went. And Marshal
Agamemnon abandoned Bienor and Oileus
with glistening bare chests when he had stripped them.
Onward he went to kill two sons of Priam,
Isus and Antiphus, one bastard stripling,
one in the royal line – both brothers riding
a single chariot. Isus held the reins
with Antiphus, the gently bred, beside him.
These two one day, while they were tending flocks
in Ida's vales, Achilles took and bound
with willow shoots, but later freed for ransom.
Now the Lord of the Great Plains, Agamemnon,
hit one with a spear-cast in the chest
above the nipple; the other, Antiphus,
he struck with his long sword beside the ear,
toppling him from his car. He bent to take
their arms and knew them: he had seen them once
in the encampment by the ships, that day

Achilles brought them down the mountainside.
A lion, discovering a forest bed,
and picking up in his great fangs the fawns
of a swift doe, will shake and break their backs
and rend their tender lives away with ease,
while she is powerless to help, though near,
but feels a dreadful trembling come upon her;
bolting the spot, she leaps through underbrush
at full stretch, drenched in sweat, before the onset
of the strong beast of prey. Just so, not one
among the Trojans could prevent those two
from being destroyed: the rest, too, turned and ran.
Next came Peisander and Hippolochus,
sons of Antimachus. Expecting gold
and gifts from Alexandrus, luxuries,
Antimachus had harangued against returning
Helen to Menelaus. Now his sons
were caught by Agamemnon. Both were driving
a single chariot, when the shining reins
ran out of their limp hands, and panic shook them:
Agamemnon, bounding like a lion,
faced them.

    But they begged him from the car:
'O son of Atreus, take us alive! Be sure
you shall have fitting ransom! Treasures lie
by hundreds in Antimachus' great hall,
things made of bronze and gold and hard-wrought iron.
Our father would not count the cost in these,
if he could know we are still alive
amid the Achaean ships!'

      So they appealed to him
in tears, and begged for mercy from the king,
but heard a voice beyond appeal: 'Ah, you are
Antimachus' sons? On Troy's assembly ground
when Menelaus went there with Odysseus
to make our argument, Antimachus
held out for killing both men then and there
and no safe-conduct back to the Achaeans.
That is the infamy you'll pay for now!'
 With this he hit Peisander in the chest
with a spear-thrust that threw him from the chariot
and smashed him on his back. Hippolochus leapt,
but Agamemnon caught him on the ground
with one sword-cut, then slashed his arms away

and sent him rolling out amid the mêlée
like a round mortar-stone. He left them there.
And now, wherever Trojans in the mass
were thrown most into confusion, there he charged,
and soldiers of Achaea ran along
behind him. Infantry killed infantry
in forced retreat,, and chariot-fighters killed
chariot-fighters. Dust rose underfoot
as thudding hooves of horses shook the plain
and men plied deadly bronze. King Agamemnon,
calling the Argives in the chariot's wake,
pressed on, slaughtering. As a fire catches
in parching brushwood without trees, and wind
this way and that in a whirl carries the blaze
to burn off crackling thickets to the root,
so under Agamemnon's whirling charge
the routed Trojans fell. Mettlesome teams
drew empty clattering cars down lanes of war,
bereft of drivers. These lay on the field,
more lovable to kites than to their wives.
But Zeus mysteriously guided Hector
out of the spears and dust, out of the slaughter,
out of the blood and tumult – while Atreides
led the chase and cheered the Danaans on.
Past the old tomb of Ilus in mid-plain
the Trojans streamed, and past the wild fig-tree,
fighting to reach the city; and Agamemnon
followed with battle-cries, attacking ever,
bloodying his inexorable hands.
At last they reached the West Gate and the oak
and halted there, awaiting one another,
as those behind in mid-plain struggled on
like cows a lion terrifies at dusk
into a stampede. One cow at a time
will see breathtaking death: clamped on her neck
with powerful fangs, the lion crunches her
to make his kill, then gulps her blood and guts.
Even so in pursuit was Agamemnon,
forever killing laggards as they fled.
Dozens fell, thrown head first from the chariots,
or on their backs, as with his spear he ran
around them and ahead.

                Now, in the end,
when he was near the city and the wall,

to earth from heaven the father of gods and men
descended and sat down on Ida's crests
amid her springs, bearing his jagged lightning.

He made Iris of golden wings his herald,
saying: 'Away with you who walk the wind,
tell this to Hector: while he still can see
Lord Marshal Agamemnon in the forefront,
devastating the ranks, let him retire
and call on other troops to fight, to bear
the brunt of battle with his enemies.
But when spear-cast or bowshot hits the man
so that he mounts his chariot again,
at that point I give Hector power of massacre
down to the deep-sea ships of the Achaeans,
till the sun dips and starry darkness comes.'

Iris who walks on the swift wind obeyed him,
running down Ida's hills to Ilium.

There godlike Hector, son of Priam, stood
amid the horses and the welded cars,
and swooping down like wind Iris addressed him.
'Son of Priam, Hector, great in craft
of battle, Zeus commissioned me to tell you:
while you can see Lord Marshal Agamemnon
in the forefront, devastating the ranks,
you must retire, and call on other troops
to bear the brunt of battle with your enemies.
But when the man is hit, by spear or bowshot,
so that he takes to his chariot again,
at that point Zeus will give you power of massacre
as far as the deep-sea ships of the Achaeans,
till the sun dips and starry darkness comes.'

When she had said this, Iris veered away,
and from his chariot Hector vaulted down,
shaking his whetted spears, making the rounds
to put fight into Trojans everywhere
and rouse a bloody combat. Now they turned
and held a line again against Achaeans,
whom on their side new companies reinforced.
They closed up ranks for action hand to hand
and Agamemnon strove to outstrip them all.

Heaven-dwelling Muses of Olympus,
tell me who first, among allies or Trojans,
braved Agamemnon?

                          It was young Iphidamas,

Antenor's brawny and athletic son,
who had been reared in Thrace, that fertile country,
billowy grassland, nourisher of flocks.
Cisseus, father of Theano, his mother,
brought up the child, and when he reached the stage
of promising manhood tried to hold him there,
betrothing to him a daughter. But he left
his bridal chamber for the Achaean war
when the word came. Twelve ships put out with him,
and these he duly beached at Percote,
making his way to Ilium on foot.
Now it was he who tackled Agamemnon.
When they came near each other, Agamemnon
thrust but missed as the haft turned in his hand.
Iphidamas' point went home below the cuirass
hard on the belt. He put his weight on it
with heavy thews, leaning after the blow,
but could not pierce the armoured loin-guard. Rather,
his point was turned, like lead on silver bent.
The Lord of the Great Plains now took hold and drew
the weapon toward him, raging, lionlike,
wrenching it from the Trojan's hands; then struck him
with a sword-cut across the neck and killed him.
Down he dropped into the sleep of bronze.
Sad that he fought for the townsmen of his bride
and died abroad before he could enjoy her,
lavish though he had been for her: he gave
one hundred beeves, and promised a thousand head
of sheep and goats, for myriads grazed his land.
Now Agamemnon stripped his corpse and bore
amid the Achaean host his beautiful armour.

   Coon saw him: Coon, a notable fighter,
eldest son of Antenor; and cruel grief
clouded his eyes at the downfall of his brother.
Taking Agamemnon on the flank
he hit his arm below the elbow: straight
through skin and tendon passed the bright spearpoint.
Now the Lord Marshal Agamemnon shuddered –
not that he quit the battle, not at all,
but swung on Coon with gale-hardened spear –
the man by now furiously pulling his brother,
Iphidamas, by the foot, calling his peers.
But as he pulled the corpse to the Trojan side
Agamemnon sent home his polished spear

and mortally wounded him under his shield.
He moved in to behead him, and the head
rolled on Iphidamas. Thus Antenor's sons
had met their destiny at Atreides' hands,
entering the gloom of Death.

        And still the victor
roamed back and forth along the living ranks
with spear and sword attacking, or with stones,
as long as hot blood gushed from his wound. But when
his blood no longer flowed, and the gash dried,
then rays of pain lacerated Agamemnon.
Comparable to the throes
a writhing woman suffers in hard labour
sent by the goddesses of Travail, Hera's
daughters, Twisters, mistresses of pangs,
the anguish throbbed in Agamemnon now.
 Mounting his chariot, he told the driver:
'Make for the ships!' – and sore at heart he was,
but raised a piercing cry to the Danaans:

 'Friends, nobles, captains of Argives, now
the fight is yours, to beat the tide of battle
back from our ships – for Zeus
who views the wide world would not give me leave
to battle against Trojans all this day.'
 His driver whipped the beautiful chariot-horses
back to the ships, and willingly they ran
with foaming chests, and dust coating their bellies,
to bear the wounded king out of the battle.
 Hector had kept his eyes on this departure
and gave a shout to Trojans and Lycians:
'Trojans, Lycians, and Dardan spears,
remember valour, friends, and fight like men.
Their champion has left the field! Oh, here,
here is my great chance, granted me by Zeus!
Now forward with your teams into the centre
and win the highest prize of all!'

          He stirred them,
rallying each man's courage. As a hunter
would send his hounds against a lion or boar
so Hector sent his Trojans headlong in
against the Achaeans: Hector, Priam's son,
hard as the war-god – now in pride and zeal
this hunter led his fighters on. He fell
on the battle-line like a high-screaming squall

that blows down on the purple open sea!
And who were the adversaries that he killed
when Zeus accorded him this rush of glory?
Asaeus first, Autonous and Opites,
Dolops Clytides, Opheltius, Agelaus,
Aesymnus, Orus, rugged Hipponous –
these leaders of Danaans he destroyed,
then turned on the rank and file. A lashing gale
out of the west will rift high snowy clouds
the south wind piled, as big seas rise and roll
with foam and spindrift from the whistling wind:
so were Achaean masses rent by Hector.

   Ruin was near, irreparable defeat,
Achaeans all but driven on the ships,
had not Odysseus called to Diomedes:
'Son of great Tydeus, what has come over us?
Have we lost all our power of attack?
Come here and stand with me, old horse. Dishonour
lies ahead if Hector fires the ships.'

   Diomedes answered him: 'I'll stand with you
and take what comes, by heaven! Only small
good it will do us! Lord Zeus, master of cloud,
wills them the upper hand, and not ourselves.'

   At this he knocked Thymbraeus from his chariot
with a direct hit on the left breast. Odysseus
killed Molion, the squire to that lord.
From these who were out of action, they turned round
against the pursuing pack – you would have said
two boars that turned on hounds – and charging back
did slaughter among Trojans. Thus the Achaeans
had some relief, a respite, as they yielded
before magnificent Hector. Next, the two
destroyed a Trojan pair in their war-car –
sons of Merops Percosius, clairvoyant
beyond all men, who had denied his sons
permission to join man-wasting war. But they
paid him no heed: dark death-spirits led them on;
and now the incomparable spearman Diomedes
ripped them out of life and took their gear.
Hippodamas besides Hypeirochus
went down before Odysseus, who stripped them.
For a short time, downgazing out of Ida,
Zeus kept the battle doubtful, tense and even,
as each side made its kills.

Now Diomedes
fighting Agastrophus, a son of Paeon,
gave him a hip-wound, but the warrior's chariot
was not at hand to save him – a bad error;
his driver held it far away. On foot
Agastrophus went limping through the fight
until he perished.

           Looking across at this,
Hector attacked the Achaeans with a yell
while Trojan companies fell in behind.
  Diomedes shivered as he watched him come
and turning said to Odysseus beside him:
'We are the ones this wave is heading for –
a black wave, too; here is Hector in his power.
Come, let's brace for it and defend ourselves.'

  He whirled and cast, and the long spear trailed swift shadow
straight to the mark he aimed for, the helm-crest;
but it rebounded, clanging, bronze from bronze,
and never reached or broke his handsome skin:
the ridged and triple-welded helm
Apollo gave him was impervious.
But Hector swerved in shock and, running wide,
rejoined his men. Then fallen on his knees
he leaned on his great hand, and a black swoon
veiled his eyes. While Diomedes went
a long way down the line, tracking his weapon
to where it lay, Hector got back his breath
and, once more mounted on his chariot,
he rode among the other cars and shunned
the shadow of death.

           Diomedes shook his spear
and called: 'You dodged away from death again,
you dog, and a close thing, too; Phoebus Apollo
pulled you through. He it must be you pray to
whenever you go near the jolt of spears!
One more throw, by heaven, will finish you,
if there is any god on my side, too.
Now I'll face any others I can find.'

  He leaned over to strip the son of Paeon,
and then the lord of Helen, Alexandrus,
resting against the gravestone on the mound
of Ilus, patriarch son of Dardanus,
bent his bow at the Lord Marshal Diomedes.
Imagine Diomedes taking the dead man's

cuirass from his ribs, and from his shoulders
the shield all glimmering, and his heavy helm,
even as the adversary drew his bow
to the grip and shot – and not in vain the arrow
sprang from his fist, but through the right foot bonework
of Diomedes into the earth it punched.

Alexandrus jumped out of ambush laughing
and called to him vaunting: 'Hit you are, and hard!
No wasted shot, that! But I should have hit you
under the ribs and brought you down.
That would relieve the Trojans from their ordeal.
You spook them as a lion does bleating goats.'

Undaunted, Diomedes answered:
'You bow-and-arrow boy, you curly-head,
all eyes for little girls, I wish you'd try me
face to face with pike and shield: your archery
would do you no good then. You brag this way
for having scratched my instep. It is nothing,
a woman's shot, or a silly little boy's.
A weak-kneed half-wit's arrow has no point!
By heaven, arrows of mine are whetted differently.
One that grazes a man will stretch him dead.
His woman's cheeks are torn with grief,
his children orphaned. He must soak the earth
and rot, with kites for company, not women!'

As he said this, Odysseus moved over
and stood in front of him. Then, sitting back,
Diomedes pulled the arrow from his foot
and dragged agony with it through his flesh.
He climbed his chariot and told his driver,
'Make for the ships!' And he was grieved at heart.

Odysseus now, the good spear, stood alone;
no Argive held that ground with him, as fear
had gripped them all. And grimly vexed,
he spoke to his own valour: 'Here is trouble.
What will become of me? A black day, this,
if I show fear and run before this crowd;
but worse if I am captured, being alone.
Zeus routed all the rest of the Danaans.
But why this bandying inward words, my friend?
Cowards are men who leave the front in war.
The man who will be worth respect in battle
holds on, whether he's hit or hits another.'

During these meditations, on they came,

the lines of Trojan infantry, and broke
around and hemmed him in – hemmed in their peril.
As when around a wild boar lusty hunters
and hounds deploy, until the beast trots out
from heavy thicket, whetting his white tusks
against his lower jaws; the hounds go circling
in to attack, and under the hue and cry
a gnashing sound of tusks and teeth is heard;
even so now, around rugged Odysseus,
the Trojans ran. Deiopites was the first
Odysseus wounded, on the slope of shoulder,
making a spring with his sharp spear; and next
he hit Thoon and Ennomus and killed them;
then Chersidamas, who had vaulted down
out of his car, he caught square in the navel
under his bulging shield; the man fell hard
in dust and with his hand spread gripped the earth.
Leaving them there, he hit Hippasides
Charops, a brother of the rich man, Socus –
and Socus gallantly ran up to shield him,
taking a stand before the attacker, saying:

'Odysseus, great in all men's eyes, unwearied
master of guile and toil, today the sons
of Hippasus will be your claim to glory:
either you kill and strip such men as these
or die, hit by my spear.'

                    Even as he spoke,
he let fly at the round shield, and his weapon
pierced the shining surface, pierced the bright
elaborate cuirass with his weight behind it,
flaying Odysseus' ribs. Athena barred
all access to her hero's heart and lungs.

Odysseus knew the wound had not been mortal,
and yielding ground he said to Socus: 'Ah,
poor soldier, your own death-plunge into the dark
lies before you now: you crippled me
for any further fight today with Trojans,
but as for you, I say a bloody death,
a black nightmare of death, is close upon you;
my spear kills you. You'll give up the fight
to me, your soul to that strong driver, Death.'

This made the other turn as if to run,
but as he turned the spear crashed in his back
between the shoulders, driving through his chest,

and down he went with clanging gear.
                                          Odysseus
made his boast over the fallen: 'Son
of Hippasus, that fighting man and horseman,
death ran ahead to meet you: no escape.
Poor soldier, father and mother will not bend
to close your eyes in death, but carrion birds
will tear them out and clap their wings around you.
My own corpse will be fired by the Achaeans
if in fact I die.'
                    On this he drew
Socus' hard weapon from his flesh and through
his convex shield. After the extracted spearhead
blood welled up in streams and grieved his heart.
Elated when they saw Odysseus' blood
flow out, the Trojans yelled, converging on him.
Now he gave ground, backing away, and called
his own companions. Three tremendous shouts
he gave, as loud as a man's head could hold,
and each time he was heard by Menelaus,
who turned and said to Aias at his side:

'Son of Telamon and the gods of old,
Lord Aias of the army, a faint shout
has reached my ears – Odysseus' voice it is,
as though the man were in trouble, and great trouble,
with Trojans who had cut him off alone.
We must get through the mêlée; better save him.
I am afraid some hurt will come to him,
and loss irreparable to the Achaeans.'

At this he led the way, and Aias followed,
godlike, formidable, and before long
they found Odysseus: Trojans had closed round him
as tawny jackals from the hills will ring
an antlered deer, gone heavy with his wound.
After the hunter's arrow strikes, the deer
goes running clean away: he runs as long
as warm blood flows and knees can drive him on.
Then when at last the feathered arrow downs him,
carrion jackals in a shady grove
devour him. But now some power brings down
a ravenous lion, and the shrinking jackals
go off cowering: he must have their prey.
Just so around Odysseus, man of war
with versatile wits, the Trojans closed. But he

by stabbing out and feinting with his spear
averted death's hard hour for that day.
And now came Aias with his tower of shield
to stand beside him. This way and that the Trojans
shrank away, and soldierly Menelaus led
their quarry by the hand out of the fight
to where his driver brought his chariot up.
Now Aias, charging, brought down Doryclus,
a bastard son of Priam; then he wounded
Pandocus, Lysander, and Pyrasus,
Pylartes, too. As when a river in flood
from mountain snowfields reaches the flat land
whipped by a storm of rain, it sweeps away
hundreds of withered oaks, hundreds of pines,
and casts black tons of driftwood in the sea,
so Aias in his glory swept the field,
wrecking both chariots and men. But Hector
had no report of it, being in a fight
along Scamander bank on the left wing
amid great slaughter, where a battle-cry
indomitable had risen around Nestor
and soldierly Idomeneus. These Hector
faced in battle; he performed prodigies
in spearmanship and chariot-handling, making
havoc in the young men's ranks. And yet
the Achaeans might not yet have given him passage
had not the husband of Helen, Alexandrus,
put a stop to Machaon's gallantry
with one bowshot, an arrow triple-barbed,
in the right shoulder. And the grimmest Achaeans
feared for him, feared the enemy might take him
now that the tide of war had turned.

                                    Idomeneus
called over at once to Nestor: 'Son of Neleus,
glory of Achaeans, quick! Remount
your car and let Machaon come aboard,
and make your team race to the ships. A surgeon
is worth an army-full of other men
at cutting shafts out, dressing arrow wounds.'

Nestor, Gerenian lord of horse, complied,
regaining his own chariot as Machaon, son
of the healer Lord Asclepius, came aboard.
Nestor flicked his team, and willingly
they ran for their safe haven at the ships.

At Hector's side Cebriones made out
the mêlée's pattern: 'You and I,' he said,
'are fighting, Hector, on the outer edge
of a great deafening battle. Other Trojans
are in confusion, chariots and men.
Telamonian Aias flurries them.
I know him well: he is the one who bears
the wide shield round his shoulders. Why not guide
our horses toward him where the charioteers
and infantry are locked in deadly combat,
putting each other in the dust; their cries
are never still.'
        At this, he shook out reins
to his glossy team with blowing manes, and used
the cracking whip. And when they felt the lash,
they drew the nimble chariot briskly on
through Trojans and Achaeans, trampling shields
and bodies of the dead. The axle-tree
beneath was blood-bespattered; round the car
the rails were spattered; from the horses hooves
and from the wheel-rims blood flew up in spray.
Into the man-eating moil Hector now longed
to plunge and make a breach; he pressed the Achaeans,
never gave way an inch to any spear,
but ranged among the ranks of other fighters,
using his javelin, longsword, and big stones,
and shunning only Aias in the combat:
Zeus took it ill when he engaged his betters.
Now Father Zeus, benched high on Ida, moved
great Aias to retreat. He stood stock-still
and tossed his sevenfold shield over his shoulder,
dazed with dread. With half-closed eyes
he glared at the crowd, a wild thing brought to bay,
turning a little, shifting knee past knee.
So formidable in his fear he was –
like a dun lion from a stable yard
driven by hounds and farmhands: all night long
they watch and will not let him take his prey,
his chosen fat one. Prowling, craving meat,
he cannot make a breakthrough. Volleying javelins
are launched against him by strong arms, firebrands
bring him to heel, for all his great élan,
and heartsick he retreats at dawn. So Aias,
heartsick before the Trojans, foot by foot

retreated grudgingly for the ships' sake.
An ass that plods along a field will be
too much for attacking boys; on his dumb back
stick after stick may break; still he will enter
standing grain and crop it, even as boys
are beating him – so puny is their strength,
and barely will they drive him from the field
when he is gorged on grain. In the same way
the confident Trojans and their best allies
continuously made the son of Telamon
their target, with direct hits on his shield.
Remembering his power in attack,
sometimes he turned at bay and held the advance
of Trojan squadrons, then resumed retreat,
but kept them from the straight path to the ships
while he himself, between Achaeans and Trojans,
forged his way. Spears thrown by brawny hands
at times would stick in his great shield; the rest
stood fixed midway in earth before they reached
the white flesh they were famished for.

         Eurypylus,
Euaemon's great son, realized his danger,
seeing him hard pressed by the missile hail,
and moved over beside him. Stabbing out
with his bright spear he hit Phausius' son,
Apisaon, a marshal, in the liver
under his midriff and unstrung his knees,
then bent to take the armour from his shoulders.
Godlike Alexandrus had seen him come,
now saw him strip Apisaon: in all haste
he drew his bow upon Eurypylus
and hit him in the right thigh with an arrow,
splintering the shaft, weighting the leg.

 Retiring now to bleed among his men
and shun black death, Eurypylus cried sharply:
'Friends, lords and nobles of the Argives, halt!
turn round and try to keep off death's hard hour
from Aias; he is driven back by spears.
I would not say for sure he will survive
the grinding war! Go form a wedge for Aias,
the son of Telamon!'

       So, with his leg wound,
Eurypylus begged them. And they formed the wedge
for Aias, moving near, shoulder to shoulder,

leaning shield on shield, with spears held high,
while Aias gave way toward them. When he joined them
he turned and took his stand.
                              That way they fought
as the very body of fire strives and bends,
while out of battle Nelean horses foaming
carried Nestor, carried Machaon. And
Achilles the great runner saw Machaon!

He had been standing on his ship's high stern
to view the moil of war, over the rampart,
heart-rending struggle and pursuit. But now
he called to Patroclus from the after-deck,
and hearing in the hut, the other came,
rugged, it seemed, as Ares – though his doom
was fixed that instant.
                         He it was spoke first:
'Why call me out, Achilles? How can I help you?'

And the great runner answered: 'Son of Menoetius,
dear to my heart, the Achaeans now will come
to beg and pray, I think, around my knees!
Inexorable need presses upon them.
Only go now, Patroclus, and ask Nestor
who is this wounded man he ferries back
out of the battle. All his gear behind
looks like the gear of Machaon –
but I could not get a good look at the man;
the chariot shot beyond me at full gallop.'

Doing as his companion willed, Patroclus
ran off along the Achaean huts and ships.
Now Nestor and the wounded man, arriving
at Nestor's hut, dismounted on the turf,
and Eurymedon, the squire, unhitched the team.
Standing against the sea-breeze on the beach
they cooled off, letting sweat-soaked chitons dry,
then entering Nestor's hut they took their seats
in armchairs. Mulled drink was prepared for them
by softly braided Hecamede, Nestor's
prize from Achilles' plundering of Tenedos –
Arsinous' daughter. The Achaeans
had chosen her for Nestor, honouring excellence
in council. First the girl pushed up before them
a beautiful table with enamelled legs,
then she set out a basket all of bronze,
an onion to give relish to their wine,

pale yellow honey, sacred barley-meal,
beside a cup of wondrous beauty, brought
from Pylos by the old king: golden nails
it had for studding, and four handles on it,
each adorned by a pair of golden doves
who perched to drink, with double stems beneath.
Another man would strain to budge this cup
once full, clear of the table. But not Nestor:
old though he was, he lifted it with ease.
Now mixing Pramnian wine for them in this,
the servant like a goddess in demeanour
grated a goat's milk cheese over the wine
upon a brazen grater, and sifted in
white barley-meal. Her potion thus prepared,
she called on both to drink.
                                              Now the two men
drank long to rid themselves of burning thirst.
In their relief they were exchanging talk
when at the door Patroclus, like a god,
appeared and stood. Old Nestor left his chair
to take his hand, to lead him in and seat him.

But from the door Patroclus shook his head
and said: 'No time to take a chair, your grace:
I will not be persuaded: he that sent me
is worthy of respect and quick to anger,
and sent me here to learn who that man was
you brought in wounded. But I see myself
it is Machaon, marshal of troops. I'll bear
this word back to Achilles. Well you know
how dangerous the man can be, your grace!
In a flash he could accuse me without cause.'

Lord Nestor of Gerenia replied:
'How is this, that Achilles cares for any
Achaeans who are hit? He has no notion
of what distress has come upon the army.
Wounded and out of action, our best men
are lying by the ships: Lord Diomedes;
Odysseus, the great spearman; Agamemnon;
Eurypylus, hit by an arrow in the thigh;
and this man whom I brought just now from war,
disabled by an arrow from a bowstring.
Splendid Achilles pities no Danaans,
waiting – is he not – until the ships
on the sea-verge are fanned by billowing fire,

whether we Argives will or not, and we
ourselves are killed off one by one.

                                    'My strength is
not what it was, in my bent leg or arm.
If I were only young and had my powers
intact, as when the quarrel rose between
the Eleans and ourselves for cattle-raiding!
I killed Itymoneus, Hypeirochus' son,
a champion then in Elis, and drove home
his rustled cattle. Trying to protect them,
he met a javelin from my hand and fell,
his bumpkin herdsmen panicking around him.
Prizes out of the plain we drove together
in a great host: of cows there were fifty herds,
as many flocks of sheep and droves of swine
and roaming herds of goats: and chestnut horses —
one hundred and fifty tawny horses,
mares every one, many with suckling foals.
We drove them into Pylos, Neleus' land,
up to the town, at night. And Neleus' pride
was pleased that spoil so great had fallen to me,
a green hand at war. Loud in the dawnlight,
heralds announced that all men who had claims
on ancient Elis should present themselves,
and on their assembling, leading men of Pylos
made the apportionment — for there were many
to whom the Epeians were in debt. We suffered
wrongs in Pylos, being a scanty people.
Heracles in the years before had come
with depredation, and death upon our best.
Twelve, for example, were the sons of Neleus,
and I alone was left, the rest were killed.
These exploits puffed the Epeians up; they showed
their insolence devising crimes against us.
Now our old king sequestered for himself
a herd of oxen and a flock of sheep,
three hundred beasts with herdsmen — for in Elis
a great debt was his due: a four-horse team
of racing-horses and their chariot
that once would have contended in the games
and raced to win the tripod, but Augeias,
lord of Eleans, kept them, and sent home
the empty-handed, grieving charioteer.
In his long anger for these words and deeds

the old king now made choice
of plenty for himself, and to the people
gave all the rest to be distributed,
seeing to it that no man lacked his share.
We were proceeding with all this, and making
sacrifice around the town
when on the third day the Epeians came
in multitudes, with horses driven hard,
with them two boys, the Moliones, armed,
though still untrained in warfare.

                      'There's a city,
Thryoessa, on a beetling hill
above the Alpheius at the verge of Pylos.
This they besieged, in fury to pull it down,
and scoured the whole plain, but Athena bore
a warning for us, running from Olympus
by night, to take up arms, and she assembled
troops of Pylos keen to fight. Now Neleus
would not hear of my arming, hid my horses,
denied I had ever learned the arts of war!
Yet even so I made my mark among
our charioteers, foot-soldier though I was,
Athena so conducted that affray.
A stream called Minyeius joins the sea
near Arene. Horsemen of Pylos there
awaited the unearthly dawn, while infantry
flowed up to join us. Arming with all speed,
by noon we reached Alpheius' ancient waters,
making our offerings there, to Zeus all-powerful,
to Alpheius and to Poseidon, bulls,
a heifer to Athena, Hope of Soldiers.
Afterward we took our evening meal
along the column by companies, and slept
each man in his own gear beside the river.
Meanwhile the bold invading Epeians kept
the town besieged. They burned to pull it down,
but first had sight of Ares' handiwork!
For as the flaming sun rose on the land
we met them in battle, calling on Lord Zeus
and on Athena. Pylians and Epeians
contended. I was the first to kill a man
and take his horses – the spearman Mulius.
He was Augeias' son-in-law, his consort
russet-haired Agamede, she who knew

all medicinal herbs the wide world bears.
This man I hit with my bronze-bladed spear
as he came on, and he tumbled into the dust.
Then I mounted his war-car, and I stood
amid our forward fighters. The Epeians
shrank away, this way and that: they saw
their captain charioteer, splendid in battle,
fallen. And my hour had come: I drove
into them like a black storm-cloud and captured
fifty chariots. Two men bit the dust
alongside each, overpowered by my spear.
Then, too, I would have pillaged the two sons
of Actor and Moliones – but their true sire
who rules the wide sea and sets earth a-tremble
hid them in cloud and saved them from the war.
After that, Zeus gave power into the hands
of Pylians, and we pursued our enemy
through all the great plain, taking many lives,
amassing their fine armour, till we brought
our horses to the grainland, Buprasium,
Olenia Rock, and the hill called Alesius.
There, as Athena made our troops turn back,
I killed and left my last foe.
                            'The Achaeans
withdrew briskly and turned their horses' heads
toward Pylos. Among gods, they prayed to Zeus,
to Nestor among men.

                    'So was I then,
if that was I and not a dream. Not so
Achilles, who alone gains by his valour.
Ah, but I can prophesy his weeping
after his people perish!

                        'My dear fellow,
Menoetius made your duty doubly clear
when he sent you from Phthia to Agamemnon!
Standing inside, Odysseus and I
overheard him, every word, so clearly!
We had arrived at Peleus' great house
on our recruiting journey through Achaea,
and found the old soldier, Menoetius, there with you
at Achilles' side. Then Peleus, master of horses,
burned thigh-bones to Zeus, lord of the lightning,
in the enclosure of his court, and held
a cup of smooth gold, pouring dusky wine

on the burnt offerings. You two were carving,
right and left, the carcass of the ox,
when we two reached the entrance-way. Achilles
rose in surprise, and taking both our hands
required us to rest, then placed before us
all that a guest should have. We were refreshed
by food and drink, and thereupon I spoke,
inviting both to go with us. Most heartily
you wished to go. And now your fathers both
repeatedly enjoined your duties on you.
The old man, Peleus, urged his child, Achilles,
to do none but great feats, to be distinguished
above the rest. As for Menoetius,
the son of Actor, these were his words to you:
"My child, Achilles is a higher being
by his immortal blood; but you are older.
He is more powerful, but your part should be
to let him hear close reasoning and counsel,
even commands. He will be swayed by you
for his own good."

              'These were your father's words,
although you now forget them. Ah, but now,
late though it is, tell all this to Achilles,
hoping he may come round. Who knows what power
may help a plea from you to stir his heart!
There's sweetness in persuasion by a friend.
If in his own mind he is keeping clear
of an oracle: if her ladyship, his mother,
declared to him some prophecy from Zeus,
all right: then let him send you into battle!
Let the battalion of Myrmidons follow you!
Victory light for Danaans you may be!
And let him give you all his beautiful armour
to wear in battle. Taking you for him
the Trojans may retire from the field
and let the young Achaeans have a respite
exhausted as they are. War gives brief rest!
You and your soldiers, fresh against tired men,
might easily throw them back upon the town
away from our encampment and our ships.'

  At this, Patroclus' heart bounded within him
and he went running back along the shipways
towards Achilles. Just as he passed the ship
of great Odysseus, where the assembly ground

and place of justice were, and gods' altars,
there came Eurypylus, the wounded man,
Euaemon's noble son, struck by the arrow,
limping out of combat. Sultry sweat
ran down his shoulders and his face, dark blood
still trickled from his wound, but he limped on,
unshaken spirit.
                         Seeing him, Patroclus,
moved to compassion, said: 'Poor soldiers!
Captains, lords of Danaans, how you all
were fated here, across the sea from home,
to glut wild dogs in this rich realm of Troy!
But tell me this, Eurypylus, your grace,
are the Achaeans holding Hector still
or will they perish, downed by his spear?'
                                         Eurypylus
replied: 'Noble Patroclus, there will be
no longer any defensive line of Achaeans.
They will fall back on the black ships soon. Our best
in other combats lie now in the camp
with missile wounds or gashes made by spears
in Trojan hands. Enemy power grows.
As for myself, give me a hand here, take me
down to your ship and cut this shaft away
from my leg wound; then wash the black blood out
with warm water, and sift into the wound
that anodyne you learned of from Achilles –
a drug that, people say, the very best
of centaurs, Cheiron, taught him. We have surgeons,
Podaleirius and Machaon, but the one
I think is lying wounded in his hut,
himself in need of a healer, and the other
faces the Trojan charge, still in the plain.'
    The staunch son of Menoetius replied:
'How can this be? What action can we take,
Eurypylus? I am on my way to give
Achilles counsel from old Nestor of Gerenia,
lord of the western approaches to Achaea.
But not for that will I neglect or fail you,
badly hurt as you are.'
                         Supporting him
with one arm round him, under his chest, he led him
into the hut. A squire put oxhides out
on which he laid the wounded man, then took

his sheath-knife and laid open the man's thigh
to excise the biting arrow. With warm water
he washed the black blood flowing from the wound,
then rubbed between his hands into a powder
over the wound a bitter yarrow root,
that dulled all pangs of pain. Now the gash dried
as the blood and powder clotted.

BOOK XII

THE RAMPART BREACHED

AFTER this fashion
in his own hut Menoetius' gallant son
tended Eurypylus, the wounded man,
while Argives fought the Trojan mass attack
their moat no longer could contain – nor could
the rampart they had built to save the ships,
carrying the moat around it. To the gods
they gave no hecatombs that might have won them
to guard the wall as shield for the deep-sea craft
and plunder that it ringed. The immortal gods
had never willed it, and its time was brief.
While Hector lived and while Achilles raged,
and while Lord Priam's town lived on, unsacked,
so long the Achaeans' rampart stood. But after
the flower of Troy went down, with many Argives
fallen or bereft, when Priam's Troy
was plundered in the tenth year, and the Argives
shipped again for their dear homeland – then
Poseidon and Apollo joined to work
erosion of the wall by fury of rivers
borne in flood against it, all that flow
seaward from Ida: Rhesus, Heptaporus,
Caresus, Rhodius, Granicus, Aesepus,
Scamander's ancient stream, and Simois
round which so many shields and crested helms
had crashed in dust with men who were half gods.
These rivers were diverted at their mouths
and blent into one river by Apollo,
who sent that flood nine days against the rampart.
Zeus let his rain fall without pause, to bring
the wall more quickly under inshore water;
as for the god who shakes the islands, he
in person with his trident in his hands
led on the assault. Foundation logs and stones
the Achaeans toiled to lay he shunted seaward,
levelling all by the blue running sea.
In sand again he hid the long seashore
when he had washed the wall down, and he turned

the rivers to their old, fair watercourses.
Thus before long Poseidon and Apollo
settled this earthwork. Now, though, on both sides
tumult and combat raged around the wall
whose tower-beams rang from battering. The Argives
under Zeus's lash were beaten back
upon the long ships, all in fear of Hector,
master of rout that day. Aye, as before,
furious as a high wind when it strikes,
he wheeled and fought — boarlike, or like a lion
that rounds in mighty joy on dogs and men:
the hunters close ranks in a wall and face him
to make a broadside volley of javelins,
but his high heart will neither quail nor flee;
his own courage kills him; everywhere
he turns to test the ranks, and when he charges
all give way.
        So forward into the mêlée
Hector charged and turned and called his men
to cross the moat. But his own chariot-team
dared not, but on the very brink arrested,
whinnied and reared away in panic, seeing
the ditch could not be taken in a leap
or passed through easily. On either side
banks overhung it with stakes pointing inward,
sharp and long and close together, set
by the Achaeans as a ground defence
against their dire attackers. No beast drawing
a nimble car could easily descend there,
and men on foot thought hard if they could pass.
    At this, Polydamas at Hector's elbow
said: 'Hector, and the rest of you, our captains,
captains of auxiliaries: we are fools
to drive our teams into the moat, so rough
it is to get across — the stakes inside
like fangs against us — and then comes the wall.
There is no chance at all with chariots
to get down in the place and fight — no room;
impaled there, I can see us now.

           'If Zeus
in thunder will make havoc of Achaeans,
if he is hot in the Trojans' cause,
by heaven, I wish this fight were over soon —
the Achaeans wiped out, distant far from Argos,

winning no glory!
                              'If they once re-form,
braced on the ships, and counter-attack, while we
are trapped here in the ditch, then I foresee
not even a messenger will reach the town;
no one escapes the Achaeans, once they rally.
Well, then, everyone do as I propose:
charioteers pull up at the moat's edge
while we ourselves in harness and on foot
follow Hector in closed ranks. The Achaeans
cannot hold, if now their ultimate
destruction is at hand.'

     Polydamas' counsel to avoid the risk
won Hector over, and he vaulted down
with weapons from his chariot. Other Trojans
stayed no longer huddled behind their teams
but, seeing that Hector had dismounted, each
commanded his charioteer to keep in line
outside the ditch, with a tight rein on his horses,
while fighting-men moved out ahead. They formed
five companies under leaders, each in column.
Those who deployed with Hector and Polydamas
were bravest and most numerous, grimly bent
on carrying battle to the long ships
when they had breached the wall. Cebriones
joined them, third in command, and in his place
as driver Hector left a weaker man.
Paris headed a second company
whose officers were Alcathous and Agenor.
A third was under Helenus and Deiphobus,
two of Priam's sons, and Asius
Hyrtacides, whose great roan horses brought him
from Arisbe and the Selleis river.
Over the fourth Aeneas held command,
Anchises' powerful son, whom Lord Antenor's
two sons joined: Archelochus and Acamas,
trained in every fighting skill. Sarpedon
held command of the allies; he chose
for officers Glaucus and Asteropaeus,
far and away the best men, he thought,
of the auxiliaries, after himself, who stood
high in the whole army.
                              Bull's-hide shields
being dressed in line, they rushed at the Danaans,

certain that these could not resist the charge
that swept now on the black ships. And all Trojans,
all allies, obeyed the battle plan
of cool Polydamas: all except Asius
Hyrtacides. He did not care to leave
his team and driver but, still mounted, rode
to attack the Achaean ships – the idiot,
he would not give his own hard fate the slip
or ride in glory from the beach-head back
to windy Ilium in his war-car.
Miserable death would shroud him, by the spear
of Idomeneus, Deucalion's noble son.
Asius drove to the left around the ships
to a place where the Achaeans were withdrawing
chariots and horses from the plain.
Here he swerved for the wall, and found the gates
of planking with great bolts as yet unshut;
men held them open to admit and save
stray fugitives from battle. Straight ahead
he drove his team, while after him his men
ran yelling – for they thought the Achaeans could not
hold but had to fall back on the ships.
All a delusion: at the entrance-way
they met two Lapith spearmen, champions,
Polypoetes, the son of Peirithous,
and Leonteus, tough as the war-god. These
outside the tall gates held their ground like oaks
that tower on high hills, enduring wind
and rain through all their days, with roots deep down,
tenacious of the earth. Like oaks indeed
the two stood fast and trusted their right arms,
their fighting power, against great Asius.
On came the Trojans toward the wall with shields
uplifted, with a long-drawn battle-cry
around Lord Asius, Iamenus, Orestes,
Adamas Asiades, Thoon, and Oenomaus.
    Until just now the Lapiths, the defenders,
had been inside the wall issuing orders
to Achaean troops to form around the ships,
but when they saw the Trojans charge, and when
a cry came from the Danaans in retreat,
they bounded through the gateway to give battle.
Think of two savage boars in a mountain-place
awaiting a loud rabble of dogs and men:

they swing their heads from side to side and rip
through underbrush, snapping the twigs off short,
with a sharp noise of gnashing tusks
until some hunter makes the kill. Just so,
the bright bronze breastplates clanged
as these two took their blows. Prodigiously
they fought, putting their trust in their own power
and in the marksmen on the wall above.
In fact, now from high places, in defence
of camp and ships and their own lives, the men
were pitching stones: and the stones showered to earth
like snow driven by a storm-wind thick and fast
in a murky veil swept over pastureland.
So missiles came in torrents, from Achaean
hands as well as Trojan. Helmets rang
and bossed shields rang with hits.

                                        But Asius
Hyrtacides pummeled his thighs and groaned
and bit his lip and said: 'O Father Zeus,
you, even you, turn out to be a liar.
I thought destiny was against the Achaeans
holding before our drive and our spear-arms
unleashed. Now see, like agile-waisted hornets
or bees who build their hives on a stony road –
hornets that will not leave their homes but wait
for hunters, and in fury defend their young –
those two men, two men only, at the gate
will not give way. For them, kill or be killed!'
    But Asius' complaint left Zeus unmoved:
it pleased him to award the day to Hector.
    Now there was fighting at the various gates –
a difficult thing for me to tell it all
as though I were a god! Around the rampart
at every point, blaze upon blaze of war
leapt upward. Out of savage need the Argives
fought on bitterly to save the ships,
and all the gods who took their part were grieved;
still the two Lapiths dealt terrific blows.
Polypoetes, son of Peirithous,
hit Damasus' helm hard on a cheek-plate,
bronze too frail to take the blow. Straight through
into the skull the spearhead crunched its way,
demolishing the brain. Down went the man.
Then Polypoetes killed Pylon and Ormenus.

War-bred Leonteus killed Hippomachus
with a spear-thrust at the loin-guard, drew his sword,
and at close quarters, leaping through the press,
ran through Antiphates, who went down backward;
next at Menon and Iamenus he lunged
and at Orestes, taking their lives away.
Now while the Lapiths made these kills and took
the dead men's flashing armour, those who followed
Polydamas and Hector – their young troops
in number and valour greatest, sworn to breach
the Achaean wall and set the ships afire –
halted hesitant at the moat. Just then
as they desired to cross, a bird flew by them,
heading to the left across the army,
an eagle beating upward, in its claws
a huge snake, red as blood, alive and jerking,
full of fight: it doubled on itself
and struck the captor's chest and throat. At this
the eagle in its agony let go
and veered away screaming downwind. The snake
fell in the mass of troops, and Trojans shuddered
to see the rippling thing lie in their midst,
a portent from Lord Zeus who bears the stormcloud.
   Polydamas at Hector's elbow said:
'Hector, you always manage to rebuke me
when I talk well to assemblies: it won't do
at all to cross you, peace or war, in council;
only to confirm you. Well, once more,
I intend to speak as I think best.
Let us not carry the fighting to the ships!
The end, I think, is what the bird portended –
if a true portent – when we wished to cross,
the eagle bearing left across the army,
beating upward, grappling this great snake,
alive. She dropped it here, she never gained
her own nest with it, never had her will
to give it to her nestlings. Ah, we too
are grappling danger! Granted we break the gates
and force a breach in the Achaean wall,
granted they fall back, we shall never make it
intact to the ships by these same paths,
but many a Trojan must we leave behind
lacerated with bronze by the defenders.
That is what you'd hear from a diviner

learned in signs and heeded by the troops!'

Hector in the bright helm frowned and said:
'This time I have no liking for your counsel.
You must have other and braver things to say.
If this comes from the heart, why, then the gods
themselves have wrecked your wits! You try to tell me
I should forget what Zeus of the long thunder
planned and promised with his nod to me!
You – you would have me put my faith in birds
whose spreading wings I neither track nor care for,
whether to the right hand sunward they fly
or to the left hand, westward into darkness.
No, no, I say, rely on the will of Zeus
who rules all mortals and immortals. One
and only one portent is best: defend
our fatherland! And why should you turn pale
at war and combat? Even if the rest of us
are killed to a man beside the Argive ships,
no fear that you will be: you lack ability
for warfare, and you lack the nerve to face it!
I tell you, though, that if you hold off now
or make one soldier falter in this battle,
you are a dead man on the spot
with my own spearblade in you!'
                                        So he finished,
turning to go forward, as the others
followed him with a blood-curdling cry,
and from the slopes of Ida Zeus who plays
in thunder roused a gale against the ships,
blowing a dustcloud to bewilder spent
Achaeans, while to Trojans and to Hector
he made his gift of glory. Trustful now
of Zeus's omens and their own right arms,
they made trial of the wall to break it down.
Layers of earth and stone they undermined,
and the revetments of the fighting-wall
they tore away by prying loose the posts
the Achaeans drove to hold the earthwork in.
They pulled these up, thinking when they were gone
to breach the wall. But even now the Danaans
would not yield free passage: jamming oxhide
bags of earth into the gaping dyke,
they cast stones from above on the attackers.
   Everywhere along the parapet

one Aias and the other, acting marshals,
roamed and cheered the Achaeans on: at times
with pleading and at other times with iron
words of rebuke, if they caught sight of anyone
hanging back from the fight.

              'Friends,' one would say,
'whether you are among the best, or fair,
or a poor fighter – all men cannot be
equal in war – this challenge is for everyone;
you see it for yourselves. Now not one man
may let himself be turned back on the ships
by any baying enemy he hears.
Keep your shots going forward, cheer each other,
so Zeus who is Olympian lord of lightning
may let us throw them back upon the town.'

    With words like these, and urgent battle-cries,
both men cheered the Achaeans on.

                   Imagine
flakes of snow that come down thick and fast
on a winter day when Zeus who views the wide world
brings on a fall of snow, showing mankind
his means of making war. He lulls the winds
and sifts white flakes in stillness hour by hour
until hilltop and foreland are all hid
as are the farmers' meadow-lands and fields,
while snow comes down over the hoary sea,
on harbours and on shores. Though running surf
repel it, all things else are muffled white,
weighed down by snow from heaven, a storm of Zeus.
So thick and fast the stones flew. Here they fell
on Trojans, there from Trojans on Achaeans,
by all hands thrown and thudding along the wall.

    But even so, and even now, the Trojans
led by great Hector could not yet have breached
the wall and gate with massive bar, had not
Lord Zeus impelled Sarpedon, his own son,
against the Argives like a lion on cattle.
Circular was the shield he held before him,
hammered out of pure bronze: aye, the smith
had hammered it, and riveted the plates
to thick bull's hide on golden rods rigged out
to the full circumference. Now gripping this,
hefting a pair of spears, he joined the battle,
formidable as some hill-bred lion, ravenous

for meat after long abstinence. His valour
summons him to attempt homesteads and flocks
and though he find herdsmen on hand with dogs
and spears to guard the sheep, he will not turn
without a fling at the stockade. One thing
or the other: a mighty leap and a fresh kill,
or he will fall at the spearmen's feet, brought down
by a javelin thrown hard. So valour drove
Sarpedon to the wall to make a breakthrough.

  Turning to Glaucus, Hippolochus' son, he said:
'What is the point of being honoured so
with precedence at table, choice of meat,
and brimming cups, at home in Lycia,
like gods at ease in everyone's regard?
And why have lands been granted you and me
on Xanthus bank: to each his own demesne,
with vines and fields of grain?

               'So that we two
at times like this in the Lycian front line
may face the blaze of battle and fight well,
that Lycian men-at-arms may say:
"They are no common men, our lords who rule
in Lycia. They eat fat lamb at feasts
and drink rare vintages, but the main thing is
their fighting power, when they lead in combat!"

  'Ah, cousin, could we but survive this war
to live forever deathless, without age,
I would not ever go again to battle,
nor would I send you there for honour's sake!
But now a thousand shapes of death surround us,
and no man can escape them, or be safe.
Let us attack – whether to give some fellow
glory or to win it from him.'

                 Glaucus
listened and moved only to obey,
and leading the great Lycian tribe the two men
charged. Now Menestheus shivered, seeing them come
with menace for him against the wall. He glanced
around him at the battlements of Achaeans,
looking for some chief who might repel
destruction from his men. Aias the Tall
and Aias the Short he saw, avid for war,
both standing there, and Teucer, from his hut
this moment come to join them: all were near,

and yet he could not reach them with a shout,
so loud the clangour that went up to heaven,
clash of shields and helms that rang with blows
and blows upon the gates, now all were shut,
besieged by Trojans trying to break them down.
    In haste he sent Thootes off to Aias,
telling him: 'Run to Aias; call him here;
or call both, rather: that is best by far,
since sure destruction is upon me here.
The Lycian captains bring such weight to bear
in battle, as in the past; they are formidable.
If our two on the wall there are hard pressed,
get Aias Telamonius alone
and with him Teucer, who knows bowmanship.'
    When he had heard him out, the messenger
darted along the wall manned by Achaeans
to halt by those named Aias. He said at once:
'Aias and Aias, marshals of the Argives,
the son of Peteos, reared under heaven, begs
your presence for a time at least, to share
the danger – both of you, if possible;
that would be best by far, as sure destruction
comes upon him there. But you can see
the Lycian captains bring such weight to bear
in battle, as in the past; they are formidable.
But if the fight is hot here, too, then Aias
Telamonius alone can go,
and the good bowman, Teucer, with him.'

                                   Tall
Aias, son of Telamon, complied,
first saying swiftly to the son of Oileus:
'Aias, you and Lycomedes hold
your ground here, and keep shouting at Danaans
to put their hearts into the fight. Meanwhile
I will go lend a hand there in the battle.
But I should soon be back, when I have given
our men support.'
                       So off he went,
and Teucer, too, his brother, went along.
Passing inside the wall, they found Menestheus'
tower and those who manned it hard beset,
as now the Lycian chiefs like a thunder-squall
loomed at the rampart. These two hurled themselves
into the fight against the attacking line,

and a great shout went up.
                              Telamonian Aias
made the first kill – Sarpedon's brave companion,
Epicles – by heaving a jagged block,
the topmost of a pile that lay inside
against one of the battlements. Not easily
could any mortal now alive
hold it in both hands, even in his prime;
but Aias raised it high and hurled it down,
shattering helmet, skull, and brains
at one blow. Down the Lycian dropped
headlong from the wall's height like a diver,
as warm life ebbed from his bones.
                                   Then Teucer shot
Glaucus, powerful son of Hippolochus,
with an arrow as he rushed the wall – a bow-shot
just where he saw his arm bared. Joy in battle
left the young fighter; off the wall he leapt,
not to be seen and taunted by Achaeans.
Glaucus' withdrawal made Sarpedon grieve
the instant he perceived it; still the battle
gave him joy. He pierced Alcmaon, son
of Thestor, and drew the spearblade out, as doubling
forward after the spear the man fell hard,
his brazen gear clanging. Then Sarpedon,
grasping a battlement with massive hands,
wrenched – and the parapet came toppling down,
so men could mount by it to the stripped wall.
Aias and Teucer met him now together.
Teucer put a shaft in the bright belt
on which his shield hung, but Zeus brushed away
death's shadow from his child: his fate was not
to die abaft the ship. Though Aias lunged
and hit the shield, his point would not pass through;
it only stopped Sarpedon.
                          He fell back
a little from the crumbled battlement –
not in retreat, though, but still craving honour –
and whirled and called his godlike countrymen:
'Lycians, why are you lagging, slackening off
your driving power? It is hard for me
alone, strong as I am, to make a breakthrough,
clear a way to the ships. Come up alongside!
More hands here will do a better job!'

Inwardly shrinking from their lord's rebuke,
they bunched around him and attacked in force.
The Argives, for their part, inside the wall,
reinforced their companies. Both found it
heavy work, for neither could the Lycians
breach the wall and clear a way to the ships,
nor could Danaan spears dislodge
the Lycians from the wall once they had reached it.
Think of two men contending over boundary stones,
each with his measuring rod, in the common field,
in a narrow place, disputing what is fair:
so here the parapet divided these,
and for the parapet they tore each other's
chest-protecting, oxhide-aproned shields.
Many were gashed by the cold-hearted bronze –
every man who left his back uncovered,
turning, and some men through the shield itself,
and everywhere, towers and battlements
were blood-bespattered from both sides. But still
the attacking Trojans could not rout the Achaeans.
They held. Think of an honest cottage spinner
balancing weight in one pan of the scales
and wool yarn on the other, trying to earn
a pittance for her children: evenly poised
as that were these great powers making war,
until at last Lord Zeus conferred on Hector,
Priam's son, the glory of bursting through
the Achaean wall.
                    In a piercing voice he called:
'On, on, Trojans, horse-breakers, breach
the Argive wall and pitch a hell of fire
into the ships!'
                    The listening troops obeyed
and surged in a great throng against the wall
to clamber between towers, carrying spears.
Now Hector picked a boulder that had stood,
broad-bottomed, sharp on top, before the gate.
The strongest pair of men in the whole realm,
as men are now, could not with ease heave up
this boulder from the ground into a wagon.
Lightly Hector handled it alone,
for Zeus, the son of crooked-minded Cronos,
made it a trifling weight for him. A shepherd
will carry easily, in either hand,

a new-shorn ram's fleece – no great weight for him;
so Hector, lifting up the stone, went forward
to the high double doors of heavy timber
closing the gateway. Two crossbars inside
were rammed in place and one pin fastened them.
He took a stance before the doors and braced,
with feet apart, for full force in the blow,
then smashed down at the centre. Hinges cracked
on both sides as the great mass tumbled through,
the doors groaned inward, bars gave way, the planks
were splintered by the impact right and left,
and through the breach in glory Hector leapt,
his visage dark as nightfall, though he shone
terribly from the bronze that he was dressed in,
carrying a brace of spears.

                No one could stop him,
none but the gods, as he leapt through the gate,
his eyes burning. Then he wheeled and called
the mass of Trojans to come charging on
across the wall. And they obeyed him, some
by swarming over, others pouring through
the very gateway. And the Danaans broke
for their long ships in an uproar always rising.

BOOK XIII

ASSAULT ON THE SHIPS

WHEN Zeus had brought great Hector and his Trojans
into the beach-head by the ships, he left them
to cruel toil of battle, and to grief,
while he himself with shining eyes turned north,
gazing on the far lands of Thracian horsemen,
Mysians, hand-to-hand fighters, Hippemolgi,
who live on mare's milk, nomads, Abii,
most peaceable and just of men. And Zeus
now kept his shining eyes away from Troy,
confident that no other god would come
to take a hand for Trojans or Danaans.

But the strong god who makes the mainland shake
had not been blind. Enthralled, watching the battle,
he sat on woody Samos' highest ridge
off Thrace, whence Ida could be seen entire
and Priam's town and the Achaean ships.
He had climbed up from the salt sea, and now
he pitied Achaeans beaten down by Trojans.
Rancour within him deepened against Zeus.
Then from the stony mountain down he went
with mighty strides; a tremor shook the crags
and forest under Poseidon's immortal feet.
Three giant steps, then four, and he was home
at Aegae, where his golden chambers glimmer
in the green depth and never wash away.
Here he entered; into his chariot-shafts
he backed his racing-team with golden manes,
put on his golden mantle, took his whip
of pliant gold, stepped up into his car,
and rolled out on the waves. Great fish beneath him
gambolled from every quarter of the deep,
aware their lord rode overhead; in laughter .
whitecaps parted, and the team full tilt
airily drew unwetted the axle-tree;
with leap on leap they bore him toward the beach-head.
There is a cavern deep in the deep sea
midway between the rocky isle of Imbros
and Tenedos: here he who shakes the islands

drove his horses down, unharnessed them,
tossed them heavenly fodder, looped their hocks
with golden hobbles none could break or slip –
that they should abide here their lord's return;
and off he went to the Achaean army.

    Now like a storm or prairie fire, swarming
steadily after Hector son of Priam,
the Trojans roared as one man – on the verge,
they thought, of capturing the Achaean ships
and dealing death to the best men around them.

    But now from the deep water,
girdler of earth and shaker of earth, Poseidon
came to arouse new spirit in the Argives.
Calchas he seemed, with his unwearied voice,
addressing first those two, fiery as he,
the men named Aias: 'Aias and Aias, fight
to save the Achaean army! Joy of action
is what you must remember, and have done
with clammy dread. Elsewhere I do not fear
the free spear-arms of Trojans, though they've crossed
our big rampart in force. They can be held,
all of them, by Achaeans! Only here,
in this one place, I am most afraid
it will go badly for us. Here this madman,
Hector, like a conflagration leads them,
bragging he is a child of almighty Zeus.
I wish you were inspired by some god
to hold the line hard, clamped hard here, you two,
rallying others: you could block and turn
his whirlwind-rush away from the long ships,
even if the Olympian sets him on.'

    The god who girdles earth, even as he spoke,
struck both men with his staff, instilling fury,
making them springy, light of foot and hand.
Then upward like a hawk he soared – a hawk
that, wafted from a rock-point sheer and towering
shoots to strike a bird over the plain:
so arrowy in flight Poseidon left them.

    The son of Oileus knew his nature first
and turned to say to the son of Telamon:
'That was one of the gods who hold Olympus,
here in the seer's shape telling us to fight
abaft the ships. It was not Calchas, not
the reader of bird-flight; from his stride, his legs

as he went off, I knew him for a god.
The gods are easily spotted! As for me,
I feel more passion to do battle now;
I tingle from the very soles of my feet
to my finger tips!'

        And Telamonian Aias
answered: 'So it is with me:
my hands itch to let the spearshaft fly!
Power is rising in me; I can feel
a springing freshness in my legs. I long
to meet this implacable Hector face to face!'

So they assured each other, in that joy
of battle which the god inspired; and he
meanwhile put heart in the Achaean soldiers
rearward, taking a respite among the ships.
Dead on their feet from toil of war, these men
were losing heart; now they could see the Trojans
massing as they crossed the rampart. Watching,
in silence the Achaeans' eyes grew wet;
they saw no way to escape the evil hour.

But he who makes the islands tremble, passing
lightly among them, stiffened the backbone
of all those rugged companies. Teucer first
and Leitus he commanded as he came,
and Peneleos and Thoas, Deipyrus,
and last Meriones and Antilochus,
clarion in battle. Urgently and swiftly
he cried to them:

        'Shame, Argives, shame, young men!
By fighting you can save our ships,
but if you shirk the battle, then we face
defeat this day at the Trojans' hands.
By heaven, what a thing to see! I never
dreamed the war would come to this: our beach-head
raided by Trojans! Until now those men
were timorous as greenwood deer, light fare
for jackals, leopards, wolves – wandering deer
with no fight in them and no joy in battle.
Trojans in other days would never meet
Achaean power on the attack – not they!
Far from the city now, they press the combat
to the very ships – by our commander's fault
and by our soldiers' fault in giving in.
At odds with him, our men will not hold fast

beyond the ships, but die around them!
                                        'Call it
proved and true beyond a doubt
that Agamemnon, Lord of the Great Plains,
caused this by contempt shown to Achilles.
Are we to break off battle, then? How can we?
Rather, find a remedy; good men's hearts
respond to remedies! You must no longer
hang back, but attack, for honour's sake,
as every one of you is a first-rate soldier.
Would I now quarrel with one who shunned the war
if he were a man unfit for it? No. With you,
I am full of anger. Soldiers, you'll bring on
worse things yet by your half-heartedness.
Let each man get a fresh grip on his pride
and look to his standing. The great contest begins,
Hector begins his drive along the ships
in force: he has broken the gate-bar and the gate.'

    In terms like these Poseidon stirred the Achaeans,
and round the two named Aias they made stand,
hard companies the war-god would not scorn,
nor would Athena, Hope of Soldiers. Gathering,
picked men faced the Trojan charge. faced Hector,
spear by spear and shield by shield in line
with shield-rims overlapping, serried helms,
and men in ranks packed hard – their horsehair plumes
brushed one another when the shining crests
would dip or turn; so dense they stood together,
as from bold hands the spearshafts, closing up,
were pointed, quivering. And the men looked ahead,
braced for battle.
                    Trojans massed and running
charged them now, with Hector in the lead
in furious impetus, like a rolling boulder
a river high with storm has torn away
from a jutting bank by washing out what held it;
then the brute stone upon the flood
goes tossed and tumbling, and the brush gives way,
crashing before it. It must roll unchecked
as far as level ground, then roll no more,
however great its force had been. So Hector
threatened at first to sweep clear to the sea
through the huts and ships of the Achaeans, killing
along the way – but when he reached the line

of packed defenders he stopped dead in his tracks.
His adversaries lunging out with swords
and double-bladed spears beat him away,
so that he stepped back, shaken.

                      Then he cried:
'Trojans, Lycians, Dardans, fight hard here!
They cannot hold me, not for long,
by making bastion, closed in line together!
No, I can see them break before the spear,
if it is sure I have the first of gods
behind me, Hera's consort, lord of thunder!'
    Shouting, he cheered them on to the attack,
and Priam's son, Deiphobus, inflamed
by a great hope, moved out ahead, his round shield
forward as he trod, catlike, compact
behind it. Then Meriones took aim
and cast his shining spear. A direct hit
on the round shield of bull's hide – but no breakthrough;
the long haft snapped off at the blade. Deiphobus
had held his shield before him at arm's length
to counter that hard blow. And now Meriones
retired amid his company, full of rage
to see spearhead and victory broken off.
Rearward he went, along the huts and ships,
to get a long spear left inside his hut.
    The rest fought on, with long-drawn battle-cries,
and Telamonian Teucer drew first blood
by killing a son of Mentor, herder of horses,
Imbrius the pikeman. He had lived
at Pedaeum before the Achaeans came
and had a young wife, Medesicaste, born
of a slave to Priam. When the rolling ships
of the Danaans beached, he journeyed back
to Ilium, stood high, and lived near Priam,
who ranked him with him own sons. Teucer gashed
Imbrius under the ear with his long weapon,
then withdrew it. Down the Trojan went,
as on a hilltop, visible far and wide,
an ash hewn by an axe puts down its verdure
shimmering on the ground. So he went down,
and round him clanged his harness wrought in bronze.
Teucer rushed in to strip him; as he did so,
Hector aimed a thrust with his bright spear,
but the alert man swerved before the point,

escaping by a hair's breadth. Hector hit
a son of Cteatus Actorides,
Amphimachus, with a spear-thrust in the chest
just as he joined the fight. He thudded down
and his armour clanged upon him. Hector lunged
to pull away the brave man's fitted helm,
and Aias reached for Hector with his spear –
but nowhere shone his bare flesh, all concealed
by his grim armour. Aias hit his shield-boss
hard and forced him backward, making Hector
yield the dead. Achaeans drew them off.
Stichius and Menestheus, in command
of the Athenians, bore Amphimachus
amid the Achaeans. As for Imbrius,
one Aias and the other, fast and bold,
took him as lions carry off a goat
under the noses of a biting pack
into a forest undergrowth: aloft,
clear of the ground, they lug him in their jaws.
Just so, with tossing plumes like manes, these two
lugged Imbrius, and stripped him of his gear.
Then from his tender neck Aias Oiliades,
in anger for Amphimachus, lopped his head
and bowled it through the mêlée till it tumbled
in dust at Hector's feet.
                          Poseidon, too,
grew hot over Amphimachus, his grandson.
Passing amid the huts and ships, he kindled
fire in Danaans and devised Trojans' woe.
Idomeneus now crossed his path, just come
from a fellow-captain slashed behind the knee,
who had been helped by others from the battle.
Idomeneus had commended him to the surgeons
and made his way now to his hut; he longed
once more to join the fighting. The Earthshaker
addressed him in the form and voice of Thoas,
Andraemon's son, who ruled all Pleuron, all
that steep land, Calydon of Aetolians,
where country folk revered him as a god.

As Thoas, now Poseidon said: 'Idomeneus,
marshal and mind of Cretans, what has become
of those Achaean threats against the Trojans?'

The Cretan captain in reply said: 'Thoas,
the blame cannot be pinned on any man,

so far as I know, up to now. Our people
understand war, none is unmanned by fear,
not one has lagged or slipped away from carnage.
Only it must be somehow to the pleasure
of arrogant Zeus, that here ingloriously
far from Argos the Achaeans perish!
Ah, Thoas!
before this you have shown courage in danger,
and when you see a man go slack, you brace him.
No quitting now! Let every soldier hear it!'

    Poseidon answered him: 'Idomeneus,
let that man never voyage home from Troy
but be a carcass for the dogs to play with
who would give up the fight this day! Come on,
and bring your gear; no time to lose; we must
hit hard and hit together, both of us,
if we are going to make our presence felt.
When feeble men join forces, then their courage
counts for something. Ours should count for more,
since we can fight with any.'
           So the god
took part with men once more in toil of combat.
When he had reached his hut, Idomeneu
bound on his handsome armour, took two spears,
and ran out like a lightning-bolt, picked up
by Zeus to handle flickering on Olympus
when he would make a sign to men – the jagged
dance of it blinding bright. So as he ran
bronze flashed about his breast.
               Meriones,
his valiant aide, came up, still near the hut,
on his way to get a bladed spear to carry,
and mighty Idomeneus said: 'Meriones,
Molus' dear son, good runner, best of friends,
how is it that you left the battle?
Have you been hit? Some arrow grinding in you?
Or were you bringing word to me? No sitting
still in huts for me: I long to fight!'

    The cool man said: 'Idomeneus, counsellor
of battle-craft to Cretans under arms,
I came to see if any spear is left here
I can use. I shattered mine just now
against Deiphobus' shield.'

    Idomeneus answered: 'Spears? All you desire,

twenty-one spears, you'll find inside, arrayed
against the bright wall of the entrance-way –
all Trojan; I win weapons from the dead.
I do not hold with fighting at long range,
therefore I have the spears, and shields as well,
and helms as well, and bright-faced cuirasses.'

    Meriones the cool man in reply
said: 'In my quarters, at my ship, I too
have plenty of Trojan gear; not near at hand, though.
I say I am not – not, I say – a man
to pass up any attack. I take my place
in the front rank for action and for honour
whenever battle's joined. There may be others
who have not seen me fight, but I believe
you know me.'

             And the captain of Cretans answered:
'Know you, and how you stand. Why need you say it?
Suppose amid the ships we picked our best
for a surprise attack: that is the place
where fighting qualities in truth come out,
and you can tell a brave man from a coward.
This one's face goes greener by the minute;
he is so shaky he cannot control himself
but fidgets first on one foot, then the other,
his teeth chattering, his heart inside him pounding
against his ribs at shapes of death foreseen.
As for the brave man, his face never changes,
and no great fear is in him, when he moves
into position for an ambuscade;
his prayer is all for combat, hand to hand,
and sharp, and soon. Well, no man then
would look down on your heart and fighting skill!
And were you hit by a missile or a thrust
in the toil of war, the blow would never come
from behind on nape or back, but in the chest
or belly as you waded in
to give and take at the battle-line.
But no more talk or dawdling here like children!
Someone might sneer and make an issue of it.
Go to my hut and choose a battle-spear.'

    Meriones, peer of Ares, in a flash
picked from the hut a bladed spear and ran
after Idomeneus, athirst for battle.
Imagine Ares, bane of men, when he

goes into combat with Rout close behind,
his cold and powerful son,
who turns the toughest warrior in his tracks.
From Thrace these two take arms against Ephyri
or gallant Phlegyes; but not for them
to heed both sides: they honour one with glory.
Just so, Meriones and Idomeneus,
helmed in fiery bronze, captains of men,
made their way to battle.
                            But Meriones
asked his friend: 'Son of Deucalion, where
do you say we join the combat? On the right,
or in the centre, or on the left? I find
the Achaeans there, if anywhere, shorthanded
in this attack.'
                    And the Cretan captain said:
'The middle ships have their defenders:
Aias Telamonius, Aias Oiliades,
Teucer, our best hand with a bow – and brave
at close quarters. They will give Hector
more than he can handle in this battle,
hot as he is for war. He's powerful, yes,
but he will find it uphill work to conquer
these sharp fighters, formidable hands,
and set our ships aflame – unless Lord Zeus
should toss a firebrand aboard himself.
No mortal nourished on Demeter's meal,
none vulnerable to bronze or stones will make
great Telamonian Aias yield. He would not
in a stand-up fight give ground to dire Achilles –
whom in a running fight no man can touch.
This way for us, then, to the army's left:
to see how soon we'll give some fellow glory
or win it from him.'
                        Swift as the god of war,
Meriones was off, and led the way
to that part of the line his friend required.
When the Achaeans saw Idomeneus
in fresh strength, like a flame, with his companion,
richly armed, all gave a shout and grouped
about him: and a great fight, hand to hand,
arose at the ship-sterns. Gusts of crying wind
on days when dust lies thickest on the lanes
will wrestle and raise a dustcloud high: so spread

this mêlée as men came together, sworn
with whetted bronze to kill and strip each other.
Bristling spines of long flesh-tearing spears
went home in the deadly press; and a man's eyes
failed before the flash of brazen helmets,
cuirasses like mirrors, and bright shields
in sunlight clashing. Only a man of iron
could have looked on light-hearted at that fight
and suffered nothing.
                          At cross-purposes,
the sons of Cronos in their power brought on
bitter losses and death for brave men. Zeus
on the one hand willed for Hector and the Trojans
victory, to vindicate Achilles;
at the same time, he willed no annihilation
of the Achaeans before Troy, but only
honour to Thetis and her lion-like son.
Poseidon for his part now roused the Argives,
moving among them, after he emerged
in secret from the grey sea; being grieved
by Argive losses at the Trojans' hands,
he felt bitter indignation against Zeus.
Both gods were of the same stock, had one father,
but Zeus had been first-born and knew far more.
In giving aid, Poseidon therefore would not
give it openly: always under cover,
in a man's likeness, he inspired the ranks.
These gods had interlocked and drawn
an ultimate hard line of strife and war
between the armies; none
could loosen or break that line
that had undone the knees of many men.
    Idomeneus belied his grizzled head
and, calling on Danaans, with a bound
scattered the Trojans, for he killed Othryoneus
of Cabesus, a guest of Troy. This man
had come, on hearing lately of the war,
and bid for Cassandra, the most beautiful
of Priam's daughters. Though he had brought no gifts,
he promised a great feat: to drive from Troy
the army of Achaeans, willy-nilly.
Then old Priam had agreed to give her,
nodding his head on it; so the man fought
confident in these promises. Idomeneus

aimed at him with long spear flashing bright
and caught him in mid-stride. His plate of bronze
could not deflect the point driven in his belly,
and down he crashed.

            The other taunted him:
'Othryoneus, I'll sing your praise
above all others, if you do your part
for Priam! He had promised you his daughter.
Well, we could promise, and fulfil it, too,
to give you Agamemnon's loveliest daughter
brought out of Argos for you as your bride –
if you would join to plunder Troy.
Come, and we'll make the marriage-bond
aboard the long ships. There's no parsimony
in us when it comes to bridal gifts.'

                    With this,
he dragged him by one foot out of the combat.
Asius, now dismounted, moved up fast
to fight over the body, while his driver
held the horses panting at his shoulders.
Putting his heart into the cast, he tried
to hit Idomeneus; but the Achaean whipped
his missile in ahead and struck his throat
under the chin, running him through with bronze.
Tall Asius fell the way an oak or poplar
falls, or a towering pine, that shipbuilders
in mountain places with fresh-whetted axes
fell to make ship's timber. So, full length,
he lay before his team and chariot,
wheezing, clutching at the bloody dust.
His stunned driver had lost what wits he had
and did not dare to break from his enemies
by wheeling his team around. Antilochus
put a spear into him. The bronze he wore
could not deflect the point driven in his belly,
and with a gasp he pitched down from the car.
His team was taken by Antilochus,
great-hearted Nestor's son, amid the Achaeans.

    Enraged at Asius' fall, Deiphobus
went for Idomeneus with a hard spear-cast,
but he foresaw the blow and dodged the point
by disappearing under his round shield
of bull's hide, fitted on two struts or bars,
and plated with concentric rings of bronze.

Under this he packed himself, as over it
the bronze-shod spear passed; and his shield rang out
under the glancing blow. But not for nothing
thrown by Deiphobus' brawny hand,
the spear hit a high officer, Hypsenor
son of Hippasus, in the liver under
the diaphragm, and brought him tumbling down.

Deiphobus gave a great shout and exulted:
'Asius is down, but there's revenge!
On his journey to Death's iron gate
he will be glad I gave him company.'

This went home to the Argives, most of all
Antilochus, whose heart was stirred,
but in his grief he still bethought himself
for his companion. On the run he reached him,
straddled him and held his shield above him.
Two other friends, Mecisteus, Echius' son,
and brave Alastor, bent to lift and carry him
groaning deeply to the sheltering ships.

Idomeneus' passion for battle never waned:
he strove to shroud some Trojan in hell's night
or else himself to fall, as he fought off
the black hour for Achaeans.

                                    Now he met
Alcathous, Aesyetes' noble son,
Anchises' son-in-law. This man had married
Hippodameia, eldest of the daughters,
dearest to her father and gentle mother
in their great hall. In beauty, skill, and wit,
she had excelled all girls of her own age.
For this reason, too, the man who won her
had been the noblest suitor in all Troy.
Now it was he that by Idomeneus' hand
Poseidon overcame. The god entranced
his shining eyes and hobbled his fine legs,
so that he could not turn back or manœuvre,
but like a pillar or a full-grown tree
he stood without a tremor. Square in the chest
Idomeneus caught him, sundering the cuirass
that until now had saved his flesh from harm.
And now at last he cried aloud, the rending
spear between his ribs, and down he crashed,
his heart, being driven through, in its last throes
making the spear-butt quake. The mighty war-god

then extinguished all his force.
　　Idomeneus yelled and exulted savagely:
'Ah, then, Deiphobus, shall we call it quits
when three are downed for one? You counted first!
Bright soul, come forward now, yourself, and face me!
Learn what I am! I come in the line of Zeus,
who fathered Minos, lord of the Cretan seas,
and he in turn fathered Deucalion
who fathered me, commander of many fighters
in the wide land of Crete. Then here to Troy
my ships brought me to plague you and your father
and all the Trojans.'
　　　　　　　　　　　Challenged so, Deiphobus
weighed the choice before him: should he pair
with some brave Trojan – going back to get him –
or take Idomeneus on alone? It seemed
more promising to him to join Aeneas,
whom he discovered in the battle's rear,
standing apart, resentful against Priam,
as Priam slighted him among his peers.
　　Deiphobus reached his side and said to him swiftly:
'Counsellor of Trojans, you must come
defend your kinsman, if his death affects you.
Follow me, to rescue Alcathous,
your sister's husband, who made you his ward
when you were still a small child in his house.
The great spearman, Idomeneus, brought him down.'
The appeal aroused Aeneas. Craving battle,
he charged Idomeneus; and he, no child
to be overtaken by a qualm of fear,
steadily waited, like a mountain boar
who knows his power, facing a noisy hunt
in a lonely place: his backbone bristles rise;
both eyes are fiery; gnashing his tusks
he waits in fury to drive back dogs and men.
Idomeneus, great spearman, so awaited
without a backward step Aeneas' onset.
　　But to his friends he called out, looking back
at Aphareus, Ascalaphus, Deipyrus,
and those two masters of the battle-cry,
Meriones and Antilochus; he sent
an urgent cry to alert them: 'This way, friends!
Give me a hand here, I am alone!
I have a nasty fear of the great runner,

Aeneas, now upon me: he has power
to kill, and has the bloom
of youth that is the greatest strength of all.
If we were matched in age as in our spirit
in single fight, then quickly he or I
should bear away the glory.'

As he spoke,
with one mind all the others closed around him,
taking position, shields hard on their shoulders.
Aeneas, too, on his side turned and called
Deiphobus and Paris and Agenor,
fellow-captains of Trojans. Troops moved up
behind him now, as a flock out of a pasture
follows a ram to drink – and the shepherd's heart
rejoices: so did Aeneas' heart rejoice
to see the men-at-arms follow his lead.
Both masses came together, hand to hand,
pressing on Alcathous, long polished spearshafts
crossing, and the bronze on the men's ribs
rang like anvils from the blows they aimed
at one another. Most of all, those peers
of Ares, Aeneas and Idomeneus,
strove with heartless bronze to rend each other.
Aeneas made the first throw, but his adversary
saw the aim and twisted to elude it,
so that Aeneas' point went home in earth
and stuck with quivering shaft, the force he gave it
with his great arm spent on the air. Idomeneus
for his part thrust at Oenomaus and hit him
mid-belly, breaking through his cuirass-joint,
and the bronze lance-head spilt his guts like water.
Dropping in dust, the Trojan clawed the ground.
Idomeneus pulled his long spear out, but could not
strip the Trojan's shoulders of his gear,
being driven back by spear-throws. And then, too,
he was no longer certain of his footwork
in lunging or recovery, but fought
defensively against the evil hour,
his legs no longer nimble in retreat.
Now as he gave way step by step, Deiphobus,
implacable against him, made a throw
but missed again; he hit Ascalaphus,
a son of the god Ares, running him through
the shoulder with his heavy spear. He fell

in dust and clawed the ground. And roaring Ares
heard no news as yet that his own son
died in that mêlée – no, for he was sitting
on high Olympus under golden clouds,
restrained by the will of Zeus, as were the other
immortal gods, all shut away from war.
But hand to hand around Ascalaphus
the fight went on: Deiphobus took the dead man's
helm, but Meriones, fast as the war-god,
leaped and speared the Trojan's outstretched arm.
The crested helm fell with a hollow clang,
and with a falcon's pounce Meriones
regained his spear and jerked it from Deiphobus'
upper arm at the shoulder-joint, then back
he turned to merge into his company.
A brother of the wounded man, Polites,
putting an arm around his waist, withdrew him
out of the battle-din to where his team
stood waiting in the rear, with car and driver.
Away to Troy they bore Deiphobus,
who groaned in his distress, while blood ran down
his arm from the open wound.

                              And still the others
fought as the long-drawn battle-cry arose.
Lunging at Aphareus, son of Caletor,
Aeneas hit his throat as he turned toward him
and cut it with his sharp spearpoint: the head
fell to one side as shield and helm sank down
and death, destroyer of ardour, flooded him.
Antilochus' sharp eye on Thoon saw him
turn away, and in one leap he slashed
the vein that running up the back comes out
along the neck; he sheared it from the body,
so that the man fell backward in the dust
with arms out to his friends. Antilochus
closed to take the harness from his shoulders
watchfully, as the Trojans from all sides
moved up and struck at his broad glittering shield.
But none with his cold-hearted bronze could scratch
Antilochus' tender skin – because Poseidon
protected him amid those many blows.
And never out of range of them he turned
and turned upon his enemies: the spearshaft
swerving, never still, with his intent

to throw it and bring someone down
or to close in and kill.

                    Now Asius' son
Adamas caught him as he aimed and struck him,
stepping in close, driving his point mid-shield,
but felt the spearshaft broken by Poseidon,
who grudged him this man's life. One half the spear
hung like a fire-hardened stake impaled
in the shield of Antilochus, while on the ground
the other half lay. Adamas then backed
into his throng of friends, away from death,
but as he drew away, Meriones
went after him and hit him with a spear-throw
low between genitals and navel, there
where pain of war grieves mortal wretches most.
The spear transfixed him. Doubled up on it,
as a wild bullock in the hills will writhe
and twitch when herdsmen fetter and drag him down,
so did the stricken man – but not for long
before Meriones bent near and pulled out
spearhead from flesh. Then night closed on his eyes.

   Now with his Thracian broadsword Helenus
cut at Deipyrus' head and broke his helm off:
buffeted to the ground and underfoot
it rolled till an Achaean fighter caught it,
but black night closed upon Deipyrus' eyes.
Grief at his death took great-lunged Menelaus,
and menacing with hefted spear he bore
down on Lord Helenus, while Helenus
drew arrowhead to handgrip. All at once
one made his cast, the other man let fly,
and Priam's son hit Menelaus' breast
upon his armour's rondure – but the barbed
shaft went skittering.

                    On a threshing floor
one sees how dark-skinned beans or chickpeas leap
from a broad shovel under a sharp wind
at the toss of the winnower: just so
from shining Menelaus' cuirass now
the bitter arrow bounced up and away.
Meanwhile the son of Atreus, clarion
in battle, struck the hand that held the bow:
he drove his brazen spearhead through the knuckles
into the bowstave. Helenus recoiled

amid his countrymen, eluding death,
his dangling left hand dragging the ashwood spear.
Great-hearted Agenor drew the spearhead out
and bound his hand in sheep's wool from a sling
an aide supplied him. Then came Peisander
in a rush at the great figure of Menelaus –
impelled by fatal destiny to fall
before you in the mêlée, Menelaus –
and when the range narrowed between these two
Menelaus missed: the spear was turned aside:
Peisander, though, got home his stroke upon
Menelaus' shield. Only, he could not
drive his metal in and through: the shield
held fast; the shaft below the spearhead broke,
yet even so in joy he hoped for victory.
By the silver-studded hilt Menelaus drew
his longsword as he leapt upon Peisander
who now brought out from underneath his shield
a double axe on a long polished helve.
In one great shock both men attacked at once,
axe-head on helmet ridge below the crest
came hewing down, but the sword-stroke
above the nose on the oncoming brow
went home; it cracked the bone, and both his eyes
were spilt in blood into the dust at his feet
as he bent over and fell.

                    Menelaus followed
to spurn the man's chest with his foot and strip
his gear away. And glorying over him
he said: 'Here is the way back from the ships!
This way you'll leave our beach-head,
Trojans who have not yet enough of war.
You don't lack vileness otherwise, or crime
committed against me, you yellow dogs;
you knew no fear of Zeus in his high thunder,
lord of guests – no forethought of his anger
harshly rising! He will yet destroy
your craggy city for you. My true queen
you carried off by sea with loads of treasure
after a friendly welcome at her hands.
This time you lust to pitch devouring fire
into our deep-sea ships, and kill Achaeans.
You will be stopped somehow, though savage war
is what you crave!'

Then in a lower tone
he said: 'O Father Zeus, incomparable
they say you are among all gods and men
for wisdom; yet this battle comes from you.
How strange that you should favour the offenders –
favour the Trojans in their insolence
ever insatiable for war! All things
have surfeit – even sleep, and love, and song,
and noble dancing – things a man may wish
to take his fill of, and far more than war.
But Trojans will not get their fill of fighting.'

Menelaus as he spoke had ripped away
and given his men the dead man's bloodstained arms.
Now once more, yet again, he entered combat.
Here in a surge against him came
Harpalion, King Pylaemenes' son,
who journeyed with his father to make war
at Troy – never thereafter to come home.
At close quarters this fighter hit the shield
of Menelaus, but he could not drive the bronze
onward and through it. Backward in recoil
he shrank amid his people, shunning death,
with wary glances all around
for anyone whose weapon might have nicked him.
After him, though, Meriones
let fly a bronze-shod arrow, and it punched
through his right buttock, past the pelvic bone,
into his bladder. On the spot he sank
down on his haunches, panting out his life
amid the hands of fellow-soldiers: then
he lengthened out like an earthworm
as dark blood flowing from him stained the ground.
Falling to work around him, Paphlagonians
lifted him in a car and drove him back
to Troy in sorrow. And his father, weeping,
walked behind; there was no retribution
for the dead son. But the death angered Paris,
because among the Paphlagonians
the man had been his guest and his great friend.
In anger now he let an arrow fly.

There was a young Achaean named Euchenor,
noble and rich, having his house at Corinth,
a son of the visionary, Polyidus.
When he took ship he knew his destiny,

for Polyidus had foretold it often:
he was to die of illness in his megaron
or else go down to death at Trojan hands
amid the Achaean ships. Two things at once
he had therefore avoided: the heavy fine
men paid who stayed at home, and the long pain
of biding mortal illness. Paris' arrow
pierced him below jaw and ear, and quickly
life ebbed from his body, the cold night
enwrapped him.

        And the rest fought on like fire's
body leaping. Hector had not learned
that Trojans on their left flank near the ships
were being cut to pieces; victory there
was almost in Achaean hands, Poseidon
urged them on so, and so lent them strength.
But Hector held that ground where first he broke
through gate and wall and deep ranks of Danaans —
there where the ships of Aias and Protesilaus
were drawn up on the grey sea-beach, and landward
the parapet had been constructed lowest.
Here in chariots or on foot
the Achaeans fought most bitterly: Boeotians,
Ionians in long chitons, men of Locris,
men of Phthia, illustrious Epeians
fought off Hector from the ships, but could not
throw him back as he came on like flame.
Athenians, picked men, were here, their chief
Peteos' son, Menestheus, and his aides,
Pheidas and Stichios, rugged Bias. Next
the Epeian leaders, Meges, son of Phyleus,
Amphion and Dracius; of Phthia then,
Medon and staunch Podarces. Aye, this Medon,
noble Oileus' bastard son and Aias'
brother, lived in Phylace
far from his fatherland, as he had killed
a kinsman of Oileus' second lady,
Eriopis. As for the Lord Podarces,
he was a son of Iphiclus Phylacides.
These, then, in arms before the men of Phthia,
fought for the ships at the Boeotians' side.
But Aias, Oileus' quick son, would never,
not for a moment, leave Telamonian Aias.
These two men worked together, like dark oxen

pulling with equal heart a bolted plough
in fallow land. You know how, round the base
of each curved horn, the sweat pours out, and how
one smooth-worn yoke will hold the oxen close,
cutting a furrow to the field's edge? So
these toiling heroes clove to one another.
Surely the Telamonian had retainers –
many and courageous countrymen –
who took his shield when weariness came on him
and sweat ran down his knees. No Locrians
backed up the other Aias, Oïleus' son:
they could not have sustained close-order combat,
having no helms of bronze with horsehair crests,
no round shields and no spears of ash. In fact,
when they took ship together for Ilium,
they put their faith in bows and braided sheep's-wool
slings, with which they broke the Trojan lines
by pelting volleys.

               Now the men in armour
fought with Trojans in the front lines, fought
with Hector, hand to hand, but in the rear
the bowmen shot, being safely out of range –
and Trojans lost their appetite for battle
as arrows drove them in retreat.

                     At this,
they might have left the ships and the encampment
wretchedly to return to windy Troy,
had not Polydamas moved close to Hector,
saying: 'You are a hard man to persuade.
Zeus gave you mastery in arms; therefore
you think to excel in strategy as well.
And yet you cannot have all gifts at once.
Heaven gives one man skill in arms, another
skill in dancing, and a third man skill
at gittern-harp and song; but the Lord Zeus
who views the wide world has instilled clear thought
in yet another. By his aid men flourish,
and there are many he can save; he knows
better than any what his gift is worth.
Let me tell you the best thing as I see it,
now everywhere around you in a ring
the battle rages.

              'Ever since the Trojans
crossed the wall, some have hung back, though armed,

while others do the fighting – and these few,
outnumbered, are dispersed along the ships.
Give way, call all our captains back, we'll test
their plans of actions, every one. Shall we
attack the deep-sea ships, can we assume
god wills to grant the day to us? And could we
retire from the ships without a slaughter?
As for me, I fear
the Achaeans may still pay the debt they owe
for yesterday, as long as the man we know,
famished for battle, lingers on the beach-head:
I doubt he'll keep from fighting any longer.'

This wariness won Hector's nod. At once
down from his chariot he swung to earth,
with all his weapons, and commanded swiftly:
'Polydamas –
it is up to you to call and hold our captains
while I take on the battle over there.
I will come back as soon
as I have made my orders clear to them.'

And towering like a snow-peak off he went
with a raucous cry, traversing on the run
Trojans and allied troops. Their officers
collected near Polydamas on hearing
new commands from Hector. Deiphobus,
Lord Helenus, Adamas, son of Asius,
and Asius, Hyrtacus' son, were those
he looked for down the front. Safe and unhurt
he scarcely found them. Those who lost their lives
at Argive hands were lying near the sterns;
others were thrown back on the wall with wounds.
But one man he soon found, on the left flank
of grievous battle: Alexandrus, prince,
husband of Helen of the shining hair.

He stood there cheering on his company,
and stepping near him Hector spoke to him
in bitterness: 'Paris, you bad-luck charm,
so brave to look at, woman-crazed, seducer,
where is Deiphobus? And Helenus?
Asius, Hyrtacus' son? Adamas, his son?
Where is Othryoneus? If these are gone,
tall Ilium is crumbling, sure disaster
lies ahead.'

And Alexandrus answered:

'Hector, since you are moved to blame the blameless,
there may be times when I break off the fighting,
but I will not now. My mother
bore me to be no milksop. From the hour
you roused our men to battle for the ships
we have been here engaging the Danaans
without respite. As for the friends you look for,
some are dead. Deiphobus and Helenus
went off, I think, with spear-wounds in the hand,
but the Lord Zeus has guarded them from slaughter.
Lead us now, wherever your high heart
requires. We are behind you, we are fresh
and lack no spirit in attack, I promise,
up to the limit of our strength.
Beyond that no man fights, though he may wish to.'
    With these mild words he won his brother over.
Into the thick of battle both men went,
round Cebriones, Polydamas, and Phalces,
Orthaeus, godlike Polyphetes, Palmys,
and the sons of Hippotion, Ascanius
and Morys. These had come the day before
at dawn, replacements from Ascania's ploughland.
    Zeus now intensified the fight. Men charged
like rough winds in a storm launched on the earth
in thunder of Father Zeus, when roaring high
the wind and ocean rise together; swell
on swell of clamorous foaming sea goes forward,
snowy-crested, curling, ranked ahead
and ranked behind: so line by compact line
advanced the Trojans glittering in bronze
behind their captains.
                        Hector in the lead,
peer of the man-destroying god of war,
held out his round shield, thick in bull's hide, nailed
with many studs of bronze, and round his temples
his bright helmet nodded. Feinting attack
now here, now there, along the front, he tried
the enemy to see if they would yield
before his shielded rush – but could not yet
bewilder the tough hearts of the Achaeans.
Aias with a giant stride moved out
to challenge him: 'Come closer, clever one!
Is this your way to terrify the Argives?
No, we are not so innocent of battle,

only worsted by the scourge of Zeus.
And now your heart's desire's to storm our ships,
but we have strong arms, too, arms to defend them.
Sooner your well-built town shall fall
to our assault, taken by storm and plundered.
As for yourself, the time is near, I say,
when in retreat you'll pray to Father Zeus
that your fine team be faster than paired falcons,
pulling you Troyward, making a dustcloud boil
along the plain!'

           At these words, on the right
an eagle soared across the sky. 'Iache!'
the Achaean army cried at this.

                    In splendour
Hector shouted: 'Aias, how you blubber;
clumsy ox, what rot you talk! I wish
I were as surely all my days
a son of Zeus who bears the storm-cloud, born
to Lady Hera, honoured like Athena
or like Apollo – as this day will surely
bring the Argives woe, to every man.
You will be killed among them! Only dare
stand up to my long spear! That fair white flesh
my spear will cut to pieces: then you'll glut
with fat and lean the dogs and carrion birds
of the Trojan land! You'll die there by your ships!'

    He finished and led onward. The front rank
moved out after him with a wild cry,
and from the rear the troops cheered. Facing them,
the Argives raised a shout; they had not lost
their grip on valour but now braced to meet
the Trojan onslaught. Clamour from both sides
went up to the pure rays of Zeus in heaven.

BOOK XIV

BEGUILEMENT ON MOUNT IDA

NOW Nestor heard that tumult while he drank,
but finished drinking. Then he turned and said
to Asclepius' son: 'Consider now, Machaon,
what had best be done here. Battle-cries
of young fighters are louder, near the ships.
As for yourself, be easy, drink my wine,
till Hecamede has a cauldron warmed
and bathes your clotted blood away. For my part,
I'll go outside and find a lookout point.'

He picked up in the hut a shield that lay there
all aglow with bronze – one that belonged
to a son of his, the horseman Thrasymedes,
who bore that day his father's shield. Then Nestor
chose a burly newly whetted spear,
and stepping out he saw that grim day's work:
Achaeans driven back, at bay; elated
Trojans pressing on; the wall torn down.

As when the open ocean
rises in a leaden smooth groundswell,
forerunner of high winds; a rocking swell,
directionless, that neither rolls nor breaks
until the blow comes on from Zeus: just so
the old man pondered, with divided mind,
whether to turn toward the Danaan mass
or find and join Lord Marshal Agamemnon.
Then he decided; it seemed best to him
to join the son of Atreus. In the line,
soldiers meanwhile fought on to strip each other,
metal upon their bodies clanging loud
with sword-blows and the double-bladed spears.

But now to Nestor's side the princes came
along the shipways, those who had been hit:
Diomedes, Odysseus, Agamemnon,
leaving the rear where, distant from the fighting,
ships were beached along the wash of surf –
higher inland were those first dragged ashore
around whose sterns the wall was built. In rows
they kept the ships drawn up; even that wide shore

could not contain the fleet in one long line;
they hauled them up, therefore, wave after wave,
and filled the beach between two promontories.
Now headed inland, eyes upon the mêlée,
the princes came that way, leaning on spears,
with aching hearts; and the advent of Nestor
gave their hearts a new twinge.
                              Agamemnon
hailed him, saying: 'Nestor, son of Neleus,
pride of Achaeans! Why turn this way, seaward,
away from the battle-danger? Now I fear
their champion, Hector, will make good his word,
the threat he made in his harangue to Trojans,
not to return to Ilium from the beach-head
until he fired our ships and killed our men.
So he proclaimed; now it is coming true.
My god, it seems the rest of the Achaeans,
like Achilles, hold a grudge against me!
They have no will to fight, to save the ships.'
    Lord Nestor of Gerenia replied:
'What you describe is all too clear. High-thundering
Zeus himself could not now otherwise
dispose the fight: those walls are overthrown
we put our trust in as impregnable,
a bulwark for the ships and for ourselves.
The enemy have brought the battle down
hard on the ships; you could not if you tried
make out whether from left or right our troops
are harried most and thrown into confusion.
Men go down on every hand; their death-cries
rise in air. We must think what to do,
if any good can be achieved by thinking.
I do not say that we should enter combat;
hurt men cannot fight.'
                          And the Lord Marshal
Agamemnon said: 'Since now they press the fight
around the ships' sterns, neither wall nor moat
made any difference, though painful labour
built them, and Danaans dearly hoped
they'd make a shield to save our ships and men –
this must be somehow satisfactory
to the high mind of Zeus, that far from Argos
Achaeans perish here without a name.
I knew it when he favoured us and saved us,

I know it now, when he glorifies our enemies,
treating them like gods! He tied our hands,
he took the heart out of us.

                    'Come, everyone
do as I say: haul down the line of ships
nearest the sea to launch on the bright breakers,
moor them afloat till starry night comes on
and Trojans break off battle. Under cover
of darkness we may launch the rest.
There's no disgrace in getting away from ruin,
not by a night retirement. Better a man
should leave the worst behind him than be caught.'

    Odysseus, the great tactician, frowned
and looked at him and answered: 'Son of Atreus,
what kind of talk is this?
Hell's misery! I'd put you in command
of some disordered rabble, not an army
strong as our own. Our lot from youth to age
was given us by Zeus: danger and war
to wind upon the spindle of our years
until we die to the last man.

                    'Would you, then,
quit and abandon for ever the fine town
of Troy that we have fought for all these years,
taking our losses? Quiet! or some other
Achaeans may get wind of this. No man
who knew what judgement is in speech could ever
allow that thought to pass his lips – no man
who bore a staff, whom army corps obeyed,
as Argives owe obedience to you.
Contempt, no less, is what I feel for you
after the sneaking thing that you propose.
While the two armies are in desperate combat,
haul our ships into the sea? You'd give
the Trojans one more thing to glory over –
and they are winning out, god knows, already!
As for ourselves, sheer ruin is what it means.
While our long ships are hauled down, will the soldiers
hold the line? Will they not look seaward
and lose their appetite for battle? There,
commander, is your way to wreck us all.'

    Lord Marshal Agamemnon answered him:
'You hit hard, and the blow comes home, Odysseus.
Let it be clear I would not urge the troops

to launch, against their will and yours, not I.
Whoever has a better plan should speak,
young man or old; I would be glad to hear it.'
   Now Diomedes of the great war-cry
spoke up: 'Here's one. No need to go afield for it.
If you are willing to be swayed, and are not
irritated with me, the youngest here.
                   'I, too,
can claim a brave and noble father, Tydeus,
whom funeral earth at Thebes has mounded over.
To Portheus three excellent sons were born,
who lived in Pleuron and in Calydon –
Agrius, Melas, and the horseman Oeneus,
bravest of all and father of my father.
Oeneus remained there, while my wandering father
settled in Argos. It was the will of Zeus
and of the other gods.
              'He took Adrastus'
daughter as bride and founded a great house:
grain-lands enough he owned, and he owned orchards
thick with trees, and herds and flocks aplenty.
Beyond that, he was best of all Achaeans
in handling a spear: you must have heard this
and know the truth of it. My lineage
therefore is noble. If what I say's well said
you may not disregard it.
             'Let us go
this way to battle, wounded as we are;
we have no choice. There in the field we may
keep clear of missiles, not to be hit again,
but put heart in the rest. Just as before
they save themselves, and shirk the fight.'
                   To this
the others listening hard gave their assent.
They turned, and Agamemnon led them forward.
   This was not lost on the god who shakes the earth,
who now appeared as an old man and walked
beside them, taking Agamemnon's hand,
saying to him in a clear voice rapidly:
'Son of Atreus, think how the fierce heart
must sing now in Achilles' breast,
to see the slaughter and rout of the Achaeans!
Compassion is not in him. Let him rot, then!
Some god crush him! But the gods in bliss

are not unalterably enraged with you.
Somehow the hour will come when Trojan captains
make the wide plain smoke with dust, in chariots
racing from camp and ships back to the city!'

Launching himself upon the field of war,
he broke into a shout nine or ten thousand
men who yelled in battle might have made,
meeting in shock of combat: from his lungs
the powerful Earthshaker sent aloft
a cry like that. In every Achaean heart
he put the nerve to fight and not be broken.

Now Lady Hera of the Golden Chair
had turned her eyes upon the war. She stood
apart upon a snow-crest of Olympus
and recognized her brother-in-law, her brother,
striving in battle, breathing hard – a sight
that pleased her. Then she looked at Zeus, who rested
high on the ridge of Ida bright with springs,
and found him odious.

                         Her ladyship
of the wide eyes took thought how to distract
her lord who bears the storm-cloud. Her best plan,
she thought, was this: to scent and adorn herself
and visit Ida, hoping hot desire
might rise in him – desire to lie with her
and make love to her nakedness – that so
she might infuse warm slumber on his eyes
and over his shrewd heart.

                              She entered then
the chamber built for her by her own son,
Hephaestus, who had fitted door to doorpost
using a secret bolt no god could force.
These shining doors the goddess closed behind her,
and with ambrosia cleansed all stain away
from her delectable skin. Then with fine oil
she smoothed herself, and this, her scented oil,
unstoppered in the bronze-floored house of Zeus,
cast fragrance over earth and heaven. Hera,
having anointed all her graceful body,
and having combed her hair, plaited it shining
in braids from her immortal head. That done,
she chose a wondrous gown, worked by Athena
in downy linen with embroideries.
She caught this at her breast with golden pins

and girt it with a waistband, sewn all around
with a hundred tassels. Then she hung
mulberry-coloured pendants in her ear-lobes,
and loveliness shone round her. A new head-dress
white as the sun she took to veil her glory,
and on her smooth feet tied her beautiful sandals.
Exquisite and adorned from head to foot
she left her chamber.

               Beckoning Aphrodite,
she spoke to her apart from all the rest:
'Will you give heed to me, and do as I say,
and not be difficult? Even though you are vexed
that I give aid and comfort to Danaans
as you do to the Trojans.'

                      Aphrodite,
daughter of Zeus, replied: 'Hera, most honoured
of goddesses, being Cronos' own daughter,
say what you have in mind!
I am disposed to do it if I can,
and if it is a thing that one may do.'

   And Lady Hera, deep in her beguilement,
answered: 'Lend me longing, lend me desire,
by which you bring immortals low
as you do mortal men!

                 'I am on my way
to kind Earth's bourne to see Oceanus
from whom the gods arose, and Mother Tethys.
In their great hall they nurtured me, their gift
from Rhea, when Lord Zeus of the wide gaze
put Cronos down, deep under earth and sea.
I go to see them and compose their quarrel:
estranged so long, they have not once made love
since anger came between them. Could I coax them
into their bed to give and take delight,
I should be prized and dear to them for ever.'

   Aphrodite, lover of smiling eyes,
replied to her: 'It is not possible
and not expedient, either, to deny you,
who go to lie in the great arms of Zeus.'

   Now she unfastened from around her breast
a pierced brocaded girdle. Her enchantments
came from this: allurement of the eyes,
hunger of longing, and the touch of lips
that steals all wisdom from the coolest men.

This she bestowed in Hera's hands and murmured:
'Take this girdle, keep it in your breast.
Here are all suavities and charms of love,
I do not think you will be ineffective
in what you plan.'
                    Then wide-eyed Hera smiled
and smiling put the talisman in her breast.
Aphrodite entered her father's house,
but Hera glided from Olympus, passing
Pieria and cherished Emathia,
flashing above the snowy-crested hills
of Thracian horsemen. Never touching down,
she turned from Athos over the sea-waves
to Lemnos, to the stronghold of old Thoas.

Here she fell in with Sleep, brother of Death,
and took his hand and held it, saying warmly:
'Sleep, sovereign of gods and all mankind,
if ever you gave heed to me before,
comply again this time, and all my days
I shall know well I am beholden. Lull
to sleep for me the shining eyes of Zeus
as soon as I lie down with him in love.
Then I shall make a gift to you, a noble,
golden, eternal chair: my bandy-legged
son Hephaestus by his craft will make it
and fit it with a low footrest
where you may place your feet while taking wine.'

But mild sweet Sleep replied: 'Most venerable
goddess, daughter of Cronos, great of old,
among the gods who never die, I might
easily lull another to sleep – yes, even
the ebb and flow of cold Oceanus,
the primal source of all that lives.
But Zeus, the son of Cronos? No, not I.
I could not venture near him, much less lull him.
One other time
you taught me something, giving me a mission,
when Heracles, the prodigious son of Zeus,
had plundered Ilium and come away.
That day indeed I cast my spell
on the Father's heart; I drifted dim about him,
while you prepared rough sailing for the hero.
In the open sea you stirred a gale that drove
Heracles on Cos Island, far from friends.

Then Zeus woke up and fell into a fury
and hurled the gods about his hall, in quest
of me above all. Out of heaven's air
into deep sea to be invisible for ever
he would have plunged me, had not Night preserved me,
all-subduing Night,
mistress of gods and men. I fled to her,
and he for all his rage drew back, for fear
of doing a displeasure to swift Night.
A second time you ask me to perform
something I may not.'

                But to this she answered:
'Why must you dwell on that unhappy day?
Can you believe that Zeus who views the wide world
will be as furious in defence of Trojans
as for his own son, Heracles? No, no.
Come. I should add, my gift to you will be
one of the younger Graces for a mistress,
ever to be called yours.'

                In eager pleasure,
Sleep said: 'Swear by Styx' corroding water!
Place one hand on earth, grassland of herds,
and dip your other hand in dazzling sea:
all gods with Cronos in the abyss, attest
that I shall marry one of the younger Graces,
Pasithea, the one I have desired
all my living days.'

                Without demur,
Hera whose arms shone white as ivory
took oath as he demanded. Each by name
she called on all the powers of the abyss,
on all the Titans. Then, when she had sworn,
these two departed in the air from Lemnos,
putting on veils of cloudrack, lightly running
toward Ida, mother of beasts and bright with springs.
At Lectum promontory, from the sea
they veered inland and upland. At their passage
tree-tops were in commotion underfoot.
But Sleep soon halted and remained behind
before he came in range of Zeus's eyes.
He mounted a tall pine, the tallest one
on Ida, grown through mist to pierce the sky.
Amid the evergreen boughs he hid and clung
and seemed that mountain-thrush of the clear tone,

called 'chalcis' by the gods, by men 'cymindis.'

Hera swept on to Gargaron, Ida's crest,
and there Zeus, lord of cloud, saw her arrive.
He gazed at her, and as he gazed desire
veiled his mind like mist, as in those days
when they had first slipped from their parents' eyes
to bed, to mingle by the hour in love.
He stood before her now and said: 'What brings you
down from Olympus to this place?
The chariot you ride is not in sight.'

The Lady Hera answered him in guile:
'I go my way to the bourne of Earth, to see
Oceanus, from whom the gods arose,
and Mother Tethys. In their distant hall
they nourished me and cared for me in childhood.
Now I must see them and compose their strife.
They live apart from one another's bed,
estranged so long, since anger came between them.
As for my team, it stands at Ida's base
ready to take me over earth and sea.
On your account I came to see you first,
so that you will not rage at me for going
in secret where Oceanus runs deep.'

The lord of cloud replied: 'But you may go there
later, Hera. Come, lie down. We two
must give ourselves to love-making. Desire
for girl or goddess in so wild a flood
never came over me! Not for Ixion's bride
who bore that peerless hero, Peirithous;
or Danae with her delicious legs,
illustrious Perseus' mother; or Europa,
daughter of Phoenix, world-renowned, who bore me
Minos and magnificent Rhadamanthys;
Semele or Alcmene, Theban ladies –
one bore the rugged hero Heracles,
the other Dionysus, joy of men –
or Demeter, the queen in her blond braids;
or splendid Leto; or yourself! No lust
as sweet as this for you has ever taken me!'

To this the Lady Hera in her guile
replied: 'Most formidable son of Cronos,
how impetuous! Would you lie down here
on Ida's crest for all the world to see?
Suppose one of the gods who never die

perceived us here asleep and took the story
to all the rest? I could not bear to walk
directly from this love-bed to your hall,
it would be so embarrassing. But if you must,
if this is what you wish, and near your heart,
there is my own bedchamber. Your dear son,
Hephaestus, built it, and he fitted well
the solid door and door-jamb. We should go
to lie down there, since bed is now your pleasure.'

But the lord marshal of storm-cloud said: 'No fear
this act will be observed by god or man,
I shall enshroud us in such golden cloud.
Not even Helios could glimpse us through it,
and his hot ray is finest at discerning.'

At this he took his wife in his embrace,
and under them earth flowered delicate grass
and clover wet with dew; then crocuses
and solid beds of tender hyacinth
came crowding upward from the ground. On these
the two lay down and drew around them purest
vapour of golden cloud; the droplets fell
away in sunlight sparkling. Soon the Father,
subjugated by love and sleep, lay still.
Still as a stone on Gargaron height he lay
and slumbered with his lady in his arms.

The god of sleep went gliding to the beach-head
bearing word to the god who shakes the earth.
He halted at his side and swiftly said:
'Warm to your work now, comfort the Danaans,
even award them glory in the fight –
for a while at any rate – while Zeus is sleeping,
now that I've wrapped him in a night of sleep.
Hera beguiled him into making love.'

And he was gone into far lands of fame
when he had stirred Poseidon to fight harder.

The god now gained the line in a single bound
and called out: 'Argives, shall we yield to Hector
once again? And let him take the ships,
let him win glory? He would have it so
because Achilles lingers by his ships,
anger in his heart.

            'Well, that great man
need not be missed too badly, if the rest of us
rally each other to defend ourselves.

Come, every man, and act on what I say:
the army's best and biggest body-shields
are those that we should wear, our heads encased
in helms that flash on every side, our hands
upon the longest spears! And then attack!
I will myself go first. My life upon it,
Hector for all his valour cannot hold us!
Any fresh man who bears against his shoulder
a light shield, give it now to a tired fighter,
and slip his own arm in a heavier one.'

    The attentive soldiers acted on his words,
while Diomedes, Odysseus, and Agamemnon,
wounded as they were, kept all in order.

    Down the ranks they made exchange of gear,
good gear to good men, poor to the inferior,
and when hard bronze was fitted to their bodies
all moved out. Poseidon took the lead,
in his right fist a blade fine-edged as lightning
that mortals may not parry in grievous war –
for blinding fear makes men stand back from it.
Hector drew up the Trojan lines opposing,
and now the blue-maned god of sea and Hector
brought to a dreadful pitch the clash of war,
one giving heart to Trojans, one to Argives.
Waves of the sea ran berserk toward the Argive
huts and ships as the two armies closed
with a great cry. No surge from open sea,
whipped by a norther, buffets down on land
with such a roar, nor does a forest fire
in mountain valleys blazing up through woods,
nor stormwind in the towering boughs of oaks
when at its height it rages, make a roar
as great as this, when Trojans and Achaeans
hurled themselves at one another.

                         Hector
drove at Aias first with his great spear,
as Aias had swung round at him. He hit him
at that point where two belts crossed on his chest,
one for his shield, one for his studded sword,
and both together saved his skin. In rage
because the missile left his hand in vain,
Hector fell back in ranks away from danger,
but as he drew away Telamonian Aias
picked up one of the wedging stones for ships

rolled out there, many, at the fighters' feet,
and smote him in the chest, above his shield-rim,
near his throat. The impact spun him round
reeling like a spent top. As an oak tree
under the stroke of Father Zeus goes down,
root and branch, and deadly fumes of brimstone
rise from it, and no man's courage keeps him
facing it if he sees it – Zeus's bolt
being rough indeed – so all Hector's élan
now dropped in dust. He flung his spear, his shield
and helm sank down with him, his blazoned armour
clanged about him.
                     Yelling Achaean soldiers
ran toward him, hoping to drag him off,
and they made play with clumps of spears. But none
could wound or hit the marshal of the Trojans,
being forestalled by the Trojan peers,
Aeneas, Polydamas, and Agenor,
Sarpedon, chief of Lycians, and Glaucus.
None of the rest neglected him, but over him
all held up their round shields. Fellow-soldiers
lifted him in their arms to bear him off
out of the grind of battle to his horses.
These were waiting in the battle's rear
with painted chariot and driver. Now
toward Troy they carried Hector, hoarsely groaning.
Reaching the ford of Xanthus, the clear stream
of eddying water that immortal Zeus
had fathered, from the car they laid him down
on the river-bank and splashed cool water on him.
Taking a deep breath, opening his eyes wide,
he got to his knees and spat dark blood, then backward
sank again as black night hooded him,
stunned still by the hurled stone.
                              But the Argives,
seeing Hector leave the field, were swift
to step up their attacks upon the Trojans,
taking new joy in battle. Out in front,
the runner, Aias, son of Oileus, lunged
and wounded Satnius Enopides,
whom by the banks of Satnioeis river
a flawless naiad bore the herdsman, Enops.
This Satnius the famous son of Oileus,
coming in fast, speared in the flank. He tumbled,

and then around him Trojans and Danaans
clashed in bitter combat. Polydamas
took the lead, shaking his spear to guard him,
and struck Areilycus' son,
Prothoenor, square on the right shoulder,
his spear passing through. Into the dust
he fell and clutched at earth with his spread hand.
   Then Polydamas gloried, shouting high:
'By god, this time the spearshaft from the hand
of Panthous' son leapt out to some effect.
One of the Argives caught it in his flesh;
I can see him now, using it for a crutch,
as he stumps to the house of Death!'
                    His boasting brought
anguish to Argives, most of all to Aias,
veteran son of Telamon: beside him
the dying man fell. Now with his shining spear
he thrust at the withdrawing enemy,
but he, Polydamas, with a sidewise leap
avoided that dark fate. Another got it –
Archelochus, for the gods had planned his ruin.
Just at the juncture of his neck and skull
the blow fell on his topmost vertebra
and cut both tendons through. Head, mouth, and nostrils
hit the earth before his shins and knees.
   Now Aias in his turn to Polydamas
shouted: 'Think now, Polydamas, tell me truly
if this man was not worthy to be killed
for Prothoenor? as he seemed to me
no coward nor of cowards' kind, but brother
to Lord Antenor, master of horse, or else
his son, for he was very nearly like him.'
   He said this knowing the answer well. And pain
seized Trojan hearts. Standing above his brother,
Acamas brought down Promachus, a Boeotian,
as he was tugging at the dead man's feet.
   Then gloating over him with a wild cry
Acamas said: 'You Argive arrow-boys,
greedy for the sound of your own voices,
hardship and grief will not be ours alone!
You'll be cut down as he was! Only think,
the way your Promachus has gone to sleep
after my spear downed him – and no delay
in the penalty for my brother's death. See why

a soldier prays that a kinsman left at home
will fight for him?
                        And this taunt hurt the Argives.
Most of all, it angered Peneleos
and he attacked Acamas, who retired
before his charge. Peneleos, instead,
brought down Ilioneus, a son of Phorbas,
the sheepherder, whom of all Trojans Hermes
favoured most and honoured with possessions,
although Ilioneus' mother bore the man
that son alone. Peneleos drove his spearhead
into the eye-socket underneath the brow,
thrusting the eyeball out. The spearhead ran
straight through the socket and the skull behind,
and throwing out both hands he sat down backward.
Peneleos, drawing his long sword, chopped through
the nape and set the severed helmeted head
and trunk apart upon the field. The spear
remained in the eye-socket.
                            Lifting up
the head by it as one would lift a poppy,
he cried out to the Trojans, gloating grimly:
'Go tell Ilioneus' father and his mother
for me, Trojans, to mourn him in their hall.
The wife of Promachus, Alegenor's son,
will not be gladdened by her husband's step,
that day when we Achaeans make home port
in the ships from Troy.'
                        And the knees of all the Trojans
were shaken by a trembling as each one
looked for a way to escape breath-taking death.
    Muses in your bright Olympian halls,
tell me now what Achaean most excelled
in winning bloodstained spoils of war
when the Earthshaker bent the battle line.
Aias Telamonius cut down
the Mysian leader, Hyrtius Gyrtiades;
Antilochus killed Mermerus and Phalces;
Meriones Morys and Hippotion;
Teucer Prothoon and Periphetes.
After that, Menelaus hit Hyperenor's
flank, and the spearhead spilt his guts like water.
By the wound-slit, as by a doorway, life
left him in haste, and darkness closed his eyes.

But Aias the swift runner, son of Oileus,
killed more than any: none could chase as he could
a soldier panicked in that god-sent rout.

BOOK XV

THE LORD OF STORM

RUNNING among the stakes, crossing the moat,
many of them were cut down by Danaans;
the remnant reached the chariots and stood there,
pale with fear, beaten.
                              And now Zeus
on Ida's top by Hera's queenly side
awoke and rose in a single bound. He saw
the Trojans and Achaeans – Trojans routed,
pressed by Achaeans whom Poseidon joined;
saw Hector stretched out on the battlefield,
brothers-in-arms around him, squatting down
where he lay, faint and fighting hard for breath,
vomiting blood. The man who knocked him out
was not the weakest of Achaeans.
                                      Watching,
the father of gods and men was moved to pity.
He turned with a dark scowl and said to Hera:
'Fine underhanded work, eternal bitch!
putting Lord Hector out of action,
breaking his fighting men! I should not wonder
if this time you will be the first to catch it,
a whip across your shoulders for your pains!
Do you forget swinging so high that day?
I weighted both your feet with anvils,
lashed both arms with golden cord
you couldn't break, and there you dangled
under open heaven amid white cloud.
Some gods resented this,
but none could reach your side or set you free.
Any I caught I pitched head first
over our rampart, half-dead, down to earth!
Yet even so my heartache for the hero,
Heracles, would not be shaken off.
You and the north wind had connived, sent gales
against that man, brewed up sea-perils for him,
driven him over the salt waste to Cos Island.
I set him free, I brought him back
from all that toil to the blue-grass land of Argos.

'These things I call to mind once more
to see to it that you mend your crooked ways.
Learn what you gain by lechery with me,
tricking me into it! That's why you came,
apart from all the gods!'

                  Now Hera shuddered
answering in a clear low tone, protesting:
'Earth be my witness, and the open sky,
and oozing water of Styx – the gods can take
no oath more solemn or more terrifying –
and by your august person, too, I swear
as by our sacred bed – how could I lightly
swear by that? – no prompting word of mine
induced the god who makes the mainland shake
to do harm to the Trojans and to Hector,
backing their enemies. It cannot be
anything but his own heart that impels him.
Seeing the tired Achaeans in retreat
upon their own ships' sterns, he pitied them.
But I – I too – should counsel him to go
where you command him, lord of darkening cloud.'

    At this he smiled, the father of gods and men,
and lightly came his words upon the air:
    'Then in the time to come, my wide-eyed lady,
supposing you should care to sit with me
in harmony among the immortal gods,
for all Poseidon's will to the contrary,
he must come round to meet your wish and mine.
If what you say is honest, then rejoin
the gods' company now, and call for Iris,
call for Apollo with his wondrous bow.
Iris will go amid the mailed Achaeans
with my word to Poseidon: *Quit the war,
return to your own element.* Apollo
must then brace Hector for the fight and breathe
new valour in him, blot from his memory
the pangs that now wear out his spirit. Let him
shatter the Achaeans into retreat,
helpless, in panic, till they reach the ships
of Peleus' son, Achilles. Then that prince
will send Patroclus, his great friend, to war,
and Hector in glory before Ilium
by a spear-cast will bring Patroclus down,
though he destroy a host of men, my son,

Sarpedon, being among them. Aye, for this
the Prince Achilles in high rage
will kill heroic Hector. From that moment
I'll turn the tide of battle on the beach
decisively, once and for all,
until the Achaeans capture Ilium,
as Athena planned and willed it. But until
that killing I shall not remit my wrath.
Nor shall I let another god take part
on the Danaans' side – no, not before
the heart's desire of the son of Peleus
shall have been consummated. So I promised,
so with a nod I swore, that day when Thetis
touched my knees and begged me to give honour
to Achilles, raider of cities.'
                When he finished,
Hera took pains to follow his command:
from Ida's crests she flashed to high Olympus
quick as a thought in a man's mind.
Far and wide a journeying man may know
the earth and with his many desires may dream,
'Now let me be in that place or that other!'
Even so instantaneously Queen Hera
passed to steep Olympus. She appeared
in the long hall of Zeus amid the immortals,
who rose, lifting their cups to her.
                She passed,
ignoring all the rest, but took a cup
from rose-cheeked Themis, who came running out
to meet her, crying: 'Hera,
why have you come back? Oh, how dazed you look!
Your husband must have given you a fright!'
    To this the beautiful goddess with white arms
replied: 'No need to ask, my lovely Themis.
You know how harsh and arrogant he is.
Preside now at our feast,
here in the hall of gods, and with the rest
you'll hear what cruelty he shows.
Among mortals or gods, I rather think
not everyone will share his satisfaction,
although one still may feast and be at ease.'
    The Lady Hera finished and sat down,
and all turned sullen in the hall of Zeus.
Her lips were smiling, but the frown remained

unsmoothed upon her brow.

                    Then she broke out
in her bad temper: 'Oh, what mindless fools
to lay plans against Zeus! And yet we do,
we think we can be near him, and restrain him,
by pleading or by force. But there he sits
apart from us, careless of us, forever
telling us he is quite beyond us all
in power and might, supreme among the gods!
So each must take what trouble he may send.
And this time grief's at hand
for Ares; yes, his son died in the fighting,
dearest of men to him: Ascalaphus.
The strong god Ares claimed that man for son.'

    Now Ares smote his thighs with open hands
and groaned: 'You must not take it ill, Olympians,
if I go down amid the Achaean ships
to avenge my son – and so I will, though fate
will have me blasted by the bolt of Zeus
to lie in bloody dust among the dead!'

    He called to Terror and Rout to yoke his horses
while he put on his shining gear. Now soon
another greater and more bitter fury
would have been roused in Zeus against the gods,
had not Athena, gravely fearing for them,
left the chair she sat on, and come forward
out of the forecourt. She removed the helm
from Ares head, the great shield from his shoulder,
and laid his spear down, lifted from his hand.

    Then she spoke to rebuke the angry god:
'You've lost your mind, mad one, this is your ruin!
No use your having ears to listen with –
your self-possession and your wits are gone.
Have you not taken in what Hera says,
who just now came from Zeus? Do you desire
to have your bellyful of trouble first
and find yourself again upon Olympus,
rage as you will, brought back by force, moreover
bringing a nightmare on the rest of us?
In a flash he'll turn from Trojans and Achaeans
and create pandemonium on Olympus,
laying hands on everyone alike,
guilty or not. Therefore I call on you
to drop your anger for your son. By now

some better man than he in strength and skill
has met his death in battle, or soon will.
There is no saving the sons of all mankind.'

Then in his chair she seated burly Ares.
Hera now called Apollo from the hall
with Iris, messenger of the immortals.
Lifting her voice, addressing both, she said:
'Zeus commands you with all speed to Ida.
Once you are there and face him, you'll perform
whatever mission he may set for you.'

With this the Lady Hera turned away
and took her chair again, as off they soared
toward Ida, bright with springs, mother of beasts.
On Gargaron height they found him at his ease,
the broad-browed son of Cronos, garlanded
by fragrant cloud. The two gods took their stand
before him who is master of the storm —
and he regarded them, unstirred by anger,
seeing their prompt obedience to his lady.

Then to Iris he said: 'Away with you,
light-foot, take my message to Poseidon,
all of it; do not misreport it; say
he must give up his part in war and battle,
consort with gods or else go back to sea.
But if he disobeys or disregards me,
let him remember: for all his might,
he does not have it in him to oppose me.
I am more powerful by far than he,
and senior to him. He has forgotten this,
claiming equality with me. All others
shrink from that.'

                    Then running on the wind
swift Iris carried out his order. Down
from Ida's hills she went to Ilium,
as snow or hail flies cold from winter cloud,
driven by north wind born in heights of air.

So Iris flew in swiftness of desire,
halting beside the Earthshaker to say:
'O girdler of the earth, sea-god, blue-maned,
I bear a message from the lord of storm.
You must give up the battle, must retire
amid the gods, or else go back to sea.
But if you disobey or disregard him,
he warns you he will take a hand in war

against you, coming here himself. You would
do well to avoid that meeting, he advises,
seeing he's far more powerful than you
and senior to you. You have overlooked this,
claiming equality with him. All others
shrink from that.'

                 His face grown dark with rage,
the great Earthshaker said: 'The gall of him!
Noble no doubt he is, but insolent, too,
to threaten me with forcible restraint
who am his peer in honour. Sons of Cronos
all of us are, all three whom Rhea bore,
Zeus and I and the lord of those below.
All things were split three ways, to each his honour,
when we cast lots. Indeed it fell to me
to abide for ever in the grey sea water;
Hades received the dark mist at the world's-end,
and Zeus the open heaven of air and cloud.
But Earth is common to all, so is Olympus.
No one should think that I shall live one instant
as he thinks best! No, let him hold his peace
and power in his heaven, in his portion,
not try intimidating me –
I will not have it – as though I were a coward.
Better to roar and thunder at his own,
the sons and daughters he himself has fathered!
They are the ones who have to listen to him.'

   Wind-swift Iris answered: 'Shall I put it
just that way, god of the dark blue tresses,
bearing this hostile message back to Zeus?
Or will you make some change? All princely hearts
are capable of changing. And, you know,
the Furies take the part of elder brothers!'

   Poseidon made reply: 'Excellent Iris,
very well said; that is a point well taken;
it is a fine thing when a messenger
knows what is fitting.

                 'But it irks me
his being so quarrelsome, railing at me
who am his peer in destiny and rank.
I yield, though – but I take it ill, by heaven.
And there is more to say: with all my power
I warn him, if without me and Athena,
Hera and Hermes and the Lord Hephaestus,

he should make up his mind alone
to spare steep Ilium, and will not sack it,
will not give the Argives the upper hand,
then he incurs our unappeasable anger.'
    When he had said this, turning from the Achaeans,
into the deep he plunged, and the soldiers missed him.
    Then, to Apollo, Zeus who gathers cloud
said: 'Go, dear Phoebus, to the side of Hector,
now that the god who shakes the earth has gone
into the salt immortal sea. He shunned
our towering anger. Had he not, some others
might have had lessons in the art of war –
even the gods below, round fallen Cronos.
But it is better far for both
that even though he hates it he give way
before my almighty hands. Not without sweat
would that affair have been concluded.
                        'Well,
take for yourself my tasseled shield of storm-cloud,
and shake it hard with lightning overhead
to rout the Achaean soldiers. God of archery,
make Hector your own special charge.
Arouse his utmost valour till, in rout,
the Achaeans reach the ships and Helle's waters.
There I myself shall conjure word and act
to give once more a respite to Achaeans.'
    Without demurring at his father's words
Apollo glided from the heights of Ida,
like that swiftest of birds, the peregrine.
He found Prince Hector, Priam's son,
no longer supine but just now recovered,
sitting up, able to see and know
his friends' faces around him; his hard panting
and sweating had been eased. The mind of Zeus,
master of cloud, reanimated him.
    And standing near the man, Apollo said:
'Hector, why do you sit here, weak and sick,
far from the rest? What has come over you?'
    And Hector of the shining helmet answered,
whispering hoarsely: 'Excellency, who are you?
A god? What god, to face and question me?
Do you not know that near the Achaean sterns
where I had killed his friends, formidable
Aias hit my chest with a great stone

and knocked the fighting spirit out of me?
In fact I thought this day I'd see the dead
in the underworld – I thought I had breathed my last!'
    Apollo, lord of archery, replied:
'Be of good heart. The god you see, from Ida,
the Lord Zeus sent to fight with you in battle.
I am Apollo of the golden sword;
I rescued you before, you and your city.
Up, then; tell your host of charioteers
to charge the deep-sea ships. I shall go first
and cut a passage clean for chariot-horses,
putting Achaean soldiery to rout.'
    This inspired a surge of fighting spirit
in the commander's heart. As when a stallion,
long in the stall and full-fed at his trough,
snaps his halter and goes cantering off
across a field to splash in a clear stream,
rearing his head aloft triumphantly
with mane tossed on his shoulders, glorying
in his own splendour, and with driving knees
seeking familiar meadow-land and pasture:
just so Hector, sure-footed and swift,
sped on the chariots at the god's command.
    And the Achaeans? Think of hunting dogs
and hunters tracking a wild goat or a stag
to whom steep rock and dusky wood
give cover, so the hunters are at a loss
and by their cries arouse a whiskered lion
full in their path, at which they all fall back,
eager as they have been for prey: just so,
Danaans thronging in pursuit, and drawing
blood with swords and double-bladed spears,
when they caught sight of Hector coming on
toward their front rank, turned round in sudden terror,
courage ebbing to their very feet.
    But now they heard from Thoas, son of Andraemon,
bravest of the Aetolians, a tough man
at spear-throwing and in close combat, too;
and few Achaeans bested him in assembly
when the young vied in argument: 'Bad luck,'
he cried, 'this marvel that I see ahead:
Hector escaped from death, he's on his feet.
God knows, each one of us had hoped and prayed
he died from Aias' blow! But no, some god

protected him and saved him. This same Hector
broke the strength of many a Danaan,
and now he will again. Without some help
from Zeus who thunders in high heaven
he could not lead this charge so furiously.
Come, then, everyone do as I advise:
the rank and file we'll order to the rear,
back to the ships. But we who count ourselves
as champions in the army will stand fast.
We may contain him if we face him first
with ranked spears. Wild as he is, I think
that in his heart he fears to mix with us.'
    Assenting to this speech they acted on it.
Those with Aias and Idomeneus,
Teucer, Meriones, the veteran Meges,
formed for close-order combat, calling first-rate
spearmen to face Hector and the Trojans.
Meanwhile the rank and file fell back
upon the Achaean ships.
                All in a mass
with jutting spears the Trojans came, as Hector
strode in command. Apollo, leading him,
was cloaked in a white cloud, and held the shield
of ominous storm-cloud, with its trailing fringe.
The smith Hephaestus gave this shield to Zeus
to carry and strike fear in men. Apollo
handled it now as he led on the Trojans.
All in a mass the Argive captains stood,
and a sharp cry rose from both sides; then arrows
bounded from bowstrings; then from bold men's hands
a rain of spears came. Some stuck fast in agile
fighters' bodies; many between the ranks
fell short of the white flesh and stood a-quiver,
fixed in earth, still craving to be sated.
As long as Phoebus held the shield of storm-cloud
motionless, from both sides missiles flew,
men fell on both. But when he made it quake
with lightning, staring Danaans in the face,
and gave, himself, a deafening battle-cry,
he stunned them all and they forgot their valour.
As when a pair of wild beasts in the dusk
stampedes a herd of cows or a flock of sheep,
by a sudden rush, and no herdsman is near,
so the Achaeans lost their nerve and panicked.

Apollo sent the soul of rout among them,
but glory to the Trojans and to Hector.

Each man slew his man in the broken field:
Hector killed Stichius and Arcesilaus,
one a Boeotian captain, and the other
comrade of brave Menestheus; then Aeneas
dispatched Medon and Iasus: the first-named
a bastard son of Oileus, and half-brother
of Aias: he had lived in Phylace
in exile from his own land, having murdered
a kinsman of his stepmother, Eriopis.
Iasus was a captain of Athenians
and son, so called, of Sphelus Bucolides.
Polydamas killed Mecisteus – Echius,
his father, fell in the early battle-line
before Polites – and heroic Agenor
killed Clonius. Then as Deiochus ran,
Paris hit his shoulder from behind
and drove the brazen spearhead through his chest.

While Trojans stripped these dead, Achaeans
crowding into the ditch among the stakes
were forced in a wild scramble across the wall.

So Hector with a great shout called his men:
'Sweep on the ships! Let bloodstained gear alone!
The man I see on the wrong side of the wall,
away from the ships, will die there by my hand.
They won't be lucky enough to burn his corpse –
his women and his kin; wild dogs will drag him
before our city.'
                              Swinging from the shoulder
he whipped his horses on, and called the Trojans
after him into the enemy's ragged ranks,
and all together, guiding the chariot horses,
gave a savage cry. Far in the lead
Apollo kicked the embankment of the ditch
into the middle and so made a causeway,
wide as a spear-throw when a powerful man
puts his back into throwing. Over this
they poured in column, led on by Apollo
holding the dusky splendid shield of cloud.
As for the Achaean rampart, in one sweep
he levelled it, as a boy on the sea-shore
wipes out a wall of sand he built
in a child's game: with feet and hands, for fun,

he scatters it again. Just so,
bright Phoebus, you threw down the Argive wall,
so long and hard to build, and terrified
the Argives. Backed up on the ships, they waited,
crying out to each other, lifting prayerful
hands to all the gods.
                              Gerenian Nestor,
lord of the western approaches to Achaea,
stretching his hands out to the sky of stars,
prayed: 'Father Zeus, if someone long ago
in Argos of the grain-fields offered up
fat haunches of a cow or sheep in fire
and begged you for a safe return from Troy,
winning your promise and your nod, remember
now, Olympian! Defend us
against this pitiless day! Do not allow
Achaeans to be crushed this way by Trojans!'
    Fervently he prayed, and the lord of wisdom
thundered a great peal, hearing the old man's prayer.
And at that peal of Zeus's thunder, Trojans
thrilled with joy of battle, running harder
after the Argives. Like a surging wave
that comes inboard a ship when a gale blows –
wind giving impetus to sea – the Trojans
crossed the rampart with a mighty cry
and whipped their chariots toward the sterns. Once there,
they fought close-up with double-bladed spears,
attackers from the chariots, defenders
high on the black hulls, thrusting down long pikes
that lay aboard for sea-fights, double-length
in fitted sections, shod with biting bronze.
    As long as both sides fought around the rampart
still remote from the ships, Patroclus stayed
inside the shelter with Eurypylus
to give him pleasure, talking, and to treat
his aching wound with salve against the pain;
but when he knew the Trojans had crossed over,
knew by their cry the Danaans were in rout,
he groaned and smote his thighs with open hands,
and miserably he said:
                              'Eurypylus,
I cannot linger with you here,
much as you need me. The big fight begins.
One of your men can keep you company,

but I must go to Achilles in a hurry
to make him join the battle. Who can say
if with god's help I may convince and move him?
A friend's persuasion is an excellent thing.'

Even as he spoke, he strode out. The Achaeans
meanwhile held position at the ships
against the Trojan rush, but they could not
repel the Trojans, even outnumbering them,
nor could the Trojans break the Danaan line
to penetrate amid the huts and ships.
But as a chalk-line in a builder's hands –
a man who learned his whole craft from Athena –
makes a deck-beam come out straight, just so
the line of battle had been sharply drawn.

Fighting went on around the various ships.
Hector headed for Aias, and these two
fought hard for a single ship; neither could Hector
dislodge his enemy and fire the ship,
nor could the other force his attacker back –
for Hector had Apollo on his side.
But Aias downed Caletor, Clytius' son,
as he bore fire against the ships. He hit him
full in the chest, and down with clanging arms
he tumbled, as the torch fell from his hand.

When Hector saw his cousin fall
before the black ship in the dust, he cried
in a loud voice to Trojans and Lycians:
'Trojans, Lycians, Dardani, all soldiers,
now is no time to yield even an inch
here in the narrow ways! Defend Caletor,
or they will take his arms! He died fighting
to win the ships!'

With this he aimed a cast
of shining spear at Aias, but he missed him,
aimed then a second cast at Lycophron,
a son of Mastor, and a squire to Aias,
native of Cythera, but Aias' guest
on Salamis, for he had killed a Cytheran.
Now Hector cleft this man above the ear
with his sharp spearhead as he stood by Aias.
Down in the dust upon his back he fell,
down from the ship's stern, flopping, all undone.

Then Aias shivered and called out to his brother:
'Teucer, old soul, our friend Mastorides,

our faithful friend, is dead. When he left Cythera
and lived with us, we loved and honoured him
as much as our own parents. And now Hector
has killed the man. Where are your deadly arrows?
Where is the tough bow that Apollo gave you?'

    Teucer took it all in, and on the run
he came to join his brother. In his hand
he held the strung bow and a quiver of arrows.
Shooting, he made them flash upon the Trojans,
and hit Cleitus, Peisenor's brilliant son,
companion of Polydamas Panthoides,
as he held hard his reins
in trouble with his horses, trying to hold them
close in where the wheeling lines were packed,
to do his best for Hector and the Trojans.
Now in a flash his evil moment came,
and no one by his strength of will could stop it:
a quill of groaning pierced his neck behind.
He dropped out of the car. The horses reared,
then jerked the empty chariot backward rattling.
Lord Polydamas noticed it at once
and ran to catch the horses. These he gave
to Astynous, Protiaon's son,
commanding him to hold the chariot near
and keep his eyes open. He himself
went back to join the mêlée.

                 One more arrow
Teucer drew for Hector helmed in bronze,
and would have stopped the battle for the ships
if that shot had dispatched him in his triumph.
But Zeus perceived it, and he guarded Hector –
wrested that boon from Telamonian Teucer,
who as he pulled the smooth bow snapped the string.

    The heavy-headed shaft went wide, the bow
dropped from his hands, and with a shiver Teucer
said to his brother: 'Damn the luck. Some god
is cutting off our prospects in this fight.
He forced the bow out of my hand and broke
the new gut I had whipped on it this morning
to stand the spring of many shafts.'

                    To this
Telamonian Aias answered: 'Well, old friend,
just let the bow and sheaf of arrows lie,
since a god wrecked them, spiting the Danaans.

Take up a long pike, get a shield, and fight
the Trojans that way, make the soldiers fight.
If the enemy is to take the ships,
they'll know they are in a battle. Let us hold on
to joy of combat!'

Teucer put his bow
inside his hut. He took his four-ply shield
hard on his shoulder, pulled on a well-made helm,
picked out a strong shaft shod with cutting bronze,
and ran out, taking his stand at Aias' side.

Hector had seen that weaponry undone,
and now he shouted to Trojans and Lycians:
'Trojans, Lycians, Dardani, all soldiers,
friends, be men, take a fresh grip on courage
here by the decked ships. I have just seen
how Zeus crippled their champion's archery!
Easy to see how men get strength from Zeus:
on the one hand, when he gives them glory,
on the other, when he saps their enemies.
Taking the heart out of the Argives now,
he reinforces us. Fight for the ships
as one man, all of you! And if one finds
his death, his end, in some spear-thrust or cast,
then that is that, and no ignoble death
for a man defending his own land. He wins
a peaceful hearth for wife and children later,
his home and patrimony kept entire,
if only the Achaeans sail for home.'

He put fresh heart in every man by this.
But from the opposing line Aias called out
to his companions:

'Argives, where is your pride?
Isn't it clear enough? Either we perish
or else fight off this peril and are saved.
If Hector burns our ships, will you get home
on foot, do you think? Maybe you cannot hear him
calling his whole army on, already
mad to fire the ships? No invitation
to dance, that shouting, but to a fight.

'No plan,
no cleverness can serve us now but this:
to close with them and fight with all we have.
Better to win life or to lose it fighting
now, once and for all, than to be bled

to death by slow degrees in grinding war
against these ships, by lesser men than we.'

This aroused and stiffened them. Then Hector
slaughtered Schedius, son of Perimedes,
chief of Phocians, but Aias slaughtered
Laodamas, a captain of infantry,
Antenor's brilliant son. And Polydamas
killed the Cyllenian, Otus, comrade-in-arms
of Meges and a captain of Epeians.
Seeing this, Meges rushed, but Polydamas
dodged aside and the spear-thrust missed. Apollo
would not allow him, Panthous' noble son,
to perish in that mêlée. Meges wounded
Croesmus instead, full in the chest, and down
he tumbled, thudding. Meges stripped his gear.
Against him then came Dolops, a good spearman,
skilled in warfare, valorous,
fathered by Lampus, best of men, a son
of Laomedon. Dolops at close quarters
broke through the centre of Meges' shield,
but his close-woven battle-jacket saved him,
one that he wore all fitted with bronze plates,
a cuirass Phyleus, his father, brought
out of Ephyra, from the Selleis river.
Marshal Euphetes, host and friend, had given it
to wear as a defence against attackers
in war; this time it saved from mortal hurt
the body of his son. Now that son, Meges,
thrust at the crown of Dolops' helm. He broke
the horsehair plume away, and down it fell,
resplendent with fresh purple, in the dust.
While Dolops kept his feet and went on fighting,
hoping for victory, the formidable
Menelaus came to Meges' aid,
obliquely and unseen, and hit the Trojan's
shoulder from behind. The famished spearhead,
driven hard, passed through his chest, and down
head first he sprawled. The two Achaeans bent
to strip his shoulders of his gear. Then Hector
called to Dolops' kinsmen, first of all
to Melanippus, Hicetaon's son,
who pastured shambling cattle in the old days
in Percote, Troy's foes being far away,
but when the ships of the Danaans came

he went again to Ilium, and grew
distinguished among Trojans, lived with Priam
on equal terms with Priam's sons.

                          Now Hector
called to him, called him by name, rebuked him,
saying: 'Melanippus, are we slackening?
Are you not moved at all by your cousin's death?
See how they make for Dolops' armour! Go in
after them! No fighting at a distance
now, until we kill them – or they'll storm
Troy's height and lay her waste with all her sons.'

    With this he plunged ahead, and the godlike man,
Melanippus, kept at his side.

                          Great Aias
tried to put fighting spirit in the Argives:
'Friends,' he cried, 'respect yourselves as men,
respect each other in the moil of battle!
Men with a sense of shame survive
more often than they perish. Those who run
have neither fighting power nor any honour.'

    The men themselves wished to put up a fight
and took his words to heart. Around the ships
they formed a barrier of bronze. But Zeus
rallied the Trojans.

                          Then Lord Menelaus,
clarion in war, said to Antilochus:
'Antilochus, of all the young Achaeans
no one is faster on his feet than you,
or tough as you in combat: you could make
a sortie and take out some Trojan soldier.'

    He himself hastened on, but roused the man,
who ran out with his shining javelin poised
and scanned the battle-line. Trojans gave way
before the javelin-thrower, but his throw
was not wasted. He hit proud Melanippus,
Hicetaon's son, beside the nipple
as he moved up to battle. Down he went
slumping to earth, and darkness hid his eyes.
Antilochus broke forward like a hound
on a stricken deer that a hunter met and shot
on its way out of a thicket: even so,
Antilochus threw himself upon you,
Melanippus, to take your gear. But Hector
made for him on the run along the line,

and fighter though he was, and fast, Antilochus
would not resist but fled him – as a beast
that has done some depredation, killed a dog
or cowherd near the cattle, slinks away
before a crowd can gather. Nestor's son
ran off like that, while Hector and the Trojans,
shouting high, rained javelins after him.
Once in the mass again, he turned and stood.

And now like lions, carnivores, the Trojans
hurled themselves at the ships. They brought to pass
what Zeus commanded, and he kept their valour
steadily awake. He dazed the Argives,
wresting glory away from them. That day
the purpose of his heart was to confer
the glory on Hector, Priam's son, enabling him
to cast bright tireless fire on the ships
and so fulfil the special prayer of Thetis.
Zeus the lord of wisdom awaited that,
to see before his eyes the lightning-glare
of a ship ablaze: for from that moment on
he had in mind reversal for the Trojans
and glory for Danaans. Knowing all this,
he sent against the deep-sea ships a man
who longed to burn them: Priam's son,
Hector, furious in arms as Ares
raging, his spear flashing, or as fire
that rages, devastating wooded hills.
His mouth foamed with slaver, and his eyes
were flaming under dreadful brows, the helm
upon his temples nodded terribly
as he gave battle. From the upper air
Lord Zeus himself defended him and gave him
honour and power alone amid the host –
for he would be diminished soon: a day
of wrath for him at Lord Achilles' hands
was being wrought even then by Pallas Athena.

Hector, attacking, tried to break the lines
at that point where the Achaean soldiery
was thickest, and their gear the best.
But not with all his ardour could he break them.
They held hard, locked solid, man to man,
like a sheer cliff of granite near the sea,
abiding gale-winds on their shrieking ways
and surf that climbs the shingle with a roar:

so the Danaans bore the Trojan rush
and kept their feet and would not flee. But Hector
ran with a flashing torch and tried them, first
from one side, then the other, and he plunged
the way a billow whipped up by a gale
beneath dark scud descends upon a ship,
and she is hidden stem to stern in foam,
as a great gust of wind howls in the sail
and sailors shake in dread; by a hair's breadth
are they delivered from their death at sea:
just so Achaean hearts were rent. And Hector
was like a pitiless lion coming down
on cattle, gone to graze in a great meadow,
hundreds of them, tended by a herdsman
not yet skilled at fighting a wild beast
to prevent the slaughter of a cow: poor fellow,
either at the forefront of the herd
or at the rear he keeps pace with his cattle,
but into their midst the lion leaps to take one
as all the rest stampede. Now the Achaeans,
under attack by Hector and Father Zeus,
broke and ran like cattle. One man only
Hector killed: Periphetes, a Mycenaean,
son of Copreus, who went back and forth
announcing labours that Eurystheus set
for brawny Heracles. A poorer man
by far was Copreus, and the son superior
in every gift, as athlete and as soldier,
noted for brains among the Mycenaeans.
Now he afforded Hector glory: twisting
back, he tripped upon the body-shield
he bore full-length, shoulder to foot, a tower
against all weapons. On the rim he tripped
and, hindered, fell down backward, and his helm
rang out around his temples as he fell.
Hector's sharp eye perceived this. On the run
he reached Periphetes, halted at his side,
and speared him through the chest, killing him there
with all his friends nearby. They could not help him,
bitterly as they grieved for him, their dread
of Hector being so great.

                    The Achaeans now
were driven back within the line of ships,
those that were first drawn inland: prow and stern

enclosed them. Trojans poured into the shipways,
forcing the Argives back from the first ships.
Then by the huts they made a stand, massed there,
and would not scatter through the camp, constrained
by pride and fear, but ceaselessly called out
to one another.

           Nestor of Gerenia,
lord of the western approaches to Achaea,
implored the soldiers for their children's sake:
'Be men, dear friends, respect yourselves as men
before the others! All of you, remember
children and wives, possessions, and your parents,
whether they be alive or dead! I beg you,
on their account, although they are not here,
to hold your ground: no panic and no rout!'

  So Nestor rallied them. Athena now
dispelled the nebulous haze before their eyes,
and light burst shining on them, front and rear,
from ships and from the battle. They saw clearly
Hector of the war-cry and his soldiery,
those in reserve who had not joined the fight
and those in combat, storming the long ships.

  Now the stout heart of Aias cared no longer
to stay where others had withdrawn; he moved
with long strides on the ships' decks, making play
with his long polished pike, the sections joined
by rivets, long as twenty-two forearms.
Think of an expert horseman, who has harnessed
a double team together from his string
and rides them from the plain to a big town
along the public road, where many see him,
men and women both; with perfect ease,
he changes horses, leaping, at a gallop.
That was Aias, going from deck to deck
of many ships with his long stride, his shout
rising to heaven, as in raging tones
he ordered the Danaans to defend them.
Neither would Hector stay amid the ruck
of battle-jacketed Trojans. Like an eagle
flashing down on a flock of long-winged birds
who feed at a riverside – white geese or cranes
or long-necked swans – so Hector struck ahead
and charged a ship with its black prow, for Zeus
behind him drove him on with his great hand

and cheered on soldiers with him.
                                    Now again
there was a sharp fight near the ships: you'd say
that iron men, untiring, clashed in battle,
so fiercely they fought on. And to what end?
There was no way to escape, the Achaeans thought,
sure they would be destroyed. But every Trojan's
heart beat fast against his ribs with hope
of firing ships and killing Achaean soldiers.
These were their secret thoughts as they gave battle.

   Hector gripped the stern of a deep-sea ship,
a fast sailer, a beauty, which had brought
Protesilaus to Troy but would not bring him
back to his own land. Around this ship
they slaughtered one another in close combat,
Trojans and Achaeans. Neither side
could stand a hail of arrows or javelins,
but for like reasons moved toward one another,
hewing with battle-axe and hatchet, wielding
longsword and double-bladed spear. The swords
were many and beautiful, black-sheathed and hilted,
that fell to earth out of the hands of men
or off their shoulders. Earth ran dark with blood.

   Once Hector had the stern-post in his hands,
he kept a deathgrip on the knob and gave
command to the Trojans: 'Fire now! Bring it up,
and all together raise a battle-shout!
Zeus gave this day to us as recompense
for everything: now we may burn the ships
that came against the gods' will to our shore
and caused us years of siege – through cowardice
of our old counsellors who held me back
when I said "Battle at the ships' sterns!"
They held back soldiers, too. In those days, ah,
if Zeus who views the wide world blocked our hearts,
now it is he who cheers and sends us forward!'

   At this they all attacked more furiously,
and Aias could no longer hold. The missiles
forced him back, he yielded a few paces,
thinking his time had come, and left the deck
of the trim ship for the seven-foot bench amidships.

   There he stood fast, alert, with his long pike
to fend off any Trojan with a torch,
and kept on shouting fiercely to Danaans:

'Friends, Danaan soldiers, hands of Ares,
take a fresh grip on courage! Fight like men!
Can we rely on fresh reserves behind us?
A compact wall, to shield our men from death?
Not that, nor any town with towers where
we might defend ourselves and find allies
enough to turn the tide. No, here we are,
on the coastal plain of Trojans under arms,
nothing but open sea for our support,
and far from our own country. Safety lies
in our own hands, not going soft in battle.'

    Saying this, he made a vicious lunge
with his sharp-bladed pike. And any Trojan
bound for the decked ships with a blazing torch
for Hector's satisfaction would be hit
by Aias, waiting there with his long pike.
He knocked down twelve, close in, before the ships.

BOOK XVI

A SHIP FIRED, A TIDE TURNED

THAT was the way the fighting went
for one sea-going ship. Meanwhile Patroclus
approached Achilles his commander, streaming
warm tears – like a shaded mountain-spring
that makes a rock-ledge run with dusky water.
Achilles watched him come, and felt a pang for him.

Then the great prince and runner said: 'Patroclus,
why all the weeping? Like a small girl-child
who runs beside her mother and cries and cries
to be taken up, and catches at her gown,
and will not let her go, looking up in tears
until she has her wish: that's how you seem,
Patroclus, winking out your glimmering tears.
Have you something to tell the Myrmidons
or me? Some message you alone have heard
from Phthia? But they say that Actor's son,
Menoetius, is living still, and Peleus,
the son of Aeacus, lives on
amid his Myrmidons. If one of these
were dead, we should be grieved. Or is this weeping
over the Argives, seeing how they perish
at the long ships by their own bloody fault!
Speak out now, don't conceal it, let us share it.'

And groaning, Patroclus, you replied:
'Achilles, prince and greatest of Achaeans,
be forbearing. They are badly hurt.
All who were the best fighters are now lying
among the ships with spear or arrow wounds.
Diomedes, Tydeus' rugged son, was shot;
Odysseus and Agamemnon, the great spearman,
have spear wounds; Eurypylus
took an arrow-shot deep in his thigh.
Surgeons with medicines are attending them
to ease their wounds.

　　　　　　　　But you are a hard case,
Achilles! God forbid this rage you nurse
should master me. You and your fearsome pride!
What good will come of it to anyone, later,

unless you keep disaster from the Argives?
Have you no pity?
Peleus, master of horse, was not your father,
Thetis was not your mother! Cold grey sea
and sea-cliffs bore you, making a mind so harsh.
If in your heart you fear some oracle,
some word of Zeus, told by your gentle mother,
then send me out at least, and send me quickly,
give me a company of Myrmidons,
and I may be a beacon to Danaans!
Lend me your gear to strap over my shoulders;
Trojans then may take me for yourself
and break off battle, giving our worn-out men
a chance to breathe. Respites are brief in war.
We fresh troops with one battle-cry might easily
push their tired men back on the town,
away from ships and huts.'
                    So he petitioned,
witless as a child that what he begged for
was his own death, hard death and doom.
                              Achilles
out of his deep anger made reply:
'Hard words, dear prince. There is no oracle
I know of that I must respect, no word
from Zeus reported by my gentle mother.
Only this bitterness eats at my heart
when one man would deprive and shame his equal,
taking back his prize by abuse of power.
The girl whom the Achaeans chose for me
I won by my own spear. A town with walls
I stormed and sacked for her. Then Agamemnon
stole her back, out of my hands, as though
I were some vagabond held cheap.
                         'All that
we can let pass as being over and done with;
I could not rage for ever. And yet, by heaven, I swore
I would not rest from anger till the cries
and clangour of battle reached my very ships!
But you, now, you can strap my famous gear
on your own shoulders, and then take command
of Myrmidons on edge and ripe for combat,
now that like a dark storm-cloud the Trojans
have poured round the first ships, and Argive troops
have almost no room for manœuvre left,

with nothing to their rear but sea. The whole
townful of Trojans joins in, sure of winning,
because they cannot see my helmet's brow
aflash in range of them. They'd fill the gullies
with dead men soon, in flight up through the plain,
if Agamemnon were on good terms with me.
As things are, they've outflanked the camp. A mercy
for them that in the hands of Diomedes
no great spear goes berserk, warding death
from the Danaans! Not yet have I heard
the voice of Agamemnon, either, shouting
out of his hateful skull. The shout of Hector,
the killer, calling Trojans, makes a roar
like breaking surf, and with long answering cries
they hold the whole plain where they drove the Achaeans.
Even so, defend the ships, Patroclus.
Attack the enemy in force, or they
will set the ships ablaze with whirling fire
and rob Achaeans of their dear return.
Now carry out the purpose I confide,
so that you'll win great honour for me, and glory
among Danaans; then they'll send me back
my lovely girl, with bright new gifts as well.
Once you expel the enemy from the ships,
rejoin me here. If Hera's lord,
the lord of thunder, grants you the day's honour,
covet no further combat far from me
with Trojan soldiers. That way you'd deny me
recompense of honour. You must not,
for joy of battle, joy of killing Trojans,
carry the fight to Ilium! Some power
out of Olympus, one of the immortal gods,
might intervene for them. The Lord Apollo
loves the Trojans. Turn back, then, as soon
as you restore the safety of the ships,
and let the rest contend, out on the plain.
Ah, Father Zeus, Athena, and Apollo!
If not one Trojan of them all
should get away from death, and not one Argive
save ourselves were spared, we two alone
could pull down Troy's old coronet of towers!'

    These were the speeches they exchanged. Now Aias
could no longer hold: he was dislodged
by spear-throws, beaten by the mind of Zeus

and Trojan shots. His shining helm rang out
around his temples dangerously with hits
as his helm-plates were struck and struck again;
he felt his shoulder galled on the left side
hugging the glittering shield – and yet they could not
shake it, putting all their weight in throws.
In painful gasps his breath came, sweat ran down
in rivers off his body everywhere;
no rest for him, but trouble upon trouble.

Now tell me, Muses, dwellers on Olympus,
how fire first fell on the Achaean ships!
Hector moved in to slash with his long blade
at Aias' ashwood shaft, and near the spearhead
lopped it off. Then Telamonian Aias
wielded a pointless shaft, while far away
the flying bronze head rang upon the ground,
and Aias shivered knowing in his heart
the work of gods: how Zeus, the lord of thunder,
cut off his war-craft in that fight, and willed
victory to the Trojans. He gave way
before their missiles as they rushed in throwing
untiring fire into the ship. It caught
at once, agush with flame, and fire lapped
about the stern.

            Achilles smote his thighs
and said to Patroclus: 'Now go into action,
prince and horseman! I see roaring fire
burst at the ships. Action, or they'll destroy them,
leaving no means of getting home. Be quick,
strap on my gear, while I alert the troops!'

Patroclus now put on the flashing bronze.
Greaves were the first thing, beautifully fitted
to calf and shin with silver ankle-chains;
and next he buckled round his ribs the cuirass,
blazoned with stars, of swift Aeacides;
then slung the silver-studded blade of bronze
about his shoulders, and the vast solid shield;
then on his noble head he placed the helm,
its plume of terror nodding high above,
and took two burly spears with his own handgrip.
He did not take the great spear of Achilles,
weighty, long, and tough. No other Achaean
had the strength to wield it, only Achilles.
It was a Pelian ash, cut on the crest

of Pelion, given to Achilles' father
by Cheiron to deal death to soldiery.
He then ordered his war-team put in harness
by Automedon, whom he most admired
after Prince Achilles, breaker of men,
for waiting steadfast at his call in battle.
Automedon yoked the fast horses for him –
Xanthus and Balius, racers of wind.
The storm-gust Podarge, who once had grazed
green meadowland by the Ocean stream, conceived
and bore them to the west wind, Zephyrus.
In the side-traces Pedasus, a thoroughbred,
was added to the team; Achilles took him
when he destroyed the city of Eetion.
Mortal, he ran beside immortal horses.
Achilles put the Myrmidons in arms,
the whole detachment near the huts. Like wolves,
carnivorous and fierce and tireless,
who rend a great stag on a mountainside
and feed on him, their jaws reddened with blood,
loping in a pack to drink spring water,
lapping the dark rim up with slender tongues,
their chops a-drip with fresh blood, their hearts
unshaken ever, and their bellies glutted:
such were the Myrmidons and their officers,
running to form-up round Achilles' brave
companion-in-arms. And like the god of war
among them was Achilles: he stood tall
and sped the chariots and shield-men onward.

Fifty ships there were that Lord Achilles,
favoured of heaven, led to Troy. In each
were fifty soldiers, shipmates at the rowlocks.
Five he entrusted with command and made
lieutenants, while he ruled them all as king.
One company was headed by Menesthius
in his glittering breastplate, son of Spercheius,
a river fed by heaven. Peleus' daughter,
beautiful Polydora, had conceived him
lying with Spercheius, untiring stream,
a woman with a god; but the world thought
she bore her child to Perieres' son,
Borus, who married her in the eyes of men
and offered countless bridal gifts. A second
company was commanded by Eudorus,

whose mother was unmarried: Polymele,
Phylas' daughter, a beautiful dancer
with whom the strong god Hermes fell in love,
seeing her among singing girls who moved
in measure for the lady of belling hounds,
Artemis of the golden shaft. And Hermes,
pure Deliverer, ascending soon
to an upper room, lay secretly with her
who was to bear his brilliant son, Eudorus,
a first-rate man at running and in war.
When Eileithyia, sending pangs of labour,
brought him forth to see the sun-rays, then
strong-minded Echecles, Actor's son,
led the girl home with countless bridal gifts;
but Phylas in his age brought up the boy
with all kind care, as though he were a son.
Company three was led by Peisander
Maemalides, the best man with a spear,
of all Myrmidons after Patroclus.
Company four the old man, master of horse,
Phoenix, commanded. Alcimedon, son
of Laerces, commanded company five.
     When all were mustered under their officers,
Achilles had strict orders to impart:
'Myrmidons, let not one man forget
how menacing you were against the Trojans
during my anger and seclusion: how
each one reproached me, saying, "Iron-hearted
son of Peleus, now we see: your mother
brought you up on rage, merciless man,
the way you keep your men confined to camp
against their will! We might as well sail home
in our sea-going ships, now this infernal
anger has come over you!" That way
you often talked, in groups around our fires.
Now the great task of battle is at hand
that you were longing for! Now every soldier
keep a fighting heart and face the Trojans!'
     He stirred and braced their spirit; every rank
fell in more sharply when it heard its king.
As when a builder fitting stone on stone
lays well a high house-wall to buffet back
the might of winds, just so
they fitted helms and studded shields together:

shield-rim on shield-rim, helmet on helmet, men
all pressed on one another, horsehair plumes
brushed on the bright crests as the soldiers nodded,
densely packed as they were. Before them all
two captains stood in gear of war: Patroclus
and Automedon, of one mind, resolved
to open combat in the lead.

               Achilles
went to his hut. He lifted up the lid
of a sea-chest, all intricately wrought,
that Thetis of the silver feet had stowed
aboard his ship for him to take to Ilium,
filled to the brim with shirts, wind-breaking cloaks,
and fleecy rugs. His hammered cup was there,
from which no other man drank the bright wine,
and he made offering to no god but Zeus.
Lifting it from the chest, he purified it
first with brimstone, washed it with clear water,
and washed his hands, then dipped it full of wine.
    Now standing in the forecourt, looking up
toward heaven, he prayed and poured his offering out,
and Zeus who plays in thunder heard his prayer:
'Zeus of Dodona, god of Pelasgians,
O god whose home lies far! Ruler of wintry
harsh Dodona! Your interpreters,
the Selli, live with feet like roots, unwashed,
and sleep on the hard ground. My lord, you heard me
praying before this, and honoured me
by punishing the Achaean army. Now,
again, accomplish what I most desire.
I shall stay on the beach, behind the ships,
but send my dear friend with a mass of soldiers,
Myrmidons, into combat. Let your glory,
Zeus who view the wide world, go beside him.
Sir, exalt his heart,
so Hector too may see whether my friend
can only fight when I am in the field,
or whether single-handed he can scatter them
before his fury! When he has thrown back
their shouting onslaught from the ships, then let him
return unhurt to the shipways and to me,
his gear intact, with all his fighting men.'
    That was his prayer, and Zeus who views the wide world
heard him. Part he granted, part denied:

he let Patroclus push the heavy fighting
back from the ships, but would not let him come
unscathed from battle.
               Now, after Achilles
had made his prayer and offering to Zeus,
he entered his hut again, restored the cup
to his sea-chest, and took his place outside –
desiring still to watch the savage combat
of Trojans and Achaeans. Brave Patroclus'
men moved forward with high hearts until
they charged the Trojans – Myrmidons in waves,
like hornets that small boys, as boys will do,
the idiots, poke up with constant teasing
in their daub chambers on the road,
to give everyone trouble. If some traveller
who passes unaware should then excite them,
all the swarm comes raging out
to defend their young. So hot, so angrily
the Myrmidons came pouring from the ships
in a quenchless din of shouting.
              And Patroclus
cried above them all: 'O Myrmidons,
brothers-in-arms of Peleus' son, Achilles,
fight like men, dear friends, remember courage,
let us win honour for the son of Peleus!
He is the greatest captain on the beach,
his officers and soldiers are the bravest!
Let King Agamemnon learn his folly
in holding cheap the best of the Achaeans!'
   Shouting so, he stirred their hearts. They fell
as one man on the Trojans, and the ships
around them echoed the onrush and the cries.
On seeing Menoetius' powerful son, and with him
Automedon, aflash with brazen gear,
the Trojan ranks broke, and they caught their breath,
imagining that Achilles the swift fighter
had put aside his wrath for friendship's sake.
Now each man kept an eye out for retreat
from sudden death. Patroclus drove ahead
against their centre with his shining spear,
into the huddling mass, around the stern
of Protesilaus' burning ship. He hit
Pyraechmes, who had led the Paeones
from Amydon, from Axius' wide river –

hit him in the right shoulder. Backward in dust
he tumbled groaning, and his men-at-arms,
the Paeones, fell back around him. Dealing
death to a chief and champion, Patroclus
drove them in confusion from the ship,
and doused the tigerish fire. The hull half-burnt
lay smoking on the shipway. Now the Trojans
with a great outcry streamed away; Danaans
poured along the curved ships, and the din
of war kept on. As when the lightning-master,
Zeus, removes a dense cloud from the peak
of some great mountain, and the look-out points
and spurs and clearings are distinctly seen
as though pure space had broken through from heaven:
so when the dangerous fire had been repelled
Danaans took breath for a space. The battle
had not ended, though; not yet were Trojans
put to rout by the Achaean charge
or out of range of the black ships. They withdrew
but by regrouping tried to make a stand.

                                        In broken

ranks the captains sought and killed each other,
Menoetius' son making the first kill.
As Areilycus wheeled round to fight,
he caught him with his spearhead in the hip,
and drove the bronze through, shattering the bone.
He sprawled face downward on the ground.

                                        Now veteran

Menelaus thrusting past the shield
of Thoas to the bare chest brought him down.
Rushed by Amphiclus, Meges on the alert
got his thrust in first, hitting his thigh
where a man's muscles bunch. Around the spearhead
tendons were split, and darkness veiled his eyes.
Nestor's sons were in action: Antilochus
with his good spear brought down Atymnius,
laying open his flank; he fell head first.
Now Maris moved in, raging for his brother,
lunging over the dead man with his spear,
but Thrasymedes had already lunged
and did not miss, but smashed his shoulder squarely,
tearing his upper arm out of the socket,
severing muscles, breaking through the bone.
He thudded down and darkness veiled his eyes.

So these two, overcome by the two brothers,
dropped to the underworld of Erebus.
They were Sarpedon's true brothers-in-arms
and sons of Amisodarus, who had reared
the fierce Chimaera, nightmare to many men.
Aias, Oileus' son, drove at Cleobulus
and took him alive, encumbered in the press,
but killed him on the spot with a sword-stroke
across his nape – the whole blade running hot
with blood, as welling death and his harsh destiny
possessed him. Now Peneleos
and Lycon clashed; as both had cast and missed
and lunged and missed with spears,
they fought again with swords. The stroke of Lycon
came down on the other's helmet-ridge
but his blade broke at the hilt. Peneleos
thrust at his neck below the ear and drove
the blade clear in and through; his head toppled,
held only by skin, and his knees gave way.
Meriones on the run overtook Acamas
mounting behind his horses and hit his shoulder,
knocking him from the car. Mist swathed his eyes.
Idomeneus thrust hard at Erymas' mouth
with his hard bronze. The spearhead passed on through
beneath his brain and split the white brain-pan.
His teeth were dashed out, blood filled both his eyes,
and from his mouth and nostrils as he gaped
he spurted blood. Death's cloud enveloped him.
There each Danaan captain killed his man.
As ravenous wolves come down on lambs and kids
astray from some flock that in hilly country
splits in two by a shepherd's negligence,
and quickly wolves bear off the defenceless things,
so when Danaans fell on Trojans, shrieking
flight was all they thought of, not of combat.
Aias the Tall kept after bronze-helmed Hector,
casting his lance, but Hector, skilled in war,
would fit his shoulders under the bull's-hide shield,
and watch for whizzing arrows, thudding spears.
Aye, though he knew the tide of battle turned,
he kept his discipline and saved his friends.
As when Lord Zeus would hang the sky with storm,
a cloud may enter heaven from Olympus
out of crystalline space, so terror and cries

increased about the shipways. In disorder
men withdrew. Then Hector's chariot-team
cantering bore him off with all his gear,
leaving the Trojans whom the moat confined;
and many chariot-horses in that ditch,
breaking their poles off at the tip, abandoned
war-cars and masters. Hard on their heels
Patroclus kept on calling Danaan fighters
onward with slaughter in his heart. The Trojans,
yelling and clattering, filled all the ways,
their companies cut in pieces. High in air
a blast of wind swept on, under the clouds,
as chariot-horses raced back toward the town
away from the encampment. And Patroclus
rode shouting where he saw the enemy mass
in uproar: men fell from their chariots
under the wheels and cars jounced over them,
and running horses leapt over the ditch –
immortal horses, whom the gods gave Peleus,
galloping as their mettle called them onward
after Hector, target of Patroclus.
But Hector's battle-team bore him away.
    As under a great storm black earth is drenched
on an autumn day, when Zeus pours down the rain
in scudding gusts to punish men, annoyed
because they will enforce their crooked judgements
and banish justice from the market place,
thoughtless of the gods' vengeance; all their streams
run high and full, and torrents cut their way
down dry declivities into the swollen sea
with a hoarse clamour, headlong out of hills,
while cultivated fields erode away –
such was the gasping flight of the Trojan horses.
    When he had cut their first wave off, Patroclus
forced it back again upon the ships
as the men fought toward the city. In between
the ships and river and the parapet
he swept among them killing, taking toll
for many dead Achaeans. First,
thrusting past Pronous' shield, he hit him
on the bare chest, and made him crumple: down
he tumbled with a crash. Then he rushed Thestor,
Enops' son, who sat all doubled up
in a polished war-car, shocked out of his wits,

the reins flown from his hands – and the Achaean
got home his thrust on the right jawbone, driving
through his teeth. He hooked him by the spearhead
over the chariot rail, as a fisherman
on a point of rock will hook a splendid fish
with line and dazzling bronze out of the ocean:
so from his chariot on the shining spear
he hooked him gaping and face downward threw him,
life going out of him as he fell.
                                        Patroclus
now met Erylaus' rush and hit him square
mid-skull with a big stone. Within his helm
the skull was cleft asunder, and down he went
head first to earth; heart-breaking death engulfed him.
Next Erymas, Amphoterus, Epaltes,
Tlepolemus Damastorides, Echius,
Pyris, Ipheus, Euippus, Polymelus,
all in quick succession he brought down
to the once peaceful pasture-land.
                                        Sarpedon,
seeing his brothers-in-arms in their unbelted
battle-jackets downed at Patroclus' hands,
called in bitterness to the Lycians:
'Shame, O Lycians, where are you running?
Now you show your speed! I'll take on this one,
and learn what man he is that has the power
to do such havoc as he has done among us,
cutting down so many, and such good men.'
   He vaulted from his car with all his gear,
and on his side Patroclus, when he saw him,
leapt from his car. Like two great birds of prey
with hooked talons and angled beaks, who screech
and clash on a high ridge of rock, these two
rushed one another with hoarse cries.
                                        But Zeus,
the son of crooked-minded Cronos, watched,
and pitied them. He said to Hera: 'Ai!
Sorrow for me, that in the scheme of things
the dearest of men to me must lie in dust
before the son of Menoetius, Patroclus.
My heart goes two ways as I ponder this:
shall I catch up Sarpedon
out of the mortal fight with all its woe
and put him down alive in Lycia,

in that rich land? Or shall I make him fall
beneath Patroclus' hard-thrown spear?'

                                    Then Hera
of the wide eyes answered him: 'O fearsome power,
my Lord Zeus, what a curious thing to say.
A man who is born to die, long destined for it,
would you set free from that unspeakable end?
Do so; but not all of us will praise you.
And this, too, I may tell you: ponder this:
should you dispatch Sarpedon home alive,
anticipate some other god's desire
to pluck a man he loves out of the battle.
Many who fight around the town of Priam
sprang from immortals; you'll infuriate these.
No, dear to you though he is, and though you mourn him,
let him fall, even so, in the rough battle,
killed by the son of Menoetius, Patroclus.
Afterward, when his soul is gone, his lifetime
ended, Death and sweetest Sleep can bear him
homeward to the broad domain of Lycia.
There friends and kin may give him funeral
with tomb and stone, the trophies of the dead.'
    To this the father of gods and men agreed,
but showered bloody drops upon the earth
for the dear son Patroclus would destroy
in fertile Ilium, far from his home.
When the two men had come in range, Patroclus
turned like lightning against Thrasymelus,
a tough man ever at Sarpedon's side,
and gave him a death-wound in the underbelly.
Sarpedon's counterthrust went wide, but hit
the trace-horse, Pedasus, in the right shoulder.
Screaming harshly, panting his life away,
he crashed and whinnied in the dust; the spirit
left him with a wing-beat. The team shied
and strained apart with a great creak of the yoke
as reins were tangled over the dead weight
of their outrider fallen. Automedon,
the good soldier, found a way to end it:
pulling his long blade from his hip
he jumped in fast and cut the trace-horse free.
The team then ranged themselves beside the pole,
drawing the reins taut, and once more,
devoured by fighting madness, the two men clashed.

Sarpedon missed again. He drove his spearhead
over the left shoulder of Patroclus,
not even grazing him. Patroclus then
made his last throw, and the weapon left his hand
with flawless aim. He hit his enemy
just where the muscles of the diaphragm
encased his throbbing heart. Sarpedon fell
the way an oak or poplar or tall pine
goes down, when shipwrights in the wooded hills
with whetted axes chop it down for timber.
So, full length, before his war-car lay
Sarpedon raging, clutching the bloody dust.
Imagine a great-hearted sultry bull
a lion kills amid a shambling herd:
with choking groans he dies under the claws.

So, mortally wounded by Patroclus
the chief of Lycian shieldsmen lay in agony
and called his friend by name: 'Glaucus, old man,
old war-dog, now's the time to be a spearman!
Put your heart in combat! Let grim war
be all your longing! Quickly, if you can,
arouse the Lycian captains, round them up
to fight over Sarpedon. You, too, fight
to keep my body, else in later days
this day will be your shame. You'll hang your head
all your life long, if these Achaeans take
my armour here, where I have gone down fighting
before the ships. Hold hard; cheer on the troops!'

The end of life came on him as he spoke,
closing his eyes and nostrils. And Patroclus
with one foot on his chest drew from his belly
spearhead and spear; the diaphragm came out,
so he extracted life and blade together.
Myrmidons clung to the panting Lycian horses,
rearing to turn the car left by their lords.

But bitter anguish at Sarpedon's voice
had come to Glaucus, and his heart despaired
because he had not helped his friend. He gripped
his own right arm and squeezed it, being numb
where Teucer with a bowshot from the rampart
had hit him while he fought for his own men,
and he spoke out in prayer to Lord Apollo:
'Hear me, O lord, somewhere in Lycian farmland
or else in Troy: for you have power to listen

the whole world round to a man hard pressed as I!
I have my sore wound, all my length of arm
a-throb with lancing pain; the flow of blood
cannot be stanched; my shoulder's heavy with it.
I cannot hold my spear right or do battle,
cannot attack them. Here's a great man destroyed,
Sarpedon, son of Zeus. Zeus let his own son
die undefended. O my lord, heal this wound,
lull me my pains, put vigour in me! Let me
shout to my Lycians, move them into combat!
Let me give battle for the dead man here!'

    This way he prayed, and Phoebus Apollo heard him,
cutting his pain and making the dark blood dry
on his deep wound, then filled his heart with valour.
Glaucus felt the change, and knew with joy
how swiftly the great god had heard his prayer.
First he appealed to the Lycian captains, going
right and left, to defend Sarpedon's body,
then on the run he followed other Trojans,
Polydamas Panthoides, Agenor,
and caught up with Aeneas and with Hector,
shoulder to shoulder, urgently appealing:

    'Hector, you've put your allies out of mind,
those men who give their lives here for your sake
so distant from their friends and lands: you will not
come to their aid! Sarpedon lies there dead,
commander of the Lycians, who kept
his country safe by his firm hand, in justice!
Ares in bronze has brought him down: the spear
belonged to Patroclus. Come, stand with me, friends,
and count it shame if they strip off his gear
or bring dishonour on his body – these
fresh Myrmidons enraged for the Danaans
cut down at the shipways by our spears!'

    At this, grief and remorse possessed the Trojans,
grief not to be borne, because Sarpedon
had been a bastion of the town of Troy,
foreigner though he was. A host came with him,
but he had fought most gallantly of all.
They made straight for the Danaans, and Hector
led them, hot with anger for Sarpedon.

    Patroclus in his savagery cheered on
the Achaeans, first the two named Aias, both
already aflame for war: 'Aias and Aias,

let it be sweet to you to stand and fight!
You always do; be lion-hearted, now.
The man who crossed the rampart of Achaeans
first of all lies dead: Sarpedon. May we
take him, dishonour him, and strip his arms,
and hurl any friend who would defend him
into the dust with our hard bronze!'
    At this they burned to throw the Trojans back.
And both sides reinforced their battle lines,
Trojans and Lycians, Myrmidons and Achaeans,
moving up to fight around the dead
with fierce cries and clanging of men's armour.
Zeus unfurled a deathly gloom of night
over the combat, making battle-toil
about his dear son's body a fearsome thing.
At first, the Trojans drove back the Achaeans,
fiery-eyed as they were; one Myrmidon,
and not the least, was killed: noble Epeigeus,
a son of Agacles. Over Budeum,
a flourishing town, he ruled before the war,
but slew a kinsman. So he came as suppliant
to Peleus and to Thetis, who enlisted him
along with Lord Achilles, breaker of men,
to make war in the wild-horse country of Ilium
against the Trojans. Even as he touched the dead man,
Hector hit him square upon the crest
with a great stone: his skull split in the helmet,
and he fell prone upon the corpse. Death's cloud
poured round him, heart-corroding. Grief and pain
for this friend dying came to Lord Patroclus,
who pounced through spear-play like a diving hawk
that puts jackdaws and starlings wildly to flight:
straight through Lycians, through Trojans, too,
you drove, Patroclus, master of horse,
in fury for your friend. And Sthenelaus
the son of Ithaemenes was the victim:
Patroclus with a great stone broke his nape-cord.
    Backward the line bent, Hector too gave way,
as far as a hunting-spear may hurtle, thrown
by a man in practice or in competition
or matched with deadly foes in war. So far
the Trojans ebbed, as the Achaeans drove them.
Glaucus, commander of Lycians, turned first,
to bring down valorous Bathycles, the son

of Chalcon, one who had his home in Hellas,
fortunate and rich among the Myrmidons.
Whirling as this man caught him, Glaucus hit him
full in the breastbone with his spear, and down
he thudded on his face. The Achaeans grieved
to see their champion fallen, but great joy
came to the Trojans, and they thronged about him.
Not that Achaeans now forgot their courage,
no, for their momentum carried them on.
Meriones brought down a Trojan soldier,
Laogonus, Onetor's rugged son,
a priest of Zeus on Ida, honoured there
as gods are. Gashed now under jaw and ear
his life ran out, and hateful darkness took him.
Then at Meriones Aeneas cast
his bronze-shod spear, thinking to reach his body
under the shield as he came on. But he
looked out for it and swerved, slipping the spear-throw,
bowing forward, so the long shaft stuck
in earth behind him and the butt quivered;
the god Ares deprived it of its power.

Aeneas raged and sneered: 'Meriones,
fast dodger that you are, if I had hit you
my spearhead would have stopped your dance for good!'

Meriones, good spearman, answered him:
'For all your power, Aeneas, you could hardly
quench the fighting spirit of every man
defending himself against you. You are made
of mortal stuff like me. I, too, can say,
if I could hit you square, then tough and sure
as you may be, you would concede the game
and give your soul to the lord of nightmare, Death.'

Patroclus said to him sharply: 'Meriones,
you have your skill, why make a speech about it?
No, old friend, rough words will make no Trojans
back away from the body. Many a one
will be embraced by earth before they do.
War is the use of arms, words are for council.
More talk's pointless now; we need more fighting!'

He pushed on, and godlike Meriones
fought at his side. Think of the sound of strokes
woodcutters make in mountain glens, the echoes
ringing for listeners far away: just so
the battering din of those in combat rose

from earth where the living go their ways – the clang
of bronze, hard blows on leather, on bull's hide,
as longsword-blades and spearheads met their marks.
And an observer could not by now have seen
the Prince Sarpedon, since from head to foot
he lay enwrapped in weapons, dust, and blood.
Men kept crowding around the corpse. Like flies
that swarm and drone in farmyards round the milk-pails
on spring days, when the pails are splashed with milk:
just so they thronged around the corpse. And Zeus
would never turn his shining eyes away
from this mêlée, but watched them all and pondered
long over the slaughter of Patroclus –
whether in that place, on Sarpedon's body,
Hector should kill the man and take his gear,
or whether he, Zeus, should augment the moil
of battle for still other men. He weighed it
and thought this best: that for a while Achilles'
shining brother-in-arms should drive his foes
and Hector in the bronze helm toward the city,
taking the lives of many. First of all
he weakened Hector, made him mount his car
and turn away, retreating, crying out
to others to retreat: for he perceived
the dipping scales of Zeus. At this the Lycians
themselves could not stand fast, but all turned back,
once they had seen their king struck to the heart,
lying amid swales of dead – for many
fell to earth beside him when Lord Zeus
had drawn the savage battle line. So now
Achaeans lifted from Sarpedon's shoulders
gleaming arms of bronze, and these Patroclus
gave to his soldiers to be carried back
to the decked ships.
              At this point, to Apollo
Zeus who gathers cloud said: 'Come, dear Phoebus,
wipe away the blood mantling Sarpedon;
take him up, out of the play of spears,
a long way off, and wash him in the river,
anoint him with ambrosia, put ambrosial
clothing on him. Then have him conveyed
by those escorting spirits quick as wind,
sweet Sleep and Death, who are twin brothers. These
will set him down in the rich broad land of Lycia,

and there his kin and friends may bury him
with tomb and stone, the trophies of the dead.'

Attentive to his father, Lord Apollo
went down the foothills of Ida to the field
and lifted Prince Sarpedon clear of it.
He bore him far and bathed him in the river,
scented him with ambrosia, put ambrosial
clothing on him, then had him conveyed
by those escorting spirits quick as wind,
sweet Sleep and Death, who are twin brothers. These
returned him to the rich broad land of Lycia.

Patroclus, calling to his team, commanding
Automedon, rode on after the Trojans
and Lycians – all this to his undoing,
the blunderer. By keeping Achilles' mandate,
he might have fled black fate and cruel death.
But overpowering is the mind of Zeus
forever, matched with man's. He turns in fright
the powerful man and robs him of his victory
easily, though he drove him on himself.
So now he stirred Patroclus' heart to fury.

Whom first, whom later did you kill in battle,
Patroclus, when the gods were calling deathward?
First it was Adrastus, Autonous,
and Echeclus; then Perimus Megades,
Eristor, Melanippus; afterward,
Elasus, Mulius, Pylartes. These
he cut down, while the rest looked to their flight.
Troy of the towering gates was on the verge
of being taken by the Achaeans, under
Patroclus' drive: he raced with blooded spear
ahead and around it. On the massive tower
Phoebus Apollo stood as Troy's defender,
deadly toward him. Now three times Patroclus
assaulted the high wall at the tower-joint,
and three times Lord Apollo threw him back
with counterblows of his immortal hands
against the resplendent shield. The Achaean then
a fourth time flung himself against the wall,
more than human in fury.

                        But Apollo
thundered: 'Back, Patroclus, lordly man!
Destiny will not let this fortress town
of Trojans fall to you! Not to Achilles,

either, greater far though he is in war!'
Patroclus now retired, a long way off
and out of range of Lord Apollo's anger.
Hector had held his team at the Scaean Gates,
being of two minds: should he re-engage,
or call his troops to shelter behind the wall?
While he debated this, Phoebus Apollo
stood at his shoulder in a strong man's guise:
Asius, his maternal uncle, brother
of Hecabe and son of Dymas, dweller
in Phrygia beside Sangarius river.

Taking his semblance now, Apollo said:
'Why break off battle, Hector? You need not.
Were I superior to you in the measure
that I am now inferior, you'd suffer
from turning back so wretchedly from battle.
Action! Lash your team against Patroclus,
and see if you can take him. May Apollo
grant you the glory!'
                           And at this, once more
he joined the mêlée, entering it as a god.
Hector in splendour called Cebriones
to whip the horses toward the fight. Apollo,
disappearing into the ranks, aroused
confusion in the Argives, but on Hector
and on the Trojans he conferred his glory.
Letting the rest go, Hector drove his team
straight at Patroclus; and Patroclus faced him
vaulting from his war-car, with his spear
gripped in his left hand; in his right
he held enfolded a sparkling jagged stone.
Not for long in awe of the other man,
he aimed and braced himself and threw the stone
and scored a direct hit on Hector's driver,
Cebriones, a bastard son of Priam,
smashing his forehead with the jagged stone.
Both brows were hit at once, the frontal bone
gave way, and both his eyes burst from their sockets
dropping into the dust before his feet,
as like a diver from the handsome car
he plummeted, and life ebbed from his bones.
You jeered at him then, master of horse, Patroclus:
'God, what a nimble fellow, somersaulting!
If he were out at sea in the fishing-grounds

this man could feed a crew, diving for oysters,
going overboard even in rough water,
the way he took that earth-dive from his car.
The Trojans have their acrobats, I see.'

With this, he went for the dead man with a spring
like a lion, one that has taken a chest-wound
while ravaging a cattle pen – his valour
his undoing. So you sprang, Patroclus,
on Cebriones. Then Hector, too, leapt down
out of his chariot, and the two men fought
over the body like two mountain-lions
over the carcass of a buck, both famished,
both in pride of combat. So these two
fought now for Cebriones, two champions,
Patroclus, son of Menoetius, and Hector,
hurling their bronze to tear each other's flesh.
Hector caught hold of the dead man's head and held,
while his antagonist clung to a single foot,
as Trojans and Danaans pressed the fight.
As south wind and the south-east wind, contending
in mountain groves, make all the forest thrash,
beech trees and ash trees and the slender cornel
swaying their pointed boughs toward one another
in roaring wind, and snapping branches crack:
so Trojans and Achaeans made a din
as lunging they destroyed each other. Neither
considered ruinous flight. Many sharp spears
and arrows trued by feathers from the strings
were fixed in flesh around Cebriones,
and boulders crashed on shields, as they fought on
around him. And a dust-cloud wrought
by a whirlwind hid the greatness of him slain,
minding no more the mastery of horses.
Until the sun stood at high noon in heaven,
spears bit on both sides, and the soldiers fell;
but when the sun passed toward unyoking time,
the Achaeans outfought destiny to prevail.
Now they dragged off gallant Cebriones
out of range, away from the shouting Trojans,
to strip his shoulders of his gear. And fierce
Patroclus hurled himself upon the Trojans
in onslaughts fast as Ares, three times, wild
yells in his throat. Each time he killed nine men.
But on the fourth demonic foray, then

the end of life loomed up for you, Patroclus.
Into the combat dangerous Phoebus came
against him, but Patroclus could not see
the god, enwrapped in cloud as he came near.
He stood behind and struck with open hand
the man's back and broad shoulders, and the eyes
of the fighting man were dizzied by the blow.
Then Phoebus sent the captain's helmet rolling
under the horses' hooves, making the ridge
ring out, and dirtying all the horsehair plume
with blood and dust. Never in time before
had this plumed helmet been befouled with dust,
the helmet that had kept a hero's brow
unmarred, shielding Achilles' head. Now Zeus
bestowed it upon Hector, let him wear it,
though his destruction waited. For Patroclus
felt his great spearshaft shattered in his hands,
long, tough, well-shod, and seasoned though it was;
his shield and strap fell to the ground; the Lord
Apollo, son of Zeus, broke off his cuirass.
Shock ran through him, and his good legs failed,
so that he stood agape. Then from behind
at close quarters, between the shoulder blades,
a Dardan fighter speared him: Panthous' son,
Euphorbus, the best Trojan of his age
at handling spears, in horsemanship and running:
he had brought twenty chariot-fighters down
since entering combat in his chariot,
already skilled in the craft of war. This man
was first to wound you with a spear, Patroclus,
but did not bring you down. Instead, he ran back
into the mêlée, pulling from the flesh
his ashen spear, and would not face his enemy,
even disarmed, in battle. Then Patroclus,
disabled by the god's blow and the spear-wound,
moved back to save himself amid his men.
But Hector, seeing that his brave adversary
tried to retire, hurt by the spear-wound, charged
straight at him through the ranks and lunged for him
low in the flank, driving the spearhead through.
He crashed, and all Achaean troops turned pale.
Think how a lion in his pride brings down
a tireless boar; magnificently they fight
on a mountain-crest for a small gushing spring –

both in desire to drink – and by sheer power
the lion conquers the great panting boar:
that was the way the son of Priam, Hector,
closed with Patroclus, son of Menoetius,
killer of many, and took his life away.

    Then glorying above him he addressed him:
'Easy to guess, Patroclus, how you swore
to ravage Troy, to take the sweet daylight
of liberty from our women, and to drag them
off in ships to your own land – you fool!
Between you and those women there is Hector's
war-team, thundering out to fight! My spear
has pride of place among the Trojan warriors,
keeping their evil hour at bay.
The kites will feed on you, here on this field.
Poor devil, what has that great prince, Achilles,
done for you? He must have told you often
as you were leaving and he stayed behind,
"Never come back to me, to the deep-sea ships,
Patroclus, till you cut to rags
the bloody tunic on the chest of Hector!"
That must have been the way he talked, and won
your mind to mindlessness.'

                    In a low faint voice,
Patroclus, master of horse, you answered him:
'This is your hour to glory over me,
Hector. The Lord Zeus and Apollo gave you
the upper hand and put me down with ease.
They stripped me of my arms. No one else did.
Say twenty men like you had come against me,
all would have died before my spear.
No, Leto's son and fatal destiny
have killed me; if we speak of men, Euphorbus.
You were in third place, only in at the death.
I'll tell you one thing more; take it to heart.
No long life is ahead for you. This day
your death stands near, and your immutable end,
at Prince Achilles' hands.'

                      His own death
came on him as he spoke, and soul from body,
bemoaning severance from youth and manhood,
slipped to be wafted to the underworld.

    Even in death Prince Hector still addressed him:
'Why prophesy my sudden death, Patroclus?

Who knows, Achilles, son of bright-haired Thetis,
might be hit first; he might be killed by me.'
   At this he pulled his spearhead from the wound,
setting his heel upon him; then he pushed him
over on his back, clear of the spear,
and lifting it at once sought Automedon,
companion of the great runner, Achilles,
longing to strike him. But the immortal horses,
gift of the gods to Peleus, bore him away.

BOOK XVII

CONTENDING FOR A SOLDIER FALLEN

IN the midst of the great fight
the eye of Menelaus, dear to the wargod,
had seen Patroclus brought down by the Trojans.
Now he came forward in his fiery bronze
through clashing men to stand astride the body –
protective as a heifer who has dropped
her first-born calf: she stands above it, lowing,
never having known birth-pangs before.
So, over dead Patroclus, Menelaus
planted his heels, with compact shield and spear
thrust out to kill whoever might attack him.

One whose heart leaped at Patroclus' fall
was Panthous' son, Euphorbus.
Halting nearby, he said to Menelaus:
'Son of Atreus, nobly bred, Lord Marshal,
yield, leave the corpse, give up his bloody gear!
No Trojan hit Patroclus in the fight
before I hit him. Let me have my glory.
Back, or I'll take your sweet life with one blow.'

Hot with anger, red-haired Menelaus
growled: 'Father Zeus, this vanity and bragging
offends the air! A lion or a leopard
could not be so reckless; or a boar,
baleful with pounding fury in his ribcage:
Panthous' sons are bolder,
more headlong than these. But youth and brawn
brought no triumph or joy to Hyperenor,
when he sneered at me and fought me. Feeblest of all
Danaans he called me! Never on his own feet, I swear,
did he return to gladden wife and kin.
Aye, and you – I'll break your fighting heart
if you stand up to me. Give way!
Don't challenge me, get back into the ruck
before something happens to you! Any fool
can see a thing already done.'

                              The other
took no heed but answered: 'Now, by god,
you will give satisfaction for my brother,

the man you killed and boast of having killed,
leaving his bride lonely in her new chamber,
his parents harrowed by the loss!
I might become a stay against their grief
if I could put your head and shield and helm
in Panthous' hands, in the fair hands of Phrontis.
Come on, no more delay in fighting out
the test of this – we'll see who holds his ground,
who backs away.'
            And at these words he struck
the other's shield. The bronze point failed to break it,
bending at impact on the hard plate. Then
in his turn Menelaus made his lunge,
calling on Zeus. The spearhead pierced the young man's
throat at the pit as he was falling back,
and Menelaus with his heavy grip
drove it on, straight through his tender neck.
He thudded down, his gear clanged on his body,
and blood bathed his long hair, fair as the Graces',
braided, pinched by twists of silver and gold.
Think how a man might tend a comely shoot
of olive in a lonely place, well watered,
so that it flourished, being blown upon
by all winds, putting out silvery-green leaves,
till suddenly a great wind in a storm
uprooted it and cast it down: so beautiful
had Panthous' son, Euphorbus, been,
when Menelaus killed him and bent over
to take his gear.
            And as a mountain-lion
cuts out a yearling from a grazing herd –
the plumpest one – clamping with his great jaws
upon her neck to break it, and then feeds
on blood and vitals, rending her; around him
dogs and herdsmen raise a mighty din
but keep away, unwilling to attack,
as pale dread takes possession of them all:
so not one Trojan had the heart to face
Menelaus in his pride. He might with ease
have borne Euphorbus' gear away, had not
Apollo taken umbrage and aroused
Hector, peer of the swift war-god, against him.
    In a man's guise, in that of Mentes, Lord
of Cicones, Apollo said: 'Lord Hector,

here you are chasing what cannot be caught,
the horses of Achilles! Intractable
to mortal men they are, no one could train them
except their master, whom a goddess bore.
Meanwhile Menelaus, dear to Ares,
stands guard over Patroclus. He has killed
a princely Trojan, Panthous' son
Euphorbus, putting an end to his audacity,
his high heart.'

             Turning back, once more the god
entered the moil of men. But heavy pain
bore down on Hector's darkened heart, and peering
along the ranks in battle he made out
one man loosing the armour of the other,
prone on the field, his gashed throat welling blood.
Then Hector shouldered through the fight, his helmet
flashing, and his shout rose like the flame
of Hephaestus' forge, unquenchable.

                        It blasted
Menelaus, and cursing in his heart
the Achaean said to himself: 'What now? If I
abandon this good armour, leave Patroclus,
who lies here for my honour's sake, I hope
no Danaans may see me to my shame!
But it I fight alone in pride, they may
surround me, Hector and the other Trojans –
god forbid – many against one man.
And now Hector is leading the pack this way!
Why go on arguing with myself? To enter
combat when the will of god's against you –
to fight a man god loves – that's doom, and quickly.
No Danaan will lift his brows at me
for giving ground to Hector: Hector goes
under god's arm to war. If I could only spot
Aias anywhere, we two might brace
in joy of battle, and contend once more,
even against god's will, to bring the body
back to Achilles – somehow. That would be
making the best of it.'

                  But while he pondered,
Trojan ranks came on, as Hector led them.
Backward at last he turned, and left the body,
facing about at every step, the way
a bearded lion does when dogs and men

with spears and shouts repel him from a farmyard,
and hatred makes his great heart turn to ice
as he is forced from the cattle-pen. Just so,
forced from Patroclus, tawny Menelaus
step by step retired, then stood fast
on reaching the main body of his men.
Meanwhile he kept an eye out for great Aias,
the son of Telamon, and all at once
he saw him, on the far left of the battle,
cheering his men, to make them stand and fight,
for Apollo put wild fear into them all.
   Menelaus ran to his side and said:
'Aias, come, good heart, we'll make a fight of it
near Patroclus, try to bring his body
back to Achilles, though he lies despoiled,
his gear in Hector's hands.'

               This call went straight
to the fighting heart of Aias, and he followed
Menelaus down the field.

            Meanwhile
when he had stripped Patroclus of his armour,
Hector pulled at the corpse: now to behead it
and give the trunk to Trojan dogs! But Aias
came up then, his great shield like a tower,
and Hector fell back on the waiting ranks
to mount his car. The splendid arms of Achilles
he gave to soldiers to be borne to town,
his trophies, his great glory.

             And still Aias
extending his broad shield above Patroclus,
stood as a lion will above his cubs
when a hunting-party comes upon the beast
in underbrush, leading his young; he narrows
eyes to slits, drawing his forehead down.
So Aias took his stand above Patroclus,
while Menelaus, dear to the war-god, stood
nearby and let his grief mount up.

             Now Glaucus,
Hippolochus' son, captain of Lycians,
glaring at Hector, had harsh words for him:
'Hector, you are a great man, by the look of you,
but in a fight you're far from great.
That's how it goes, a big name, and a craven!
Put your mind on how to save your town

with troops born here at Ilium, no others!
Not one Lycian goes into combat
after this for Troy! What have we gained,
battling without rest against hard enemies?
How would you save a lesser man in war,
you heartless fraud, if you could quit Sarpedon,
comrade-in-arms and guest as well, and leave him
to be the Argives' prey and spoil? In life
he was a great ally to you and Troy,
and yet to keep the scavenging dogs from him –
you had no heart for that! Here's what I say,
if any of the Lycians obey me,
we are for home, and let doom fall on Troy!
If the Trojans had spirit – had that unshakeable
will that rightly comes to men who face
for their own land the toil and shock of war,
we'd pull Patroclus into Ilium quickly!
And were he brought in death to the great town
of Priam, if we dragged him from the fury,
the Argives would return Sarpedon's arms,
his body, too, for us to carry home
to Ilium in fair exchange.
For he who perished here was the dear friend
of a great prince, greatest by far of those
who hold the beach and their tough men-at-arms.
But as for you, you did not dare
meet Aias, face to face and eye to eye,
in the din of battle, or engage him. Why?
Because he is a better man than you are.'

    Hector in his shimmering helmet frowned
and answered him: 'So young, and yet so insolent?
Old son, I had thought you a steady man,
coolest of those who live in Lycia.
Now I despise your thought. Nonsense to say
I would not meet huge Aias. When have I
shown fear of sword-play, or of trampling horses?
Strongest of all, though, is the mind of Zeus
who bears the storm-cloud: he can turn back
a champion, and rob him of his triumph,
even when he incites the man. Come here,
my friend, stand by me, watch me in action. All
day long I'll be the coward you describe,
or else you'll see me stop the enemy cold
no matter how he fights to shield Patroclus.'

To the Trojans now he gave a mighty shout:
'Trojans, Lycians, hard-fighting Dardani,
be men, old friends, remember your own valour,
while I put on Achilles' beautiful arms,
taken from Patroclus when I killed him.'
Then in his shimmering helmet Hector turned
to leave the deadly fight, and running hard
he caught up soon with his platoon of soldiers;
they were not far, bearing the great man's armour
up to the city. Hector stood there then,
apart from all the dolorous war, and changed.
He who had given those arms to be carried back
into the proud town, to the folk of Troy,
now buckled on the bright gear of Achilles,
Peleus' son – that gear the gods of heaven
granted his father. He, when old, bestowed it
on a son who would not wear it into age.
    And Zeus who gathers cloud saw Hector now
standing apart, in the hero's shield and helm,
and nodded, musing over him: 'Ah, poor man,
no least presage of death is in your mind,
how near it is, at last. You wear the gear
of a great prince. Other men blanch before him.
It is his comrade, gentle and strong, you killed,
and stripped his head and shoulders of helm and shield
without respect. Power for the time being
I will concede to you, as recompense,
for never will Andromache receive
Achilles' arms from you on your return.'
    He bent his great head, over his black brows,
and made the arms fit Hector.
                                    Then fierce Ares
entered the man, his bone and sinew thrilled
with power and will to fight. Among his men
he shouldered forward with a mighty shout,
flashing in the armour of Achilles,
and stirred each man he came abreast of –
Mesthles, Glaucus, Medon, Thersilochus,
Asteropaeus, Deisenor, Hippothous,
Phorcys, Chromius, and the seer of birds,
Ennomus.
                In a swift speech he urged them:
'Hear me, hosts of neighbours and allies,
not from desire for numbers or display

did I enlist you, bring you from your cities
here to Troy. You were to save our wives
and children from the Achaeans, our besiegers.
And I deprive my people to that end
with requisitioning for you – supplies,
to build your strength and strength of heart. Go forward,
every man, therefore, to meet destruction
or to come through: these are the terms of war.
Patroclus has been killed indeed. Whoever
pulls his body to our charioteers –
if Aias can be made to yield to him –
that man wins half our spoils
when I allot them. I myself take half,
so glory equal to my own is his.'

   At this they surged ahead and bore down hard
with lifted spears on the Danaans. High hopes
they had of dragging off the corpse from Aias –
fools, for he took their lives, many, upon it.

   To Menelaus, clarion in battle,
Aias now said: 'Old-timer, Menelaus,
I see no hope for us of getting back,
all on our own, out of this fight. My fear
is less for the dead body of Patroclus –
glutting the dogs and birds he may be, soon –
than for my life and yours, in mortal peril.
Hector's a battle-cloud, covering everything.
Our death looms in that cloud.
Call to our champions, if they can hear you.'

   Menelaus complied, and high and clear
made himself heard by the Danaans: 'Friends,
captains and lords of Argives, all who drink
with Agamemnon and with Menelaus
wine of the peers, and all those in command
of men-at-arms – glory from Zeus attend you –
I find it hard to pick out single men,
the action being so hot,
but let each one come forward on his own
against the shame of seeing Trojan dogs
sport with Patroclus!'

                           Aias the runner, son
of Oileus, heard distinctly and came first
through battle on the run; Idomeneus
came next, and his retainer, Meriones,
peer of the murderous war-god. Then the rest;

and who could name so many in his mind,
who came up afterward to rouse the action?
　　Now the Trojans charged, all in a mass,
led by Hector. As at a river mouth
a big sea thunders in against the stream,
high banks resound, and spume blows from the surf,
so came the Trojans shouting. The Achaeans
formed a line in singleness of heart
around Patroclus, walled by brazen shields.
And Zeus the son of Cronos poured thick mist
about their shining helms, for in the past
Patroclus never had offended him
while he lived on as the comrade of Achilles;
now he hated to see him prey to dogs
and stirred his friends to fight for him.

　　　　　　　　　　　　　　　　　　First, though,
the Trojan impetus bent the Achaean line
back from the dead man, wavering, though not one
could Trojan spearmen kill, for all their passion.
Now they pulled at the corpse, but not for long
were the Achaeans to be parted from it:
Aias made them spring back, he whose bulk
and feats of war surpassed all the Achaeans
after Prince Achilles. Plunging ahead,
he broke the Trojans, valorous as a boar
in mountain land who scatters dogs and men
with ease, wheeling upon them in a glade.
Even so the son of Telamon,
magnificent Aias, whirled about and broke
the clump of Trojans that had ringed Patroclus
thinking now surely to drag away the body
to their own town, and win acclaim for it.
Aye, the illustrious son of the Pelasgian
Lethus, Hippothous, looping his sword-belt
around the tendons at the ankles, drew
the body backward on the field of war
to win favour with Hector and the Trojans.
Black fate came to him; none could deflect it.
Aias leaping through the mêlée struck
his helm with brazen cheek-plates; round the point
the ridge that bore the crest crumpled at impact,
cleft by a great spear in a massive hand.
His brains burst, all in blood, out of the wound
as far as the spearhead socket. On the spot

his life died out in him and from his hands
he let Patroclus' foot fall to the ground
as he pitched forward head first on the body,
far from Larisa's rich farmland; nor ever
would he repay his parents for their care,
his life being cut short by the spear of Aias.

There and then, with spearpoint flashing, Hector
lunged at Aias; Aias saw it coming
and dodged the bronze point by a hair. Instead
the shock came to the son of Iphitus,
Schedius, a Phocian hero, who had lived
as lord of many in renowned Panopeus.
Now the spear caught him under the collar-bone;
the bronze point cut through to his shoulder-blade,
and down he crashed, his war-gear clanging on him.
For his part, Aias hit the son of Phaenops,
veteran Phorcys, in the middle belly
just as he came up to Hippothous.
The spearhead broke his cuirass at the joint
and pierced his abdomen. Fallen in the dust,
he clutched the earth with hand outspread. His men
fell back, then; so did Hector; and the Argives
gave a loud cry as they dragged off
the bodies, those of Phorcys and Hippothous,
ripping from their shoulders gear of war.

At that point, under pressure from Achaeans
and overcome by their own weakness, Trojans
might have re-entered Ilium; beyond
the limit set by Zeus the Argives might
have won the day by their own heart and brawn.
Not so: Apollo now inflamed Aeneas,
taking the form of Epytus' son, Periphas,
a crier, and a kind man, who had aged
in the crier's duty, serving old Anchises.

In that disguise Apollo son of Zeus
said: 'How could men like you save Ilium,
Aeneas, overriding heaven's will?
In other days I've seen men put their trust
in their own strength and manhood, or in numbers,
and hold their realms, beyond the will of Zeus.
And now in fact Zeus wills the victory
far more for us than for Danaans. Amazing,
the way you shrink from battle!'
                                        Facing him,

Aeneas recognized the archer, Apollo,
and shouted then to Hector: 'Hector! all
captains of Trojans and allies; what shame
to go back into Ilium, spent and beaten!
Here, standing near me, is a god who tells me
Zeus on high is our defender, Zeus,
master of battle! Come, we'll cut our way
through the Danaans; and god forbid they take
Patroclus' corpse aboard ship at their leisure!'
     At this he leapt ahead and took position
forward of his line: the rest swung round
and faced the Achaeans. With his spear Aeneas
hit Arisbas' son, Leocritus,
comrade of Lycomedes, and the heart
of Lycomedes grieved as he went down.
He moved in range, thrust out, and hit
Apisaon Hippasides, a captain,
in the liver under the ribs. His knees
buckled, and he who had come from Paeonia,
the best at warfare after Asteropaeus,
fell to earth. Asteropaeus grieved
as he went down, and now with generous heart
he too attacked but failed to break the Danaans,
whose line of shields made them a barrier,
spearpoints advanced, compact around Patroclus.
     Aias it was who passed from man to man
saying: 'No one retreats a step; but no one
fights out of line, either, before the rest.
Close in around him, fight on, hand to hand.'
     These were great Aias' orders. Now the earth
grew stained with bright blood as men fell in death
close to one another: Trojans, allies,
and Danaans, too, for they, too, bled,
although far fewer died – each one remembering
to shield his neighbour from the fatal stroke.
So all fought on, a line of living flame.
And safe, you'd say, was neither sun nor moon,
since all was darkened in the battle-cloud –
as were the champions who held and fought
around the dead Patroclus.
                                        The main armies,
Trojans and Achaeans under arms,
were free to make war under the open sky
with sunlight sharp about them: not a cloud

appeared above the whole earth or the hills.
The armies fought, then rested, pulling back
to a good distance, out of range
of one another's arrows, quills of groaning.
Those in the centre, though, endured the cloud
with toil of war; and they lost blood as well
to heartless bronze, those champions.

                     Two fine men,
Thrasymedes and Antilochus, famous both,
were unaware of Prince Patroclus' death,
thinking he still fought in the forward line.
Vigilant to deal with death and rout, these two
gave battle on the flank, as Nestor ordered,
urging them from the black ships into action.
For the other heroes all day long the bout
of bitter striving raged: fatigue and sweat,
with never a pause; all knees and shins and feet
and hands and eyes of fighters were bespattered,
around the noble friend of swift Achilles.
A man will give his people a great ox-hide
to stretch for him, having it soaked in grease:
and grasping it, on all sides braced around it,
they pull it till the moisture goes, the oil
sinks in, with many tugging hands, and soon
the whole expanse is dry and taut. Just so,
this way and that way in a little space
both sides kept tugging at the body: Trojans
panting to drag it off toward Ilium,
Achaeans to the decked ships. Round about,
wild tumult rose. Ares, Frenzy of Soldiers,
would not have scorned that fight, nor would Athena,
even in deadly rage, so murderous
the toil of men and chariots for Patroclus
that Zeus prolonged that day.

                     Not yet, remember,
had Prince Achilles word of his friend's death.
Far from the ships this action had gone on
under the Trojans' wall, and no clear foresight
came to him: Patroclus would, he thought,
approach the gates but then turn back; he could not
hope alone to take the town by storm.
Often Achilles, listening in secret,
had learned things from his mother as she foretold
the will of mighty Zeus for him. This time

she gave no word to him of what calamity
had come, that his great friend had been destroyed.
But hour by hour the rest fought for the body,
gripping whetted spears, dealing out death.
    And some Achaean veteran might say:
'Old friends, no glory in our taking ship
again for home; sooner may black earth here
embed us all! That would be better far
than giving up this body to the Trojans,
a trophy for them, and a glory won!'
    And of the Trojans there were some to say:
'Old friends, if in the end we are cut down
alongside this one – just like him – the lot of us,
still not a man should quit the fight!'
                                That way
the Trojans talked and cheered each other on.
And that was how that battle went – a din
of iron-hearted men through barren air
rose to the sky all brazen.
                        Out of range,
the horses of Achilles, from the time
they sensed their charioteer downed in the dust
at the hands of deadly Hector, had been weeping.
Automedon, the son of Diores,
laid often on their backs his flickering whip,
pled often in a low tone – or he swore at them –
but neither toward the shipways and the beach
by Helle's waters would they budge, nor follow
Achaeans into battle. No: stock-still
as a gravestone, fixed above the tomb
of a dead man or woman, they stood fast,
holding the beautiful war-car still: their heads
curved over to the ground, and warm tears flowed
from under eyelids earthward as they mourned
their longed-for driver. Manes along the yoke
were soiled as they hung forward under yoke-pads.
    Seeing their tears flow, pitying them, Lord Zeus
bent his head and murmured in his heart:
'Poor things, why did I give you to King Peleus,
a mortal, you who never age nor die,
to let you ache with men in their hard lot?
For of all creatures that breathe and move on earth
none is more to be pitied than a man.
Never at least shall Hector, son of Priam,

ride behind you in your painted car.
That I will not allow. Is it not enough
that he both has the gear and brags about it?
I shall put fire in your knees and hearts
to rescue Automedon, bear him away
from battle to the decked ships. Glory of killing,
even so, I reserve to his enemies
until they reach the ships, until sundown,
until the dusk comes, full of stars.'

                With this
he sent a fiery breath into the horses.
Shaking the dust to earth from their long manes,
they bore the war-car swiftly amid the armies.
Automedon gave battle as he rode,
though grieving for his friend. Behind the horses
in foray like a hawk on geese, with ease
he doubled back, out of the Trojan din,
then quickly drove full tilt upon the mass,
but made no kills, though whipping in pursuit,
being single-handed in his car – unable
to thrust well with a spear, needing both hands
to guide the horses.

                  One of his men at last
caught on: one Alcimedon, son of Laerces
Haemonides: he halted just behind
and called out: 'Automedon,
this futile plan of action – which of the gods
put you up to it? He took your wits away –
fighting alone like this against the Trojans,
and in the line! – though your companion fell,
and Hector himself has got Achilles' arms
to swagger in.'

                And to this Automedon,
son of Diores, answered: 'Alcimedon,
what other Achaean has your knack
for guiding the divine fire of these horses?
Only Patroclus, matchless when he lived,
but destiny and death have come upon him.
Come then, take the whip and the bright reins,
while I step from the chariot into battle!'

    Alcimedon, mounting the swift war-car,
caught up whip and reins, and Automedon
vaulted down.

                Hector noticed all this,

and to Aeneas, near at hand, he said:
'Counsellor of the Trojans mailed in bronze,
I've seen that team, Achilles' team, re-enter
battle with poor drivers. I might hope
to capture it, if you, for one, were with me;
against the two of us, closing upon it,
they would not make a stand or dare give battle.'

Anchises' noble son nodded, and both
went forward, shoulders cased in hardened oxhide
shields, all plated with a wealth of bronze,
and at their heels went Chromius and Aretus,
hoping to kill that pair of charioteers
and drive the haughty team away. But they were
fooled in this: from Automedon's stroke
they would not come unbloodied.

                              Calling on Zeus,
he felt new power surge about his heart,
and cried to Alcimedon, his loyal friend:
'Not at a distance from me! Keep the team
close up, aye, keep them breathing on my back!
I do not think Hector Priamides
will quit until he mounts this car
behind the beautiful horses of Achilles,
killing us both, routing the Argive line;
else in the front line he must fall himself.'

To those called Aias, and to Menelaus
he shouted: 'Aias and Aias, captains of Argives,
and you, Menelaus: turn the body over
to your best men; let them stand by and hold
the enemy back. But come yourselves, defend
the living, too – the pair of us – ward off
our evil hour! Hector and Aeneas,
Trojan champions, have put their weight
into the painful battle. Now, by heaven,
the issue lies upon the gods' great knees,
and as for me, I'll make my throw. Let Zeus
look after all the rest.'

                              Rifling the spear
over its long slim shadow, he let fly
and hit Aretus' circular shield. The surface
failed to hold, and the bronze point drove on
straight through his belt into the lower belly.
As when a rugged fellow with an axe
has cleft an ox behind the horns, and cut

through all the hump, so the beast rears and falls,
Aretus reared and tumbled back, undone
by the long spear still quivering in his bowels.
Now with his spearhead flashing, Hector cast
at Automedon, who foresaw the cast
and doubled forward, dodging under the point.
The great shaft punched into the earth behind him,
sticking there, vibrating. Burly Ares
deprived it of its force there. Now with swords
the men made for each other, hand to hand,
but soon the two named Aias broke them apart,
shouldering at their friend's call through the press.
Flurried by these two, Hector and Aeneas,
Chromius, too, backed off again,
leaving Aretus lying there, his life
slashed out of him.
                    Then Automedon, peer
in speed of the war-god, took the dead man's armour,
and vaunting cried: 'By heaven now I've eased
my heart somewhat of anguish for Patroclus,
tearing out a man's guts; but no such man as he.'

Lifting the bloodstained gear into his car,
he stepped aboard, his legs and forearms wet
with blood, like a lion sated on a bull.

Over Patroclus the rough combat widened,
loud with oaths and sobs; and from the sky
Athena came, kindling the fight, for Zeus
who views the wide world, as his humour changed,
had sent her down to stiffen the Danaans.
As when from storm-lit heaven he bends a rainbow,
omen of war to mortal men, or omen
of a chill tempest, pelting flocks and herds,
and ending the field work of countrymen,
so, folded in a ragged cloud of storm-light,
Athena entered the Achaean host.

She braced each soldier's will to fight, but first
to the son of Atreus, massive Menelaus,
she spoke, as he stood near to her. Her form
seemed that of Phoenix, her strong voice his voice:
'The shame of it will make you hang your head,
Menelaus, if glorious Achilles'
faithful friend is dragged under Troy wall
by ravening dogs! Call on your own strength,
and put fight in the army!'

Menelaus,
the deep-lunged man of battle, answered her:
'Phoenix, yes – old timer, full of years –
and may Athena give me force, may she
deflect the spears. My will is to defend
Patroclus. When he died, it touched my heart.
But Hector is a devouring flame: he will not
pause, laying about him: Zeus exalts him!'

At this the grey-eyed goddess secretly
took pleasure, that of all the gods he chose
to make his prayer to her. Power in his shoulders
she instilled, and gristle in his knees,
and in his heart the boldness of a shad-fly,
fiercely brushed away but mad to bite,
as human blood is ambrosial drink to him.
So furious daring swelled in Menelaus'
dark chest-cave, and he regained his place
above Patroclus, levelling his spear.

There was a Trojan, son of Eetion,
Podes by name, a rich and noble man,
whom Hector honoured most in all the realm
as his convivial friend. This was the fighter
tawny Menelaus hit in the belt
as he recoiled, and drove the spearhead through.
He went down with a crash. The son of Atreus
pulled his body from amid the Trojans
over to his own line.

Now Apollo
standing at Hector's elbow spurred him on.
Phaenops Asiades he seemed, who came
from Abydos and held first place with Hector
of all his foreign friends.

In this man's guise
the archer Apollo said: 'Would any Achaean
fear you now? How openly you shrank
from Menelaus – in the past, at least,
no tough man with a spear! Just now, alone,
he carried off a dead man from the Trojans,
a faithful friend of yours whom he had killed,
a brave man in attack, Podes, the son
of Eetion.'

Then a cloud of pain
darkened the heart of Hector. Amid attackers
he went forward, helmed in the fiery bronze.

And now the son of Cronos took in hand
the storm-cloud with its fringe and fitful glare,
and hid in cloud Mount Ida. Flash on flash
he let his lightning fall, with rumbling thunder,
shaking the earth. To the Trojans now he gave
clear victory, and he routed the Achaeans.
First to panic was Peneleos
the Boeotian: as he turned, face to the front,
he took a spear-wound in the shoulder – just
a grazing wound, but one that nicked the bone –
from Polydamas' point, thrust close at hand;
and at close quarters Hector wounded Leitus,
great Alectryon's son, on the forearm
and put him out of action. He retreated,
thinking no longer with one useless hand
to fight the Trojans. And as Hector chased him,
Idomeneus cast at the Trojan's cuirass,
hitting him near the nipple, but the shaft
broke off below the point. A cry went up
from the Trojan side, and Hector threw in turn
at Idomeneus, the son of Deucalion,
mounted now in his chariot. By a hair
he missed him, but the spear brought down
Meriones' friend and driver, Coeranus.
From Cretan Lyctus Coeranus had come
along with Meriones. At first, that day,
Idomeneus had left the camp and ships
on foot, in peril, offering the Trojans
a triumph, had not Coeranus driven up
full speed and come abreast to be his saviour,
shielding him from his evil hour. Coeranus
now lost his life to Hector, killer of men,
who speared him under jaw and ear and prized
his teeth out, roots and all, splitting his tongue.
Down from his chariot he fell, dropping
the reins to earth.

> Meriones bent to take them
in his own hands, then said to Idomeneus:
'Use your whip to make it to the camp!
You know as well as I, there's no fight left
in the Achaeans.'

> Away, and toward the ships,
Idomeneus lashed his horses with long manes,
for fear had entered him at last.

Great Aias
and Menelaus were not blind: they saw
that Zeus accorded victory to the Trojans.
Telamonian Aias bowed before it.
'Damn this day,' he said. 'A fool would know
that Zeus had thrown his weight behind the Trojans.
All their stones and javelins hit the mark,
whoever flings them, good soldier or bad!
As for ourselves, no luck at all, our shots
are spent against the ground. We two, alone,
may think what's best to do – somehow to try
dragging the body back, as we ourselves
return alive to comfort friends of ours.
There they are, desperately looking toward us,
hopeless now of a pause in Hector's rage,
his uncontainable handiwork: they see
he'll break in on our black ships. Now if only
there was a man to run for it, to bring word
to Peleus' son! I think he can't have heard
the black report that his dear friend is dead.
I cannot anywhere see a runner, though,
in this cloud, covering men and chariots.
O Father Zeus, come, bring our troops from under
the dustcloud: make clear air: give back our sight!
Destroy us in daylight – as your pleasure is
to see us all destroyed!'
                                    The Father pitied him,
seeing his tears flow. He dispersed the cloud,
rolled back the battle-haze, and sunlight shone,
so the whole fight became abruptly clear.
    Then Aias said to Menelaus: 'Will you
use your eyes now, royal friend,
to spot, if you can, Antilochus, Nestor's son
and a good fighter. Send him on the run
to tell Achilles of his dear friend's death.'
    Menelaus complied, but slowly, as a lion
goes from a farmyard, lagging, tired out
with worrying dogs and men who watched all night
to keep him from his choice of fatted cattle.
Avid for meat, he bounds in to attack
but has no luck: a hail of javelins
thrown by tough cowherds comes flying out at him,
and brands of flame from which he flinches, roaring.
At dawn he trails away with sullen heart.

So Menelaus, lord of the great war-cry,
left Patroclus, hating to go, afraid
the panicking Achaeans would abandon him
to be their enemies' prey.

                He lingered long,
bidding Meriones and the two named Aias:
'Remember poor Patroclus, each of you,
his warmth of heart. He had a way of being
kind to all in life. Now destiny and death
have overtaken him.'

                Then Menelaus
turned to search the field, keen as an eagle
who has, they say, of all birds under heaven
the sharpest eyes: even at a great height
he will not miss a swift hare gone to earth
under a shady bush; he plummets down
straight on him, catches him, and tears his life.
So your bright eyes, Prince Menelaus,
glanced everywhere amid the crowd of soldiers,
looking for Nestor's son, if he lived still.

    And soon enough he found him, on the left flank,
cheering his men, sending them into action,
and as he reached him red-haired Menelaus
cried: 'Antilochus, come here, young prince,
and hear sad news. Would god it had not happened!
You yourself have seen, I think, by now
that god sends ruin surging on our army.
Victory goes to the Trojans. Our best man,
Patroclus, fell – irreparable loss
and grief to the Danaans.

                'Here is your duty:
run to the ships, tell all this to Achilles,
in hope that he can make all haste to save
the disarmed corpse, and carry it aboard –
though Hector has his armour.'

              Hearing these words
appalled and sick at heart, Antilochus
lost for a time his power of speech: his eyes
brimmed over, and his manly voice was choked.
Yet even so he heeded Menelaus,
handing over his armour to his friend,
Laodocus, who turned his team and chariot
near to him. Then he set off on the run.

    And so in tears Antilochus left the battle

with evil news for Achilles Peleides.
As for you, Menelaus, you did not
lend a hand to his friends, when he had gone,
leaving a great void for the men of Pylos.
Rather, Menelaus sent Thrasymedes
and ran back to Patroclus.

                    There he stood
by those named Aias telling them: 'I found him.
Then I sent him shoreward. He will report
to our great runner, Achilles. But I doubt
Achilles will appear, even though he'll be
insane with rage at Hector. Can he come
to make war on the Trojans without armour?
No, we had better plan it for ourselves,
how best to save the dead man, and how best
escape death in the hue and cry of Trojans.'

    Telamonian Aias answered: 'All you say
is reasonable, excellency. Be quick,
you and Meriones, get good leverage
under the body, lift it, and lug it back
out of the line. We two will stay behind
to engage the Trojans and Prince Hector – being
alike in name and heart. Often in the past
we've waited side by side for slashing Ares.'

    At this Menelaus and Meriones
got their arms under the dead man and gave
a great heave upward. From the Trojan mass
a cry broke out, as they perceived the Achaeans
lifting the body, and they set upon them
like a dog-pack chasing a wounded boar
ahead of young men hunting. For a while
they stream out in full cry, ready to rend him,
but when he wheels to take them on, staking
everything on his own valour, they recoil
and swerve this way and that. The Trojans, too,
came harrying behind them in a pack
with cut and thrust of sword and bladed spear,
but when the two named Aias wheeled and stood
to menace them, their faces changed: not one
dared charge ahead for a contest over the body.
Guarded so, the bearers, might and main,
strove on to bring it to the ships. Around them
battle spread like a fire that seethes and flares
once it has broken out upon a city;

houses fall in with flame-bursts, as the wind
makes the great conflagration roar: so now
incessant din of chariots and spearmen
beset them on their way. Grim as a mule-team
putting their strong backs into hauling, down
a rocky footpath on a mountainside,
a beam or a ship's timber; and their hearts
are wearied out, straining with toil and sweat:
so these with might and main carried the body.
And, close behind, the two named Aias fought
their rearguard action. As a wooded headland
formed across a plain will stem a flood
and hold roiled currents, even of great rivers,
deflecting every one to wander, driven
along the plain; and not one, strongly flowing,
can wash it out or wear it down: just so
the two named Aias held the fighting Trojans
and threw them back. Still they pressed on, and most
of all Aeneas Anchisiades
with brilliant Hector. As a cloud of starlings
or jackdaws shrieking bloody murder flies
on seeing a hawk about to strike; he brings
a slaughter on small winged things: just so
under pursuit by Hector and Aeneas
Achaean soldiers shrieked and fled, their joy
in combat all forgotten. Routed Achaeans'
gear of war piled up along the moat,
and there was never a respite from the battle.

BOOK XVIII

THE IMMORTAL SHIELD

WHILE they were still in combat, fighting seaward
raggedly as fire, Antilochus
ran far ahead with tidings for Achilles.
In shelter of the curled, high prows he found him
envisioning what had come to pass,
in gloom and anger saying to himself:
'Ai! why are they turning tail once more,
unmanned, outfought, and driven from the field
back on the beach and ships? I pray the gods
this may not be the last twist of the knife!
My mother warned me once that, while I lived,
the most admirable of Myrmidons
would quit the sunlight under Trojan blows.
It could indeed be so. He has gone down,
my dear and wayward friend! I told him,
Push their deadly fire away, I told him,
then return! You must not fight with Hector!'

And while he called it all to mind,
the son of gallant Nestor came up weeping
to give his cruel news: 'Here's desolation,
son of Peleus, the worst news for you –
would god it had not happened! – Lord Patroclus
fell, and they are fighting over his body,
stripped of armour. Hector has your gear.'

A black storm-cloud of pain shrouded Achilles.
On his bowed head he scattered dust and ash
in handfuls and befouled his beautiful face,
letting black ash sift on his fragrant chiton.
Then in the dust he stretched his giant length
and tore his hair with both hands.

From the hut
the women who had been spoils of war to him
and to Patroclus flocked in haste around him,
crying loud in grief. All beat their breasts,
and trembling came upon their knees. Antilochus
wept where he stood, bending to hold the hero's
hands when groaning shook his heart: he feared
the man might use sharp iron to slash his throat.

And now Achilles gave a dreadful cry. Her ladyship
his mother heard him, in the depths offshore
lolling near her ancient father. Nymphs
were gathered round her, all the Nereids
who haunted the green chambers of the sea.
Glauce, Thaleia, and Cymodoce,
Nesaea, Speio, Thoe, Halie
with her wide eyes, Cymothoe, Actaea,
Limnoreia, Melite, and Iaera,
Amphithoe, Agaue, Doto, Proto,
Pherousa, Dynamene, Dexamene,
Amphinome, Callianeira, Doris,
Panope, and storied Galatea,
Nemertes and Apseudes, Callianassa,
Clymene, Ianeira, Ianassa,
Maera, Oreithyia, Amatheia,
and other Nereids of the deep salt sea,
filling her glimmering silvery cave.

                                    All these
now beat their breasts as Thetis cried in sorrow:
'Sisters, daughters of Nereus, hear and know
how sore my heart is! Now my life is pain
for my great son's dark destiny! I bore
a child flawless and strong beyond all men.
He flourished like a green shoot, and I brought him
to manhood like a blossoming orchard tree,
only to send him in the ships to Ilium
to war with Trojans. Now I shall never see him
entering Peleus' hall, his home, again.
But even while he lives, beholding sunlight,
suffering is his lot. I have no power
to help him, though I go to him. Even so,
I'll visit my dear child and learn what sorrow
came to him while he held aloof from war.'
     On this she left the cave, and all in tears
her company swam aloft with her. Around them
a billow broke and foamed on the open sea.
As they made land at the fertile plain of Troy,
they went up one by one in line to where,
in close order, Myrmidon ships were beached
to right and left of Achilles.

                                Bending near
her groaning son, the gentle goddess wailed
and took his head between her hands in pity,

saying softly: 'Child, why are you weeping?
What great sorrow came to you? Speak out,
do not conceal it. Zeus
did all you asked: Achaean troops,
for want of you, were all forced back again
upon the ship-sterns, taking heavy losses
none of them could wish.'

                                    The great runner
groaned and answered: 'Mother, yes, the master
of high Olympus brought it all about,
but how have I benefited? My greatest friend
is gone: Patroclus, comrade in arms, whom I
held dear above all others – dear as myself –
now gone, lost; Hector cut him down, despoiled him
of my own arms, massive and fine, a wonder
in all men's eyes. The gods gave them to Peleus
that day they put you in a mortal's bed –
how I wish the immortals of the sea
had been your only consorts! How I wish
Peleus had taken a mortal queen! Sorrow
immeasurable is in store for you as well,
when your own child is lost: never again
on his home-coming day will you embrace him!
I must reject this life, my heart tells me,
reject the world of men,
if Hector does not feel my battering spear
tear the life out of him, making him pay
in his own blood for the slaughter of Patroclus!'

      Letting a tear fall, Thetis said: 'You'll be
swift to meet your end, child, as you say:
your doom comes close on the heels of Hector's own.'

      Achilles the great runner ground his teeth
and said: 'May it come quickly. As things were,
I could not help my friend in his extremity.
Far from his home he died; he needed me
to shield him or to parry the death-stroke.
For me there's no return to my own country.
Not the slightest gleam of hope did I
afford Patroclus or the other men
whom Hector overpowered. Here I sat,
my weight a useless burden to the earth,
and I am one who has no peer in war
among Achaean captains – though in council
there are wiser. Ai! let strife and rancour

perish from the lives of gods and men,
with anger that envenoms even the wise
and is far sweeter than slow-dripping honey,
clouding the hearts of men like smoke: just so
the marshal of the army, Agamemnon,
moved me to anger. But we'll let that go,
though I'm still sore at heart; it is all past,
and I have quelled my passion as I must.

'Now I must go to look for the destroyer
of my great friend. I shall confront the dark
drear spirit of death at any hour Zeus
and the other gods may wish to make an end.
Not even Heracles escaped that terror
though cherished by the Lord Zeus. Destiny
and Hera's bitter anger mastered him.
Likewise with me, if destiny like his
awaits me, I shall rest when I have fallen!
Now, though, may I win my perfect glory
and make some wife of Troy break down,
or some deep-breasted Dardan woman sob
and wipe tears from her soft cheeks. They'll know then
how long they had been spared the deaths of men,
while I abstained from war!
Do not attempt to keep me from the fight,
though you love me; you cannot make me listen.'

Thetis, goddess of the silvery feet,
answered: 'Yes, of course, child: very true.
You do no wrong to fight for tired soldiers
and keep them from defeat. But still, your gear,
all shining bronze, remains in Trojan hands.
Hector himself is armed with it in pride! —
Not that he'll glory in it long, I know,
for violent death is near him. Patience, then.
Better not plunge into the moil of Ares
until you see me here once more. At dawn,
at sunrise, I shall come
with splendid arms for you from Lord Hephaestus.'

She rose at this and, turning from her son,
told her sister Nereids: 'Go down
into the cool broad body of the sea
to the sea's Ancient; visit Father's hall,
and make all known to him. Meanwhile, I'll visit
Olympus' great height and the lord of crafts,
Hephaestus, hoping he will give me

new and shining armour for my son.'

At this they vanished in the offshore swell,
and to Olympus Thetis the silvery-footed
went once more, to fetch for her dear son
new-forged and finer arms.

                     Meanwhile, Achaeans,
wildly crying, pressed by deadly Hector,
reached the ships, beached above Helle's water.
None had been able to pull Patroclus clear
of spear and sword-play: troops and chariots
and Hector, son of Priam, strong as fire,
once more gained upon the body. Hector
three times had the feet within his grasp
and strove to wrest Patroclus backward, shouting
to all Trojans – but three times the pair
named Aias in their valour shook him off.
Still he pushed on, sure of his own power,
sometimes lunging through the battle-din,
or holding fast with a great shout: not one step
would he give way. As from a fresh carcass
herdsmen in the wilds cannot dislodge
a tawny lion, famished: so those two
with fearsome crests could not affright the son
of Priam or repel him from the body.
He might have won it, might have won unending
glory, but Iris running on the wind
came from Olympus to the son of Peleus,
bidding him gird for battle. All unknown
to Zeus and the other gods she came, for Hera
sent her down.

                    And at his side she said:
'Up with you, Peleides, who strike cold fear
into men's blood! Protect your friend Patroclus,
for whom, beyond the ships, desperate combat
rages now. They are killing one another
on both sides: the Achaeans to defend him,
Trojans fighting for that prize
to drag to windy Ilium. And Hector
burns to take it more than anyone –
to sever and impale Patroclus' head
on Trojan battlements. Lie here no longer.
It would be shameful if wild dogs of Troy
made him their plaything! If that body suffers
mutilation, you will be infamous!'

Prince Achilles answered: 'Iris of heaven,
what immortal sent you to tell me this?'

And she who runs upon the wind replied:
'Hera, illustrious wife of Zeus,
but he on his high throne knows nothing of it.
Neither does any one of the gods undying
who haunt Olympus of eternal snows.'

Achilles asked: 'And now how shall I go
into the fighting? Those men have my gear.
My dear mother allows me no re-arming
until I see her again here.
She promises fine arms from Lord Hephaestus.
I don't know whose armour I can wear,
unless I take Aias' big shield.
But I feel sure he's in the thick of it,
contending with his spear over Patroclus.'

Then she who runs upon the wind replied:
'We know they have your arms, and know it well.
Just as you are, then, stand at the moat; let Trojans
take that in; they will be so dismayed
they may break off the battle, and Achaeans
in their fatigue may win a breathing-spell,
however brief, a respite from the war.'

                                        At this,
Iris left him, running downwind. Achilles,
whom Zeus loved, now rose. Around his shoulders
Athena hung her shield, like a thunderhead
with trailing fringe. Goddess of goddesses,
she bound his head with golden cloud, and made
his very body blaze with fiery light.
Imagine how the pyre of a burning town
will tower to heaven and be seen for miles
from the island under attack, while all day long
outside their town, in brutal combat, pikemen
suffer the war-god's winnowing; at sundown
flare on flare is lit, the signal fires
shoot up for other islanders to see,
that some relieving force in ships may come:
just so the baleful radiance from Achilles
lit the sky. Moving from parapet
to moat, without a nod for the Achaeans,
keeping clear, in deference to his mother,
he halted and gave tongue. Not far from him
Athena shrieked. The great sound shocked the Trojans

into tumult, as a trumpet blown
by a savage foe shocks an encircled town,
so harsh and clarion was Achilles' cry.
The hearts of men quailed, hearing that brazen voice.
Teams, foreknowing danger, turned their cars
and charioteers blanched, seeing unearthly fire,
kindled by the grey-eyed goddess Athena,
brilliant over Achilles. Three great cries
he gave above the moat. Three times they shuddered,
whirling backward, Trojans and allies,
and twelve good men took mortal hurt
from cars and weapons in the rank behind.
Now the Achaeans leapt at the chance
to bear Patroclus' body out of range.
They placed it on his bed,
and old companions there with brimming eyes
surrounded him. Into their midst Achilles
came then, and he wept hot tears to see
his faithful friend, torn by the sharp spearhead,
lying cold upon his cot. Alas,
the man he sent to war with team and chariot
he could not welcome back alive.

                                        Her majesty,
wide-eyed Hera, made the reluctant sun,
unwearied still, sink in the streams of Ocean.
Down he dropped, and the Achaean soldiers
broke off combat, resting from the war.
The Trojans, too, retired. Unharnessing
teams from war-cars, before making supper,
they came together on the assembly-ground,
every man on his feet; not one could sit,
each being still in a tremor – for Achilles,
absent so long, had once again appeared.
Clearheaded Polydamas, son of Panthous,
spoke up first, as he alone could see
what lay ahead and all that lay behind.
He and Hector were companions-in-arms,
born, as it happened, on the same night; but one
excelled in handling weapons, one with words.
   Now for the good of all he spoke among them:
'Think well of our alternatives, my friends.
What I say is, retire upon the town,
instead of camping on the field till dawn
here by the ships. We are a long way

from our stone wall. As long as that man raged
at royal Agamemnon, we could fight
the Achaeans with advantage. I was happy
to spend last night so near the beach and think
of capturing ships today. Now, though, I fear
the son of Peleus to my very marrow!
There are no bounds to the passion of that man.
He will not be contained by the flat ground
where Trojans and Achaeans share between them
raging war: he will strive on to fight
to win our town, our women. Back to Troy!
Believe me, this is what we face!
Now, starry night has made Achilles pause,
but when day comes, when he sorties in arms
to find us lingering here, there will be men
who learn too well what he is made of. Aye,
I dare say those who get away will reach
walled Ilium thankfully, but dogs and kites
of Troy will feed on many. May that story
never reach my ears! If we can follow
my battle-plan, though galled by it, tonight
we'll husband strength, at rest in the market place.
Towers, high gates, great doors of fitted planking,
bolted tight, will keep the town secure.
Early tomorrow we shall arm ourselves
and man the walls. Worse luck then for Achilles,
if he comes looking for a head-on fight
on the field around the wall! He can do nothing
but trot back, after all, to the encampment,
his proud team in a lather from their run,
from scouring every quarter below the town.
Rage as he will, he cannot force an entrance,
cannot take all Troy by storm. Wild dogs
will eat him first!'
                         Under his shimmering helmet
Hector glared at the speaker. Then he said:
'Polydamas, what you propose no longer
serves my turn. To go on the defensive
inside the town again? Is anyone
not sick of being huddled in those towers?
In past days men told tales of Priam's city,
rich in gold and rich in bronze, but now
those beautiful treasures of our home are lost.
Many have gone for sale to Phrygia

and fair Maeonia, since the Lord Zeus
grew hostile towards us.
                'Now when the son of Cronos
Crooked Wit has given me a chance
of winning glory, pinning the Achaeans
back on the sea – now is no time to publish
notions like these to troops, you fool! No Trojan
goes along with you, I will not have it!
Come, let each man act as I propose.
Take your evening meal by companies;
remember sentries; keep good watch; and any
Trojan tired of his wealth, who wants
to lose everything, let him turn it over
to the army stores to be consumed in common!
Better our men enjoy it than Achaeans.
At first light we shall buckle armour on
and bring the ships under attack. Suppose
the man who stood astern there was indeed
Achilles, then worse luck for him,
if he will have it so. Shall I retreat
from him, from clash of combat? No, I will not.
Here I'll stand, though he should win; I might
just win, myself: the battle-god's impartial,
dealing death to the death-dealing man.'

  This was Hector's speech. The Trojans roared
approval of it – fools, for Pallas Athena
took away their wits. They all applauded
Hector's poor tactics, but Polydamas
with his good judgement got not one assent.
They took their evening meal now, through the army,
while all night long Achaeans mourned Patroclus.

  Achilles led them in their lamentation,
laying those hands deadly to enemies
upon the breast of his old friend, with groans
at every breath, bereft as a lioness
whose whelps a hunter seized out of a thicket;
late in returning, she will grieve, and roam
through many meandering valleys on his track
in hope of finding him; heart-stinging anger
carries her away. Now with a groan
he cried out to the Myrmidons:
                   'Ah, god,
what empty prophecy I made that day
to cheer Menoetius in his megaron!

I promised him his honoured son, brought back
to Opoeis, as pillager of Ilium
bearing his share of spoils.
But Zeus will not fulfil what men design,
not all of it. Both he and I were destined
to stain the same earth dark-red here at Troy.
No going home for me; no welcome there
from Peleus, master of horse, or from my mother,
Thetis. Here the earth will hold me under.
Therefore, as I must follow you into the grave,
I will not give you burial, Patroclus,
until I carry back the gear and head
of him who killed you, noble friend.
Before your funeral pyre I'll cut the throats
of twelve resplendent children of the Trojans —
that is my murdering fury at your death.
But while you lie here by the swanlike ships,
night and day, close by, deep-breasted women
of Troy, and Dardan women, must lament
and weep hot tears, all those whom we acquired
by labour in assault, by the long spear,
pillaging the fat market towns of men.'

     With this Achilles called the company
to place over the camp-fire a big tripod
and bathe Patroclus of his clotted blood.
Setting tripod and cauldron on the blaze
they poured it full, and fed the fire beneath,
and flames licked round the belly of the vessel
until the water warmed and bubbled up
in the bright bronze. They bathed him then, and took
sweet oil for his anointing, laying nard
in the open wounds; and on his bed they placed him,
covering him with fine linen, head to foot,
and a white shroud over it. So all that night
beside Achilles the great runner,
the Myrmidons held mourning for Patroclus.

     Now Zeus observed to Hera, wife and sister:
'You had your way, my lady, after all,
my wide-eyed one! You brought him to his feet,
the great runner! One would say the Achaean
gentlemen were progeny of yours.'

     And Hera with wide eyes replied: 'Dread majesty,
Lord Zeus, why do you take this tone? May not
an ordinary mortal have his way,

though death awaits him, and his mind is dim?
Would anyone suppose that I, who rank
in two respects highest of goddesses –
by birth and by my station, queen to thee,
lord of all gods – that I should not devise
ill fortune for the Trojans whom I loathe?'

So ran their brief exchange. Meanwhile
the silvery-footed Thetis reached Hephaestus'
lodging, indestructible and starry,
framed in bronze by the bandy-legged god.
She found him sweating, as from side to side
he plied his bellows; on his forge were twenty
tripods to be finished, then to stand
around his megaron. And he wrought wheels
of gold for the base of each, that each might roll
as of itself into the gods' assembly,
then roll home, a marvel to the eyes.
The cauldrons were all shaped but had no handles.
These he applied now, hammering rivets in;
and as he toiled sure-handedly at this,
Thetis arrived. Grace in her shining veil
just going out encountered her – that Grace
the bow-legged god had taken to wife.

                                        She greeted
Thetis with a warm handclasp and said:
'My lady Thetis, gracious goddess, what
has brought you here? You almost never honour us!
Please come in, and let me give you welcome.'

Loveliest of goddesses, she led the way,
to seat her guest on a silver-studded chair,
elaborately fashioned, with a footrest.

Then she called to Hephaestus: 'Come and see!
Thetis is here, in need of something from you!'

To this the Great Gamelegs replied:
'Ah, then we have a visitor I honour.
She was my saviour, after the long fall
and fractures that I had to bear, when Mother,
bitch that she is, wanted to hide her cripple.
That would have been a dangerous time, had not
Thetis and Eurynome taken me in –
Eurynome, daughter of the tidal Ocean.
Nine years I stayed, and fashioned works of art,
brooches and spiral bracelets, necklaces,
in their smooth cave, round which the stream of Ocean

flows with a foaming roar: and no one else
knew of it, gods or mortals. Only Thetis
knew, and Eurynome, the two who saved me.
Now she has come to us. Well, what I owe
for life to her ladyship in her soft braids
I must repay. Serve her our choicest fare
while I put up my bellows and my tools.'

At this he left the anvil block, and hobbled
with monstrous bulk on skinny legs to take
his bellows from the fire. Then all the tools
he had been toiling with he stowed
in a silver chest. That done, he sponged himself,
his face, both arms, bull-neck and hairy chest,
put on a tunic, took a weighty staff,
and limped out of his workshop. Round their lord
came fluttering maids of gold, like living girls:
intelligences, voices, power of motion
these maids have, and skills learnt from immortals.
Now they came rustling to support their lord,
and he moved on toward Thetis, where she sat
upon the silvery chair.

                              He took her hand
and warmly said: 'My Lady Thetis, gracious
goddess, why have you come? You almost never honour us.
Tell me the favour that you have in mind,
for I desire to do it if I can,
and if it is a thing that one may do.'

Thetis answered, tear on cheek: 'Hephaestus,
who among all Olympian goddesses
endured anxiety and pain like mine?
Zeus chose me, from all of them, for this!
Of sea-nymphs I alone was given in thrall
to a mortal warrior, Peleus Aeacides,
and I endured a mortal warrior's bed
many a time, without desire. Now Peleus
lies far gone in age in his great hall,
and I have other pain. Our son, bestowed
on me and nursed by me, became a hero
unsurpassed. He grew like a green shoot;
I cherished him like a flowering orchard tree,
only to send him in the ships to Ilium
to war with Trojans. Now I shall never see him
entering Peleus' hall, his home, again.
But even while he lives, beholding sunlight,

suffering is his lot. I have no power
to help him, though I go to him. A girl,
his prize from the Achaeans, Agamemnon
took out of his hands to make his own,
and ah, he pined with burning heart! The Trojans
rolled the Achaeans back on the ship-sterns,
and left them no escape. Then Argive officers
begged my son's help, offering every gift,
but he would not defend them from disaster.
Arming Patroclus in his own war-gear,
he sent him with his people into battle.
All day long, around the Scaean Gates,
they fought, and would have won the city, too,
had not Apollo, seeing the brave son
of Menoetius wreaking havoc on the Trojans,
killed him in action, and then given Hector
the honour of that deed.

                 'On this account
I am here to beg you: if you will, provide
for my doomed son a shield and crested helm,
good legging-greaves, fitted with ankle clasps,
a cuirass, too. His own armour was lost
when his great friend went down before the Trojans.
Now my son lies prone on the hard ground in grief.'

  The illustrious lame god replied: 'Take heart.
No trouble about the arms. I only wish
that I could hide him from the power of death
in his black hour – wish I were sure of that
as of the splendid gear he'll get, a wonder
to any one of the many men there are!'

  He left her there, returning to his bellows,
training them on the fire, crying, 'To work!'
In crucibles the twenty bellows breathed
every degree of fiery air: to serve him
a great blast when he laboured might and main,
or a faint puff, according to his wish
and what the work demanded.

                  Durable
fine bronze and tin he threw into the blaze
with silver and with honourable gold,
then mounted a big anvil on his block
and in his right hand took a powerful hammer,
managing with his tongs in his left hand.

  His first job was a shield, a broad one, thick,

well-fashioned everywhere. A shining rim
he gave it, triple-ply, and hung from this
a silver shoulder-strap. Five welded layers
composed the body of the shield. The maker
used all his art adorning this expanse.
He pictured on it earth, heaven, and sea,
unwearied sun, moon waxing, all the stars
that heaven bears for garland: Pleiades,
Hyades, Orion in his might,
the Great Bear, too, that some have called the Wain,
pivoting there, attentive to Orion,
and unbathed ever in the Ocean stream.

  He pictured, then, two cities, noble scenes;
weddings in one, and wedding feasts, and brides
led out through town by torchlight from their chambers
amid chorales, amid the young men turning
round and round in dances: flutes and harps
among them, keeping up a tune, and women
coming outdoors to stare as they went by.
A crowd, then, in a market place, and there
two men at odds over satisfaction owed
for a murder done: one claimed that all was paid,
and publicly declared it; his opponent
turned the reparation down, and both
demanded a verdict from an arbiter,
as people clamoured in support of each,
and criers restrained the crowd. The town elders
sat in a ring, on chairs of polished stone,
the staves of clarion criers in their hands,
with which they sprang up, each to speak in turn,
and in the middle were two golden measures
to be awarded him whose argument
would be the most straightforward.

                         Wartime then;
around the other city were emplaced
two columns of besiegers, bright in arms,
as yet divided on which plan they liked:
whether to sack the town, or treat for half
of all the treasure stored in the citadel.
The townsmen would not bow to either: secretly
they armed to break the siege-line. Women and children
stationed on the walls kept watch, with men
whom age disabled. All the rest filed out,
as Ares led the way, and Pallas Athena,

figured in gold, with golden trappings, both
magnificent in arms, as the gods are,
in high relief, while men were small beside them.
When these had come to a likely place for ambush,
a river with a watering-place for flocks,
they there disposed themselves, compact in bronze.
    Two look-outs at a distance from the troops
took their posts, awaiting sight of sheep
and shambling cattle. Both now came in view,
trailed by two herdsmen playing pipes, no hidden
danger in their minds. The ambush party
took them by surprise in a sudden rush;
swiftly they cut off herds and beautiful flocks
of silvery-grey sheep, then killed the herdsmen.
When the besiegers from their parleying-ground
heard sounds of cattle in stampede, they mounted
behind mettlesome teams, following the sound,
and came up quickly. Battle-lines were drawn,
and on the river-banks the fight began
as each side rifled javelins at the other.
Here then Strife and Uproar joined the fray,
and ghastly Fate, that kept a man with wounds
alive, and one unwounded, and another
dragged by the heels through battle-din in death.
This figure wore a mantle dyed with blood,
and all the figures clashed and fought
like living men, and pulled their dead away.
    Upon the shield, soft terrain, freshly ploughed,
he pictured: a broad field, and many ploughmen
here and there upon it. Some were turning
ox-teams at the ploughland's edge, and there
as one arrived and turned, a man came forward
putting a cup of sweet wine in his hands.
They made their turns-around, then up the furrows
drove again, eager to reach the deep field's
limit; and the earth looked black behind them,
as though turned up by ploughs. But it was gold,
all gold – a wonder of the artist's craft.
    He put there, too, a king's field. Harvest-hands
were swinging whetted scythes to mow the grain,
and stalks were falling along the swath
while binders girded others up in sheaves
with bands of straw – three binders, and behind them
children came as gleaners, proffering

their eager armfuls. And amid them all
the king stood quietly with staff in hand,
happy at heart, upon a new-mown swath.
To one side, under an oak-tree his attendants
worked at a harvest banquet. They had killed
a great ox, and were dressing it; their wives
made supper for the hands, with barley strewn.

A vineyard then he pictured, weighted down
with grapes: this all in gold; and yet the clusters
hung dark purple, while the spreading vines
were propped on silver vine-poles. Blue enamel
he made the enclosing ditch, and tin the fence,
and one path only led into the vineyard
on which the loaded vintagers took their way
at vintage-time. Light-hearted boys and girls
were harvesting the grapes in woven baskets,
while on a resonant harp a boy among them
played a tune of longing, singing low
with delicate voice a summer dirge. The others,
breaking out in song for the joy of it,
kept time together as they skipped along.

The artisan made next a herd of longhorns,
fashioned in gold and tin: away they shambled,
lowing, from byre to pasture by a stream
that sang and rippled in a reedy bed.
Four cowherds all of gold were plodding after
with nine lithe dogs beside them.

                                   On the assault,
in two tremendous bounds, a pair of lions
caught in the van a bellowing bull, and off
they dragged him, followed by the dogs and men.
Rending the belly of the bull, the two
gulped down his blood and guts, even as the herdsmen
tried to set on their hunting-dogs, but failed:
no trading bites with lions for those dogs,
who halted close up, barking, then ran back.

And on the shield the great bow-legged god
designed a pasture in a lovely valley,
wide, with silvery sheep, and huts and sheds
and sheepfolds there.

                       A dancing floor as well
he fashioned, like that one in royal Cnossus
Daedalus made for the Princess Ariadne.
Here young men and the most desired young girls

were dancing, linked, touching each other's wrists,
the girls in linen, in soft gowns, the men
in well-knit chitons given a gloss with oil;
the girls wore garlands, and the men had daggers
golden-hilted, hung on silver lanyards.
Trained and adept, they circled there with ease
the way a potter sitting at his wheel
will give it a practice twirl between his palms
to see it run; or else, again, in lines
as though in ranks, they moved on one another:
magical dancing! All around, a crowd
stood spellbound as two tumblers led the beat
with spins and handsprings through the company.

 Then, running round the shield-rim, triple-ply,
he pictured all the might of the Ocean stream.

 Besides the densely plated shield, he made
a cuirass, brighter far than firelight,
a massive helmet, measured for his temples,
handsomely figured, with a crest of gold;
then greaves of pliant tin.
        Now when the crippled god
had done his work, he picked up all the arms
and laid them down before Achilles' mother,
and swift as a hawk from snowy Olympus' height
she bore the brilliant gear made by Hephaestus.

BOOK XIX

THE AVENGER FASTS AND ARMS

DAWN in her yellow robe rose in the east
out of the flowing Ocean, bearing light
for deathless gods and mortal men. And Thetis
brought to the beach her gifts from the god of fire.
She found her dear son lying beside Patroclus,
wailing, while his men stood by
in tears around him.

               Now amid that throng
the lovely goddess bent to touch his shoulder
and said to him: 'Ah, child, let him lie dead,
for all our grief and pain, we must allow it;
he fell by the gods' will.
But you, now – take the war-gear from Hephaestus.
No man ever bore upon his shoulders
gear so magnificent.'

               And she laid the armour
down before Achilles, clanging loud
in all its various glory. Myrmidons
began to tremble at the sound, and dared not
look straight at the armour; their knees shook.
But anger entered Achilles as he gazed,
his eyes grown wide and bright as blazing fire,
with fierce joy as he handled the god's gifts.

   After appraising them in his delight
he spoke out to his mother swiftly: 'Mother,
these the god gave are miraculous arms,
handiwork of immortals, plainly – far
beyond the craft of men. By heaven, I'll wear them!
Only, I feel the dread that while I fight
black carrion-flies may settle on Patroclus'
wounds, where the spearheads marked him, and I fear
they may breed maggots to defile the corpse,
now life is torn from it. His flesh may rot.'

   But silvery-footed Thetis answered: 'Child,
you must not let that prey on you. I'll find
a way to shield him from the black fly hordes
that eat the bodies of men killed in battle.
Though he should lie unburied a long year,

his flesh will be intact and firm. Now, though,
for your part, call the Achaeans to assembly.
Tell them your anger against Agamemnon
is over and done with!

After that, at once
put on your gear, prepare your heart, for war!'
    Her promise gave her son whole-hearted valour.
Then, turning to Patroclus, she instilled
red nectar and ambrosia in his nostrils
to keep his body whole.

And Prince Achilles
passed along the surf-line with a shout
that split the air and roused men of Achaea,
even those who, up to now, had stayed
amid the massed ships – navigators, helmsmen,
men in charge of rations and ship stores.
Aye, even these now headed for assembly,
since he who for so long had shunned the battle,
Achilles, now appeared upon the field.
Resolute Diomedes and Odysseus,
familiars of the war-god, limped along,
leaning on spears, for both had painful wounds.
They made their way to the forefront and sat down,
and last behind them entered the Lord Marshal
Agamemnon, favouring his wound: he too
had taken a slash, from Coon, Antenor's son.
    When everyone had crowded in, Achilles,
the great battle-field runner, rose and said:
'Agamemnon, was it better for us
in any way, when we were sore at heart,
to waste ourselves in strife over a girl?
If only Artemis had shot her down
among the ships on the day I made her mine,
after I took Lyrnessus!
Fewer Achaeans would have died hard
at enemy hands, while I abstained in anger –
Hector's gain, the Trojans' gain. Achaeans
years hence will remember our high words,
mine and yours. But now we can forget them,
and, as we must, forgo our passion. Aye,
by heaven, I drop my anger now!
No need to smoulder in my heart forever! Come,
send your long-haired Achaeans into combat,
and let me see how Trojans will hold out,

if camping near the beach-head's their desire!
I rather think some will be glad to rest,
provided they get home, away from danger,
out of my spear's range!'
                                      These were his words,
and all the Achaeans gave a roar of joy
to hear the prince abjure his rage.

    Lord Marshal Agamemnon then addressed them,
standing up, not in the midst of them,
but where he had been sitting: 'Friends, fighters,
Danaans, companions of Ares: it is fair
to listen to a man when he has risen
and not to interrupt him. That's vexation
to any speaker, able though he may be.
In a great hubbub how can any man
attend or speak? A fine voice will be muffled.
While I open my mind to the son of Peleus,
Argives, attention! Each man weigh my words!
The Achaeans often brought this up against me,
and chided me. But I am not to blame.
Zeus and Fate and a nightmare Fury are,
for putting savage Folly in my mind
in the assembly that day, when I wrested
Achilles' prize of war from him. In truth,
what could I do? Divine will shapes these things.
Ruinous Folly, eldest daughter of Zeus,
beguiles us all. Her feet are soft, from walking
not on earth but over the heads of men
to do them hurt. She traps one man or another.
Once indeed she deluded Zeus, most noble
of gods and men, they say. But feminine
Hera with her underhanded ways
tricked him, the day Alcmene, in high Thebes,
was to have given birth to Heracles.
Then glorying Zeus remarked to all the gods:
"Hear me, all gods and goddesses, I'll tell you
of something my heart dwells upon. This day
the childbirth-goddess, Eileithyia, brings
into the light a man who will command
all those around him, being of the race of men
who come of my own blood!" But in her guile
the Lady Hera said: "You may be wrong,
unable to seal your word with truth hereafter.
Come, Olympian, swear me a great oath

he will indeed be lord of all his neighbours,
the child of your own stock in the race of men
who drops between a woman's legs today!"
Zeus failed to see her crookedness: he swore
a mighty oath, and mightily went astray,
for flashing downward from Olympus crest
Hera visited Argos of Achaea,
aware that the strong wife of Perseus' son,
Sthenelus, was big with child,
just entering her seventh month. But Hera
brought this child into the world's daylight
beforehand by two months, and checked Alcmene's
labour, to delay the birth of hers.
To Zeus the son of Cronos then she said:
"Zeus of the bright bolt, father, let me add
a new event to your deliberations.
Even now a superior man is born
to be a lord of Argives: Eurystheus,
a son of Sthenelus, the son of Perseus,
of your own stock. And it is not unfitting
for him to rule the Argives." This report
sharply wounded the deep heart of Zeus.
He picked up Folly by her shining braids
in sudden anger – swearing a great oath
that never to starred heaven or Olympus
Folly, who tricks us all, should come again.
With this he whirled her with one hand and flung her
out of the sky. So to men's earth she came,
but ever thereafter made Zeus groan to see
his dear son toil at labours for Eurystheus.

'So, too, with me: when in his shimmering helm
great Hector slaughtered Argives near the ships,
could I ignore my folly, my delusion?
Zeus had stolen my wits, my act was blind.
But now I wish to make amends, to give
all possible satisfaction. Rouse for war,
send in your troops! I here repeat my offer
of all that Odysseus promised yesterday!
Stay if you will, though the war-god presses you.
Men in my service will unload the gifts
from my own ship, that you may see how richly
I reward you!'

        Achilles answered: 'Excellency,
Lord Marshal Agamemnon, make the gifts

if you are keen to – gifts are due; or keep them.
It is for you to say. Let us recover
joy of battle soon, that's all!
No need to dither here and lose our time,
our great work still undone. When each man sees
Achilles in a charge, crumpling the ranks
of Trojans with his bronze-shod spear, let each
remember that is the way to fight his man!'
     Replied Odysseus, the shrewd field-commander:
'Brave as you are, and like a god in looks,
Achilles, do not send Achaean soldiers
into the fight unfed! Today's mêlée
will not be brief, when rank meets rank, and heaven
breathes fighting spirit into both contenders.
No, tell all troops who are near the ships to take
roast meat and wine, for heart and staying power.
No soldier can fight hand to hand, in hunger,
all day long until the sun goes down!
Though in his heart he yearns for war, his legs
go slack before he knows it: thirst and famine
search him out, and his knees fail as he moves.
But that man stayed with victualling and wine
can fight his enemies all day: his heart
is bold and happy in his chest, his legs
hold out until both sides break off the battle!
Come, then, dismiss the ranks to make their breakfast.
Let the Lord Marshal Agamemnon
bring his gifts to the assembly-ground
where all may see them; may your heart be warmed.
Then let him swear to you, before the Argives,
never to have made love to her, my lord,
as men and women by their nature do.
So may your heart be peaceable toward him!
And let him sate your hunger with rich fare
in his own shelter, that you may lack nothing
due you in justice. Afterward, Agamemnon,
you'll be more just to others, too. There is
no fault in a king's wish to conciliate
a man with whom he has been quick to anger!'
     And the Lord Marshal Agamemnon answered:
'Glad I am to hear you, son of Laertes,
finding the right word at the right time
for all these matters. And the oath you speak of
I'll take willingly, with all my heart,

and will not, before heaven, be forsworn.
Now let Achilles wait here, though the war-god
tug his arm; and all the rest of you
wait here assembled till the gifts have come
down from our quarters, and our peace is made.
For you, Odysseus, here is my command:
choose the finest young peers of all Achaea
to fetch out of my ship those gifts we pledged
Achilles yesterday; and bring the women.
Let Talthybius prepare for sacrifice,
in the army's name, a boar to Zeus and Helios.'

   Replied Achilles: 'Excellency, Lord Marshal,
another time were better for these ceremonies,
some interval in the war, and when I feel
less passion in me. Look, those men lie dead
whom Hector killed when Zeus allowed him glory,
and yet you two propose a meal! By god,
I'd send our soldiers into action now
unfed and hungry. Have a feast, I'd say,
at sundown, when our shame has been avenged!
Before that, for my part, I will not swallow
food or drink – my dear friend being dead,
lying before my eyes, bled white by spear-cuts,
feet turned to his hut's door, his friends in mourning
around him. Your concerns are none of mine.
Slaughter and blood are what I crave, and groans
of anguished men!'

                     But the shrewd field-commander
Odysseus answered: 'Achilles, flower and pride
of the Achaeans, you are more powerful
than I am – and a better spearman, too –
only in sizing matters up I'd say
I'm just as far beyond you, being older,
knowing more of the world. So bear with me.
Men quickly reach satiety with battle
in which the reaping bronze will bring to earth
big harvests, but a scanty yield, when Zeus,
war's overseer for mankind, tips the scales.
How can a fasting belly mourn our dead?
So many die, so often, every day,
when would soldiers come to an end of fasting?
No, we must dispose of him who dies
and keep hard hearts, and weep that day alone.
And those whom the foul war has left unhurt

will do well to remember food and drink,
so that we may again close with our enemies,
our dangerous enemies, and be tough soldiers,
hardened in mail of bronze. Let no one, now,
be held back waiting for another summons:
here is your summons! Woe to the man who lingers
beside the Argive ships! No, all together,
let us take up the fight against the Trojans!'

He took as escort sons of illustrious Nestor,
Phyleus' son Meges, Thoas, and Meriones,
and the son of Creon, Lycomedes, and
Melanippus, to Agamemnon's quarters.
No sooner was the work assigned than done:
they brought the seven tripods Agamemnon
promised Achilles, and the twenty cauldrons
shining, and the horses, a full dozen;
then they conducted seven women, skilled
in housecraft, with Briseis in her beauty.
Odysseus weighed ten bars of purest gold
and turned back, followed by his young Achaeans,
bearing the gifts to place in mid-assembly.

Now Agamemnon rose. Talthybius
the crier, with his wondrous voice, stood near him,
holding the boar. The son of Atreus drew
the sheath-knife that he carried, hung
beside the big sheath of his sword, and cut
first bristles from the boar. Arms wide to heaven
he prayed to Zeus, as all the troops kept still,
all sitting in due order in their places,
hearing their king.

                      In prayer he raised his eyes
to the broad sky and said: 'May Zeus, all-highest
and first of gods, be witness first, then Earth
and Helios and the Furies underground
who punish men for having broken oaths,
I never laid a hand on your Briseis,
proposing bed or any other pleasure;
in my quarters the girl has been untouched.
If one word that I swear is false,
may the gods plague me for a perjured liar!'

He slit the boar's throat with his blade of bronze.
Then Talthybius, wheeling, flung the victim
into the offshore water, bait for fish.

Achilles rose amid the Argive warriors,

saying: 'Father Zeus, you send mankind
prodigious follies. Never otherwise
had Agamemnon stung me through and through;
never would he have been so empty-headed
as to defy my will and take the girl!
No, for some reason Zeus had death at heart
for the Achaeans, and for many. Well:
go to your meat, then we'll resume the fighting.'

Thus he dismissed the assembly. All the men
were quick to scatter, each to his own ship.
As for the gifts, the Myrmidons took over
and bore them all to Achilles' ship, to stow
within his shelter. There they left the women
and drove the horses to the herd.

                                        The girl
Briseis, in her grace like Aphrodite,
on entering saw Patroclus lying dead
of spear wounds, and she sank down to embrace him
with a sharp sobbing cry, lifting her hands
to tear her breast, soft throat, and lovely face,
this girl, shaped like the goddesses of heaven.

Weeping, she said: 'Patroclus, very dear,
most dear to me, cursed as I am, you were
alive still when I left you, left this place!
Now I come back to find you dead, my captain!
Evil follows evil so, for me.
The husband to whom father and mother gave me
I saw brought down by spears before our town,
with my three brothers, whom my mother bore.
Dear brothers, all three met their day of wrath.
But when Achilles killed my lord, and sacked
the city of royal Mynes, not a tear
would you permit me: no, you undertook
to see me married to the Prince Achilles,
conveyed by ship to Phthia, given a wedding
among the Myrmidons. Now must I mourn
your death for ever, who were ever gentle.'

She wailed again, and women sobbed about her,
first for Patroclus, then for each one's grief.

Meanwhile Achaean counsellors were gathered
begging Achilles to take food. He spurned it,
groaning: 'No, I pray you, my dear friends,
if anyone will listen! – do not nag me
to glut and dull my heart with food and drink!

A burning pain is in me. I'll hold out
till sundown without food. I say I'll bear it.'

   With this he sent the peers away, except
the two Atreidae and the great Odysseus,
Nestor, Idomeneus, and old Lord Phoenix.
These would have comforted him, but none
could quiet or comfort him until he entered
the bloody jaws of war.

                              Now pierced by memory,
he sighed and sighed again, and said: 'Ah, once
you, too, poor fated friend, and best of friends,
would set a savoury meal deftly before us
in our field-shelter, when the Achaeans wished
no time lost between onsets against Trojans.
Now there you lie, broken in battle. Ah,
lacking you, my heart will fast this day
from meat and drink as well. No greater ill
could come to me, not news of Father's death –
my father, weeping soft tears now in Phthia
for want of that son in a distant land
who wars on Troy for Helen's sake – that woman
who makes the blood run cold. No greater ill,
even should my son die, who is being reared
on Scyros, Neoptolemus, if indeed
he's living still. My heart's desire had been
that I alone should perish far from Argos
here at Troy; that you should sail to Phthia,
taking my son aboard your swift black ship
at Scyros, to introduce him to his heritage,
my wide lands, my servants, my great hall.
In this late year Peleus may well be dead
and buried, or have few days yet to live,
beset by racking age, always awaiting
dire news of me, of my own death.'

   As he said this he wept. The counsellors groaned,
remembering each what he had left at home;
and seeing them sorrow, Zeus took pity on them,
saying quickly to Athena: 'Daughter,
you seem to have left your fighting man alone.
Should one suppose you care no more for Achilles?
There he sits, before the curving prows,
and grieves for his dear friend. The other soldiers
flock to meat; he thirsts and hungers. Come,
infuse in him sweet nectar and ambrosia,

that an empty belly may not weaken him.'
  He urged Athena to her own desire,
and like a gliding sea-hawk, shrilling high,
she soared from heaven through the upper air,
while the Achaeans armed throughout the ranks.
Nectar and ambrosia she instilled
within Achilles, that his knees be not
assailed by hollow famine; then she withdrew
to her mighty father's house. Meanwhile the troops
were pouring from the shipways to the field.
As when cold snowflakes fly from Zeus in heaven,
thick and fast under the blowing north wind,
just so, that multitude of gleaming helms
and bossed shields issued from the ships, with plated
cuirasses and ashwood spears. Reflected
glintings flashed to heaven, as the plain
in all directions shone with glare of bronze
and shook with trampling feet of men. Among them
Prince Achilles armed. One heard his teeth
grind hard together, and his eyes blazed out
like licking fire, for unbearable pain
had fixed upon his heart. Raging at Trojans,
he buckled on the arms Hephaestus forged.
The beautiful greaves, fitted with silver anklets,
first he put upon his legs, and next
the cuirass on his ribs; then over his shoulder
he slung the sword of bronze with silver scabbard;
finally he took up the massive shield
whence came a radiance like the round full moon.
As when at sea to men on shipboard comes
the shining of a camp-fire on a mountain
in a lone sheep-fold, while the gusts of night-wind
take them, loath to go, far from their friends
over the teeming sea: just so
Achilles' finely modelled shield sent light
into the heavens. Lifting his great helm
he placed it on his brows, and like a star
the helm shone with its horse-tail blowing free,
all golden, that Hephaestus had set in
upon the crest. Achilles tried his armour,
shrugging and flexing, making sure it fitted,
sure that his gleaming legs had play. Indeed
the gear sat on him light as wings: it buoyed him!
Now from a spear-case he withdrew a spear –

his father's – weighty, long, and tough. No other
Achaean had the strength to handle it,
this great Pelian shaft
of ashwood, given his father by the centaur
Cheiron from the crest of Pelion
to be the death of heroes.

                              Automedon
and Alcimus with swift hands yoked his team,
making firm the collars on the horses,
placing the bits between their teeth, and pulling
reins to the war-car. Automedon then
took in hand the shining whip and mounted
the chariot, and at his back Achilles
mounted in full armour, shining bright
as the blinding Lord of Noon.

                              In a clarion voice
he shouted to the horses of his father:
'Xanthus and Balius! Known to the world
as foals of great Podarge! In this charge
care for your driver in another way!
Pull him back, I mean, to the Danaans,
back to the main body of the army,
once we are through with battle; this time,
no leaving him there dead, like Lord Patroclus!'

    To this, from under the yoke, the nimble Xanthus
answered, and hung his head, so that his mane
dropped forward from the yoke-pad to the ground –
Hera whose arms are white as ivory
gave him a voice to say: 'Yes, we shall save you,
this time, too, Achilles in your strength!
And yet the day of your destruction comes,
and it is nearer. We are not the cause,
but rather a great god is, and mighty Fate.
Nor was it by our sloth or sluggishness
the Trojans stripped Patroclus of his armour.
No, the magnificent god that Leto bore
killed him in action and gave Hector glory.
We might run swiftly as the west wind blows,
most rapid of all winds, they say; but still
it is your destiny to be brought low
by force, a god's force and a man's!'

                                       On this,
the Furies put a stop to Xanthus' voice.
    In anger and gloom Achilles said to him:

'Xanthus, why prophesy my death? No need.
What is in store for me I know, know well:
to die here, far away from my dear father,
my mother, too. No matter. All that matters
is that I shall not call a halt today
till I have made the Trojans sick of war!'
    And with a shout he drove his team
of trim-hooved horses into the front line.

BOOK XX

THE RANGING OF POWERS

THUS on the beach-head the Achaeans armed
with you, Achilles, avid again for war,
and Trojans faced them on the rise of plain.
Zeus meanwhile, from the utmost snowy height
of ridged Olympus, gave command to Themis
to call the gods together. Everywhere
she went about and bade them to his hall.
None of the rivers failed to come, not one
except the Ocean stream; none of the nymphs
who haunt cool greenwood groves and river-heads
and inland grassy meads. All made their way
to the hall of Zeus, lord of the clouds of heaven,
taking their chairs in sunlit courts, laid out
with all Hephaestus' art in polished stone.

So these assembled. Then the god of earthquake
heeded the goddess; from the great salt sea
he came aloft to take his place among them,
asking his brother Zeus what he proposed:
'Lord of the bright bolt, why do you bring us here?
Something to do with Trojans and Achaeans,
now their lines are drawn, and the war flares?'

And Zeus who gathers cloud replied: 'You know
what plan I have in mind and why I called you,
why you are here. Men on both sides may perish,
still they are near my heart. And yet, by heaven,
here I stay, at ease upon a ridge.
I'll have an ample view here. But you others,
go into action, side with men of Troy
or with Achaeans, as each has a mind to.
Suppose Achilles takes the Trojans on
alone: not for a minute will they hold him.
In times past they used to shake to see him,
and now he's mad with rage for his friend's death,
I fear he'll break the wall down, sack the town,
before the time has come for it.'

                                        Lord Zeus
fell silent then, but kindled bitter war,
and the immortals entered it. They took

positions as they wished. Hera, Athena,
Poseidon, girdler of the earth, and Hermes,
most sharp-witted of them all; Hephaestus,
proud and brawny but with tottery shanks:
these were the sea-borne Achaeans' partisans.
  For the Trojans, Ares in a flashing helm,
beside him long-haired Phoebus, Artemis,
Leto and Xanthus, and the smiling goddess
Aphrodite. Until the gods came near
the Achaeans gloried more, now that Achilles
again had joined the fight so long forgone.
Every Trojan felt his knees atremble,
seeing the great runner armed
and flashing like the deadly god of war.
When the Olympians joined the lines arrayed,
Strife came in power, goader of fighting men.
Then standing by the moat outside the wall
or on the shore of beating surf, Athena
shrieked, and her adversary, Ares, yelled
across from her, like a pitch-black hurricane
roaring to Trojans from the heights of Troy,
or veering by the course of Simois
on Callicolone.
                    So the gods in bliss
roused the contenders, hurled them into war,
and broke in massive strife among themselves.
Out of heaven the father of gods and men
thundered crack on crack; Poseidon heaving
underground made the wide mainland quake
even to craggy mountain-peaks. On Ida,
white with watercourses, all the slopes
and crests were set atremble; so was the city,
Troy, and the grounded ships of the Achaeans.
Dread came in undergloom to Aidoneus,
lord of shades: he bounded from his throne
and gave a cry, in fear that earth, undone
by Lord Poseidon's shaking, would cave in,
and the vile mouldy kennels the gods hate
might stand revealed to mortals and immortals.
That was the measure of the shock
created by the onset of the gods.
And now, by heaven, against Lord Poseidon
Phoebus Apollo drew his feathered bolts;
against Enyalius the grey-eyed goddess

Athena stood; and like a golden shaft
the archer, Artemis, of whistling arrows,
sister of Apollo, faced great Hera.
Leto was opposed by gracious Hermes,
way-finder for souls, and the god of fire,
Hephaestus, faced a mighty eddying river,
Xanthus to the gods, to men Scamander.
These were the divine adversaries.

                               Achilles
went into that battle wild to engage
great Hector, son of Priam, with whose blood
his heart and soul desired to glut the war-god.
Straight against him, though, Apollo drove
Aeneas. He put courage in this man.

    Taking Lycaon's voice and look, he said:
'Counsellor of Trojans, Prince Aeneas, tell me:
what of your threats and promises, in wine,
before your peers, to face the son of Peleus,
Achilles, in the battle?'

                         And Aeneas
answered him: 'Lycaon, son of Priam,
why demand this, when my heart's unready
to take that formidable fighter on?
It will not be the first time: once before
I met him, and he drove me with his spear
from Ida, when he raided herds of ours
and took Lyrnessus, plundered Pedasus.
The Lord Zeus helped me out of it: he gave me
wind and legs to run, else I had fallen
under Achilles' and Athena's blows.
She went ahead of him and cast her light
of glory on him, made him with his spear
defeat and strip the Leleges and Trojans.
This is the point: no man can fight Achilles!
In every battle, one of the gods is there
to save him from destruction, while his weapon
flies unwavering till it bites its way
through some man's flesh. Would the god only bring
under equal strain both parties to the fight,
Achilles would not win so easily,
not though the man is bronze from head to foot.'

    And Lord Apollo, son of Zeus, replied:
'Come, sir, you too invoke the gods, the undying,
the ever young! One hears you are, yourself,

a child of Aphrodite.
Achilles comes of a goddess not so high –
not, like yours, a daughter of Zeus, but born
to the sea's Ancient. Come, then, bear your point
straight forward, bronze unworn, unbloodied! Never
be turned aside by taunts or threats from him!'

He breathed into the captain's heart a glow
of fighting spirit, and Aeneas shouldered
forward, helmed in fiery bronze. But Hera
glimpsed Anchises' son on the attack,
hunting Achilles through the field.

                                        She called
her two confederates, saying: 'Now take care,
Poseidon and Athena, how this action
runs its course! There is Aeneas, helmet
flashing, facing the son of Peleus;
Phoebus Apollo forced him to attack.
Why do we not, all three of us, repel him,
turn him in his tracks? Or one of us
could back Achilles, give him the edge in power,
in stamina, in valour, let him know
the high immortals love him! Those who fought
for Trojans in past days of deadly war
were unavailing as the wind. We three
have come down from Olympus to engage
in this great battle, that he take no hurt
from Trojans on this day. In time he'll suffer
all that his destiny, on his life's thread,
spun for him when his mother gave him birth.
But lacking intimation of these things –
dream-voice of gods – Achilles may feel dread
when some god comes against him in the combat.
Gods take daunting shapes when they appear.'

At this the god who makes the mainland quake,
Poseidon, said: 'No need for senseless anger.
Why should we be quick to embroil ourselves
as adversaries of the others, being
far more powerful than they are? Come,
we'll move out of the trampled plain and take
some look-out post on high. Let men make war!
Only if Ares fights, or Lord Apollo,
or if they keep Achilles from the combat,
then the clang of battle will begin
between us on the spot –

with a quick outcome, I predict: they'll be
so battered by our arms, they must fall back
on the Olympian conclave.'

                              And Poseidon
led them to the Wall of Heracles,
an earthwork, built for the mighty man by Pallas
Athena and the Trojans in times past,
as cover for him when the sea-monster
drove him from beach to plain. Now Lord Poseidon
took his ease there, followed by the others,
shoulders mantled in unbroken cloud.

On Callicolone's brow, opposing gods
were seated around Ares, breacher of walls,
with you, Archer Apollo. Resting so,
both companies were thoughtful: neither cared
to take the initiative toward wounds and war,
but Zeus from his high throne ruled over all.

The whole plain now filled up with troops and flashed
with bronze of men and chariots, as the earth
reverberated under their feet. Two fighters,
far and away the best, between the armies
made for each other, both on edge for combat,
Aeneas, son of Anchises, and Achilles.
Aeneas had gone forward first
and nodded, menacing, with heavy helm.
Well forward of his chest he held his shield,
and shook his bronze-shod spear. Opposing him
Achilles now came up like a fierce lion
that a whole countryside is out to kill:
he comes heedless at first, but when some yeoman
puts a spear into him, he gapes and crouches,
foam on his fangs; his mighty heart within him
groans as he lashes both flanks with his tail,
urging his valour on to fight; he glares
and bounds ahead, hoping to make a kill
or else himself to perish in the tumult.
That was the way Achilles' heart and spirit
drove him to meet Aeneas.

                              As they closed,
Achilles, prince and formidable runner,
spoke first: 'Why are you out of line so far,
Aeneas? Moved to challenge me in battle?
Hoping to lord it over Trojan horsemen,
heir to Priam's dignity as king?

Ha! Even if you kill me, not for that
will Priam put his honour in your hands!
Has he not sons, is he not sound, is he
so bird-witted? Or have the Trojans parcelled
garden-land, their choicest, in your name,
vineyard and ploughland, rich, for you to tend
in case you kill me? Rough work that will be,
let me predict. At spear-point once before
I think I made you skip. Don't you remember
the time I chased you from your herd, alone
down Ida's hills, fast as your legs would take you?
You ran without a backward look, ran on
into Lyrnessus; but I broke that town
in one charge, with Athena and Lord Zeus,
making its women spoil, taking their day
of freedom from them. As for you, Zeus moved
to save your life; so did the other gods,
but there will be no saving you this time,
I think, though luck like that is what you pray for.
Now enough. Here's my command: retire
on your own people, make no pass at me,
or you'll be hurt. A child or fool can see
what's done when it is done.'
                              Aeneas answered:
'Son of Peleus, use words to frighten
a small boy, not me. I am well able
to bandy cutting words and insults too.
Each knows about the other's birth and parents
from the old tales of mortals that we've heard;
you'll never see my parents nor I yours.
Royal Peleus' son, you are said to be,
and the salt-sea goddess Thetis was your mother.
My own claim is that I was born the son
of Anchises, the hero, and my mother
is Aphrodite. Of these four, one pair
will mourn a son today – as not by bragging
can this quarrel be resolved, I'd say,
so that we two may be relieved of battle.
But if you wish to learn such things as well,
to know the story of our race, already
known to many soldiers: Zeus, cloud-master,
fathered Dardanus and built the town
Dardania, since Ilium's stronghold
was not yet walled or peopled on the plain,

and men still made their home on Ida's hills.
Dardanus begot King Erichthonius,
richest of mortals in his time: he owned
three thousand mares that grazed his pasture-land
and gloried in their frisking colts. These mares
Boreas the north wind loved as they grazed,
and in the likeness of a black-maned stallion
chose his brood-mares. They conceived and bore
twelve colts, that in their gallop over farmland
ran without trampling on the tips of grain,
and running on the sea's broad back they clipped
the white-caps doffing foam on grey salt water.
Erichthonius was the father of Tros,
lord of the Trojans. Three fine sons he had:
Ilus, Assaracus, and Ganymedes,
handsomest of mortals, whom the gods
caught up to pour out drink for Zeus and live
amid immortals for his beauty's sake.
Ilus begot Laomedon, Laomedon
Tithonus, Priam, Lampus, Clytius,
and Hicetaon, wild sprig of the war-god.
Assaracus fathered Capys, he Anchises,
Anchises fathered me. Priam begot
Prince Hector. These are the blood-lines I claim.
But Zeus gives men more excellence or less
as he desires, being omnipotent.
Come, no more childish talk, here at the heart
of a great battle. Each side has a mass
of bitter words to say: no deep-sea ship
could take that load, even a hundred-bencher.
Men have twisty tongues, and on them speech
of all kinds; wide is the grazing-land of words,
both east and west. The manner of speech you use,
the same you are apt to hear. By what necessity
must we goad one another face to face
with provocations? like two city-women
ruffling into the middle of a street
to wrangle, bitten by rage,
with many a true word – and some false, for anger
calls out those as well. My mind is set
on honour. Words of yours cannot throw me off,
not till our spears have crossed. Come, on with it!
We'll have a taste of one another's bronze!'
        At this he drove hard with his massive spear

against the marvellous shield: a great clang
resounded at the impact of the spearhead.
Achilles with his big fist held the shield
at arm's length, instinctively, for fear
Aeneas' shaft might cleave it and come through –
a foolishness; he had not learned as yet
how slim the chance is that the splendid gifts
of gods will crack or yield to mortal fighters.
In fact, this time Aeneas' well-aimed spear-thrust
could not breach the shield. The fire-god's plate
of gold contained it. Though it pierced two layers,
there were three more: the bandy-legged smith
had wrought five all together, two of bronze,
two inner ones of tin, and the gold plate
by which the ashwood spear was now contained.
Achilles in his turn rifled his spear
and hit Aeneas' round shield near the rim
where bronze was thinnest, and the bull's hide thinnest.
Straight through drove the Pelian ash. The plate
gave way screeching. Down Aeneas crouched
and held his shield away from him in fear.
The spearshaft cleared his back and then stuck fast
in the battlefield, hurled with such force; it broke
asunder two disks of the covering shield.
But he ducked under it, then stood, and pain
in a rush came over him, clouding his eyes,
for dread of the spear implanted close at hand.
Achilles closed with him, drawing his sword,
with a wild war-cry. But Aeneas bent
for a boulder, a huge weight, that, as men are
in our day, two men could not carry: this
he hefted easily alone. Aeneas
might have smashed his lunging adversary
either on the helm or on the shield
that had protected him from rending death;
Achilles with his sword-stroke at close quarters
might have slashed the other's life away,
had not Poseidon's sharp eye caught the danger.
    Instantly to his immortal friends
he said: 'Here's trouble for Aeneas' sake!
He goes to dark Death at Achilles' hands
and soon: being gullible he listened
to Apollo, but that god will not protect him
against a foul close. Why must the blameless man

be hurt to no good end, for the wrongs of others?
His gifts were always pleasing to the gods
who hold wide heaven. Come now, we ourselves
may take him out of danger, and make sure
that Zeus shall not be angered by his death
at Achilles' hands. His fate is to escape,
to ensure that the great line of Dardanus
may not unseeded perish from the world.
For Zeus cared most for Dardanus, of all
the sons he had by women, and now Zeus
has turned against the family of Priam.
Therefore Aeneas and his sons, and theirs,
will be lords over Trojans born hereafter.'

The Lady Hera answered with wide eyes:
'Earthshaker, put your own mind on Aeneas,
whether to save him or to let him die.
By heaven, Pallas and I have taken oath
before the immortals many times: we shall not
keep the evil day from any Trojans,
even when all Troy catches fire, with flames
the fighting Achaeans light!'
                                    On hearing this,
Poseidon, shaker of the earth, made off
along the battle-line, through press of spears,
until he reached Aeneas and Achilles.
Instantly over Achilles' eyes he cast
a battle-haze, and pulled his ashwood shaft
out of the round shield of Aeneas; then
he laid the spear down at Achilles' feet,
but swept Aeneas off the ground and upward.
Lifted aloft by the god's hand, he soared,
traversing many lines of men and chariots,
until he reached the flank of the wild field
where the Caucones entered combat.
                                    There
Poseidon swiftly said into his ear:
'Aeneas, what god has commanded it –
this recklessness of challenging Achilles,
a man more powerful than you are, dearer
to the immortal gods? No, no,
stay clear of meeting him, or else you'll drop
before your time into the house of Death.
Remember, after Achilles meets his doom
you may be daring; then go forward, then

take on the leaders, for there is no other
Achaean who can slay you on the field.'

    With this, since all was said, he left him there,
and from Achilles' eyes he blew away
the magic battle-haze.

                    With all his might
the man stared, and then full of bitterness
said to himself: 'By god, here is a wonder
wrought before my eyes! Here on the ground
my spear lies, and there's no man to be seen
where one stood and I made my cast to kill him!
Aeneas has been dear to the gods then, sure
enough, though I had thought his boasts were wind.
To hell with him! He'll never have the heart
to stand up to me now, glad as he was
to slip away from death. Come on, I'll lead
Danaans who love war; we'll press the fight
against the rest, to see what they are made of!'

    At this he bounded back on the first line,
calling on every fighter: 'Soldiers, Achaeans,
no more waiting out of range of Trojans!
Every man make up his mind to fight
and move on his enemy! Strong as I am,
it's hard for me to face so many men
and fight with all at once. Not even Ares,
god though he is, immortal, nor Athena
could face the opening jaws of such a battle
and bear the toil alone. And yet I will,
so far as I have power in arms and legs,
and stamina. I'll not ease off, I swear,
not for an instant. No. I'll break their line.
I think no Trojan crossing spears with me
will burn with joy for it!'

                  So he cheered them on.
And splendid Hector shouted to the Trojans
to go against Achilles; 'Trojans, fighters,
have no fear of the son of Peleus. Using
words, I too could fight the gods. The test
is harder with a spear; gods are far stronger.
Achilles cannot accomplish all he says.
One thing he'll do, another leave half done.
I'll face him, though he thrusts like fire, bladed
fire, and though he has a heart like iron!'

    He cheered the Trojans, and they lifted spears

against Achilles, all in a clump, in valour
closing ranks, while a battle-cry went up.
    And then at Hector's side Apollo said:
'Do not attack Achilles yet: wait for him
deep in the mass, out of the front-line shouting,
else he may down you with his long shaft thrown
or with a sword-cut close at hand.'
                          Once more
afraid when he had heard the god's voice speaking,
Hector drew back amid the crowded troops.
Achilles rushed upon them in his might
with a blood-curdling shout, and first he killed
the son of Otrynteus, brave Iphition,
born by a naiad to the raider of cities
under snow-covered Tmolus, in the fertile
townland of Hyde. As this young man strove
to meet him, Prince Achilles struck his head
square in the middle, and it split in two.
He thudded down.
                  Achilles then sang out:
'Terror of all soldiers, there you lie!
Here is your place of death! So far away
your birthplace, near Gygaea lake, and there
your father's royal parkland on the trout-stream
Hyllus and the eddying Hermus river!'
    So he exulted, while the other's eyes
were veiled in night. Then chariots of Achaeans
cut the body asunder with sharp wheels
in the advancing battle. And Achilles
killed a second man, Demoleon,
Antenor's son, a good defensive fighter.
He hit him on the temple through the helmet
fitted with bronze cheek-pieces, and the metal
could not hold; the driven
spearhead cleft it, broke the temple-bone,
so that his brains were spattered in the helm.
For all his fighting heart, Achilles downed him.
Then Hippodamas: he had left his car
to run before Achilles, but the Achaean
speared him in the back. He gasped his life out,
bellowing, like a bull dragged up before
Poseidon, lord of Helice, by boys
who yank his halter – and the god of earthquake
takes joy watching them. Bellowing so,

the rugged soul left Hippodamas' bones.
Achilles turned his spear on Polydorus,
Priam's son. The father had refused
permission to this boy to fight, as being
youngest of all his sons and dearest, one
who could outrun the rest.

             Just now, in fact,
out of pure thoughtlessness, showing his speed,
he ran the front line till he met his end.
The great battle-field runner, Prince Achilles,
hit him square in the back as he flashed by —
hit where the golden buckles of his belt
and both halves of his cuirass linked together.
Passing through the man, out at the navel
the spearhead came, and on his knees he fell
with a loud cry. The blinding cloud of death
enveloped him as he sprawled out, his entrails
held in his hands before him. Hector saw
his brother Polydorus fallen aside
against the earth, his entrails in his hands;
and mist of death veiled Hector's eyes as well.
He could not hang at a distance any longer,
but shook his spear and ran upon Achilles
like a wild flame.

             When the Achaean saw him
he gave a start and prayed: 'The man is near
who most has hurt my heart; he took the life
of the friend I had so cherished. May we two
not shrink from one another any longer
upon the open ground of war!'

                    He glared
under his brows at Hector and gave a shout:
'Come on, come on straight! You will make it
all the sooner to the edge of doom!'

    But Hector answered without fear: 'Achilles,
why suppose you can frighten me with words
like a small boy? I, too, have some gift
for jeers and insults. You are strong, I know,
and I am far from being a match for you.
But on the gods' great knees these matters lie.
Poorest of men, compared to you, by heaven,
I still may take your life with one spear-cast.
My spearhead, too, has had its cutting-power!'
    Even as he spoke he hefted and let fly,

and with a puff of wind Athena turned
the spearhead from Achilles in his glory –
a wind-puff like a sigh. The spear came back
to Hector, falling at his feet. Achilles
put all his heart into a lunge to kill him,
raising a wild cry. But Apollo caught
the Trojan up, god-fashion, with great ease
and hid him in a white cloud.

                      Then three times
the great battle-field runner, Prince Achilles,
lunged with his spear, three times he cleft the cloud,
but when, beside himself, he lunged a fourth time,
then he vented a blood-chilling cry:
'You got away from death again, you dog!
The evil hour came near you, but Apollo
saved you again: I'm sure you pray to him
on entering spear-play. Even so, I'll kill you
later, on sight, if I too have a god
beside me. I can tackle others now,
whatever Trojan I may find.'

                        With this,
he jabbed and wounded Dryops in the neck,
then left him, fallen at his feet, and turned
on Demuchus, Philetor's rugged son,
whom he checked with a spear-thrust at the knees,
then killed with a swinging blow of his long sword.
Next he took on Laogonus and Dardanus,
Bias' sons, and forced them from their chariot,
one with a spear-cast, one slashed by the sword.
Then Tros, Alastor's son, sank at his knees
and begged the Achaean to take him prisoner,
to spare a man his own age, not to kill
but pity him. How witless, to imagine
Achilles could be swayed! No moderate temper,
no mild heart was in this man, but harsh
and deadly purpose. Tros embraced his knees,
beseeching him, but with his blade he opened
a wound below the liver. Out it slipped,
with red blood flowing downward from the wound,
filling his lap. Then darkness veiled his eyes
and spirit failed him. But Achilles moved
toward Mulius and hit him with a spear-thrust
square on the left ear; the bronze point at once
punched through and out the ear on the right side.

Then he chopped Echeclus, Agenor's son,
with his long, hilted sword, straight through his head,
and all the blade grew hot with blood, as dusky
death and destiny overcame the man.
Deucalion next he speared where elbow-tendons
held together, and the spearpoint pierced
through the man's arm. Standing with arm inert,
Deucalion waited, seeing death before him.
Achilles aimed a sword-cut at his neck
and knocked both head and helmet far away.
The fluid throbbed out of his vertebrae
as he lay stretched upon the earth. Achilles
turned to the noble son of Peires, Rhigmus,
one who had come from the rich land of Thrace.
He jabbed him in the belly, and the spearhead
stuck in his bowels; he dropped from his chariot.
Just as his driver swung the team around
Achilles hit him with his spear between
the shoulder-blades, jolting him from the car
as the horses panicked.
                        A forest fire will rage
through deep glens of a mountain, crackling dry
from summer heat, and coppices blaze up
in every quarter as wind whips the flame:
so Achilles flashed to right and left
like a wild god, trampling the men he killed,
and black earth ran with blood. As when a countryman
yokes oxen with broad brows to tread out barley
on a well-bedded threshing-floor, and quickly
the grain is husked under the bellowing beasts:
the sharp-hooved horses of Achilles just so
crushed dead men and shields. His axle-tree
was splashed with blood, so was his chariot-rail,
with drops thrown up by wheels and horses' hooves.
And Peleus' son kept riding for his glory,
staining his powerful arms with mire and blood.

BOOK XXI

THE CLASH OF MAN AND RIVER

As they came down to a ford in the blue Xanthus,
eddying and running, god-begotten
wondrous river, there Achilles drove
amid the rout and split them, left and right –
scattering half toward Troy over the plain
where yesterday Achaeans broke and ran
when Hector raged. Now Trojans ran that way,
and Hera spread a cloud ahead to slow them.
The other half were forced into the stream
now running high with foam on whirlpools. Down
they plunged, smacking the water, and the banks
and gullied beds echoed their hurly-burly.
This way and that they swam, shouting, spun round
and round by eddies. As when locusts flitter
before a prairie fire into a river,
tireless flames, leaping abruptly higher,
scorch them, and they crumple into the water:
so the currents rushing before Achilles
now grew choked with men and chariot-teams.

    He left his spear propped on a tamarisk
by the river-bank, then like a wild god
he leapt in savagely for bloody work
with sword alone, and struck to right and left,
as cries and groans went up from men he slashed
and dark blood flushed the stream.

                      As darting fish,
in flight before a dolphin, crowd the bays
of a great roadstead, terrified, for he
engorges all he catches; so the Trojans
cowered down the dangerous river's course
and under overhanging banks. Arm-wearied
by butchery, Achilles from the stream
picked twelve young men alive to pay the price
for dead Patroclus. He led these ashore,
startled as fawns, and bound their hands behind them,
using the well-cut thongs they wore as belts
round braided combat-shirts. He turned them over
to men of his command to be led back

to the decked ships, then launched himself again
on furious killing.
                    At this point he met
a son of Priam, Prince Lycaon,
scrambling from the river. Achilles once
on a night-raid had captured this young man,
forced him out of his father's orchard, where
with a bronze knife he had been cutting boughs
of a wild fig for chariot-rails: the raider
came like a ghost upon him, unforeseen.
That time Achilles sold him overseas
to Lemnos. Jason's son had purchased him,
but he was freed by an old family friend,
Eetion of Imbros, who gave passage
to the fair town Arisbe, whence in flight
he reached his father's hall. Being come again
from Lemnos, he enjoyed eleven days
with friends at home. On the twelfth day a god
returned him to the rough hands of Achilles,
who would dispatch him to the realm of Death.
The great battle-field runner, Prince Achilles,
found the man disarmed: he had no helm,
no shield, not even a spear; all were thrown down
when heat and sweat oppressed him as he toiled
to leave the stream, his knees sapped by fatigue.
    Taken aback, grimly Achilles said
in his great heart: 'God, here is a strange thing
to have before my eyes! Trojans I've killed
will stand up in the western gloom of death
if this one could return, his evil day
behind him – after I sold him, shipped him out
to Lemnos island. The great grey salt sea
that balks the will of many could not stop him.
Well, let him taste our spearhead now. Let me
absorb the answer: can it be he'll come
back from the grave, or will the fertile earth
detain him, as it does the strongest dead?'
    Thus he reflected, waiting, and the other
came in a rush to clasp his knees, confused,
but mad with hope to escape the pain of death
and the black shape of destiny. Achilles
raised his long spear aiming to run him through.
Lycaon ducked and ran and took his knees
even as the driven spear passed over, starved

for blood and raw man-flesh, and stuck in earth.
  Grasping one knee, the unarmed man held on
with his left hand to the spearshaft of Achilles,
and pled with him:

                              'I come before your knees,
Achilles: show respect, and pity me.
Pleader and plea are worth respect, your grace.
You were the first Achaean at whose hands
I tasted the bruised barley of Demeter,
upon that day when, among orchard trees,
you captured me, then shipped me out to Lemnos
away from father and friends. I earned for you
a hundred bulls' worth. Triple that I'll bring
as ransom, this time. Twelve days have gone by
since I returned from my hard life abroad
to Ilium. But now sinister fate
has put me in your hands a second time:
in hate, somehow, Zeus guided me to you.
A man of short life – so my mother bore me,
Laothoe, daughter of old Altes, lord
of the fighting Leleges, who holds the rock
of Pedasus upon the Satnioeis.
Priam, lover of many, loved his daughter,
and two of us were born of her; both men
you will have slaughtered. Aye, you killed my brother
amid foot-soldiers, noble Polydorus –
brought him down with a spear-throw. And here
my evil hour has come. I see I cannot
get away from you; the will of heaven
forced us to meet. But think of one thing more:
don't kill me, since the belly where I grew
never held Hector, never held the man
who killed your friend, that gentle and strong soldier.'
  In these terms Priam's son pled for his life,
but heard a voice of iron say:
'Young fool, don't talk to me of what you'll barter.
In days past, before Patroclus died
I had a mind to spare the Trojans, took them
alive in shoals, and shipped them out abroad.
But now there's not a chance – no man that heaven
puts in my hands will get away from death
here before Ilium – least of all a son
of Priam. Come, friend, face your death, you too.
And why are you so piteous about it?

Patroclus died, and he was a finer man
by far than you. You see, don't you, how large
I am, and how well-made? My father is noble,
a goddess bore me. Yet death waits for me,
for me as well, in all the power of fate.
A morning comes or evening or high noon
when someone takes my life away in war,
a spear-cast, or an arrow from a bowstring.'
     At this the young man's knees failed, and his heart;
he lost his grip upon the spear
and sank down, opening his arms. Achilles
drew his sword and thrust between his neck
and collar-bone, so the two-edged blade went in
up to the hilt. Now face down on the ground
he lay stretched out, as dark blood flowed from him,
soaking the earth. Achilles picked him up
by one foot, wheeled, and slung him in the river
to be swept off downstream.
                         Then he exulted:
'Nose down there with fishes. In cold blood
they'll kiss your wound and nip your blood away.
Your mother cannot put you on your bed
to mourn you, but Scamander whirling down
will bear you to the sea's broad lap,
where any fish that jumps, breaking a wave,
may dart under the dark wind-shivered water
to nibble white fat of Lycaon. Trojans,
perish in this rout until you reach,
and I behind you slaughtering reach, the town!
The god-begotten river swiftly flowing
will not save you. Many a bull you've offered,
many a trim-hooved horse thrown in alive
to Xanthus' whirlpools. All the same, you'll die
in blood until I have avenged Patroclus,
paid you back for the death-wounds of Achaeans
cut down near the deep-sea-going ships
far from my eyes.'
                         On hearing this, the river
darkened to the heart with rage. He cast
about for ways to halt prodigious Achilles'
feats of war and keep death from the Trojans.
Meanwhile the son of Peleus took his spear
and bounded straight ahead for Asteropaeus,
burning to kill this son of Pelegon,

whom the broad river Axius had fathered
on Periboea, eldest of the daughters
of Acessamenus. Whirling, deep-running
river that he was, Axius loved her.
And now Achilles made for Asteropaeus,
who came up from the stream-bed to confront him,
holding two spears. And Xanthus, in his anger
over all the young men dead, cut down
by Achilles pitilessly in the stream,
gave heart to this contender.

                   As they drew near,
the great runner and prince was first to speak:
'Who are you, soldier? Where do you come from,
daring to challenge me? Grief comes to all
whose sons meet my anger.'

                          Pelegon's
brave son replied: 'Heroic son of Peleus,
why do you ask my birth? I am a native
of rich farmland, Paeonia; Paeones
are the spearmen I command. Today the eleventh
dawn came up since I arrived at Ilium.
My line began, if you must know, with Axius,
mover of beautiful water over land,
who fathered the great spearman, Pelegon,
and Pelegon is said to have fathered me.
But now again to battle, Lord Achilles.'

   That was his prideful answer. Then Achilles
lifted his Pelian ash. His enemy,
being ambidextrous, cast both spears at once
and failed. With one he hit Achilles' shield
but could not pierce it, for the gold plate held,
the god's gift; with his other spear he grazed
the hero's right forearm. Dark blood ran out,
but, craving man-flesh still, the spear passed on
and fixed itself in earth. In turn, Achilles,
putting his heart into the cast to bring down
Asteropaeus, rifled his ashwood spear.
He missed him, hitting the high bank of the river,
where the long shaft punched in to half its length.
The son of Peleus, drawing sword from hip,
lunged forward on his enemy, who could not
with his big fist work the spear loose: three times
he tried to wrench it from the arching bank,
three times relaxed his grip, then put his weight

into a fourth attempt to break the shaft,
and bent it; but Achilles closed
and killed him with a sword-stroke. Near the navel
he slashed his belly; all his bowels dropped out
uncoiling to the ground. He gasped, and darkness
veiled his eyes.
            Upon the chest Achilles
mounted, and then bent to strip his armour,
gloating: 'This way you'll rest. It is rough work
to match yourself with children of Lord Zeus,
river's offspring though you are. You claimed
descent from a broad river; well, I claim
descent from Zeus almighty. My begetter,
lord over many Myrmidons, was Peleus,
the son of Aeacus, a son of Zeus.
Zeus being stronger than the seaward rivers,
so are his offspring than a river's get!
Here's a big river for you, flowing by,
if he had power to help you. There's no fighting
Zeus the son of Cronos. Achelous
cannot rival him; neither can the might
of the deep Ocean stream – from whom all rivers
take their waters, and all branching seas,
all springs and deep-sunk wells. And yet he too
is terrified by the lightning flash of Zeus
and thunder, when it crashes out of heaven.'
    With this he pulled from the bank's overhang
his bronze-shod spear, and, having torn the life
out of the body, left it there, to lie
in sand, where the dark water lapped at it.
Then eels and fish attended to the body,
picking and nibbling kidney fat away.
    As for Achilles, he ran onward, chasing
spearmen of Paeonia in their rout
along the eddying river: these had seen
their hero vanquished by the hand and blade
and power of Achilles. Now he slew
Thersilochus, Mydon, and Astypylus,
Mnesus, Thrasius, Aenius, Ophelestes,
and would have killed far more, had not the river,
cold with rage, in likeness of a man,
assumed a voice and spoken from a whirlpool:
   'O Achilles, you are first in power
of all men, first in waywardness as well,

as gods forever take your side. If Zeus
has given you all Trojans to destroy,
destroy them elsewhere, do your execution
out on the plain! Now my blue watercourses
back up, filled with dead; I cannot spend
my current in the salt immortal sea,
being dammed with corpses. Yet you go on killing
wantonly. Let be, marshal of soldiers.'

Achilles the great runner answered: 'Aye,
Scamander, child of Zeus, as you require,
the thing shall be. But as for killing Trojans,
arrogant enemies, I take no rest
until I back them on the town and try out
Hector, whether he gets the best of me
or I of him.'

At this he hurled himself
upon the Trojans like a wild god.

The deep
and swirling river then addressed Apollo:
'All wrong, bow of silver, child of Zeus!
You have not worked the will of Zeus. How often
he made you free to take the Trojan side!
You could defend them until sunset comes,
till evening darkens grain-land.'

As he spoke,
the great spearman Achilles in a flash
leapt into midstream from the arching bank.
But he, the river, surged upon the man
with all his currents in a roaring flood,
and swept up many of the dead, who jostled
in him, killed by Achilles. He ejected
these to landward, bellowing like a bull,
but living men he kept in his blue streams
to hide them in deep places, in backwaters.
Then round Achilles with an ominous roar
a wave mounted. It fell against his shield
and staggered him, so that he lost his footing.
Throwing his arms around a leafy elm
he clung to it; it gave way, roots and all,
and tore the bank away, and dipped its branches
in the clear currents, damming up the river
when all had fallen in. The man broke free
of swirling water, turned into the plain
and ran like wind, in fear. But the great god

would not be shaken off: with his dark crest
he reared behind to put the Prince Achilles
out of action and protect the Trojans.
Achilles led him by a spear-throw, running
as fast as the black eagle, called the hunter,
strongest and swiftest of all birds: like him
he flashed ahead, and on his ribs the bronze
rang out with a fierce clang. At a wide angle
he fled, and the river with tremendous din
flowed on behind. Remember how a farmer
opens a ditch from a dark reservoir
to water plants or garden: with his mattock
he clears away the clods that dam the stream,
and as the water runs ahead, smooth pebbles
roll before it. With a purling sound
it snakes along the channel, going downhill,
outrunning him who leads it: so the wave
sent by the river overtook Achilles
momently, in spite of his great speed,
as gods are stronger than men are. Each time
the great battle-field runner, Prince Achilles,
turned to make a stand – to learn if all
the immortal gods who own the sweep of heaven
chased him – every time, the rain-fed river's
crest buffeted his back, and cursing
he leapt high in the air. Across his knees
the pressure of swift water tired him,
and sand was washed away under his feet.
  Lifting his eyes to heaven, Achilles cried:
'Father Zeus, to think that in my travail
not one god would save me from the river –
only that! Then I could take the worst!
None of the gods of heaven is so to blame
as my own mother, who beguiled me, lying,
saying my end would come beneath Troy's wall
from flashing arrows of Apollo. Ah,
I wish Hector had killed me; he's their best.
Then one brave man would have brought down another.
No, I was fated to ignoble death,
whelmed in a river, like a swine-herd's boy
caught by a winter torrent as he crosses.'
  Now as he spoke, Poseidon and Athena,
taking human form, moved near and stood,
and took his hands to tell him what would calm him.

Poseidon was the speaker: 'Son of Peleus,
do not be shaken overmuch or fearful,
seeing what gods we are, your two allies,
by favour of Zeus – myself and Pallas Athena.
The river is not destined to pull you down.
He will fall back, and you will soon perceive it.
Meanwhile here's good counsel, if you'll take it.
Do not allow your hands to rest from war –
from war that treats all men without distinction –
till you have rolled the Trojan army back
to Ilium, every man of them who runs,
and shut them in the wall. Then when you've taken
Hector's life, retire upon the ships.
We give you glory; it is yours to win.'
    At this the two went off to join the gods.
Achilles, as their great directive stirred him,
crossed the plain, filled with flood-water now,
where beautiful gear of slain men was afloat
and corpses, too. With high and plunging strides
he made his way in a rush against the current,
and the broad-flooded river could not check him,
fired as he was with power by Athena.
    Scamander, though, did not give up; his rage
redoubled, and he reared his foaming crest
with a hoarse shout to Simois: 'My own brother,
if we both try, can we not hold this man?
If not, he'll storm Lord Priam's tower soon;
the Trojans all in tumult won't resist him.
Give me a hand now, fill your channels up
with water from the springs, make dry beds brim,
and lift a wall of water: let it grind
and thump with logs and stones; we'll halt this madman,
powerful at the moment though he is,
with his intent to match the gods. I say
neither his great brawn nor his splendid form
will pull him through, nor those magnificent arms.
They will be sunk in mud under flood water.
As for the man, I'll roll him up in sand
and mound a ton of gravel round about him.
Achaeans who would gather up his bones
will have no notion how, in all the slime
I'll pack him in. And that will be his tomb;
no need for them to heap a barrow for him
when soldiers make his funeral.'

Now Xanthus
surged in turbulence upon Achilles,
tossing his crest, roaring with spume and blood
and corpses rolling, and a dark wave towering
out of the river fed by heaven swept
downward to overwhelm the son of Peleus.

Hera cried aloud in dread for him
whom the great raging stream might wash away,
and called to her dear son Hephaestus: 'Action,
Gamelegs, my own child! We thought you'd be
a match for whirling Xanthus in the battle.
Lend a hand, and quickly. Make your fire
blaze up. I'll be raising from the sea
a rough gale of the west wind and the south wind,
able to carry flames to burn the heads
and armour off the Trojans. Kindle trees
by Xanthus' banks, hurl fire at the river,
and do not let him put you off with threats
or honeyed speech. No slackening your fury!
Only when I call out, with a long cry,
withhold your living fire then.'

Hephaestus
brought heaven's flame to bear: upon the plain
it broke out first, consuming many dead men
there from the number whom Achilles killed,
while all the plain was burned off and the shining
water stopped. As north wind in late summer
quickly dries an orchard freshly watered,
to the pleasure of the gardener, just so
the whole reach of the plain grew dry, as fire
burned the corpses. Then against the river
Hephaestus turned his bright flame, and the elms
and tamarisks and willows burned away,
with all the clover, galingale, and rushes
plentiful along the winding streams.
Then eels and fish, in backwaters, in currents,
wriggled here and there at the scalding breath
of torrid blasts from the great smith, Hephaestus,
and dried away by them, the river cried:

'Hephaestus, not one god can vie with you!
Neither would I contend with one so fiery.
Break off the quarrel: let the Prince Achilles
drive the Trojans from their town. Am I
a party to that strife? Am I their saviour?'

He spoke in steam, and his clear current seethed,
the way a cauldron whipped by a white-hot fire
boils with a well-fed hog's abundant fat
that spatters all the rim, as dry split wood
turns ash beneath it. So his currents, fanned
by fire, seethed, and the river would not flow
but came to a halt, tormented by the gale
of fire from the heavenly smith, Hephaestus.
    Turning in prayer to Hera, Xanthus said:
'Hera, why did your son pick out my stream
from others to attack? You know
I merit this less than the other gods
who intervened for Trojans. Yet by heaven
if you command it, I'll give up the fight;
let the man, too, give up, and in the bargain
I swear never to interpose between
the Trojans and their day of wrath, that day
when all Troy blazes with consuming fire
kindled by the warriors of Achaea.'
    Hera whose arms are white as ivory
listened to this, then told her son Hephaestus:
'Hold now, splendid child. It will not do
to vex an immortal river so, for men.'
    At this Hephaestus quenched his heavenly fire,
and back in its blue channels ran the wave.
And now that Xanthus had been overcome,
the two gods dropped their combat: Hera, still
angry, checked them. Heavy and harsh strife,
however, came upon the rest, whose hearts
grew stormy on both sides against each other.
Now they attacked in uproar. The broad earth
resounded, and great heaven blared around them,
and Zeus, who heard from his Olympian seat,
laughed in his heart for joy, seeing the gods
about to meet in strife.
                         And not for long
were they apart, now Ares the shield-cleaver
led them; first he lunged against Athena,
gripping his bronze-shod spear and roaring at her:
'Why do you drive the gods to quarrel once more,
dog-fly, with your bold and stormy ways,
and the violent heart that sets you on? Remember
telling Diomedes to hit me hard?
Remember: you yourself, taking the spear

quite openly, made a thrust at me, and gashed
my noble flesh? Now in your turn, for that
and all you've done, I think you'll have to pay!'

  With this he struck hard at the storm-cloud shield
that trails the rain of heaven: even a bolt
from Zeus will not undo it. Blood-encrusted
Ares hit it with his giant spear.
Recoiling, in her great hand she picked up
a boulder lying there, black, jagged, massive,
left by the men of old as a boundary stone,
and hurling it hit Ares' neck. His knees
gave way and down he went on seven hundred
feet of earth, his long mane in the dust,
and armour clanged upon him.

                                    Laughing at him,
Athena made her vaunt above him: 'Fool,
you've never learned how far superior
I'm glad to say I am. Stand up to me?
Lie there: you might fulfil your mother's curse,
baleful as she is, incensed at you,
because you switched to Trojans from Achaeans.'

  Now Aphrodite, Zeus's daughter, taking
Ares' hand, began to help him away,
as he wheezed hard and fought to get his breath.

  But Hera saw her. She called out to Athena:
'Daughter of Zeus the Storm-king, what a couple!
There that dog-fly goes, escorting Ares,
bane of mankind, out of the deadly war
amid the battle din. Go after them!'

  Athena followed, in a flash, with joy,
and from the side struck Aphrodite's breast
with doubled fist, so that her knees went slack,
her heart faint, and together she and Ares
lay in a swoon upon the earth.

                                    Athena
said derisively:

                        'If only
all the gods who would assist the Trojans
came to fight the Argives with such power!
If only they were bold as these, and tough
as Aphrodite was, rescuing Ares
under my nose! In that case, long ago
we should have dropped the war – for long ago
we should have carried Ilium by storm.'

At this Queen Hera smiled. And the Earthshaker
said to Apollo: 'Phoebus, must we two
stay out of it? That isn't as it should be,
when others enter into action. More's
the pity if we go back without fighting
to Olympus, to the bronze door-sill of Zeus.
You take the lead, you are younger: it would be
awkward of me, since I was born before you,
know more than you do.

                     'Idiot, but how
forgetful you have been! Don't you remember
even now, what troubles over Ilium
we alone among the gods have had,
when from the side of Zeus we came to serve
the strong man Laomedon all one year
for a stated wage? Then he assigned our work,
no trifle for my own: I walled the city
massively in well-cut stone, to make
the place impregnable. You herded cattle,
slow and dark amid the upland vales
of Ida's wooded ridges. When the Seasons
happily brought to an end our term of hire,
barbaric Laomedon kept all our wages
from us, and forced us out, with vile threats:
to bind us hand and foot, he said, and send us
in a slave-ship to islands overseas –
but first to crop our ears with a bronze knife!
So we departed, burning inwardly
for payment he had promised and not made.
For this you coddle his people now ? You are not
willing, like the rest of us, to see
the Trojans in their pride, with wives and children,
come utterly to ruin and to grief.'

     The lord of distant archery, Apollo,
answered: 'Lord of earthquake, sound of mind
you could not call me if I strove with you
for the sake of mortals, poor things that they are.
Ephemeral as the flamelike budding leaves,
men flourish on the ripe wheat of the grain-land,
then in spiritless age they waste and die.
We should give up our fighting over men.
Let men themselves contend with one another.'

     On this he turned away. He would not face
his father's brother, hand to hand.

And now he was derided by his sister,
Lady Artemis, huntress of wild beasts,
who had her stinging word: 'In full retreat
are you, yielding victory to Poseidon,
making him pay nothing for his glory.
Idiot, why do you have your useless bow?
I'll never let you brag again
in Father's hall, among the gods,
that you'll oppose Poseidon in the battle.'

To this, Archer Apollo made no answer,
but Hera, Zeus's consort, did, in anger:
'How can you think to face me, shameless bitch?
A hard enemy I'll be for you, although
you carry a bow, and Zeus has made of you
a lioness to women. You have leave
to put to death any you choose. No matter:
better to rend wild beasts on mountainsides,
and woodland deer, than fight a stronger goddess.
If you want lessons in war, then you can learn
how I excel you, though you face me—'

                                     Here
she took hold of the wrists of Artemis
in her left hand; with her right hand she snatched
her quiver and bow and boxed her ears with them,
smiling to see her duck her head, as arrows
showered from the quiver. Artemis
ran off in tears, as a wild dove, attacked
by a diving hawk, will fly to a hollow rock,
a narrow cleft where she cannot be taken.
So, weeping, she took flight and left her bow.

Then Hermes the Way-finder said to Leto:
'I would not dream of fighting you, so rough
seem the Cloud-master's wives in fisticuffs.
No, you may make your boast quite happily
to all the immortal gods that you have beaten me!'

Leto retrieved the bow of Artemis
and picked her arrows up where they had veered
and landed in a flurrying of dust.
Then she retired with her daughter's weapons.
Artemis reached Olympus, crossed the bronze
door-sill of Zeus, and at her father's knees
sank down, a weeping girl, her fragrant gown
in tremors on her breast.

                             Her father hugged her,

asking with a mild laugh: 'Who in heaven
injured you, dear child? Pure wilfulness!
As though for a naughty act!'
                              To this the mistress
of baying packs, her hair tied back, replied:
'Your lady, Hera, buffeted me, father.
She of the snow-white arms, by whom the gods
are plagued with strife and bickering.'
                              While these two
conversed, Phoebus Apollo entered Ilium,
concerned for the wall, to keep the Danaan men
from storming it this day, before their time.
The other deathless ones went to Olympus,
some in anger, others enjoying triumph,
and took their chairs beside their father, lord
of storm-cloud. But Achilles all that time
wrought havoc with the Trojans and their horses.
As a smoke-column from a burning town
goes heavenward, propelled by the gods' anger,
grief to many a townsman, toil for all,
Achilles brought the Trojans harrowing grief.
    Erect on Troy's great tower, ageing Priam
gazed at huge Achilles, before whom
Trojans in tumult fled, and no defence
materialized.
                      Then groaning from the tower
Priam descended. For the gatekeepers,
known as brave soldiers, he had urgent words:
'Keep the gates open, hold them, till the troops
retiring from battle are in the town.
There is Achilles, harrying them. Too near.
I fear we'll have a slaughter. When our soldiers
crowd inside the wall to get their breath,
close both your timbered gates, bolt them again.
I fear this murderous man may leap the wall.'
    At this they pushed the bolts, opening the gates,
and the gateway made a refuge. Then Apollo
flashed out to avert death from the Trojans,
headed as they were for the high wall,
men grown hoarse in thirst, covered with dust
out of the plain where they had run. Achilles,
wrought to a frenzy, pressed them with his spear,
all his great heart bent on winning glory.
Troy of the high gates might have fallen now

to the Achaean soldiers, but Apollo
stirred the Prince Agenor, strong and noble
son of Antenor. Into this man's heart
the god sent courage, and stood near him, leaning
on an oak-tree, concealed in heavy mist,
to guard him from the shapes and weight of death.

Agenor halted when he saw the raider
of cities, Achilles, and his heart grew large
as he awaited him, saying to himself
grimly: 'This is the end of me. If I break
and run before Achilles like the others,
he'll take me, even so: I'll have my throat
cut like a coward for my pains. What if
I let them go in panic toward the town
ahead of him, while I run at a tangent
leaving the wall, to cross the plain
until I reach the mountain slopes of Ida,
taking cover in undergrowth? This evening,
after a river-bath to cleanse my sweat,
I might return to Ilium. Why say it?
God forbid he sees me cutting away
from Troy into the open; in one sprint
he'll have me. After that, there's no escape
from my last end of death, so powerful
the man is, far beyond us all. Suppose
I meet him here, on the west approach to Troy?
Surely his body, even his, can be
wounded by sharp bronze; he can live but once;
men say he's mortal, though the son of Cronos,
Zeus, awards him glory.'

Even as he spoke,
he pulled himself together to face Achilles,
blood surging to his heart before the fight.
And as a panther out of underbrush
will go to meet a hunter, and have no fear,
and never falter when it hears the hounds;
and even though the hunter draw first blood,
the beast trailing the spear that wounded it
will not give up, until it close with him
or else go down: just so the Prince Agenor,
son of Antenor, would not now retreat
until he put Achilles to the test.

With round shield held before him, and his spear
aimed at the man, he gave a battle shout

and cried: 'You hoped today at last to storm
the city of the Trojans. A rash hope.
Grief and wounds are still to be suffered for her.
Inside there, we are many fighting men.
For our dear parents, wives, and sons, we'll hold
the city and defend it. You come here
to meet your doom, prodigious though you are,
sure as you are in warfare.'

                              He let fly
the sharp spear from his heavy hand and struck
the shin below the kneecap square and hard.
Around his leg the new shin-guard of tin
rang out deafeningly; back from the point
of impact sprang the spearhead, piercing nothing,
buffeted back by the god's gift.

                              Then Achilles
struck in turn at his princely enemy,
Agenor, but Apollo
would not let him win this glory now.
He whisked away Agenor, hid him in mist,
and quietly removed him from the war.
By trickery then he kept the son of Peleus
away from Trojan soldiers: taking Agenor's
likeness to the last detail, he halted
within range of Achilles, who set off
to chase him. For a long time down the plain
of grain-land he pursued him, heading him
along Scamander, as the god kept a bare lead –
for so Apollo teased him on; Achilles
thought to catch his quarry with a sprint.
Meanwhile the other Trojans in their panic
reached the walled town, thanking heaven, and all
the city filled up, jammed with men. They dared not
wait outside the wall for one another,
to learn who died in battle, who came through,
but all whose legs had saved them now took cover,
in hot haste entering the city.

BOOK XXII

DESOLATION BEFORE TROY

ONCE in the town, those who had fled like deer
wiped off their sweat and drank their thirst away,
leaning against the cool stone of the ramparts.
Meanwhile Achaeans with bright shields aslant
came up the plain and nearer. As for Hector,
fatal destiny pinned him where he stood
before the Scaean Gates, outside the city.

Now Achilles heard Apollo calling
back to him: 'Why run so hard, Achilles,
mortal as you are, after a god?
Can you not comprehend it? I am immortal.
You are so hot to catch me, you no longer
think of finishing off the men you routed.
They are all in the town by now, packed in
while you were being diverted here. And yet
you cannot kill me; I am no man's quarry.'

Achilles bit his lip and said:
'Archer of heaven, deadliest
of immortal gods, you put me off the track,
turning me from the wall this way. A hundred
might have sunk their teeth into the dust
before one man took cover in Ilium!
You saved my enemies with ease and stole
my glory, having no punishment to fear.
I'd take it out of you, if I had the power.'

Then toward the town with might and main he ran,
magnificent, like a racing chariot-horse
that holds its form at full stretch on the plain.
So light-footed Achilles held the pace.
And ageing Priam was the first to see him
sparkling on the plain, bright as that star
in autumn rising, whose unclouded rays
shine out amid a throng of stars at dusk –
the one they call Orion's dog, most brilliant,
yes, but baleful as a sign: it brings
great fever to frail men. So pure and bright
the bronze gear blazed upon him as he ran.
The old man gave a cry. With both his hands

thrown up on high he struck his head, then shouted,
groaning, appealing to his dear son. Unmoved,
Lord Hector stood in the gateway, resolute
to fight Achilles.

              Stretching out his hands,
old Priam said, imploring him: 'No Hector!
Cut off as you are, alone, dear son,
don't try to hold your ground against this man,
or soon you'll meet the shock of doom, borne down
by the son of Peleus. He is more powerful
by far than you, and pitiless. Ah, were he
but dear to the gods as he is dear to me!
Wild dogs and kites would eat him where he lay
within the hour, and ease me of my torment.
Many tall sons he killed, bereaving me,
or sold them to far islands. Even now
I cannot see two sons of mine, Lycaon
and Polydorus, among the Trojans massed
inside the town. A queen, Laothoe,
conceived and bore them. If they are alive
amid the Achaean host, I'll ransom them
with bronze and gold: both I have, piled at home,
rich treasures that old Altes, the renowned,
gave for his daughter's dowry. If they died,
if they went under to the homes of Death,
sorrow has come to me and to their mother.
But to our townsmen all this pain is brief,
unless you too go down before Achilles.
Come inside the wall, child; here you may
fight on to save our Trojan men and women.
Do not resign the glory to Achilles,
losing your own dear life! Take pity, too,
on me and my hard fate, while I live still.
Upon the threshold of my age, in misery,
the son of Cronos will destroy my life
after the evil days I shall have seen –
my sons brought down, my daughters dragged away,
bedchambers ravaged, and small children hurled
to earth in the atrocity of war,
as my sons' wives are taken by Achaeans'
ruinous hands. And at the end, I too –
when someone with a sword-cut or a spear
has had my life – I shall be torn apart
on my own doorstep by the hounds

I trained as watch-dogs, fed from my own table.
These will lap my blood with ravenous hearts
and lie in the entrance-way.
                                    'Everything done
to a young man killed in war becomes his glory,
once he is riven by the whetted bronze:
dead though he be, it is all fair, whatever
happens then. But when an old man falls,
and dogs disfigure his grey head and cheek
and genitals, that is most harrowing
of all that men in their hard lives endure.'

  The old man wrenched at his grey hair and pulled out
hanks of it in both hands, but he moved
Lord Hector not at all.

                          The young man's mother
wailed from the tower across, above the portal,
streaming tears, and loosening her robe
with one hand, held her breast out in the other,
saying: 'Hector, my child, be moved by this,
and pity me, if ever I unbound
a quieting breast for you. Think of these things,
dear child; defend yourself against the killer
this side of the wall, not hand to hand.
He has no pity. If he brings you down,
I shall no longer be allowed to mourn you
laid out on your bed, dear branch in flower,
born of me! And neither will your lady,
so endowed with gifts. Far from us both,
dogs will devour you by the Argive ships.'

  With tears and cries the two implored their son,
and made their prayers again, but could not shake him.
Hector stood firm, as huge Achilles neared.
The way a serpent, fed on poisonous herbs,
coiled at his lair upon a mountainside,
with all his length of hate awaits a man
and eyes him evilly: so Hector, grim
and narrow-eyed, refused to yield. He leaned
his brilliant shield against a spur of wall
and in his brave heart bitterly reflected:

  'Here I am badly caught. If I take cover,
slipping inside the gate and wall, the first
to accuse me for it will be Polydamas,
he who told me I should lead the Trojans
back to the city on that cursed night

Achilles joined the battle. No, I would not,
would not, wiser though it would have been.
Now troops have perished for my foolish pride,
I am ashamed to face townsmen and women.
Someone inferior to me may say:
"He kept his pride and lost his men, this Hector!"
So it will go. Better, when that time comes,
that I appear as he who killed Achilles
man to man, or else that I went down
fighting him to the end before the city.
Suppose, though, that I lay my shield and helm
aside, and prop my spear against the wall,
and go to meet the noble Prince Achilles,
promising Helen, promising with her
all treasures Alexandrus carried home
by ship to Troy – the first cause of our quarrel –
that he may give these things to the Atreidae?
Then I might add, apart from these, a portion
of all the secret wealth the city owns.
Yes, later I might take our counsellor's oath
to hide no stores, but share and share alike
to halve all wealth our lovely city holds,
all that is here within the walls. Ah, no,
why even put the question to myself?
I must not go before him and receive
no quarter, no respect! Aye, then and there
he'll kill me, unprotected as I am,
my gear laid by, defenceless as a woman.
No chance, now, for charms from oak or stone
in parley with him – charms a girl and boy
might use when they enchant each other talking!
Better we duel, now at once, and see
to whom the Olympian awards the glory.'
    These were his shifts of mood. Now close at hand
Achilles like the implacable god of war
came on with blowing crest, hefting the dreaded
beam of Pelian ash on his right shoulder.
Bronze light played around him, like the glare
of a great fire or the great sun rising,
and Hector, as he watched, began to tremble.
Then he could hold his ground no more. He ran,
leaving the gate behind him, with Achilles
hard on his heels, sure of his own speed.
When that most lightning-like of birds, a hawk

bred on a mountain, swoops upon a dove,
the quarry dips in terror, but the hunter,
screaming, dips behind and gains upon it,
passionate for prey. Just so, Achilles
murderously cleft the air, as Hector
ran with flashing knees along the wall.
They passed the look-out point, the wild fig-tree
with wind in all its leaves, then veered away
along the curving wagon-road, and came
to where the double fountains well, the source
of eddying Scamander. One hot spring
flows out, and from the water fumes arise
as though from fire burning; but the other
even in summer gushes chill as hail
or snow or crystal ice frozen on water.
Near these fountains are wide washing-pools
of smooth-laid stone, where Trojan wives and daughters
laundered their smooth linen in the days
of peace before the Achaeans came. Past these
the two men ran, pursuer and pursued,
and he who fled was noble, he behind
a greater man by far. They ran full speed,
and not for bull's hide or a ritual beast
or any prize that men compete for: no,
but for the life of Hector, tamer of horses.
Just as when chariot-teams around a course
go wheeling swiftly, for the prize is great,
a tripod or a woman, in the games
held for a dead man, so three times these two
at full speed made their course round Priam's town,
as all the gods looked on.

                    And now the father
of gods and men turned to the rest and said:
'How sad that this beloved man is hunted
around the wall before my eyes! My heart
is touched for Hector; he has burned thigh-flesh
of oxen for me often, high on Ida,
at other times on the high-point of Troy.
Now Prince Achilles with devouring stride
is pressing him around the town of Priam.
Come, gods, put your minds on it, consider
whether we may deliver him from death
or see him, noble as he is, brought down
by Peleus' son, Achilles.'

Grey-eyed Athena
said to him: 'Father of the blinding bolt,
the dark storm-cloud, what words are these? The man
is mortal, and his doom fixed, long ago.
Would you release him from his painful death?
Then do so, but not all of us will praise you.'

Zeus who gathers cloud replied: 'Take heart,
my dear and honoured child. I am not bent
on my suggestion, and I would indulge you.
Act as your thought inclines, refrain no longer.'

So he encouraged her in her desire,
and down she swept from ridges of Olympus.
Great Achilles, hard on Hector's heels,
kept after him, the way a hound will harry
a deer's fawn he has startled from its bed
to chase through gorge and open glade, and when
the quarry goes to earth under a bush
he holds the scent and quarters till he finds it;
so with Hector: he could not shake off
the great runner, Achilles. Every time
he tried to spring hard for the Dardan gates
under the towers, hoping men could help him,
sending missiles down, Achilles loomed
to cut him off and turn him toward the plain,
as he himself ran always near the city.
As in a dream a man chasing another
cannot catch him, nor can he in flight
escape from his pursuer, so Achilles
could not by his swiftness overtake him,
nor could Hector pull away. How could he
run so long from death, had not Apollo
for the last time, the very last, come near
to give him stamina and speed?

                                                Achilles
shook his head at the rest of the Achaeans,
allowing none to shoot or cast at Hector –
none to forestall him, and to win the honour.
But when, for the fourth time, they reached the springs,
the Father poised his golden scales. He placed
two shapes of death, death prone and cold, upon them,
one of Achilles, one of the horseman Hector,
and held the mid-point, pulling upward. Down
sank Hector's fatal day, the pan went down
toward undergloom, and Phoebus Apollo left him.

Then came Athena, grey-eyed, to the son
of Peleus, falling in with him, and near him,
saying swiftly: 'Now at last I think
the two of us, Achilles loved by Zeus,
shall bring Achaeans triumph at the ships
by killing Hector – unappeased
though he was ever in his thirst for war.
There is no way he may escape us now,
not though Apollo, lord of distances,
should suffer all indignity for him
before his father Zeus who bears the storm-cloud,
rolling back and forth and begging for him.
Now you can halt and take your breath, while I
persuade him into combat face to face.'

    These were Athena's orders. He complied,
relieved, and leaning hard upon the spearshaft
armed with its head of bronze.

                    She left him there
and overtook Lord Hector – but she seemed
Deiphobus in form and resonant voice,
appearing at his shoulder, saying swiftly:
'Ai! Dear brother, how he runs, Achilles,
harrying you around the town of Priam!
Come, we'll stand and take him on.'

                      To this,
great Hector in his shimmering helm replied:
'Deiphobus, you were the closest to me
in the old days, of all my brothers, sons
of Hecabe and Priam. Now I can say
I honour you still more
because you dared this foray for my sake,
seeing me run. The rest stay under cover.'

    Again the grey-eyed goddess spoke:
'Dear brother, how your father and gentle mother
begged and begged me to remain! So did
the soldiers round me, all undone by fear.
But in my heart I ached for you.
Now let us fight him, and fight hard.
No holding back. We'll see if this Achilles
conquers both, to take our armour seaward,
or if he can be brought down by your spear.'

    This way, by guile, Athena led him on.
And when at last the two men faced each other,
Hector was the first to speak.

He said:
'I will no longer fear you as before,
son of Peleus, though I ran from you
round Priam's town three times and could not face you.
Now my soul would have me stand and fight,
whether I kill you or am killed. So come,
we'll summon gods here as our witnesses,
none higher, arbiters of a pact: I swear
that, terrible as you are,
I'll not insult your corpse should Zeus allow me
victory in the end, your life as prize.
Once I have your gear, I'll give your body
back to Achaeans. Grant me, too, this grace.'

   But swift Achilles frowned at him and said:
'Hector, I'll have no talk of pacts with you,
for ever unforgiven as you are.
As between men and lions there are none,
no concord between wolves and sheep, but all
hold one another hateful through and through,
so there can be no courtesy between us,
no sworn truce, till one of us is down
and glutting with his blood the war-god Ares.
Summon up what skills you have. By god,
you'd better be a spearman and a fighter!
Now there is no way out. Pallas Athena
will have the upper hand of you. The weapon
belongs to me. You'll pay the reckoning
in full for all the pain my men have borne,
who met death by your spear.'

                              He twirled and cast
his shaft with its long shadow. Splendid Hector,
keeping his eye upon the point, eluded it
by ducking at the instant of the cast,
so shaft and bronze shank passed him overhead
and punched into the earth. But unperceived
by Hector, Pallas Athena plucked it out
and gave it back to Achilles.

                              Hector said:
'A clean miss. Godlike as you are,
you have not yet known doom for me from Zeus.
You thought you had, by heaven. Then you turned
into a word-thrower, hoping to make me lose
my fighting heart and head in fear of you.
You cannot plant your spear between my shoulders

while I am running. If you have the gift,
just put it through my chest as I come forward.
Now it's for you to dodge my own. Would god
you'd give the whole shaft lodging in your body!
War for the Trojans would be eased
if you were blotted out, bane that you are.'

    With this he twirled his long spearshaft and cast it,
hitting his enemy mid-shield, but off
and away the spear rebounded. Furious
that he had lost it, made his throw for nothing,
Hector stood bemused. He had no other.
Then he gave a great shout to Deiphobus
to ask for a long spear. But there was no one
near him, not a soul.

               Now in his heart
the Trojan realized the truth and said:
'This is the end. The gods are calling deathward.
I had thought
a good soldier, Deiphobus, was with me.
He is inside the walls. Athena tricked me.
Death is near, and black, not at a distance,
not to be evaded. Long ago
this hour must have been to Zeus's liking
and to the liking of his archer son.
They have been well disposed before, but now
the appointed time's upon me. Still, I would not
die without delivering a stroke,
or die ingloriously, but in some action
memorable to men in days to come.'

    With this he drew the whetted blade that hung
upon his left flank, ponderous and long,
collecting all his might the way an eagle
narrows himself to dive through shady cloud
and strike a lamb or cowering hare: so Hector
lanced ahead and swung his whetted blade.
Achilles with wild fury in his heart
pulled in upon his chest his beautiful shield —
his helmet with four burnished metal ridges
nodding above it, and the golden crest
Hephaestus locked there tossing in the wind.
Conspicuous as the evening star that comes,
amid the first in heaven, at fall of night,
and stands most lovely in the west, so shone
in sunlight the fine-pointed spear

Achilles poised in his right hand, with deadly
aim at Hector, at the skin where most
it lay exposed. But nearly all was covered
by the bronze gear he took from slain Patroclus,
showing only, where his collar-bones
divided neck and shoulders, the bare throat
where the destruction of a life is quickest.
Here, then, as the Trojan charged, Achilles
drove his point straight through the tender neck,
but did not cut the windpipe, leaving Hector
able to speak and to respond. He fell
aside into the dust.
                    And Prince Achilles
now exulted: 'Hector, had you thought
that you could kill Patroclus and be safe?
Nothing to dread from me; I was not there.
All childishness. Though distant then, Patroclus'
comrade in arms was greater far than he –
and it is I who had been left behind
that day beside the deep-sea ships who now
have made your knees give way. The dogs and kites
will rip your body. His will lie in honour
when the Achaeans give him funeral.'

Hector, barely whispering, replied:
'I beg you by your soul and by your parents,
do not let the dogs feed on me
in your encampment by the ships. Accept
the bronze and gold my father will provide
as gifts, my father and her ladyship
my mother. Let them have my body back,
so that our men and women may accord me
decency of fire when I am dead.'

Achilles the great runner scowled and said:
'Beg me no beggary by soul or parents,
whining dog! Would god my passion drove me
to slaughter you and eat you raw, you've caused
such agony to me! No man exists
who could defend you from the carrion-pack –
not if they spread for me ten times your ransom,
twenty times, and promise more as well;
aye, not if Priam, son of Dardanus,
tells them to buy you for your weight in gold!
You'll have no bed of death, nor will you be
laid out and mourned by her who gave you birth.

Dogs and birds will have you, every scrap.'
Then at the point of death Lord Hector said:
'I see you now for what you are. No chance
to win you over. Iron in your breast
your heart is. Think a bit, though: this may be
a thing the gods in anger hold against you
on that day when Paris and Apollo
destroy you at the Gates, great as you are.'
Even as he spoke, the end came, and death hid him;
spirit from body fluttered to undergloom,
bewailing fate that made him leave his youth
and manhood in the world.

                            And as he died
Achilles spoke again. He said:
'Die, make an end. I shall accept my own
whenever Zeus and the other gods desire.'
At this he pulled his spearhead from the body,
laying it aside, and stripped
the blood-stained shield and cuirass from his shoulders.
Other Achaeans hastened round to see
Hector's fine body and his comely face,
and no one came who did not stab the body.
Glancing at one another they would say:
'Now Hector has turned vulnerable, softer
than when he put the torches to the ships!'
And he who said this would inflict a wound.
When the great master of pursuit, Achilles,
had the body stripped, he stood among them,
saying swiftly: 'Friends, my lords and captains
of Argives, now that the gods at last have let me
bring to earth this man who wrought
havoc among us – more than all the rest –
come, we'll offer battle around the city,
to learn the intentions of the Trojans now.
Will they give up their strong point at this loss?
Can they fight on, though Hector's dead?
                            'But wait:
why do I ponder, why take up these questions?
Down by the ships Patroclus' body lies
unwept, unburied. I shall not forget him
while I can keep my feet among the living.
If in the dead world they forget the dead,
I say there, too, I shall remember him,
my friend. Men of Achaea, lift a song!

Down to the ships we go, and take this body,
our glory. We have beaten Hector down,
to whom as to a god the Trojans prayed.'

Indeed, he had in mind for Hector's body
outrage and shame. Behind both feet he pierced
the tendons, heel to ankle. Rawhide cords
he drew through both and lashed them to his chariot,
letting the man's head trail. Stepping aboard,
bearing the great trophy of the arms,
he shook the reins, and whipped the team ahead
into a willing run. A dust-cloud rose
above the furrowing body; the dark tresses
flowed behind, and the head so princely once
lay back in dust. Zeus gave him to his enemies
to be defiled in his own fatherland.
So his whole head was blackened. Looking down,
his mother tore her braids, threw off her veil,
and wailed, heart-broken to behold her son.
Piteously his father groaned, and round him
lamentation spread throughout the town,
most like the clamour to be heard if Ilium's
towers, top to bottom, seethed in flames.
They barely stayed the old man, mad with grief,
from passing through the gates.

                                        Then in the mire
he rolled, and begged them all, each man by name:
'Relent, friends. It is hard; but let me go
out of the city to the Achaean ships.
I'll make my plea to that demonic heart.
He may feel shame before his peers, or pity
my old age. His father, too, is old,
Peleus, who brought him up to be a scourge
to Trojans, cruel to all, but most to me,
so many of my sons in flower of youth
he cut away. And, though I grieve, I cannot
mourn them all as much as I do one,
for whom my grief will take me to the grave –
and that is Hector. Why could he not have died
where I might hold him? In our weeping, then,
his mother, now so destitute, and I
might have had surfeit and relief of tears.'

These were the words of Priam as he wept,
and all his people groaned.

                                        Then in her turn

Hecabe led the women in lamentation:
'Child, I am lost now. Can I bear my life
after the death of suffering your death?
You were my pride in all my nights and days,
pride of the city, pillar to the Trojans
and Trojan women. Everyone looked to you
as though you were a god, and rightly so.
You were their greatest glory while you lived.
Now your doom and death have come upon you.'

These were her mournful words. But Hector's lady
still knew nothing; no one came to tell her
of Hector's stand outside the gates. She wove
upon her loom, deep in the lofty house,
a double purple web with rose design.
Calling her maids in waiting,
she ordered a big cauldron on a tripod
set on the hearth-fire, to provide a bath
for Hector when he came home from the fight.
Poor wife, how far removed from baths he was
she could not know, as at Achilles' hands
Athena brought him down.

                              Then from the tower
she heard a wailing and a distant moan.
Her knees shook, and she let her shuttle fall,
and called out to her maids again: 'Come here.
Two must follow me, to see this action.
I heard my husband's queenly mother cry.
I feel my heart rise, throbbing in my throat.
My knees are like stone under me. Some blow
is coming home to Priam's sons and daughters.
Ah, could it never reach my ears! I die
of dread that Achilles may have cut off Hector,
blocked my bold husband from the city wall,
to drive him down the plain alone! By now
he may have ended Hector's deathly pride.
He never kept his place amid the chariots
but drove ahead. He would not be outdone
by anyone in courage.'

                              Saying this, she ran
like a madwoman through the megaron,
her heart convulsed. Her maids kept at her side.
On reaching the great tower and the soldiers,
Andromache stood gazing from the wall
and saw him being dragged before the city.

Chariot-horses at a brutal gallop
pulled the torn body toward the decked ships.
Blackness of night covered her eyes; she fell
backward swooning, sighing out her life,
and let her shining head-dress fall, her hood
and diadem, her plaited band and veil
that Aphrodite once had given her,
on that day when, from Eetion's house,
for a thousand bridal gifts, Lord Hector led her.
Now, at her side, kinswomen of her lord
supported her among them, dazed and faint
to the point of death.

                              But when she breathed again
and her stunned heart recovered, in a burst
of sobbing she called out among the women:
'Hector! Here is my desolation. Both
had this in store from birth – from yours in Troy
in Priam's palace, mine by wooded Placus
at Thebe in the home of Eetion,
my father, who took care of me in childhood,
a man cursed by fate, a fated daughter.
How I could wish I never had been born!
Now under earth's roof to the house of Death
you go your way and leave me here, bereft,
lonely, in anguish without end. The child
we wretches had is still in infancy;
you cannot be a pillar to him, Hector,
now you are dead, nor he to you. And should
this boy escape the misery of the war,
there will be toil and sorrow for him later,
as when strangers move his boundary stones.
The day that orphans him will leave him lonely,
downcast in everything, cheeks wet with tears,
in hunger going to his father's friends
to tug at one man's cloak, another's chiton.
Some will be kindly: one may lift a cup
to wet his lips at least, though not his throat;
but from the board some child with living parents
gives him a push, a slap, with biting words:
"Outside, you there! Your father is not with us
here at our feast!" And the boy Astyanax
will run to his forlorn mother. Once he fed
on marrow only and the fat of lamb,
high on his father's knees. And when sleep came

to end his play, he slept in a nurse's arms,
brimful of happiness, in a soft bed.
But now he'll know sad days and many of them,
missing his father. 'Lord of the lower town'
the Trojans call him. They know, you alone,
Lord Hector, kept their gates and their long walls.
Beside the beaked ships now, far from your kin,
the blowflies' maggots in a swarm will eat you
naked, after the dogs have had their fill.
Ah, there are folded garments in your chambers,
delicate and fine, of women's weaving.
These, by heaven, I'll burn to the last thread
in blazing fire! They are no good to you,
they cannot cover you in death. So let them
go, let them be burnt as an offering
from Trojans and their women in your honour.'
    Thus she mourned, and the women wailed in answer.

BOOK XXIII

A FRIEND CONSIGNED TO DEATH

THAT was the way they grieved at Troy. Retiring
shoreward to the beach and Helle's waters,
each to his ship, Achaeans turned away,
but not the Myrmidons.

                   Achilles held them
undismissed, and spoke among these fighters:
'Chariot-skirmishers, friends of my heart,
we'll not unharness our good horses now
but in our war-cars filing near Patroclus
mourn him in line. That is fit honour paid
to a captain fallen. When we've gained relief
in lamentation, we can free the teams
and take our evening meal here.'

                   With one voice
they all cried out in sorrow, and he led them,
driving their teams with wind-blown manes three times
around the body, weeping, and among them
Thetis roused their longing to lament.
The sandy field, the gear of men grew wet
with salt tears, for they missed him bitterly,
the man who turned the battle-tide.

                       Achilles
led them in repeated cries of grief,
laying his deadly hands upon his friend:
'Patroclus, peace be with you in the dark
where Death commands, aye, even there. You see
I shall have done soon all I promised you:
I dragged Hector this far, to give wild dogs
his flesh and let them rend it among themselves,
and I have brought twelve radiant sons of Troy
whose throats I'll cut, to bloody your great pyre,
such fury came upon me at your death.'

    Shameless abuse indeed he planned for Hector,
and laid the body face down in the dust
beside Patroclus' bed of death. His soldiers
now unbuckled all their brazen gear,
freed the whinnying horses of their harness,
and sat down, in their hundreds, all before

Achilles' ship. Then to their heart's desire
he made the funeral feast. Sleek oxen, many,
bellowed and fell slack on the iron blade
in slaughter; many sheep and bleating goats
and tuskers ruffed in fat. These beasts were singed,
then held out spitted in Hephaestus' flame,
and blood ran streaming down around the body.

    Achaean peers induced Achilles now –
barely prevailing on his grief and rage –
to visit the Lord Agamemnon;
and when they came up to the Marshal's hut
they bade the clear-voiced criers there
set out a tripod cauldron on the fire,
thinking Achilles might wash off the blood
that stained his body.

                     He would not hear of it,
but swore: 'By Zeus, I will not! By that god
best and all-highest, it is not in order
to bring hot water near me, till I lay
Patroclus on his pyre, and heap his barrow,
and shear my hair. No burden like this grief
will come a second time upon my heart,
while I remain among the living.

                          'Now,
by heaven, we'll consent to the grim feast.
At first light turn the men out, my Lord Marshal,
to bring in all the firewood required
that the dead man may reach the gloomy west;
then let strong fire hide and consume the corpse;
and let the troops return to duty.'

    So he spoke, and they listened and obeyed him,
busied themselves with dinner, took their meat,
and no one lacked his portion of the feast.
When they had put their hunger and thirst away,
the rest retired, each man to his hut,
but on the sea beach near the wash and ebb
Achilles lay down groaning among his men,
his Myrmidons, on a bare open place
where breakers rolled in spume upon the shore.
Pursuing Hector around windy Troy
he had worn out his legs. Now restful floods
of sleep, dissolving heartache, came upon him,
and soon forlorn Patroclus' shade came near –
a perfect likeness of the man, in height,

fine eyes, and voice, and dressed in his own fashion.

   The image stood above him and addressed him:
'Sleeping so? Thou hast forgotten me,
Achilles. Never was I uncared for
in life but am in death. Accord me burial
in all haste: let me pass the gates of Death.
Shades that are images of used-up men
motion me away, will not receive me
among their hosts beyond the river. I wander
about the wide gates and the hall of Death.
Give me your hand. I sorrow.
When thou shalt have allotted me my fire
I will not fare here from the dark again.
As living men we'll no more sit apart
from our companions, making plans. The day
of wrath appointed for me at my birth
engulfed and took me down. Thou too, Achilles,
face iron destiny, godlike as thou art,
to die under the wall of high-born Trojans.
One more message, one behest, I leave thee:
not to inter my bones apart from thine
but close together, as we grew together,
in thy family's hall. Menoetius
from Opoeis had brought me, under a cloud,
a boy still, on the day I killed the son
of Lord Amphidamas – though I wished it not –
in childish anger over a game of dice.
Peleus, master of horse, adopted me
and reared me kindly, naming me your squire.
So may the same urn hide our bones, the one
of gold your gracious mother gave.'
                                        Achilles
spoke in answer, saying: 'Dear old friend,
why comest hither, and why these demands?
I shall bring all to pass for thee; I shall
comply with all thy bidding. Only stand
nearer to me. For this little time
may we embrace and take our fill of tears.'

   He stretched his arms out but took hold of nothing,
as into earth Patroclus' shade like smoke
retreated with a faint cry.
                                    Then Achilles
rose in wonderment and clapped his hands,
and slowly said: 'A wisp of life remains

in the undergloom of Death: a visible form,
though no heart beats within it. All this night
the shade of poor Patroclus bent above me
grieving and weeping, charging me with tasks.
It seemed to the life the very man.'

                       At this
the Myrmidons were stirred again to weep.
Then Dawn with rose-red fingers in the east
began to glow upon them as they mourned
around the pitiful body.

                    Agamemnon
ordered out mules and men from every hut
to forage firewood. As overseer
went that good man Meriones, lieutenant
of staunch Idomeneus. The troops filed out
with loggers' axes and tough plaited rope,
while mules plodded ahead of the working party.
Up hill and down, and cutting across the slopes,
they tramped until they came to Ida's valleys.
There at once they pitched in, hewing hard
with whetted axes at the towering oaks
until they came down crashing. The Achaeans
trimmed and split the trunks and lashed the logs
on muleback. Laden mules broke up the ground
and trod out paths through underbrush, descending
eagerly to the plain, while all the axe-men
carried logs as well; Meriones
had so commanded. On the shore they stacked
their burdens in a woodpile, where Achilles
planned Patroclus' barrow and his own;
then, having heaped a four-square mass of timber,
all sat down together. Now Achilles
ordered his veteran Myrmidons to arm
and yoke their horses to the chariots.
They rose and put their gear on. Chariot-fighters
mounted with drivers in the cars, and these
moved out ahead; behind, a cloud of infantry
followed. In between, his old companions
bore Patroclus, covering the corpse
with locks of hair they sheared off and let fall.
Achilles held the head in grief; his friend
he would consign now to the world of Death.
When they had reached the place Achilles chose
they put the body down and built the pyre

of timber, high as they could wish. Achilles
turned to another duty now. Apart
from the pyre he stood and cut the red-gold hair
that he had grown for the river Spercheius.

Gazing over the wine-dark sea in pain,
he said: 'Spercheius, Peleus my father's vow
to you meant nothing, that on my return
I'd cut my hair as an offering to you,
along with fifty sheep ungelded, slain
at your headwaters, where your park and altar
fragrant with incense are. The old man swore it,
but you would not fulfil what he desired.
Now, as I shall not see my fatherland,
I would confer my hair upon the soldier
Patroclus.'

                    And he closed his dear friend's hands
upon it, moving all to weep again.

The sun would have gone down upon their weeping
had not Achilles quickly turned and said
to Agamemnon: 'Sir, troops act at once
on your command. Men may grow sick of tears.
Dismiss these from the pyre to make a meal,
and we who are closest to the dead will care
for what is to be done now. Let each captain
stay with us here.'

                    On hearing this, the Marshal
Agamemnon made the troops disperse
at once to their own ships. Close friends remained.
They added timber and enlarged the pyre
to a hundred feet a side. On top of it
with heavy hearts they laid the dead man down.
Sheep and shambling cattle, then, in droves
they sacrificed and dressed before the pyre.
Taking fat from all, splendid Achilles
sheathed the body head to foot. He piled
flayed carcasses around it. Amphorae
of honey and unguent he arranged in order,
tilted against the bier. He slung the bodies
of four fine horses on the pyre, and groaned.
Nine hunting-dogs had fed at the lord's table;
upon the pyre he cut the throats of two,
but as for the noble sons of Troy, all twelve
he put to the sword, as he willed their evil hour.

Then in the midst he thrust the pitiless might

of fire to feed upon them all, and cried
upon his dead companion: 'Peace be with you
even in the dark where Death commands, Patroclus.
Everything has been finished as I promised.
Fire will devour twelve noble sons of Troy
along with you, but I will not restore
Hector to Priam; he shall not be eaten
by fire but by wild dogs.'

               That was his boast,
but no dogs nosed at Hector: Zeus's daughter
Aphrodite kept them from his body
night and day, anointing it with oil
ambrosial, rose-fragrant, not to let
rough dragging by Achilles rip the skin.
Phoebus Apollo, too, from heaven sent down
a black cloud to the plain, shading the spot
the body lay on – that the power
of burning sun should not invade and parch
the flesh of limbs and sinews.

                    And now, too,
Patroclus' pyre would not flame up. Achilles
thought of another way. He drew apart
and prayed to the two winds of the north and west,
assuring them of sacrificial gifts.
Then from a golden cup he made libation
copiously, praying the two to come,
so that the dead might quickly be consumed
by conflagration of the great logs. Iris
heard his prayers and went to tell the winds,
at that time gathered indoors, in the home
of the blustering west wind, for a drinking bout.
Iris ran down to stand upon the doorstone,
and, when they saw her, all the winds uprose
with invitations, each one for himself.
But she refused and said: 'I must not stay;
I'm bound onward, across the streams of Ocean,
to the country of the Sunburned: hecatombs
they'll make the gods; I must attend the feast.
Achilles begs the winds of north and west
to blow toward him; he promises fine offerings
if you will fan and set aflame the pyre
Patroclus lies on, mourned by all Achaeans.'
That said, she soared away. The north and west winds
issued with a wondrous cry, both driving

cloud before them. Over open sea
they blew in a rush and took their gusty way,
as seas grew rough under the gale-wind wailing.
Then to the fertile plain of Troy they came
and fell upon the pyre. The flame roared,
blazing up terribly, and all night long
they joined to toss the crest of fire high
with keening blasts. And all night long Achilles
dipped up wine from a golden bowl and poured
his double cupfuls down, soaking the earth,
and calling Patroclus' feeble shade. He mourned him
as a father mourns a newly married son
whose death is anguish to his kin. Just so
Achilles mourned his friend and gave his bones
to the great flame to be devoured; with dragging
steps and groans he moved about the pyre.
Now when the star of morning eastward rose
to herald daylight on the earth, and Dawn
came after, yellow-robed, above the sea,
the pyre died down, the flame sank, and the winds
departed, veering homeward once again
by sea for Thrace, as the ground swell heaved and foamed.

Achilles left the pyre and lay down spent,
and sweet sleep overtook him at a bound.
But when the rest returned round Agamemnon,
voices and trampling feet awoke the sleeper.

Up he sat, then spoke out: 'Son of Atreus,
noblemen of Achaea's host, begin
by wetting down the pyre with tawny wine
to quench whatever fire hangs on. Then come,
we'll comb the ashes for Patroclus' bones!
They will be easy to pick out: he lay
alone, in the pyre's middle, and the rest
were burnt apart from him, around the edge,
all jumbled in no order, men and horses.
Then we'll pack his bones in a golden urn
with sheep-fat in a double fold, to keep
until I too go hid in undergloom.
No heavy labour at a heavy tomb
I ask – only a fitting one; in due course
build it wide and high, you who are left
behind me in the long ships of the oarsmen.'

They did his will: dampened the pyre with wine
in every part where flame had licked its way

and a bed of ashes fallen. Shedding tears
for their mild-hearted friend they gathered up
his bones into a golden urn and added
a double fold of fat, then within doors
they set the urn and veiled it with fine linen.
Next they drew a circle for a mound
around the pyre, and laid stones on the line,
and made a mound of earth.
                              When they had done,
they were all ready to be gone, but now
Achilles held the troops upon the spot
and seated them, forming a wide arena.
Prizes out of the ships, cauldrons and tripods,
horses and mules and oxen he supplied,
and softly-belted girls, and hoary iron.
First for charioteers he set the prizes:
a girl adept at gentle handicraft
to be taken by the winner, and a tripod
holding twenty-six quarts, with handle-rings.
For the runner-up he offered a six-year-old
unbroken mare, big with a mule foal.
For third prize a fine cauldron of four gallons,
never scorched, bright as on casting day,
and for the fourth two measured bars of gold;
for fifth, a new two-handled bowl.

He stood erect and spoke to all the Argives:
'Son of Atreus, soldiers of Achaea,
these rewards await the charioteers
in this arena. If our competition
were held in honour of another man,
I'd carry off the first prize in this race.
You know how far my team outpoints the rest
in form and breeding, being divine: Poseidon
gave them to Peleus, he in turn to me.
But I am out of it, so are my horses,
now they have lost their splendid charioteer,
the kind man, who so often glossed their manes
with oil when he had scrubbed their bodies down.
Now where they stand they droop their heads for him,
their manes brushing the ground, and grieve at heart.
Get ready, any others of the army
confident in your teams and rugged cars!'

Achilles finished, and the drivers gathered,
first of all Admetus' dear son, Lord

Eumelus, best at management of horses;
then powerful Diomedes, son of Tydeus,
yoking the Trojan horses he had taken
from Aeneas when Apollo saved the man.
After him tawny-headed Menelaus,
Atreus' noble son, with his fast team,
his own Podargus, Agamemnon's Aethe –
a mare that Echepolus Anchisiades
gave Agamemnon, to avoid the toil
of serving under him at windy Troy,
and to enjoy his days at home. For Zeus
had made him wealthy, living at Sicyon
where dancing-floors are spacious. Menelaus
harnessed the mare, all quivering for the run.
Antilochus, the fourth, readied his team –
resplendent son of the heroic Lord
Nestor Neleiades. Horses of Pylos
drew his war-car.
                          At his elbow now
his father halted, with a word to the wise:
'Antilochus, by heaven, even as a youngster
Zeus and Poseidon cared for you and taught you
every kind of horsemanship. No need
for me to add instruction, when you know
so well the trick of making turns. However,
these are slow horses, and they may turn in
a second-rate performance. The other teams
are faster. But the charioteers
know no more racing strategy than you do.
Work out a plan of action in your mind,
dear son, don't let the prize slip through your fingers.
Astuteness makes a forester, not brawn,
and by astuteness on the open sea
a helmsman holds a ship on the right course
though roughed by winds. One driver beats another
thinking it out beforehand. Many a one
will trust his team and chariot so far
that he wheels wide on turns, and carelessly,
to one side, then the other, and his horses
career over the track, not kept in hand.
But a skilled charioteer with slower horses,
keeping his eye on the turning post,
will cling to it as he takes the curve, remembering
to give his horses rein into the stretch

but with a sure hand, watching the front-runner.
As to the mark, it stands out; you can't miss it:
a dry stump, a man's height above the ground,
of oak or pine, not rotted by the rain,
where the outward course turns home. Around this mark
there is smooth footing. It may be a memorial
of a man dead long ago, or a turning-post
built in the old days. Now the Prince Achilles
makes it our half-way mark. As you drive near it,
hug it with car and horses; you yourself
in the chariot-basket lean a bit to the left
and at the same time lash your right-hand horse
and shout to him, and let his rein run out.
Your left-hand horse should graze the turning-post
so that your wheel-hub seems to scrape the edge.
But mind there's no collision with the stump:
you'll hurt the horses and destroy the car,
and that will bring joy to your adversaries,
humiliation to you. No, son, be cool and watchful.
If on the turn you overtake and pass,
there's not a chance of someone catching you –
not if he drove the great horse of Adrastus,
fleet Arion, born of the gods, or those
of Laomedon, magnificent ones bred here.'
    When he had told his son the ultimate arts
of charioteering, Nestor sat down again.
The fifth competitor was Meriones,
and he now yoked his team. All drivers mounted,
then the pebbles marked by each were dropped
in a helmet, and Achilles churned it round
till one bounced out: the token of Antilochus,
second, that of Eumelus, as it chanced,
then came the master-spearman Menelaus,
then Meriones took his appointed place,
and Diomedes, greatest of them all,
came last of all in order of the start.
Reining in line they waited, while Achilles
showed the mark far off on the flat plain
and stationed near it, as a referee,
Phoenix, the lord companion of his father,
to judge the race and to report the truth.
All the drivers raised their whips at once
above their teams, then lashed, with reins as well,
and cheered the horses as they broke away.

Over the plain they covered distance quickly,
running at full stretch, leaving the ships behind,
as dust rose under the barrels of the horses
like a cloud raised by a whirlwind, and their manes
flew backward in the wind-stream as they ran.
The cars went rocketing, now on the level field,
now through the air on rises. Charioteers
kept their feet, and each man's heart beat hard
with passion to be first. All cheered their teams,
and horses raised a dust-cloud in their flight.
Now when they turned into the home stretch
back to the grey sea, each man's quality
appeared as the horses went all out. The mares
of Pheres' son had pulled ahead, behind him
Diomedes' Trojan horses kept the pace
and not a length behind, but hard upon him.
Always about to mount his car, they seemed,
and his broad back and shoulders felt their breath
in warm gusts, as they seemed at every stride
to rest their heads upon him. Diomedes
would have passed him now, or pulled up even,
had not Apollo in a fit of anger
struck the flashing whip out of his hands.
Now Diomedes' eyes welled tears of rage.
He saw the mares ahead still, going away,
as running without a lash his team slowed down.
Athena, though, had noticed how Apollo
cheated him. She darted after him
to give the whip back, and revive his horses,
then in anger overtook Eumelus
and cracked his yoke in two. The horses parted,
swerving on the track; the chariot-pole
swung earthward; and the man himself was thrown
out of his car to roll beside the wheel.
His elbows, mouth, and nose were skinned,
his forehead battered at his brows, his eyes
clouded with tears, his big voice choked.
But Diomedes passed him wide and drove
in a spurt ahead of all the rest. Athena
fired his team and awarded him the glory.
After him, tawny-headed Menelaus
now ran second.

                    As for Antilochus,
he called to his father's horses: 'Move, you two!

Stretch yourselves, and do it now! By god,
I don't expect you to contest the lead
of Diomedes' team: Athena gave them
speed, gave him his glory. Only catch
Menelaus' horses, don't be left behind!
Will Aethe put you both to shame, a filly?
Why eat her dust, you champions?
Here's what I promise, and it will be done:
You'll get no grooming and no feed from Nestor;
far from it; he'll butcher you on the spot
if you lose form and we bring up the rear.
Press that chariot, and put on speed.
I'll manage it, I know the way to pass
at the narrow point ahead: I can't go wrong.'

    Stung to fear by their master's angry voice,
the team put on a burst of speed, and suddenly
Antilochus saw the narrowing track ahead.
A gully ran there, where storm-water massed
had broken off the edge and made a landslide.
Driving for the passage, Menelaus
tried to keep his wheels clear, but Antilochus
swung to one side to pass, and drove his team
outside the track, sheering a little toward him.

    Then Menelaus was afraid. He yelled:
'Antilochus, you're driving like a madman!
Pull up! The track's too narrow here. Ahead
it widens, you can pass there! Keep away,
or you'll collide and wreck us both!'

                         Antilochus
only drove harder, lashing at his team,
like a man deaf and blind. About as far
as a discus flies, whirled out from wheeling shoulders,
when a young athlete tries his form, so far
the two teams raced each other. Then Menelaus'
mares fell back; he leaned back on the reins,
not to let the chariots lock wheels
and overturn and pile up on the track,
while drivers, mad to win, sprawled in the dust.

    His opponent passed, and tawny Menelaus
growled at him: 'Antilochus, no man
in the world is a more dangerous pest than you are.
Pass, and be damned to you. The rest of us
were wrong to think you had a grain of sense.
But you can't have the prize this way, unless

you take oath for it.'
                              And he called his horses:
'Don't hold back, don't falter, moping there.
The others' knees and fetlocks will be tired
before your own: they have no youth like yours.'

Fearing their master's tone, his horses now
recovered speed, and gained upon the others.

Meanwhile the Argives on the measured field
sat watching as the chariots coursed the plain,
raising plumes of dust. The Cretan captain
Idomeneus caught sight of the horses first,
headed for home; he sat outside the field
high up, on a look-out point. Hearing a shout
from someone far away, he knew the voice
and recognized the stallion in the lead –
all chestnut-coloured, save that on his forehead
he wore a blaze of white, round as the moon.

Up stood Idomeneus and shouted down:
'Friends, lords and captains of the Argives, am I
the only one who can make out the horses,
or do you too? A new team has the lead,
as I see it, another charioteer
is coming into view. Eumelus' horses
must have been hurt along the way: they had
the edge on the outward lap.
By god, the ones I saw rounding the turn
I cannot see now anywhere, though I
have strained my eyes to scan the plain of Troy.
The driver lost his reins, or couldn't guide
his team full circuit, so he failed the turn.
His chariot broke down, he must have fallen,
and the stampeded mares ran off. Stand up
and look, the rest of you! I can't be sure
I recognize him, but he seems that man,
Aetolian by birth and lord of Argives,
son of Tydeus, rugged Diomedes!'

A rude reply he got from the runner, Aias,
Oileus' son, who said: 'Idomeneus,
why this rash talk too soon? Those running horses
are still far off and have the plain to cover.
Not by a long shot are you youngest here
or the one who has the best eyes in his head.
But you always have to say something. No point
in blurting it out now; sharper men are here.

The leading team is the one that led before:
Eumelus' team, and he's the one who rides
behind and holds the reins.'

        The Cretan captain
answered him in anger: 'No one like you
for picking fights and giving foolish counsel;
otherwise you rank last among the Argives,
having a mind like a hoof. Here, let me wager
a tripod or a cauldron and appoint
Agamemnon arbiter between the two of us
as to which team is first. You'll know, all right,
when you have to pay!'

        Aias got up at once
in hot anger, to make a rough reply,
and more and louder bickering was in prospect,
had not Achilles towered up and said:
'No more of this, no railing back and forth,
Aias, Idomeneus! Not on this occasion!
If someone else behaved so, you'd resent it.
Sit down, both of you, and watch the race.
The chariot-teams are coming this way fast,
whipped on to win. Before long, you will know
who's first and who's behind.'

        Even as he spoke,
Diomedes came on racing for the finish,
laying on his whip with shoulder-strokes,
so that his horses lifted their hooves high
at every furious track-devouring stride.
A constant spray of dust rained on the man
as the chariot, overlaid with gold and tin,
ran on the horses' heels. Behind the tyres
no deep wheel-mark was left in the fine dust.
The team stormed to the finish. He pulled up
in the arena, as a bath of sweat
poured to the ground from horses' necks and chests.
Then he swung from the glittering car and propped
his long whip on the yoke. And his lieutenant,
Sthenelus, took the prizes without delay.
He handed the woman over to his men
and let them carry the tripod by its rings,
while he unyoked the team. In second place
Antilochus Nestorides drove in,
by guile, not speed, outrunning Menelaus,
who finished, even so, close on his heels:

close as a chariot-wheel to a horse that pulls
his master at a dead run on the plain:
tips of his tail-hairs whisk at the wheel-rim
as he runs just ahead, with no expanse
between, and all the plain beyond to cover.
Just so close, Menelaus came in behind
Antilochus. At first by a discus-throw
he had been outrun, but then he caught up fast,
helped by the valour of Agamemnon's mare,
silken-coated Aethe. A longer race
and Menelaus would have passed, to win
decisively, and no dead heat. In fourth place
Meriones, Idomeneus' right-hand man,
came after Menelaus by a spear-cast.
His were the slowest horses of them all,
and he least fit for driving on a racecourse.
Last of all the son of Admetus came,
on foot, pulling his car, driving his horses
before him at a walk. And beholding him
swift Prince Achilles felt a pang of pity.

Sharply he spoke out, standing amid the Argives:
'The best man is the last to bring his team in.
Come, we'll award him second prize, in fairness.
Let Diomedes have the first.'

Then all the soldiers shouted 'Aye' to this,
and as they had approved, he would have given
the prize mare to Eumelus; but Antilochus
made his claim in protest: 'O Achilles,
if you go through with this thing you've announced,
I'll be furious! You mean to take my prize,
considering that his chariot and team
were hurt, and he, too, the brave fellow. Well,
he should have prayed the immortals! If he had,
he would have finished far from last. Granted
that you are sorry for him, fond of him,
there's gold aplenty in your hut, and bronze,
and you have cattle, serving-maids, and horses.
Take some later; give him a greater prize;
or take them here and now. You'll have the Achaeans'
praise for it. *I will not yield the mare.*
And any man who cares to fight for her
can try me, hand to hand.'
                                              At this
the Prince Achilles, the great runner, smiled,

enjoying Antilochus, as he liked the man.
He warmly answered him: 'Antilochus,
if you invite me to find something else
to award Eumelus, I'll be glad to do it.
The cuirass that I took from Asteropaeus,
bronze with a casting of bright tin around it:
that he shall have, and worth a great sum, too.'

He told his close companion, Automedon,
to bring the cuirass from the hut. He did so,
and Achilles handed it over to Eumelus,
who took it gladly.

                But now Menelaus
faced them all, still sore at heart, his anger
grimly set against Antilochus. A herald
handed him a staff and called for silence.
Then he spoke among them as a king:
'Antilochus, you were clear-headed once.
How have you acted now? Mocked at my skill
and fouled my horses, pushing your own ahead,
although they were inferior by far.
Come now, lords and captains of the Argives,
judge between us – and no favouring me.
Never let any Achaean soldier say:
"Menelaus got the upper hand by lies
against Antilochus; he takes the prize,
because although his horses were slower far
he himself prevailed by power and rank."
Here: I'll conduct the case, and not one man
will take exception; it will be justly done.
Antilochus, come here, sir, as good discipline
requires; stand there before your team and car.
Pick up the slim whip that you used in driving;
touch your horses; by the god of earthquake
swear you did not mean to foul my car.'

     Clear-headed Antilochus answered: 'Wait a bit, sir.
Surely I'm younger than you are, my Lord
Menelaus; you stand higher in age and rank.
You know a young man may go out of bounds:
his wits are nimble, but his judgement slight.
Be patient, then. The mare I won I'll give you,
and any other and greater thing of mine
you might request I'd wish to give at once,
rather than fall in your esteem, my lord,
for all my days, and live as an offender

before the unseen powers.'

               When he had spoken,
the son of Nestor led the mare across
and put the bridle in Menelaus' hands.
And Menelaus was refreshed at heart
as growing grain is, when ears shine with dew,
and the fields ripple. So the heart within you,
Menelaus, was refreshed.

               And happily
the older man said to the younger: 'Now,
Antilochus, I am coming round to you,
after my anger. You were never thoughtless
before this. Youth prevailed over your good sense.
The next time, have a care not to pull tricks
on higher officers. Truly, no other
Achaean could so quickly win me over,
but you've fought hard, and toiled long years,
as your father and brave brother have, for me.
I shall comply with what you asked at first
and give the mare to you, though she is mine,
so these men too may know
my temper is not cruel and overbearing.'

    Then to Noemon, squire of Antilochus,
he gave the mare to lead away, and took
instead the shining cauldron. Meriones,
as fourth to cross the finish line, picked up
the measured bars of gold. But the fifth prize,
the bowl with handles on both sides, remained.

    Achilles carried it across the field
to make a gift of it to Nestor, saying:
'Here is a keepsake, venerable sir,
for you, too, from Patroclus' funeral day.
You'll never see him again among the Argives.
Prize though it is, I give this bowl, since you
will not contend in boxing or in wrestling,
nor will you enter for the javelin-throw
or run the quarter-mile. Stiffness of age
encumbers you even now.'

               And he gave the bowl.
Nestor received it and was pleased. He said:
'You've put the matter very well, my son.
My legs are strong no longer, as you say;
I am not fast on my feet; my hands no longer
move out fast to punch or throw. Would god

I had my young days back, my strength entire,
as when the Epeians buried Amarynceus
at Buprasium, and his sons
held contests in his honour. That day, no one
gave me a match – no man of the Epeians,
Pylians, or brave Aetolians.
In boxing I defeated Clytomedes,
the son of Enops; in the wrestling-bout
I threw my man, Ancaeus the Pleuronian;
in the quarter-mile I beat an excellent runner,
Iphiclus; and in the javelin-throw
I out-cast both Phyleus and Polydorus.
Only in chariot-racing, Actor's sons
pulled out ahead. By being two against one
they pushed their team in front, hating to see me
win again when the greatest prize remained.
Those two were twins: one held the reins alone –
the reins alone – while the other used the whip.
That was the man I was. Now let the young
take part in these exertions: I must yield
to slow old age, though in my time I shone
among heroic men.

                          'Well, carry on
the funeral of your friend with competitions.
This I take kindly, and my heart is cheered
that you remember me as well-disposed,
remembering, too, the honour that is due me
among Achaeans. May the gods
in fitting ways reward you for it all.'

    Achilles bent his head to Nestor's praise
and then returned across the field of Achaeans.

    Now as first prize for the bruising fist-fight
he led a mule to tie it in the ring,
a beast of burden, six years old, unbroken,
that would be hard to break. And for the loser
he set out a two-handled cup, then stood
and said to the Argives: 'Excellency, Agamemnon,
and other Achaeans under arms, I call
on two of our most powerful men to try
for these awards of boxing.
The one Apollo helps to keep his feet –
if all Achaeans will concede the winner –
may take this working-animal for his own,
while a two-handled cup goes to the loser.'

At this a huge man got to his feet at once,
huge but compact, clever with his fists,
Epeius, a son of Panopeus.

He laid hold of the stubborn mule and said:
'Step up, one of you men, and take the cup!
I think no other here will take the mule
by whipping me. I'm best, I don't mind saying.
Enough to admit I'm second-rate at war;
no man can be a master in everything.
Here is my forecast, and it's dead sure.
I'll open his face and crack his ribs. His friends
should gather and stand by to take him off
after my left and right have put him down.'

At this they all grew silent. Euryalus
alone stood up to face him, well-built son
of Lord Mecisteus Talaionides,
who in the old days came to Thebes when Oedipus
had found his grave. At that time, Mecisteus
defeated all the Cadmeians. His son
had Diomedes to attend him now
and cheer him on, wishing him victory.
First he cinched around him a fighter's belt
and then bound rawhide strips across his knuckles.
Both men, belted, stepped into the ring
and, toe to toe, let fly at one another,
hitting solid punches. Heavy fists
then milled together as they worked in close
with a fierce noise of grinding jaws. Their bodies
ran with sweat. Then Epeius leapt out
with a long left hook and smashed the other's cheek
as he peered out through puffed eyes. He could keep
his feet no longer, but his legs gave way
and down he went – the way a leaping fish
falls backward in the offshore sea when north wind
ruffles it down a beach littered with sea-wrack:
black waves hide him. So the man left his feet
and dropped at the blow. Gallantly Epeius
gave him a hand and pulled him up; his friends
with arms around him helped him from the ring,
scuffing his feet and spitting gouts of blood,
his head helplessly rolling side to side.
They sat him down, addled, among themselves,
and took charge of the double-handled cup.

Achilles now at once put on display

before the troops a third array of prizes –
those for the grinding wrestling-bout. The winner
was to acquire a fire-straddling tripod
valued at twelve oxen by the Achaeans.
As for the loser, in their midst Achilles
placed a woman versatile at crafts,
whose value was four oxen.
                                    Standing there,
he said to the Argives: 'Up with you, the pair
who will contend for this one.'
                                    Up they stood,
huge Aias Telamonius, then Odysseus,
the calculating and resourceful man.
Wearing their belts, the two leaned toward each other
in the arena, and with oaken hands
gripped one another's elbows. Think of timbers
fitted at a steep angle for a roof
a master-builder makes to break the winds!
The bones in each man's back creaked at the strain
put on him by their corded thews, and sweat
ran down in rills. Around their ribs and shoulders
welts were raised by the holds they took, all scarlet
where the blood gathered. Without pause they strove
to win the tripod: neither could Odysseus
throw his man and pin him, nor could Aias,
countered by Odysseus' brawn.
                                    At last
when the tied match began to bore the soldiers,
Aias muttered: 'Son of Laertes, royal
Odysseus, master mariner and soldier,
hoist me, or I'll hoist you. What happens then
is god's affair.'
                                    At this he heaved him up.
But Odysseus had his bag of tricks: he kicked
behind the knee, knocking his legs from under him,
and down went Aias backward, as Odysseus
dropped on his chest. The onlookers came alive,
looked hard and marvelled at the fall. The wrestlers
got to their feet for a fresh try, and Odysseus
heaved in turn, but could not budge the big man
even a half-inch off the ground. He bent
his knee behind him, and then both went down
locked together: both got coats of dust.
    They would have roused and tried for a third fall,

had not Achilles held them back. He said:
'No more of this bone-cracking bout.
The victory goes to both. Take equal prizes.
Off with you, so the rest here can compete.'

They broke and turned away as he commanded,
wiped off the dust, and pulled their chitons on.

For the next event, the quarter-mile, Achilles
offered a silver winebowl of six gallons.
Never a mixing bowl in all the world
could match its beauty: artisans of Sidon
had lavished art upon it. Phoenicians
had brought it out by sea and, mooring ship
in a roadstead, had conferred the bowl on Thoas.
Euneos, son of Jason, later gave it
as ransom to Patroclus for Lycaon,
son of Priam. Now at his old friend's funeral
Achilles put the bowl down, as first prize,
for that man who should prove the faster runner.
Second prize he made a giant ox,
and, for the hindmost, half a bar of gold.

Towering there, he gave the word to Argives:
'Step up, if you will try for this award.'

Aias the runner, son of Oileus,
at once came forward; then that canny man,
Odysseus, and then Nestor's son, Antilochus,
fastest man of them all among the young.
They toed the line, Achilles showed the finish,
then from the starting-line the race began,
and Aias quickly took the lead. Beside him
noble Odysseus pressed him hard. As close
as to a weaving woman's breast the bar
of warp is drawn, when accurately she passes
shuttle and spool along the meshing-web
and holds to her breast one weighted bar, so close
in second place Odysseus ran: his feet
came sprinting in the other's tracks before
the dust fell, and on Aias' nape he blew
hot breath as he ran on. All the Achaeans
cheered for Odysseus, the great contender,
and called to him as he ran with labouring heart.

But entering the last hundred yards, Odysseus
prayed in his heart to the grey-eyed one, Athena:
'Hear me, goddess: come, bless me with speed!'

That was his prayer, and Pallas Athena heard him,

lightened his legs, lightened his feet and arms,
and when they all came fighting for the finish
Aias on the dead run slipped – Athena
tripped him – at a point where dung had dropped
from lowing oxen that Achilles killed
in honour of Patroclus. Aias' mouth
and nose were plastered, plugged with muck.
But Prince Odysseus, the long-enduring,
bore off the winebowl, having finished first,
while Aias took the ox.

He stood a moment,
holding the beast's horns in his hands, and spat
the dung out of his mouth before he said:
'Damn the luck: she did for me, that goddess
always beside him, like a coddling mother!'
At this the crowd laughed at him, full of glee.

Antilochus took the last prize with a smile
and said to the Argives: 'Every man here knows,
but anyway I'll say it, friends: the immortals
honour the older men as much as ever.
Aias has it over me in age
by only a few years, but the captain here
belongs to an earlier generation of men.
Fresh in age, they call him. He's a tough one
for any runner to match himself against,
except Achilles.'

By these final words
he gave due honour to the son of Peleus.
Achilles in return said: 'Antilochus,
that word of praise will not go unrewarded.
I'll add another half-bar to your prize.'
This he bestowed, and the young man took it gladly.

Then Achilles brought a battle-spear,
a shield and helm, and laid them on the field –
the armour of Sarpedon, which Patroclus
took for spoil.

He stood and told the Argives:
'Now I invite two men to fight for these –
two of our bravest, in full battle-gear,
equipped with cutting-weapons, too. They are
to take one another on before the crowd.
And that one of the two who first shall hit
the good flesh of the other, draw his blood,
making a stroke through helm or shield – to him

I'll give this handsome broadsword, silver-hilted,
Thracian, that I took from Asteropaeus.
The armour shall belong to both in common
and in our hut we'll make them a good feast.'

Huge Aias rose, the son of Telamon,
and rugged Diomedes rose as well.
On one side and the other of the crowd
they put their gear on, then paced to the centre,
hot for combat, glaring while a hush
of admiration ran through all the troops.
As they came near, with lightning feints three times
they all but charged each other, and then Aias
hit Diomedes hard on the round shield.
He came short of his body, as the breastplate
safely enclosed it. Over the tower shield
Diomedes now with flickering point at play
endangered Aias' throat, and in commotion,
fearing for Aias, the Achaeans cried:
'Break off this duel, and pick up equal prizes!'

Achilles, though, awarded the big sword,
scabbard, and well-cut belt to Diomedes.

Then he set out a meteorite, a missile
Eetion in power used to hurl –
before Achilles brought him down and took
this fused iron with plunder in his ships.

Now he stood and told the men: 'Step forward,
those who will try for this one. A man's fields
may lie far from his town, but five long years
this lump will last: neither shepherd nor ploughman
need go up to town for want of iron,
he'll be supplied at home.'

                            Then Polypoetes,
a man who stood his ground in battle, rose,
then stalwart, sturdy-hearted Leonteus,
then Aias Telamonius and Epeius
moved into place. Epeius took the iron,
and heaved it – and the crowd of Achaeans laughed.
The good fighter, Leonteus, made his try,
and then, as third man, Telamonian Aias
hurled the iron from his massive hand
beyond the others. But when Polypoetes
took the lump in turn, he made it hurtle
as far as a herdsman throws a cattle-staff,
rifling it clear across a herd: so far

beyond the ring he hurled it, and the soldiers
roared applause. Men of his company
carried the royal prize down to the ships.
    Wrought iron for the archers now – ten axe-heads
double-bladed, ten with single blades –
Achilles laid in order in the ring.
He set a mast up from a black-hulled ship
at the sand's edge, and tethered by a cord
around one foot a rock-dove.
                                    'Shoot at that!'
said he. 'The man who hits the fluttering dove
may carry all the double-axes home.
If someone cuts the cord he'll miss the bird:
call it a poor shot! Second prize for him!'
    At this the kingly archer Teucer rose,
followed by Idomeneus' lieutenant,
staunch Meriones. And choosing lots
they rolled them in a helmet. Teucer's pebble
had the luck: he drew and shot his arrow
without a pause, also without a vow
of rams in hecatomb to Lord Apollo.
He missed the bird, begrudged him by Apollo,
hitting instead the cord that tethered her.
The cutting arrowhead parted the cord,
and skyward the bird flew, as the frayed length
of cord dangled to earth. All the Achaeans
breathed a mighty sigh – but in one motion
Meriones whipped the bow out of his hands.
He held an arrow ready for his shot
and now vowed to Apollo, archer of heaven,
to offer first-born lambs in hecatomb.
Aloft, dark against cloud, he saw the dove,
and as she wheeled he shot her through the body
under the wing. His arrow, passing through,
plummeted back and stuck before his feet.
The wounded rock-dove settled on the mast
with hanging head and drooping wings, and soon,
as life throbbed from her body, she fell down
far from the bowman. All the troops looked on
and marvelled at the shooting. Then Meriones
picked up the double-blades, Teucer the single,
to carry to the ships.
                        Finally, Achilles
furnished a throwing-spear and a new cauldron

chased with floral figures, worth an ox.
The javelin-throwers advanced: first Agamemnon,
ruler of the great plains, then Meriones,
lieutenant to Idomeneus.

                    But Achilles
had a proposal for them: 'Son of Atreus,
considering that you excel us all –
and by so much – in throwing-power, I'd say
that you should simply carry off this prize.
We'll give the spear, though, to Meriones,
if you agree. That is what I propose.'

   Lord Marshal Agamemnon gave consent,
so the bronze-shod spear went to Meriones.
Then to his crier, Talthybius,
Agamemnon entrusted the beautiful cauldron.

BOOK XXIV

A GRACE GIVEN IN SORROW

THE funeral games were over. Men dispersed
and turned their thoughts to supper in their quarters,
then to the boon of slumber. But Achilles
thought of his friend, and sleep that quiets all things
would not take hold of him. He tossed and turned
remembering with pain Patroclus' courage,
his buoyant heart; how in his company
he fought out many a rough day full of danger,
cutting through ranks in war and the bitter sea.
With memory his eyes grew wet. He lay
on his right side, then on his back, and then
face downward – but at last he rose, to wander
distractedly along the line of surf.
This for eleven nights. The first dawn, brightening
sea and shore, became familiar to him,
as at that hour he yoked his team, with Hector
tied behind, to drag him out, three times
around Patroclus' tomb. By day he rested
in his own hut, abandoning Hector's body
to lie full-length in dust – though Lord Apollo,
pitying the man, even in death,
kept his flesh free of disfigurement.
He wrapped him in his great shield's flap of gold
to save him from laceration. But Achilles
in rage visited indignity on Hector
day after day, and, looking on,
the blessed gods were moved. Day after day
they urged the Wayfinder to steal the body –
a thought agreeable to all but Hera,
Poseidon, and the grey-eyed one, Athena.
These opposed it, and held out, since Ilium
and Priam and his people had incurred
their hatred first, the day when Alexandrus
made his mad choice and piqued two goddesses,
visitors in his sheep-fold: for he praised
a third, who offered ruinous lust.
    Now when Dawn grew bright for the twelfth day,
Phoebus Apollo spoke among the gods:

'How heartless and how malevolent you are!
Did Hector never make burnt offering
of bulls' thigh-bones to you, and unflawed goats?
Even in death you would not stir to save him
for his dear wife to see, and for his mother,
his child, his father, Priam, and his men:
they'd burn the corpse at once and give him burial.
Murderous Achilles has your willing help –
a man who shows no decency, implacable,
barbarous in his ways as a wild lion
whose power and intrepid heart
sway him to raid the flocks of men for meat.
The man has lost all mercy;
he has no shame – that gift that hinders mortals
but helps them, too. A sane one may endure
an even dearer loss: a blood-brother,
a son; and yet, by heaven, having grieved
and passed through mourning, he will let it go.
The Fates have given patient hearts to men.
Not this one: first he took Prince Hector's life
and now he drags the body, lashed to his car,
around the barrow of his friend, performing
something neither nobler in report
nor better in itself. Let him take care,
or, brave as he is, we gods will turn against him,
seeing him outrage the insensate earth!'

    Hera whose arms are white as ivory
grew angry at Apollo. She retorted:
'Lord of the silver bow, your words would be
acceptable if one had a mind to honour
Hector and Achilles equally.
But Hector suckled at a woman's breast,
Achilles is the first-born of a goddess –
one I nursed myself. I reared her, gave her
to Peleus, a strong man whom the gods loved.
All of you were present at their wedding –
you too – friend of the base, forever slippery! –
came with your harp and dined there!'

                                    Zeus the storm-king
answered her: 'Hera, don't lose your temper
altogether. Clearly the same high honour
cannot be due both men. And yet Lord Hector,
of all the mortal men in Ilium,
was dearest to the gods, or was to me.

He never failed in the right gift; my altar
never lacked a feast
of wine poured out and smoke of sacrifice –
the share assigned as ours. We shall renounce
the theft of Hector's body; there is no way;
there would be no eluding Achilles' eye,
as night and day his mother comes to him.
Will one of you now call her to my presence?
I have a solemn message to impart:
Achilles is to take fine gifts from Priam,
and in return give back Prince Hector's body.'

At this, Iris who runs on the rainy wind
with word from Zeus departed. Midway between
Samos and rocky Imbros, down she plunged
into the dark grey sea, and the brimming tide
roared over her as she sank into the depth –
as rapidly as a leaden sinker, fixed
on a lure of wild bull's horn, that glimmers down
with a fatal hook among the ravening fish.
Soon Iris came on Thetis in a cave,
surrounded by a company of Nereids
lolling there, while she bewailed the fate
of her magnificent son, now soon to perish
on Troy's rich earth, far from his fatherland.

Halting before her, Iris said: 'Come, Thetis,
Zeus of eternal forethought summons you.'

Silvery-footed Thetis answered: 'Why?
Why does the great one call me to him now,
when I am shy of mingling with immortals,
being so heavy-hearted? But I'll go.
Whatever he may say will have its weight.'

That loveliest of goddesses now put on
a veil so black no garment could be blacker,
and swam where wind-swift Iris led. Before them
on either hand the ground swell fell away.
They rose to a beach, then soared into the sky
and found the viewer of the wide world, Zeus,
with all the blissful gods who live for ever
around him seated. Athena yielded place,
and Thetis sat down by her father, Zeus,
while Hera handed her a cup of gold
and spoke a comforting word. When she had drunk,
Thetis held out the cup again to Hera.

The father of gods and men began: 'You've come

to Olympus, Thetis, though your mind is troubled
and insatiable pain preys on your heart.
I know, I too. But let me, even so,
explain why I have called you here. Nine days
of quarrelling we've had among the gods
concerning Hector's body and Achilles.
They wish the Wayfinder to make off with it.
I, however, accord Achilles honour
as I now tell you – in respect for you
whose love I hope to keep hereafter. Go, now,
down to the army, tell this to your son:
the gods are sullen toward him, and I, too,
more than the rest, am angered at his madness,
holding the body by the beaked ships
and not releasing it. In fear of me
let him relent and give back Hector's body!
At the same time I'll send Iris to Priam,
directing him to go down to the beach-head
and ransom his dear son. He must bring gifts
to melt Achilles' rage.'
                              Thetis obeyed,
leaving Olympus' ridge and flashing down
to her son's hut. She found him groaning there,
inconsolable, while men-at-arms
went to and fro, making their breakfast ready –
having just put to the knife a fleecy sheep.

    His gentle mother sat down at his side,
caressed him, and said tenderly: 'My child,
will you forever feed on your own heart
in grief and pain, and take no thought of sleep
or sustenance? It would be comforting
to make love with a woman. No long time
will you live on for me: Death even now
stands near you, appointed and all-powerful.
But be alert and listen: I am a messenger
from Zeus, who tells me the gods are sullen toward you
and he himself most angered at your madness,
holding the body by the beaked ships
and not releasing it. Give Hector back.
Take ransom for the body.'
                              Said Achilles:
'Let it be so. Let someone bring the ransom
and take the dead away, if the Olympian
commands this in his wisdom.'

So, that morning,
in camp amid the ships, mother and son
conversed together, and their talk was long.
  Lord Zeus meanwhile sent Iris to Ilium.
'Off with you, lightfoot, leave Olympus, take
my message to the majesty of Priam
at Ilium. He is to journey down
and ransom his dear son upon the beach-head.
He shall take gifts to melt Achilles' rage,
and let him go alone, no soldier with him,
only some crier, some old man, to drive
his wagon-team and guide the nimble wagon,
and afterward to carry home the body
of him that Prince Achilles overcame.
Let him not think of death, or suffer dread,
as I'll provide him with a wondrous guide,
the Wayfinder, to bring him across the lines
into the very presence of Achilles.
And he, when he sees Priam within his hut,
will neither take his life nor let another
enemy come near. He is no madman,
no blind brute, nor one to flout the gods,
but dutiful toward men who beg his mercy.'
  Then Iris at his bidding ran
on the rainy winds to bear the words of Zeus,
until she came to Priam's house and heard
voices in lamentation. In the court
she found the princes huddled around their father,
faces and clothing wet with tears. The old man,
fiercely wrapped and hooded in his mantle,
sat like a figure graven – caked in filth
his own hands had swept over head and neck
when he lay rolling on the ground. Indoors
his daughters and his sons' wives were weeping,
remembering how many and how brave
the young men were who had gone down to death
before the Argive spearmen.
                                    Zeus's courier,
appearing now to Priam's eyes alone,
alighted whispering, so the old man trembled:
'Priam, heir of Dardanus, take heart,
and have no fear of me; I bode no evil,
but bring you friendly word from Zeus,
who is distressed for you and pities you

though distant far upon Olympus. He
commands that you shall ransom the Prince Hector,
taking fine gifts to melt Achilles' rage.
And go alone: no soldier may go with you,
only some crier, some old man, to drive
your wagon-team and guide the nimble wagon,
and afterward to carry home the body
of him that Prince Achilles overcame.
Put away thoughts of death, shake off your dread,
for you shall have a wondrous guide,
the Wayfinder, to bring you across the lines
into the very presence of Achilles.
He, for his part, seeing you in his quarters,
will neither take your life nor let another
enemy come near. He is no madman,
no blind brute, nor one to flout the gods,
but dutiful toward men who beg his mercy.'

Iris left him, swift as a veering wind.
Then Priam spoke, telling the men to rig
a four-wheeled wagon with a wicker box,
while he withdrew to his chamber roofed in cedar,
high and fragrant, rich in precious things.

He called to Hecabe, his lady: 'Princess,
word from Olympian Zeus has come to me
to go down to the ships of the Achaeans
and ransom our dead son. I am to take
gifts that will melt Achilles' anger. Tell me
how this appears to you, tell me your mind,
for I am torn with longing, now, to pass
inside the great encampment by the ships.'

The woman's voice broke as she answered: 'Sorrow,
sorrow. Where is the wisdom now that made you
famous in the old days, near and far?
How can you ever face the Achaean ships
or wish to go alone before those eyes,
the eyes of one who stripped your sons in battle,
how many, and how brave? Iron must be
the heart within you. If he sees you, takes you,
savage and wayward as the man is,
he'll have no mercy and no shame. Better
that we should mourn together in our hall.
Almighty fate spun this thing for our son
the day I bore him: destined him to feed
the wild dogs after death, being far from us

when he went down before the stronger man.
I could devour the vitals of that man,
leeching into his living flesh! He'd know
pain then – pain like mine for my dead son.
It was no coward the Achaean killed;
he stood and fought for the sweet wives of Troy,
with no more thought of flight or taking cover.'
　　In majesty old Priam said: 'My heart
is fixed on going. Do not hold me back,
and do not make yourself a raven crying
calamity at home. You will not move me.
If any man on earth had urged this on me –
reader of altar smoke, prophet or priest –
we'd say it was a lie, and hold aloof.
But no: with my own ears I heard the voice,
I saw the god before me. Go I shall,
and no more words. If I must die alongside
the ships of the Achaeans in their bronze,
I die gladly. May I but hold my son
and spend my grief; then let Achilles kill me.'
　　Throwing open the lids of treasure-boxes
he picked out twelve great robes of state, and twelve
light cloaks for men, and rugs, an equal number,
and just as many capes of snowy linen,
adding a dozen chitons to the lot;
then set in order ten pure bars of gold,
a pair of shining tripods, four great cauldrons,
and finally one splendid cup, a gift
Thracians had made him on an embassy.
He would not keep this, either – as he cared
for nothing now but ransoming his son.
　　And now, from the colonnade,
he made his Trojan people keep their distance,
berating and abusing them: 'Away,
you craven fools and rubbish! In your own homes
have you no one to mourn, that you crowd here,
to make more trouble for me? Is this a show,
that Zeus has crushed me, that he took the life
of my most noble son? You'll soon know what it means,
as you become child's play for the Achaeans
to kill in battle, now that Hector's gone.
As for myself, before I see my city
taken and ravaged, let me go down blind
to Death's cold kingdom!'

                                        Staff in hand,
he herded them, until they turned away
and left the furious old man. He lashed out
now at his sons, at Helenus and Paris,
Agathon, Pammon, Antiphonus,
Polites, Deiphobus, Hippothous,
and Dius – to these nine the old man cried:
  'Bestir yourselves, you misbegotten whelps,
shame of my house! Would god you had been killed
instead of Hector at the line of ships.
How curst I am in everything! I fathered
first-rate men, in our great Troy; but now
I swear not one is left: Mestor, Troilus,
laughing amid the war-cars; and then Hector –
a god to soldiers, and a god among them,
seeming not a man's child, but a god's.
Ares killed them. These poltroons are left,
hollow men, dancers, heroes of the dance,
light-fingered pillagers of lambs and kids
from the town pens!
                              'Now will you get a wagon
ready for me, and quickly? Load these gifts
aboard it, so that we can take the road.'
  Dreading the rough edge of their father's tongue,
they lifted out a cart, a cargo-wagon,
neat and manœuvrable, and newly made,
and fixed upon it a wicker box, then took
a mule yoke from a peg, a yoke of boxwood
knobbed in front, with rings to hold the reins.
They brought out, too, the band nine forearms long
called the yoke-fastener, and placed the yoke
forward at the shank of the polished pole,
shoving the yoke-pin firmly in. They looped
three turns of the yoke-fastener round the knob
and wound it over and over down the pole,
tucking the tab-end under. Next, the ransom:
bearing the weight of gifts for Hector's person
out of the inner room, they piled them up
on the polished wagon. It was time to yoke
the mule-team, strong in harness, with hard hooves,
a team the Mysians had given Priam.
Then for the king's own chariot they harnessed
a team of horses of the line of Tros,
reared by the old king in his royal stable.

So the impatient king and his sage crier
had their animals yoked in the palace yard
when Hecabe in her agitation joined them,
carrying in her right hand a golden cup
of honeyed wine, with which, before they left,
they might make offering.

                       At the horses' heads
she stood to tell them: 'Here, tip wine to Zeus,
the father of gods. Pray for a safe return
from the enemy army, seeing your heart is set
on venturing to the camp against my will.
Pray in the second place to Zeus the storm-king,
gloomy over Ida, who looks down
on all Troy country. Beg for an omen-bird,
the courier dearest of all birds to Zeus
and sovereign in power of flight,
that he appear upon our right in heaven.
When you have seen him with your own eyes, then,
under that sign, you may approach the ships.
If Zeus who views the wide world will not give you
vision of his bird, then I at least
cannot bid godspeed to your journey,
bent on it though you are.'

                      In majesty
Priam replied: 'My lady, in this matter
I am disposed to trust you and agree.
It is an excellent thing and salutary
to lift our hands to Zeus, invoking mercy.'

The old king motioned to his housekeeper,
who stood nearby with a basin and a jug,
to pour clear water on his hands. He washed them,
took the cup his lady held, and prayed
while standing there, midway in the walled court.

Then he tipped out the wine, looking toward heaven,
saying: 'Zeus, our Father, reigning from Ida,
god of glory and power, grant I come
to Achilles' door as one to be received
with kindliness and mercy. And dispatch
your courier-bird, the nearest to your heart
of all birds, and the first in power of flight.
Let him appear upon our right in heaven
that I may see him with my own eyes
and under that sign journey to the ships.'

Zeus all-foreseeing listened to this prayer

and put an eagle, king
of winged creatures, instantly in flight:
a swamp eagle, a hunter, one they call
the dusk-wing. Wide as a doorway in a chamber
spacious and high, built for a man of wealth,
a door with long bars fitted well, so wide
spread out each pinion. The great bird appeared
winging through the town on their right hand,
and all their hearts lifted with joy to see him.
In haste the old king boarded his bright car
and clattered out of the echoing colonnade.
Ahead, the mule-team drew the four-wheeled wagon,
driven by Idaeus, and behind
the chariot rolled, with horses that the old man
whipped into a fast trot through the town.
Family and friends all followed weeping
as though for Priam's last and deathward ride.
Into the lower town they passed, and reached
the plain of Troy. Here those who followed after
turned back, sons and sons-in-law. And Zeus
who views the wide world saw the car and wagon
brave the plain.

        He felt a pang for Priam
and quickly said to Hermes, his own son:
'Hermes, as you go most happily
of all the gods with mortals, and give heed
to whom you will, be on your way this time
as guide for Priam to the deep-sea ships.
Guide him so that not one of the Danaans
may know or see him till he reach Achilles.'

    Argeiphontes the Wayfinder obeyed.
He bent to tie his beautiful sandals on,
ambrosial, golden, that carry him over water
and over endless land on a puff of wind,
and took the wand with which he charms asleep –
or, when he wills, awake – the eyes of men.
So, wand in hand, the strong god glittering
paced into the air. Quick as a thought
he came to Helle's waters and to Troy,
appearing as a boy whose lip was downy
in the first bloom of manhood, a young prince,
all graciousness.

        After the travellers
drove past the mound of Ilus, at the ford

they let the mules and horses pause to drink
the running stream. Now darkness had come on
when, looking round, the crier
saw Hermes near at hand.

　　　　　　　　　He said to Priam:
'You must think hard and fast, your grace;
there is new danger; we need care and prudence.
I see a man-at-arms there – ready, I think,
to prey on us. Come, shall we whip the team
and make a run for it? Or take his knees
and beg for mercy?'

　　　　　　　　　Now the old man's mind
gave way to confusion and to terror.
On his gnarled arms and legs the hair stood up,
and he stared, breathless.

　　　　　　　　　But the affable god
came over and took his hand and asked: 'Old father,
where do you journey, with your cart and car,
while others rest, below the evening star?
Do you not fear the Achaeans where they lie
encamped, hard, hostile outlanders, nearby?
Should someone see you, bearing stores like these
by night, how would you deal with enemies?
You are not young, your escort's ancient, too.
Could you beat off an attacker, either of you?
I'll do no hurt to you but defend you here.
You remind me of my father, whom I hold dear.'

　　Old Priam answered him: 'Indeed, dear boy,
the case is as you say. And yet some god
stretched out his hand above me, he who sent
before me here – and just at the right time –
a traveller like yourself, well-made, well-spoken,
clear-headed, too. You come of some good family.'

　　The Wayfinder rejoined: 'You speak with courtesy,
dear sir. But on this point enlighten me:
are you removing treasure here amassed
for safety abroad, until the war is past?
Or can you be abandoning Ilium
in fear, after he perished, that great one
who never shirked a battle, your own princely son?'

　　Old Priam replied: 'My brave young friend, who are you?
Born of whom? How nobly you acknowledge
the dreadful end of my unfortunate son.'

　　To this the Wayfinder replied: 'Dear sir,

you question me about him? Never surmise
I have not seen him with my very eyes,
and often, on the field, I saw him chase
Argives with carnage to their own shipways,
while we stood wondering, forbidden war
by the great anger that Achilles bore
Lord Agamemnon. I am of that company
Achilles led. His own ship carried me
as one of the Myrmidons. My father is old,
as you are, and his name's Polyctor; gold
and other wealth he owns;
and I am seventh and last of all his sons.
When I cast lots among them, my lot fell
to join the siege against Troy citadel.
Tonight I've left the camp to scout this way
where, circling Troy, we'll fight at break of day;
our men are tired of waiting and will not stand
for any postponement by the high command.'

    Responded royal Priam: 'If you belong
to the company of Achilles, son of Peleus,
tell me this, and tell me the whole truth:
is my son even now beside the ships?
Or has Achilles by this time dismembered him
and thrown him to the wild dogs?'

                       The Wayfinder
made reply again: 'Dear sir,
no dogs or birds have yet devoured your son.
Beside Achilles' ship, out of the sun,
he lies in a place of shelter. Now twelve days
the man has lain there, yet no part decays,
nor have the blowfly's maggots, that devour
dead men in war, fed on him to this hour.
True that around his dear friend's barrow-tomb
Achilles drags him when dawn-shadows come,
driving pitilessly; but he mars him not.
You might yourself be witness, on the spot,
how fresh with dew he lies, washed of his gore,
unstained, for the deep gashes that he bore
have all closed up – and many thrust their bronze
into his body. The blest immortal ones
favour your prince, and care for every limb
even in death, as they so cherished him.'

    The old king's heart exulted, and he said:
'Child, it was well to honour the immortals.

He never forgot, at home in Ilium –
ah, did my son exist? was he a dream? –
the gods who own Olympus. They in turn
were mindful of him when he met his end.
Here is a goblet as a gift from me.
Protect me, give me escort, if the gods
attend us, till I reach Achilles' hut.'

    And in response Hermes the Wayfinder
said: 'You are putting a young man to the test,
dear sir, but I may not, as you request,
accept a gift behind Achilles' back.
Fearing, honouring him, I could not lack
discretion to that point. The consequence, too,
could be unwelcome. As for escorting you,
even to Argos' famous land I'd ride
a deck with you, or journey at your side.
No cutthroat ever will disdain your guide.'

    With this, Hermes who lights the way for mortals
leapt into the driver's place. He caught up
reins and whip, and breathed a second wind
into the mule-team and the team of horses.
Onward they ran toward parapet and ships,
and pulled up to the moat.

                  Now night had fallen,
bringing the sentries to their supper fire,
but the glimmering god Hermes, the Wayfinder,
showered a mist of slumber on them all.
As quick as thought, he had the gates unbarred
and open to let the wagon enter, bearing
the old king and the ransom.

                 Going seaward
they came to the lofty quarters of Achilles,
a lodge the Myrmidons built for their lord
of pine-trees cut and trimmed, and shaggy thatch
from mowings in deep meadows. Posts were driven
round the wide courtyard in a palisade,
whose gate one crossbar held, one beam of pine.
It took three men to slam this home, and three
to draw the bolt again – but great Achilles
worked his entryway alone with ease.
And now Hermes, who lights the way for mortals,
opened for Priam, took him safely in
with all his rich gifts for the son of Peleus.
Then the god dropped the reins, and stepping down

he said: 'I am no mortal wagoner,
but Hermes, sir. My father sent me here
to be your guide amid the Achaean men.
Now that is done, I'm off to heaven again
and will not visit Achilles. That would be
to compromise an immortal's dignity –
to be received with guests of mortal station.
Go take his knees, and make your supplication:
invoke his father, his mother, and his child;
pray that his heart be touched, that he be reconciled.'

Now Hermes turned, departing for Olympus,
and Priam vaulted down. He left Idaeus
to hold the teams in check, while he went forward
into the lodge. He found Achilles, dear
to Zeus, there in his chair, with officers
at ease across the room. Only Automedon
and Alcimus were busy near Achilles,
for he had just now made an end of dinner,
eating and drinking, and the laden boards
lay near him still upon the trestles.

Priam,
the great king of Troy, passed by the others,
knelt down, took in his arms Achilles' knees,
and kissed the hands of wrath that killed his sons.

When, taken with mad Folly in his own land,
a man does murder and in exile finds
refuge in some rich house, then all who see him
stand in awe. So these men stood.

Achilles
gazed in wonder at the splendid king,
and his companions marvelled too, all silent,
with glances to and fro.

Now Priam prayed
to the man before him: 'Remember your own father,
Achilles, in your godlike youth: his years
like mine are many, and he stands upon
the fearful doorstep of old age. He, too,
is hard pressed, it may be, by those around him,
there being no one able to defend him
from bane of war and ruin. Ah, but he
may none the less hear news of you alive,
and so with glad heart hope through all his days
for sight of his dear son, come back from Troy,
while I have deathly fortune.

'Noble sons
I fathered here, but scarce one man is left me.
Fifty I had when the Achaeans came,
nineteen out of a single belly, others
born of attendant women. Most are gone.
Raging Ares cut their knees from under them.
And he who stood alone among them all,
their champion, and Troy's, ten days ago
you killed him, fighting for his land, my prince,
Hector. It is for him that I have come
among these ships, to beg him back from you,
and I bring ransom without stint.

'Achilles,
be reverent toward the great gods! And take
pity on me, remember your own father.
Think me more pitiful by far, since I
have brought myself to do what no man else
has done before – to lift to my lips the hand
of one who killed my son.'

Now in Achilles
the evocation of his father stirred
new longing, and an ache of grief. He lifted
the old man's hand and gently put him by.
Then both were overborne as they remembered:
the old king huddled at Achilles' feet
wept, and wept for Hector, killer of men,
while great Achilles wept for his own father
as for Patroclus once again; and sobbing
filled the room.

But when Achilles' heart
had known the luxury of tears, and pain
within his breast and bones had passed away,
he stood then, raised the old king up, in pity
for his grey head and greybeard cheek, and spoke
in a warm rush of words:

'Ah, sad and old!
Trouble and pain you've borne, and bear, aplenty.
Only a great will could have brought you here
among the Achaean ships, and here alone
before the eyes of one who stripped your sons,
your many sons, in battle. Iron must be
the heart within you. Come, then, and sit down.
We'll probe our wounds no more but let them rest,
though grief lies heavy on us. Tears heal nothing,

drying so stiff and cold. This is the way
the gods ordained the destiny of men,
to bear such burdens in our lives, while they
feel no affliction. At the door of Zeus
are those two urns of good and evil gifts
that he may choose for us; and one for whom
the lightning's joyous king dips in both urns
will have by turns bad luck and good. But one
to whom he sends all evil – that man goes
contemptible by the will of Zeus; ravenous
hunger drives him over the wondrous earth,
unresting, without honour from gods or men.
Mixed fortune came to Peleus. Shining gifts
at the gods' hands he had from birth: felicity,
wealth overflowing, rule of the Myrmidons,
a bride immortal at his mortal side.
But then Zeus gave afflictions too – no family
of powerful sons grew up for him at home,
but one child, of all seasons and of none.
Can I stand by him in his age? Far from my country
I sit at Troy to grieve you and your children.
You, too, sir, in time past were fortunate,
we hear men say. From Macar's isle of Lesbos
northward, and south of Phrygia and the Straits,
no one had wealth like yours, or sons like yours.
Then gods out of the sky sent you this bitterness:
the years of siege, the battles and the losses.
Endure it, then. And do not mourn for ever
for your dead son. There is no remedy.
You will not make him stand again. Rather
await some new misfortune to be suffered.'

    The old king in his majesty replied:
'Never give me a chair, my lord, while Hector
lies in your camp uncared for. Yield him to me
now. Allow me sight of him. Accept
the many gifts I bring. May they reward you,
and may you see your home again.
You spared my life at once and let me live.'

    Achilles, the great runner, frowned and eyed him
under his brows; 'Do not vex me, sir,' he said.
'I have intended, in my own good time,
to yield up Hector to you. She who bore me,
the daughter of the Ancient of the sea,
has come with word to me from Zeus. I know

in your case, too – though you say nothing, Priam –
that some god guided you to the shipways here.
No strong man in his best days could make entry
into this camp. How could he pass the guard,
or force our gateway?
                        'Therefore, let me be.
Sting my sore heart again, and even here,
under my own roof, suppliant though you are,
I may not spare you, sir, but trample on
the express command of Zeus!'
                              When he heard this,
the old man feared him and obeyed with silence.
Now like a lion at one bound Achilles
left the room. Close at his back the officers
Automedon and Alcimus went out –
comrades in arms whom he esteemed the most
after the dead Patroclus. They unharnessed
mules and horses, led the old king's crier
to a low bench and sat him down.
Then from the polished wagon
they took the piled-up price of Hector's body.
One chiton and two capes they left aside
as dress and shrouding for the homeward journey.
Then, calling to the women slaves, Achilles
ordered the body bathed and rubbed with oil –
but lifted, too, and placed apart, where Priam
could not see his son – for seeing Hector
he might in his great pain give way to rage,
and fury then might rise up in Achilles
to slay the old king, flouting Zeus's word.
So after bathing and anointing Hector
they drew the shirt and beautiful shrouding over him.
Then with his own hands lifting him, Achilles
laid him upon a couch, and with his two
companions aiding, placed him in the wagon.
    Now a bitter groan burst from Achilles,
who stood and prayed to his own dead friend: 'Patroclus,
do not be angry with me, if somehow
even in the world of Death you learn of this –
that I released Prince Hector to his father.
The gifts he gave were not unworthy. Aye,
and you shall have your share, this time as well.'
    Then Prince Achilles turned back to his quarters
He took again the splendid chair that stood

against the farther wall, then looked at Priam
and made his declaration:

> 'As you wished, sir,
the body of your son is now set free.
He lies in state. At the first sight of Dawn
you shall take charge of him yourself and see him.
Now let us think of supper. We are told
that even Niobe in her extremity
took thought for bread – though all her brood had perished,
her six young girls and six tall sons. Apollo,
making his silver longbow whip and sing,
shot the lads down, and Artemis with raining
arrows killed the daughters – all this after
Niobe had compared herself with Leto,
the smooth-cheeked goddess. "She has borne two children,"
Niobe said, "How many have I borne!"
But soon those two destroyed the twelve.

> 'Besides,
nine days the dead lay stark, no one could bury them,
for Zeus had turned all folk of theirs to stone.
The gods made graves for them on the tenth day,
and then at last, being weak and spent with weeping,
Niobe thought of food. Among the rocks
of Sipylus' lonely mountainside, where nymphs
who race Achelous river go to rest,
she, too, long turned to stone, somewhere broods on
the gall immortal gods gave her to drink.

> 'Like her we'll think of supper, noble sir.
Weep for your son again when you have borne him
back to Troy; there he'll be mourned indeed.'

In one swift movement now Achilles caught
and slaughtered a white lamb. His officers
flayed it, skilful in their butchering
to dress the flesh; they cut bits for the skewers,
roasted, and drew them off, done to a turn.
Automedon dealt loaves into the baskets
on the great board; Achilles served the meat.
Then all their hands went out upon the supper.
When thirst and appetite were turned away,
Priam, the heir of Dardanus, gazed long
in wonder at Achilles' form and scale –
so like the gods in aspect. And Achilles
in his turn gazed in wonder upon Priam,
royal in visage as in speech.

Both men
in contemplation found rest for their eyes,
till the old hero, Priam, broke the silence:
'Make a bed ready for me, son of Thetis,
and let us know the luxury of sleep.
From that hour when my son died at your hands
till now, my eyelids have not closed in slumber
over my eyes, but groaning where I sat
I tasted pain and grief a thousandfold,
or lay down rolling in my courtyard mire.
Here for the first time I have swallowed bread
and made myself drink wine. Before, I could not.'

Achilles ordered men and serving-women
to make a bed outside, in the covered forecourt,
with purple rugs piled up and sheets outspread
and coverings of fleeces laid on top.
The girls went out with torches in their hands
and soon deftly made up a double bed.
Then Achilles, defiant of Agamemnon,
told his guest: 'Dear venerable sir,
you'll sleep outside tonight, in case an Achaean
officer turns up, one of those men
who are forever taking counsel with me –
as well they may. If one should see you here
as the dark night runs on, he would report it
to the Lord Marshal Agamemnon. Then
return of the body would only be delayed.
Now tell me this, and give me a straight answer:
How many days do you require
for the funeral of Prince Hector? – I should know
how long to wait, and hold the Achaean army.'

Old Priam in his majesty replied:
'If you would have me carry out the burial,
Achilles, here is the way to do me grace.
As we are penned in the town, but must bring wood
from the distant hills, the Trojans are afraid.
We should have mourning for nine days in hall,
then on the tenth conduct his funeral
and feast the troops and commons;
on the eleventh we should make his tomb,
and on the twelfth give battle, if we must.'

Achilles said: 'As you command, old Priam,
the thing is done. I shall suspend the war
for those eleven days that you require.'

He took the old man's right hand by the wrist
and held it, to allay his fear.
                                    Now crier
and king with hearts brim-full retired to rest
in the sheltered forecourt, while Achilles slept
deep in his palisaded lodge. Beside him,
lovely in her youth, Briseis lay.
And other gods and soldiers all night long,
by slumber quieted, slept on. But slumber
would not come to Hermes the Good Companion,
as he considered how to ease the way
for Priam from the camp, to send him through
unseen by the formidable gatekeepers.
    Then Hermes came to Priam's pillow, saying:
'Sir, no thought of danger shakes your rest,
as you sleep on, being great Achilles' guest,
amid men fierce as hunters in a ring.
You triumphed in a costly ransoming,
but three times costlier your own would be
to your surviving sons – a monarch's fee –
if this should come to Agamemnon's ear
and all the Achaean host should learn that you are here.'
The old king started up in fright, and woke
his herald. Hermes yoked the mules and horses,
took the reins, then inland like the wind
he drove through all the encampment, seen by no one.
When they reached Xanthus, eddying and running
god-begotten river, at the ford,
Hermes departed for Olympus. Dawn
spread out her yellow robe on all the earth,
as they drove on toward Troy, with groans and sighs,
and the mule-team pulled the wagon and the body.
And no one saw them, not a man or woman,
before Cassandra. Tall as the pale-gold
goddess Aphrodite, she had climbed
the citadel of Pergamus at dawn.
Now looking down she saw her father come
in his war-car, and saw the crier there,
and saw Lord Hector on his bed of death
upon the mule-cart.
                              The girl wailed and cried
to all the city: 'Oh, look down, look down,
go to your windows, men of Troy, and women,
see Lord Hector now! Remember joy

at seeing him return alive from battle,
exalting all our city and our land!'

Now, at the sight of Hector, all gave way
to loss and longing, and all crowded down
to meet the escort and body near the gates,
till no one in the town was left at home.
There Hector's lady and his gentle mother
tore their hair for him, flinging themselves
upon the wagon to embrace his person
while the crowd groaned. All that long day
until the sun went down they might have mourned
in tears before the gateway.

But old Priam
spoke to them from his chariot: 'Make way,
let the mules pass. You'll have your fill of weeping
later, when I've brought the body home.'

They parted then, and made way for the wagon,
allowing Priam to reach the famous hall.
They laid the body of Hector in his bed,
and brought in minstrels, men to lead the dirge.
While these wailed out, the women answered, moaning.
Andromache of the ivory-white arms
held in her lap between her hands
the head of Hector who had killed so many.

Now she lamented: 'You've been torn from life,
my husband, in young manhood, and you leave me
empty in our hall. The boy's a child
whom you and I, poor souls, conceived; I doubt
he'll come to manhood. Long before, great Troy
will go down plundered, citadel and all,
now that you are lost, who guarded it
and kept it, and preserved its wives and children.
They will be shipped off in the murmuring hulls
one day, and I along with all the rest.

'You, my little one, either you come with me
to do some grinding labour, some base toil
for a harsh master, or an Achaean soldier
will grip you by the arm and hurl you down
from a tower here to a miserable death –
out of his anger for a brother, a father,
or even a son that Hector killed. Achaeans
in hundreds mouthed black dust under his blows.
He was no moderate man in war, your father,
and that is why they mourn him through the city.

Hector, you gave your parents grief and pain
but left me loneliest, and heart-broken.
You could not open your strong arms to me
from your deathbed, or say a thoughtful word,
for me to cherish all my life long
as I weep for you night and day.'

                       Her voice broke,
and a wail came from the women.

                           Hecabe
lifted her lamenting voice among them:
'Hector, dearest of sons to me, in life
you had the favour of the immortal gods,
and they have cared for you in death as well.
Achilles captured other sons of mine
in other years, and sold them overseas
to Samos, Imbros, and the smoky island,
Lemnos. That was not his way with you.
After he took your life, cutting you down
with his sharp-bladed spear, he trussed and dragged you
many times round the barrow of his friend,
Patroclus, whom you killed – though not by this
could that friend live again. But now I find you
fresh as pale dew, seeming newly dead,
like one to whom Apollo of the silver bow
had given easy death with his mild arrows.'

  Hecabe sobbed again, and the wails redoubled.
Then it was Helen's turn to make lament:
'Dear Hector, dearest brother to me by far!
My husband is Alexandrus,
who brought me here to Troy – God, that I might
have died sooner! This is the twentieth year
since I left home, and left my fatherland.
But never did I have an evil word
or gesture from you. No – and when some other
brother-in-law or sister would revile me,
or if my mother-in-law spoke to me bitterly –
but Priam never did, being as mild
as my own father – you would bring her round
with your kind heart and gentle speech. Therefore
I weep for you and for myself as well,
given this fate, this grief. In all wide Troy
no one is left who will befriend me, none;
they all shudder at me.'

                        Helen wept,

and a moan came from the people, hearing her.
  Then Priam, the old king, commanded them:
'Trojans, bring firewood to the edge of town.
No need to fear an ambush of the Argives.
When he dismissed me from the camp, Achilles
told me clearly they will not harass us,
not until dawn comes for the twelfth day.'
  Then yoking mules and oxen to their wagons
the people thronged before the city gates.
Nine days they laboured, bringing countless loads
of firewood to the town. When Dawn that lights
the world of mortals came for the tenth day,
they carried great-hearted Hector out at last,
and all in tears placed his dead body high
upon its pyre, then cast a torch below.
When the young Dawn with fingertips of rose
made heaven bright, the Trojan people massed
about Prince Hector's ritual fire.
All being gathered and assembled, first
they quenched the smoking pyre with tawny wine
wherever flames had licked their way, then friends
and brothers picked his white bones from the char
in sorrow, while the tears rolled down their cheeks.
In a golden urn they put the bones,
shrouding the urn with veiling of soft purple.
Then in a grave dug deep they placed it
and heaped it with great stones. The men were quick
to raise the death-mound, while in every quarter
look-outs were posted to ensure against
an Achaean surprise attack. When they had finished
raising the barrow, they returned to Ilium,
where all sat down to banquet in his honour
in the hall of Priam king.
                              So they performed
the funeral rites of Hector, tamer of horses.

GLOSSARY AND INDEX OF NAMES

THE following list aims at no more than to identify persons and places named in the *Iliad* and to show how their names are pronounced. (An acute accent indicates where stress falls; a hyphen is used to separate two syllables otherwise mistakable for one; a bar above a vowel marks it as long – and, if it immediately follows another vowel, as separately pronounced.)

The Greek patronymic, although most often rendered explicitly, is sometimes retained in this translation. It was a kind of surname, whereby a man might be designated by his father's name in epithetical form: e.g. Diomedes as Tydides (son of Tydeus), Odysseus as Laertiades (son of Laertes); or in simple adjectival form, e.g. Aias son of Telamon as Telamonius (Telamonian). Each of the brothers Agamemnon and Menelaus might be called Atreides (son of Atreus), or together the Atreidae.

In general, page-references are given wherever a name or a description that stands for it occurs. But the group-names of the contending armies and place-names at the centre of action are entered in detail only until they have become familiar; a few of the most constantly named princ·᠆l characters are entered whenever they do or suffer somethin.. significant, but not invariably where the mention is no more than incidental; and a few names, mentioned only once and then for decoration rather than active function, are omitted altogether.

Readers who seek fuller information than this glossary provides are referred to books such as Lemprière's *Classical Dictionary*, or the *New Larousse Encyclopedia of Mythology*.

Place-names mentioned may be found on the maps on pages 468–70, excepting some whose importance is minimal or their reality doubtful.

ACHELÓ-US, a river of western Greece, 369, 438

ACHÍLLĒS, son of Peleus (hence Pelides) and Thetis, grandson of Aeacus (Aeacides), leader of the Myrmidons vii, xiii, xiv, xv, xvi, xvii, xviii, 1, 2–7, 9–12, 14, 16, 24, 28, 37, 39, 71, 109, 116, 139, 148, 149, 151–5, 160, 161, 182–3, 196, 197, 201, 226, 249, 257, 276–8, 279, 280–2, 298, 321–4, 326–7, 329–30, 339–40, 341–9, 351, 352, 354, 355–63, 364–73, 378–80, 381–2, 383–92, 393, 396–403, 405, 409–11, 412–13, 414–16, 417–20, 421, 423, 424–5, 433, 434–40

ÁCTŌR, (1) father of Astyoche, 32; (2) grandfather of Patroclus, 200, 276

ÁDAMAS, a Trojan ally, 207, 232, 237

ADMĒTUS, a Thessalian king, father of Eumelus, 38, 403

ADRASTEÍA, a town in Mysia, 41

ADRÁSTUS, (1) king of Sicyon, 33, 243; (2) son of Merops, a Trojan ally, 41; (3) name of two unspecific Trojans, 99, 294

AÉACUS, grandfather of Achilles, 276, 369

AÉGAE, a town in Achaea proper, 132, 217

AEGIALEÍA, wife of Diomedes, 84

AÉGIALUS, (1) coastland of Achaea, 34; (2) a district in Paphlagonia, 42

AEGÍNA, an island off the Peloponnese, 33

AÉGIUM, a town in the realm of Agamemnon, 34

AENÉ-AS, son of Anchises (Anchisiades) and Aphrodite, leader of the Dardanians, 41, 77–81, 84–5, 86–7, 88, 100, 129, 181, 206, 229, 230–1, 251, 264, 290, 292, 308–9, 313–14, 320, 352–9, 404

AÉNUS, a Thracian town, 72

AÉPYTUS, an Arcadian hero, 34

AESÉPUS, a Trojan river, 41, 59, 204

AESYÉTĒS, (1) a Trojan hero, 40; (2) father of Alcathous, 228

AÉTHĒ, Agamemnon's mare, 404, 407, 410

AÉTHICES, a people of northern Greece, 38

AÉTHON, a horse of Hector's, 132

AÉTHRA, handmaid to Helen, 47

AETOLIANS, the people of Aetolia in western Greece, 35, 158–9, 413

AGAMĒDĒ, wife of Mulius, 199

AGAMÉMNŌN, son of Atreus (hence Atrides) and brother of Menelaus, king of Mycenae and chief commander of the Achaeans, vii, xiii, xiv, xv, xvi, xvii, 1–7, 8–9, 18–21, 24–5, 28–31, 34, 45, 46, 48, 50–1, 56, 61–9, 74, 87, 98, 99, 114, 116, 117, 121, 124, 129, 132–3, 134, 143, 145, 146–7, 152, 162, 164–7, 170, 180–1, 182–7, 197, 240–4, 250, 276, 324, 339–44, 346, 397, 399, 400, 402, 420, 439

AGAPÉNŌR, commander of the Arcadians, 35

AGÁSTHENĒS, son of Augeias and father of Polyxeinus, 35

AGÁSTROPHUS, a Trojan, 189

AGATHŌN, a son of Priam, 428

AGELÁ-US, (1) a Trojan, 133; (2) a Greek, 188

AGÉNŌR, son of Antenor, a leading fighter on the Trojan side, 70, 181, 206, 230, 233, 251, 264, 290, 379–80

AÍAS, (1) son of Telamon of Salamis, ix, xiii, xvi, 4, 5, 29, 33, 39,

MAPS OF REAL PLACES

OF the many places and geographical features – some real, some mythical, and some an amalgam of fact and fiction – that figure largely in the story of the *Iliad*, only those whose existence and location are reasonably certain are included on the following maps of Greece and The Troad in the classical period.

GREECE AND THE AEGEAN

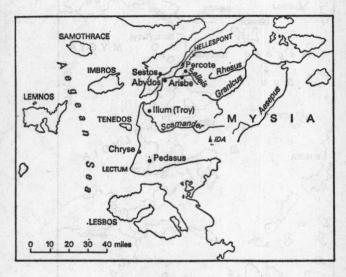

THE TROAD

THE WORLD'S CLASSICS

A Select List

HANS ANDERSEN: Fairy Tales
Translated by L. W. Kingsland
Introduction by Naomi Lewis
Illustrated by Vilhelm Pedersen and Lorenz Frølich

ARTHUR J. ARBERRY (Transl.): The Koran

LUDOVICO ARIOSTO: Orlando Furioso
Translated by Guido Waldman

ARISTOTLE: The Nicomachean Ethics
Translated by David Ross

JANE AUSTEN: Emma
Edited by James Kinsley and David Lodge

Northanger Abbey, Lady Susan, The Watsons,
and Sanditon
Edited by John Davie

Persuasion
Edited by John Davie

WILLIAM BECKFORD: Vathek
Edited by Roger Lonsdale

KEITH BOSLEY (Transl.): The Kalevala

CHARLOTTE BRONTË: Jane Eyre
Edited by Margaret Smith

JOHN BUNYAN: The Pilgrim's Progress
Edited by N. H. Keeble

FRANCES HODGSON BURNETT: The Secret Garden
Edited by Dennis Butts

FANNY BURNEY: Cecilia
or Memoirs of an Heiress
Edited by Peter Sabor and Margaret Anne Doody

THOMAS CARLYLE: The French Revolution
Edited by K. J. Fielding and David Sorensen

TOBIAS SMOLLETT: The Expedition of Humphry Clinker
Edited by Lewis M. Knapp
Revised by Paul-Gabriel Boucé

ROBERT LOUIS STEVENSON:
Treasure Island
Edited by Emma Letley

ANTHONY TROLLOPE: The American Senator
Edited by John Halperin

GIORGIO VASARI: The Lives of the Artists
Translated and Edited by Julia Conaway Bondanella and Peter Bondanella

VIRGINIA WOOLF: Orlando
Edited by Rachel Bowlby

ÉMILE ZOLA: Nana
Translated and Edited by Douglas Parmée

A complete list of Oxford Paperbacks, including The World's Classics, OPUS, Past Masters, Oxford Authors, Oxford Shakespeare, and Oxford Paperback Reference, is available in the UK from the Arts and Reference Publicity Department (BH), Oxford University Press, Walton Street, Oxford OX2 6DP.

In the USA, complete lists are available from the Paperbacks Marketing Manager, Oxford University Press, 200 Madison Avenue, New York, NY 10016.

Oxford Paperbacks are available from all good bookshops. In case of difficulty, customers in the UK can order direct from Oxford University Press Bookshop, Freepost, 116 High Street, Oxford, OX1 4BR, enclosing full payment. Please add 10 per cent of published price for postage and packing.